# RHETORICAL INVESTIGATIONS

# RHETORICAL INVESTIGATIONS

*Studies in Ordinary Language Criticism*

Walter Jost

University of Virginia Press
Charlottesville and London

University of Virginia Press
© 2004 by the Rector and Visitors of the University of Virginia
All rights reserved
Printed in the United States of America on acid-free paper
*First published 2004*

9 8 7 6 5 4 3 2 1

Library of Congress Cataloging-in-Publication Data
Jost, Walter, 1951–
  Rhetorical investigations : studies in ordinary language criticism / Walter Jost.
      p.    cm.
Includes bibliographical references and index.
  ISBN 0-8139-2249-6 (alk. paper)
  1. Rhetoric. 2. Criticism—History—20th century. 3. Frost, Robert, 1874–1963—Criticism and interpretation. I. Title.
PN175 .J64 2004
808—dc22

                                                            2003016076

For Charles Altieri, for Stanley Cavell
for showing a way (not *the* way)

For Walter J. Ong, S. J., for Gerald L. Bruns

For Paul Delanty for Junior English

It is ... of the essence of our investigation that we do not seek to learn anything *new* by it. We want to *understand* something that is already in plain view. For *this* is what we seem in some sense not to understand.

—Ludwig Wittgenstein, *Philosophical Investigations*

When in Rome, do as the Greeks.

—Kenneth Burke, *Counter-Statement*

This is how philosophers should salute each other: "Take your time!"

—Ludwig Wittgenstein, *Culture and Value*

CONTENTS

| | |
|---|---|
| Acknowledgments | ix |
| List of Abbreviations | xi |
| Introduction | 1 |

**Book I. Rhetoric: An Advanced Primer** — 25

1. Dialectic as Dialogue: The Order of the Ordinary — 27
2. Rhetorical Invention: Notes toward an American Low Modernism — 61
3. Grammatical Judgment: It All Depends on What You Mean by "Home" — 94
4. Logical Proof: Perspicuous Representations — 122

**Book II. Four Beginnings for a Book on Robert Frost** — 157

5. Lessons in the Conversation That We Are: "The Death of the Hired Man" (Invention) — 159
6. Naming Being in "West-Running Brook": (Judgment as Acknowledgment) — 183
7. Giving Evidence and Making Evident: Civility and Madness in "Snow" (Proof) — 217
8. Ordinary Language Brought to Grief: "Home Burial" (Dialogue in Disorder and Doubt) — 243

Appendix: Frost Poems Discussed — 271
Notes — 299
Index — 339

# ACKNOWLEDGMENTS

IN SEVERAL chapters of this book the word "acknowledgment" does a kind of work beyond what it usually does in its everyday contexts, which is to register one's recognition of or gratitude for something or someone. In Wittgenstein and Cavell (and I believe this can be said of Heidegger and Gadamer), knowledge, giving evidence, hits bedrock on what we "acknowledge," conditions made evident to us not by propositional proof but by their critical involvement in everything we say and do. The work of art, like other manifestations of the world, is impossible to fit into the fixed parameters of concepts, propositions, and rules; rather, it accomplishes its work by weaving a pattern of myriad threads, a pattern that can then be seen and acknowledged in a variety of ways. So in his essay "Literature as a Projection of Desire," Italo Calvino observes that "every true book of criticism may be read like one of the texts it deals with, as a web of poetic metaphors." Like the work of art in a small way, then—I mean in my attempt to make something manifest beyond propositional knowledge—my own acknowledgment of the people who have helped and encouraged me must be this book as a whole, not merely these few poor sentences up front.

Many generous colleagues have given time and encouragement, and I am deeply grateful to Charles Altieri, Ed Block Jr., Wayne C. Booth, Tony Cascardi, Stanley Cavell, Ken Dauber, Richard Eldridge, Jamie Ferreira, Michael Fischer, Michael Hyde, Wayne Lesser, Michael Levenson, Jerry McGann, Saul Morson, Richard Poirier, David Lee Rubin, Allen Scult, John Shotter, Steve Smith, Patricia Spacks, and Chip Tucker. My special thanks go to my friend and colleague Wendy Olmsted at the University of Chicago for her careful reading of the entire manuscript. I thank those groups who heard earlier versions of some of these chapters at Marquette, Northwestern, Villanova, Wake Forest, and the University of Virginia. I also thank the last named for two Sesquicentennial research fellowships and for summer grants, as well as Ralph Cohen and others at the Commonwealth Center for Literary and Cultural Change at the University of Virginia for intellectual and monetary support, and Susan Brady, my excellent copy editor and proofreader.

This book has grown up alongside my now grown children, Alex and Alison, and has dogged the heels of my wife, Marcella, Lo! these many years: for their love, interest, and forbearance, my love back.

Perhaps like many authors at the end of a long labor, I identify with the words Wittgenstein uses to conclude his preface to *Philosophical Investigations*: "I should have liked to produce a good book. This has not come about, but the time is past in which I could improve it."

## ACKNOWLEDGMENTS

SOMETIMES in slightly different forms, parts of this book appear elsewhere: Parts of chapters 3 and 4 are reprinted from *Robert Frost at the Millennium: New Essays*, ed. Earl J. Wilcox and Jonathan N. Barron (Columbia: University of Missouri Press, 2000). By permission of the University of Missouri Press. Copyright 2000 by the Curators of the University of Missouri. Another part of chapter 4 appeared in *American Literature* 60 (May 1988): 226–40 (reprinted in *On Frost: The Best of "American Literature,"* ed. Louis Budd and Edwin Cady [Durham: Duke University Press, 1991], 207–21). Copyright 1988, Duke University Press. All rights reserved. Used by permission of the publisher. Still another part of chapter 4 appeared in *A Companion to Rhetoric*, ed. Walter Jost and Wendy Olmsted (Oxford: Blackwell, 2004), reprinted by permission of the publisher. Chapter 5 first appeared in *College English* 58 (April 1996): 397–422. Copyright 1996 by the National Council of Teachers of English. Reprinted with permission. Chapter 6 was published in *Texas Studies in Literature and Language* 36 (spring 1994): 5–50, and also chapter 7, 39 (spring 1997): 27–64. Reprinted by permission of the publisher. Chapter 8 appeared in *Ordinary Language Criticism: Literary Thinking after Cavell after Wittgenstein*, ed. Kenneth Dauber and Walter Jost (Northwestern University Press, 2003), 77–114. Reprinted by permission of the publisher.

"THE DEATH of the Hired Man," "West-Running Brook," "Snow," "Home Burial," "The Black Cottage," "The Code," "Leaves Compared with Flowers," "Two Tramps in Mud Time," "Dust of Snow," "Nothing Gold Can Stay," "Beech," "There Are Roughly Zones," "Revelation," excerpt from "Iris by Night" by Robert Frost from *The Poetry of Robert Frost*, ed. Edward Connery Lathem. Copyright 1923, 1928, 1930, 1934, 1939, © 1969 by Henry Holt and Co., copyright 1936, 1942, 1944, 1951, 1956, 1958, 1962 by Robert Frost, copyright 1964, 1967 by Lesley Frost Ballantine. Reprinted by permission of Henry Holt and Company, LLC.

# ABBREVIATIONS

| | |
|---|---|
| *BBB* | Ludwig Wittgenstein. *The Blue and Brown Books.* New York: Harper and Row, 1958. |
| *BT* | Martin Heidegger. *Being and Time.* Translated by John Macquarrie and Edward Robinson. New York: Harper and Row, 1962. In citations of this work, the pages of the English translation are followed by the pages of the German edition (*Sein und Zeit.* 7th ed. [Tübingen: Max Niemeyer Verlag, n.d.]). |
| *Cambridge* | Ludwig Wittgenstein. *Lectures: Cambridge 1932–1935.* Edited by A. Ambrose. Totowa, N.J.: Littlefield and Adams, 1979. |
| *CHU* | Stanley Cavell. *Conditions Handsome and Unhandsome: The Constitution of Emersonian Perfectionism.* Chicago: University of Chicago Press, 1990. |
| *CJ* | Immanuel Kant. *Critique of the Power of Judgment.* Edited by Paul Guyer. Translated by Paul Guyer and Eric Matthews. Cambridge: Cambridge University Press, 2000. |
| *CPPP* | Robert Frost. *Collected Poems, Prose, and Plays.* Edited by Richard Poirier and Mark Richardson. New York: Library of America, 1995. |
| *CPR* | Immanuel Kant. *Critique of Pure Reason.* Translated by Norman Kemp Smith. New York: St. Martin's Press, 1965. |
| *CR* | Stanley Cavell. *The Claim of Reason.* Oxford: Oxford University Press, 1979. |
| *CT* | Stanley Cavell. *Contesting Tears: The Hollywood Melodrama of the Unknown Woman.* Chicago: University of Chicago Press, 1996. |
| *CV* | Ludwig Wittgenstein. *Culture and Value.* Edited by G. H. von Wright with Heikki Nyman. Translated by Peter Winch. Chicago: University of Chicago Press, 1984. |
| *De orat* | Marcus Tullius Cicero. *De oratore.* 2 vols. Translated by E. W. Sutton. 1975. Reprint, Cambridge: Harvard University Press, 1979. |
| *Ethics* | Ludwig Wittgenstein. "A Lecture on Ethics." *The Philosophical Review* 74 (January 1965): 3–12. |
| Evans | William R. Evans, ed. *Robert Frost and Sidney Cox: Forty Years of Friendship.* Hanover, N.H.: University Press of New England, 1981. |

| | |
|---|---|
| GM | Kenneth Burke. *A Grammar of Motives.* Berkeley and Los Angeles: University of California Press, 1969. |
| *Interviews* | *Interviews with Robert Frost.* Edited by Edward Connery Lathem. New York: Holt, Rinehart, and Winston, 1966. |
| IQO | Stanley Cavell. *In Quest of the Ordinary: Lines of Skepticism and Romanticism.* Chicago: University of Chicago Press, 1994. |
| *Lectures* | Ludwig Wittgenstein. *Lectures and Conversations on Aesthetics, Psychology, and Religious Belief.* Compiled from notes taken by Yorick Smythies, Rush Rhees, and James Taylor. Edited by Cyril Bennet Berkeley. Berkeley and Los Angeles: University of California Press, n.d. |
| LLU | *The Letters of Robert Frost to Louis Untermeyer.* New York: Holt, Rinehart, and Winston, 1963. |
| MWM | Stanley Cavell. *Must We Mean What We Say?* Cambridge: Cambridge University Press, 1969. |
| NE | Aristotle. *Nichomachean Ethics.* Translated by David Ross. Revised by J. O. Urmson and J. L. Ackrin. Oxford: Oxford University Press, 1998. |
| NYUA | Stanley Cavell. *This New Yet Unapproachable America: Lectures after Emerson after Wittgenstein.* Albuquerque: Living Batch Press, 1989. |
| OC | Ludwig Wittgenstein. *On Certainty.* Edited by G. E. M. Anscombe and G. H. von Wright. Translated by Denis Paul and G. E. M. Anscombe. New York: Harper and Row, 1969. |
| PEL | Michel de Certeau. *The Practice of Everyday Life.* Berkeley and Los Angeles: University of California Press, 1984. |
| PI | Ludwig Wittgenstein. *Philosophical Investigations.* Translated by G. E. M. Anscombe. New York: Macmillan, 1953. |
| *Poetry* | *The Poetry of Robert Frost: The Collected Poems.* Edited by Edward Connery Lathem. New York: Henry Holt, 1969. |
| PP | *Robert Frost: Poetry and Prose.* Edited by Edward Connery Lathem and Lawrance Thompson. New York: Henry Holt, 1972. |
| *Rhet* | Aristotle. *On Rhetoric.* Edited and translated by George A. Kennedy. New York: Oxford University Press, 1991. |
| RM | Kenneth Burke. *A Rhetoric of Motives.* Berkeley and Los Angeles: University of California Press, 1950. |

| | |
|---|---|
| *RPP2* | Ludwig Wittgenstein. *Remarks on the Philosophy of Psychology.* Vol. 2. Edited by G. H. von Wright and Heikki Nyman. Translated by C. G. Luckhardt and M. A. E. Aue. Chicago: University of Chicago Press, 1980. |
| *SL* | *Selected Letters of Robert Frost.* Edited by Lawrance Thompson. New York: Holt, Rinehart, and Winston, 1964. |
| *SP* | *Selected Prose of Robert Frost.* Edited by Hyde Cox and Edward Connery Lathem. New York: Holt, Rinehart, and Winston, 1966. |
| *SW* | Stanley Cavell. *The Senses of Walden.* Expanded ed. Chicago: University of Chicago Press, 1992. |
| *Themes* | Stanley Cavell. *Themes Out of School: Effect and Causes.* Chicago: University of Chicago Press, 1984. |
| Thompson 1 | Lawrance Thompson. *Robert Frost: The Early Years, 1874–1915.* New York: Holt, Rinehart, and Winston, 1966. |
| Thompson 2 | Lawrance Thompson. *Robert Frost: The Years of Triumph, 1915–1938.* New York: Holt, Rinehart, and Winston, 1970. |
| Thompson 3 | Lawrance Thompson with R. H. Winnick. *Robert Frost: The Later Years: 1938–1963.* Holt, Rinehart, and Winston, 1976. |
| *TM* | Hans-Georg Gadamer. *Truth and Method.* 2d rev. ed. Translated by Joel Weinsheimer and Donald G. Marshall. New York: Continuum, 1993. |
| *Walden* | Henry D. Thoreau. *Walden.* Edited by J. Lyndon Shanley. Princeton: Princeton University Press, 1971. |
| *WV* | Stanley Cavell. *The World Viewed: Reflections on the Ontology of Film.* Enlarged edition. Cambridge: Harvard University Press, 1979. |
| *Zettel* | Ludwig Wittgenstein. *Zettel.* Edited by G.E.M. Anscombe and G. H. von Wright. Translated by G.E.M. Anscombe. Berkeley and Los Angeles: University of California Press, 1970. |

RHETORICAL INVESTIGATIONS

# INTRODUCTION

"To Speke of Wo That Is in Mariage."

ALL GOOD marriages are marriages of inconvenience—if by inconvenience we mean an ongoing willingness to take pains. Even a marriage that exists only on paper—that is, in words—if it is a good one, will often be trying. For better or worse, the union of rhetoric and philosophy framed in different ways in this book, a union widely celebrated and bemoaned of late across the arts and humanities under a variety of names—grammar and rhetoric, philosophy and literature, reason and desire, reference and semiotics, truth and antifoundationalism, nature and narrative—is complex and conflicted, and has been, as is well known, inconvenient for a very long time. In fact, notwithstanding rumors about last year's elopement of metaphor and epistemology, there has been a lover's quarrel between them from their distant, pre-Socratic beginnings, so that meddling once more in their affairs ought not to be taken to evince any illusion of critical daring on my part. On the contrary: as one of the prodigal issue of such parents myself, I am trying in this book to articulate "something more felt than known" (*SP* 45) about their home life, found (as it happens in my case) in the poetry of Robert Frost. In *Tolstoy or Dostoyevsky* (1959), George Steiner notes that "literary criticism should arise out of a debt of love," and so it has here, with the understanding that no code or formula can keep love from being inconvenient all around.[1]

On reflection, I see that I have written parts of this book after the manner of what Steiner, in the 1996 preface to the second edition of his first book, calls the "Old Criticism." My new Old Criticism combines aspects of an Empsonian interest in the verbal density of literary texts with attention to, on the one hand, the standard, everyday contextual uses and circumstances that all literary uses of language presuppose, and, on the other, the nonstandard, grammatical (philosophical) and rhetorical matters that help make some literature significant and for some people attractive. My sort of reading runs roughly parallel to what Richard Poirier has called "reading pragmatically," aiming at what contemporary phenomenological hermeneutics calls the practical meaning projected "in front of" the text, which I further take to align with, for example, "language games," "form of life," and the "everyday and ordinary" in Wittgenstein; with "art as experience" and "dramatic rehearsal" in Dewey and Gadamer; and with the "*sensus communis*" of the rhetorical tradition.

None of these positions, I should say up front, depends upon strictly defining the term "literature," if by strictly we mean identifying common empirical characteristics of texts across all cases falling under the term (even while we conveniently

marginalize bothersome exceptions). After Wittgenstein we know that much of our language, including many of our concepts, simply does not work by way of logical definition, ostensive or otherwise. In *Language, Thought, and Logic* (1993), John M. Ellis gives the wonderful example of the word "weed," a perfectly workable notion but one delimited by changeable criteria of preference and use rather than by fixed extensional properties belonging to all instances.[2] Similar efforts in post-Saussurean linguistics and philosophy, in contemporary rhetorical theory, and in related disciplines have arrived at results that approximate or complement Wittgenstein's well-known dictum, "Ask not for the meaning, but for the use" (*PI* § 43; also § 20, 120, 138, 179). In his earlier *The Theory of Literary Criticism* (1974), Ellis shows that we act, we use, we do things with what we have historically called literature, things that we do not do, for a variety of reasons and causes, with other modes of speech and language: "Whenever the ordinary [everyday] use of language to communicate to someone in a specific context is no longer evident, and the piece of language is no longer regarded as one having interest *only* for its original utterer, those addressed by him, and those (present or future) who have interest in the whole [original] situation, it is being treated as literature. And here, 'being treated as literature' means . . . actually 'established as a literary text': the class of literary texts is the class of those to which we respond in this way."[3]

This fails as a definition of a well-marked class since the content Ellis gives to "respond in this way" is noticeably minimal and vague—just as the diverse phenomenon that is "literature" requires, I will argue, if the account is to prompt inquiry rather than impose theoretical norms. In the present book, therefore, no more straightforward (or no less vague) an account will be necessary to distinguish literature from what is not literature.

To anticipate, consider several distinctions regarding language and literature to be developed in the four chapters comprising book 1 of the present volume. First, following the first part of *Philosophical Investigations* (1953), I will distinguish "ordinary language" from language that is not ordinary because it is used absolutely or metaphysically in traditional ways or, in the shadow of metaphysics, used skeptically in fairly radical ways, when language is said to be "idling" (*PI* § 132; cf. *OC* § 117), in the sense that its alleged meaning has no actual use, as ordinary language does, no traction, so to speak (*PI* § 107) in "this complicated form of life" of ours (*PI* p. 174).

Second, following the second part of Wittgenstein's book (on "seeing aspects" and "continuous seeing-as"), we can distinguish "standard" uses, featuring the "primary" meanings of ordinary words in specific contexts of use, from "nonstandard" uses and their "secondary" meanings. *Standard use* is practical use, directed to people's actions and intentions when they speak or write and to conventional techniques for using words for specific purposes. Standard use includes the criteria of our concepts and the circumstances in which they apply, and it ranges, in

turn, from "everyday" pursuits (shopping for apples, going to work, working at home, playing a game) to "noneveryday," let us say more specialized, pursuits of engaging complex matters of fact in the world (performing a biological experiment, measuring planetary motions, drafting federal regulations, testing for the presence of anthrax, and so on).

By contrast, *nonstandard use* ("secondary meanings"; "the *experience* of meaning"; *PI* pp. 214e–16e) differs from standard use in being directed *away* from empirical matters of fact *as empirical,* away from how things operate in the real world in order to effect quite different techniques.[4] The forms of nonstandard speech vary, as is well known, ranging from, for example, *ritual* uses of language in religious ceremonies to (our concern here) *grammatical* uses of language, for example, language as it is displayed in literary works or investigated in (certain kinds of) philosophy and literary criticism.

Anthony Cascardi's *The Bounds of Reason: Cervantes, Dostoyevsky, Flaubert* (1986) and James Guetti's *Wittgenstein and the Grammar of Literary Experience* (1993) offer lucid articulations of literature and literary criticism as nonstandard uses of ordinary language, as "grammatical displays" or performances of what Wittgenstein calls "secondary" meanings, which is another way of saying language prised apart from specific contexts and purposes aimed at matters of fact.[5] The philosopher Stephen Mulhall, a close student of Wittgenstein, Cavell, and Heidegger, among others, makes much the same point: "The original or primary employment of [a] term relates to questions of use and purpose, to the particular technique of using a word and the particular intentions of a speaker in a specific context; but in 'experiences of meaning,' words are uttered in isolation, forming no part of linguistic interchange and divorced from specific purposes—and yet we are inclined to use the word 'meaning' here too. Literature furnishes analogous experiences with language."[6] I will revisit these distinctions—especially that between empirical use and grammatical display or performance—in different contexts throughout this book, not so much "proving" their coherence philosophically as showing or displaying or performing their possibilities in poetry, philosophy, and criticism.

In an academic and cultural climate more or less inhospitable to such an emphasis on shared ordinary, practical, and grammatical matters, as distinct from more narrowly conceived empirical causes, pronounced political differences, and historicist conflicts, I offer in a modest way what Wittgenstein calls "reminders" of what is in circulation *before* it gets terminally theorized, reminders of how we speak, what the grammar of our language allows us to say, how we establish or project the senses of words, on what basis we know each other and express ourselves in the face of skepticism, and the nature and scope of human limits. Again, as one of the epigraphs to this book suggests, such reminding is less a matter of sheerly empirical recovery or polemic than of the "dawning of an aspect" and

"seeing-as" and "continuous meaning perception" (as in Wittgenstein's duck/rabbit stereogram). That is, we learn to recontextualize how we see objects and events of ordinary language, including some poems, and then more competently go on with what we have unwittingly been neglecting all along: "The problems are solved, not by giving new information, but by arranging what we have always known" (*PI* § 109).

For these reasons, the present book is more about exemplifying a specific kind of critical inquiry, interpretation, argument, and community activity than it is about a particular poet, historical trajectory, literary period, or cultural moment.[7] Frost's poems present me with an occasion to rethink a nexus of questions about the everyday and ordinary, language, experience, common sense, judgment, and exemplarity; to question our assumptions about the grammatical and rhetorical possibilities of literary criticism; and to reexamine what I take to be underappreciated resources for criticism to be found in the traditions of rhetoric, hermeneutic phenomenology, pragmatism, and so-called ordinary language philosophy and criticism.[8]

I expect this fact may frustrate experts within more than one field who will be impatient for me to get to their point. But then the value of ideas like the everyday and ordinary resides in part in their potential to act as "retardation devices," as stop signs whose repetition disrupts the drive toward theoretical acquisitiveness and the exploitation of intellectual capital.[9] Everyday matters remind us of our more commonly held responsibilities, and they can help temper the residual modernist disdain for ideas and images such as home, for the timely word *play*, for modest claims for the practical efficacy of literature, and for a better-balanced diet of reading. Were I to reduce my interests to a single question, it would be: What happened to rhetoric after romanticism? Such reduction, however, would be but a prolegomenon to the contemporary abundance, the rhetorician's (and romantic's) *copia*, of possibilities for rhetorical investigations across disciplines.

As a rhetorician myself, I approach philosophy off-center and awry, as do many academics these days. Many North American philosophers—among them Bernstein, Cavell, MacIntyre, Putnam, Rorty, Rosen, Taylor, and Toulmin—have, like many of their European counterparts, adjusted their discipline to a new axis of rotation around the concrete and particular. Although George Steiner is probably right to say that any notable work of literature at least implies a metaphysics, the deterministic Taine, in his essay on Balzac, laments the fact that most authors fail to achieve anything like a full philosophic vision. Yet I imagine that few of us are prepared to agree that the ideas of literature necessitate, in Lionel Trilling's words, either the "completeness" or the "*hardness*" of systematic thought."[10] Of course it all depends on what we mean by or what we want in something we might call "full vision" or "completeness" or "metaphysics" or "hardness." In Frost's *A Masque of Mercy* (1947), Job's wife is characteristically content (characteristic

for Frost) to inquire after "unsystematic / Stray scraps of palliative reason" (lines 141–42) to live by. What matters to me about Frost is that he manages to put into practice an unsystematic rhetorical metaphysics conceived as "equipment for living" (Kenneth Burke's terms—what Stanley Cavell calls "our transcendental impositions; *CR* 153), both within and against several currents of his time, which run still, in my view, in our own. This is a metaphysics whose chief virtue is rhetorical agility, an adaptability, even quickness, of connection—what was once known as mother-wit—rather than some supposed or imposed rigor or hardness.

The present work makes no attempt, then, to explore systematically the Frost oeuvre; this study must not be taken as complete or full in one ordinary sense. Instead, I have tried to select what Wittgenstein calls "perspicuous representations" (*PI* § 122) of Frost's own rhetorical and philosophical methods to enable others to go on with their own investigations of Frost and other writers, in prose as well as in poetry.[11] For better and for worse, this is teaching by example, not by doctrine, and hence it is fraught with the usual dangers of leading astray by an apparent randomness in the selections. Montaigne observes in his concluding essay, "Of Experience," that "tout exemple cloche" [every example limps], never quite manages to instantiate a determinate rule. Yet I think such an approach is necessary, as Frost, Trilling, Empson, and the early Steiner also believed, given the nature of the problems on the table. For his epigraph to *The Claim of Reason* (1979), Stanley Cavell cites Emerson in a similar spirit: "Truly speaking, it is not instruction, but provocation, that I can receive from another soul."

In addition to patience and an ear for verse, the rhetorical student of such blurred genres could use a sense of humor and an ear for the adverse, for one may fail to feel, as in a marriage or family, just when bonds are breaking and need to be bridged or when boundaries need to be reasserted or reimagined. All of the primary and most of the secondary dramatis personae in this book are amply supplied with all three. Frost possessed a Keatsian patience and was, like Montaigne, almost juvenile in his taste for trouble. What has been said of Mark Twain also applies to Frost: "His great gift was his humor, which was not simply a comic tactic but a vernacular clarity and moral skepticism which he could deploy against respectable Eastern pretension and moral convention."[12] "I suppose," Frost said in a lecture, "a poem is a kind of fooling" (*PP* 818), which fooling he also shrewdly meant to be a kind of—that is, kindred to—philosophic inquiry: "I myself, since forty, have had a great leaning toward the philosophy department" (*PP* 374).[13]

Similarly, Frost's cross-Atlantic near-contemporary Ludwig Wittgenstein worked on the premise that philosophy, which is not literature, could be written *both* as poetry and as jokes, and also as questions,[14] while yet another distant connection, Martin Heidegger, called for a "poetic thinking" that promised liberation from the metaphysical superseriousness of traditional philosophy. Back at home, although there is little of William James's charm or humor to be found in

the pragmatist philosopher John Dewey, nevertheless, in *Art as Experience* (1934), Dewey considered the consummations possible to art to be as happily freeing, satisfying, and instructive as those in everyday life, which he reported to be great. Also in 1934, the equally pragmatic, far more comedic Kenneth Burke himself brought poetic and philosophic ideas and methods together again, now under the sign of ancient tragedy ("dramatism") and the study of words ("logology")—additional variations on the romance of rhetoric, poetry, and philosophy. More recently, when Stanley Cavell ends *The Claim of Reason* by asking, "But can philosophy become literature and still know itself?" his pun on "become" is a kind of fooling to remind us that this marriage of minds has been something of a mismatch from the start. For that disjunctive "But" is the last of many hard knocks throughout Cavell's book, and the issues appear likely to remain contentious: "[T]he reader would have to ask himself or herself, 'Do I know what philosophy can—and cannot—do?'"[15] Do we always know when we encounter philosophy or what it looks like?

In these postmodern times, needless to say, not everyone has found intellectual occupation in this fashion nor embraced any one of the conflicting versions of this alliance (or dalliance). On the one hand, some insist on reading the tensions and tragedies between philosophy (reason, reference, proof) and rhetoric (language, literature, persuasion) less as signs of hope than of instability pointing down the road to divorce, when philosophy will shake off rhetoric like a loose woman or rhetoric slip out of philosophy's unfeeling grasp. In different ways, both the high modernists, such as Pound and Eliot, and a late-blooming rationalist, such as Yvor Winters, sought a historical or philosophic or theological rationale for poetry, and either condescended to or condemned Frost's poetic-rhetorical drift. More recently, historian John Patrick Diggins, who otherwise appreciates the role that rhetoric broadly conceived has played throughout the century in American pragmatist thought, nevertheless fears for the fate of history, facts, and our general ability to judge claims of any sort should these be superseded by the rhetorical, here meaning willfully interest-driven and strictly linguistic (Nietzschean, Rortyan) "redescriptions" of our being-in-the-world. For Diggins, as for Henry Adams before him, "modernism" betokens a "crisis of knowledge and authority" that a rhetoricized pragmatism has not resolved and never will.[16] And while philosophers Newton Garver and Seung-Chong Lee embrace a "philosophy based on rhetoric" rather than on logic, even they hesitate when Stanley Cavell elevates what appears to them to be baggy rhetorical texts over crisper philosophic problems.[17] On the other hand, on behalf of those for whom it is *rhetoric* and *narrative*—the local and linguistically indeterminate—that is in need of being protected from an abusive ontotheological metaphysics, it may be sufficient to cite Richard Rorty's suggestion, similar to those made by Stanley Fish and others, to the effect that we consider the philosophic enterprise annulled and get on with our practical

lives, that is, with edifying conversations directed to our own human (if only local) solidarity.

Of course, it may happen that philosophy and rhetoric are rent asunder yet again, or that one is allowed to control the other, in the way (for example) that a destabilizing rhetoric still tends to drive literary theory and criticism in much deconstructive, new historicist, and related cultural studies. On the other hand, I am suggesting that those in the various camps just mentioned are quietly being challenged by others who, perhaps more patient, would bring aspects or versions of philosophy and rhetoric into closer—which is to say more equally helpful and respectful—union. Part of my previous contribution to this cooperative competition or competitive cooperation between rhetoric and reason, belief and authority, concentrated on John Henry Newman. For it was just this neglected and unlikely figure who offered the first modern(ist) turn of the rhetorical wheel away from romantic universalism, preceding even Kierkegaard and Nietzsche.[18] In an earlier book, I worked out Newman's use of Aristotelian practical philosophy and Ciceronian rhetoric to inform what the nineteenth century called "philosophy" in the round (theology, science, history, literature, education). My aim was twofold: (1) to use the history of rhetorical philosophy, what Eugene Garver terms "the history of prudence," to illuminate Newman's thought, and Newman's thought to illuminate the history of rhetoric, and (2) to describe the ways in which one nonprofessionalized philosopher and theologian cast apprehension, inference, and assent as means of facing the crisis of belief toward the end of the nineteenth century.[19]

In this book, I am interested in how a philosophically minded poet—one with rhetorical tools, problems, and strategies similar to Newman's—faces that same crisis of belief and culture (even as he demystifies claims about crisis) at the beginning of the twentieth century. Because neither literary theory generally nor even the main line of Frost criticism in particular has undertaken to coordinate Frost's interests in poetry and philosophy in anything resembling the ways, much less at the depth they have for Stevens, Eliot, and others, I try to give evidence that, and to make evident how, the likes of Wittgenstein, Kenneth Burke, and Stanley Cavell extend in the twentieth century the rhetorical investigations of figures such as Emerson and Newman in the nineteenth, with the poet Robert Frost as one possible middle term connecting the extremes. If we take literature (here poetry) and philosophy as the termini of our discussion, then *rhetoric* becomes a new middle term, inasmuch as it is rhetoric's ability to *find* (invent) "middle terms" of various sorts that others may come to acknowledge as the *ligamen* connecting extremes.[20]

It follows from such a twinned vision (poetry as philosophy, philosophy as poetry) that I do not intend this book exclusively for students of Frost's poetry, or of modern poetry, literature, philosophy, or rhetoric. I do, of course, aim to contribute directly to the study of Frost in several ways. First, I intend to help repair

what DiBattista and McDiarmid identify as the breach between "high" culture and "the raw energies of common, ordinary life" as these are distributed in what I call literary low modernism.[21] Second, my version of rhetorical criticism can contribute to what Rita Felski and other feminist theorists see as the inadequate theorizing of modernity, in the present case by indicating what Frost rather uniquely contributes to the age.[22] And third, I offer new rhetorical-philosophical readings and aesthetic estimates of Frost's achievement in some of his most subtle yet powerful poems.

That said, however, I am equally on the lookout for ways to juxtapose, to project the senses of certain critical terms—in Wittgenstein's phrase, to "go on" with—certain matters of thought and belief across literary, cultural, and rhetorical disciplines, in what was once called a liberal arts, or humanistic, education, laying out what Wittgenstein calls some of the "'*possibilities*' of [the] phenomena" (*PI* § 90) of philosophy, rhetoric, and literature. In doing so I extend the concerns of my previous work, showing what an expansive, contemporary sense of rhetorical thought looks like and can do, in a manner that will, I hope, interest some readers no matter what academic discipline or intellectual premises they happen to call home.

### Ordinary Language Criticism

Said another way, this book might be considered a contribution to the indeterminate area of studies Ezra Pound once alluded to as "logopoetics," that Angus Fletcher inaugurates, more recently, as "noetics" (Gr. *noein,* to think), that Gary Saul Morson, Caryl Emerson, and others widen further as "prosaics,"[23] and that Kenneth Dauber and I elsewhere have called "ordinary language criticism," loosely derived from so-called ordinary language philosophy.[24]

For Fletcher, "*Noetics* names the field and the precise activity occurring when the poet introduces thought as a discriminable dimension of the form and meaning of a poem. . . . [Noetics] shows us how thoughts, ideas, reflections, memories, judgments, intuitions, and visions are involved in the fundamental process of the making of the poem."[25] For Morson and Emerson, the unnoticed speech and actions of our everyday practices are easily overlooked by theorists intent on establishing systemic causal connections. As a result, "what [such] methods fail to see is the rich texture of prosaic life that conditions everything about the [literary] work, from its language, to its 'devices,' to its complex layers of meaning."[26] What then of the kind of ordinary language criticism practiced here?

In the tradition of ordinary language philosophy, particularly as it is continued by Cavell, we learn concepts against an existential background form of life—in Erich Auerbach's phrase, we learn things "fraught with background"[27]—not, that is, by logical definitions (which have their own uses in our language games) but by situated criteria, the features and functions of things, the behaviors and actions of people in certain circumstances in which we operate with our words.

Traditionally, philosophy has asked how a world "is," or how a world so much as comes to be conceived, what its "conditions" are, or what the powers and limits of understanding must be. Cavell reminds us that conditions etymologically signify what we *speak-with*, the ordinary language with which we articulate a world and ourselves. Cavell further argues that criteria come to an end, that they establish identity, not existence—hence they can not defeat, yet need not succumb to, skepticism. And so Cavell, in extending Wittgenstein, suggests that the truth of our fundamental concepts—not just what they are or mean but whether we are to take them as real (since criteria alone cannot determine that)—depends less on notions of knowledge than on what we accept or "acknowledge."

Ordinary language philosophy thus differs from theory construction in the sciences to the extent that the latter, unlike philosophy, extends largely empirical claims about what something is, how it developed, its agency, how it works, what its real-life consequences are likely to be, and so on.[28] Ordinary language philosophy adds nothing to such methods and results but rather shows how they are possible by displaying the structure of the grammar out of which they arise in the first place. Hence ordinary language philosophy (and thus criticism) also differs from contemporary cultural critique *to the extent* that such critique is theoretical and/or directed to explanation alone rather than to an "aesthetic" (grammatical-rhetorical) appreciation and criticism of language, of which explanations may play only a small part. Both theory and cultural criticism ultimately sanction their fundamental concepts through philosophical considerations of *some* kind; hence they may (must) be scrutinized from the position, for Cavell, of ordinary language philosophy. But note well that "philosophy" here has pretenses to no authority beyond *ourselves*. Thus Cavell's own uses of Rousseau and Freud, for example, are philosophically somewhat generic (grammatical), *not* empirical and theoretical, which is to say that Cavell appeals to how certain concepts work in a given time and place, in a human form of life.

It follows that ordinary language criticism of, for example, literary works, in being consistent though not necessarily coextensive with ordinary language philosophy, uses the critical methods of the latter in addition to its own methodologies in order to illuminate a range of operations: from study of fundamental philosophic problems, to study of the phenomena of language as these concern the cultural ramifications of fundamental concepts, to examination of grammatical, rhetorical, logical, and dialectical communicative transactions and their relationships to ordinary language in everyday life. Fletcher includes these and similar matters under the activity of "thinking the poem":

> Thinking the poem implies such things as taking the poem as an occasion for thought; thinking through the poem; being aware of one's thoughts as one reads the poem; looking for some logic in the poem; allowing the poem

to trigger certain lines of thought; looking in the poem for what Coleridge called its "implicit metaphysic"; asking if what one is experiencing is Heidegger's "what is called thinking"; thinking about whether the poem is getting one to think.[29]

The purpose of such study is aesthetic in a broad way, meaning that an ordinary language critic seeks, following Kant (in my case, by way of Dewey and Gadamer), to articulate communal grounds of judgment regarding the meaning and quality (the "beauty" in an extended sense) of an experienced artifact or event or performance. It is this last move—the turn to an aesthetics grounded in ordinary language and to "exemplary knowledge"[30]—that makes ordinary language criticism something other than a nostalgic return to romantic expressivism or New Critical formalism. In ordinary language criticism, as Wittgenstein puts it, "aesthetics and ethics are one and the same,"[31] meaning not that important differences do not distinguish the discourses of the two but rather that both derive from ordinary language and ordinary life, hence must be returned to them, as it were, above all in scholarship and in teaching. Dewey puts this succinctly: "Domestic utensils, furnishings of tent and house, rugs, mats, jars, pots, bows, spears, were wrought with such delighted care that today we hunt them out and give them places of honor in our art museums. Yet in their own time and place, such things were enhancements of the processes of everyday life."[32]

It should come as no surprise, then, that ordinary language criticism names an array of critical practices, not a determinate set of principled theories or methods. For it investigates literary thinking across or askew to fields and theoretical specialisms, attending to the background complexity of everyday life and ordinary language as they shape the form and content of literary works.[33] In addition to Morson, Fletcher, and others, critics as diverse (and now relatively neglected) as William Empson, Kenneth Burke, and Paul Goodman were all "ordinary language critics" intent on various aspects of the extraordinary complexity in literary uses of ordinary language.

More specifically, the present book studies modes of *rhetorical* thinking and their sometimes unique social locations and uses. Of course my title, *Rhetorical Investigations*, is intended to recall Wittgenstein's *Philosophical Investigations*,[34] although the two can differ in their intended orientation and scope in several ways. Philosophical investigations explore the context-dependent criteria and grammar of our concepts, seeking to evoke and to question "general norms" (*MWM* 32), as well as to show the possibilities of new meanings and uses by flushing out our grammatical (conceptual) confusions and errors. The effort aims at earning what Wittgenstein called "peace" from doing philosophy and what Frost called "a momentary stay against confusion": "peace" or a "stay against confusion" because the confusion disappears and we are again attuned with each other and our

world; "momentary," because criteria belong to language games and form of life, and both change.³⁵ Rhetorical investigations stand closer to unique circumstances of action and language use, are more fluid in their persuasive argumentation, more keyed to the variety of discursive practices, and more focused on problems of communication, with the aim of enriching our common sense of the complexity of our conceptual and imaginative webs of possibility and judgment.

In spite of these differences, the area of overlap between rhetoric and philosophy is finally crucial, I believe, to an understanding of either kind of investigation, since each conceptually involves the other. Philosophic grammar possesses an inalienable rhetorical dimension, for it investigates words/concepts *in use,* in ordinary language bonded both to more specialized, nonstandard practices (for example, art) as well as to their everyday contexts. Rhetoric, in turn, presupposes complex grammars involving changing conceptual criteria and rules, examples and prototypes, categories and their rough zones of meaning, and an "order" or "ordering" as a continuing moral project that allows for centrifugal social and linguistic forces against order. And both grammatical and rhetorical investigations are ordinary rather than traditionally metaphysical, theoretically principled, or scientifically empirical. The terms and concepts of rhetorical investigations are not fetishized or reified beyond all contrasts; nor imposed onto experience from without, as a requirement; nor found as if ready-made within experience—not, at least, to the extent that we reader-participants are willing to acknowledge. And for this, again, there is no convenient formula or fixed protocol.³⁶

The image that Conrad's narrator in *Heart of Darkness* offers to evoke the relation of story and meaning in Marlowe's tale—"a glow that brings out a haze"—is not inappropriate to the grammatical and rhetorical investigations of ordinary language criticism, for the contextual background that each provides for the other eventually becomes the warrant for our attention while still remaining a mist or haze. Dewey says that "to the being fully alive, the future is not ominous but a promise; it surrounds the present as a halo."³⁷ Stanley Cavell calls Emerson's prose "a kind of mist or fog" (*NYUA* 78). And Thoreau says our words are perspiration off a body (*Walden* 325), as it were the glowing haze illuminating and blinding human beings hovering between abstract codes, rules, and dicta (reflective theory) and concrete facts and actions (practice). While the poet Derek Walcott rightly describes Frost's poetry as "pragmatic and commonplace as a Dutch interior," what has been said about the painter Pieter Bruegel's oxymoronic and skeptical *Children's Games*—that it is as preoccupied with the everyday and ordinary as it is with play—is apposite to Frost's poems: "The painting's 'aboutness' can be made manifest, but only as the tacit dimension of an inquiry that keeps producing what Blake calls 'particular knowledge.'"³⁸

(Something like the negative of this picture is present within those interior, bright-dark adult games perpetrated by Vladimir Nabokov, one of whose narrators'

destructive flailings against Haze [Delores: "Lo-lee-ta"] is summarized by fellow-novelist Martin Amis: "Humbert's sin is biological, a sin against the ordinary. He has made ordinary biology impossible: marriage, childbirth, a daughter, ordinary happiness, ordinary health."[39])

In a similar vein, the philosopher Ludwig Wittgenstein notes: "Perhaps what is inexpressible (what I find mysterious and am not able to express) is the background against which what I could express has its meaning" (*CV* 16e), a remark that helps to explain his insatiable desire for "perspicuous representations."[40] And so Frost: "The background in hugeness and confusion shading away from where we stand into black and utter chaos; and against the background any small man-made figure of order and concentration. What pleasanter than that this should be so?" (*SP* 107). Among others, these Tolstoyan sentiments stand behind everything that interests me here.

## Trivial Pursuit

> It's knowing what to do with things that counts
> "At Woodward's Gardens"

To investigate commonplace matters—which is to say not settled beliefs so much as shared resources out of which contested beliefs arise—we will need to reflect on our own everyday life, to occupy as it were a middle position between the *sensus communis* of a community and its traditions on the one hand and its exemplifications, descriptions, contradictions, and corrections in art, philosophy, criticism, and the like on the other. To do this rhetorically, we need to select and organize (to "invent") critical terms and to generate topical catalogs of skepticism and belief, of American literary modernism and its sense of crisis, of Frost's interest in home and being-away-from-home, and of a variety of related matters. And to accomplish these ends, we need a working sense of what "rhetoric" signifies as well as some sort of schema capable of organizing new terms—or new meanings for old terms—suitable for elucidating Frost's rhetorical approach to a poetry of the everyday and ordinary. These tasks I take up in turn here.

If we glance momentarily at a hundred pages or so of Kenneth Burke's *A Rhetoric of Motives* (1950), we get not only the handiest brief description but perhaps the closest thing in our own time to a recognizably Ciceronian "oratory" or rhetoricized philosophy (itself rooted in the Greek sophistic thought of Isocrates and the skepticism of Sextus Empiricus), now appropriately reinvented in response to radical philosophical as well as historical and social changes in modern times.[41] If we consider rhetoric as a first-order discursive activity for influencing attitude (belief) or action in indeterminate matters (*rhetorica utens*), as well as a second-order reflection on the nature and scope of such first-order discourse (*rhetorica*

*docens*), its contemporary dimensions become easier to identify. Burke provides an introductory summary of the rhetorical motive wherever it may appear: "persuasion, exploitation of opinion . . . a work's nature as addressed, literature for use . . . verbal deception . . . the 'agonistic' generally . . . formal devices, the art of proving opposites (as 'counterpart' of dialectic)" (*RM* 64). This is all familiar enough, falling in line with Aristotle's distinctions between the art of rhetoric and other arts (for example, dialectic) and the art of rhetoric and principled subject matters, probable or apodictic (for example, ethics and politics, psychology, metaphysics). By the time Burke has finished his little handbook, however, the nature and scope of ancient and traditional rhetorical studies have been so transformed—so inextricably entangled in his previous *Grammar of Motives* (1945) concerned with substance and identity, and (in the last section of *A Rhetoric of Motives*, on "Order") anticipating the later logological-dialectical studies of *The Rhetoric of Religion* (1961)—that any local "art" or "craft" of rhetoric as simple persuasion has long since given way to studies of the ways *all* linguistic acts of understanding and interpretation are tied to the practical interests and values of people.[42]

For Burke, the meanings achieved through grammatical-rhetorical "identification" now subsume "persuasion" as rhetoric's architectonic principle ("Wherever there is persuasion, there is rhetoric. And wherever there is 'meaning,' there is 'persuasion'"; *RM* 172), which involves at least the following: (1) our active identifying the nature (or "properties") of some situation, action, person, event—some indeterminacy—from a given evaluative and always temporal, even everyday, perspective, as when one calls modern philosophical skepticism a "crisis"; (2) our organizing our own moral growth in terms of such identifications, that is, identifying ourselves with those identifications, as when a modern crisis of reason and belief becomes *my* crisis, or at least the scene of my response; (3) our recognizing that such identifications create disagreement and discord between ourselves and others in a specific time and place, as when Frost resists the high modernist account of his cultural moment *as* a crisis; and (4) our attempting, in our efforts to identify some person, situation, event, problem, to get others to identify *their* interests—hence their identities or moral and political characters (however fragmented they may be)—with our own, even if we, or they, do so without conscious intent, as when Cavell and Wittgenstein rechristen the crisis of reason and belief as a constitutive part of the finite human being's predicament in the world.[43] In an ongoing dialectic of merger and division, universal and particular, the one and the many, persuasion and refutation, "You persuade a man only insofar as you can talk his language by speech, gesture, tonality, order, image, attitude, idea, identifying your ways with his" (*RM* 55).[44]

To persuade a person one needs to talk her language, but to analyze persuasive identifications one needs a method to talk about that talk. Rhetoric is such a method, so long as we include not only the history of the discipline as it is conventionally

written but the widespread uses to which that method has been put throughout history as an intellectual, even architectonic, means of thought and judgment. In the latter sense, as architectonic method, rhetorical thinking in any subject matter field is used to discriminate different plausible perspectives on any topic and to arrive at specific and general judgments, however provisional. For the purpose of structuring the present work, therefore, I propose to borrow the traditional, broad discriminations of the liberal arts—namely *grammar, rhetoric, logic,* and *dialectic*—and to repostulate these terms, now as an ordered schema of rhetorical topoi that can open new areas of thought and new lines of argument to explore everyday life and talk as these reappear in the poems of Robert Frost.[45] (Analytically separable, all four of these arts may be, of course, operative at any one time in a given poem.)

In investigating Frost in this way I am engaged in a "trivial pursuit," recalling trivial or commonplace matters (etymologically, *"trivium"* signified the intersection of three roads, where people meet) and rethinking parts of the ancient trivium of grammar, rhetoric, and logic/dialectic for contemporary use.[46] I propose that the traditional arts of discourse can be rediscovered in Frost as both problematic areas of everyday action and as intellectual and linguistic abilities held in common (though hardly equally) by ordinary people outside of technical or specialized pursuits. Thus *grammar* can help us to specify the particular grounds of, the "judgments" underwriting, human life in a certain place and time and the general means by which speakers organize conceptual parts into wholes. *Rhetoric* can show us the specific circumstances surrounding our acts and words and the ways we invent new words and actions in new circumstances.[47] *Logic* can lead us to particular sequences of people's words and actions and to the general gestalt patterns that connect actions to other actions, beliefs to further beliefs, judgments to further judgments. And *dialectic* can help us to see how people, how *we,* cohere in communities or fail to, how we participate in the ordering of the ordinary or are prevented from or fail at doing so. For expository purposes, and because it is the architectonic principle ordering this book, I start with rhetoric here, even while the book begins and ends with the questions of dialectic, that is, of order and community.

Rhetoric: Invention

In the classical tradition of Aristotle and Cicero, *heuresis,* or *inventio*—often translated in the Renaissance as "investigation"—is the primary office or task of rhetoric. In order for a speaker to persuade, he or she must first become aware of the particulars of some problematic situation to speak about, including an audience involved enough in the problem and its resolution to speak to. When the process is controlled, becoming aware is creative or inventive rather than merely reactive or serendipitous because, while there may be innumerable facts at hand,

just what those facts are and mean, how to demonstrate their connections to issues and values, which positions are most probable to the speaker and audience, which should be changed or substituted—these and related matters must be sorted out, formulated, and interpreted by marshalling a variety of rhetorical prompts or "reminders" known as topics (*topoi*, lit. "places") or commonplaces *(loci communes)*. Topics are discursive means of provisionally organizing relatively indeterminate facts, premises, and myriad other considerations to justify a claim (if only retrospectively) or otherwise lead someone to "get" or "see" something in a way that others do, or might, contest. Topics are "headings" or "regions" that organize these materials, although for the purposes of my own investigations, a distinction needs to be drawn here. The difference is that between (1) "formal" topics as *forms or patterns of inference* (for example, argument from genus, species, cause, effect, division, opposites, related things, and many others) common to most argumentation;[48] and (2) "material" (substantive) common topics *(koina)* and, more important, "special" topics *(eide)*, that is, historically situated sources from which semantic content can be drawn to argue and amplify persuasively. The latter are funded social categories, specific to certain subject matters or interests and constantly replenished by new funds and new uses.[49]

Used to organize that largely inexpressible, everyday background of "circumstances" *(Umstände)* that Wittgenstein so frequently speaks of, "first-stage" topics operate without artful or even conscious control, part of our natural standing background. When organized and made available, however, by rhetorical theorists and other thinkers in subject-matter fields, "second-stage" topics of the sort that concern me (in particular, material, special topics), though they have taken changing and often perplexing forms throughout the ages with no two lists exactly the same, provide discursive resources for invention.[50] Francis Bacon follows Aristotle and Cicero in construing topics as I will throughout these investigations, as "place[s] for inquiry and invention." Topics serve for recollecting or reminding ourselves of what we rightly or wrongly already say or value or believe, useful in public argumentation and solitary thought alike for discovering what to say, or not say, or confute, in a specific case.[51] In Vico's *On the Study Methods of Our Times* (1708), "traditional 'topics' is the art of finding 'the *medium*,' i.e., the middle term: in the conventional language of scholasticism, 'medium' indicates what the Latins call *argumentum*."[52] For Vico, it is not inference as such but rather the ability to establish *connections* among thoughts, statements, and acts that is central in rhetoric, an ability that eventually becomes second nature: "Those who know all the *loci*, i.e., the lines of argument to be used, are able (by an operation not unlike reading the printed elements on a page) to grasp extemporaneously the elements of persuasion inherent in any question or case."[53]

In fact, Vico too, much like Boethius in the Middle Ages, is following Cicero (and Quintilian), for whom invention is "the development of loci, their amplification,

and the graceful *connections* made in it among the particulars of the case."⁵⁴ His method also resembles that of Erasmus, who, "however severe the split of reality[,] made every effort to find a middle link that would throw a bridge across the gap. The discovery of a connection between opposites established some kind of similarity and [raised] the possibility of rapprochement. . . . With a third element inserted between two previously exclusive sides, the static structure of opposition yielded to a dynamic pattern of development, whereby the middle now functioned as progress between start and finish."⁵⁵ Over the last two centuries, however, topics in general have all but disappeared in rhetorical studies in favor of more determinate (logical or scientific) means of arguing, and in the last two decades, they have been displaced altogether in literary discussions of rhetoric by Derrida's and others' Nietzschean concerns with conceptual binaries and tropes. In "The Rhetoric of Temporality," it is well known, Paul de Man perceives an antinomy in romantic rhetoric between a purportedly stable symbol and a pervasive and unstable allegory ultimately aligned with tropes, above all irony. In de Man's view, all of us are constrained to subordinate systematic or traditional topoi to the service of those disorienting and disruptive figures and tropes.⁵⁶ Against what I want to suggest is most important in the rhetorical tradition, de Man reduces "rhetoric" to an unstable figurality in which binary topics and proofs ("ideas") are subordinated to and subsumed by tropes and figures ("images").

Less well known is that Kenneth Burke travels a parallel but considerably different route from de Man.⁵⁷ Burke too explores the interplay of "idea" and "image" but in a manner consistent with the pragmatic bent of the rhetorical tradition rather than the metaphysical turn of romantic expressivism and its reversal in some forms of the reactionary skepticism of much deconstruction, or the dogmatic commitments of much Marxist and psychoanalytic theorizing. Burke writes: "In keeping with the genius of Hazlitt's expression, 'ideas of the imagination,' we began thinking that there should be a term for ideas and images both. 'Titles' (or 'epithets') seemed to meet the requirement. For the rhetorician uses 'titles' (either imaginal or ideological) to *identify* a person or a cause with whatever kinds of things will, in his judgment, call forth the desired response. He will select such titles in accordance with the bias of his intention and the opinions of his audience. But what are such titles (or 'entitlings' or 'identifications') but another term for the Aristotelian 'topics,' which shift so easily and imperceptibly between ideas and images that you wonder how the two realms could ever come to be at odds?" (*RM* 86; my emphasis).⁵⁸ In this view, topics are not mere memory places whose images enable systematic storing of information, as de Man suggests, nor are they exclusively generators of commonsense opinions *(doxa)* and probable arguments *(endoxa)*. Rather they are intellectual means of identification that open onto diverse problems, ranging from urgently practical to philosophical, and diverse materials, extending from concepts and arguments whose purpose it

is to support claims and whose excellence is *phronesis* or *prudentia*, to images, tropes, and figures whose purpose it is to evoke or "show forth" *(epi-deixis)* thought, including the temporal grounds of thought, and whose excellence is not *phronesis* but *kairos*, the "appropriateness" and "timeliness" of situated speech. In order to stay close to Frost's *substantive* rather than more strictly inferential or logical interests, therefore, and in order to avoid *listing* generic formal topics ahead of time in favor of concentrating on what Frost actually says and does, my chief focus throughout is both "inductive" invention via comparisons, as in Frost's "Leaves Compared with Flowers" in chapter 2, and "ratiocinative" invention via special topics, as in all of the extended analyses in book 2.[59]

A further, equally neglected way to conceive of rhetorical invention as a connective power irreducible to nature or artifice or genius alone but importantly related to all three is to recall that *"ingenium,"* Vico's term for imagination, reaches back to Renaissance conceptions of wit, and specifically to what C. S. Lewis calls "wit-*ingenium*."[60] Wit-*ingenium* is not the knack for "ingenious jokes" of the sort that appear in much eighteenth-century verse (Lewis calls this sort of thing "wit-demoted"; we might identify it as the clever shit that Frost is rightly lampooned for sometimes stepping into: the ordure of the ordinary). Nor is wit-*ingenium* an account of what goes on in the creative mind or imagination (*PI* § 196). Rather, it is the ability to *find* what is at stake in a discussion, to *negotiate* resemblances or "connectives" for *this* particular group, at *this* time, in *this* place. It is, or should be, a central category of description for Frost's work, for it is a marker distinguishing his version of modernism from virtually all others, as Frost himself suggested in his 1960 *Paris Review* interview with Richard Poirier: "Somebody has said that poetry among other things is the marrow of wit. That's probably way back somewhere—marrow of wit. There's got to be wit. And that's very, very much left out of this labored [high modernist] stuff" (*CPPP* 890).

For Frost, emotions in poetry "must be dammed back and harnessed by discipline to the wit mill" (*CPPP* 807), a witty enough expression transforming the experiential stream of perception into the grinding work of making one's daily bread. Frost's image, in other words (like Burke's account), presents a *continuum* of inner and outer forces: the enthusiasm inherent in the mill stream is met with the deliberated resistance of the mill, resistance that transforms natural energy into a poetic product by way of a middle term, the contrived mechanism of the millstone and mill wheel. This is an ironic image, I take it, clearly at variance, for example, with Wordsworth's quasi-metaphysical "emotions recollected in tranquility" and all the more with Pope's "what oft was thought." The millstone/mill wheel is at once an ancient apparatus and an operation whose effect turns on (in the senses of "requires," "electrifies," as in a turbine, and "turns against") the *copia* of natural resources. The image is apt, I think, for what Cicero and Vico had in mind when speaking of the operations (including the political) of rhetoric in art.

In other words, the central expression here is that easily overlooked prepositional phrase "by discipline" ("dammed back and harnessed by discipline to the wit mill"). For discipline looks to an outward set of activities of constructing machines, harnessing natural forces, negotiating social conditions of time, space, buyers and sellers, and so on.

### Grammar: Judgment ("We Use Judgments as Principles of Judgments")

The weakness in relying on invention alone to prop up rhetorical (or poetic, or philosophical) theorizing is not that there is no end to what might be invented or posited but rather that, paradoxically, there can be no beginning. This is because invention alone possesses no means to discriminate among the possible middle terms one might locate—that is, to tell what counts and what doesn't count in a real or fictional world. Invention in some contemporary cultural theorizing has become a blindman's buff, or bluff. Jean-François Lyotard asserts that "one judges without criteria" and that judgment itself resolves into "the power to invent criteria."[61] But such claims presuppose all sorts of conceptual criteria and stand or fall according to something other than imagination and will, as Lyotard himself seems to allow in aligning himself with Aristotle's ethical thought.[62] He means, in other words, without *definitive* or fixed and unequivocal criteria. As Nelson Goodman has put the point: "The many stuffs—matter, energy, waves, phenomena—that worlds are made of are made along with the worlds. But made from what? Not from nothing, after all, but from other worlds. Worldmaking as we know it always starts from worlds already on hand; the making is a remaking."[63] For the purpose of stabilizing my own rhetorical thinking theoretically, therefore, "invention" presupposes something to operate on and with, and a situation within which to bring it to a (provisional, momentary) end, so that I am constrained to inquire into rhetoric's materials—that is, the *logoi*, the language and concepts—used to invent in the first place or to conclude at all. In the rhetorical tradition deriving chiefly from Cicero, topical invention works on the *copia verborum ac rerum*, the "storehouse" of words and things in the collective memory of a group—its *sensus communis*—and aims at a conclusion or judgment.[64] Rhetorical investigations, in short, are stabilized in the *sense* of a community, and the question becomes what it means to use or trust that sense or senses (cf. *SW*).

Of course, merely to assert that it is somehow obvious (common sense) that what is called common sense is important, true, useful; or, conversely, that skepticism of (say) material objects is "excessive" just because people naturally live their lives unskeptically and because, after all, our senses must be "trusted" in order to formulate doubt at all, begs all of the big questions, as Cavell has noted (*CR* 134). Wittgenstein states the issue succinctly: "There is no common sense answer to a philosophical problem" (*BBB* 58–59). The temptation to attack common sense derived, in Wittgenstein's view, from traditional philosophers' conviction that their

own principles and methods could *correct* the perceived incompetence of common sense, for example, its variability, contradictoriness, vagueness; for Wittgenstein, what Emerson called "the common, familiar and low"—what Wittgenstein refers to as the everyday and ordinary—appeals to how a *network* of beliefs and real-life practices go together in how we speak. The temptation to defend common sense directly, so to speak, by listing its (allegedly) universal contents—as Thomas Reid attempted to do in the eighteenth century in reaction to Hume's skeptical attack on common sense—derived, understandably but misguidedly, from the felt unfairness of the attack.[65]

In fact, neither position held: traditional philosophy could not sustain its own attack on common sense and the everyday and ordinary in the face of advances in anthropological linguistics, anthropology, and other fields, while eighteenth-century and later philosophic defenses of common sense played into their opponents' hands by contradictorily insisting that we do "know" (or can, anyway, achieve "moral certainty" about) what nevertheless could not, in the event, be logically proved.[66] For his part, Wittgenstein reacted against the Scottish common sense philosophy of Reid and G. E. Moore, both of whom fought Humean skepticism by offering, after the fashion of traditional rhetoricians, *"lists"* of foundational truths—for example, that there is a world beyond our bodies; that every event has a cause; that moral judgments are not merely expressions of personal preference; that "this is my hand"; that there are other human beings in the world besides myself.[67] In this regard, we may emphasize that Wittgenstein was *not* a traditional defender of common sense, if by that term we mean either a community's general beliefs or some laundry list of alleged foundational truths. As Kant expressed it, "For what is [common sense] but an appeal to the opinion of the multitude, of whose applause the philosopher is ashamed, while the popular charlatan glories and confides in it?"[68] Unlike Kant, however—or rather, unlike the Kant of the first two *Critiques* and like Kant, but far exceeding him, in the third *Critique*—Wittgenstein *does* defend common sense, after a fashion, as linguistically transcendental, doing so under the provisions of his interest in "ordinary language" and our experience in a form of life: "One can defend common sense against the attacks of philosophers only by solving their puzzles, i.e., by curing them of the temptation to attack common sense; not by restating the views of common sense" (*BBB* 58–59; *CR* 33–34).[69] But how, then, does one "defend" common sense in the absence of knock-down logic or, in any case, *some* kind of proof?

## Logic (Proof): "A Better Wildness of Logic"

The problem I am tracking here is caught by another American *grammaticus-rhetoricus*, Stanley Cavell: "My interest, it could be said, lies in finding out what my beliefs mean, and learning the particular ground they occupy. This is not the same as providing evidence for them. One could say it is a matter of making

them evident" (*MWM* 241). "In such a context," in Nelson Goodman's terms, "I am not so much stating a belief or advancing a thesis or a doctrine as proposing a categorization or scheme of organization, calling attention to a way of setting our nets to capture what may be significant likenesses and differences."[70] Both providing evidence for and making evident are matters of logic in certain senses, but Cavell is suggesting that we need to extend the concept of proof from syllogistic inference or truth-functional logic to seeing and evoking patterns in disparate phenomena, as in metaphors, examples, parables, artworks, jokes, and projections of concepts. Elsewhere he observes: "Before giving a name to [Emerson's and Thoreau's] foreign rigor I have at least to indicate some way to avoid, or postpone, a standing and decisive consideration that professional philosophers will have for refusing to hear out an articulation of the intuition that Emerson and Thoreau warrant the name of philosophy—the consideration that no matter what one may mean by, say, conceptual accuracy, a work like *Walden* has nothing in it to call *arguments*" (*IQO* 14). This aligns with Wittgenstein's resistance, in the *Philosophical Investigations*, to the standing temptation to want to clean up a messy reality by imposing idealized concepts or calculi onto what is grammatically indeterminate and contingent. Grammar itself is not rule-governed but rather a matter of judgment predicated on our ability to "see" what is what in specific cases. The criteria of many of our concepts, in other words, are relatively stable and recognizable without, however, being abstractable from the situation and its (relevant) circumstances, themselves a function in part of the innumerable other concepts in play in any determination of the real and in principle open to changes in any particular *Lebensform*.

Thus when Wittgenstein writes, "A main source of our failure to understand is that we do not *command a clear view* [*übersehen*] of the use of our words. Our grammar is lacking in this sort of perspicuity" (*PI* § 122), he is pointing out not a deficiency in our language to be made good by stricter logical controls via definition and inference but rather a fact of our language and thus of our world: ordinary language in everyday use is not fundamentally predictable according to a priori theories. But then the question resurfaces: just what "logic" is it that will produce the sort of judgments involved in, for example, obeying a rule? Wittgenstein continues: "A perspicuous representation produces just that understanding which consists in 'seeing connexions.' Hence the importance of finding and inventing *intermediate cases* [*des Findens und des Erfindens "Zwischenliedern"*]. The concept of a perspicuous representation is of fundamental significance for us. It earmarks the form of account we give, the way we look at things" (*PI* § 122). There are at least two comments I need to make here.

First, by "perspicuous representation," Wittgenstein means finding or constructing samples, or examples, by means of which grammatical distinctions and rhetorical comparisons and connections can be brought about. Such a pursuit is

on a continuum with Vichian "invention" of middle terms mentioned earlier (hence the overcoming of binaries by triads), but now the task is considerably more involved than in Vico since we are not relying on general propositions or preexisting allegorical or propositional frameworks but rather on often complex "cases" whose terms may be multiple and whose connections (differences and similarities) are not so much inferential as systemic, as in a gestalt. Wittgenstein does not have a name for the sort of grammatical connections organizing our conceptual grasp of a problem—it is certainly neither deductive nor inductive—but whether we call it "reflective thought" or "coduction" or "abduction" or "natural inference" or something else, one makes many kinds of claims and "proves" them by a process more akin to metaphor than to logical inference, by an "evocation" *(epideixis)* of their field of employment, by "projecting the sense of a word" (*CR* 180ff.), and by a "confession" regarding or "witnessing to" their truth. Metaphor by itself is hardly sufficient to capture philosophically the interplay of freedom and constraint here, since many of the connections and projections of a concept are not metaphorical but narratively embedded in a whole form of life, a fact that brings me to my second point.

About Wittgenstein's methods, Cavell notes that "there are questions, jokes, parables, and propositions so striking (the way lines are in poetry) that they stun mere belief" (*MWM* 71). Or again, more specifically, there is "'finding and inventing intermediate cases' (PI § 122) '[inventing] fictitious natural history' ([*PI*] II, p. 230), investigating one expression by investigating a grammatically related expression . . . and so on" (*MWM* 66). Similarly, about Cavell's own methods it has been observed that "his philosophy is not made of arguments; instead it is composed of descriptions, readings, musings, fantasies, puzzles about words, imaginary conversations, improvisatory flights."[71] In short, once that which is thought of as philosophy veers away from universal, once-and-for-all answers to the question, "What is philosophy?" philosophy itself becomes a non-rule-governed discourse or transcendental language game or "voice," open to its own ongoing reinvention by means of a wide (wild) range of discursive tools. This range comprises a variety of "polydictory logics"[72] whose validity depends on whether or not what I can find to say about the concepts I use is in attunement with the community whose concepts I wish or think they are or might become. And this means facing the threats of irrationalism, of empty oracularity, and of skepticism.[73]

## Dialectic: Community Dialogue (Orderings)

As I have begun to suggest, what has accompanied the historical and linguistic turns in pragmatism, hermeneutics, and ordinary language philosophy, but has been eclipsed by powerfully sophisticated theories of knowledge, power, and skepticism in literary studies, is the turn to the everyday and ordinary. In Frost's language, "Maturity is no object except perhaps in education where you might

think from all the talk the aim and end of everything was to get sophisticated before educated."[74] Here sophistication and maturity are equated with a drive to totality, specialization, and thoroughness, to system and expert knowledge. What Frost *wants* to develop is not (not at first) theoretical sophistication ("training") but the ability to handle "the metaphors of poetry" present in "all thinking, scientific and philosophic" (*SP* 49). This last notion—that metaphor, broadly conceived, is present in all thought—may seem to erase the intended contrast between the trained and the untrained, but a better rendering is that the primary and grounding value in all thinking is not specialized expertise but the developed capacity to *see connections* (hence distinctions) across the whole of life: "It certainly belongs as much to the composer, the musician, the general, and I'm told the mathematician and the scientist. And it probably belongs to the scholar" (*SP* 50). Waving aside that last tongue-in-cheek, we can propose that the capacity to see and/or make connections that count for some group comprises the order, or ordering, of the ordinary, whether in poetry or philosophy or everyday life.

When a phenomenon like our ordinary lives is indeterminate and mediated by interests and experience, "how we look at things" is not a matter of rules but of juxtapositions of our choices and interests, our real-life practices and values. To be relied on and developed without being "sophisticated" or confined to expertise, therefore, is the ability—conceptual and linguistic at once, belonging in principle to everyone—to "command a view" by offering constructions that order some part of our world-making. Genius, art, the judgment of taste: in teaching us that these matters are not rule-governed, Kant also importantly suggested that we seek a "universality" of acceptance of their products, that we appeal to the fellow next to us, to the woman down the street, to the man on the Clapham omnibus, to the effect that our way of seeing things and making connections *does*, in fact, coherently order some part or aspect of a shareable world.

All of this, however, is only to gesture at what is meant by the ordinary in Frost and others, so that we need to proceed with these matters in the following chapters. Meanwhile Wittgenstein also serves to remind me here that, in pursuing indeterminacies, what earmarks my own method is making "connections" *(Zusammenhänge)*,[75] the "continuum-thinking" characteristic, as Sacvan Bercovitch has noted, of "American intermediate selfhood."[76] It is not knowledge that we seek but the development of an ability to command "a view" of our grammar and rhetoric—which is to say our world—by selecting or inventing examples and metaphors, stories, jokes, and the rest, especially those intermediate cases and gradations (*Zwischenstufen*; *BT* 201/158) that elucidate the continuum between extremes. "Maturity"—here, thoroughness and systematic expert knowledge—is "no object," then, in two senses: it is not our goal in itself, and it is (or ought to be for the painstaking thinker) no obstacle. "It is, rather, of the essence of our

investigation that we do not seek to learn anything *new* by it. We want to *understand* something that is already in plain view. For *this* is what we seem in some sense not to understand" (*PI* § 89).

BOOK 1 OF this work backs away from (one kind of) detailed ordinary language criticism (the middle of chapter 4, on "Two Tramps in Mud Time," is an exception) to map out a rhetorical practice as we go, one that locates Frost in various intellectual contexts and situations. My claim for it is not originality of thought but rather reinvention of some traditional materials and the perspicuousness of an organized rationale of the relevant data. Chapter 1 attempts to gather a community from which it can draw the words to go on. Chapter 2 selects from and organizes those words as windows and doorways into Frost's poetry. Chapter 3 roughs out a house around them. And chapter 4 is a preliminary hearing or audition of the claims made thus far for the everyday and ordinary, for rhetorical investigations, and for Robert Frost.

Book 2 presents extended examples of ordinary language criticism conceived here as rhetorical investigations designed to "show forth" (rhetorically, an *epi-deixis*) what is stated more abstractly in book 1. Each chapter is intended as a possible way of going on with the chapter in book 1 correlated with it—that is, chapter 1 read in tandem with chapter 8, chapter 2 with 5, chapter 3 with 6, and chapter 4 with 7. All together, however, are not intended to accumulate to anything more (or less) than guides or prompts for further thought, rhetorical topoi for invention and judgment, unfinished arcs and not closed circles, as the title of book 2 is meant to indicate. Chapter 5 is a lesson in how the life of a farming couple, of lyric poetry, of a culture's language, gets renewed by being reinvented. Chapter 6 asks what we mean by (human) life as temporal. Chapter 7 meditates on time and proof as matters, in good measure, of timing. And chapter 8 comes to grief in its own ambivalent desire to dissent from, and to reconvene senses of, community.

# BOOK

# I

# RHETORIC
## *An Advanced Primer*

>The daily papers talk of everything except the daily. The papers annoy me, they teach me nothing. What they recount [*racontent*] doesn't concern me, doesn't ask me questions and doesn't answer the questions I ask or would like to ask.
>
>What's really going on, what we're experiencing, the rest, all the rest, where is it? How should we take account of [*comment en rendre compte*], question, describe what happens every day and recurs every day: the banal, the quotidian, the obvious, the common, the ordinary, the infra-ordinary, the background noise, the habitual? ...
>
>How are we to speak of these "common things," how to track them down rather, flush them out, wrest them from the dross in which they remain mired, how to give them a meaning, a tongue, to let them, finally, speak of what is, of what we are [?]
>
>...Not the exotic any more, but the endotic.
>
>—Georges Perec, "Approches de quoi?" (Approaches to what?), from *L'Infra-ordinaire*

CHAPTER

1

# DIALECTIC AS DIALOGUE
*The Order of the Ordinary*

We want to establish an order in our knowledge of the use of language; an order with a particular end in view; one out of many possible orders; not *the* order.

—Ludwig Wittgenstein, *Philosophical Investigations*

The philosophical appeal to what we say, and the search for our criteria on the basis of which we say what we say, are claims to community.

—Stanley Cavell, *The Claim of Reason*

Sherlock Holmes and Dr. Watson went on a camping trip. After a meal and a good bottle of wine they went to their tent, retired for the night, and fell fast asleep. Some hours later, Holmes awoke and nudged his faithful assistant. "Watson," he said, "look up at the sky and tell me what you see."

Watson replied, "I see millions and millions of stars."

"What does that tell you?"

Watson pondered for a moment. "Well, astronomically it tells me there are potentially millions and even billions of planets. Astrologically, I observe that Saturn is in Leo. Horologically, I deduce that the time is approximately quarter past three. Theologically, I infer a Creator who is all-powerful and a Creation in comparison to which we are small and insignificant. And meteorologically, I expect that we will have a beautiful day tomorrow. Why, what does it tell you?"

Holmes replied, "Watson, you idiot, some bastard has stolen our tent."

## Conditions of Telling

### Recounting Criteria

CONSTANT, though not unvarying, in the systematic philosophizing of the West from ancient times to our own has been the assumption, that because everyday life presents endlessly diverse and shifting scenes of opinion and custom expressed in equally impermanent and equivocal words of ordinary language ("mere rhetoric"), both the everyday and ordinary are—the assumption is that they *must* be, more or less—illusory. Stanley Cavell observes that "philosophers find it their intellectual birthright to distrust the everyday, as in Descartes' second meditation:

'... words impede me, and I am nearly deceived by the words of ordinary language. For we say that we see the same wax'" (*NYUA* 32).[1] Here "seeing" is a concept of our natural or ordinary language ostensibly used in the way people use it every day, while the wax provides what Cavell calls a best case example for knowing: if one doesn't really "see" something so obvious as *that* (a ball of wax), then one can't really be said to *know* anything about the external world at all. Of course, Descartes manages to overcome his own skeptical doubt about the external world, not because the ordinary somehow rises to vindicate itself but because the cogitating philosopher intuits "pure natures" whose existence in the external world is guaranteed by a benevolent God—in other words, through a variety of interlocking metaphysical proofs.

From the pre-Socratics onward, most traditional philosophers have argued that the appearances of everyday life and their articulation in ordinary language depend upon, even while they distract our attention from, notions of eternal Platonic forms or Kantian categories, or natural or providential order, or metaphysical substance, each of these understood as stable foundations. In our own time, the everyday and ordinary still gets formulated, though less frequently, in different but equally deflationary ways, made out, for example, to be systematically distorted by institutionalized modes of power (Habermas's "systematically distorted communication") or driven by unconscious desire (Freud's "psychopathology of everyday life"). Whether too rational (read "ideologically tainted") or too irrational, the results are much the same: ordinary language and everyday life serve, with what are ostensibly very good reasons, as merely necessary points of departure for genuine philosophical thinking.

As we know, such thinking has imagined itself in many guises: Platonic, and later Plotinian, Hegelian, Marxist, and Husserlian dialectics; rationalist and transcendental metaphysics; categorical, propositional, and symbolic logic; and so on. What underwrites these modes of knowledge is not only their preoccupation with ontological or epistemological foundations and the quest for certainty but shared assumptions about the obvious inadequacy of everyday life and ordinary language to tell us what the world is. Historian of ideas Isaiah Berlin gives tongue-in-cheek expression to the dangerous practical implications of traditional, theory-driven accounts of the Human Mess: "Since I know the only true path to the ultimate solution of the problems of society, I know which way to drive the human caravan; and since you are ignorant of what I know, you cannot be allowed to have liberty of choice even within the narrowest limits, if the goal is to be achieved."[2]

In contemporary times, such long-standing assumptions and goals have not themselves withstood close critical scrutiny. Berlin's parody is silent about the more positive, post-Enlightenment rise of freedom and plurality in nation-states, and about the recognition of individual and political autonomy—all products of tra-

ditional philosophizing. But the point is that unless *those* values are stabilized in a conception of "order" that answers to further emerging needs of human beings, freedom and plurality can be sublimed into the Will of a One, most often a political sovereign or the State as Grand Inquisitor, whose manner of inquiry is seductive or violent, indifferently.[3] In "New Year Letter (January 1, 1940)," W. H. Auden wryly summarizes one version of this recurring error of our handing over our lives part and parcel to abstract thought:

> We hoped; we waited for the day
> The State would wither clean away,
> Expecting the Millennium
> That theory promised us would come:
> It didn't. Specialists must try
> To detail all the reasons why;
> Meanwhile at least the layman knows
> That none are so lost as those
> Who overlook their crooked nose,
> That they grow small who imitate
> The mannerisms of the great,
> Afraid to be themselves, or ask
> What acts are proper to their task.[4]

"Disillusion," as Cavell points out, "is what fits us for reality, whether in Plato's terms or D. W. Winnicott's. But then we must be assured that this promise is based on a true knowledge of what our illusions are."[5]

Of course the problem remains as to what we might mean by order, knowledge, and illusion. On most traditional epistemological models, again, we do not "know" unless we can give a principled account of the object-in-view from the position of an informed and disinterested spectator overseeing life's confused appearances in order to make manifest its real (its metaphysical or empirical) form or substance. By contrast, in some modern and contemporary versions of philosophy from Hume on, we need instead to acknowledge our inability to achieve—or, alternately, we need to celebrate our liberation from—those principled accounts themselves. Recently and most radically, some have tried to free us through demystification of accounting *as such*, on the grounds that critical reflection in even the strongest truth claims is but a further shadow-play of the skepticism that always dogs foundationalist theories. Given this contemporary attitude, the traveling caravan of man is then seen to have been scattered to the four corners, every manservant for himself, with or without a tent.

Consider, as a particularly telling example of such an attitude, the minister in Frost's "The Black Cottage" (1914), considered later in this chapter. Frost's self-absorbed cleric can be seen to possess all of the qualities of the modern skeptic more than a little unsure of his ideas and methods, casually but obsessively doubting

the tenets of his own fundamental religious and political creeds by holding or rejecting them in indifferent alternation—that is, as circumstances, relevant or not, dictate. Like many others in his time and place, the minister, we will see, operates in the absence of any hope of shared criteria or standards for even probable judgment. In the end, this Browningesque doubter, this poor man's Bishop Bloughram, lapses into what he fantasizes to be his own private language, in reality a desert solitaire of the mind ("My cowering caravans"; line 124), while his heart remains passive-aggressive in defense of its self-defeating, pseudo-self-affirmations.

All of which, in any case, leaves untouched the assumption, perhaps endemic to human beings, that their own everyday and ordinary scene of behavior is one either of unsystematic (hence unrationalized or ungovernable) action, opinion, or desire; or of systematic, overrationalized distortion of these forces or powers by co-opting ideologies. Of the traditional ways out of this dilemma, one leads straight to metaphysics, dogmatic or transcendental, the other to skeptical doubt. What happens, however, when we entertain alternate routes by setting those assumptions aside—not dismissing them, but feeling our way toward a larger context or order in which they can be placed?

Two objections immediately come to mind. First, it is very dubious that anything we might call "everyday life in ordinary language" might count in philosophy (much less in poetry) as not only the first but the highest court of appeal just as it stands. The claim is dubious in view not only of the tedium, confusions, exclusions, self-contradictions, and violence of everyday life but also of what is repeatedly exposed as the patently self-serving "common sense" of the so-called reasonable man. By the everyday here I mean the tasks and conflicts in front of our noses, what we already think we know, or know how to do or know how to operate: our kitchens and clocks, computers and cars, the roles we button into each morning for school and work, the norms of behavior we blithely disobey on the way home each night. This is the living space of regular trash pickup and vacations and 7-Eleven holdups, television theme songs and internet pop-up ads: in a word, our Everyman's daily quota of head-, tooth-, and heartaches.[6] Alternately, the everyday and ordinary also appears to us as, in Heidegger's terms, what is "present-at-hand" *(Vorhanden)* in the cornucopia of both our material possessions and our objectifying concepts, as well as "ready-to-hand" *(Zuhanden)* in equally abundant, readily available, and ready-made meanings, often an endless Beckettian "chatter" *(Gerede)* threatening to absorb us beyond all accounting for anything at all. Behold the Big Box nonarchitecture of yet another Wal-Mart, the increasing personal danger posed by SUVs, destruction of the global climate, the banal *copia* of network national news, suburban sprawl, the war on terrorism. Any gesture in this book toward relying on such clichés as the source of actual answers to serious questions would be antecedently improbable, to say the least.

Second, to assume anything about the everyday and ordinary is to *assume*

something. In the joke I use as one of this chapter's epigraphs, for example, it is to assume what even Holmes's sleepy assistant Watson takes for granted in availing himself of various scientific disciplines in answer to Holmes's question, "What does that tell you?" For at least part of the skepticism ingredient in this joke is that Watson's specialized disciplinary perspectives effectively blind him to the everyday right before his eyes (in Greek, *"idiotes"* signifies a separate, even isolated, person. Like so many of us in and out of academia, Watson is star-struck). Conversely, part of the philosophic truth of this joke is that "telling" what our situation is involves publicly available discriminations of our shared contexts, of what "counts" as what, and shared narratives about what counts *to us* engaged in the accounting. And the joke, tellingly, leaves both unspoken, untold, *assumed:* what a tent is, what camping is, how tents get staked down, what it is to steal something, how impressive it would be to steal a staked-down tent, how shaming it might be to someone to find himself not only (as it were) homeless but nakedly so, perhaps at the very moment when he was dreaming of hearth and home.[7] Hence, at the end, Holmes's clarifying what it is that Watson overlooks at the tip of his own nose promises to prove as improvably circular, as bedded down with assumptions, as any other traditional or modern disciplinary defense or subversion of meaning or truth.[8]

Seeing no way past this double bind of necessity and defeasibility of assumptions, finding ourselves as it were homeless and borne down by our baggage, we may further allow that such assumptions, in being not only unavoidable after all but themselves idiosyncratic and contingent, resist and even elude systematic theoretical articulation. Indeed, in many ways our everyday background is more difficult to discern than Watson's guiding ideas and methods just because the virtually endless possibilities for discrimination and narration, being contextual if not yet necessarily communal, are far more richly sensed than seen.

Rather than speaking in terms of theoretical judgment of right and wrong, therefore, this fact might lead us to reformulate our attitude about our own hermeneutic horizons in terms of pragmatic loss and gain.[9] Here the point is not that assumptions are metaphysically self-evident or dialectically or transcendentally or logically deducible, or (conversely) that all are skeptically motivated exclusively by desire, ideology, or power, but rather what we, as it were epistemically, lose and gain in giving credence—but is "giving credence" the right phrase? (*CR* 242–43)— to our everyday life and language, however conflicted and even "eclipsed," to use John Dewey's term, they may be.[10] Allow me briefly to expand on these reflections about these fundamental assumptions partly constituting "our" everyday life, and then to suggest what we gain in acknowledging them in a positive though still critical way.

At one point in his writings about Ralph Waldo Emerson, first of all, in translating Wittgenstein's term *"Umgangssprache"* as "colloquial speech," Stanley

Cavell concedes the potential of that phrase to mislead, although he also indicates how to avoid the slippery slope toward which it beckons us: "What I [have] in mind in alluding to some 'danger' in translating *Umgangssprache* as colloquial speech is that it may make words appear as fashions of speech, dictates of sociability, manners of putting something that are more or less evanescent or arbitrary and are always to be passed beyond philosophically into something more permanent and precise. . . . it leaves out the German word's extraordinary representation of everyday language as a form of circulation, communication as exchange" (*NYUA* 33). What interests me here is that Cavell's interest in "communication as exchange" and "circulation" recalls one of Wittgenstein's images for language as an ancient city whose center is a maze of twisting alleys and streets as it were doubling back onto each other (*PI* § 18), and as "a complicated network of similarities overlapping and criss-crossing" (*PI* § 66). Not just space but time circulates here in the suggestion that life's everyday tasks and rounds move forward and back in an ongoing recycling and renewing, in what Heidegger calls a "retrieval" *(Wiederholung)* of our words and thus ourselves.[11] Wittgenstein and Cavell are thinking of the everyday and ordinary as fundamental yet evolving cares and commitments of human beings in community with and against each other—hence of everyday language as a human habitat and even "home" in which we dwell, the linguistic hub of activities constitutive of the human form of life. Communication minimally requires media, in which voices can be heard articulating abiding interests and activities.

As for loss and gain, second, I am thinking of how inquiry is promoted into collectively accessible connections in our conceptions of the world. This is what I take William James to have meant in one of his accounts of truth as "agreement with reality": "To 'agree' in the widest sense with a reality can only mean to be guided either straight up to it or into its surroundings [or "circumstances," Wittgenstein's *Umstände*], or to be put into such working touch with it as to handle [Heidegger's *Vorhanden*, Cavell's "unhandsomeness"] either it or something connected with it better than if we disagreed. . . . Any idea that helps us to deal, whether practically or intellectually, with either the reality or its belongings, that doesn't entangle our progress in frustrations, that *fits*, in fact, and adapts our life to the reality's whole setting, will agree sufficiently to meet the requirement. It will hold true of that reality."[12] How, then, might *starting* from or appealing to reality as "everyday experience in our criteria of ordinary language" allow us to do more than is commonly thought possible when we reject it or them?

Well, first, what happens when the everyday *is* somehow taken away or eclipsed (when "home" becomes, to make prescient F. Scott Fitzgerald's terms for the lower Manhattan of our own times, a "valley of ashes")?: "The power of [the] recognition of the ordinary for philosophy is bound up with the recognition that refusing or forcing the order of the ordinary is a cause of philosophical emptiness

(say avoidance) and violence" (*NYUA* 33). Thinkers like Emerson, Cavell, and Wittgenstein have proposed that analyzing everyday experience by means of empirical or transcendental methods eventuates in what Dewey calls "isolation," the alienation of being from becoming, fact from value, ordinary language from philosophical expression, our interests from our acts, acts from judgments, leaving us abstractly committed to dogmatic or ideological results but existentially unconnected to any sense of persons or community or cosmos, making self-reflection increasingly exposed to what a proliferating number of experts, like our medical friend Watson, can "tell," and "tell us."[13] A related loss when we do *not* believe (believe in? know?)[14] our own everyday experience is our sacrificing our capacity to talk about meaning and values in art, ethics, or politics as anything other than epiphenomena of "power" or "will" or "capital" or ad hoc "interpretive communities."[15]

By contrast there may be gains in trying to theorize the everyday and ordinary as grounds for what has been called the "mysterious indeterminacy" of the real,[16] although we need to take care that our angle of refraction doesn't blind us, as it did Watson, to the ever-moving range of their possibilities. For what we stand to gain in crediting the everyday and ordinary as something other than necessary error or grist to the critical theorist's mill—seeing it as the central primary place or seat (*topos, sedes*) of our condition—is, first, an accommodating set of regulative practices and ideals by which values and facts, concepts and their criteria, criteria and their situations, mutually constitute ourselves and our world; and, second, a more realistic and capacious attitude toward the variety of ways of talking about art and similar human pursuits as on a continuum with—neither the same as nor unavoidably alienated from—the words and actions of everyday life.

This is, in Thomas Dumm's words, "another sense of the ordinary" from that which has become commonplace in much modern political and modernist cultural theory, one about which Dumm, in commenting on Cavell's repeated invocations of Emerson's "the common, the familiar, the low,"[17] observes that "we need to understand the uneventfulness of the ordinary [as] the inevitable ground from which we may come to a better appreciation of events."[18] In *Art as Experience,* Dewey similarly emphasizes that "about every explicit and focal object there is a recession into the implicit and vague which is not intellectually grasped. In reflection we call it dim and vague. But in the original experience it is not identified as . . . vague. It is a function of the whole situation." Hence, in art, "the sense of the including whole implicit in ordinary experiences is rendered intense within the frame of a painting or poem. It, rather than any special purgation, is that which reconciles us to the events of tragedy":

> We are, as it were, introduced into a world beyond this world which is nevertheless the deeper reality of the world in which we live in our ordinary experiences. We are carried out beyond ourselves to find ourselves. I can

see no psychological ground for such properties of an experience save that, somehow, the work of art operates to deepen and to raise to great clarity that sense of an enveloping undefined whole that accompanies every normal experience.[19]

Like Emerson and Cavell, Dumm is understandably interested in the ordinary as a site of resistance to the routine and normal as well as to the "eventful." But Dumm tends to overlook Dewey's point, namely that background routines, norms, rituals, and the like *can* be individually and collectively enabling and not just crippling, can be cognitively meaningful and not just emotionally cathartic.[20] For this reason, Cavell, in one of his earliest essays, writes that "recognizing what we say, in the way that is relevant in philosophizing, is like recognizing our present commitments and their implications; to one person a sense of *freedom* will demand an escape from them, to another it will require their more total *acceptance*. Is it obvious that one of these positions must, in a given case, be right?" (*MWM* 57; my emphasis).

In a related vein of argument about theorizing the everyday, Gerald Bruns has noted that "strategic thinking—getting the right angle on things, finding the right theoretical ideas and methods of approach or attack—is *useless* when it comes to things like shame or sense of worth," whether found in everyday experience, art, philosophy, or (presumably) jokes: "To say what shame is, or pride, one must be able to understand and interpret one's own situation—the standards one acknowledges and lives by: [Heidegger's] 'significance conditions' . . . under which one acts. It is this understanding and interpretation which is constitutive of the emotion. What justifies an emotion is not how things are but how things matter—a neutral, monological [theoretical] observer is just not going to see the point, certainly not going to feel its force, because there is nothing intrinsic, nothing observable, that calls for the response of shame. Mattering [like 'telling'] is situated and dialogical."[21]

Stanley Rosen endorses similar pragmatic, hermeneutic, and ordinary language commitments when he writes that "ordinary experience is not a first principle; it is just ourselves, . . . the speeches and deeds with which we exhibit the regularity that underlies and encompasses our pursuit of the extraordinary. Ordinary experience [is not] an infallible criterion of philosophical investigation. It is on my view a necessary but not sufficient condition for a philosophy to be worthy of serious consideration that it offer a plausible response to the needs elicited in human beings by the everywhere compelling features of everyday life."[22] "The needs elicited in human beings" is another way of pointing to that communicative recirculation at the heart of Wittgenstein's and Cavell's image of language. The question here is how does "mattering" (or, for that matter, "matter")—that is, how does a *world*—come to be in the first place? What is meant, or what do I, or

we, mean by "everyday life" or "ordinary language?" How do we conceptualize our everyday world and thus ourselves?

Of course, how that question gets answered all depends—on circumstances of time, place, occasion, audience, purpose. It is, again, generally understood that traditional models of thought and language rely on various standard measures to plot out a world: clear and distinct ideas (Descartes), or immediate sensations or impressions and corresponding ideas (Locke, Hume), or transcendental regulative "forms" (Plato), or "ideas" (Berkeley), or "conditions of the possibility of knowing" (Kant), or even "common sense" (Reid and, up to a point, Hume himself). Any of these approaches can elicit our awareness of the real, even if the real is only the apparent or the phenomenal. To express that awareness, moreover, we require, on all of these models, a value-neutral language understood to correlate, much as a container holds the contained, our thoughts and the things to which they refer lest we succumb to a helpless relativism or skepticism. Thus, starting either from objectively given simples or from complex judgments, we build up or deduce or logically extrapolate or work our way back to or intuit bases of the world in which we exist. Hence empirical observation, or rationally certified primitive but certain ideas, or transcendental deductions—*and* a disinterested language—are of first importance.

In a rhetorical investigation such as my own, however, how we answer the question about the everyday and ordinary "all depends" on "circumstances" in a more serious way than traditional models have allowed, in the sense that circumstances inform, help to constitute (affect the substance of) the answer and not merely occasion it. (This is what was meant earlier by our being bedded down with assumptions: we may be wayward or even homeless in our changing circumstances, but we are not lacking resources altogether to adapt.) Here I want to sketch a Wittgensteinian and Cavellian line of thinking about the everyday and ordinary starting *in medias res*, that is, with ourselves precisely as creatures of circumstance. Most important and abiding of these circumstances is the fact that we happen to be creatures who have a voice, who can speak. What counts here, then, is *how* things matter or mean, how fundamental interests and needs are not only elicited in human beings by their everyday lives but also help constitute those lives in the first place through language. Of course, language too can fail, so that in approaching modern poetry in general and Robert Frost in particular, we will need to be on the lookout for problems of skeptical doubt about the external world, indeed about all "beliefs" (as Frost puts it in "Education by Poetry"; *SP* 44–46) in self, others, art, nation, and God.

## Five Red Apples

If we consider once more that simile from *Philosophical Investigations* (1953) of language as an ancient city, we can begin to distinguish and connect concepts of the "everyday" and "ordinary" important for the remainder of this book. Wittgenstein

writes: "Our language can be seen as an ancient city: a maze of little streets and squares, of old and new houses, and of houses with additions from various periods; and this surrounded by a multitude of new boroughs with straight regular streets and uniform houses" (*PI* § 18). Here "our language" means simply language, the language we naturally speak—"ordinary" language, which therefore includes (using this picture) not only our "everyday" words and speech, as it were the central and oldest part of the city, but our "noneveryday" language, in particular specialized uses of language, for example "the symbolism of chemistry and the notation of the infinitesimal calculus . . . for these are, so to speak, the suburbs of our language" (*PI* § 18). The latter are often more uniform, though they may lie far distant from city life, while the former comprise "an immense network of easily accessible wrong turnings" (*CV* 18e) in which we (sometime suburbanites) may easily lose our way: "A philosophical problem has the form: 'I don't know my way about'" (*PI* § 123).

Thus my first point is that what is meant by "ordinary language" here includes our everyday *and* noneveryday purposeful uses, what Wittgenstein calls "primary" uses and meanings that sometimes overlap or converge on each other and sometimes are far apart and opposed. "Ordinary" is thus distinguished from empiricist and metaphysical conceptions of language that evade the temporality of their use, as it were timelessly correlating words with objects, essences, impressions or ideas, or absolutes from the perspective of a private, perceiving consciousness. When Descartes doubts whether the objecthood of the world can be distinguished from his own dreaming or delusion, the mind is conceived as a self-enclosed mechanism and language as merely the vehicle of its transmission; when perception is called into doubt, the words that express perception (for example, "seeing," "wax") dissipate along with it.

But note then that *this* question—is use-X ordinary or metaphysical (or skeptical) language?—asks for a distinction that must be drawn in this book *not* as a generalization but only *as specific cases arise,* since such a judgment depends on how words are functioning in a given time or place. (Sometimes a Descartes, Hume, or Kant is working in perfectly ordinary ways, in ordinary language, sometimes not; and it is not always obvious which is which.) Apart from such absolutism (and its skeptical black dog), there is no language use—including the language use we call literature—that is *not* "ordinary" in my sense, though there are "circumstances" that are nonlinguistic, and there are *uses* of language that disconnect words from just those circumstances that help give them meaning. When Cavell shows how we "project" words into new circumstances (*CR* 180ff.), he is fighting that model of language in which all particulars fall under universal concepts, proposing instead, after Wittgenstein, that concept and circumstance (not concept and percept) are mutually constitutive.

Again using Wittgenstein's picture for language (old and new houses together, houses with additions from various periods), my second point is that we will find

in the present book no exact line of demarcation between everyday and noneveryday language use. Though these terms, everyday and noneveryday, will receive fuller treatment in subsequent chapters, here we can think of a *continuum* of language use in which complex sets of more specialized activities radiate outward from less specialized cares and commitments, activities, and purposes belonging to some people, or (with respect to some concepts) to people as such. Just as suburbs "depend on"—in the sense that they grow up only because there is an older center of—the city, so specialized language use "depends on" or presupposes our more everyday uses of language even while specialized uses can help us clarify what those everyday uses are.

Said otherwise, everyday as well as noneveryday language use and their meanings are "taken up" in philosophy, literary criticism, or critical theory to help us get clearer about the grammar of standard and nonstandard speech precisely by performing their possibilities: "When I talk about language (words, sentences, etc.) I must speak the language of everyday [*die Sprache des Alltags*]. Is this language somehow too coarse and material for what we want to say? *Then how is another one to be constructed?* (*PI* § 120). When criticism or philosophy abstracts itself entirely from the standard uses of words, it is no longer part of *any* polis—no longer part of the language or life of the community; non-sense.

As a perspicuous example of a philosophical problem, then—philosophical in the sense of involving not knowing one's way about the everyday; perspicuous because reduced to a few features of the grammar of our language about which Wittgenstein wants to help us get clear—consider the language game of "five red apples" that begins *Philosophical Investigations:*

> I send someone shopping. I give him a slip marked "five red apples." He takes the slip to the shopkeeper, who opens the drawer marked "apples"; then he looks up the word "red" in a table and finds a colour sample opposite it; then he says the series of cardinal numbers—I assume that he knows them by heart—up to the word "five" and for each number he takes an apple of the same colour as the sample out of the drawer.—It is in this and similar ways that one operates with words. (*PI* § 1)

"Apples" and "red" seem straightforward enough, but what, or how, does "five" mean if we approach this concept/word as we are inclined to do with the other two, that is on the traditional model of ostensive definition? By having us say "five" as we point to five apples, Wittgenstein is just beginning to position us to see that *unless* complex sets of other concepts and behaviors are already in place, it will be unclear just what this pointing-to is all about: "Explanations come to an end somewhere" (*PI* § 1). For Wittgenstein, that end resides in the cares, commitments, and activities at the very heart of the ancient life of language, which is to say our life. Absent shared purposes in specific contexts embedded in potentially

vast networks of other concepts, purposes, activities—not merely status quo "lifestyles" or ephemeral public opinion polls but something more like "life works," fundamental, if changing, human needs and judgments—the very notions of "counting" or "number" (not to mention "apple" or "red") cannot arise at all. For Wittgenstein in effect is inter alia inviting us to wonder: What (for instance) prevents me from taking "five" as an *adverb* modifying "red," as if it referred to an indefinite scale of the color: "X is a 'five red,' but Y is a 'four red,' and what I want are five red apples"? In my imagined account of his language game, numbers simply do not isolate objects nor evince "characteristics" supposedly held in common across all cases of number use. In Wittgenstein's language game, numbers *could* refer to such a color scale; but in his narrative telling of "five red apples," they do not. And the concept of "number" as such *could* refer to common characteristics across all cases, but on investigation, it does not. Why not? Well, what are we humans interested in and what do we care about? How do we *use* the concept of "number" or "five?"[23]

The question is not an empirical one but—this is my third point—a grammatical, and *therefore* rhetorical, matter: "[Philosophical] problems are solved, not by giving new information, but by arranging what we have always known" "by looking into the workings of our language" (*PI* § 109; also *CR* 14ff.). We don't settle the question of the meaning of "five" empirically—say by usage polls or statistical analyses of public opinions about the word—but by *descriptions* of how all of us use such a concept, of how our concepts fit, or fail to fit, the circumstances of their use, of what circumstances need to be in place for a given concept to function in the way it does, to what group of people—and much else besides. Unlike the natural sciences—which are empirical and proceed by means of hypotheses and observation and seek explanatory theory—so-called ordinary language investigations set about describing the grammar of our natural language, not the causal conditions of their existence: "Essence is expressed by grammar" (*PI* § 371); "Philosophy simply puts everything before us, and neither explains nor deduces anything. —Since everything lies open to view there is nothing to explain" (*PI* § 126). By "seeing connexions" (*PI* § 122) between something on the one hand as everyday and ordinary as shopping for five red apples, and, on the other, our philosophical and rhetorical problems of conceptualization and communication, the nonstandard activity of philosophizing may illuminate hidden lanes and alleyways of our ordinary life in speech: cul-de-sacs, dead ends, shortcuts, private paths behind hedges, bridges we had not known or do not recognize when we come upon them from a different direction.[24] Education in language is education in a form of life; and investigation as ordinary language criticism might therefore illuminate literature as well as philosophy.

A further example or two may help here. One can define a word such as "greeting" ("gestures or words of welcome," *American Heritage Dictionary*) so that

the definition holds across all cases; this is what we have dictionaries for. We name or define in this way for the convenient recall of things we wish to treat as the same. But on analysis, such a labeling definition presupposes our familiarity with what *counts* as a greeting in specific situations, to specific people, and with the activities within which it has its function. We don't, for example, high-five at funerals, nor do we slow to a halt and solemnly nod our heads when we encounter acquaintances at hockey games. In other words, though both of these things satisfy the terms of the definition, they are not what we would call (not what is meant by) "greeting," that is, not in *those* circumstances. (But then, who is "we?" And do "we" never do these things? *Normally* we do not.)

One can see this better if we rewrite the definition as a rule: "When you meet someone, give gestures or words of welcome." Like many rules ("Do not walk on the grass"), this one is vague: May I *run* on the grass? Eat the daisies? The rule is an abstraction and simplification, as it were an abbreviation, of the larger contexts out of which it is abstracted and within which it is expected to function. And though such rules and definitions most certainly (obviously) have their uses, *that* is the point: these definitions and rules are themselves particular situated uses appropriate to certain situations, activities, purposes. They are not, on investigation, *the* paradigm, "*the* order," for how concepts as such come to mean.

Traditionally philosophy's account of language has long obscured this larger scope of operations (Wittgenstein famously begins the *Investigations* by citing Augustine as representative). On Augustine's account, we seem to establish a world by first recognizing truths in the mind or facts outside the body, then matching them up with words as defining labels or names or "representations." The model is self-confidently value-free, since what are named are similar characteristics across cases. What this model hides is that the object categorized assumes the identity it does for us only because we have attended to particular features; have allowed those features to count as significant, emotionally interesting, and engaging; have treated dissimilar characteristics "as" similar, and so on. All of us learn to refer to a "lamp" as an (as *one*) object because, as it happens, people (we) do not normally wear lampshades on our heads as we go about our day. If we did, we might learn "lamp" as *two* objects, or perhaps as five, not one. In other words, what is primary in our acquisition and use of concepts and language is our situated placement in the world, the always already shared background of interests, values, activities, and purposes comprising the times and places when we learn to use those concepts—in a word, their grammar. Different types of greetings are thus "conventional" in the sense that they might be otherwise in a different time and place, but they are also fully "natural" in the sense that they belong to human beings *as such,* to the human "form of life." In this way, then, Wittgenstein is, and is not, normative. Inasmuch as grammatical description includes knowing all of the circumstances of appropriate concept use, it enables moral and political (even

religious) self-reflection (cf. *PI* § 373). But the philosopher's job is not to *tell* us what to do but rather "tell" us how things stand, what our situation is now, what is confused or incoherent, and how we might go on and make sense.[25]

More specifically, philosophic investigations specify the linguistic "criteria" behind, in J. L. Austin's terms, "what we say when" we encounter some particular setting with a particular purpose, some set of circumstances, the hazy standing "background" which, by definition, it is impossible fully to articulate. Criteria provide an alternative accounting from the traditional models for what happens when we conceptualize: "The criteria which we accept for 'fitting,' 'being able to,' 'understanding,' are much more complicated than might appear at first sight. That is, the game with these words, their employment in the linguistic intercourse that is carried on by their means, is more involved—the role of these words in our language other—than we are tempted to think" (*PI* § 182). The importance of criteria not only to Wittgenstein but to Cavell is signaled in the latter's beginning *The Claim of Reason* (1979) with the notion of criteria as comprising (part of) ordinary language, and with related notions of the common and familiar as central both to Wittgenstein's and Austin's ways of philosophizing and to Cavell's way of going on with them. For Cavell, criteria are "the means by which we learn what our concepts are and hence 'what kind of object anything is' (*[Philosophical Investigations]* 373)" (*CR* 16), constituting a large part of how we speak about our most basic concepts, such as "five" or "pain" or "understanding" or "knowledge" or "soul" or even "apple" (when I ask you to "please hand me an apple," I don't complain that you've handed me an apple *and* a stem). Criteria are that by which we identify instances of our concepts in terms of certain objects, behaviors, activities, persons, uses, and the like in certain circumstances.[26] Frequently criteria perform like fixed definitions, but perhaps more frequently they do not, telling us rather "what counts" in our use of concepts in *specific* times and places, both in the sense of counting as an instance *of* something (of "justice," of "understanding," of "'seeing' the same wax") and counting *to* specific people who use these words in the ways they do (this might called their rhetorical dimension): "This explicitly makes our agreement in judgment, our attunement expressed through criteria, agreement in valuing. So that what can be communicated, say a fact, depends upon agreement in valuing, rather than the other way around" (*CR* 94).

Think of concepts, then, as also on a continuum, ranging from the relatively uncontested, fixed and stable, to the hotly contested and indeterminate. And consider that it is people, it is *we,* who are sometimes faced with deciding, or who decide to face, whether or not we want to make *that* kind of sense or, it may be, speak that kind of nonsense. Thus Cavell calls the criteria of ordinary language nothing less than the "conditions of intelligibility" of our understanding of and living in or coping with the world:[27] "Criteria are criteria of judgment; the underlying idea is one of discriminating or separating cases, of identifying by means of

differences.... All I want from these considerations... is a prospective attention to Wittgenstein's emphasis upon the idea of judgment" (*CR* 17).

When Austin probes the concept of "excuses," he discovers a neglected variety of situations and employments of the term that illuminate problems in moral philosophy and "linguistic phenomenology" (his term for ordinary language philosophy). In more determinate disciplines, criteria can be complex but relatively straightforward, what Thomas Kuhn calls "normal science"—for instance, the defining criterion for "angina" is not some vague pain experienced in the chest region but a specific kind of bacillus found in the bloodstream. Even in philosophy, as P.M.S. Hacker notes, much of what Wittgenstein undertakes to establish are those "normal regularities of phenomena ... the gravitational force that holds our language-games stable."[28] But often in philosophy and related areas of political theory, ethics, or literary studies, the criteria of a concept (of "intention," "lyric," "freedom," "interpretation," "meaning," "beauty," "responsibility," "pretense"), while they *may* be stable, may also be or easily become multiple, shifting, and contested—in a word, relatively indeterminate or overdetermined. In *The Hedgehog and the Fox*, for example, Isaiah Berlin relates Tolstoy's rejection of accepted understandings of history as "scientific": "But why should Napoleon, or Mme de Stael or Baron Stein or Tsar Alexander, or all of these people, plus the *Contrat social*, 'cause' Frenchmen to behead or drown each other? Why is *this* called an 'explanation'?"[29] The question is a good one and not to be dismissed, as Austin notes: a "disagreement as to what we should say is not to be shied off, but to be pounced upon: for the explanation of it can hardly fail to be illuminating."[30]

The recognition that debate and skepticism, rightly taken, do not deny the world helps us to see that the existence of the world and others is a matter for responsibility and response, not disengaged knowledge, and can be likened, to come at this from another direction, to how Heidegger understands human being-in-the-world as a "primordial" function of differential relations of "significance" *(Bedeutsamkeit)*. "World" signifies more than a collocation of objects; it is a series not of interlocking metaphysical proofs but of interlocking "involvement wholes" *(Bewandtnisganzheiten)* and "equipmental wholes" *(Zeugganzen)* and "referential wholes" *(Verweisungsganzheiten)*. These are various hermeneutic or interpretive "as-structures" by means of which Dasein signifies at all, and within which the "Being" of beings—the different modes by which beings appear—becomes manifest in the first place. (And in this regard recall that Heidegger, in *Being and Time* [1928], refers to Aristotle's *Rhetoric* as "the first systematic hermeneutic of the *everydayness [Alltäglichkeit]* of being with one another"; *BT* 178/138; my emphasis.) For Heidegger, as-structures constitute the "involvement wholes" that organize the human mode of being within its changing cultural manifestations, not as founding certainties of metaphysics but as funded-yet-dynamic commitments about which we primordially "care" and toward whose possibilities and claims we

are drawn forward in time. Things, people, beings, always already "count" for us not first as objects but as *going concerns*: to perceive them as isolated objects (as in a laboratory) takes effort and requires a determined diminution of what is present from the beginning, namely the full range of our interpretive understanding, including the linguistic structures for "seeing-something-as-something," what Wittgenstein means by "seeing-as" (*PI* pt. 2).

For this and other reasons to be pursued, "the everyday and ordinary" is not a residue remaining after science has extracted its essence; instead, it signifies the prior, fuller conditions out of which essence is a function of grammatical identification postulated for certain purposes. In *Being and Time*, it is true, Heidegger speaks as though our initial conditions of understanding somehow precede not only logic but language altogether, whereas the later Wittgenstein abandons any search for explanations deeper than the grammar of our language.[31] But what both Wittgenstein and Heidegger (and Cavell and Frost) insist on, I think, is that scientific or theoretical (disciplinary) uses of fixed concepts derive from a richer existential nexus of activities and interests, of already-articulated discriminations or "judgments" *(Urteile)*, of projections of our existing words into novel situations, of metaphor and other tropes. In my asking a student to "take a chair" in class, for example, one of the criteria for "chair" is that one can sit *in* it (what is meant is not a two-inch plastic chair for a doll house), while criteria for "take" include one's knowing that one is to *sit* in it, hence knowing what it is in general for a human being "to sit" and not drape oneself across it; knowing not to remove it altogether (perhaps by stealing it); and knowing that one is not to remove another student from his or her chair in order to be able to "take" it. (And as we all further know, this account of "take a chair" is not the half of it.)

I want to conclude this brief explanation of how the everyday and ordinary are matters of "experience" (conceived here as relying on and/or recounting criteria) by shifting out of everyday language games such as "five red apples" and "take a chair" and approaching from a different direction. When, in the following chapters, we consider poetry generally and Frost's poetry specifically, grammatical criteria will still be seen to function to help us identify instances of our concepts, but they will do so differently than they do in the matters of fact of life, and sometimes very differently. This is itself a grammatical remark, not only about criteria but about poems. I take it as given, for instance, that we "get" a weather report differently than we get a chair, a joke, or a poem. Although it is obvious that some or even much of our standard use of ordinary language employs "literary" or rhetorical tropes and figures and, it may be, every other device we call literary or rhetorical, nevertheless critics *can* (and sometimes do) "get" or "take" those language uses differently in poems. In taking poems grammatically and rhetorically, standard use is not discarded but subsumed under the less specific function

of displaying, even "showing off," the grammatical possibilities of speech. As Wittgenstein suggests: "Do not forget that a poem, even though it is composed in the language of information, is not used in the language-game of giving information" (*Zettel* § 160). So, while the poem as a whole can be referred to various criteria of genre, author, historical period, and so on, the work as a unique form (borrowing Aristotle's term) or experience (Dewey's) or act (Kenneth Burke's) is not subsumable without remainder under absolutely fixed class concepts. What is variously included under the rubric "literature" thus involves ordinary language used not only with all sorts of everyday (and perhaps even noneveryday) meanings but also with "*experiencing* a meaning" (*PI* 175e; my emphasis), that is, of possibilities of meaning not exhausted by a specific, standard, practical use. And thus ordinary language philosophy and criticism can also be taken as nonstandard uses of ordinary language to investigate ordinary language "on display" in literature.

In my own investigations, accordingly, I want to make perspicuous some aspects of the linguistic situations we encounter in construing the ordering and breakdown of their grammar, rhetoric, logic, and dialectic. Such analysis is different from conceiving of poetic language *totaliter* as, say, the Russian formalists and American New Critics did, and as some deconstructionists still do, as *necessarily* disruptive, strange, deforming, "defamiliarizing" of everyday life, as though art necessarily emptied life of its claims on us while life itself was incapable of form altogether. Art sometimes does this, but is it always clear, in a given work, when or to what effect? By the same token, analysis of this sort is a way of conceiving "order" that is the opposite of that found, for example, in allegory, where it is traditionally a relatively complete organization of unmoving parts. For us (for me) order is a dynamic and fluid organizing or ordering of the environment by willful agents.[32]

In *Colors of the Mind: Conjectures on Thinking in Literature* (1991), Angus Fletcher quotes Wittgenstein against totalizing responses to the questions of order and defamiliarization, summarizing the point on which I am staking my own claims and interest: "'A poet's words go through and through us.' And that's connected causally with the use they have in our life. And it is also connected with the way in which, *conformably* to this use, we let our thoughts roam up and down [*schweifen*] in the familiar surroundings of the words' (*Zettel* § 155)" [my emphasis]. And Fletcher observes: "In effect, poetry and fiction and plays . . . get their piercing power from their contextual affiliation with the most ordinary uses our words have 'in our life.'"[33] The difference, then, between plotting empirical connections and investigating grammatical and rhetorical situations and conditions is to be shown in the way this book "roams up and down" familiar surroundings without dodging the difficulty of knowing what they are. And roaming up and down with respect to a work of art means, among other things, consulting (witnessing to,

confessing, acknowledging, showing, displaying, making evident) how the words function outside of poems in our everyday lives, lives with which they are "affiliated" but not identical.

## Who's Doing the Recounting? An Ethics and Politics of the Ordinary in First-Person Singular and Plural

I have suggested that in their major works Wittgenstein and Cavell are responding to traditional philosophical rejections of the everyday and ordinary to be found in metaphysical, empiricist, or skeptical arguments. This fact tends to make these works *appear* to be focused on specialized epistemological questions rather than on (what they might better be said to be) first and foremost hermeneutical matters of being-in-the-world. Said another way, traditional skepticism of the external world can also extend to the existence of the self and other people, thence to the status of the knowledge claims we make in practical matters of ethics and politics. When faced with questions of the good or of obligation, skeptics have usually fallen back on probability or practical ("moral") certainty to protect their (or our) interests. In this section, I propose that *all* matters of existence for Cavell—the material world, other minds, and moral knowledge—are ultimately ethical and political, that the problem of knowledge of the world and others is ultimately a kind of evaluating that Cavell calls "acknowledgement."[34] In the latter part of this chapter, I will look at an example from Frost of the skeptic's refusal or inability to acknowledge.

It is easy, for example, to be baffled by or to ignore Cavell's advertence to Rousseau in the early going of *The Claim of Reason* (*CR* 22–28). There, in the midst of his prosaic discussion of criteria, Cavell suddenly invokes "a natural outcropping of concepts which will later come more centrally or thematically into play" (*CR* 23), and then turns in passing—as though feeling obligated to show us some famous landmark—to point to Rousseau's *Social Contract* (1762). What does Rousseau, that mid-Enlightenment, protoromanticist figure, have to do with concepts, criteria, grammar, Frost? The question gestures toward my earlier query about "what we say when," for Cavell's invocation of others (here, Rousseau) and what *they* say we say when, is one way to begin to establish the (ordinary, everyday) criteria for identifying both the self who philosophizes and the ethical and political responsibilities of that self in, and out of, the activity of philosophizing. For my part, Dewey's *The Public and Its Problems* (1927) can serve a similar function in identifying a critically neglected aspect of poems of Robert Frost and others. My question then is: What, briefly, can Rousseau and Dewey make clearer regarding the "conditions of telling" in philosophy, poetry, and everyday life?

For Cavell, what is of chief interest in Rousseau's version of the social contract is that it is precisely *not* a historical claim about political origins, much less (what Hume took it to be; *CR* 23) a circular response to the question, "Why

should I obey the government?" (To answer this by saying, "because there is a contract in force" sounds like a bad joke.) Rousseau's interest in the contract is a philosophical, not historical, attempt to specify the relationship between self and others, the citizen and his or her community. The use of these possessive pronouns here is telling (it is criterial), for in Rousseau's analysis the individual, in consenting to give up her freedom to others, receives back from others—by means of the general will—that same freedom in fuller form. In other words, *consent* to membership is consent to equality with others in a community that is freely willed and for which, therefore, one is (I am) responsible. In embodying *my* will, the community offers me the ongoing opportunity to discover who I am among others, so to speak the social and political parts of myself, even while it requires my active dissent if I am to dissociate myself from what it does in my name. (And of course dissent *can* appropriately take passive forms—silence, digression, filibuster, and so on.) In effect, the social contract gives me a claim to speak and act for others and others for me.

Of course, Rousseau is aware that the general will is never perfectly realized, that it is frustrated by selfishness, oppression, intolerance, terror (man is born free and everywhere in chains), so that Cavell's interest in consent centers on the fact that the individual must *explore* his relationships in order to discover, in society's laws and in the activities of its members, his own identity: "the philosophical significance of [Rousseau's] writing lies in its imparting of philosophical education":

> it is philosophical because its method is an examination of myself by an attack upon my assumptions; it is political because the terms of this self-examination are the terms which reveal me as a member of a polis; it is education not because I learn new information but because I learn that the finding and forming of my knowledge of myself requires the finding and forming of my knowledge of that membership (the depth of my own and the extent of those joined with me). (*CR* 25)

The existence of the social contract, then, does not explain *why* we consent; rather our consent, our being *already* contracted with others in innumerable enterprises, defines, "it is a condition for the possibility of, political speech *per se.*"[35] This does not mean that some sheer ability to speak is a precondition for consent, but, on the contrary, that granting consent, in the senses of choosing and acting as always already bound with others, as invested in their cares and commitments, is itself a (grammatical, philosophical) "condition" of being able to speak as a person at all—to tell what's what. This is how Rousseau contributes to the grammar of political philosophy, by defining humans as bonded under the authority, and responsibility, not of a sovereign or a church but of their *own* will and the search for their own political voices in the everyday and ordinary.

(Put another way: if my own appeal earlier to "home" seemed too convenient, convention-bound, nostalgic, or repressive, communication understood as Wittgenstein's "circulation" and Rousseau's "search" may enable us to "embrace a kind of homelessness, a condition that could make the idea of home more palpable by showing more clearly the character of what home lacks. The play of home and homelessness is a process of a politics of the ordinary."[36] As used throughout the present book, in other words, "home" is the unending *process of exploring our own premises*. Put rhetorically, the general will is just the search for common and special topics of a political community.)

In order to extend Rousseau's discussion of specific moral and political experience to more general problems of skepticism of others and of a politically competent community, and in order to begin to make these points more concrete and historically more specific to Robert Frost's cultural situation in America between 1900 and 1930, I want briefly to recall John Dewey's response, in *The Public and Its Problems* (1927), to Walter Lippmann's popular and influential indictment of democratic common sense in *Public Opinion* (1922).[37] While Frost is well known for his individualist (anti–New Deal) politics, I want to call on Cavell's Rousseau for a different line of thought. Rather in the way that Kierkegaard's stress on "the single individual" has led critics to overlook his equally strong, albeit tacit, rhetorical preoccupation with his reading audience, or in the way Rousseau's use of the social contract has been obscured by literalist over rhetorical interpretations, or in the way Wittgenstein's and Cavell's use of the term "ordinary language" has led critics to demand empirical evidence of usage rather than rely on their (the critics') own grammatical senses of their use of their own language, so have narrow accounts of Frost as "self-reliant" and as political "conservative"—though perfectly true as far as they go—long overshadowed his *philosophical* commitments to an American political modernism deeply concerned with the first-person *plural* as well as singular—that is, with showing not just what "I" say, but what "we" say when.

For Lippmann in the opening decades of the twentieth century, rhetorical substance and style, everyday common sense (public opinion) and public speech, were not and never had been appropriate tools of competent representation for the purposes of self-government. Lippmann's was a political skepticism that lifted to the level of public policy the more generalized battle between popular and aristocratic modes of speech among all strata of society throughout the nineteenth century. Lippmann's position had three central supports. First, as modern society grows more fragmented and its problems and the agencies to deal with them more complex, modern democracies must turn to social science "experts" to supply accurate reporting of the facts of people's environment. Second, these experts should operate apart from the decision makers, meaning here epistemologically apart: "the power of the expert depends upon separating himself from those who

make the decisions, upon not caring, in his expert self, what decision is made."[38] And last, the experts' reporting would be fed to decision makers who would, effectively, *be* the nation, choosing its interests, problems, and directions. From out of its vast resources of skepticism, such a theory generously seeks to dispose (or impose) the requirements of science onto the waywardness of poor unscientific ("ordinary") man.

By contrast, Dewey undertook, by way of philosophical rather than empirical inquiry, to show that however great a role experts should play in the so-called machinery of government, and whatever harsh truths reside in Hobbes's struggle of all against all or in Machiavelli's atomization of the members of the polis and the superiority of the prince, or indeed in Rousseau's outright dismissal of democratic forms of government, "no government by experts in which the masses do not have the chance to inform the experts as to their needs can be anything but an oligarchy managed in the interests of the few."[39] Again, I want to isolate three elements of Dewey's position in *The Public and Its Problems,* not to try to address political questions at stake here or to hook them up with specific political interests of Frost but rather to connect Dewey's philosophic concerns regarding the commonsense interests of ordinary people—that is, the ways people normally understand and communicate *as* a community—with the similar but neglected concerns of Cavell's Rousseau and of (my own accounting of) Frost.

First, for Dewey, communication as dialogue and discussion, as conversation, is *philosophically* and not just empirically central to what it means to be human, it is part of the philosophic grammar of the concept "human being": "To learn to be human is to develop through the give-and-take of communication an effective sense of being an individually distinctive member of a community; one who understands and appreciates its beliefs, desires and methods, and who contributes to a further conversion of organic powers into human resources and values" (154). Second, it follows that the political value of democracy involves the "consultation and discussion which uncover [not merely parrot what are said to be] social needs and troubles." De Tocqueville, Dewey relates, "pointed out in effect that popular government is educative as other modes of political regulation are not. It forces a recognition that there are common interests, even though the recognition of what they are is confused ["in eclipse"; 110ff.]; and the need it enforces of discussion and publicity brings about some clarification of what they are" (207–8). Third, the centrality of these common interests, beliefs, and values to democratic (read human) existence have been eclipsed by the complexity of modern life and capitalist commodification of culture, so that "the essential need . . . is the improvement of the methods and conditions of debate, discussion and persuasion. That is *the* problem of the public" (208).[40] For Dewey, this "rhetorical turn" does not mean banishing scientific experts (as Plato, in the *Republic,* co-opted the rhetoricians and exiled the poets altogether) but rather putting the experts in their place,

or better, reconfirming and extending the role of ordinary language and the methods of rhetoric to *locate* as well as communicate common interests.[41] This elevation of the everyday and ordinary is something experts qua specialists can not do and that extreme skeptics, anyway, near fatally forbid themselves.

Now the provisional conclusions I want to make, at this stage of my argument, are also threefold. First, I will have occasion to note in the following chapter that rhetorical methods of inquiry, discussion, and judgment had been under suspicion at least since the time of the Enlightenment, not only in the academic abstract but concretely and urgently, as practical questions of social identity and political life, in France, England, and America, and in widely discussed forums ranging from newspapers to popular books as well as academic treatises and plays (for example, Shaw's *Pygmalion* [1919]), to poems such as Frost's early "The Tuft of Flowers" (written in 1897) and late "Beech" (published in 1942), to the landmarks of high modernism. In theoretically distinguishing metaphysical or scientific methods of proof from rhetorical appeals in politics and art, Dewey, unlike Lippmann, trusts both, giving what Hilary Putnam calls priority to the practical: "The dilemma facing classical defenders of democracy arose because all of them presupposed that we already know our nature and our capabilities. In contrast, Dewey's view is that we don't *know* what our interests and needs are or what we are capable of until we engage in politics,"[42] until, that is, we give voice to our interests. In another guise this is, of course, just that struggle between philosophic "experts" and the ordinary man in everyday life with which I started the chapter. In needing to discover *our* interests, democracy is not promoted by fixed beliefs (however commonsensical), much less by the reification of the ordinary as the normal, but rather by the transformation of the everyday. Ordinary language expresses interests that are always to some extent *emerging,* as knowledge and events change; hence it expresses the "romance" of the ordinary situated among the suffocating normal and routine and the distracting (or violent) eventful and the self-regarding heroic and stellar.

Such a position as Dewey's, second, comes close to what these days is called political communitarianism,[43] but, more important, it involves a turn to debate and discussion and, we will see, a Ciceronian interest in argument and persuasion as modes of both prudential reasoning and of philosophical inquiry and judgment. Contrary to most critical estimates, philosophical appeal to dialogue, conversation, to what Frost called "gossip" ("our interest in each other"), is of central moment in Frost's poems, performing a normative function for him of the sort that the search for the general will does for Rousseau and that "acknowledgement" does for Cavell: we engage the "truth" of skepticism (and thereby sidestep what is misleading in skepticism) not by knowing but by *acknowledging* our responsibility to the cares and commitments of others, of people who are not "proved" to exist but whom we acknowledge by caring for and responding to them. As we have said,

the idea of acknowledgment, like that of the social contract, is not intended as an epistemological proof or historical explanation to justify ethical or political obedience in the present but rather as the reverse: by appealing to the nature of man "as" self-defining only within a community, Rousseau argues that man must use his capacity for considerations beyond self-interest (the general will, the cares and commitments of others) to forge his chains into shared bonds. Like Rousseau and Dewey, Frost posits such social bonds or links without forgetting the requirement that they be constantly challenged in the name of continually emerging moral and political regulative ideals never finally defined, what Cavell in later writings calls "Emersonian perfectionism." Said otherwise, Dewey democratizes Rousseau in ways both Frost and Cavell would approve:

> Symbols . . . depend upon and promote communication. The results of conjoint experience are considered and transmitted. Events cannot be passed from one to another, but meanings may be shared by means of signs. Wants and impulses are then attached to common meanings. They are thereby transformed into desires and purposes, which, since they implicate a common or shared meaning, present new ties converting a conjoint activity into a community of interest and endeavor. Thus there is generated what, metaphorically, may be termed a general will and social consciousness.[44]

"Conditions of telling" thus involve both criteria of communal *discriminations* of concepts and the emerging and changing *narratives* of concrete individuals within whose lives and stories criteria emerge and have their being in a community. Such a stance combines traditional Enlightenment liberalism and contemporary postmodern communitarianism in a way that typifies, in my view, Frost's most philosophically intuitive moments.

Third, I want to reposition Dewey's analysis, in chapter 6 of *The Public and Its Problems*, of the cultural forces involved in the "eclipse" of the public in America in the early twentieth century ("It is not that there is no public. . . . There is too much public, a public too diffused and scattered and too intricate in composition"; 137), by reminding us that Dewey's analysis is but part of the much larger story of philosophical and religious skepticism pervasive in European cultural life from Descartes forward. So-called external world and other minds skepticism occupies, of course, the center of Cavell's interpretation of Wittgenstein's *Philosophical Investigations* and stands behind Dewey's *The Public and Its Problems* and much of his other work, for Lippmann's political skepticism is but a symptom of more serious doubts about what we can know with any kind of certainty, whether "logical" or "moral." We might say that for Dewey, "eclipse" is a *grammatical* criterion of the concepts of "community" and "communication" themselves, inasmuch as "experience," as using or accounting with criteria, is necessarily pitched forward into the absent unknown (eclipsed) future. Rather in

the way (and during the same period) that Freud made the "unconscious" the repressed part of the concept of the ego, and the later Heidegger and Derrida made "Nichtigkeit" or "différance" a criterion of Dasein and the structure of signs, Dewey and Cavell are aware that knowledge and experience—like political democracy itself—depend upon inventing agencies to bring it out of eclipse *not* once and for all but over and over again, foregrounding what is background and vice versa, allowing for and even requiring repression, différance, absence, eclipse. The problems of the public do not constitute a brand-new crisis but are part and parcel of the human as well as the democratic condition. In Rousseau's terms, selfish resistance not just to finding but even to seeking the general will is not only historical and social but also ontological. In this regard it is not insignificant, I think, that the title of Frost's first book is *A Boy's Will* (1913), for a boy—as in Wittgenstein's quotation of Augustine—stands in need of linguistic, hence political and philosophical, education, lacking which he remains willful in a self-centered way. In lieu of expanding on the complex problem of skepticism here (select aspects of which will be treated in later chapters), I offer instead a perspicuous example of Frost's own preoccupation with responding to—not defeating but as it were handling—the problem of skepticism of other minds and its concomitant eclipse of one of the conditions of telling anything, namely community and communication.

### "They Suffered from a General Onslaught": Skepticism and Dogmatism in "The Black Cottage"

So far I have only hinted that thinkers such as Dewey, Wittgenstein, and Cavell, in resisting accounts of knowledge and language as ultimately resting on empiricist, idealist, or rationalist foundations, also resist various forms of skepticism barking at the heels of all such accounts. The history of skepticism extends back far beyond Descartes, of course, to the ancient Pyrrhonians and the Academic Skeptics of Plato's school. But Descartes's answer to skepticism in the Cogito, and his proofs for the existence of God in the *Meditations* (1641), mark the beginnings of the best-known strand of the modern period and its quest for certainty outside the bounds of religious or institutional authorities. What Richard Bernstein has called "Cartesian anxiety," the (negatively incapable) quest for certainty in knowledge, surfaces again and again not only in philosophy but, more loosely, in literature and, even more broadly, in the culture at large.[45] Frost's "The Black Cottage" (1914) ought to serve well as a beginning example of skepticism, for the minister in the poem embodies both the traditional quest for certainty and the modern refusal of foundations—at the cost, naturally, of oscillating between dogmatism on the one hand and skepticism on the other.

"The Black Cottage" is, moreover, one of those poems of Frost about which

he asserted, "So many of them have literary criticism in them—*in* them. And yet I wouldn't admit it. I try to hide it."[46] That is, the minister's skeptical dilemma here is resolved only in our experience of the poem itself, in *our* recounting of the criteria we use in the evaluation of its action and form and in the acknowledgments we rely on in doing so. Critics have entirely overlooked not only this poem's oblique commentary on, but its own exemplifications of, reading and speaking as constitutive parts of everyday praxis and experience, of those "conditions of telling" what is in front of our noses—including, in this case, poems. It is not coincidental, in other words, that "The Black Cottage"—written in a post-Arnoldian world of doubt at the very start-up of American literary high modernism and the latter's flight from the everyday and ordinary—features the *search* for a more stable conception of "experience" as words-in-action. This is a search that preoccupied Dewey in his reconstruction of philosophy as well as Wittgenstein and Cavell in their response to Descartes's extreme skeptical doubt. To introduce these matters, Robert Langbaum's seminal modern study of what Dilthey was the first to call *"Erlebnisdichtung,"*[47] or the "poetry of experience," will provide us with a useful point of departure for our understanding of Frost.[48]

According to Robert Langbaum in *The Poetry of Experience* (1957), the genre of the dramatic monologue is better defined by family resemblances of effect than by fixed external criteria of form.[49] Conceived by Browning and Tennyson chiefly as a reaction against the one-sidedly subjective or self-revelatory impulse of romantic lyric, looking instead to blend lyric and dramatic, subjective and objective impulses (81), the genre offers, as Langbaum explains, sympathy of understanding for "reprehensible" or otherwise marginal characters, offering readers an increase not in knowledge but in "experience," which is to say a net gain in our self-awareness and imaginative understanding of the other. To Langbaum, the genre is an "excellent vehicle for the 'impossible' case" (86), for example, the "combination of villain and aesthete" who stalks through Browning's "My Last Duchess" or "The Bishop Orders His Tomb" (86). In each of these poems, the "extraordinary point of view" (42) of the duke or bishop gets explored in the dramatic melding of character, situation, and idea, its effects a result of the tensions between our fascination with, and consequent sympathy for, the character, and our moral resistance to what he represents. Inasmuch as "the utter outrageousness of the duke's behavior makes condemnation the least interesting response" (83), however, we are in effect invited by the poet to suspend the moral impulse in order to allow ourselves instead to *understand* the duke, "the end being to establish the reader's sympathetic relation to the poem, to gain 'facts from within'" (78). Again, to Langbaum this is what the "poetry of experience" is all about: appropriating what is not ourselves into what we already are, as it were extending our own horizons and boundaries.

Among Frost's poems, the clearest example of monologic marginality is "A

Servant to Servants" (1914), although "The Black Cottage"—notwithstanding the presence of an unidentified narrator at the beginning and end—also probably belongs to the genre. Read in the context of Tennyson's dramatic monologues, for example, which frequently deal "with an emotional perversity that verges on the pathological" (87), and specifically with "a certain life-weariness, a longing for rest through oblivion" (89) (Ulysses, I suppose, would be the purest case), the minister in "The Black Cottage," in his fantasy of a desert waste, also longs for oblivion, at least briefly (but then *can* one, grammatically speaking, "long" "briefly?" ["Could someone have a feeling of ardent love or hope for the space of one second—no matter what preceded or followed this second?"; *PI* § 583]):

> "As I sit here, and oftentimes, I wish
> I could be monarch of a desert land
> I could devote and dedicate forever
> To the truths we keep coming back and back to.
> So desert it would have to be, so walled
> By mountain ranges half in summer snow,
> No one would covet it or think it worth
> The pains of conquering to force change on."
>
> (lines 111–18)

And otherwise the minister evinces a perverse blend of charming volubility and passive aggression:

> "Do you know but for her there was a time
> When, to please younger members of the church,
> Or rather say non-members in the church,
> Whom we all have to think of nowadays,
> I would have changed the Creed a very little?
> Not that she ever had to ask me not to;
> It never got so far as that; but the bare thought
> Of her old tremulous bonnet in the pew,
> And of her half asleep was too much for me.
> Why, I might wake her up and startle her.
> It was the words 'descended into Hades'
> That seemed too pagan to our liberal youth.
> You know, they suffered from a general onslaught.
> And well, if they weren't true why keep right on
> Saying them like the heathen? We could drop them."
>
> (lines 84–98)

As in many poems by Browning, moreover, we encounter in "The Black Cottage" a lone speaker whose words, not entirely motivated by his interlocutor, present us with his own highly motivated "facts from within," his unique autobiographical constellation of thoughts and feelings about faith and doubt, race

and equality, time and eternity, war and peace, talk and silence, almost incoherently inviting us to identify with his point of view on the one hand while, on the other, bracketing altogether the larger issues of morality, politics, perhaps even humanness itself, offering a kind of Zarathustrean aestheticism beyond good and evil: "'No one would covet it [his imaginary desert world] or think it worth / The pains'" (lines 117–18); and earlier: "'Pretty . . . Come in. No one will care'" (line 11). Thus William Pritchard concludes that Frost's interest in this poem is "psychological."[50]

In light of Langbaum's criteria, then, "The Black Cottage" is a dramatic monologue but, it would seem, a flawed one, perhaps even an outright failure, for many of the same reasons that Langbaum finds "Hohenstiel-Schwangau" and "Fifine" unsuccessful: "because no outline of character emerges from the intricacy of the argument, there is no one to sympathize with and we are therefore not convinced. . . . Arguments cannot make the case in the dramatic monologue but only passion, power, strength of will and intellect, just those existential virtues which are independent of logical and moral correctness and are therefore best made out through sympathy and when clearly separated from, even opposed to, the other virtues" (86). Turn the poem this way or that, it is impossible to attribute to the minister in "The Black Cottage" either passion, power, or strength of will or intellect; no coherent character emerges here to sympathize with. Rightly or wrongly, on the other hand, the threat of argument hums constantly in the background:

> "And she liked to talk. She had seen Garrison
> And Whittier, and had her story of them.
> One wasn't long in learning that she thought,
> Whatever else the Civil War was for,
> It wasn't just to keep the States together,
> Nor just to free the slaves, though it did both.
> She wouldn't have believed those ends enough
> To have given outright for them all she gave.
> Her giving somehow touched the principle
> That all men are created free and equal.
> And to hear her quaint phrases—so removed
> From the world's view today of all those things."
>
> (lines 52–63)

As for passion, power, or strength of will: the minister vaguely dismisses the Civil War that swept off the widow's husband, condescends to the personal force of "innocence" the widow manifests ("'Strange how such innocence get its own way'"; line 81), and shows utter deficiency of a general will both in his readiness to change the Creed "'to please the younger members of the church'" (line 85) (!), and in his decision *not* to change it after all out of cravenness at offending the widow (!!)—all of which is in line with his earlier doubts about the Constitution.

In short, like Browning's duke and bishop, the minister is what some would consider a proto-high modernist aesthete (lines 9–11), holding his story of the widow "at arm's length" (line 9), trying in effect "to convert otherness into aesthetic identity."[51] Far from being in any way extraordinary, however, much less a pathological villain—in fact Frost wrote at the time that he had insinuated "no villains" into *North of Boston* (1914), in which "The Black Cottage" appears[52]—the minister is a homegrown skeptic about the home of the everyday and ordinary, a skeptic of the most everyday and ordinary sort for his time, and for that reason he is easy to confuse with a skeptically minded (but not mindlessly skeptical) author like Frost.

As for strength of intellect, finally, Reuben Brower has astutely observed that the minister "is made to sound like a young man who has swallowed William James too hastily"[53]—in a word, thoughtful but no thinker:

> "She had some art of hearing and yet not
> Hearing the latter wisdom of the world.
> White was the only race she ever knew.
> Black she had scarcely seen, and yellow never.
> But how could they be made so very unlike
> By the same hand working in the same stuff?
> She had supposed the war decided that.
> What are you going to do with such a person?"
>
> (lines 73–80)

But then, what are *we* going to do with such an engaging character so adrift as the minister, someone who keeps his national history straight ("'Fredericksburg wasn't Gettysburg, of course'"; line 33) but can't recall one of his parishioner's pertinent facts of loss ("'I *ought* to know'"; line 32; my emphasis) to make that history count here. In the abstract, to be sure, the minister professes a fairly sophisticated view of both history and facts. You can tell this by the way he considers the interpretation of texts—the Constitution, the Bible—as contextual matters historically interpretable according to changing frameworks of understanding:

> "That's a hard mystery of Jefferson's.
> What did he mean? Of course the easy way
> Is to decide it simply isn't true.
> It may not be. I heard a fellow say so.
> But never mind, the Welshman got it planted
> Where it will trouble us a thousand years.
> Each age will have to reconsider it."
>
> (lines 64–70)

It may be difficult to understand the exact meaning of his later nostrum that "'Most of the change we think we see in life / Is due to truths being in and out of

favor'" (lines 109–10), but at least it sounds vaguely okay, possibly even cutting-edge, and we can hear a defensible pragmatist claim in such lines.

Such, anyway, is his theory. In practice, things do not go so well, for, on scrutiny, the minister engages in the most arrant reductivist thinking: he pigeonholes the widow as simpleminded and childish (lines 81, 102) when his own evidence shows her thoughtful forthrightness (line 54), independence and backbone (lines 40–42, 58, 71ff.), and courageous ability to suffer personal loss (line 59). And he otherwise dismisses not only the widow but his own congregation—and here he begins to show his stripes with his precious "dear me" (line 104)—as variable winds blowing warm and cold, rhetorical crowds whose "favor" one must curry and whose variability one escapes, briefly, perhaps, but *"oftentimes"* (line 111; my emphasis), either in solipsistic soliloquy or (afterward, vis-à-vis his interlocutor) repressed violence: "'There are bees in this wall.' He struck the clapboards" (line 125).

The point about currying favor is pivotal, for it signals that his skepticism about something so basic as Jeffersonian human rights might generalize: if he doesn't know the most basic things about one human being, how can he or anyone else know anything about others at all? Here a kind of abject posing upstages even the "general onslaught" the minister mentions having tried to address in line 96, that is, the general onslaught of religious doubt and general skepticism so prevalent in the late nineteenth century, of which the minister becomes an even more generalized, secular as well as religious, victim and exemplar.

We can determine this skepticism by considering *how*, and how poorly, the minister plays the language game of credal statements, questioning claims in the Creed and Constitution not only as to their *meaning* (which questioning acceptably follows from the minister's allusion to interpretive frameworks) but as to their *truth* (which questioning does not follow, anyway not in the same way). For it is one thing, a hermeneutic and even pragmatic thing (*OC* § 422), to interpret statements of people in light of interpretive frameworks; it is another matter altogether to interpret interpretive frameworks solely in the light of further statements of people, as if the statements themselves, in being *words*, sieved out all certainty about the *world*—as if criteria were stabilized in nothing at all. The reason these acts of interpretation differ is that the latter option blurs the different grammatical roles that credal statements play compared to other kinds of statements: "Think of the tools in a tool-box: there is a hammer, pliers, a saw, a screw-driver, a rule, a glue-pot, glue, nails and screw.—The functions of words are as diverse as the functions of these objects" (*PI* § 11). The minister speaks as if all statements were tools to be used in the same way, whether as equally negotiable or equally doubtable, simply because one can *say* that one doubts them: "That is to say, the *questions* that we raise and our *doubts* depend on the fact that *some propositions are exempt from doubt, are as it were like hinges on which those turn*" (*OC* § 341; my emphasis), or, in another image, like railroad cars "shunted onto an

unused siding" (OC § 210).⁵⁴ This is just what the minister, both clergyman and citizen, fails to grasp: "'Of course the easy way / Is to decide it simply isn't true. / It may not be. I heard a fellow say so'" (lines 65–67).

Taken alone, the minister's doubt is, again, logically unexceptionable on the minister's own pragmatist grounds: our fundamental credal statements are *not* logically certain. But rhetorically and philosophically the minister interprets the Constitution and Creed "the easy way," as though one's "decision" about such statements is to be fashioned in the light of popular sentiments, of alternative opinions considered *apart* from firmer considerations of the grammar of our speech. Here grammar includes the criteria of concepts (including the everyday situations to which and in which it speaks) *and* the acknowledgment of others as creatures who have cares and commitments of their own. By changing his mind about changing the Creed, on the specious ground that it may upset the widow (an appeal, in sum, to his own fear of her), the minister practices the moral relativism that Cavell has under view in the crucial part 3 of *The Claim of Reason*: "what such a theory says, in effect, is that there is no theoretical difference between persuading someone to do something by convincing him that he ought to, *using reasons which convince you,* and by persuading him by appeals to his fears, your prestige, or another's money." Here, in other words, "persuading" is prised loose from convincing, rhetorical desire from the interests of grammar, so that the end of speech is, in effect, doing or getting what one wants:

> "Why not sit down if you are in no haste?
> These doorsteps seldom have a visitor.
> The warping boards pull out their own old nails
> With none to tread and put them in their place."
>
> (lines 47–50)

Cavell continues: "It may in fact be the case that the latter grounds [doing or getting what one wants] are always decisive, that no such practice is manifest in the practice of a given society; Thrasymachus and Marx, among others, thought that. But then they *knew* they were attacking morality and society as a whole" (*CR* 278). The difference between titans like Thrasymachus and Marx and our well-intentioned, cringing little minister is that the latter knows *not* what he is doing, and so veers half-madly between skepticism here and insular dogmatism at the end ("'So desert . . . so walled / By mountain ranges . . . / No one would covet it'"; lines 115–17).

For Wittgenstein, by contrast, credal statements serve as the "bedrock" on which all of our concepts and arguments ultimately turn (*PI* § 217), or, alternatively, the banks within which the river of everyday life flows without themselves flowing away (*OC* § 96–99), *not* because they provide some *fundamentum incon-cussam veritatis,* but because they may move or change and yet still manage the

Heraclitean flow. In short, they are fallible but nevertheless fundamental "acknowledgments" in natural language and ordinary life underwriting the criteria and grammatical rules organizing concepts like "human," "world," "certainty," "experience," and the like, concepts and actions that *make possible* other activities of everyday life and their innumerable language games—in a phrase, our "conditions of telling." While those conditions *can* change, change is not achieved by fiat but by rearranging one's whole world. When the minister questions them instead the *easy* way, overlooking or ignoring their role as grammatical hinges, he confuses the different roles our words pragmatically perform in our lives. Then his only remedy is to hold the world and others at arm's length and ultimately to drop out of everyday language games altogether—though he cannot, as we see, sustain this retreat, and he returns to his interlocutor (as he returns, longing "briefly" but *often*, to the cottage—it is no "chance" their being there [line 1]—in a pathetic repetition-compulsion).

Hence Wittgenstein writes: "As if giving grounds did not come to an end sometime. But the end is not an ungrounded presupposition. It is an ungrounded way of *acting*" (*OC* § 110; my emphasis). In a 1915 letter to Louis Untermeyer, written hard on the heels of publishing "The Black Cottage," Frost gives his own version of Wittgenstein's commitment to action: "Nothing is true except as a man or men adhere to it," a dictum that sounds like the minister's but only superficially: "to live for it, to spend themselves on it, to die for it. Not to argue for it!"

> There's no greater mistake than to look on fighting as a form of argument. To *fight* is to leave words and act as if you believed—to *act* as if you believed. Sometimes I leave my doubts of words altogether and I ask myself what is the place of them. They are worse than nothing unless they do something, unless they amount to deeds as in ultimatums and war crys [*sic*]. . . . My definition of literature would be just this: words that have become deeds." (*LLU* 10; cf. *PI* § 546: "Words are also deeds.")

The remainder of this book may be read as a sustained commentary on these notes of Wittgenstein and Frost, and on Rosen's earlier emphasis on "speeches and deeds." For even though, as Frost puts it, he does sometimes "*leave my doubt of words altogether*," he is not naïvely denying skepticism its constitutive role in thought and language so much as putting it in its place, as something already held relatively steady by virtue of what words *do* in practice rather than merely say in theory, by how a person lives (and dies) with others in contexts near and far. Thus experience here means not individual *consciousness* so much as participation in a public nexus of words and actions, while life is not logically stated in propositions or proved by argument so much as tested by one's own character in a shared form of life, quite as it was for Isocrates and Cicero, and indeed for Chaucer: "Experience, though noon auctorite / Were in this world, is right ynough for

me." In *Art as Experience,* Dewey stresses the central importance in experience of the authority of our suffering or undergoing reversals of expectation: "There is ... an element of undergoing, of suffering in its large sense, in every experience. Otherwise there would be no taking in of what preceded. For 'taking in' in any vital experience is something more than placing something over what was previously known. It involves reconstruction which may be painful."[55] Thus we must search for our premises.

Such a provisional conclusion speaks directly, of course, to the claims about experience and character, hence about community, in Langbaum. Granted that lack of coherence of character in the minister means no sympathy in the reader, hence no experience as Langbaum defines it. But then, if it is not Frost's dramatic goal to delineate someone else's character, he cannot be said to fail at extending our capacity for sympathy, for experience as *Erlebnis*. On the contrary, suppose that Frost is offering an experience as *Erfahrung,* aiming at something else, at "character" or "virtues" *not,* in fact, separable from intelligence, passion, and strength of will or from the grammar of these concepts. As Frost wrote to another friend at the time: "The language [of the poems] is appropriate to the virtues I celebrate. At least I am sure I can count on you for knowing what I am about" (*SL* 83–84). But then, what *is* he about? What virtues? *Whose* character?

We can take one more step toward an answer if, in keeping with the notion that "words are deeds" (*CV* 46e, 31e; *PI* § 546), we ask what we ourselves have to do to read this poem well, what Frost requires of us if we want to go on with such things. In "The Dramatic Monologue and Related Lyric Forms," Ralph W. Rader generalizes the specific point I am after in "The Black Cottage": "My more particular claim is that we register the figures in these dramatic poems as projected in various kinds of specific significant relationship to the author which we grasp not through some special poetic way of knowing [what I have identified as Langbaum's Diltheyan *Erlebnis*] but by extension of the means by which we have been equipped by evolution to understand, through our bodies, ourselves, and by tacit inference, the human others like ourselves, in the context of the world of which we are part."[56] Thus what Frost requires of us centrally includes our coming to see how the minister is playing with a false but commonly held opposition: "*either* absolute openness *or* absolute fixity," saying in so many words that he does not believe such an opposition but acting as if, showing us, he does. The experience of reading this poem is thus not one of extending our own fixed character by absorbing a new character to a further fixed universal, thereby intensifying our own inner feelings or knowledge, but of engaging in what genuinely counters and even foils us: "we seek not another version of ourselves, but a set of tangents that help to clarify our lives by maintaining differences enabling us to feel we can engage others, both for what they become as expressive beings and for the sake of how those beings become capable of influencing and judging us."[57] All of which

is pretty much the central support of Gadamer's Hegelian notion of "experience" as *Erfahrung* and what Hegel called "skepticism in action" and Cavell "living our skepticism": "If we thus regard experience in terms of its result, we have ignored the fact that experience is a process. In fact, this process is essentially negative. It cannot be described as simply the unbroken generation of typical universals. Rather, this generation takes place as false generalizations are continually refuted by experience and what was regarded as typical is shown not to be so" (*TM* 353).

But then Frost's skepticism, like Hegel's and Gadamer's, is nevertheless not the same as the minister's ("it makes a difference which"; line 32), for in this case, at least, the negativity of experience, Frost's challenge to our expectations as readers, *includes* a challenge to the wholesale skepticism so tempting, and fashionable, in his time as in ours. This challenge is not to the effect that we have, after all, *sure* grounds for our beliefs but rather that our ungrounded beliefs are ultimately tested as ethical-political *actions*, committed discriminations between credal principles and the variety of language games they contain and make possible. What Victorians learned to expect of the genre of the dramatic monologue from Browning and Tennyson is almost entirely overthrown in "The Black Cottage" (calling into question the rubric itself), leaving us constrained to negotiate a series of agons whose members are ambiguously attractive and unattractive: minister and widow, Jefferson and his doubters, the widow and the racists, the minister and his liberal youth, fickle audiences and the sounds of silence, texts and contexts, and many others—in sum, the topoi structuring the innumerable lines of argument, the patterns and collage, that compose the experience of the poem. In fact, rhetorical arguments *do* "make the case" here, in the sense that the reader must carefully connect and differentiate complex lines of thought and feeling within the overarching topoi of "possible" and "impossible." "The Black Cottage" may be a dramatic monologue, but Frost requires us to take up, ourselves, a middle position in a *dialogue* between him and the minister, turning soliloquy into conversation and even some measure of heteroglossia, cultivating our power (our *virtù* and our virtues) to invent and judge by seeing *through* poses—*with* them as well as *past* them—and in that way locating our own moral-intellectual position.[58] And while all literature can and (at least for Gadamer) should be read this way, my own argument throughout this book will be that Frost himself strategically endorses such an approach to experience, in books as well as out.

As we have seen, however, experience is always of limits and refusal. What good is it, then, to us readers and writers of criticism? Can this sort of thing be *taught*? Similarly, Wittgenstein asks: "Can one learn this knowledge?" "Yes; some can. Not, however, by taking a course in it, but through *"experience"* [*Erfahrung*].— Can someone else be a man's teacher in this? Certainly. From time to time he gives him the right *tip* [*den richtigen Wink*]. This is what "learning" and "teaching" are like here.—What one acquires here is not a technique; one learns correct

judgments" (*PI* p. 227). Correct judgments collect a character and critical community around them the way an experienced person collects negative examples of what Kant called reflective judgments (not just positive or confirming examples of determinant judgments) by attending to the surprises he or she suffers. By attending to small things dismissed or overlooked that make a difference, that "count" or "tell," as Cavell puts it, a community gathers itself together, creates and re-creates its ethos or character, and finds or makes an order among the ordinary that is nevertheless continually renewed, an invention out of and toward new judgments.

But, then, as is well known, Frost is a consummate trickster figure. For (in his words again) to "*act* as if one believed" in such a community is, after all, "to act *as if* one believed," hence perhaps not to believe at all, even to act without any conscious commitment. (And, in fact, for neither Wittgenstein, Frost, Burke, nor Cavell is a world supported by beliefs or even knowledge. Cavell writes that "the human creature's basis in the world as a whole, its relation to the world as such, is not that of knowing, anyway not what we think of as knowing" [*CR* 324; see also *IQO* 4]. Isn't this skepticism, after all?)

Otherwise said, to "act as if" is to posture and pose, sometimes to pretend, or to impersonate, to give a pretense of something, a simulacrum. It has been said of Lionel Trilling that "the coherent intellectual community and clearly defined cultural situation that Trilling addresses were partly a rhetorical invention . . . a counter-historical ideal community."[59] What, then, are such posing and posturing *for,* and how should we credit, and why should we trust, impostors like Frost? To address that question I propose that we start over, using our conclusions here as a beginning to reconsider what we mean by invention and judgment and logic in literature, trying to determine what counts for Frost, and trying to see what counts for ourselves.

CHAPTER

# 2

# RHETORICAL INVENTION
*Notes toward an American Low Modernism*

> The subjects of the other arts are derived from hidden and remote sources while the whole art of oratory lies open to view, and is concerned in some measure with the common practice, custom and speech of mankind, so that, whereas in all other arts that is most excellent which is farthest removed from the understanding and mental capacity of the untrained, in oratory the very cardinal sin is to depart from the language of everyday life and the usage approved by the sense of the community.
> —Cicero, *De oratore*

## Positions, Impositions, Poses

### Positions

IF WE TAKE the "art of oratory," so confidently surveyed in the quotation from Cicero above, too literally or too historically, it will likely appear impossibly anachronistic for contemporary literary studies. Today's literary Theorists-with-a-capital-T will more likely equate oratory or eloquence with "the meat-chopping gesture and rhetorical bark of the demagogue," as Vladimir Nabokov, in *Speak, Memory,* so memorably puts it, than with whatever it was Cicero had in mind.[1] While the words Nabokov discreetly inscribes on his own pages can and often do "speak" to us, it is not, at least not obviously, because those words depend on "approved usages" of style or some static *sensus communis* of a people (which common sense, as it happens, Nabokov famously forswears in various novels and lecture-essays). On the contrary, if such words speak to us, perhaps it is because—this has long been a commonplace of romantic and modern art—they seem to have been spirited away from common sense and ordinary language altogether.[2] If we were now even to try to reconnect with "oratory-as-formal-public-eloquence" on native grounds, in the American literary grain, we would need to go all the way back to Ralph Waldo Emerson, who was, among other things, an orator in the high genteel tradition of Edward T. and William Ellery Channing, exploiting "the usage approved by the sense of the community." Yet Emerson, like other serious writers around him, was already well on his way toward a different model of speech, later working (as did William James and Mark Twain) a sweeping lecture circuit through the 1870s. In his *Journals,* Emerson contrasts those "pulpits

tame and ineffectual," "with their cold, mechanical preparation for a delivery most decorous—fine things, pretty things, wise things," hence with "no transpiercing, no loving, no enchantment," to what is newly possible on the secular podium: "Here is all the true orator will ask, for here is a convertible audience & here are no stiff conventions that prescribe a method, a style, a limited quotation of books.... No, here everything is admissible, philosophy, ethics, divinity, criticism, poetry, humor, fun, mimicry, anecdotes, jokes, ventriloquism . . . it is a panharmonicon."[3]

What I will call "Emerson's list" of admissibles will itself prove convertible, returning in different guises as we go.[4] Here I want merely to note that by the time Robert Frost began his own publishing career a bit later (1890 to be exact, the year of publication of Emily Dickinson's works), Emersonian informal talk and conversation—freely used by Lincoln in his normal "middling" style of speech and increasingly introduced in popular grammars and rhetorics from 1850 onward—and *not* formal oratory presented a more plausible model for a democratic nation of increasingly crowded, often unacculturated, urban dwellers on the move and make.[5] In fact, worry over appropriate modes of talk in politics, religion, commerce, and virtually all public and private venues had been considerable (as our discussion of Lippmann and Dewey earlier attest) throughout the nineteenth century in America and remained so even into the 1930s. The genre of the public lecture had become little more than "an episode in a narrative of conflicts" no longer adequate to contemporary experience, while the demands of a democratic polity were increasingly clashing with the privatization of experience in the emerging communication technologies of telephone and moving pictures.[6] As late as 1905, in reaction to this general shift, William James's brother Henry can be heard scolding the aspiring alumnae at Bryn Mawr for the growing laxity of their everyday talk and bearing in "The Question of Our Speech."[7] Yet Frost's high school sweetheart, covaledictorian, and wife-to-be, Elinor, in her own commencement address at their high school ten years earlier, celebrated "Conversation as a Life Force," and Frost himself would develop a career as writer and speaker around an anti-oratorical, personal conversation, himself nominating, as one of the three great things in life along with religion and science, nothing more or less prepossessing than "gossip." And what can conversational gossip have to do with the lofty eloquence and stable common sense of ancient rhetoric?

The question would not have ruffled Cicero (or Aristotle), who observed, "the same rules that we have for words and sentences in [oratory] will apply also to conversation."[8] Though Cicero is speaking here of stylistic matters, we can effect such an easy transition between styles and genres because oratory or rhetoric, in addition to being a social attitude adapted to the needs of a larger community, models an intellectual method of thinking as well as speaking about substantive problems, and not merely a manual of style, grace, or social propriety.[9] For him,

as for much of the rhetorical tradition afterward (Todorov calls Cicero "the last of the ancients and the first of the moderns"),[10] rhetoric more fully conceived offers large-scale discursive strategies and tactics, enunciated and given effect in *De oratore* (itself written as a conversation), which can be used as intellectual re-sources for serious engagement in matters ranging from practical affairs of everyday life to practical (we now say pragmatic or hermeneutic or rhetorical) philosophy.[11] As discussed in the introduction and first chapter, rhetoric comprises word and thought, image and idea, speech and reason, imagination and discursive invention practiced on "common" places (topoi or *loci communes*), turning or troping them toward the novel circumstances of people's changing interests, and the judgment of such inventions, seeing them as more or less useful or true for some community.

In the epigraph to this chapter, therefore, the "language of everyday life," "the usage approved by the sense of the community," and "the common practice, custom and speech of mankind," were conceived differently from the way we commonly conceive them now, namely as fearful clingings to popular beliefs and conventions, or as settled dispositions toward fixed concepts, or as courting fashion, praise, or power for their own sake. And though it is true that the Greek polis and Roman Republic were far more homogeneous than modern societies; that both Aristotle and Cicero considered their beliefs firmly anchored in first principles; and that the Roman Republic was ruled by educated and political elites; nevertheless for Cicero such expressions as he gives to the materials of "oratory" denote conflicting possibilities, not fixed positions, suggesting that what stabilizes lives are publicly accessible arguments and appeals framed within a background of "natural" linguistic criteria, rules, and social practices in public space and contained by a moderate ("Academic") skepticism. Rhetoric is thus, in Cicero's language, "open to view" in the specific sense that, although considerable experience, knowledge, and skill may be needed to engage an intelligent conversation, argue matters of law, or write history or a poem, no determinate theory, single subject matter, or training in a "remote" expertise is required to become an eloquent human being.

In a similar way for Robert Frost, himself a better Latinist than either Eliot or Pound, "the living part of a poem is the intonation entangled somehow in the syntax idiom [*sic*] and meaning of a sentence. It is only there for those who have heard it previously in conversation" (*SL* 107); "I was under twenty when I deliberately put it to myself one night after good conversation that there are moments when we actually touch in talk what the best writing can only come near" (*SL* 159). For Frost, the important point is not stylistic preferences but the fact that conversation or gossip serves as shorthand for people's interest in each other, indeed that it signifies nothing less than the matrix of literature as such. In a kind of paraphrase of Kant's "all thinking must ultimately . . . refer to perceptions"

(*CPR* 33), Frost holds that "all our literature has got to come down, sooner or later, to the talk of everyday life" (*CPPP* 694). The modern literary thinker who probably comes closest to this attitude, notwithstanding his dismissal of poetry as nonpolyphonic, is Mikhail Bakhtin: "In real life we very keenly and subtly hear all those nuances in the speech of people surrounding us, and we ourselves work very skillfully with all these colors on the verbal palette. We very sensitively catch the smallest shift in intonation, the slightest interruption of voices in anything of importance to us in another person's practical everyday discourse. All those verbal sideward glances, loop-holes, hints, thrusts do not slip past our ear, are not foreign to our lips. All the more astonishing, then, that up to now all this has found no precise theoretical cognizance, nor the assessment it deserves!"[12]

Conversation and literature meet, for Frost, on the grounds of practical problems, tensions, conflicts, and interests, and the everyday talk used to explore them thoughtfully or avoid them cannily, giving voice to what Richard Poirier has identified as Frost's "work of knowing" and what the poet Derek Walcott calls "the practicality of poetry, its workday occupation."[13] For Frost, everyday life, *hence* poetry, is inter alia a matter of negotiating indefinite symbolic exchanges within a complex environment, that is to say, it is a matter of "oratory" (read rhetoric) in Cicero's expandable sense. Poetry is public and useful. In an early letter (1913) to his friend John Bartlett, Frost wrote: "I could never make a merit of being caviare to the crowd the way my quasi-friend Pound does. I want to reach out, and would if it were a thing I could do by taking thought" (*SL* 98). How easy to miss that unprepossessing prepositional phrase at the end.

Even on the most casual encounter with Frost's poems, one can hear the language (style, structure, grammar, rhetoric) of practical problem solving, commonsense reasoning and beliefs, the rhetoric of the everyday and ordinary—"the common, the familiar, the low"—often intermingled with philosophic meditations on their origins and ends. Such language is certainly "open to view" and ordinary; in fact, it has appeared to most critics and theorists so wide-eyed and ordinary as not to require sophisticated study at all—the preeminence of the everyday and ordinary in twentieth-century philosophy notwithstanding.[14] Like Gertrude Stein and (to an extent) Wallace Stevens, Frost's *virtù* or power, as Robert Kern has put it, "consists in his radical renewal and revision of the Wordsworthian project of appropriating the language of everyday life for poetry."[15] Unlike them, Frost was committed to exploiting the overdeterminations of semantic meanings rather than the opacities of syntax and language, and to rhetorical dramas of ideas rather than those chiefly of desire or gnomic unknowing.[16]

Frost conducts, for example, "a lover's quarrel with the world" ("The Lesson for Today") by way of being "made to believe" ("The Fear") or "verily [to] believe" ("Happiness Makes Up in Height for What It Lacks in Length"), though often "too ready to believe the most" ("A Boundless Moment"), "invest[ing] with reasons"

("Brown's Descent"), with "reason enough" ("The Housekeeper"), and "reason why" ("My November Guest"), "'furnishing the reasons'"("From Plane to Plane"), and "debating" ("On a Tree Fallen across the Road") with "good arguments" ("The Death of the Hired Man"), with "persuasion" ("The Subverted Flower"), with "precedent" ("The Onset"), and with myriad kinds of "saying" ("The Hill Wife"), what "we" or "some say" ("Revelation," "Fire and Ice," "Paul's Wife"); "taking for a proof" ("Pauper Witch of Grafton"), or "putting off the proof" ("Dust in the Eyes"), or "demanding proof" ("On Taking from the Top to Broaden the Base"), "if there needed proof" at all ("The Valley's Singing Day"), even if only "gentle proof" ("Not Quite Social"), or just plain "proof" ("In the Home Stretch") or "evidence" ("A Hundred Collars"). The ubiquity of such language offers at least a preliminary sign of Frost's being preoccupied with rhetorical matters, even as he secularizes what has been called the "religious rhetoric" of high modernist poets like Eliot and Yeats, rendering poetry fitter for engagement with—rather than estrangement from—everyday experience, that is, the criteria people habitually use to cope with the world.[17]

As a way of locating some of the generic features of Frost's rhetorical posture without my insisting here on its philosophic qualities, consider briefly his later lyric, "Leaves Compared with Flowers" (1935),[18] which begins almost in sing-song:

> A tree's leaves may be ever so good,
> So may its bark, so may its wood.
> But unless you put the right thing to its root
> It never will show much flower or fruit.
>
> (lines 1–4)

On a first pass we encounter nothing very serious here, barely enough in the title to hint at the need for arguing on either side of a question—Leaves compared with flowers: so which are better? Quite characteristically for Frost, however, the poem soon comes to recast a meditative introspection into the form of a quasi-public debate, all but belying Mill's claim that rhetoric is (merely) heard while poetry is (mysteriously) overheard, as if telepathically eavesdropped upon.[19] In other words, not only is the reader being directly addressed here, but she also is required to participate in an argument by intellectually weighing alternatives. The debate gets obliquely introduced in the first two stanzas in alternating voices— the narrator's double-voicing of the commonplaces of others (of our own) in lines 1–4, followed by, in lines 5 and 6, the poet's own counterstatement:

> But I may be one who does not care
> Ever to have tree bloom or bear:
> Leaves for smooth and bark for rough,
> Leaves and bark may be tree enough.
>
> (lines 5–8)

This line of argument is then extended with further exempla:

> Some giant trees have bloom so small
> They might as well have none at all.
> Late in life I have come on fern.
> Now lichens are due to have their turn.
>
> (lines 9–12)

And then the controversy is given overt rhetorical status and sharpened to a point in the penultimate fourth quatrain:

> I bade men tell me, which in brief,
> Which is fairer, flower or leaf?
> They did not have the wit to say
> Leaves by night and flowers by day.
>
> (lines 13–16)

Frost enjoys nothing more than to invite his readers to consider some deliberative or judicial question—which, A or B, is better, fairer?—and then to make the question seem to disappear by showing how inadequate monovocal argument on one side or the other is to such a matter ("They did not have the wit to say"), only to finish with a rhetorical flourish by reinstating the issue but on a different intellectual and emotional (imaginative) plane. By the end, "leaves," "bark," "petals," and "flowers" have become what rhetoricians call material, or special, topics, more or less specific terms whose meanings have accrued beyond whatever stable, determinate uses the poet has made of them:

> Leaves and bark, leaves and bark
> To lean against and hear in the dark.
> Petals I may have once pursued.
> Leaves are all my darker mood.
>
> (lines 17–20)

In other words, the rhetorical genre of this poem drifts, as it were, from ersatz-deliberation and conclusive judgment on an indefinite issue (what Cicero and other rhetoricians called a "thesis," itself traditionally turning, as in Renaissance lyric and drama, on some kind of comparison)[20] to a more inclusive if nonstandard "epideictic" celebration in praise of antithetical virtues ("Leaves by night and flowers by day"; or again, in "Fire and Ice," "I hold with those who favor fire," but "Ice is also great"; and elsewhere, "Nothing I should care to leave behind"). It also develops from a misleadingly synchronic comparison to a fuller diachronic sense of the appropriateness of all things great and small, according, that is, to their respective *"circumstantiae"* (cf. also "The Master Speed"); and from the evocation of "wit," noted (in contrary ways) by both Kant and Shaftesbury in the eighteenth century as an important part of the *sensus communis* by virtue of its appeal to recognizable

public connections,[21] to a notably nineteenth-century private "mood," a mood transformed at the end, however, to *include* its more moralizing and moralized predecessor (wit) in a uniquely twentieth-century, ironic admixture of both.[22] In this poem, I want to suggest, our own *sensus communis* comes to be rethought, not least our sense about speech itself: a comparison of what were once called the "flowers" of rhetoric (its figures and tropes), admired as a product of wit by the learned, with Whitman's democratic "leaves of grass" (ordinary things), accessible to learned and unlearned alike. Neither is seen as an objective social orientation nor yet a subjective personal preference or mood; both are synthesized as a practical awareness of the value of what is often overlooked in life *and* art: the everyday and ordinary refigured, rethought. From this perspective, "Leaves Compared with Flowers" is an especially self-conscious, rhetorical performance—an epideictic celebration—of many of the themes and tactics historically and intellectually considered central to rhetoric.[23]

I have featured this poem because its discrimination and joining of both sides of a question is a further characteristic of Frost's thinking. A similar inquiry and celebration occurs not only in "The Black Cottage," as we have seen, but in "Two Tramps in Mud Time" (analyzed in chapter 4), in which unity of vision is similarly managed from a dual perspective: "as my two eyes make one in sight" (line 68) = as my (Frost's) two "I's" (the narrator's and the tramps') make one insight. Philosophically the method is neither a Platonic nor Hegelian nor a looser Emersonian transcendence to a higher unity; rather, it is what Richard McKeon would call a Ciceronian operationalism, in which "struggle or strife or conflict or contention or competition or debate" is central.[24] Hence it is a method by virtue of which one may as soon end with only one side of a pair of terms as another, with disunion as soon as unity, or with a unity or generalization or rule quite different from what one might have expected on starting: "The Ciceronian debate does not move dialectically from communities and oppositions to an assimilation of lesser truths in the greater. It is controversy, and the debate is only resolved insofar as anyone chooses to adopt one of the conflicting positions or to modify it or to formulate a new position with elements from the alternatives as components. One begins and ends with perspectival diremptions. . . . Philosophy is constituted by this on-going conversation, the clash of statements and judgments, and the value of the method lies precisely in this discrimination of perspectives and the differentiation of frames of reference . . . as devices for invention and judgment."[25] In "Two Tramps in Mud Time," the topical perspectives of "invention" and "judgment" appear as "play" and "work." Here they are imaged as "flowers" and "leaves," elsewhere as "fire" and "ice," freedom and constraint, working together and working apart, self and neighbor, and so on. In the abstract, these topoi may ring hollow, but in the materiality of their respective poems, Frost keeps complex concepts in play, and at work, without reducing their tensions within some more

stable *tertium quid.* Topical invention deploys and fills up terms and arguments on both sides of a question circumstantially, while judgment ends provisionally, often by making room for both sides.

Equally important, "Leaves Compared with Flowers" presents a mild sending-up, a subtle satire, of classical rhetorical argument and persuasion, as well as a subtle parody of antirhetorical (read romantic) moods, for both classicism and neoclassicism as well as romanticism presuppose an undivided self in poet and reader, a self that Frost's rhetorical stance belies.[26] For "Leaves" is replete with humorous verbal deception (for example, prosopopoeia subverting the subject position in the first stanza) and characteristic rhetorical showing-off ("wit"), and it embodies a further-reaching rhetoric than even the intellectually promiscuous Cicero knew. In outward form and parodic purpose, it resembles a good many of Frost's most famous poems, in which explicit argument contends with implicit ridicule or subversion of argument: "Fire and Ice," with its "Some say . . . Some [others] say" exploitation of common opinion; "Design," an almost gloating trope of standard eighteenth-century theological debate over one of the standard proofs for God; the ongoing arguments heard or implied in "From Plane to Plane," "The Death of the Hired Man," and many similar dramatic dialogues; and the recurrence of questions of interpretation throughout the poems and other writings.

If we think about this for a moment, there should be little surprise that such preoccupation with reason, truth, dialogue, persuasion, argument, emotion, debate, audience, proof, judgment, wit, humor, deception, and even jokes—Emerson's list in a later incarnation—has been so consistently missed, or dismissed, for such a long time.[27] While such a claim as Cicero's regarding the virtually limitless scope of rhetoric as continuous with practical moral action and thought, and with history and its alleged *sensus communis,* has been for some anachronistic at best, for others it has been resisted as either intellectually presumptuous (substantively and methodologically inferior to science; sophistical) or fatuous (stylistic and ornamental; "mere" rhetoric). As the intellectual and cultural historian Walter Ong has observed: "With the advent of the age which from one point of view we call the technological age and from the other point of view the romantic age, rhetoric was not wiped out or supplanted, but rather disrupted, displaced, and rearranged. It became a bad word . . . for those given to technology because it represented 'soft' thinking [sophistry], thinking attuned to unpredictable human actuality and decisions. . . . Rhetoric was also a bad word for those given to romanticism because it seemed to hint that the controlling element in life was a contrivance rather than freedom in the sense of purely 'spontaneous' or unmotivated action, sprung up unsolicited from the interior wells of being."[28] One of the leading problems in this chapter, therefore, is to ask what Cicero's imperious claims for rhetoric entail for American literary modernism—or, more broadly, since "rhetoric" here is a moving target related by family resemblances—what it

might mean for a contemporary Ciceronian rhetoric to be concerned in some measure with "the manners, minds, and lives of mankind" (*De orat* 3.20), at least as these appear in a specific historical community.

Greater clarity on these matters will enable us to do several things. First, we can illuminate shaded aspects of Frost's poetry, reevaluating his relatively weak standing among his more celebrated literary peers. Second, we can widen the approach to the Anglo-American scene of modernist, and specifically "low modernist," poetics, opening up the latter as "a relatively recent discovery [that] constitutes not simply another kind of modernism . . . but rather a deliberate and often polemic disturbance within the canonical version."[29] That is, where high modernism often explicitly flees from—often in order to try to "purify"—everyday life, low modernism shows us the overlooked possibilities in everyday life and language themselves.[30] Third, we can rethink the many easy dismissals of "common sense," the "ordinary," "community," and even "taste" in poetry and criticism. For when these concepts are understood to name not settled propositional beliefs or untroubled communications between autonomous agents but rather rich grammatical and rhetorical re-sources for invention and judgment among agents as "divided selves," then their aura of simplicity and vagueness may seem less the liability it has been made out to be.[31] Not all low modernists think rhetorically, but rhetoric offers untapped resources for reading low, and rereading high modernists alike.

## Impositions

Of course, matters of communication (and community) are not, as we know, readily taken as live options in our own time. To take an interest, therefore, in the principles of rhetoric in its contemporary post-Enlightenment and postromantic forms and functions—as increasing numbers of academics these days profess to do—requires that we discriminate further possibilities of the term here. For the fact is that, as anachronistic and presumptuous as defenses of oratory have appeared at least from the Renaissance on, for still others rhetoric has become part of our postmodern business-as-usual. Here "rhetoric" is equivalent now to the metaphorical (tropistic) play of language, as in many reductive versions of Nietzsche and Derrida, and the concomitant indeterminacy of meaning and its general consequences for politics and society, especially the ideological critique of authority in much literary theory and criticism. Thus de Man writes that "Nietzsche moves the study of rhetoric away from techniques of eloquence and persuasion *[Beredsamkeit]* by making these dependent on a previous theory of figures of speech or tropes."[32] Where many philosophers and scientists (and scientist-types, such as Lippmann) have resisted rhetorical methods as unsound, and many romantic and modernist authors have dismissed rhetoric as convention-bound and unreal, postmodern "rhetorical man"[33] raids disciplinary borders and

dismantles textual boundaries and in general causes whatever rhetorical unrest is necessary. But necessary for what?

The answer to this question depends in part on how one reads postmodernism in the arts and poststructuralism in critical theory. Shall we take them as liberating impulses against the hegemonic political and aesthetic powers of modernism, as earlier in pop art or in recent new historicist, Marxist, postcolonial, and feminist criticism? Or are they repetition-compulsions of modernist thinking, in which textual liberation from the metaphysics of presence expresses in a new guise the familiar modernist "anxiety of contamination" from everyday life, history, society? Or are they part of an erotics of reading in need of no specific end beyond themselves? In light of the rage for deconstructive play even when doing cultural studies work, Richard Lanham's profile of the rhetorician as a kind of courtly Renaissance mover and shaker preoccupied with manipulating the powers-that-be to arrive at predetermined political ends ("winning") has tacitly assumed something of a default value:

> Rhetorical man is an actor; his reality public, dramatic. His sense of identity, his self, depends on the reassurance of daily histrionic reenactment. He is thus centered in time and concrete local event. The lowest common denominator of his life is a social situation. And his motivations must be characteristically ludic, agonistic. He thinks first of winning, of mastering the rules the current game enforces. He assumes a natural agility in changing orientations. He hits the street already street-wise. From birth, almost, he has dwelt not in a single value-structure but in several. He is thus committed to no single construction of the world; much rather, to prevailing in the game at hand. . . . Reality is what is accepted as reality, what is useful.

And Lanham concludes, with a rhetorical flourish (and unintended irony?): "*Homo rhetoricus* cannot, to sum up, be serious."[34]

In some hands this has become not just a moderate but a radically skeptical, debunking version of the rhetoricity of language, texts, and the world, as a wide range of theoretically invested rhetorical studies—by Barthes, Stanley Fish, Sara Suleri, Marjorie Levinson, and many others, including most recently Katherine Kearns in *Robert Frost and a Poetic of Appetite* (1994)—have shown to considerable effect. As Kearns comments on Frost: "To believe"—though this is not quite what the poet said—"that all ages are equally dark for the soul is incipient nihilism."[35] To be sure, in such claims as Lanham's and Kearns's there is much that belongs to Cicero, even to the quite schoolteacherly Quintilian—and to Robert Frost also. Lanham's "daily histrionic enactment," for example, speaks to Frost's fascination with the Goffmanesque modern self as dramatic, posed, opportunistic role-player, hence a self more energized and motivated than the ennervated Prufrock or the

alienated Mauberly (whose own makers covet at times a lost transcendental self). In a talk at Bread Loaf in 1955, Frost summed up his lifelong position toward a more fluid rhetorical posing (for poses can also be positions):

> I keep running into the idea of what's your pose? See. What's your pose? Who do you think you are? See. Now there's a nice way of saying that: who the hell do you think you are? [*Laughter*] ... That just means you know you aren't so much.... But when you say, what is your pose? Yeats says somewhere you have a choice of seven poses. Only seven poses possible—which is yours? Are you putting on airs as a don or a teacher, you know, or are you putting on airs as what—as a farmer, or as a common man, see? (*CPPP* 827)

Although Frost neglects the important point that such a posing of identity is always, in part, sanctioned and guaranteed by institutional practices,[36] he is nevertheless implicitly redefining Renaissance courtly *sprezzatura* all over again, meaning in part that he poses his own understanding of others in broadly social terms of power, that is, as ways of winning over ("putting on airs"). This is so much the case that Seamus Heaney can describe Frost as "demonically intelligent, as acute about his own masquerades as he was about others'," a veritable Machiavel.[37]

And yet, allowing for that aspect of Frost, there are, in Lanham's picture of the rhetorician as poser, background hints and allegations that do *not* resonate with either Cicero *or* Frost: for example, rhetoric's putative opposition to "seriousness," or its derogatory alignment with the "useful," works with only the narrowest senses of those words. Moreover, Frost himself does not always think or speak like a rhetorician of any kind. Although, as any close reader of his letters or occasional prose is aware, he never really sheds his ready rhetorical commitments, he tries bravely enough: "Clash is all very well for coming lawyers politicians and theologians. But I should think that there must be a whole realm or plane above that—all sight and insight, perception, intuition, rapture" (*SL* 324). Or again: "Refuse to be rushed to market or forum. Don't come as a product until you have turned yourself under many times. We don't have to be afraid we won't be social enough.... The trouble with everybody's mind is that everybody is caught out in the big forum" (*SL* 387). And elsewhere more emphatically: "Having ideas that are neither pro nor con is the happy thing. Get up there high enough and the differences that make controversy become"—but here he cannot quite sustain his Hegelian position aloft and quickly turns (as one of his poems oddly phrases it) "to earthward"—"only the two legs of a body the weight of which is on one in one period, on the other in the next." In practice, this image privileges *disputatio* and moral inquiry, for in fact we always live in one period or another, with Frost and ourselves ever playing both sides: "Democracy monarchy; puritanism paganism; form content; conservatism radicalism; systole diastole; rustic urbane; literary colloquial; work play. I should think too much of myself to let any teacher fool

me into taking sides on any one of those oppositions.... Mind you I would fight. This is no pacifism.... Don't let me oversay my position (*SL* 324–25).

Bracketing, then, further comments on community and communication, we may conclude for now that the two more familiar positions regarding rhetoric in our time, at least in literary studies, have been that of earlier romantics and moderns for whom rhetoric is anachronistic, naïve, or pretentious for professional intellectual purposes, and that of a specific kind of postmodernist for whom it is rhetoric's sole cunning to destabilize, by intellectually outwitting, all epistemological self-satisfactions across the disciplines, in and out of academe, from a position (this aspect fully shared by high modernism) of superior knowledge and expertise.[38]

In my view, such a stark option is at once imposing and impoverishing, indicating, by its conspicuous absence of a middle term, a different way for us to go about studying a figure such as Frost. For I propose that, for Frost himself, what I am calling rhetoric, what Frost called "the strife-method" (*SL* 325), is neither anachronistic or naïvely presumptuous on the one hand nor incipiently nihilistic (radically skeptical) on the other. Frost *is* skeptical about unduly bridling thinking, and his version of the strife-method seeks to avoid any such grim ontotheological fate. But it is no less true that Frost bridles against unthinking skepticism (see his poem "Voice Ways"), and again rhetorical thinking offers means to avoid *that* fate. What I call rhetorical thought in Frost's poetry is a paradox uneasily poised between Janus-faced possibilities of invention and judgment: rhetoric as an instrument for disseminating invention in a modern world, and rhetoric as a means of taste and judgment of the *"sensus communis"* (Cicero) or the "ordinary" (Wittgenstein) in an increasingly postmodern world.

## Poses

I want briefly to resurvey some of the ground I have just covered in order to get a better view of these crisscrossing paths, coordinating a literary-aesthetic perspective to help place in context earlier observations of the social scene in which a poet like Frost was working, and looking out as well for a literary response to the rejection of rhetoric, that is, an alternative (or anyway better balanced) response to the narrow deconstructive option noted above. My broader aim in this chapter, again, is inventive, juxtaposing Frost with appropriate possibilities of rhetoric, in that way adumbrating certain "*possibilities*' of [the] phenomena" (*PI* § 90) of literature (poetry) and philosophy in a low modernist vein.

The ostensible reasons, at least, why Frost's literary and artistic predecessors and contemporaries rejected rhetoric as a repertoire of intellectual methods of practical reasoning and appeal are usefully recapitulated for us in another context by Terry Eagleton: "The decline of rhetoric ... was the overdetermined effect of a number of factors: the dwindling of the 'public sphere' of political life with the

growing power of a complex, bureaucratized 'civil society'; the correlative power of script in the exercise of class rule; the puritan, rationalist, and empiricist distrust of verbal 'ornamentation' in the name of rigorous denotation; the bourgeois-democratic suspicion of rhetoric as 'aristocratic' manipulation and discursive authoritarianism; the emergence of a political science relatively sealed from the turmoil of political practice."[39] In addition, however, by reminding ourselves in passing of certain post-Cartesian, romantic, and modernist ideas forged in reaction to what Eliot usefully called the "dissociation of sensibility," we can give a small turn of the dial to familiar literary histories of modernism and recent postmodern accounts and uses of rhetoric so-called. Here I want briefly to isolate how several rationalist and empiricist doctrines, alluded to by Eagleton, motivated later romantic and modernist literary elites to repress a critical (and not, as they thought, a merely naïve) "common sense" and its rhetorical methods.

Consider Stéphane Mallarmé's imposing dictum: "Poetry is the language of a state of crisis."[40] As a thought experiment, let me rephrase this. Rather than "Poetry is," we will say (in the old-fashioned postmodern way), "Poetry was defined, at a specific historical period from 18— to 19—, as 'in essence' the language of [or, "language responding to"]"; and, better to specify "a state of crisis," we will say, "the state of a dissociation of sensibility." These substitutions, I propose, enable us to note that it was inter alia—this is widely understood—with an *epistemological* crisis ("dissociation of sensibility") that writers from Wordsworth to Mallarmé to Eliot (from Flaubert to Conrad, Woolf, and Nabokov) mentally wrestled; and that it was—this is often simply assumed—said to be an epistemological and cultural *crisis*, which is to say not only a historical turning-point, culminating in the notion of a wilderness or wasteland devoid of spiritual or religious value, but a *hypothesis*, something of a thought-experiment itself, embraced by leading thinkers and artists and yet remaining, even now, at least partly resistible on the grounds that it can be considered hyperbolic.[41] In one of the better accounts of the notion of cultural crisis, which he deems "the most widely-held assumption of twentieth-century thought," the intellectual historian Allan Megill observes that, in opposition to early romantic notions of "unity" symbolized in the image of the "circuitous journey," later continental thinkers such as Nietzsche, Heidegger, and Derrida posit the present as a state of "absolute dereliction" (33) traceable to the death of God, the rise of science, and the technologization of modern society, alienation from authentic existence in the modern city, and the other usual suspects: "The belief that all continuity had been lost and that in consequence new and unexpected possibilities had, for good or ill, been opened up was shared by many in the prewar period. But it would be a mistake to regard this feeling of crisis as merely a 'period' concept. On the contrary, it underlies the whole of modernist and postmodernist art and literature" (112). Thus, in a review of a new Pléiade edition of Mallarmé's *Oeuvres Complètes*, Charles Rosen writes:

"His [Mallarmé's] work is only in part a reaction to the deterioration of language in journalism and public life. It is fundamentally a despairing protest against ordinary life, made void by the irrelevance of all religious faith, by the corruption of general culture, by the general decline of the prestige of art except as a commodity."[42] Later Frank Lentricchia observes that "modernist poetics in the United States began with the great problem of the bourgeois world: the anatagonism between duty [money, work] and happiness [pleasures such as poetry]."[43]

Certainly the foremost component behind Mallarmé's attitude is the Enlightenment reaction against tradition and authority prevalent among seventeenth-century scientists and philosophers such as Newton, Galileo, and Descartes, who pioneered new methods of thought in reaction to medieval scholasticism and Renaissance rhetoric. With such mechanization of thought was born a Weltanschauung whose world was despiritualized and whose inhabitants were reduced to what Charles Taylor calls a "procedural" reason and a "punctual" (objectified) self—though the gain, to be sure, was perceived for centuries as nothing short of man's freedom to control himself and his world. Eliot describes the shift from one dispensation to another: "The poets of the sixteenth century ... possessed a ... sensibility which could devour any kind of experience.... In the seventeenth century a dissociation of sensibility set in, from which we have never recovered."[44] Thereafter the ideal for thinking man was to dissociate himself from his own experience by objectifying it, analyzing the external world as a congeries of mechanical forces to be controlled by logic or by experimental hypothesis and inference, and, as mentioned earlier, to be expressed in a neutral language. It is, of course, just this dissociated worldview that burdens poets from Wordsworth on, for it becomes their problem how to bridge such divisions in human life—mind against body, fact divorced from value, meaning from its history, reason from cause, man alienated from his own felt experience: "Whatever the difference between the literary movements of the nineteenth and twentieth centuries, they are connected by their view of the [external] world as meaningless, by their response to the same wilderness. That wilderness is the legacy of the Enlightenment, of the scientific and critical effort ... which, in its desire to separate fact from the values of a crumbling tradition, separated fact from all values—bequeathing a world in which the fact is measurable quantity while value is man-made and illusory."[45] By the early nineteenth century, poet and artist had reacted by assuming the vatic personality of priest and prophet, looking not simply inward but, as it were, *through* personal experience, feeling, and insight, to effect a reunion of scattered powers, personal and cosmic, quite as Wordsworth indicates in the famous book 13 of *The Prelude* (1850):

> That Poets, even as Prophets, each with each
> Connected in a mighty scheme of truth,

> Have each his own peculiar faculty,
> Heaven's gift, a sense that fits him to perceive
> Objects unseen before . . .
>
> (lines 300–304)

As William Empson has shown, however, by "sense" Wordsworth does not mean (not here, and only rarely elsewhere) anything resembling Cicero's notion of "common sense," quite the contrary: "The effect is that, though Sensation and Imagination appear as the two extreme ends of the scale in view, so that one might expect them to be opposites, the word is so placed that it might equally apply to either. And the middle of the scale, the idea of ordinary common sense, is cut out from these uses no less firmly than the idea of sensuality."[46] Over the next hundred years and more, the leading reactions to modern life and its rationalistic, positivistic, and progressivist and capitalist tendencies, with all its well-known variations and gradations, took one of two routes: primitivist return to the natural world for the purpose of finding new modes of spiritual or psychological transcendence, or personal uniqueness edging aside common bonds without, however, eclipsing them altogether (even in Wordsworth, after all, "each [poet] with each" is "connected"); or, "as art becomes more self-consciously antisocial, so it is driven to adopt ever more extreme forms of artifice to secure its own autonomy."[47]

In this way we return to the starting point of this chapter. My argument has been that the modern philosophical and the literary high modernist rejection of rhetoric—quite like its postmodernist apotheosis across the disciplines—are both premised on the notion of epistemological (and of course religious) *crisis,* and that these commitments are at once philosophic positions, theoretical impositions, and rhetorical poses. They are philosophical *positions* because they mark out Enlightenment grounding in certainty or universality, or, in light of the latter's later deconstruction, a commitment to its endless deferral. They are theoretical *impositions* because they presuppose the requirement that knowledge, to be knowledge, must be unequivocal, transparent, and absolute, lacking which knowledge becomes Althusserian or Foucauldian Power, or realpolitik, or just good ol' American political science. (William Empson has put this succinctly: "It is a misfortune that the whole literary tradition of Symbolism has grown up so completely divorced from the tradition of fair public debate.")[48] And they are rhetorical *poses* because they serve interests and purposes that, in hindsight, are but a selection of the possibilities, hence a deflection of other realities that we will do at least as well to acknowledge. We hardly need to subscribe to the literary Marxism of Gramsci or Lukacs, much less the "scientific" Marxism of Althusser, to appreciate their keen understanding that the ideology underlying much high modernist literature turns on the construal of everyday life as a scene of breakdown and crisis, in which the everyday, normal, and comprehensible is brought

to grief as the perverse self-deceptions of the hide-bound and conventional. What is intended, after the romantics, to replace the cravenness of the mass public is a fracture of consciousness so profound as to pose everyday life as henceforth impossible as it stands, sometimes expressed in a nonrealistic or nonmimetic literature of distortion, eccentricity, nightmare, and dislocation—now not just as a historical norm but as *la condition humaine*.[49] In the American tradition, some of this gets prefigured by Sherwood Anderson's abstract sketches in *Winesburg, Ohio*, whose quotidian "grotesques," however similar in some ways to Frost's small-town folk, float ghostly free of the latter's sense of linguistic and communicational possibilities.

To whatever degree such possibilities were in eclipse at the turn of the century, Frost himself never reified any crisis of the everyday. Even if we agree with Megill, and with Stanley Cavell, that the notion of breakdown of criteria drives the whole of modernist art and literature, and even if we do think of this as some kind of major turning point or crisis, it does not necessarily follow that the consequences of such a development are paralyzing or debilitating, much less that the everyday and ordinary cannot themselves offer one way out of, or anyway through, the difficulties. For it is, I take it, broadly against, or perhaps *athwart*, this sort of presupposition about crisis (and a fortiori Katherine Kearns's distortion of him cited earlier) that Frost is reacting when he writes:

> you will often hear it said that the age of the world we live in is particularly bad. I am impatient of such talk. We have no way of knowing that this age is one of the worst in the world's history. Arnold claimed the honor for the age before this. Wordsworth claimed it for the last but one. And so on back through literature. . . . It is immodest of a man to think of himself as going down before the worst forces ever mobilized by God. . . . One can safely say after from six to thirty thousand years of experience that the evident design is a situation here in which it will always be about equally hard to save your soul. (*SP* 105–6)[50]

"In our time," as Ronald Schleifer notes in a similar fashion, "the failures of the sense and sense-making capacity, of 'progress' as a framework in which to comprehend temporality and the concomitant phenomenon of the multiplication of isolated moments of historicism[,] seem less an earthshaking crisis than they did at the beginning of the century."[51] In fact, critics invariably interpret failure—symbolized in the impoverished scenes, rural characters, and mundane activities hulking through *North of Boston, Mountain Interval,* and later books—as Frost's preoccupation with regionalism, or Whartonian realism, or merely with nostalgia for simpler days. I suggest these images magnify something considerably less documentary. Frost's scenes of everyday impoverishment, loneliness, abandonment, and drift are—but are hardly exclusively—portraits of a time and

place. Less obviously and more pointedly, they present settings for making philosophical claims about ordinary griefs regarding the fact, and fate, of loss and transition. If anything, they express the need for shedding cultural expectations (readerly tears) in order to put a new face on worn-out words. So Cavell notes of Frost's own philosophic exemplar, Emerson: "Poverty as a condition of philosophy is hardly a new idea. Emerson deploys it as an idea specifically of America's deprivations, its bleakness and distance from Europe's achievements, as constituting America's necessity, and its opportunity for finding itself" (*NYUA* 70). Frost's images of abandoned houses may evoke passing resemblance to Hawthorne's scary places, but out of Frost's houses come words and more words, either the poet's or those of someone standing in for him—for example, the Stark cousins in "The Generations of Men," who hear voices bidding them rebuild, be fruitful.

Said otherwise, and extrapolating now from these various points: if Frost's cultural scene is understood as something *other* than crisis-as-catastrophe; if the scene is seen to have been proposed (not "staged," as we would have to say if we were reading Stevens) as a place (topos) of abiding loss and renewal, then it follows that at least *one* poet's reaction to the cultural situation was something proportionally less than 180 degrees of separation. And if his contemporaries' reaction to that cultural scene was appraised by this poet to be, as it were, not altogether perfectly calibrated to the changing speed of the facts, then it may be possible for him to have written, and for us to read, somehow in sympathy with that scene, even while as seriously committed to a search (I mean a search as serious as those in more formalistic revolt) for new criteria of concepts such as "lyric" or "knowing" or "being" or "everyday" or "ordinary" or "modern" or "modernist." Wallace Stevens is reported to have told Frost that the "trouble with your poems, Frost, is that they have subjects and they make the visible world too easy to see."[52] But Stevens's dismissal only succeeds in underlining the fact that he, like so many others after, failed to appreciate how deceptively oblique is Frost's perspective, that it altogether subverts the sorts of flat-footed oppositions (high/low, easy/hard, subject/object, foreground/background, word/world) that Stevens chalks up to Frost's supposed schoolboy transparencies.

The problem, in any case, is not what it is we may want to call, or how we might define, cultural crisis (that is a side argument here), but how American poets, Frost in particular, understood their problems of belief, skepticism, artistic renewal, taste, and so on and the possible solutions to these problems. What needs to be shown is not any particular artist's or critic's penchant for high or low modernism but rather the *continuum of possibilities* open to and activated by poets like Frost, and later Auden, Bishop, Heaney, and a host of others; and novelists from Hemingway (largely low) to Woolf (high, leaning low) to Joyce (a blend, leaning high). In my view, high and low modernism ought to be taken as in apposition, not opposition (borrowing Charles Bernstein's words, "they connote

colorations more than dichotomies"),[53] the low now requiring greater theoretical definition and the high a more practical reassessment. I want to begin a small part of that task here by considering how to configure the continuum of high and low modernism—the apposition not the opposition—in the first place: first, by replacing Frank Lentricchia's now-dated Kantian approach to Frost by way of Gadamer's rereading of Kant and Poirier's Cavellian reading of Emerson; and second, by suggesting, at least, the consequences of such revision for exploring hidden recesses "out of school" of American literary modernism.

## Appositions
### Kant and Emerson

In *Robert Frost: Modern Poetics and the Landscapes of Self* (1975), in the culminating chapter on the "scope and limits of supreme fictions," Frank Lentricchia places Frost's poetic practice in a tradition of noncognitive aesthetics deriving chiefly from Kant and Schiller.[54] As the "polemical preface" to his book acknowledges, Lentricchia sets himself against those New Critics who, after Eliot, were onto-theologically motivated to follow Coleridge's theoretical account of poetry as a serious activity of transcendent knowing, hence in principle capable of expressing truths re-cognizable by others. As is well understood, in its stress on the creative powers of the secondary imagination, the Coleridgean position was also, after a fashion, Kantian. But for Lentricchia, Coleridge's exaggerated claims about poetry-as-knowledge patently distorted Kant and, in any case, never clearly explained *how* the world was knowable, knowable, that is, not in its phenomenal appearances but in its noumenal-romantic meanings, that is, as a humanly inhabited, "spiritual" place. Poetry was supposed to be a mode of knowing different from the phenomenal-causal, or scientific; but what mode, exactly? For Lentricchia, the romantic Symbol—and later that rhetorical irony and metaphor celebrated by New Critics—failed as answers to this question because neither had any basis in philosophic principles. In Lentricchia's view, this liberal-humanist, cognitivist approach badly perverted Frost's Kantian stress on the particular, subjective, psychological self of conscious fiction making. In addition, for Lentricchia the New Critical position prevented American and continental philosophic traditions from jointly illuminating Frost's stature as a major modernist poet.

Against this misappropriation of Kant, and thus of Frost, Lentricchia insisted on the private, affective, noncognitive, and "therapeutic" character of Frost's poetry. Like all art, poetry provides a "purposeless play" generating an "intransitive attention" (145) in the beholder, offering a "better nature" than external facts, through which artist and reader individually attain a fuller psychological harmony of their faculties. Accordingly, "when we grasp Frost's landscape, the personal world shaped by the poet's consciousness in and through language, a world answering

to the psychic needs of its shaper, we are *not* gaining a form of shareable knowledge of a common public reality" (144; my emphasis). On the contrary, according to Lentricchia we enter the sphere of a shaping poetic consciousness that achieves—and enables readers to participate in—a liberating wholeness of inner being in the harmony or play of all of its faculties. On this view, Frost frames the mind as a compensatory fantasy-mechanism against the uninhabitable bruteness of external fact, the world of phenomenal objects. His poems are "epistemologically unsanctioned, free-floating structures . . . peculiar to the poet who projects the unveilings of the hidden self" (152).[55]

In the last pages of his book, Lentricchia vaguely allows for a "more expansive and generous" Frost than the one he has just presented, a Frost who sought "engagement" with others (181) beyond some isolated sphere of inner experience-as-consciousness. Two decades later, in *Modernist Quartet* (1994), Lentricchia has considerably tilted his earlier views toward this more social-pragmatic Frost, but even Lentricchia's later pragmatism remains haunted by a therapeutic solipsism, just as his earlier readings of individual poems grossly overshoot the poet's abiding preoccupations with the rhetorical issues explored in the present book. While Lentricchia's concern to bring different philosophic traditions to bear on Frost is one I am obviously eager to support, nevertheless Lentricchia sails right past Frost's deepest and most abiding commitments—to belief, judgment, taste, wisdom, reason, persuasion, and truth. What needs to be shown is that Frost is, in fact, the first genuinely modern American poet—it is *this* point, in fact, that makes him not only modern but (his own version of) postmodern *avant la lettre*—the first *modernist* American poet to create an art aware that the conditions of everyday life and ordinary language have always been, relatively speaking, those of breakdown and loss of criteria in the face of skepticism ("eclipse"; "everywhere in chains"), hence also conditions of potential renewal through what I have been calling rhetoric. Too acute a formulation of "crisis," therefore, and too epistemically differentiated and psychologized an account of the response to it, overstate not only Frost's but other high and low modernists' poetic and philosophical positions and poses.

The problem with Lentricchia's Kantianism, then, and even with his later quasi-Burkean Marxism, is that these positions so resist, reject, or seek to transcend or escape the everyday and ordinary as to be unable to sound out Frost's extended, subtle movements within them. A good contrast to this wholesale sweeping away of the everyday and ordinary in the context of the aesthetic is Hans-Georg Gadamer's quite different reading of Kant in *Truth and Method* (1960). Gadamer's account is one that explicitly invokes the rhetorical tradition and offers new ways to understand what Richard Poirier (like Cavell) calls the pragmatic "Emersonian" tradition, which I consider *one* (not the only) important part of American low modernism. Although I can give only a brief sketch of Gadamer's appropriation

of Kant's aesthetic views here, it ought to be enough to begin to identify the signature preoccupations of low (and to suggest ways of rereading high) modernist writers, artists, and other cultural practitioners.

In *Truth and Method,* Gadamer sees Kant's analysis of aesthetic beauty in the *Critique of Judgment* (1790) as the unlikely source for a new understanding of historical knowledge, and thus, by extension, a new understanding of understanding and interpretation in general (including our understanding of the judgment of artworks). The *Critique* is an unlikely place to look for developments in general hermeneutics because aesthetic judgment, for Kant—though it does, like historical study, focus on particulars—refers strictly to the perceiving *subject,* evoking only that subject's perceptions, affects of pleasure or pain, and sense of beauty or sublimity regarding an event in or of nature, or of some unique, man-made object.[56] Moreover, since each artwork (to concentrate on artworks here, though such a focus does not fully occur until Hegel's *Aesthetics* [1835]) is a unique product, the work of genius, it cannot be judged in the way that we understand instances of nonaesthetic concepts (or, as Gadamer puts the point, "No one supposes that questions of taste can be decided by argument and proof"; *TM* 42).

By way of contrast: if one is to grasp that a particular creature is a dog, for instance, or a particular dog a pug, human understanding slots the perception under the relevant concept: the synthesis of percept and concept constitutes a "sensuous intuition" that, along with similar judgments, forms the basis of scientific knowledge of phenomena. In such cases, Kant calls the judgment rendered subsumptive, or "determinant," since the concept covers the percept without remainder, that is, the "schema" of the concept "dog" leaves nothing out of the judgment of a particular instance. More important, determinant judgment is cognitive inasmuch as it provides objective information about the phenomenon-in-view rather than exclusively about the reactions of the perceiving subject.

Aesthetic judgment does not work in the same manner. It is "reflective," not determinant, meaning that it is not rule-bound or subsumptive.[57] What counts now is not a concept or rule under which the particular fits, but rather the affective experience of the particular itself, where "experience" transcends mere sensation, is unadulterated by moral purpose (Kant's famous "purposiveness without purpose"), and works *toward* rather than *from* a universal. Now what the particular example is an example of—what it reflects and reflects on—is itself in its own singularity ("You might say the work of art does not aim to convey *something else,* just itself"; *CV* 58e). And what it *points* toward is not an already-fashioned concept but rather a new formulation, so to speak, of the concept it *seeks* to reflect. That is, reflective aesthetic judgment does not inform or "teach" us about the world, in spite of the fact that particulars may portray myriad aspects of the world (and thus be of moral interest); instead they give pleasure, at most provoke future acts of genius whose products, also necessarily unique, will also not be

rule-governed. The reflective judgment of "taste" deems a work beautiful or not beautiful, and beauty is that about which strict science is not possible just because it is not rule-governed.

By the same token, conversely, the aesthetic is intended to be a part of Kant's philosophical system of knowledge and not *merely* individual or personal or subjective, because, from within Kant's analysis of the powers and limits of human understanding, aesthetics ascends (pace Lentricchia) to a priori "subjective *universals*" (*CJ* 78), that is, to the recognition not merely of an individual's taste but of the nature of appropriate feeling and good taste (and even the perfection of taste) per se. Aesthetic judgment is not mere expression of the empirical fact that someone (anyone) likes something but rather is a claim that something *ought* to be liked, is or will be seen to be beautiful by those whose faculties are rightly disposed and whose affective experience is of the requisite scope and depth. Hence, in this view, affective "taste" just *is* the *sensus communis* to which one appeals.

It is in this picture, however, that Gadamer locates a disturbing contradiction and promising development of Kantian aesthetics for knowledge in general, as Joel Weinsheimer, among others, has shown.[58] For at crucial moments Kant grows ambivalent about the relationship of the particular instance to its covering law. On the one hand, the artwork-as-example is said to cultivate the taste without being able to do anything for the intellect as such (except, perhaps, impair it by distracting the understanding, offering it perhaps a misleading instance of a concept or rule). On the other hand, the particular work-as-example "gives the rule to art" (*CJ* 150), as Kant puts it, not, that is, to later geniuses but to lesser mortals (say, to artists manqué, or to critics!):

> Because a genius is a favorite of nature and must be regarded by us as a rare phenomenon, his example produces for other good heads a school, i.e., a methodical system of teaching according to rules, so far as these can be derived from the peculiarities of the products of his spirit. For such persons beautiful art is so far an imitation, to which nature through the medium of genius supplied the rule. (*CJ* 161–62)

The idea seems to be that smaller heads derive a rule from the example, precisely what reflective judgment is *not* supposed to be able to do, and Kant is on the verge of proposing a paradox in the face of a dilemma.[59]

In his compelling *Consequences of Enlightenment*, Anthony Cascardi also notes a series of related dilemmas and paradoxes.[60] For, in spite of Kant's claiming an a priori transcendental principle to render aesthetic judgment categorical (so that reflective judgment functions as a symbolic bridge between reason and man's purposive freedom), Kant remains unclear about exactly what this a priori might be. In part, this is understandable, since the principle can be neither theoretical nor practical, neither epistemological nor moral: "What remains ... difficult for

Kant is the issue of what he describes as a proof, deduction, or 'derivation' of what taste wants to claim in its *prima facie* assertions of beauty and sublimity" (68). "It is precisely a domain of knowledge that is without grounds or, as Wittgenstein would say, without criteria, that the theory of reflective judgment is meant to establish" (59). In the end, Kant himself seems to acknowledge that the form of knowledge that aesthetic judgment is intended to comprise is itself unprovable:

> As a "middle term," reflective judgment is expected to shuttle back and forth between the distinct domains of pure theoretical reason (cognition) and pure practical reason (morality), for the purpose of proving the relevance of freedom in a world of objects causally ordered and to show that nature stands ready to accommodate the ends proposed by morality. But at the same time, Kant in the third *Critique* refuses to offer any determination of this middle term. (77)

With Gadamer, Kant's various dilemmas and tensions disappear, for, in the knowledge of history, as well as in other modes of practical knowledge that are not products of rule-governed (determinant) judgments, the particular example remains unsubsumable under concepts, while reflective judgment is in no need of being provable a priori, not when Kant's differentiations of the fields of knowledge (epistemological, moral, aesthetic) are themselves rejected. Rather, on a hermeneutic and phenomenological approach, examples are taken to *re-shape* whatever concepts and laws may be evoked by them in ways not predictable by the concepts or laws themselves. Since the particular case does not fall under a concept or law without remainder, the concept or law does not exhaust the example, and Gadamer's insight becomes one that Kant might have drawn but did not (lest he admit that art possesses cognitive content), namely, that the relationship between case and rule is one of *mutual modification*.[61]

To return to trivial examples: "Do not walk on the grass" certainly suggests past behaviors (examples); but it does so without necessarily dictating exactly what the rule will mean in the future. What are we to do, for instance, with the MIT graduate student who, scooting an inch above the grass on his self-designed, nuclear-powered skateboard, destroys the grass with its lethal (though nonradioactive!) exhaust just as surely as the undergraduate who tramps in cleats across the rain-soaked quads at State? The rule alone does not decide this case, nor do past examples included under it. Rather, each modifies the other, and if we do come to *judge* that the skateboard example does belong under the rule (because it is "like" past cases of the rule enough to "count" for us), then this new example gives further shape to the rule without itself having been rule-governed and without its dictating to us how the rule shall be understood in the future.[62]

The crux of Gadamer's argument is that the aesthetic judgment (as in artworks) can and often does work in just the same way. Art provides experience for

reflective judgment that is also exemplary *knowledge* (not merely Lentricchean "consciousness" or "supreme fiction"), just as practical knowledge is often exemplary because it improves our capacity for reflective judgment beyond the realm of the aesthetic—for example, in politics, ethics, law, history, indeed in any field in which examples are used to do more than illustrate generalizations. And so, as in "Education by Poetry" (1931), Frost writes: "Suppose we stop short of imagination, initiative, enthusiasm, inspiration and originality—dread words. Suppose we don't mark [grade] in such things at all. There are still two minimal things, that we have got to take care of, taste and judgment. Americans are supposed to have more judgment than taste, but taste is there to be dealt with. That is what poetry, the only art in the college of arts, is there for" (*SP* 35–36). The particular work of art, historical event, ethical decision, political policy, or genuine experience of everyday life, *expands* our knowledge of the concept/rule/law/situation to which it is beholden but not bound. It does this by showing forth how concepts can be projected in specific circumstances (thereby suggesting similar projections in new circumstances); while our concepts, being backed by a variety of examples and their applications, suggest new ways to project their meanings. In this way, Gadamer's understanding of Kant provides a powerful extension for a rhetorical-philosophical reading not only of Frost but of high modernists generally, one that is at once resolutely ethical-political *and* cognitive *and* aesthetic (see Wittgenstein's "ethics and aesthetics are one").[63]

Lentricchia's argument (indebted as much to Schiller and to the Nietzsche of *The Birth of Tragedy* as to Kant), to the effect that objective reality is countered by the private play of mind, is transformed when we use the term "exemplary knowledge" rather than "supreme fiction." These two notions are close, it is true, inasmuch as reality never arrives unmediated for Frost any more than for Kant, and it is subject to multiple perspectives of interpretation ("fictions") for Frost as much as for any other modernist (for example, Stevens). But Gadamer's pragmatic, even Deweyan aesthetics helps us to see that poetry may be as intellectually real as any other non-rule-governed experience in and of the world, and that its "as if" character—its status as fiction, if one insists on the word—nevertheless can be as cognitively productive of belief as the strongest logical inference, scientific observation, political decision, or moral judgment. (I will take up both belief and judgment, and the logic of exemplary knowledge, in the following two chapters, suggesting that the scientific and deductive depend upon reflective judgment.)

Among critics of Frost, then, it is not Lentricchia (and a fortiori not Katherine Kearns) but rather, once again, Richard Poirier who aids us in synthesizing the explicitly rhetorical and hermeneutic aesthetics of continental philosophers—Kant and Gadamer—with the American pragmatism of the Emersonian-Jamesian tradition. Poirier writes that "Frost seems . . . of vital interest and consequence because his ultimate subject is the interpretive process itself."[64] Though I think

this is right, it remains undertheorized and overcommitted to transition and change, so that the present book works out, while it also resists, some of its considerable implications.

Poirier has intimated this connection in several of his own books over several decades. In *Robert Frost: The Work of Knowing* (1976), first of all, static and perhaps ineffable New Critical "knowledge" is replaced by the gerundive "knowing," a knowing at least tacitly allied with Heidegger's and Gadamer's phenomenological hermeneutics in its stress on the centrality of the *act* of interpretation. In *The Renewal of Literature: Emersonian Reflections* (1987), Poirier introduces other writers working on the Emerson line—Whitman and Thoreau, James, Frost, Stevens (and later Stein): "Why this grouping? First, because . . . they offer a way to think about literature and about life that seems to me a crucial alternative to the dominant modernist and so-called post-modernist ways of thinking."[65] Here Poirier shifts out of his focus on interpretation (my interest in hermeneutics) into the language (though not the resources of the tradition) of rhetoric, particularly that of "tropes." The following passages are representative: "In 'The Poet' he [Emerson] speaks of 'abandonment to the nature of things.' The word helps explain his tendency to move out of any rhetorical position he has just occupied into another one" (74); "The roots of [Emerson's obsession with language] go back at least to the fifth-century Greek sophists" (35); "Language is . . . the place wherein we can most effectively register our dissent from our fate by means of troping, punning, parodistic echoings, and by letting vernacular idioms play against revered terminologies" (72); and, speaking of troping, "I am saying that one obvious characteristic of a literary text is that its words tend to destabilize one another and to fall into conflicted or contradictory relationships" (147). Finally, in *Poetry and Pragmatism* (1996), Poirier continues his Emersonian reflections by highlighting the contribution of Jamesian pragmatism to themes of transition, indeterminacy, vague concepts and "extra-vagant" (nonsystematic) thought (and, by implication, fuzzy logic), of tradition as a resource rather than a monument, provisional truths, the limited political impact of literature's tropes, belief as effective fiction, and much else immediately pertinent to Frost and other low modernists. How, then, do we use these insights to make further discoveries (inventions) about high and low modernism?

From Crisis to Continuum: How High Becomes the Low

The many reactions to the breakdown of shared criteria and acknowledgments that high modernists characterize as a crisis, as well as the aesthetic strategies and tactics that followed from them, are by now well known enough to be revisited, questioned, and revised.[66] First, we know that those reactions pivot on the Nietzschean recognition (itself obliquely indebted to Kant)[67] of the pervasiveness of interpretation in man's views of the world, what Michael Bell calls an underlying

"contextualist metaphysics,"[68] as well as on, in my accounting, the decided resistance against identification with others, specifically with a mythicized version of the common man as philistine and of mass society as co-opted by technological modernity. Attending these are degradation of the language, runaway technology, commodity culture, Victorian sexual repression and extreme psychological naïveté in general, middle-class conventionalism, and so on.[69] Writers like Musil and Kafka follow out the logic of Angst and alienation; Mallarmé and Mondrian seek to transcend urban pathologies and uglifications to purity and beauty of forms; Nietzsche, Freud, and Marx practice a severe hermeneutics of suspicion; Joyce celebrates the modern multiplicity of perspectives by rendering the everyday and ordinary as quasi-mythical, momentous yet artistically bankrupt; Pound bewails our fate lost in the folds and abysses of history; Eliot builds bridges, never secure, over urban canyons. When foundations disappear, fiduciary frameworks fall; unities fragment, words lose their meanings in shifting surroundings; the self self-divides; the center cannot hold.

Second, the various aesthetic strategies attending upon this crisis—above all abstraction, but also the objectivization of narrator, narrative fragmentation, multiple perspectives, formalism, irony, and the rest—also rotate around the high modernist belief that art must become, as Poirier notes in "Modernism and Its Difficulties," supremely *difficult* in order to be equal to the cultural difficulty, in order that something genuine might survive.[70] Poirier notes that high modernism's celebrated difficulties of interpretation and self-relexiveness may better be taken not on their face but rather, in part, as compensatory mechanisms for the loss of the everyday world (hence the "crucial alternative" to such loss provided by the Emersonians). Rather than requiring their readers actually to master their exaggerated erudition and accumulated arcana, in other words, high modernist works offer a "primer of connoisseurship for people who are invited at the same time to pretend that they are already connoisseurs."[71] Poirier's idea is that the genuine energies of high modernist literature lie not in its ersatz erudition but in its very genuine discoveries of new forms of language.

By contrast, low modernism may be said to offer not the ersatz nostalgia for some long lost *Gemeinschaft* but rather what I call an advanced primer of rhetorical thinking and speaking. Low modernism—found perhaps most forcefully in Frost but ingredient also in Wharton and James, in Woolf and Lawrence, in Moore and Williams, sometimes in Stevens, and later in poets as diverse as Auden, Charles Olson, and Charles Bernstein[72]—speaks to those for whom everyday life has *always* been in transition, hence in need of *projection* to new situations. Low modernism praises and blames, accepts or rejects, acknowledges or refuses to acknowledge the contextual background of our words and the ordinary practices within which they operate, often symbolized by the image of "home." High and low both seek new integrations of our divided selves, but whereas high modernism

makes language (reading and writing, communication) overtly difficult and strange in order to break its readers free from the grip of an everyday perceived to be suffocating and conventionalized, low modernism makes language deceptively easy and pleasurable in order to entice us into tripping over connections we had habitually overlooked. Where the high modernist is in flight from the everyday and ordinary, seeking an epiphany of form by which to purify the language of the tribe, the low modernist provisionally "shows forth" the everyday, often by projecting home, work, talk, or marriage as possibilities (sometimes opaque, sometimes idealized) for exemplary knowledge. If high modernist formalism is read as a species of disciplined literary heroics in the face of the pervasive mediocrity of modernity, and all the more heroic because skeptical of its own forms, low modernism picks up and turns the fragments of our ruins this way and that, trying out possibilities of the phenomena. High modernism spatializes our deafness to the noise of the masses, while low modernism sounds our aspect-blindness to our own lives, reminding us that, though we already know how to talk, we must learn to listen and to adjust our words to ever-changing circumstances.

To mention just one touchstone of high modernist lyric, in "Of Modern Poetry" Wallace Stevens thematizes the overthrow of the romantic theater of identity for a new world stage in which the settings and props are self-consciously artificial: "The poem of the mind in the act of finding / What will suffice. It has not always had / To find: the scene was set . . . Then the theatre was changed / To something else" (lines 1–4). Indeed it was changed, although Charles Taylor, like Poirier, reads Stevens and other high modernists as intent on offering "epiphanies" of "lived experience," and Charles Altieri reads Stevens in particular, and "Of Modern Poetry" specifically, as offering us new "powers" and "energies" of feeling and intellection, presumably on a continuum with our normal abilities outside of poetry.[73] These energies and epiphanies, at least as Altieri, Taylor, and Poirier present them, remain very abstract, vague, and potentially bloodless, and they often end up being antiexpressivist and noncognitive altogether. Indeed, according to Gerald Bruns, for Stevens "success in experience means hearing no one's voice but your own," converting "public dialogue and social interchange into private meditation"[74]—the reverse, as it were, of the process we saw in Frost's "Leaves Compared with Flowers," and in any case no obvious solution as to how words, or mind, link up with the world. Instead, the modern artist becomes

> A metaphysician in the dark, twanging
> An instrument, twanging a wiry string that gives
> Sounds passing through sudden rightnesses, wholly
> Containing the mind, below which it cannot descend,
> Beyond which it has no will to rise.
>                It must
> Be the finding of a satisfaction, and may

> Be of a man skating, a woman dancing, a woman
> Combing. The poem of the act of the mind.
>
> (lines 19–26)

Note that Stevens's everyday figures skate and sing and even dance *alone*, while much high modernist experimental abstractionism—for all of its imposing range and intensity of exemplary linguistic and formal achievement—never escapes what might be called the skeptical drag of its own irony, namely its awareness that while romantic expressivism had reestablished the unity of the knowing subject at least "animistically," as it were, within the mediating symbol of Nature as the linguistic Sublime, the effort was nevertheless philosophically inadequate to the fragmentation of modern perspectives that it (modernist abstraction) helped disseminate and deepen, and from which it could not extricate itself. In other words, none of these traditions or reactionary movements quite manages to escape the Kantian divide, assumed in Lentricchia and Bruns, between propositionalist knowledge of phenomena and nonpropositional "play" of faculties. On the contrary, from Mallarmé and Rimbaud to postmodernists like Warhol, much of this unsuccessful straddling inevitably gave way betimes to out-and-out abandonment of the attempt to close the gap, reveling instead in aporia and paradox and perspectival multiplicity, and suspending judgment by way of the infinite play of signifiers. On such an approach not only poetry but also philosophy becomes equally (I do not say ineluctably) "dissimulative" in the sense of posing the best account of what is the case as merely what can *only* be posited, or willed, or opined, or "convened" to be (conventionalized as) true, that is, as "fiction" rather than as data still to be *judged* to be fitting or unfitting, satisfying or not satisfying, epistemically a gain or a loss. On such an account there is no cognitive judgment at all, only feeling. Nevertheless, Poirier, Taylor, and Altieri begin to step beyond the often overly narrow aesthetic conceptions that modernism subsequently fell into by the 1950s. I will leave it to others to ascertain the many complex syntheses, contrasts, contradictions, and uneasy alliances of high and low to be found in poets such as Williams, Moore, Lawrence, and others. Here it is time I try to give an account of the kind of topoi a low modernist like Frost is likely to explore.

### Possibilities of the Phenomena: A Select Topical Catalog of the Everyday

> We judge an action according to its background within human life, and this background is not monochrome, but we might picture it as a very complicated filigree pattern, which, to be sure, we can't copy, but which we can recognize from the general impression it makes.
>
> —Ludwig Wittgenstein, *Remarks on the Philosophy of Psychology*

To sidestep the modernist misunderstandings of the relations of grammar and rhetoric, philosophy and literature, truth and fiction, one recourse, we have seen,

is the Nietzsche-inspired turn to destabilizing tropes developed by many postmodernists across the disciplines and hardly in need of recapitulation here. There remains, however, the related possibility that the general reaction to the modern and later postmodern crisis was something of an over-reaction, a long-prepared-for but misleading association of rhetoric with an enfeebled sense of reason, of tradition and authority as unthinking prejudices and enthusiasm blocking the path of progressive freedom, and of public speech as merely conventionalized ornament and cliché, and a corresponding over-inflation of the epistemological claims of traditional philosophy and romantic art. Yet it *does* remain the case that the architectonic rhetoric with which to illuminate a poet like Frost owes as much to novel as to ancient modes of thinking, specifically to American pragmatism, to British ordinary language philosophy, and to German and French hermeneutics.

As anyone familiar with one or more of these movements or methods is likely to know, each one has already been shown by other theorists to be deeply interfused with more historically adequate versions of rhetoric and vice versa. This means that there exist contemporary ways of conceiving rhetoric and philosophy—and perhaps also literature—that have taken several scenic S-curves around rhetoric's historically intermittent anachronism (its epistemic naïveté) and exaggerated subversiveness (its reduction to destabilizing tropes). Between these potholes and cliff-falls it is possible to show that philosophic rhetoric can unite a method of argument and evocation with the aim of getting someone to "see" something *not* "simply-objectively-there." Thus ordinary language philosopher John Wisdom describes "*rational* persuasion" in ethics and political philosophy in a way that Cavell and others transpose to aesthetics: "this is done by drawing attention rhetorically to the features of what we are talking about, insisting upon how different it is from this, how like to that, passing insensibly from the purely factual through the semi-factual, semi-critical to the critical predicate at issue. Only this mixture is proof and the name of it is rhetoric." In literary studies, Austin Quigley has made much the same point: "Rhetorical presentation and philosophical procedure merge in the focus on exemplary instances"; "by making the activity of judging constitutive for language and culture, Wittgenstein [like Gadamer] makes what is traditionally called aesthetics a model for all philosophical activity."[75] My own aim, accordingly, is to draw attention to this and that, not (logically) to prove a thesis but by an ensemble of instances and reminders to let something shine forth in a certain light in order that we might come to acknowledge something hitherto more felt than known (or shown).

Said otherwise: at the end of his monumental volume *Mimesis*, Erich Auerbach, having commented at length on Virgina Woolf's *To The Lighthouse*, observes the emergence in the representations of modernist literature generally of "something new and elemental," something at least part of which I think we can identify, topically, in Frost:

What takes place here in Virginia Woolf's novel is precisely what was attempted everywhere in works of this kind (although not everywhere with the same insight and mastery)—that is, to put the emphasis on the random occurrence, to exploit it not in the service of a planned continuity of action but in itself. And in the process something new and elemental appeared: nothing less than the wealth of reality and depth of life in every moment to which we surrender ourselves without prejudice. To be sure, what happens in that moment—be it outer or inner processes—concerns in a very personal way the individuals who live in it, but it also (and for that very reason) concerns the elementary things which men in general have in common. It is precisely the random moment which is comparatively independent of the controversial and unstable orders over which men fight and despair; it passes unaffected by them, as daily life. The more it is exploited, the more the elementary things which our lives have in common come to light. The more numerous, varied, and simple the people are who appear as subjects of such random moments, the more effectively must what they have in common shine forth.[76]

This idea of something "shining forth" *(epi-deixis)* I will develop later. Here I am more interested in giving content to Auerbach's insight by saying something about "daily life," the everyday and ordinary, perhaps most clearly signaled in Frost by the concept of the everyday and the image of "home." The intellectual historian Jay Martin suggests that "if we turn . . . to more theoretical discussions of the idea of 'everydayness,' such as . . . Michel de Certeau's *The Practice of Everyday Life* or Agnes Heller's *Everyday Life*, it is possible to appreciate some of the complexity of the phenomenon [of everydayness] itself. For rather than being reducible to quotidian routine [mere repetition], the everyday can also be understood to contain varieties of resistances to both control from above and internalized conformity from below [that is, at the level of the everyday itself]."[77] Unlike Auerbach, Martin's focus in context is overtly political, as are those of Heller and de Certeau.[78] But for Heller at least, of whom I wish to make brief use here (I turn to de Certeau also in chapter 4), political change is effected by—only because it is, as Auerbach himself notes, implicated in—the complex moral processes by which the capabilities of normal human beings become externalized and recreated through ongoing change amidst relative constancy and repetition: "In itself and without remainder, everyday life is objectification"; or, to put it another way, "everyday activities are those in which the whole man takes shape."[79] "Everyday life" does not exhaust the concepts of "experience" or "the ordinary" or "criteria" in Wittgenstein and others, but the experience of individuals does provide a plausible point of departure for discussing a poet so enamored with the everyday and ordinary as Robert Frost.

In fact, Heller is one of the few modern theorists for whom everyday life is less like some delimited set of beliefs and biases than it is a pervasive scene of

activities within which "objectivations" of persons take place, as well as the ongoing opportunity and search for such objectivations. To think otherwise, to reify the everyday as an objective "it," is to run the risk of the grammatical error of treating as a fixed tableau what is not determinate at all. In other words, Heller's work explicitly declares itself no less a philosophical than an empirical investigation, in part phenomenological and in part Aristotelian,[80] no less interested than Wittgenstein and Heidegger (whom she cites numerous times) in investigating fundamental concepts and activities underwriting everyday life: obeying a sign, knowing when someone else has a toothache, understanding, expecting, shaming, and so on—what she calls the everyday realm of objects and tools, customs and habits, and linguistic phenomena and sign systems.[81] Like Wittgenstein and Cavell and Poirier, Heller puts us in a position to try to give equal recognition and value to what abides in the everyday as to what changes, what is stable not just subversive, what is subversive sometimes just because it *is* relatively stable, constitutive, habitual, unconscious—in short, a search for situated criteria, hence not only for individuals but for communities. Much of Heller's book can be described as a kind of *rhetorica docens*-in-miniature, a second-order topical rhetoric enabling us to read Frost with an ear out for what does not quite formulate, what is non-rule-governed, un-pre-dictable. What then, in brief, does Heller put us on the lookout for?

If we construe *Everyday Life* as we do everyday life—less as a principled theory and more as an activity of and for phenomenological investigations, and as a complex set of indeterminate rhetorical topics organizing an even more complex intricacy—then we can explore the realms of objects and tools, customs and habits, and language appearing in a writer like Frost, in the following terms: (1) their common properties and family resemblances; (2) the ways in which normal human beings "appropriate" these realms; (3) the roles played by everyday (and to an extent noneveryday) knowledge in our appropriation of these realms (both "knowing-how" and "knowing-that," also thought of as on a continuum); and (4) the media of contact through which these realms appear to us. From these we can derive a sort of rough topical catalog, one whose ultimate usefulness will be tested on the pulse of good reading as we proceed rather than on the unsatisfying mechanism of its presentation here.

Thus Heller's everyday realm can be characterized as greater or lesser indeterminacies whose ranges of interest may be delimited as follows: (1) reiterative or repetitious rather than singular, momentous, heroic, or extraordinary; (2) norm-governed and economical in effort rather than in constant need of interpretation and reinvention; and (3) situated via sign systems (chiefly language) in time and place rather than a timeless and unmediated set of activities and knowledge. Our own *appropriation* of these realms as readers can also be construed topically, inasmuch as we ourselves act, interact, speak, and know in these realms in

our lives (1) pragmatically and with probability rather than with a speculative disengagement intent on certainty; (2) through imitation and analogical extrapolation (for example, via "prototypes" in cognitive science, or Cavell's "projective imagination" [*CR* 145ff.]) rather than through strict rules and pregiven models; and (3) with general concepts and singular cases treated as it were "roughly," meaning that our concepts are—sometimes quite usefully and sometimes not—vague and fuzzy rather than unequivocal and unyielding. And it follows that everyday knowing in these realms, being pragmatic, is distinct but not hermetically sealed off its from noneveryday reflection in science, philosophy, and art, hence that everyday knowing is (1) a situated combination of knowing-how and knowing that; (2) not only repetitive and rote but inventive, inasmuch as the activity of analogical extrapolation and treatment of new, singular cases requires innovation; and (3) variously mediated in language through diverse channels ranging from parents and teachers and neighborhood to media of mass communication and now the internet. And finally (but "finally" only relatively speaking, since it is impossible to exhaust the changing everyday), our contact with each other in these realms runs the full gamut of language games, from conversation and dialogue to giving reports, informing, persuading, debating, and much else, at home and at work and in between.

As a topical catalog, such a list—as Aristotle notes of his own such lists in the *Rhetoric*—threatens endless exfoliation. "Home," for example, can function for us in our reading of Frost as both an image of a place, as a "place" (topos) in which the everyday and ordinary are explored, and as a trope for the everyday itself (for example, Holmes and Watson's tent as a home-away-from-home). Again, we know the sites of home and work are gendered spaces whose discourse will respond to awareness of that fact, so that, for example, "contact" through "conversation" can culminate in relationships like marriage or break down in divorce and death (grief), while the pragmatic attitude of "knowing-how" can flourish in the nonconceptual discourse of narrative or come to grief in the overgeneralizations of disengaged argument. Analogy or argument by example can be coordinated with deductive arguments or contrasted to them, while grammatical investigations can correct everyday knowledge by adverting to the contexts of the everyday rather than be construed as superior expertise declaimed from a place apart. And the situated aspect of the everyday, though a matter of repetition, can be construed as a timeliness sensitive to "retrieval" of the past rather than exclusively be reduced to a time past endlessly repeated. And so on.

Heller, moreover—though never mentioning rhetorical thinking as such—similarly writes that "by 'inventive' *praxis* I understand not simply the generation of novelty but rather any activity which is at the same time the solution of a problem—the *intentional* solution, that is, construed as acquisition of *experience*, broadening of opinion, the taking of decisions. And 'intentionality' is here taken not in the

narrow sense—that of the solution being present in my mind, 'envisaged' before praxis—but rather in the wider sense, i.e., as meaning teleological activity in which intention is central to action and is itself formed and articulated as the activity proceeds" (28; second inner quotation marks added). As we saw in the introduction, this is accomplished in part by use of material, special topics. While special topics take a variety of forms, they have been traditionally construed as single or paired terms or as premises (for example, maxims) more or less intrinsic to some subject matter or type of problem (for example, practical political questions) and useful for organizing the relevant circumstances of an indeterminate situation in order to frame persuasive arguments and other appeals on both sides of the question.[82]

In this way, many of Frost's poems function not only as scenes of (first-stage) topical use but also as mini (second-stage) topical catalogs to equip the reader with materials for her own invention and judgment drawn from both the case at hand and its distanciated counterparts in the changing performances of readers' readings. Such poems function didactically in a large sense of the word, as sets of "instructions" in plain language (for example, Frost's overtly rhetorical, and philosophical, "Directive"), or as conversational "primers" or "how-to" manuals ("At Woodward Gardens," alternately titled "Resourcefulness Is More Than Understanding"), and they are usually constructed as sets of related terms—fire/ice, work/play, inner/outer, self/neighbor, husband/wife, words/actions, and innumerable others—so that, as Aristotle points out, "it may not escape our notice what the real state of the case is" (*Rhet* 1355a). These are, in short, conceptual binaries, but the logical relations between terms vary from opposition to correlation to contradiction, mapping out ranges of possibilities, depending on the case at hand and the purpose in using them.

At its best, in other words, Frost's didacticism is not tied to the sort of moralism of commonplace books, traditional rhetorics, or fixed social attitudes so consistently prevalent before, and so reviled after, the eighteenth century. Nor is it tied to specific social and political commitments, from Marxist to deconstructive to traditional liberal-humanist, nowadays favored (or reviled) in American literary studies. Wordsworth's celebrated interest in the commonplace and ordinary things of life largely *contrasts* with the allegorical character of traditional rhetorical commonplaces in favor of romantic symbols and metaphors, whereas in Frost, as in Emerson, the everyday and ordinary often *coincide* with the inventional function of rhetorical topics just because Frost has invested no allegorical precommitments in them. Conversely, contemporary deconstructionists and new historicists celebrate the constructed nature of allegory, as opposed to both allegory's precommitments and symbol's mystifications, because allegory affords leverage to unfix what is seen as merely conventional, hence oppressive. But for Frost the conventional, the everyday and ordinary, are themselves taken to be

imbued with what Bakhtin calls "event potential" for creative invention, in part just *because* the fact that their topical possibilities function within contested matters has been overlooked from the romantics to our own time.[83]

Thus part of what differentiates what we may call the low modern Frost from the romantic Wordsworth and the antiromantic and better-known postmodern deconstructionists is twofold.[84] First, both the romantic *and* the antiromantic associate the commonplace tradition with fixity or artifice in opposition to creative "genius," whereas Frost loosens both artifice and genius from their historical commitments to fixed commonplaces or their subversion. Second, the romantic and antiromantic either see the common things of life as manifesting near-animistic notions of an Over-Soul or Idea, or they conveniently reduce them to materialistic notions of language or will and power, whereas a more skeptical Frost discursively manipulates the ordinary and common to manifest the sense (or nonsense) we make with the grammatical and rhetorical resources of ordinary language as it is put on display (that is, performed) in poems.[85] Topical invention allows Frost to organize perception not, or not exclusively, to "defamiliarize" the ordinary but, so to speak, to recommunalize a precarious everyday threatened by preromantic empiricism, romantic subjectivism, modernist irony, poststructuralist idealism, and the skepticisms dogging the heels of all four. Attention to topics does this in part by ferreting out philosophic and rhetorical confusions in our uses of ordinary language and in part by disclosing new paths of personal and public commitment. Since invention is never exhausted by a catalog or list, Frost's poems are better thought of as cultivating an experienced "taste" and practical "ability" or "judgment" enabling one to get on to where life happens, beneath us, under our feet, in front of our noses.

CHAPTER

# 3

# GRAMMATICAL JUDGMENT
*It All Depends on What You Mean by "Home"*

> When philosophers use a word—'knowledge,' 'being,' 'object,' 'I,' 'proposition,' 'name'—and try to grasp the *essence* of the thing, one must always ask oneself: is the word ever actually used in this way in the language-game which is its original home?
> What we do is to bring words back from their metaphysical to their everyday use.
> —Ludwig Wittgenstein, *Philosophical Investigations*

> All "homes" are in finite experience; finite experience as such is homeless.
> —William James, *Pragmatism*

## From Propositions to Utterances

### "My Proof of Being Not Unbounded"

THE TITLE of Frost's seventh book of poems, *A Witness Tree* (1942), eponymously derives from the lead poem, "Beech," whose philosophical claims, twice hedged in as they are by the speaker's skeptical "doubt" (lines 11–12), are almost but not quite squared by Sidney Cox's observation that "Frost's skepticism is a means of doubting unity enough to need another voice both to corroborate and express his own existence."[1] This is an important insight, but it begs equally important questions, for in this poem (in these lines from the spine of the poet's pen) and in related lyrics like "The Most of It" later in that book, no human voice additional to that of the poet speaks at all. Worse, in "Beech" any "witness" the tree is bearing seems as odd as if I were to try to corroborate my alibi to the police—"I was miles away in Fredericksburg"—by saying that I saw myself there in a mirror:

> Where my imaginary line
> Bends square in woods, an iron spine
> And pile of real rocks have been founded.
> And off this corner in the wild,
> Where these are driven in and piled,
> One tree, by being deeply wounded,
> Has been impressed as Witness Tree
> And made commit to memory
> My proof of being not unbounded.

> Thus truth's established and borne out,
> Though circumstanced with dark and doubt—
> Though by a world of doubt surrounded.

Here Frost hints that only against a contextual background, a "witnessing to" and by another being, can one become known at all. On beginning we might say that the tree's "being deeply wounded" ambiguates something like an outer body with an inner soul attributed to it by the one whose own existence is in doubt, as it were humanizing the stately beech as suffering witness in whose mark the poet sees only his own reflection. It is also as if such a reflective impression is supposed to impress us readers as much as it does the tree, and the speaker, simply because the speaker *says* so—and as if it is impressive only because *he* says so, warrants it to be thus ("My proof").

But what does "say" or "warrant" mean in this context? Helpful here is a reminder from Cavell's lengthy discussion of knowledge and acknowledgment in *The Claim of Reason:* "Being human is the power to grant being human" (397)—and presumably the power to withhold the grant, and something like the wisdom to realize when to exact the difference.

The tree bears witness to the separate existence of the speaker, then, but only because the speaker first grants a larger human context to the tree in his own witnessing to its mark or wound. But then it ought not to surprise us that such mutual acknowledgment is "by a world of doubt surrounded" (line 12), since his attention here seems suspiciously solipsistic and shifty. Indeed, this shiftiness is in keeping with Cavell's phrase "the power to *grant* being human": if only human beings possess the power to grant humanity, then this power logically does, after all, "prove" precisely nothing. Yet Frost assures us that "truth" has been "*established* and borne out" by virtue of a mark's being, in the poem, performatively re-marked. But how do a mere mark and a merer (mirror) remark establish *anything?* How *could* they?

Wittgenstein registers a query about such a claim as Frost makes here about the witness tree, a query regarding what might be called its epistemic status as either an opinion or a decision, or as something else less susceptible to changes of mind, fashion, will:

> "So you are saying that human agreement decides what is true and what is false?"—It is what human beings say that is true and false; and they agree in the *language* they use. That is not agreement in opinions but in form of life.
>
> If language is to be a means of communication, there must be agreement not only in definitions but also (queer [*seltsam*] as this may sound) in judgments. This seems to abolish logic, but does not do so.—It is one thing to describe methods of measurement, and another to obtain and state results of measurement. But what we call "measuring" is partly determined by a certain constancy in results of measurement. (*PI* § 241, 242)[2]

"Agreement in judgments" (in "form of life") sounds strange because we tend to think of judgment as a result of accepted *pro*ceedings—sometimes a decision, or opinion, sometimes a logical entailment accepted once premises are stated, but in any case a *specific* result that can be called true or false. However, as used by Wittgenstein here, "agreement in judgment"—agreement in what we do, how we act together, for example how what we call "measuring" is done—in altogether *pre*ceding some specific result or proof, would seem to render proof or logic irrelevant altogether. But Wittgenstein's drift has been that there is *no* proof of anything at all unless human beings are *already* taking something as settled, already in possession of a prior "constancy in results" established in their world by their actions and now taken up into the criteria of their language. (Consider the vast difference between this view and Kant's claim of the apriority of the geometry of space in his "Transcendental Aesthetic"; *CPR* 102ff.)

A constancy in human actions (not in synthetic judgments) underwrites conceptual criteria; they are fundamental "acknowledgments" regarding not what we are to call a true or false measurement but whether we will take *this* activity as exemplary, that is, take it as "measuring" in the first place.[3] Said otherwise: a particular definition presupposes a language already in place; a specific measurement presupposes the acceptance of an activity called measuring; a specific encounter with nature or with a work of art (that is, a work of art interpreted in a specific way, which is the only way we encounter works of art) presupposes an ability to imagine possibilities as acts. In all of these cases, what is *presupposed* is not "decided" upon or "agreed to" in the way we decide, by proof, that a given result is true or false, or, by agreement, that a given definition is correct or incorrect, or, by taste, that a given work of art is beautiful or not: true and false, correct and incorrect, beautiful and not beautiful, do not operate at the ontological level of founding entities, of being: they are rather the means of the "disclosure" of being ("the truth is established and borne out"). What is presupposed is always already *what we humans are doing*, how we are acting, when we define, prove a specific result, create by genius, or judge by taste.

Recall Frost again from chapter 1: "There's no greater mistake than to look on fighting as a form of argument"—that is (extrapolating now), as a form of (or a lack of) agreement. "To *fight* is to *leave words* and act as if you believed—to *act* as if you believed" (*LLU* 10; second emphasis added). (In art and criticism, the counterpart to "leaving words" in real life, which we only do relatively speaking, is leaving acts in *specific* contexts in favor of acting out *possible* acts, trying them out or on.) In "The Black Cottage," the minister is desperate to avoid presuppositions as such if he can: "to *decide*"—for example that the equality of all men "simply isn't true" (line 66; my emphasis). This is taking "the easy way" out (line 65) on both of Wittgenstein's counts: by treating the matter (acknowledgment of human equality) as if it is a decision or opinion, and by treating it as a matter that

is true or false, as if *it* depends on something to be found out about the world empirically, rather than the world as we know it depending upon how *we* act in it and thereby conceptualize it.

In "Beech," by contrast, the speaker does not so much deny or assert ("decide") truth as suggest that truth is somehow always already "proved" in the sense of its being a *commitment*, that is, a reminder, a "memory" (line 8) of the mark of the tree. If the specific result of a measurement presupposes something humans regularly do that they call measuring, then someone's specific existence presupposes that others are willing, are *committed*, to taking some things "as" human. And "humanity" is not proved or disproved, discovered to be correct or incorrect, felt to be good or bad; it is that which underwrites such concepts altogether.

Again, lest Frost's preoccupation with the grammar of "proof" continue to go unnoticed by readers and critics: in "The Most of It" the speaker in the poem repeatedly calls into the wilderness,

> And nothing ever came of what he cried
> Unless it was the embodiment that crashed
> In the cliff's talus on the other side,
> And then in the far-distant water splashed,
> But after a time allowed for it to swim,
> Instead of *proving human* when it neared
> And someone else additional to him,
> As a great buck it powerfully appeared,
>
> (lines 9–16; my emphasis)

"We want to *understand* something that is already in plain view. For *this* is what we seem in some sense not to understand" (*PI* § 89). In *The Senses of Walden*, Cavell suggests that the problem of our being-in-the-world, adumbrated in Frost's "Beech," requires our acknowledging "three of the features of the language it lives upon": "(1) that every mark of a language means something in the language, one thing rather than another; that a language is totally, systematically meaningful; (2) that words and their orderings are meant by human beings, that they contain (or conceal) their beliefs, express (or deny) their convictions; and (3) that the saying of something when and as it is said is as significant as the meaning and ordering of the words said" (*SW* 33). "Beech" toggles between the first and second features, recounting the criteria that constitute a property marker as marks of human beings; "The Most of It" exploits the ambiguity in the second and third, when "the embodiment that crashed," "instead of proving human" "as a great buck appeared"—allowing for "embodiment" and "appearance" to act as middle terms between solipsism ("He thought he kept the universe alone"; line 1) and knock-down knowledge, "proving [to be] human" by empirical seeing. The question is never empirical but rather one we make and are willing to keep as fundamentally grammatical.

Beyond these poems, in the larger context of reading Frost generally, Cavell can help us to understand such requirements of reading, marking, remarking, appearing, proving, and committing to one's own existence as human—"being not unbounded" (line 9)—by way of his response to Kant's distinction between noumena and phenomena (*CPR* 257ff.). While Cavell's reading of Kant and related matters has been dealt with from a variety of perspectives by others before me, including more than one literary theorist and critic,[4] and while the problems involved deserve far more investigation than I have space for here, we need at least a working summary of Cavell's Wittgensteinian account of Kant in order to appreciate the low modernism of poems like "Beech" and to explain why Frost remains focused on the various claims of reason and its language games of "belief," "proof," "argument," "knowledge," "truth," and the like.[5]

Among the reasons that Kant's thought is so central to Cavell's story about modernism is that by the closing decades of the eighteenth century, philosophy's problems had all but culminated in a choice between a thoroughgoing skepticism and a shaky theological or metaphysical dogmatism ("enthusiasm").[6] The choice was roughly either that (1) human beings fail really to *know* anything at all, for example, that there is an external world, or that other people exist or are "really" (not merely inferentially or analogically) human beings with feelings and minds rather than mysteriously powered machines (nowadays, aliens in human disguise); or (2) a rational metaphysics comprised of "innate" ideas (Descartes's Cogito, Leibniz's monads) underwrites not only empirical knowledge but explains and grounds all knowing, doing, and making.

As suggested in the previous chapter, the problems of epistemology and its possible skeptical defeat, and of ontology and its very real suspension, occupied the center of philosophy since Descartes and hovered like a dark angel over the efforts of artists and writers at least since the beginning of the nineteenth century. Earlier, Locke had exemplified a conservative empiricism quasi-stabilized in sensation, unaware of its skeptical implications; while Leibniz struggled to reformulate a metaphysics that would avoid an unintelligible dualism of matter and principle in his "monadology" (see *New Essays on the Human Understanding*, first published in 1765).

But it was Hume—a more thorough and consistent empiricist than Locke—who exposed these and similar attempts as equally unfounded: our knowledge of the empirical world and of other minds can only be knowledge of our own sensations and ideas, the product of psychological habit, of an association that (as it happens, happily) survives the skeptical doubts in the gloom of our dens. Hence traditional metaphysics has no basis in reason at all, as Descartes and others believed, just because such claims about the nature of reality must be empirical to be objective, and, failing to be empirical, are—all the worse for traditional metaphysics—empty. It is only then that Kant, Hercules-like, manages (by way

of a transcendental method) to hold on to a scientific, empirical objectivity with one hand and with the other to overcome the antinomies of reason by positing human freedom beyond the contingency of empirical perceptions and ideas. In this way (with the third *Critique* as intended *Mittelglied*), Kant strikes a bargain between a scientistic nihilism and a moral and religious nonsense, laying one to rest and leaving the other, properly chastened, to faith.

In "Emerson, Coleridge, Kant," Cavell summarizes Kant's *Critique of Pure Reason* ("A" edition, 1781) by way of some paragraphs of the *Prolegomena to Any Future Metaphysics* (1783), which we can paraphrase thus: in line with the objectivist quest for certainty and objectivity, knowledge of human experience is of appearances ("phenomena"), which, being appearances, (1) by definition are appearances *of* something, something that, perforce, does *not* appear ("noumena"); and (2) preclude, by virtue of the transcendental deduction of the categories of understanding, our actually *knowing* that unknown *X*, however much we may be drawn to want to know it. While reason recognizes the inevitability of its trying to think about its noumenal grounds, it cannot actually conceive them, although it *can* achieve real and certain knowledge of its own phenomenal existence (*IQO* 30). In this way, Kant maintains, or rather resuscitates, in the wake of Humean skepticism, the threatened objectivity of human knowledge—at the considerable cost, however, of severely curtailing its scope, leaving later romantic writers and thinkers thereby, in a word, horror-struck. For, while Kant posits, along with his objective account of the categories and the conditions of space and time, our moral nature in an autonomous will ("autonomy" being henceforth, as Cavell notes, one of *the* criteria of the "modern" [*MWM* 73–96]), for later thinkers and artists Kant had lost altogether the felt connection of human beings and their place in a larger "Order," what traditional metaphysics, Cartesian or otherwise, meant by an intelligible account of things, by Reason, or cosmos, or God, or Ego, and which Kant relegates to unknowable noumena. In sum, Kant finds no way to connect human freedom and purpose with the intractability of a world of deterministic causality. Cavell observes:

> The dissatisfaction with such a settlement as Kant's is relatively easy to state. To settle with skepticism (and dogmatism . . .), to assure us that we so know the existence of the world, or rather, that what we understand as knowledge is *of* the world, the price Kant asks us to pay is to cede any claim to know the thing in itself, to grant that human knowledge is not of things as they are in themselves (things as things, Heidegger will come to say). You don't—do you?—have to be a romantic to feel sometimes about that settlement: Thanks for nothing. (*IQO* 31)

The central point here turns on Kant's contradictory assumption that appearances are not self-generated and therefore are appearances *of* something, and yet

that those noumenal "things-in-themselves" of which they are appearances cannot, by definition, be thought or known as such. Ernst Cassirer warns that it is a mistake to try to take the noumenal as a realm of *objects*, but that misses the romantic worry over our ignorance of the noumenal as a loss of soul or spirit, a "disenchantment of the world," a bifurcation of scientific fact and causal relations and a metaphysical source of *value* of the world we inhabit.[7] In other words, the noumenal, constituting a realm entirely removed from human interests and concerns, is thus either (or both) unintelligible or spiritually dead. This is the point, I take it, of Cavell's advertence to Heidegger's insight that we know things as valued always already, that it is not brute sensations we feel, or even percepts conjoined with concepts, but that rather we hear (to use Heidegger's famous example) an actual motorcycle, that is, we experience an object as always already implicated in a network of significances, in an "involvement whole" (*BT* 120/87).[8]

In fact, it is for just such a motive—the perceived loss of general connection of the real world to human interest and value in Kant's attempt to defeat skepticism by transcendental deduction of the categories of understanding, pure intuitions, the categorical imperative, the apriority of reflective judgment, and so on—that led a romantic thinker like Coleridge, in chapters 8 through 13 of the *Biographia Literaria* (1815) and elsewhere, to hint at what he argues is at least implicit in Kant's philosophy, namely the view that it is the "secondary imagination," productive of the poetic Symbol, that reestablishes meaning, our human place in a (in *the*) cosmos. This is, of course, a position that Kant unremittingly resisted in his description of aesthetic judgment as a *noncognitive* middle term between the moral and critical faculties, for such a position is, once more, essentially metaphysical, as W. J. Bate among others has pointed out: "he [Coleridge] affirmed at every opportunity that reason—as in the Platonic conception of it *(nous)*—is able, as it transcends the experience and judgments drawn from the concrete world, to touch directly a reality to which it is itself the mental analogue or counterpart."[9] From this, however, it follows for Cavell that "romanticism . . . makes its own bargain with the concept of knowledge and the threat of skepticism, one which a philosopher feels may give up the game, one that accepts something like animism, represented by what still seems to be called, when it is called, the pathetic fallacy" (*IQO* 53). (Whereas Frost, in "Beech," never presumes the tree witnesses anything, so to speak, on its own: acknowledgment of the human occurs only by way of a human *practice* whose publicness is "read" off the mark of the tree, as it were in the lines of the wood, or woods.)

If Wordsworth, conversely, is innocent of Coleridge's original sin (metaphysical pride), nevertheless we make no *philosophical* headway by appealing to such things as Wordsworth's poetic reliance on metaphor, or his treatment of emotions as edifications of ethos—not, at least, *until* we possess some means of discriminating illuminative metaphors and emotional demonstrations of first-, second-, or

third-person character from those that spin in a small subjectivist pond, mirroring an empty sky.[10]

For these reasons, Cavell, in his early essays "Thinking of Emerson" and "An Emerson Mood," turns to the transcendentalism of Emerson, whose response to Kant is said to have rooted out more broadly than did the speculations of Coleridge. Thinking of Heidegger again, Cavell points to the primordiality of "mood" (*Stimmung*; *BT* 172/134ff.)—in his own terms the centrality of "attunement" and "voice"—meaning the ways in which human experience is always already mediated by interest, value, and physical embodiment: "The idea is that moods must be taken as having at least as sound a role in advising us of reality as sense-experience has" (*SW* 125), which in turn suggests that "experience" in Kant was too narrowly conceived and unequal to its reality. Equally important is Emerson's and Thoreau's turn to ordinary language, whose character is, as the former puts it in "The Poet" (1844), "to flow, and not to freeze.... for all symbols are fluxional; all language is vehicular and transitive." If this is a way of coping with skepticism, it comes not by way of discovering a locus of certainty but rather by trust, conscience, character, commitment, and a community whose words can express their claims or grants (in this way, Cavell slows down the Emersonian rush to the new). And the measure of character, commitment, and the rest lies not in a formula but in their ability to satisfy vague (but no less useful) standards of unity, coherence, simplicity, scope, diversity, and (yes) beauty.

Said otherwise, such a reading of Emerson is neither itself metaphysical nor merely supplemental to the Kantian or Coleridgean positions, for now everyday life, and the medium of its appearance in ordinary language, which is to say in conceptual criteria—in language games, and in the witnessing or "confession" involved in Cavell's expansion of the Wittgensteinian notion of "acknowledgment"—themselves function as transcendental categories or conditions (*con-ditio* = "saying-together"; *IQO* 39) of our being in the world. So that in "Beech," when the tree is said to be "deeply wounded," this is Frost's way of ambiguously stipulating that the tree stands in for something *already* human, that is, something that unseen others (that we) are willing to grant, namely the practice called "marking one's boundary lines," "placing an iron found," "recognizing someone else's mark," as a part of our human form of life. "Beech" presents the moment in which the poet's existence, through the medium of the tree, is witnessed to by others (by us) who acknowledge that the mark (and pile of rocks, or "herm," from which comes the term "hermeneutics") are together meaningful, that is, human. In other words, our practice here is neither "belief" nor "knowledge" nor "choice," since logical grounds are lacking altogether; hence it is not quite remembering or recounting criteria of the human, since the tree is not human at all. Yet the truth is established and borne out, for a ground has been present all along in the form of life in which such marking, and remarking, is practiced with others. And the poet's

"proof" is more like the "probe" it is connected to etymologically: in Cavell's language, not knowledge but "acknowledgment," a trusting thrust into the darkness.

Indeed, Frost might well have been thinking of Kant when he writes, admiringly: "Greatest of all attempts to say one thing in terms of another is the philosophical attempt to say matter in terms of spirit, or spirit in terms of matter, to make the final unity" ("Education by Poetry"; *SP* 41). On closer inspection, however, the poet's repetition of the word "attempt" in this passage makes philosophy's effort something less, it seems to me, than "final," an impression strengthened in one of Frost's letters: "we suspect them [Germans, in particular Kant] of being too philosophical and of looking for the bottom of things that haven't got a bottom or a bottom worth looking for" (*SL* 184).[11] In light of philosophy's repetition-compulsion to "bottom out," as Locke called it, to achieve finality, Frost's ironic "greatest of all attempts to say" at least hints that poetry, *unlike* traditional philosophy, may be up to something less, well, grandiose (perhaps it does not attempt to "say" so much as "show").

In order to inquire more closely into what sort of hermeneutic boundaries get "founded" rather than simply found ("Beech," line 3) in Frost, I need to show briefly that Frost's own sense of judgment at the beginning of American modernism supersedes traditional epistemological accounts while underwriting (*not* negating) the work of contemporaries such as Stevens, Williams, and Moore; and then to explain what "agreements in judgments" and form of life—what "home"— consists in. I will then be in a position to conclude the chapter by examining one of Frost's more judicious investigations of judgment, contraposing it to the minister's failure of nerve and bearing in "The Black Cottage."

## Stepping outside the Skeptic's Circle

Briefly, then, it is in Plato, and especially in Aristotle, that rationality comes to be codified in the form of the predicative proposition, for example, in scientific and dialectical syllogisms, while discursivity as such is grounded in the principle of noncontradiction, according to which, when $A$ is $B$, it is not at the same time *not-B*.[12] Since one cannot logically attack or defend this principle without begging the question (its contradictory, like its assertion, presupposes its own noncontradiction), subject-object predication defines a priori what counts as the statement of a definition, argument, or truth judgment. As we know, in practical questions Aristotle recognizes indeterminacy, the possibility that $A$ may be *either B* or *not-B* (*Metaph.* 4.7.8), and even allows for the role of metaphor in identifying possible connections among disparate phenomena. Hence his perceived need for an art of rhetoric as two-sided argumentation from the situated common sense (*doxa* and *endoxa*) of a community, in which truth-as-similitude or probability includes desire and practical choice, as in ethics, the perfection of which he terms *phronesis*, or practical wisdom (*NE* 1140a 25–1140b 8). But even in rhetoric, where persuasion

to opinion is the external end of the art, the internal end of "judgment" or "decision" *(krisis)* is nonetheless largely understood as propositional or quasi-propositional *(Rhet* 1355a3ff., 1357b13ff.), for rhetoric is an offshoot of syllogistic dialectic as much as pragmatic ethics, which is to say it is both effected chiefly by the rhetorical enthymeme (a proposition-based syllogism of a certain kind) and subordinated to the architectonic science of politics.[13] Politics, in turn, is justified ultimately in the apodicticity of metaphysics and, once more, the principle of noncontradiction.[14] Ultimately, truth is predicated only of propositional claims (judgments) thought to be adequate to a fixed natural order of enduring identities or essences.

From antiquity to the twenty-first century, some such predication theory of truth and judgment, often anchored in varying conceptions of intuition or self-evidence, has largely set the terms for rationality. Historically such theories have either bound discourses such as ethics, religion, and poetry to an allegorical framework of preexisiting truths or rendered them "nonrational" or "suprarational" because nonpropositional (one exception to both tendencies is that sixteenth-century rhetorical humanism earlier alluded to in Eliot). In the *Tractatus Logico-Philosophicus* (1922), Wittgenstein, reformulating the Kantian transcendental project, understands facts or real states of affairs to be represented only in decontextualized concepts and analytic propositions *(Sätze)*, about which, however, he would later observe: "Why do we say a proposition is something remarkable? On the one hand, because of the enormous importance attaching to it. (And this is correct). On the other hand this, together with a misunderstanding of the logic of language, seduces us into thinking that something extraordinary, something unique, must be achieved by propositions" *(PI* § 93).[15]

In more recent times, the phenomenological-hermeneutical philosopher Paul Ricoeur also centers his theory of interpretation on the proposition understood as name-plus-verb (identification and predication), although Ricoeur recognizes the need to resettle the proposition within one side of a new contrast of terms created by modern linguistics, namely within what he calls "discourse" in contrast to Saussure's and others' semiotic structuralism.[16] As is well known, on the structuralist model, in the wake of rising historical consciousness in the nineteenth century, the event-nature of the use of words *(parole)* is acknowledged but subordinated to the systematicity of a synchronic code *(langue)*, in which semantics (meaning, message) is conceived in terms of differential relations regarding the combinatorial elements of the sign (phonemic signifiers and referential signifieds). Signs, in turn, are held to be entirely immanent to the system or code, lacking reference to the external world, to what Wittgenstein calls (as Ricoeur himself notes) "forms of life."

For Ricoeur, by contrast, semantics is irreducible to semiotic codes. For where the latter all but dismissed the event-nature of *parole,* for Ricoeur "discourse" comprises a dynamic "dialectic of event and meaning," in which the event of

communication has ontological priority (inasmuch as it alone actualizes the code in reality). Language is not thereby rendered, however, an occurrence bound to its originating event, for what is actualized as event by an utterer of the sentence can be understood in other times and places as the meaning of the utterance, that is, as the propositional content of predication. Yet this move too is itself not a nostalgic return to the ancient model of the proposition, since Ricoeur calls upon the ordinary language philosophy of Austin, Ryle, and others to bind propositional content of the utterance to illocutionary (actional) and allocutionary (dialogic) effects of our words (sentences) on others. In the dialectic of event and meaning, in short, neither aspect reduces to the other: meaning itself is not merely transitory, since utterance is tied to the changing pragmatic conditions and effects of its use. Meaning has its subjective side in utterer's intention but exceeds the scene of its origination by virtue of its objective side in (now following Frege) its "sense" (what is said) and "reference" (what is referred to, the "world" pointed to by the text). This keeps the utterance practical without collapsing into utterer's intentions.

This partly Heidegger-inspired philosophy of interpretation marks an important advance on ancient conceptions of proposition-based judgment.[17] In spite of Ricoeur's allowing, however, for what he calls a "surplus of meaning" in metaphor, symbol, and the literary work of art, Ricoeur ultimately refers the meaning and truth of such texts back to the *proposition* to ground linguistic reference to the world, as though the only way to link word and world is through the notion of *predication*.[18] Isaiah Berlin summarizes the kind of quandary Ricoeur seems to be in by observing that we are "heirs today to two traditions":[19] a classical tradition of order and judgment once considered neutrally objective and grounded in universal principles (such as the law of noncontradiction) or in a priori methods (for example, reasoning *more geometrico*), later transformed into Enlightenment rationalism, empiricism, and skepticism; and a romantic tradition yoking humane liberal (Enlightenment) values with an expressivist symbolism, longing to break free of the predication theory of rationality and truth-judgment by locating spiritual powers in Nature's Sublime, or in its latter-day substitutes, and translating them into a recognizable public discourse.

Despite their often having been read as part of the problem, thinkers like Nietzsche, Dewey, Heidegger, and the later Wittgenstein affirm alternative possibilities. For them, differential but no less situated utterances ("identifications" of the Burkean kind mentioned earlier) reconfigure putatively timeless propositions without lapsing into historicist or relativistic interpretive communities. In *Philosophical Investigations,* for example, Wittgenstein demonstrates that while, in the language game of "naming" as predication, the meaning of some words is established by our ostensive pointing to an object in the world taken as a fixed and determinate referent, the meanings of many other words are established by

pointing to "samples" or "prototypes" of many different kinds, taken now not as determinate objects but as more or less indeterminate means of identification of what we want to discuss: "the *meaning* of a name is sometimes explained by pointing to its *bearer*" (*PI* § 43), where the bearer might be some complex of behavior real or imagined, or our pretending something in order to indicate what we want from someone, or a work of art, or anything else that *models the identity* (rather than "proves the existence") of what we want to establish and bear out. David Schalkwyk summarizes this insight:

> It is precisely Wittgenstein's distinction between objects in the world as things that can be represented [via predication] and objects as "instruments of language" that promises to cast some light on the vexed problem of the relationship between language, reality, and fiction. For, contrary to empiricist theories of language on the one hand, which attempt to trace meaning to the intrinsic properties or nature of objects, and Saussurean conceptions on the other, which dispense entirely with the role of the world in the constitution of signs, Wittgenstein offers a view which, while upholding the crucial tenet that "a name is no proof of the reality of the referent that bears it," nevertheless shows us that the world is always already "in" language in the form of its instruments of representation.[20]

This is a crucial point. For just as the meanings of many words *presuppose* our use of objects and the situations they appear in—so that the words function as exemplary prompts or guides or "perspicuous representations" rather than empirical descriptors—in the same way works of art can function as means of modeling the identities of things we want to discuss. Thus world and word are *already*, fundamentally, in grammatical and rhetorical, not empirical or rational, synchrony with each other, independent of questions of existence over and apart from their function as instrumentalities of human beings in a form of life and particular culture.

In "Must We Mean What We Say?" Cavell expresses much the same point by showing how the pragmatic and situational implications of our utterances impose nonlogical but no less public constraints on what we mean, as binding as any semantic content of propositions. Unless we native speakers have come to learn the kinds of situations in which assertions are asserted, or samples or models used to define what they are speaking about; unless we learn not just knowledge of codes or rules but develop the street smarts (what I have been calling the "exemplary knowledge") regarding complex and overlapping social scenes and acts within and by which our words are used and controlled, we risk *never* becoming able to judge when concepts or expressions apply (what Altieri, after Grice, calls their "expressive implicatures"). In this manner, we remove ourselves from the community attuned to such constraints and possibilities: "something *does* follow from the fact that a term is used in its usual way; it entitles you (or, using the

term, you entitle others) to make certain inferences, draw certain conclusions....
*Learning what these implications are is part of learning the language;* no less a part than learning its syntax, or learning what it is to which terms apply: they are an essential part of what we communicate when we talk" (*MWM* 11–12). On the other hand, such know-how is not only an established "being-attuned-with-others" but also a personal capacity to *project* meanings of terms as candidates for acceptance by that community (*CR* 180ff.; "Projecting a Word"). This both puts the self at risk in its judgments *and* challenges the community to reexamine its terms and commitments, its form of life, as these are expressed in the linguistic markers identifying something-as-something within specific situations (the criteria) that they use or become willing to employ. Hence self and others are morally and politically implicated in their words, for words and deeds mutually implicate each other. Frost is well aware of all of this: "How shall a man go through college without having been marked for taste and judgment? What will become of him? What will his end be? He will have to take continuation courses for college graduates. He will have to go to night schools. They are having night schools now, you know, for college graduates. Why? Because they have not been educated enough to find their way around in contemporary literature. They don't know what they may safely like in the libraries and galleries. They don't know how to judge an editorial when they see one. They don't know how to judge a political campaign" (*SP* 35).

Again, in a similar way I have suggested in the first two chapters that Robert Frost does, at least intermittently, manage to bridge the difference between the data (appearances) of existence and the situational (nonpropositional) judgments of experience in a way that moderates, and even stabilizes the grounds of, high modernist irony, even while it anticipates certain versions of postmodernist aporias. In other words, Frost's version of modernism extends the grounds of propositional truth and method within specific traditions of the everyday and ordinary and common sense, and it overcomes the perceived incommensurability of the language games of high modernism and everyday life via an evolving and open-ended conception of everyday human action and language. (Not coincidentally, Frost taught a course at Amherst in 1923 "on Judgments," as he informs Louis Untermeyer in a letter, "or less technically on Verdicts in History, Literature, and Religion—how they are made and how they stand"; Thompson 1: 251). Unlike many romantic or postromantic philosophers such as Nietzsche and Heidegger, or high literary modernist writers and thinkers—Eliot, the later Yeats, most of Pound, Joyce in *Dubliners,* even at times Williams—Frost refrains from at least overtly scolding us for lack of "authenticity" or "vitality," in favor of searching for and renewing commonly shared and ordinary sources of value, sources lost, in part, through cultural dispossession and self-neglect (and sometimes just downright personal orneriness). Yet like Frost in many ways, these same philosophers

and literary high modernists often frequently seek and find just those sources of the everyday and common even when in stated opposition to them.

Of course, it may be objected that in any case, as George Leonard has shown in his provocative *Into the Light of Things: The Art of the Commonplace from Wordsworth to John Cage* (1994), so-called ordinary and everyday people, objects, and practices have been quite prevalent in all the arts for at least two hundred years, so that, on the surface anyway, there may seem to be nothing new in the Frostian strategy, perhaps nothing that can even meaningfully be called modernist.[21] Whether it is Northumberland beggars, or the upstarts Rebecca Sharp (in "a novel without a hero") or Emma Bovary, or Bloom on Bloomsday, or Ibsen and Shaw, or urinals and Brillo boxes displayed in art galleries, or postwar confessionalist poetry, or Leslie Scalopino's beach photo-poems, "we" have been considering the so-called common and familiar in drama, prose fiction, and poetry, and in the visual and plastic arts for a long time. Outside the arts as well, what Charles Taylor has called an "affirmation of ordinary life" well predates romanticism. From the Renaissance onward, to affirm the individual, work, and marriage has been correlated with several different cultural developments: questioning social hierarchies in the early Renaissance; sacralizing the mundane in the rise of Protestantism and its work ethic; seeing everyday life as full of expressive possibilities in romanticism; rejecting ordinary conventions in the name of a more freely constructed existence in twentieth-century varieties of avant-garde; and even (as Leonard argues) overcoming the art of the ordinary altogether in the name of the real things themselves, as in the ecology movement in contemporary art. How, then, do the likes of Robert Frost and Ludwig Wittgenstein, Kenneth Burke and Stanley Cavell, help us to reenvision interest in the ordinary, and specifically in ordinary language, in art and philosophy alike? What significant new shift, if any, does their preoccupation with "grammar" as well as "rhetoric" betoken in the ways we think about such matters?

Previously I said that rhetorical invention enlarges our awareness in indeterminate issues by selectively bringing forward terms and premises, images, tropes and narratives of persuasive appeal, effectively addressing the conjectural question whether or how something appears to be the case to some interested party (*sitne?* [Is it?], for example, "Is there an intelligible method in Frost's madness, in what he sometimes calls his 'extravagance'?"). Now I want to suggest that rhetorical judgment keeps invention honest and renders its claims and appeals appropriate to human practice (our form of life). Judgment is necessary to consider the appropriateness or rightness or truthfulness of those appeals, not only to the issues and audience addressed but also to those *not* (directly) addressed, those, like ourselves, who arrive upon the text later or from afar. Judgments effectively if provisionally answer definitional (criterial) questions about *what* something is (*quid sit?* [What is it?], for example, "What shall we conclude about Frost's poetic?" or

"How do we define it, what shall we call it, what does it mean, in what does its appreciation consist?"), expressed in the form of abstract *propositions* but also of tacitly held *presuppositions* and assumptions, practical *decisions* about what identities we take on in a given situation and their effects on others, unspoken ("background") *choices* about how to conduct literary theory and criticism, judicial *sentences* (Frost's "Verdicts"), *estimations* of how to project the implications of a given artwork, unverifiable *discriminations,* and *emotions* and *acknowledgments* that are nevertheless integral parts of what is included in "the *claim* of reason," namely both the "staking out" of invention and the "staked out" of judgment. This is just what we have seen at work in "Beech": "an iron spine / And pile of real rocks have been founded" (lines 2–3).

In such a light, Frost's frequently appealed to notions in his poems of "home" and "homelessness" often operate as more or less stable images and metaphors for the "premises" and "grounds" of both rhetorical-philosophical invention and a prudential yet no less philosophical judgment, while related pairs—marriage and divorce (and remarriage), conversation and monologue, expectation and timing, skepticism and belief, and others of the sort mentioned by Heller—instantiate and/or metaphorize or project related acts of communication or its breakdown. Whence Frost's lifelong intrigue with questions of *judgment*—for example, appeals to justice and mercy in "The Death of the Hired Man"; arguments over law and equity in "The Self-Seeker"; and problems of justification (theodicy) in the two *Masques*; as well as advertence throughout his career to forms of judicial rhetoric in a great many of his lyrics. Frost's modes of rhetorical judgment—which sometimes also constitute the subject matter of the poems—range from accusation and defense (for example, "Not Quite Social," "There Are Roughly Zones") to thought experiment ("A Trial Run") and conditional verification after the fact ("On a Bird Singing in Its Sleep"), to quasi-empirical hypothesis and verification of fact ("At Woodward Gardens," where "The already known had once more been confirmed / By psychological experiment"), to discrimination of new gestalt patterns and the emotional development that comes with them ("Leaves Compared with Flowers").

A more discursive and dramatic example is "West-Running Brook" (1928), in which "naming," "calling," and "saying" are all activities of fundamental judgment-as-witnessing, investigated together but developed differently by the two speakers, who accuse and defend, hypothesize and verify, discriminate and value each other's claims about the nature of the world (about "Being"), and about themselves precisely "as" "naming [judging] beings," in ways that model for the reader both the elusiveness and the complexity—in a phrase the irreducibility to propositionality—of meaning and understanding in language. In chapter 6, I treat the rhetoric of judgment in "West-Running Brook" in detail from the perspective of a phenomenological (Heideggerian) hermeneutics, intent there on showing how accomplished Frost is at specifically ontology-inspired hermeneutic-rhetorical

reflection. Here I am more interested in laying out a parallel set of claims about the ethics and aesthetics of judgment from the perspective of a broad Wittgensteinian-Cavellian ordinary language criticism, rooted in the so-called everyday and ordinary, showing, at the end of the chapter, how these matters inform other poems, such as Frost's "There Are Roughly Zones."

## "Now We Are Getting on Together—Talking"
### Acknowledging the Limits of Criteria

I have been suggesting that many Frost poems aim at involving the reader in retrieving, interpreting, and reinterpreting the data of his or her existence as "formed experience," that is, as exemplary "as"-structures that function to increase our purchase on quotidian life, however vaguely or roughly defined, by functioning as (topical) instrumentalities or models of identificatory invention and judgment. Frost sidesteps (or better, underwrites) high modernist, epiphanic "poetry of experience" in favor of what I call (in the following chapter) an "epideictic" "poetry of process" or movement, exploring the domestic, everyday, and ordinary in ways followed by later poets from W. H. Auden to Robert Lowell to Charles Bernstein and Susan Howe. In "An Emerson Mood," Cavell adds that "something Emerson means by the common, the familiar, and the low is something I have meant, from the beginning to the end of the work I have so far accomplished, in my various defenses of proceeding in philosophy from ordinary language, from words of everyday life" (*SW* 142–43). What are those words, that life?

Broadly put, if judgments of reality, issued by us speakers of a natural or ordinary language, presuppose criteria, and if criteria in turn are a matter of cultural *agreements,* how can we be said to "know" (as distinct from merely decreeing, as if circling in a small pond) anything at all? More specifically, we may say that we know, for example, that someone is in pain by virtue of the various behaviors he or she exhibits. When the circumstances are right, we say that these are *pain* behaviors, hence criteria for recognizing pain. But the skeptic points out a problem: for it may well be that the behavior is simulated, hence offering no genuine criteria at all, and thus (it follows) that we are always left as it were with something left *out*—knowledge of that which "must" remain hidden because it is "inner," namely the *pain itself.* The skeptical argument regarding pain is then generalizable to *all* criteria for knowledge of other minds: in fact, behavior can be simulated, and thus, in principle, criteria will always fail as proof.

With this argument, Cavell, notably, agrees: criteria by themselves allow us to predicate *identity,* not to judge existence—in Burkean language, to "identify" what we call "pain" and not to prove *that* someone's particular instance of pain is, in fact, the genuine article. Our taking behavior in the appropriate context, as a criterion for pain, is thus always susceptible to error. The deeper problem, however,

is that we have no criteria telling us *when* to take something "as" pain behavior in the *first* place, that is, telling us when to take another creature as *possessed of an inner life* (*IQO* 158). Criteria of inner life, in other words, *come to an end* and presuppose a willingness (a commitment) on our part first to identify or recognize another creature "*as*" capable of feeling and thinking at all, hence empathically to identify with her and thereby "see" a human life.

If something can be said to be left out of the skeptical account of pain/inner life, then, for Cavell it is the claim that another's pain, the claim that another *as human,* makes on us. And *this* is a matter initially not of knowledge but of what we "acknowledge" (accept or affirm) in the sense that it provides us with a measure or standard of interpretation that we do in fact use by virtue of our using our natural language (*MWM* 324): "[Acknowledgment] is not a description of a given response, but a category in terms of which a given response is *evaluated*" (*MWM* 263; my emphasis).

Cavell's account of "acknowledgment" is continuous with Wittgenstein's analysis, in *On Certainty,* of our stance toward the world as such and not only toward other minds; and both positions turn on the notion of what I will call, in the following chapter, an "epideictic" rhetorical disclosure that underlies *all* argument and that invites us to identification in the first place. So Wittgenstein writes: "Where two principles really do meet which cannot be reconciled with one another, then each man declares the other a fool and a heretic. . . . I would 'combat' the other man,—but wouldn't I give him reasons? Certainly, but how far do they go? At the end of reasons comes *persuasion*" (*OC* § 611–12); "I can imagine a man who had grown up in quite special circumstances and been taught that the earth came into being 50 years ago, and therefore believed this. We might instruct him: the earth has long . . . etc.—We should be trying to give him our picture of the world. This would happen through a kind of *persuasion* (*OC* § 262). Or again, "what this proves is not that this correlation leads to this result—but that we are *persuaded* to take these appearances as models."[22] In both cases, the world and other minds are not a function of knowing but of accepting, of acknowledging that which is both *familiar* to us (because it is prior) as well as a matter of interest or *worth*. Form of life is (in a manner of speaking) the presiding *grounds* of our everyday uses of language.[23] Everyday use, in turn, points to the cultural scenes within which all manner of language games are embedded. It is this interpenetration of grammar and activity that signals the corrective dialectic of language and life. Everyday life may be understood as *that place* within and from which all language games initially exfoliate. Wittgenstein offers the following complex image: "Ask yourself whether our language is complete";

> —whether it was so before the symbolism of chemistry and the notation of the infinitesimal calculus were incorporated into it; for these are, so to

speak, the suburbs of our language. (And how many houses or streets does it take before a town begins to be a town?) Our language can be seen as an ancient city: a maze of little streets and squares, of old and new houses, and of houses with additions from various periods; and this surrounded by a multitude of new boroughs with straight regular streets and uniform houses. (*PI* § 18)

In this way, the philosophical skeptic is *not refuted*—Cavell is himself not only human but Humean in providing something resembling a skeptical solution to the problem of skeptical doubt. But the skeptic is put in his or her place, as it were subsumed by a larger "place" (topos) or circle of publicly available criteria and more deeply entrenched acknowledgments (Burke's "identifications") comprising a major part, and nonfoundationalist ground, of a dynamic *sensus communis*. Thus the skeptic's desire to prove the existence of others or the world and his disappointment at the general failure to do so are exposed as a *flight* from or "avoidance" of the human condition, a taking of our "limits" on knowing as "limitations," and, out of disappointment over not getting something "better" (complete knowledge, proof, certainty, control, concepts, rules, laws), dismissing even what stands before us, what *calls* to us (what invites us) to take responsibility both for what we have and for what we have done and might do. What is acknowledged is itself *not* a product, therefore, of rhetorical deliberation (Wittgenstein's "logic"), as Arabella Lyon has argued it is;[24] rather, as Cavell has put it, the truth of skepticism is that our relation to the world is "not one of knowing" (*CR* 241), because it is a matter of rhetorical *epi-deixis:* a "showing-forth" whose reality is not a (deliberated) conclusion but our attraction to matters that function as our standard of worth: that is, to ethos, to who we claim we are or are trying to be. As Charles Altieri has put it, "In my view, if not in Wittgenstein's, an attack on [propositional] logos that does not turn into skepticism will put an enormous burden on ethos."[25] It may be added that an equally great stress is to be placed on *kairos,* on the time and "timing" involved in someone's seeing (acknowledging) something untoward and in need of correction.

In short, resisting skepticism in literature or literary theorizing and criticism, by counting or recalling criteria of ordinary language—both in the senses of remembering them when they are forgotten and calling them back for correction and change when they are foiled or fail us—is stabilized in our acknowledgments, in what Frost alludes to as "glad recognition of the long lost" (*SP* 19). Another of Cavell's terms for the same set of concerns is "moral perfectionism," the "epistemology" of which is enacted (for example) in the works of Emerson, Thoreau, and Wittgenstein, and, I take it, of Cavell himself. Acknowledgments, moreover, are not contingent opinions or beliefs but (what is claimed) are natural human ways of acting and judging, more stable than arguable opinions and contestable claims to knowledge (*CR* 111); they require ongoing vigilance and self-transformation,

allowing us to identify the world and identify with it but requiring us also to change those identifications when we encounter various sorts of aporias, contradictions, and the like.

Attention to criteria, finally—and to the claims made on us by virtue of our own acknowledgments—revivify our interest in the world and ourselves. For these, and for their maintenance and change, we are responsible just because they remain a function of rhetorical disclosure not exclusively logical proof, which is to say what we (perforce) already use; and we listen to the call or claim of others and the world, to what Heidegger calls our "ownmost possibilities." In this way, modern skepticism helps us to discover what we now mean by the everyday and ordinary, for the everyday and ordinary just *is* that which skepticism would deny (*IQO* 170).

As Cavell has noted, the ordinary and familiar objects or activities, and the concepts and criteria under which they are subsumed in Wittgenstein—reading, understanding, following a rule, expecting something to happen, having a toothache—were chosen in order to elicit what it means to specify criteria in the first place, to show what is achieved by our mastering their grammar, including the variety of concepts we use when we speak about them (*CR* 73). But mastery also involves appropriately recognizing the vagueness and the indeterminacy of some concepts, both as to what the criteria are and whether the circumstances to which they apply are present. And this point returns us to rhetorical topics, which we have said are conceptual means of organizing criteria with respect to circumstances for particular purposes. Since circumstances vary and the application of criteria is often contested, particularly in more ethically and politically charged situations, topics are often both "dilemmatic," or two-sided, as well as vague.[26] Yet vagueness and two-sidedness can be perfectly appropriate to rhetorical problems, as John Coates, among others, has noted: "much of the work on vague concepts makes it clear that, contrary to the fears of traditional philosophy, a social science drawing on the resources of common sense and ordinary language has every claim to be considered a powerful and efficient tool of discovery [invention] and communication [judgment]."[27]

If we hearken back momentarily to "Leaves Compared with Flowers," its leading topoi are noetically interesting not (exclusively) as metaphors or symbols with fixed or even vague reference but as topical headings that urge the reader who is alert to such instrumentalities to imagine their further elements in more or less indeterminate functional relationships with each other—how it is they "flash off into wild connections" ("How Hard It Is to Keep from Being King When It's in You and in the Situation" [1951]). As Frost once stated clearly, "My ambition has been to have it said of me: He made a few connections" (*LLU* 189). Poems read rhetorically in this way are seen to prompt connections of various kinds (middle terms, similarities, distinctions, correlatives) whose "elements"—

things, people, actions, practices, consequences—are functionally related to each other and not ontologically or epistemologically fixed, so that investigating topics exceeds all mere memorization of lists and concludes only in provisional judgments open to further investigation. Readers trained to be sensitive to how such topical headings operate in their many guises (logical, phenomenological, analogical, paralogical [metaphorical], and so on) are especially agile at following out the connections that other readers miss, sometimes no doubt because the former are not distracted by a desire to impose explanatory theories. Such sensitivity correctly gauges grammatical criteria in topical use.

For these reasons, ordinary language criticism aims at being *inconsistent*—neither always suspicious nor always accepting, but (painstakingly) "fitting" or "appropriate to" whatever theoretical or critical task arises. This requires taste, practical evaluation of difference and identity turning less on logos than on ethos and *kairos* (decorum, *sprezzatura*). Rhetorical topics help tie together grammatical investigation of criteria on the one hand and the situated circumstances of their use on the other without reducing common sense to standing beliefs or practices—for an "investigation" is equally a search both for connections and for breakdowns of connections, for what fits and what does not fit.

## Rough Zones of Meaning and Acting

In his essay "The Over-Soul" (1841), Emerson invokes a romantic notion of "form of life" and the everyday contrary to what I am trying to bring into view, when he pursues a metaphysical variant on nineteenth-century philosophic holism (as in Hegel, Bradley, or Green): "the wise silence, the universal beauty, to which every part and particle is equally related; the eternal ONE."[28] Here the stress falls on the a priori and objective, as though the whole of our lives has already been given to us, as it were funded (not founded) all at once in "Nature." In good measure this is the product, I believe, of the influence of the Scottish Enlightenment, including Reid's subsumption of the moral sense under commonsense knowledge of first principles.[29] But then it is equally known that Frost rebuffs such transcendental romanticism, as in "For Once, Then, Something" (1920), whose deferral of closure anticipates later deconstructions of natural identity and identification, meta-narratives, and totalities of any kind. The now-familiar argument by which this is said to happen, hinted at earlier in Ricoeur's account of Saussurean structuralism, holds that any appeal to unit identity or a "one" commits the fallacy of the metaphysics of presence by failing to acknowledge the differential structure of identity, by which $A$ is $A$ only because we can distinguish it against a larger set of $B, C, D$ and so on. This should evoke once more the principle of contradiction, except that now $A$ is also never free of the other terms, whose endless track of traces it sustains. In this way, any whole is fragmented into parts, its relations dispersed by historically locatable convention, custom, arbitrary law, and so on.

While this argument about différance is compelling, it is difficult to understand how it is supposed to follow from it that identifications within and outside of predicative propositions disappear into contingent cultural differences altogether. For we may say, more plausibly I think, that practical reference to any "whole" is always made under the sign of différance, at least whenever the term is used functionally rather than absolutely or metaphysically. Notwithstanding his training and expertise, a military general needs to think of the "whole" army or the "entire" battle or campaign (hence the title "general"), but this is done at some specific time and locale, just as a judge in law can imagine how society "as a whole" may be affected by his or her decision in some specific case, without, that is, any illusions about his or her having exhausted some absolute totality of future thought and action. Such judgments about the whole are thus always made by specific people within a culture and from a limited viewpoint. Yet such judgments get funded or founded by further judgments taken to be necessary and somehow natural, human. How is this possible? Is it a mere *feeling* that some judgments are human, even "necessarily" so?

As it happens, Emerson—again in "The Over-Soul"—provides a different description, now of the "whole" of life under the aspect of the so-called everyday and ordinary. Employing the language of legal judgment, he calls ordinary life "one wide judicial investigation of character."[30] This is a provocative description for my purposes, helping us to consider that when we investigate the order of the ordinary, when we perform rhetorical investigations of our own lives, several things are involved.

First, the investigation is "wide"—in rhetorical terms, comprehensive; in Cicero's terms, "the practice of mankind"; in Wittgenstein's terms, "the natural history of human beings" [*PI* § 415])—without pretending to be totalistic or totalizing, in the way that a judicial proceeding is never fully in charge of the turns it will take, the nature of the facts or values it will uncover or reappraise, or the judgments or ultimate verdict it will pronounce.

Second, reflection on the everyday and ordinary is a specifically "judicial" investigation, which I take to signify a matter of judgment in both the senses of *discrimination* and *decision* (that is, in form of life as well as of opinion), made within codes of speech and behavior.

Third and most important, when we investigate the ordinary we investigate *ourselves*, our character or ethos within some social order: we become both agent and object of investigation, plaintiff and defendant, judge and jury. That this should be so is, of course, in line with Burke's account of the grammar and rhetoric of "identification" of some part or aspect of the world, for identification is at once a naming of a *thing's* properties as well as a naming from out of our *own* antecedent situation, hence a naming of *ourselves* in our identifying with or against

what is named. And this latter point accords with Cavell's notion of criteria as linking us with both the world and each other in mutual attunements.

Frost's "There Are Roughly Zones" (1939) seems to me at once a commentary on, and a kind of judicial case falling under, what I am taking to be Emerson's "constitutional" ruling about the over-soul *as* the everyday and ordinary. (Line 7 of Frost's poem even adverts sardonically to an over-soul.) As Frost puts part of what I am after: "In the final analysis it is the quality of being of a person that I care or do not care about, and, to a great extent, I feel that is entirely above, or rather beyond any code of action or manners" (*SL* 489). "There Are Roughly Zones" offers a further proving (probing) of those commonplace "leaves and bark" we often saunter past without seeing, in part by investigating our character and our world, in part by investigating the nature of such rhetorical proof and judgment themselves. Where codes presuppose forms of life to take effect, life manifests itself only within some *ordo* qua custom, which is both the ground and substance of character and community.[31]

> We sit indoors and talk of the cold outside.
> And every gust that gathers strength and heaves
> Is a threat to the house. But the house has long been tried.
> We think of the tree. If it never again has leaves,
> We'll know, we say, that this was the night it died.
> It is very far north, we admit, to have brought the peach.
> What comes over a man, is it soul or mind—
> That to no limits and bounds he can stay confined?
> You could say his ambition was to extend the reach
> Clear to the Arctic of every living kind.
> Why is his nature forever so hard to teach
> That though there is no fixed line between wrong and right,
> There are roughly zones whose laws must be obeyed?
> There is nothing much we can do for the tree tonight,
> But we can't help feeling more than a little betrayed
> That the northwest wind should rise to such a height
> Just when the cold went down so many below.
> The tree has no leaves and may never have them again.
> We must wait till some months hence in the spring to know.
> But if it is destined never again to grow,
> It can blame this limitless trait in the hearts of men.

The better or better-known Frost critics—Brower, Poirier, Lentricchia, Pritchard, Kearns—do not discuss this poem at all in their several books, so it would be unwise to attribute to them specific claims and judgments regarding interpretation and evaluation. Yet in their approaches generally there is what can be called a

"libertarian" slant, by which I mean a Kantian, Emersonian, and Nietzschean stress on autonomy and self-reliance at the cost of these terms' necessary dialectical counterparts. This is a stress that can tempt us to take the poem as asserting, in effect, the following: human beings are creatures of curiosity and desire, admirable for their ambition to transcend conventional bounds even though their courage brings them at times to grief, an excess that is but the unfortunate cost of this *all-important* drive to freedom.

Such a reading will certainly do as far as it goes, although in overlooking the poem's rhetorical action, such a reading misses the poem's contrary currents. For if we provisionally accept the fact that our nature *is* "forever so hard to teach," then any familiar commonplaces (as in the above gloss) about the necessity of constraints ("blame this limitless trait") and the value of freedom ("ambition") contradict what Frost says and does: on that approach we readers should be *easy* to teach about such matters (even though we may not follow through on what we already know is true). To get at what is *difficult* to teach and learn ("experience" as *Erfahrung*) requires a less abstract and philosophically less predetermined reading, one in which both knowledge and what we ac-knowledge are discriminated, decided, recognized, and, above all, undergone and practiced.

In "The Constant Symbol"—as in the title of his first published book, *A Boy's Will*—Frost does in fact elevate human *will*. But he does so only in the context of the poem as "a symbol great or small of the way the will has to pitch into *commitments* deeper and deeper to a rounded conclusion and then be *judged*" (*SP* 24; my emphasis). And in "Education by Poetry," Frost casually judges the judges: "How shall a man go through college without having been marked for taste and judgment?" Too many graduates "don't know how to judge an editorial when they see one. They don't know how to judge a political campaign. They don't know when they are being fooled by a metaphor, an analogy, a parable. And metaphor is, of course, what we are talking about. Education by poetry is education by metaphor," chiefly a schooling in "taste and judgment" (*SP* 35). By the poem's rhetorical action, then, I mean to include what Frost means by symbol and metaphor. Whereas others strain to equate these means with nonrational or romantic "imagination, initiative, enthusiasm, inspiration and originality" (*SP* 35), I want to follow up on Frost's interest in a less romantic and more stable and stabilizing "taste" and "judgment." On closer inspection, "There Are Roughly Zones" tropes the rhetoric of judicial argument *in utramque partem*. For, if the house and tree have long been "tried," the speaker and those inside the house undergo their own trial of sorts—if not for murder of the poor peach, then for reckless endangerment, possibly even wrongful death, and we readers are invited to render judgment about this speaker and his accomplices: Guilty, or Not Guilty? Throughout the poem, in other words, the attentive reader must initially take up the hard labor of judging

a particular case, though in the end this task is transformed into something other than the easy *ipse dixit* of decision.

I said earlier that Frost likes this rhetorical genre of accusation and defense (consider again "Not Quite Social," also from *A Further Range*, "Home Burial" [1915], "The Star-Splitter" [1923], "The Thatch" [1930]), meaning first of all that "justice" is a central topos in his work, not because justice mandates a settled code of conduct but because "character" gets exposed, its justifications probed, and its contextual limits tested. In this poem, we might say that "law and order" expresses the *ordo* of the ordinary, inasmuch as we live in zones "whose laws *must* be obeyed" (line 13; my emphasis). But note that this order is one that that holds only "roughly," or "loosely" as Frost says in "Not Quite Social," "as I would be held" (line 10)—holds, that is, not as abstract dicta or predetermined values but as *custom* holds. Yet nevertheless *holds*.[32] Said another way, that little auxiliary verb "must" in line 13 operates, I think, on the order of Stanley Cavell's "Must we mean what we say?" which is to say that it is not governed by the "'hardness of the logical must'" (*PI* § 437) but rather is exercised or flexed within the naturalness of conventions in a form of life. In the Renaissance, such "stable flexibility" was called *sprezzatura* and in Cicero *decorum*, meaning the give-and-take that does in fact restrain our ordinary lives, where what is at stake is our being human (our ethos and community) in the specific but loose circumstances in which we do, in fact, go about being human. When a cop says, "You gotta move this car," he or she means it in the way that we must move our king when he's put in check and we can't interpose another piece: it's how we go on, what we do when we play chess. Of course, we can also tip the king over, walk away—take the ticket, get towed, even suffer ourselves to be arrested, thereby ending the game. But then we can always do that, even when it's not our turn. The point is to get on with whatever it is we are doing, which is to say the kind of person we are willing to acknowledge trying to be.

After the stage is first set in the opening lines of this poem-as-legal proceeding, we begin with a concession in line 6, which, if not an outright admission of guilt ("very far north" is not necessarily too far north), is something in any event that *sounds* self-incriminating. Matters seem to turn from bad to worse in lines 7 through 13, when the defendant tries to account for his own apparent lawlessness by appeal to those age-old motives of desire and ambition. But then things get murky and confused (lines 15–18), for some agreement seems to have been in the air and has gone south, the weather has betrayed our co-conspirators, and, far from confessing, the defendant seems to be shifting the blame, first to the wind and cold, finally to some indefinite trait in "the hearts of men" (line 21) that came over them and overcame them. All of which, if I am following this correctly, could be taken ("clear to the Arctic" [line 10]) as a kind of plea of insanity.

118   RHETORIC: AN ADVANCED PRIMER

But then, remember: no malfeasance has even occurred yet (!), and if anything does happen there is no (independent, corroborating) witness or reason to think that the defendant's perfectly sane and lucid account of all this is not continuous with his previous actions. Hardly the stuff, to my ears, of an insanity defense. So we may want to reconsider. If the tree does die, the fact of the speaker's having begun to identify "ambition" (line 9) in "mind," "soul," or "heart" might just as well be taken rather as criteria of guilt, not of insanity or innocence—and then the whole case as it were goes south (perhaps clear to the Antarctic). *Unless*, of course, we choose to accept the speaker's claim that such desire and ambition mark us *all,* in which case we have some reason to think of these forces as mitigating circumstances (on the order, no doubt, of Stavrogin's epilepsy!) and of the defendant(s) as unwitting participants (or some such thing).

Naturally somebody or other's *amicus* brief will have registered the fact that a trait so pervasive in the nature of human beings, of us all, can hardly mitigate anything, at least anything much. For such desire (the objection will go) can be said to be just the sort of tendency a "reasonable person" should have been aware of and compensate for, and we are back one more time to the possibility that the speaker has, in so many words, confessed. This possibility is further witnessed to by his own talk of his having been "betrayed," hence of his having conspired (*conspiratio* = with the wind, the spirit). And while it may be retorted that this may amount to an *unwitting* confession, hence no confession at all but rather a self-betrayal, it can, in the courts of criticism, still be held against him!

I have taken some pains to lay out the to-ings and fro-ings of this poem, the way we readers are driven, or ourselves ambitiously take, now one way now another, as it were ranging from pole to pole of the poem's possibilities. I have done so to show that the judicious reader will have been very active indeed in her reading, possibly at times even too active, or anyway too eager. In any case, Frost's "zones" of moral deliberation here have become simultaneously zones of rough, undefined meaning as well—of criteria, circumstances, acknowledgments, judgments—for Frost has required us, in effect, to negotiate competing arguments, stated or implied; to try to establish the facts; to weigh the speaker's responsibility and character; to determine where we stand ourselves on what is possible and impossible; to speculate on the criteria of our concepts (just what do "mind," "soul," "heart" mean to us? what is "blame?") as well as on the pattern of the poem as a whole. As a provisional way of concluding this most curious case, therefore, let us briefly take up, in turn, Emerson's interest in character, wide investigation, and the ordinary.

Note, first, that it is *our* character, not just the speaker's character, that is in the dock here, for in negotiating those competing arguments, Frost summons *us* to act out our own ambition to get those meanings and values straight, even to take one side or the other "clear to the Arctic" (guilty, not guilty). That is *unless*,

or until, we feel the tug of the opposing side. In this way, the poet sidesteps abstract lessons about "right and wrong" and "law and order," calling, attracting us to our own activities and desires in *this* concrete situation. The poet/speaker thus stands proxy, at once counsel for the defense and witness for the prosecution, which is to say for our *own* character as reader.

But then what character do we, in fact, exhibit, as defendant, judge, and jury, as we participate in Frost's little legal drama? This question, like the poem's inquiry itself, is equally about the nature of a community's *sensus communis,* and it may eventually allow us to help answer the question with which we began the first chapter, namely whether or not Cicero's grandiose claims for rhetoric might somehow be made good. For what Frost shows, I think, are competing aspects of ourselves. First, we willingly entertain a kind of Machiavellian *virtù* or prowess— our sheer "ability to impose form on matter"—first by taking up the defense of the narrator, next by turning against him in suspicion of his conspiracy to commit. We are tempted to read as though no limits held him or us bound, as though the only point were our *own* virtuosity in argument ("Am I any good?"): willful desire abstracted from its jurisdiction, its own house and home.

Second, however, and without denying the efficacy of such desire: we enact what we might call an Aristotelian "virtue," by which an equally demanding concern with "rough zones" of right and wrong, of plausibility, meaning, fact, and value guides our discriminations and judgments of the speaker and thus of ourselves. Desire will continue to live "in the hearts of men" (line 21), which is to say in us; but desire is tempered and shaped by practical experience of the limits (the zones) of our world as we acknowledge and use those limits in our reading of the poem. In place of black-and-white judgments of the speaker's ambitions, we are left on our own recognizance, neither condemned nor exonerated so much as educated.[33] This is an aspect of our desiring nature that may, in fact, be taught, that responds as it were not to disembodied (Enlightenment) Reason but to reason's embodiment in a practical situation, in cases, problems, examples.

But why, then, is our character forever so hard to teach? I want to develop this last point, for it is significant, I think, that the speaker concludes by citing a trait "in the *hearts* of men" (line 21; my emphasis), not in their "minds" or "souls." In the history of philosophy (though not in that of rhetoric), the heart has usually been taken either as irrational and willful, at best a drive to be harnessed by man's higher nature, as in Plato or Descartes; or, on the contrary, as the locus of all things good and true, the wellspring of man's expressive nature in art and action, as in Rousseau and into our own time. There remains, however, a middle ground between these views, in which the desiderative element of man's nature—the heart—while not alone capable of reasoning, is nevertheless able to *respond* when properly trained to a "reason" suitably reformulated to *include* it as an indispensable

element of thought. Such an account approaches the very meaning of *phronesis*, or "practical wisdom," in Aristotle, Cicero, Vico, Newman and Emerson, Burke and Cavell, and Frost.

It is not much help, it is true, to call Frost an Aristotelian, if by that term we want to point to an "order" of natural forms reflected in man as a rational animal. On the other hand, Frost *does* seek to synthesize man's reasoning and desiring aspects in just the way that many thinkers after Descartes have tried to do, in ways invoking the new rhetoric alluded to earlier, by linking emotion and judgment. As Richard McKeon has noted more generally: "The invention of 'commonplaces' was [in antiquity] the provision of instrumentalities for *invention*. The investigation of 'emotions' (when Descartes produced what he claimed to be the first scientific treatment of the emotions in the seventeenth century, he makes large use of rhetorical distinctions and analyses) was to uncover the causes and structures of judgment."[34] Thus man's nature is emotional, and while emotions can run beyond reason's limits, our own emotions in reading this poem have palpably shown us that they need not, that they can respond to rough zones of meaning, plausibility, and value already established ("proved") by the practices we call on (recall) to go on. Emotions respond to factual situations and normative concerns because one mediates the other. The order of the ordinary is no longer underwritten by natural law and metaphysics, but it is possible to recognize in situations an *appropriate* emotion; and this can be called "being reasonable."

It follows that an education of the emotions requires specific cases, examples, situations, problems in order for us to learn the sorts of things we do we when we find what is "appropriate." Codes, rules, formulas, concepts, principled inquiries and theories are necessary but insufficient to respond to the complexity and dynamism of ordinary life. Cases—particularly an intermediate case such as that presented in "There Are Roughly Zones," in which we must learn to move among inner, outer, and border disputes, cases delimited (but not dictated to) by rules—offer the kind of detail we need to school our judgment. Hence the great *distance* oftentimes between Frost and a poet like Stevens, for whom "there is no authority but the poet himself, no structures of belief but the structures he makes for his own appeasement. The poet's own act of faith is: I believe in the inventions of my own productive imagination. . . . Life becomes a rhetorical situation in which you are your own audience."[35]

Second, Frost's kind of investigation is one whose processes and results cannot be simply stated or proved exclusively in propositions, not because his claims are mysterious and mystically vague but because they are a matter of practical reason and emotion, experience and example, which is to say "rough zones" of meaning and value. While such truths may usefully be discussed and analyzed, nevertheless they necessarily remain outside of focal conceptual awareness, as background illuminated by the focal case. Emerson has helped us to identify

such an investigation as "judicial," but the judgment at which we arrive through Frost's invention not only frustrates our desire (our ambition) to pronounce a verdict of guilty or not guilty, it also frustrates the desire to identify that ambition *clearly*, to name it "mind" or "soul" or even "heart." Instead, our judgment is educated to finer discriminations (telling what from what), including our ability to discriminate where (roughly) discriminations may cease as being not or no longer useful. And so Wittgenstein: "Frege compares a concept to an area and says that an area with vague boundaries cannot be called an area at all. This presumably means that we cannot do anything with it.—But is it senseless to say: 'Stand roughly there'?" (*PI* § 71).

Indeed, what proves in the event far more interesting than any metaphysical categories of explanation—"soul," "mind," or "heart," which in fact Frost treats rather indifferently—is our own sense that we can *not* attain perfect clarity about such matters, hence about ourselves (unless, of course, we tip our king and quit the game the poem opens up, a game conducted, I have been suggesting, along the lines of Emerson's definition of the ordinary). That is, we are left instead with "rough zones" of explanation, meaning, and value. Frost's real interest, and so our own, is not metaphysics but rhetorical talk ("We sit indoors and talk"; line 1)—arguments and emotions as counterparts whose reality we experience in working our way through the poem.[36]

Finally, if Frost has exercised our desire for limitlessness, hence our temptation to skepticism into running into them, he has also checked it by appeal to the *ordo* of the ordinary in which we live. That appeal was made in part through the metaphor of natural climatic zones, as though human beings are restrained by what is as undisputed as the weather—as if order were a natural law, or anyway indisputably natural. In equal part, however, Frost's appeal operates through the reader's activity of *reading* the poem, in which constraint is not natural, at least not like the weather, but is natural like culture and custom and convention and judgment—as if order were like our ordinary language. This tension (between tropes of nature and convention) is never resolved in the poem, and, though I think Frost does *not* want or require us to choose between the two, some readers will no doubt feel constrained to do so. But constrained by what? Why? Either decision—*not* to prefer and decide ("man's nature or character is *both* natural and cultural") or to prefer and choose ("man's character is *either* natural or social and contingent")—presupposes judgment, hence a process of defending and judging and a place in and from which it is defended and judged: the staking out of invention and the staked out of judgment.

CHAPTER

# 4

# LOGICAL PROOF
*Perspicuous Representations*

> *Historia* is a source of truth totally different from theoretical reason. This is what Cicero meant when he called it the *vita memoriae*. It exists in its own right because human passions cannot be governed by the universal prescriptions of reason. In this sphere one needs, rather, convincing examples, as only history can offer them. That is why Bacon describes *historia*, which supplies these examples, as virtually another way of philosophizing *(alia ratio philosophandi)*.
> —Hans-Georg Gadamer, *Truth and Method*

> Not only rules, but also examples are needed for establishing a practice. Our rules leave loop-holes open, and the practice has to speak for itself.
> —Ludwig Wittgenstein

## Emerson's List Revisited

IN *The Practice of Everyday Life,* Michel de Certeau distinguishes between hegemonic discursive "strategies" and subversive "tactics" in ways that align with our previous discussions of experience as a tension between universal and particular and between positive confirmation of the known or expected and (as in Hegel) its overthrow; of judgment as a product of practices as well as propositions, gestalt patterns as well as sentences, and values as well as facts; of the everyday as a function of repetition as well as invention; and of ordinary language as language tethered to its normal language games even when it becomes "nonstandard" by being performed in literature or put under extreme conceptual pressure in philosophy (*PEL* xix, 35–36). To put de Certeau's distinction in the language spoken in this book, tactics are rhetorical acts that place and keep relatively strategic grammatical criteria in motion by situating them with regard to relevant audiences, circumstances, authorial purposes, and the like belonging to the language game being played.

For de Certeau, strategies reify established ways of doing things; they are "the calculus of force-relationships which becomes possible when a subject of will and power (a proprietor, an enterprise, a city, a scientific institution) can be isolated from an 'environment'" in an attempt to circumscribe its interlocutors from some monumental "place" it (the subject position) can call "*propre.*" Tactics by contrast

look to preclude the listener from abstracting such practices from their inevitable social relationships. As de Certeau himself observes, "the discipline of rhetoric offers models for differentiating among the types of tactics" (*PEL* xx), presenting us with "a calculus which cannot count on a 'proper' (a spatial or institutional) location." For de Certeau, this is a rhetoric of "turning the tables," a sophistic precursor to my present Ciceronian rhetoric both in its near-limitless scope and in the crucial importance given to the notions of time as timing (*kairos*), of character and community (ethos and polis), and of propriety (*to prepon* and *decorum*).

On the whole, de Certeau's point is that strategies are largely logical and politically oppressive, while tactics are rhetorically freeing and beneficial; strategies are intransigently fixed in place, but tactics wondrously fluid in time. On this reading, not only does the tactical operate apart from the strategic, but somehow the tactical "must" (paradoxically) be subversive, nonrational, anarchical. It is as though by virtue of its very fluidity, tactical rhetoric *must* liberate. *Must* it? Is it not more plausible to think that even the most wily tactic has its strategic dimension, that some part of a tactic belongs to a larger narrative, however fragmented (and vice versa)? It is odd to say, for example, that the tactical "precludes" the speaker or reader from abstracting from circumstances, or that the rhetorical has no "proper place," since preclusion is precisely the function of strategies, not tactics, while proper places ("special topics") circumscribe the very material, the *pragmata*, of rhetoric. A given tactic is sometimes merely disorienting rather than freeing, a cliché rather than creative.

In a similar way, the contemporary poet Charles Bernstein sounds neo-Ciceronian and sophistically Frostian: "If I were to say that I conceive of myself as a tactician, I'd be saying that only in the most strategic way, because while I appreciate the distinction, I find it (fruitfully) impossible to claim either position. In this way I pursue both a strategy of tactics and a tactics of strategy, though not necessarily at the same time. In de Certeau's sense, a person operates in a tactical way because that's the only cultural and political space that is open. In poetry and poetics these are really questions of rhetoric: the issue is relationships of particular forms of rhetoric to authority and the relation of authority to power."[1]

By "relationships," I take it that Bernstein intends to point to a certain sensitiveness to (perhaps peculiarly American) circumstances, thus his reference to rhetoric. But once we recognize that strategies and tactics *both*—as universals and particulars, as rules and cases, as generalizations and future instances, as laws and their application—belong to rhetoric, then the logic overseeing them is the same as that which Oliver Wendell Holmes said governed common law: not deduction but everyday "experience," what in a previous chapter we called *Erfahrung*, the negativizing movement of foiled expectations, hence a redistribution of new and old, of positive and negative: in a phrase, the ongoing ordering of the ordinary. Against contemporary misconceptions that experience "must" be—not only in

everyday life but in art—politically or culturally shocking, "radical," "unheard-of," on the contrary "to have an experience" is indifferently both confrontative and, in Dewey's language, "consummatory," a blended tension of difference and completion.[2] Ronald Schleifer makes much the same point in *Modernism and Time:* "As Nietzsche did in philosophy, [such] lines of thought transformed the classical relationship between principle and example—a relationship of cause and effect in science and chronological systematization in philosophy—to the multi-valenced relationships between configuration and analogy."[3]

In Frost's poetry, the strategic, or *propre,* is rarely given an institutional identity and is often on its way to being undercut before it gets fully articulated: longings for order, essence, and finished formulation, or images of the nest, house, yard, and nature as "the long bead chain of repeated birth," contend with metaphors of transition, desert, boat, sand dunes, and hiking, while themes of silence, solipsism, secrecy, being framed or framed in, along with controlled prosodics, rhyme schemes, and other features of traditional form, are used by an implied author on whom it is impossible to fix specific beliefs. Thus no one can say *ahead of time* whether the strategic in Frost is oppressive or the opposite. Frost's own tactics fall into what he calls the "interstices of things ajar" ("On a Bird's Singing in Its Sleep"), as it were *cuts* across the folds of established disciplines, logics, or orders. Sometimes these are subversive acts, sometimes unexpected and even surprising retrievals of larger commitments, as when the minister in "The Black Cottage" is so hopelessly tactical as to drive us readers to a more strategic framing conversation for reassessment and provisions. As far as they go, such categories (tactics and strategies and so on) are helpful but misleading if they ask us to *choose* between the terms. Instead we need to think of them as rhetorical topoi rather than fixed conceptual binaries, as possibilities connected to each other as on a continuum and divisible *pros ton kairon,* "as circumstances call for."

From here, moreover, it is a small step to suggest that de Certeau's notions of strategy and tactics are merely expansions of the two modes of rhetorical persuasion or proof (*pistis* = conviction, belief, trust) that Aristotle calls "enthymeme" and "example" (*Rhet* 1.3). Though what Aristotle meant exactly by these modes of argument has been subject to considerable scholarly debate in recent decades, I am less interested in glossing Aristotle than in using his terms as familiar topoi to delimit a wide spectrum of rhetorical proof operating in and out of literature. Thus "enthymeme" (or "argument") encompasses the strategic end of the range, in which rule-governed arguments permit probable and sometimes even certain deductions from determinate generalizations, while "example" points to all non-rule-governed tactics enabling the rhetor to structure relatively indeterminate situations from past particulars or cases. Clearly, "non-rule-governed" here does not mean "altogether free" of strategic premises, rules, or order, since then we should be returned to de Certeau's problem of trying to conceive directionless

facts or appearances—"*example* of" with nothing for it to be "example *of*." But it does suggest that the generalizations involved will play a less-than-commanding role, functioning as topical guides or prompts rather than as rules of containment.

Aristotle typologizes examples as either nonfictional historical stories (Cicero's "*historia*" is an aggregate of such instances) or fictional stories, the latter dividing into hypothetical cases and fables or anecdotes. But of course there are many other models for examples-as-tactics, ancient and modern, rule-governed and non-rule-governed: the example as pedagogical illustration of a fixed idea or doctrine (as often requested by Socrates of his interlocutors but found in any sort of illustration strictly subordinated to a concept or rule); the related case of something synechdochically "standing-in" for some larger state of affairs (for example, "the employee of the month"); the New Testament parable as a deconstruction of human expectations, or the Kafkan parable as a representation of unrepresentable aporiae and paradox; the Wittgensteinian "sample" as a model bearing on a problematic situation (as an upholsterer's swatch exemplifies or models the upholstery without its becoming part of it). Amidst this variety, what interests me is how we are to imagine non-rule-governed examples or samples working in the absence of rules *dictating* how we are to take them. As Gerald Bruns writes, "[Experience] has the universality of proverbs rather than of principles. It is never [strictly] rule-governed."[4]

In an insightful article on Montaigne's "On Experience," for example, John D. Lyons explores the "constant slippage" in Montaigne's writing, the logical gap between general rule, law, concept and its specific instance on a vertical axis, and, on a horizontal axis, the gap *among* instances, between the exemplary case and the case to which it is applied. The slippage inheres in the fact that all things are what they are and not something else, so that individual cases, while they may resemble other cases, necessarily also differ from them. The task then is to negotiate this fissure: "Both similarity and difference generate example, and indeed both qualities must coexist for an example to be recognizable."[5]

To give another example: in legal reasoning by non-rule-governed analogy from past precedent, in case law as well as in statutory and constitutional interpretation, the horizontal axis also involves a historical gap, for the past must be *retrieved* in a present that differs from it (and here recall that Gadamer, for that very reason, affords "exemplary significance" to legal hermeneutics; *TM* 324ff.). Such gaps or distanciations can be overcome, sometimes, through a variety of judgments achieved by considering a variety of questions about sameness and difference: principled consistency among cases; relevant and significant similarities and difference to past cases and laws; comprehension of relevant "factors" of cases; application to present situations and problems; the history of application of the law; and the like. It is just this variety about which Michael Wood, also in an article on Montaigne's essay, states that it "sets out very firmly for the territory

of difference. Experience is a possible path to knowledge, Montaigne says; far from perfect, but welcome. The difficulty is in converting experience [what I earlier called "appearance" and "existence"] into sense, or what he [Montaigne] calls *consequence*—translated by [Donald] Frame as 'inference.' 'The inference that we try to draw from the resemblance of events is uncertain, because they are always dissimilar: there is no quality so universal in this aspect of things as diversity and variety.'"[6] I take it that roughly this is the reasoning behind "The Figure a Poem Makes" when Frost declares, "I tell how there may be a better wildness of logic than of inconsequence" (*SP* 19). And so Wittgenstein: "Our clear and simple language-games are not preparatory studies for a future regularization of language—as it were first approximations, ignoring friction and air-resistance. The language-games are rather set up as objects of comparison which are meant to throw light on the facts of our language by way not only of similarities, but also of dissimilarities" (*PI* § 130).

In non-rule-governed argument by example, the rhetor does not reason from universals to particulars, then, or even from particulars to universals, but from particulars to particulars, as Aristotle says about "examples" (*paradeignma*; *Rhet* 1356b). She creates by disclosing hitherto unseen similarities as she goes, formulating and reformulating rules that function more as indeterminate topics than as totalizing concepts and propositions. To use the terms of Michael Wood's essentially Aristotelian distinctions, if we think of enthymeme as "argument," then "literature is very often made of the quarrel between argument and example";[7] and if we recur to de Certeau's terms, argument-as-enthymematic strategy encompasses *all* those rhetorical moves that tilt us toward the abstract, the conceptual, the deductive, while exemplary tactics are more pliable, narratival, often metaphorical structures, sometimes disruptive and subversive, sometimes reorienting and stabilizing, which close the gap between propositional statements and everyday life beyond the work of art: "Many forms of literature thrive on just this: the risk—courted, avoided, succumbed to—of examples running away with the text . . . there is a permanent, provoked difficulty about making the example go back entirely into the argument."[8]

Of course, the continuum of argument and example, or strategies and tactics, comprises once again the poles of what I have called "Emerson's list," an indefinite repertoire that, being rhetorical, is itself ordered not by a rigid rule of essential placement, as in a proposition, but by what Aristotle called *to prepon* and other rhetoricians *"kairos," "decorum,"* and *"sprezzatura."* "The 'proper' [absolute sense of 'strategic'] is a victory of space over time. On the contrary, because it does not have a [fixed] place, a tactic *depends on time*—it is always on the watch for opportunities that must be seized" (*PEL* xix). In order, therefore, to suggest the importance of *kairos* as "time" and "timing" appropriate to situation, audience, speaker, and event in Frost's poetry, I look, in the remainder of this chapter, to lay out a

progressive line of thought. First, I borrow from, and add to, some of the larger-scale tactics that de Certeau mentions and indicate their exemplary operations in Frost generally. Second, I consider that specific tactic that Aristotle calls "example" *(paradeigma)* as found (for example) in Frost's poem "The Code." Third, I discuss briefly how another Frost poem, "Two Tramps in Mud Time," can function for us as a Wittgensteinian sample by "exemplifying" qualities and meanings regarding unforeseen, future uses ("like giants we are always hurling experience ahead of us to pave the future with"; *SP* 19). Finally, I want to suggest programmatically that the present lexicon used to describe modernist poetry (and no doubt much postmodernist art) requires the category of the "epideictic," in apposition with the "epiphanic," to help us analyze the social functions and possibilities of low modernism.

## Tactics

(1) *Games.* Games "produce differentiating events, give rise to spaces where *moves* are proportional to *situations*" (*PEL* 22). De Certeau mentions, as examples, the games of chess and go, while in Frost the game and its variants include linguistic puzzles, frequently variants of double negatives (as in "we won't say nothing is clear"; line 8 in "Voice Ways"), riddles, jokes, and paradoxes or near-paradoxes (as in "Extremes too hard to comprehend at once"; line 5 in "The Armful"), among others. In "Leaves Compared with Flowers," discussed earlier, the poet poses a riddle in keeping with the rhetorician's emphasis on circumstance, audience, and use, and there are riddles of a similar kind in "The Master Speed" and "All Revelation." In "After Apple-Picking," an elaborate puzzle of time and space is refracted though the memory-dream of a day's work, until the character's (and reader's) strategic sense of self melts and falls and all but shatters. In "The Generations of Men" and "The Telephone," games of seduction are played out with skill and cunning, melding social and sexual intercourse, what Frost gregariously calls "grex" and "sex" (*SP* 24). In "Maple," an initial certainty about a name quickly exfoliates into a puzzling analogy "to guess sometime" (line 24), one whose strangeness has "too much meaning" (line 45), amounting in the end to nearly none at all—and all to good, nontotalizing purpose: "Better a meaningless name, I should say, / As leaving more to nature and happy chance" (lines 168–69). In "Snow," Meserve challenges a paradox, "So false it is that what we haven't we can't give; / So false, that what we always say is true" (lines 149–50). Such games are tactical evasions of a strategically positioned other, as Frost explicitly avers: "We only joke about it [the world] to avoid an issue with someone to let someone know that we know he's there with his questions: to disarm him by seeming to have heard and done justice to his side of the standing argument. Humor is the most engaging cowardice. With it myself I have been able to hold

some of my enemy in play far out of gunshot" (*LLU* 166). Is all of this so far from avant-garde conceptualism?

(2) *Proverbs*. Studied by Propp and others in "strategic" (structuralist, formalist, and other) ways, proverbs have been formulated as "systems of signification" or "systems of fabrication" (*PEL* 19). Either way they have been abstracted from the historicity and rhetoricality of proverbs and its variants (the pithy formulation, *sententiae*, maxims, and so on). Perhaps more than any other tactic in Frost, these have fooled many strategically minded readers into believing that Frost himself is too self-satisfied, too conservative, too sentimental for wily tactics, hence that such sayings must be the sign- or fence-posts of fixed, time-tested strategies: "Good fences make good neighbors"; "We love the things we love for what they are"; "Only where love and need are one"; "The Road Not Taken"; "Home is the place where, when you have to go there, / They have to take you in" (lines 118–19); and innumerable others too well known to repeat. In fact, most of these sayings defeat easy systematization, for in context Frost's proverbs and adages and apothegms reverberate with the character of the hand that touches them at the time: "In the beginning was the word, to be sure, very sure, and a solid basic comfort it remains *in situ*, but the fun only begins with the spirited when you treat the word as a point of many departures. There is risk in the play" (*SP* 78). For Chinua Achebe's Igbo people, "proverbs are the palm-oil with which words are eaten." But in a close reading of Frost, proverbs are like pointed seeds, or grains of sand, in one's food.

(3) *Conversation*. "Conversation is a provisional and collective effect of competence in the art of manipulating 'commonplaces' and the inevitability of events in such a way as to make them 'habitable'" (*PEL* xxii). Of course, virtually all of Frost's poetry rotates around conversation or gossip or talk in one form or another, including talk's subcomponents such as hints, veiled allusions, "double-voicing" the speech of others, and the halts and interruptions of embarrassment or confusion, all of which, though not listed as tactics per se, overlap on de Certeau's interest in "tales" and "legends" and "accounts" of games played in the past. One of de Certeau's points is that the manipulation of rhetorical topoi makes such talk both a common and inventive enterprise. Notwithstanding what has been called Frost's "reverential monody,"[9] conversation in Frost usually manages to achieve a *social ownership* of talk. This is how Frost executes not so much a flanking move around literary high modernism as an underwriting of it—not flat-footed resistance to the experimental and dégagé, but reminders of the inventive possibilities of what we already *do* share, even if only *in potentia*, "remembering something I didn't know I knew" (*SP* 19). Poetry in the *guise* or pose of proverb-laden ordinary language, drifting conversation, achieves the triple purpose of eluding strategic modernist literary attitudes without sacrificing the serious intelligence such discourse demands; offering the accessibility required by the common reader qua

ordinary man (whose communication, we know, was "in eclipse" in the early decades of the century); and opening and exploiting fissures and gaps in a technological worldview whose very soul is strategy, called by Heidegger the "standing-reserve" (*Ge-stell*), as though nature were meant to be drunk or eaten.

(4) *La perruque* (lit. "the wig"). "*La perruque* is the worker's own work disguised as work for his employer" (*PEL* 25). Work is serious business in Frost even while it is play. Frequently Frost's characters are somehow or other skimming off the top, as when the farmer in "The Code" steals a rest as he tells his tale, or the husband in "Blueberries," out for a walk, beats Patterson to his family's own luxuriance of fruit, or the narrator in "Tuft of Flowers" never does quite get to work, or Brad burns down his farm to buy a telescope in "The Star-Splitter," or, in "The Census-Taker," the narrator is driven to "unofficial counting" for lack of anyone to count, while in "The Ax-Helve," Baptiste knows how "to make a short job long / For love of it" (lines 80–81) by discussing knowledge in view of friendship with the narrator. All of these activities circumvent expectations of governance in order to free up their agents: "It must be I want life to go on living" ("The Census-Taker"; line 64).

(5) *"Loiterature"* (hanging out, idling, wandering). By, as he puts it, "translating a pun of Maurice Blanchot's" [*"désoeuvrement"* as "idleness" and "failure to conform," absence of work], Ross Chambers coins the wonderful term "loiterature" to identify a kind of narrative concerned with socially marginalized (usually urban) characters first appearing in the early-nineteenth-century "flaneur realism" and representations of bohemia, characters such as commonly appear in Balzac, Baudelaire, Nerval, and others—beggars, prostitutes, strolling entertainers, tramps, and the like. Chambers's interest in this mode of writing, like mine in Frost, he calls philosophical, specifically epistemological: "By opposing the monumental, the sublime, and the 'ideal' in the aesthetic sphere, loiterature was simultaneously situating itself, in social terms, as a discourse of counterdisciplinarity. In doing so, it was led specifically to attempt a transvaluation of the *trivial*—something that foreshadows ... contemporary attempts such as those of Michel de Certeau to deploy the concept of the 'everyday' as a phenomenon of culture that can subvert from within—whether in art or in the domain of knowledge—the claims of *techne* [principled arts or subject matters]."[10] My only demur here is that loiterature possesses, in addition to a negative subversive charge, the ability to *order* the trivial and ordinary, provisionally to remap and stabilize activity by locating new criteria for our concepts and the acknowledgments they presuppose (see "Two Tramps in Mud Time" below).

(6) *Tropes*. "To be memorized as well as memorable, they [anecdotes and the like] are *repertories of schemas of action*" (*PEL* 23). For lack of time I have lumped together tropes and narratives, merely signaling here that the latter in particular is a central rhetorical tactic easy to overlook or dismiss as unexceptional in Frost.

I will have occasion to discuss exemplarity below, but here I want to underline de Certeau's notion of "repertoires of schemas of action." This is a way of describing what rhetoric as a whole does, namely lay out topoi or commonplaces whose function it is to excite creative thought and judgment and not merely jog memory-as-repetition. Thus tropes such as metaphor and metonymy can themselves function as "exempla" for future thought and action, while narrative examples can trope thought and behavior in ways unforeseen until employed in further use.

As presented here, in short, "tactics" cuts across the long-standing division between the "humanist" and "courtly" rhetoric deriving from the Renaissance, a distinction now usually encountered as "liberal-humanist" as opposed to "ideological" or "cultural" rhetoric: the former (for example, Scaliger's, or much of Kenneth Burke's) is given over to such things as practical knowledge and social ethics, universality, and education; the latter (for example, Machiavelli's or Castiglione's, nowadays Terry Eagleton's or Stephen Greenblatt's or Homi Bhaba's) to specific social circumstances of power and advancement or its blockage and co-optation. De Certeau's own rhetoric is a mild contemporary version of the courtly, while Frost's poetic is humanistic-with-a-twist, his tactics providing a general *practical* ethics, pedagogy, and covert politics: "Do you know, what we talked about was knowledge?" ("The Ax-Helve"; line 82).

In the end, as Charles Bernstein suggested, de Certeau's tactics as chiefly *evasive* maneuvers do not exhaust the character of Frost's rhetorical poetics. The reason is that many of Frost's "moves" are designed less to evade, less to constitute a "polemology of the weak" (*PEL* 39) (which de Certeau rightly associates with the underside of rhetoric, namely sophistic), than to concede-and-lead, or to cajole, or to supplicate, or in general to befriend a "neighborly" reader (an American, even Thoreauvian, stance) rather than to resist some "strategic" structure. Indeed, in the end it is difficult to pose Frost at all, not because he strikes a pose or wears a mask—all writers do this—but because his mask is not transparent and changes with the moment or circumstance. As *poseur extraordinaire*, Frost strikes his own poses, as farmer or as common man, making them appear common and ordinary. He exploits the ambivalence between the ordinary as known and the ordinary as scene of our knowability. In doing so, he invites us to toggle between the obvious-known and the known-neglected, feeling for ways we have wrongly posed, by imposing, ourselves theoretically or skeptically, inviting us to search out our own provisional positions and beliefs. Traditional metaphysics and contemporary theory tend to consider these matters beneath notice, even beneath contempt, but this is only misleadingly correct. The everyday and ordinary, while certainly beneath us, also offer the means of our support and direction. And confusion. The scene is "open to view," in Cicero's terms, not because our *sensus communis* is transparent or correct, much less because it is unconflicted, for it is neither. Rather, even a *sensus communis* in solution can be accessible to investigation and description

and can constitute our commitments and character, however much in process of change. Such a background scene or scenic ground is the property of the "non-expert," moreover, inasmuch as character is never a matter of expertise, nor living of professionalized training. For us, Cicero's sphere of the "untrained," the everyday and ordinary, is a realm of example and judgment. And so Wittgenstein: "What is the use of studying philosophy if all that it does for you is to enable you to talk with some plausibility about some abstruse questions of logic, etc., & if it does not improve your thinking about the important questions of everyday life?"[11]

## Exemplarity and Exemplification

> Not only rules, but also examples are needed for establishing a practice. Our rules leave loop-holes open, and the practice has to speak for itself.
>
> —Ludwig Wittgensein, *On Certainty*

Even while they manifest formal rhetorical tactics, not all of Frost's poems directly thematize rhetorical or philosophical preoccupations. Yet many poems do reflect on rhetoric understood in the broad philosophic sense in which I have been using it. A brief glance at the early dramatic dialogue "The Code" (1914), also from Frost's second book, *North of Boston* (1914), will help us further probe into how invention and judgment are linked to a logic of exemplarity and exemplification, in what I will call an epideictic search for community.

In a letter to Louis Untermeyer, Frost says of *North of Boston* that four of its poems "are almost jokes" (*LLU* 40), and surely "The Code" is one of them, its tale of an attempted homicide obviously intended to add to the fun. Here is a poem *about* persuasion, address, and unfamiliar codes of speech and behavior, in which a passing bit of phatic communication, a worker's suggesting that he and two others "take pains" to cock the hay before it rains, offends one of the workers; in which an object lesson intended to prevent future failures fails (a third farmer relates his anecdote about a former boss named Sanders); and in which the unsuspecting reader is left at the end laughing a little at the slow-witted "town-bred farmer" who misunderstands the cautionary tale, perhaps also failing, like all of the characters in the poem, sufficiently to reflect on just what has been said and done. For "The Code" is less slight, less simply a joke, or less simple a joke, than it appears. Like "Home Burial" or "The Fear," it juxtaposes the fragility of human understanding with the frigidity of mere external codes or internal emotional ellipses.

Strictly speaking, of course, a linguistic code is not a language, much less a form of life to give words direction and force, but only "devices for disguising pieces of language so that their meaning is not immediately recognizable without removal of the disguise."[12] This definition is helpful, for though Frost does not use the word strictly, the element of disguise in the form of self-hiding is crucial

to this and other poems. In "The Fear," for example, Joel is familiar with the codelike speech his wife or lover uses to allude to the difficulties between them (lines 50–54). But he fails to understand *why* a code should be needed at all, why, in effect, she is in disguise from herself and her past. Hence her repeated doubts about his ability to "understand" (lines 50, 88–89), meaning not the code itself but the motives behind it.

In "The Code," two different and distinct problems with codes are in play. The first problem is easy enough to see, the failure of a hired hand to observe a standard of behavior (a behavioral code) out of ignorance of a strange code of communication. The third hired hand has no difficulty explaining: "He [James, the worker who walked away offended] thought you meant to find fault with his work" (line 16), following which

> "You've found out something.
> The hand that knows his business won't be told
> To do work better or faster—those two things."
>
> (lines 21–23)

In this way a simple misunderstanding arises out of lack of knowledge, which lack now appears to be filled and the confusion remedied.

The second problem is more interesting but has gone entirely overlooked and unremarked by critics, namely the sheer insufficiency of codes, and more generally strategy or theory, altogether. For the joke of this poem is not, or not simply, the town-bred farmer's first innocence of the code nor even his later incomprehension of the cautionary tale about Sanders but rather how difficult it is to get anything as humanly vital as standards of life and death into something so inanimate as a linguistic or behavioral code. As it happens *this* joke may ultimately be on *us*, for we ourselves have daily occasions to learn such a lesson and yet, possessed of a nature "so hard to teach," we manage with hobgoblin consistency to miss it. Only consider: having accepted his coworker's clear account of the wrong he innocently committed, the town-bred farmer immediately proceeds further to misapprehend the cautionary tale about Sanders that follows. *Why*, since he has just been told what the code is?

The answer emerges only when we notice that we too are tempted to misunderstand this anecdote about Sanders, that we accept as reasonable the town-bred listener's question at the end, "Did he [Sanders] discharge you?" (line 113). This sounds like a question we ourselves might ask, given the astonishing fact that the tale-telling farmer who was slighted by Sanders may have tried to *kill* him. We may conceivably want to call the act depraved indifference, perhaps even attempted murder. To pursue this line of thought, however, is to fail to catch its drift by placing the story into its larger contexts. Where the town-bred farmer fails to judge the meaning and value of his coworker's conduct in the context of

unfamiliar mores (having perhaps momentarily forgotten the code?), we readers are apt to forget to ask after the larger possible contexts of this tale, Frost's outlying interests, rhetorical and philosophical.

But, then, the point cannot be the *forgetting the code* by which to judge. For once the code is recalled, one can still imagine the listener's wondering, amazed perhaps, whether the narrating coworker did, as he claims, "just right" (line 114). After all, the code does not dictate its own interpretation, and there is no end to it if we hunt for an Ur-Code to decipher this code. Nor can the point be *our* remembering any code, for we are in the same boat as he, as evidenced by the plausibility of our sharing his question at the end. Nor is it any good to suggest that there is no code after all, since there can't be an example without *some* sort of overarching project (not necessarily a concept or rule) for this tale to be an example of or for. The point is rather just our difficulty in knowing, even when we do recall the code, or recall that this poem is entitled "The Code," just how to go on to judge Frost's meaning and purpose, not merely the farmer's actions toward Sanders but the whole exemplum that just *is* these fellows talking and acting and telling stories. Not, again, that we *cannot* judge, but that knowing how, and often being able to say how we know, can be difficult.

On reflection, Frost is tempting us, in effect, to rest content, much as these fellows have rested, with, as it were, a single line of commonsense talk or judgment, namely the assumption that communication rests on our knowing or remembering a code, a rule or law, a fixed order. Such a flatfooted "moral of the story" is roughly equivalent to the town-bred farmer's assuming that his coworker got fired when, in point of fact, he did not; or to the coworker's equally self-satisfied claim that he himself did "just right" when, in principle, he may not have done so at all. For we might ask: Does the code allow you to kill your employer's wife and children, maybe the extended family too? How far is too far? (And then we may further recall: the country farmer is *not* offended when his town cousin breaks the same code, though he himself says that any man rightly should be. What then leads us to agree with the former, as of course we do, that he ought to overlook that offense, as he does, or to agree with him that he ought to respond, as he does, when the insensitive Sanders breaks the code and insults him?)

No code alone tells us such things about itself. *How* then does one know where to stop, or start, in interpreting the code? In hermeneutic terms, we are always starting over within the hermeneutic circle, repositioned in time to look and listen to what has come before us, learning how to go on in part, at least, from the exemplary everyday: "A rule stands there like a sign-post.—Does the sign-post leave no doubt about the way I have to go?" (*PI* § 84). "Washington D.C. 88 miles" doesn't tell me to stay on *this* road to get there. Frost is tempting us in order to *remind* us that temptation can lead us into confusion, that we are regularly tempted to overlook the complexity underwriting such codes, that we

are frequently confused and do not know our way about. The stay against such confusion is not rules but *practice,* as Wittgenstein suggests: "'But then doesn't our understanding reach beyond all the examples?'—A very queer expression, and a quite natural one! But is that *all?* Isn't there a deeper explanation; or mustn't at least the *understanding* of the explanation be deeper?—Well, have I myself a deeper understanding? Have I *got* more than I give in the explanation?—But then, whence the feeling that I have got more?" (*PI* § 209).

Let us briefly consider this feeling of having more, for the issues are crucial to Frost. As John Ellis has noted, much twentieth-century linguistic theory and philosophy has offered us transmission, or pipeline, models of communication, in which bits of information are en-coded in words like kernels in shells.[13] Such theories are driven by an account of conceptual categorization based on the paradigm of simple external objects whose surface similarities mandate a label to categorize them as that "kind" of thing. In contrast to these basic cases, it seems to follow that emotional, evaluative, and aesthetic terms suffer from irredeemable imperfections: vagueness of reference (for example, the word "good") or internal lack of integrity of extension, for example, the gardener's notion of "weeds." Or consider the concept of "imminent danger" in the changing common law history of product liability, a concept that evolves in surprising ways as new cases are not subsumed but presumed (or, to coin a word, "prosumed"). In sum: first we are supposed to see similar things or events, then we give them a label, then we encode them in syntactical and other conventional structures for transmission.

Following Wittgenstein, Saussure, and Pierce, Ellis shows that such theories of categorization simply *do not work,* or that *we* do not work that way. Far from starting with objective simples standing in more or less objective analogical relationships, in fact we begin with *disanalogous* objects, events, persons, and so on, with obvious surface *difference* rather than similarity. Given certain purposes, at a certain time and place, for some people and not others—given, so to speak, the standing background of our interests and activities that we "lean against and hear in the dark," our form of life—human beings *come* to group otherwise disparate things as "like" each other. This means that precise scientific or theoretical terms, putatively based on simples, are *unparadigmatic* for language use inasmuch as they derive from far richer contextual, existential placements. Given the differential contextual structure of our being in the world, what we ought rather to take as our paradigm are categories (terms) whose reference and extension may well be ragged and loose in view of the indeterminate and shifting nature of our activities and interests. Evaluative terms like "good" or vague concepts like "weed" or "poison," which, after all, are older and more basic to human existence than concepts like "quark" or "concept" itself, are constructed according to function, not according to objective characteristics, and function is usually situational and shifting. C. S. Lewis makes a similar point: "[Some words] must have begun by

having a simple, homogeneous meaning. And some words—triangle, say, or knee—may have begun life with such an equipment. It can hardly be so with the greater words."[14] Hence, for an abstract code of communication to work in the first place, "a language must *already* be in place; but for a language to be in place a form of life must be in place. For a language has nothing to say apart from the interests and purposes it bespeaks, and a code has nothing to encode and will not work apart from users who already know what to do with it, who are "master[s] of a technique" [*eine Technik beherrschen*] (*PI* § 199).

On reflection, then, any self-satisfied reading of the "The Code" as a simple joke fails to reach Frost's insight that codes alone need to be supplemented, as the code in this poem is, with specific circumstances, in this case an exemplary tale to give the codes point and direction, to teach others how to apply abstract codes or dicta, in Wittgenstein's phrase how to "go on" to connect rule and case, universal and particular, or to project further meanings of words. As in law, precedents sometimes do not merely illustrate clear rules but rather help us to interpret vague ones, and even then a past case or example may not work as intended, just as the country farmer's story does not have the intended effect on his audience in this poem. For anyone *can* easily miss the drift of an example, as the town-bred farmer does, unless he or she further enters into the form of life, that hazy, standing background the example illuminates, catching its drift.

In Frost's case, I propose, that larger context is illuminated for us by these and other characters' failures of thought and communication in *North of Boston* and other Frost books, and by others' (including our own) failures to plumb the depths of their own communication within the range of their own form of life. While "The Code" does not speak in any direct way to specific social or political matters, it does address what were pressing anxieties prevalent among both races and classes in an increasingly urban and immigrant America. In the guise of an amusing just-so story, "The Code" (like "A Hundred Collars") confronts social unease and confusion long before contemporary theorizing about difference, "the other," or postcolonialism, in a way that can remind us of what may be shared amidst what is not.

Exempla such as these, then—the talk of these workers that constitutes "The Code"; the farmer's tale about Sanders; "Leaves Compared with Flowers"; "There Are Roughly Zones"; "The Black Cottage"—can serve my initial purpose in opening up Frost as a distinctly rhetorically minded and low modernist American poet. This is not because the examples illustrate any fixed definition of rhetoric or philosophy or poetry or modernism, for we saw in chapter 2 that the new rhetoric remains undelimited as a "family of questions" rather than constituting a specific practical ability. Both concepts and examples are, in Thoreau's language, "undefined in front": "In view of the future or possible, we should live quite laxly and undefined in front, our outlines dim and misty on that side"

(*Walden* 324). And these thoughts are equally central to Frost's poetics as they are to what I am calling his rhetorical life-philosophy—only consider that Frost took anthologies to be all the criticism necessary to a poet: "For [the poet], the anthology is the best form of criticism to meddle with. It is pure example" (*CPPP* 768).[15] Like Frost, Wittgenstein is a teacher without a textbook: "'But do you really explain to the other person what you yourself understand? Don't you get him to *guess* the essential thing? You give him examples,—but he has to guess their drift'" (*PI* § 210).

## Exemplification in "Two Tramps in Mud Time"

It remains to delineate certain aspects of Frost's larger rhetorical logic by closely analyzing one of his most representative and misconstrued poems. In his ambivalent encomium "On Emerson" (1959), Frost epideictically praises the "poetic philosopher and the philosophic poet"—and then whimsically adds, "my favorite kind of both" (*SP* 112). I have suggested previously that past critics have tended to treat condescendingly Frost's interest in argument and persuasion—let us say in nondoctrinaire teaching—in favor of their own neoromantic, lyric preoccupation with Self. While the yield has been fruitful, it has been achieved at the cost of dividing what this poem itself intended to keep whole.[16] Like many of Frost's poems, "Two Tramps in Mud Time" unites divergent lines of thought by placing in tension opposed or contradictory values: self and other, the literal and the symbolic, the general and the particular, the straightforward and the ironic, and so on. Critics generally agree that at the end of the poem, Frost leaves it to his readers to apply to their own lives, to their "avocations and vocations," the maxim that love and need, work and play, can and should be one. But less agreement exists as to the meaning of this message and the value of this alleged "editorializing."[17]

Malcolm Cowley, for one, disapproved of the whole poem, calling it "an inexplicably embarrassed and apologetic effort." George Nitchie thought it a "fooling around with abstractions . . . hard to distinguish from a Thought for the Day."[18] John Kemp and Robert Berkelman admired it, and George F. Whicher called it "a fine narrative piece."[19] As for the poem's alleged message, critics have focused on whether or not the narrator-author should be understood to have surrendered his job of wood-cutting to the tramps who need the work. The woodcutting is obviously symbolic, so the matter is usually reframed as follows: Is Frost urging that we sacrifice self for others, or are we to expect those others to look out for themselves?[20]

In their pursuit of answers to these questions, critics have largely agreed on the method of establishing the poem's meaning by paraphrasing its last stanza and juxtaposing that statement with similar explicit statements in other Frost poems. The fallacy in this practice (Baudelaire once called it the "didactic heresy") is

assuming that Frost's more "direct"[21] poetry warrants, on that basis, reduction to paraphrase at the expense of asking how the poem works, as though something we might call rhetorical meaning is separable from something else we call poetic manner. Like any good postromantic, Frost denies on principle the separation of form and content, while in fact "Two Tramps in Mud Time" instances a unit of form and content in ways not yet seen or appreciated by its readers. We are enjoined as we read to see its pairs of terms as implacably opposed, but we are also schooled in rhetorically sophisticated ways to discern the ties that bind each of them and their identity-in-difference. Only by attending to what the poem is doing, however, can we learn what it is saying.

We will need to proceed patiently at first, identifying particulars, but ultimately our concern with the method of exemplification will have the dual effect of placing the critics' ideological concern over the tramps in perspective, and, more important, showing how rhetoric answers to the philosophic dimension in Frost's poetry, poetry he hoped would "begin in delight and end in wisdom."

Preliminaries

From the first stanza onward, much of the playfulness of this poem arises from its kinesthetic and visual imagery, its simple narrative line, and its familiar homespun truth about the meaning and goal of life. Together these make an engaging story. But they can also move us (Cicero's rhetorical office of *movere*) at deeper levels until we do arrive at a wisdom *(docere)* that completes our delight *(delectare)*. How is this achieved?

We can begin to move toward an answer by noting how subject matter and its manner of treatment divide the poem into several parts. Stanzas 1 through 5 introduce us to the narrator-woodcutter interrupted at his task, at his "job," which is also a giving loose to his soul. They then develop a sense of time and place, half-winter/half-spring (one of many pairs of opposites held in check in this section), when the bluebird, not blue, "wouldn't advise a thing to blossom." Each of these five stanzas falls neatly into halves, "splinterless as a cloven rock," the fourth line always end-stopped and the rhymes internally confined to the quatrains, reinforcing the feeling of opposites held balanced. Each stanza places in tension one or more pairs of images, ideas, or values, so that the very image of splitting wood, of dividing wholes, becomes a metaphor for the action of the poem itself.

The friendly tramps, for example, prove more than they seem. They have ulterior motives, and in this they are not unlike the narrator, who is "caught," as though guiltily enjoying himself under the pretense of working. Their words of encouragement have the ironic effect of throwing him off his "aim": the physical act of woodcutting that is at the same time an expression of his more spiritual self. The warm sun and the cold wind, the still air and the frozen peak, mid-May and mid-March, all are natural opposites or counterparts. And in the climactic

fifth stanza, the running water feels the "lurking frost" fasten upon it its terrible (yet delicate) "crystal teeth." Finally, a progression of verb tenses, from past to present to future, strengthens the sense of comprehensiveness and closure.

Second, stanzas 6 through 8 shift our attention back to the woodcutter and the "two hulking tramps" recently emerged "out of the woods" from the lumber camps, who reinvigorate the narrator at his task "By coming with what they came to ask," his "job for pay." Stanza 7 insinuates that in their view nothing stands between the narrator and them—"They thought all chopping was theirs by right"—an attitude that stanza 8 qualifies and brings to crisis: "Nothing on either side was said. / They knew they had but to stay their stay / And all their logic would fill my head":

> As that I had no right to play
> With what was another man's work for gain.
> My right might be love but theirs was need,
> And where the two exist in twain
> Theirs was the better right—agreed.
>
> (lines 60–64)

Now here is a curious moment in the poem, for it is the only time in which one of two opposing elements—the tramps, their ideas, and their logic—wins out over an opposing element, the narrator, or anyway the values of play and pleasure imputed to him, so the narrator supposes, by the tramps themselves (for this "exchange" of arguments is, after all, entirely mediated by the narrator alone). Though short-lived, this verbal victory has been carefully prepared for on the formal level, for each stanza of this section is noticeably differentiated from stanzas 1 through 5 by an end-stopped third line. So small a change has the significant effect of dissolving the internal integrity of the quatrains, and so of destroying the sense of opposites held in check, as though signaling a departure from the balance established previously. Now each stanza amplifies single objects of attention—the narrator in stanza 6, the tramps in 7, and the tramps' triumph of logic in 8. Values have thus continued to contend with each other across not within stanzas, but they do not remain in tension, ending up instead at the logical dissolution of one of the terms, the "right" of love or play, in eight.

But then of course it is stanza 9, not 8, that ends the poem, and here again, in this third part, we find something unique. Stanza 9 reaches back both to stanzas 1 through 5 for its symmetrical 4/4 stanzaic pattern and its featuring of opposites, and to stanzas 6 through 8 for the way it amplifies a single theme (avocation/vocation, love/need, work/play, unified "as my two eyes make one in sight"). Said otherwise, the form of section 1 and the content of section 2 are unified in section 3. More important, stanza 9 equally reconciles all of those other binaries, whose opposing terms are now, from a larger point of view, dialectically implicated as

necessary parts of some more comprehensive truth. The argument of the tramps has encountered a more potent claim to which it submits, and the poem in this way unifies what before it split apart. In fact, this new unity invites us to reconsider those oppositions as the *basis* of that unity and is the reason why we hear stanza 9 as something other than abstract commonplace and pontification.[22]

As My Two I's Make One Insight

> But yield who will to their separation,
> My object in living is to unite
> My avocation and my vocation
> As my two eyes make one in sight.
> Only where love and need are one,
> And the work is play for mortal stakes,
> Is the deed ever really done
> For Heaven and the future's sakes.
>
> (lines 65–72)

In the first quatrain of this final stanza, Frost explicitly elevates his subject matter to a higher significance, from woodcutting to the whole of life, and from pragmatic motives to the idealistic "object in living." And in the second quatrain, he superimposes onto the central topics and their meanings from stanza 8—"play," "work," "love," and "need"—a range of new meanings that give at least minimal definition to this broader scope. Previously "work" and "need" primarily meant "work for gain," for survival wages; "play" and "love" meant physical pleasure, enjoyment, diversion. Now, without losing these meanings, the words undergo indefinite expansion. Since "deed" applies to any act, and since the future is contingent and variable, the words cannot be locked into or reduced to past uses.[23] Hence the relative indeterminacy of these words, an indeterminacy that recalls past uses as examples, as possibilities, and that may thus be used as resources for the future.

While the terms can be seen as topical resources for deliberation, they also direct us retroactively to the deeds recounted in the poem, and to the poem itself as deed. If in fact we do find persuasive the claim made at the end of the poem that we need to combine work and play if we want any deed really done, perhaps it is because we have been given reasons to find it so, reasons in the work or act of the poem that lead us to believe such a unity is feasible, desirable, somehow perhaps even necessary. I believe that we have been given such reasons, although it requires looking at stanzas 1 to 8 from two different perspectives in order to see Frost's own uniting of such opposites. In this regard, the metaphor of eyesight in stanza 9, uniting different perspectives, could hardly be more apt for this hewer of wood and of large intellectual issues, identifying as it does theory with practice, the philosopher who fully sees (Gr. *theorein*, to see) with the circumspection of the pragmatic man of action.

Before we examine those reasons, however, we need to be aware that the effect of the transformation of terms in stanza 9 is such as to imply what we only sensed previously, that the tramps, like the narrator, symbolize a distinct modus vivendi, a mode justified by plain, commonsense logic or proof. And it is noteworthy that this logic or proof is prima facie as reasonable to us as it is to the tramps *and* to the narrator: work and need really do take precedence over what in the eyes of the tramps are non-necessary love and play, for if they didn't, no one would survive long enough to enjoy much of anything: "agreed." And yet this argument presupposes a principle of divide and conquer, and a need to rank divided loyalties, which may not be so acceptable when the terms of the discussion are expanded to take in life in the round. Stanza 9 in effect offers a *new* principle, of separating without dividing, which equally applies to the job of woodcutting as well as to the rest of the poem's many contradictory pairs. On reflection, in other words, the very act of splitting wood becomes emblematic of the possibility of discriminating without dividing, for it is in their having been split that the oak blocks become usable firewood, the splitting itself is a unified "deed," and the physical deed is an expression of the spiritual soul. Likewise the contending elements of warmth and cold, the bluebird's song and the earth's silence, light and dark, above all water and frost, each pair symbolizes aspects of an integrated life when seen from the vantage point of the ninth stanza.

We need to consider in some detail the art with which Frost achieves his integrated view of things, an art that is integrating of us in subtle ways and that accounts for the fact that we find stanza 9 fitting and persuasive, and no less pragmatic than the view of the tramps that it supplants.

Proving as Recounting

> Be glad of water, but don't forget
> The lurking frost in the earth beneath
>
> (lines 37–38)

Frost's admonishment to us in these lines not to forget to accommodate antithetical norms underlines the truth that we do forget, that we seek to avoid or escape oppositions of the sort found in stanzas 1 through 8, stanzas that are themselves reconciled only in stanza 9: tensions between the various contradicting images and values in one through five; between pleasures we naturally love and the reasonableness or prudence we know we need; and between one code of prudence (the tramps') and another (the narrator's). These tensions are so arranged as to arrive at a highly charged, emotional climax in the excerpt from stanza 5 above, with the images of water and frost, the pleasurable preferred to the painful (hence the narrator needs to remind us, "don't forget," and at a more intellectual level in stanza 8, with the logic of the tramps triumphing over the weaker right

attributed to the narrator, reason over feeling, prudence over pleasure; hence the easy "agreed").[24] Although diverse, these contrasting images, values, ideas align in sequences of association summarized in the topics love, need, work, and play. Love and play, for example, first represent the physical delight both in "muscles rocking soft / And smooth and moist in vernal heat" and in the other vernal images. They then represent more generally, in stanza 8, any pleasure in life or life of pleasure ("My right might be love"). Thus the topoi of *Love-Play:* narrator, woodcutting, warmth, air, brightness, bird, water, life of muscles, vernal heat—in short everything in life we are "glad of," symbolized most effectively by the vital water of "brook" and "pond" in five. By contrast, need or work first represent tactics for survival in the marketplace, and then more generally any struggle, difficulty, or necessity that "lurks" or "hulks" "out of the mud" or woods, or just out of sight. Thus the related topoi of *Work-Need:* strangers, blows, coldness, earth, darkness, silence, frost, tramps, cold logic—in short, everything in life we "dare not speak," "spare to strike," and wish to "forget."

Now the point is that these associated and related images, ideas, and values are arranged and treated by a method of disjunction and subordination, a pattern that structures and determines how we consciously react to the world presented in stanzas 1 through 8. Here it is not so much *that* we agree with what the tramps say as that we see things in the way they do, by division and negation. This is the tramps' own modus vivendi, one hardly unfamiliar to us or opposed to the way we normally act, and one that Frost exploits in the form of the poem itself. We are all adept enough in our own lives at being "glad of" what gives pleasure and at shunning ills, just as we are (on the other hand) prudent enough to subordinate pleasure to the need to survive. Thus we appreciate what in nature is pleasurable, and tend to avoid what is difficult and associated with struggle and need (the cold, dark, silent, frozen). Rhetorically, this tendency to see things as existing "in twain" (separate in the sense of opposed and contradictory) is the rhetorical "common place" we occupy at the beginning and throughout most of the poem ("yield who will to their separation"), which Frost explores for its powers and limits. Accordingly, he has us identify on the one hand with the narrator and the images associated with him, and to feel reserve toward those strangers who "put him off" and caution or fear at the images associated with them (mud, mid-March, frost, teeth). On the other hand, he has us agree with the *tramps* against the pseudonarrator's sentimentalized love and self-absorbed play. The point is that in both cases the two exist "in twain."

As a result, critics have always seen the tramps and narrator as locked into opposition. And yet, although we don't come to realize it until stanza 9, in stanza 8 we do not *know* what the narrator really believes. Actually he is not opposed to the tramps at all: his "right" only "might be love" (pleasure, etc.) and turns out not to be. Until the last, however, the narrator's true position is subordinated to the

one he imagines attributed to him by the tramps (which is then ranked below the tramps' own view). The narrator, Frost himself, is "lurking" behind a second or pseudoself, momentarily eclipsed by a worldview in which the terms of the debate are set—and, more important, by a worldview whose chief characteristic is that there *is* a debate at all. In short, Frost achieves his effects by manipulating the point of view from which we see and understand the world disclosed in the poem.

This becomes clearer in stanza 9, which not only talks about those preceding oppositions as unities but which unifies them with various rhetorical devices: paradox ("work is play"); pun ("play for mortal stakes"; simile ("as my two eyes make one in sight"); repetition of the conjunctive "and"; unity of idea (the idea of unity itself); and the unifying of form and content of the previous two sections. As a result we learn, or better are reminded of, a way of seeing oppositions as unified wholes, which resolves conflict not by avoidance or negation but by reminding us of the equal importance of the opposed parts, in nature (cold and warm, water and frost); in self (body and soul, avocation and vocation); in human relations (love and need, narrator and tramps); and in our relations with the transcendent (Heaven and the future's sakes).

Again, contrast this view and its methods with our mode of apprehension in the first two sections. Section 1 (stanzas 1–5) controls how we evaluate its images by juxtaposing opposites, presenting first what is the more obvious and pleasurable and then balancing that with the less obvious and somehow more threatening or difficult. Arrangement is crucial, for it suggests the precariousness of our satisfaction with the seemingly self-evident—the "cheery" tramps, the "unimportant" wood, the sun, the bluebird, the water, the "right" of love. It does so by juxtaposing these with the need to provide ("don't forget") for what is no less real for being less obviously pleasant or present. But note that this is accomplished with our attention directed, not to this one-sidedness of ours, but to the emotional pleasure of act and scene; the implications of inadequacy are only "lurking."

Similarly, section 2 (stanzas 6–8) brings this pattern to its logical conclusion by sharpening the differences between the pseudonarrator and the tramps, and by sacrificing one of those "sides"—love and play—to the need to work. Here again our attention is elsewhere, on the prudential over the pleasurable, and again the explicit view is that these elements are at odds. Hence throughout both sections elements are joined only by the disjunctive "but": "But if you so much as dare to speak"; "But he wouldn't advise a thing to blossom"; "My right might be love / But theirs was need"; "The sun was warm but the wind was chill." In sum, careful selection and arrangement of images and actions analogically related to each other and connoting good and bad, the separation of emotion and reason, and various syntactical and stanzaic divisions dichotomize the reader's perceptions and responses, leading her to see the world as the tramps do—dualistically. This is so successfully accomplished, in fact, that we have to ask ourselves how it

is that we come to find the claims about unity in stanza 9 persuasive at all. Why not agree with Cowley that stanza 9 is a sententious sermon, or with Poirier that the poem is a "failure?" Surely stanza 9 alone does not overcome the worldview enacted in the preceding eight: why then accept it?

The answer lies, I think, in the fundamental ambiguity of the poem's images, actions, terms, and methods of dividing and uniting. Frost does counter each of these with its opposite, but he does so ambiguously, encouraging us in effect to see the elements of each pair not simply as separated but also as united.[25] This means that Frost does not simply rely in the ninth stanza on abstract sermonizing extraneous to the rest of the poem, as Cook and others allege, but rather recommends at the end of the poem what he has been surreptitiously effecting all along, uniting opposites.

Consider how this works. Logically, stanza 8 is compelling in itself, that is, the enthymeme is valid: (Major premise) Where love and need exist in twain, need is superior; (Minor) Love and need oppose each other here; (Conclusion) Theirs (need) is the better right. Materially, however, emotionally and prudentially, the argument is incomplete, somehow unacceptable. After all, having just been admonished in stanza 5 "not to forget" *both* sides of life, we intuitively reject its rejection of its dialectical partner. By contrast, stanza 9 comes to us as a recognition, a reminder, of something we forgot we knew. Its maxim—that only when love and need, work and play are one is the deed ever really done for Heaven and man—unites emotion and reason, pleasure and prudence, and articulates that lurking experience of wholeness we only half-knew as we read the poem. For while we had been led to see the world diremptively, we were also moved on a deeper level to accept as equally important and valid each neglected side of the various pairs, and to do so because those sides were only ambiguously or tenuously unattractive or undesirable.

For example, in stanza 8 we agreed with the tramps to reject a sentimentalized love. Yet at the same time, we implicitly allowed for a love that was not pleasure simply but pleasure invested with the dignity of being "for mortal stakes," inasmuch as the woodchopping, with which "play" and "love" were associated, was a "loosing of the soul," a vehicle for the expression of deeper values. Similarly, the "frost" we fear in stanza 5 threatens with its "crystal teeth," but ambivalently, since teeth of crystal must be, after all, quite delicate, while the image itself in context excites and attracts. Or consider the half-frozen earth in stanza 4, which nevertheless promises so much life that a bluebird's song might "excite" it to bloom, and which (the absent is so far forth ambiguously present) it must "advise" to wait. So with the cold, the snow, even the *sensus communis* of the tramps: we intuitively feel the inadequacy of our own one-sidedness by having to confront what is equally natural, necessary, and attractive a part of scene, symbol, and poem. What we originally avoided we recall that we love and need. We enjoy and value

the frost as much as we do the water, which, after all—this is the point—frost is. Hence "frost / Frost" conflates the narrator with whom we first identify and the crystal teeth and tramps we fear, replacing this fear or caution with the love and need of both, which the narrator himself espouses and enacts. The "lurking frost" is thus not merely a pun on the author's name but a comment on and exemplification of the poem itself.

From this perspective we can now grasp the poem as an argument whose conclusion is drawn in stanza 9. Past disjunctive pairs can now be understood as so many *examples* of unity-in-division, related to each other by analogy, which simultaneously, but on different levels of the reader's awareness (1) show the powers and limits of the tramps' view and, more important, (2) "prove" in its patterning the maxim with which the poem ends.[26] We are persuaded, rhetorically moved to a new "place" (topos), by virtue of our having experienced several plausible examples, whose terms then become, in Kenneth Burke's formulation, "equipment for living." And this finally explains, I think, why Frost refrains from *telling* us how he responded to the tramps' putative request. It is not that this request is insignificant or irrelevant, as one critic has suggested,[27] since this situation is morally as real as any other we might imagine. Rather, Frost has us answer our own question for ourselves by requiring us to apply the experience we learned from the poem. And, speaking now for myself, I suggest that the narrator morally ought to give the work because, to put it negatively, not to give would be to ignore that "common good" and those "mortal stakes" now before him in the persons of the needy tramps. To imagine the speaker's, or Frost's, or our, refusing this unity of "self" and "other" in the act of giving is simply to have missed the point, failed to "catch the drift" of what the examples in the poem have enacted. To put this more positively, to give the woodcutting to the tramps is itself a creative "deed" that unites the narrator's love and need just as the act of woodcutting itself had been doing for him. Indeed, the narrator has been giving, precisely by denying himself, for a long time:

> The blows that a life of self-control
> Spares to strike for the common good,
>
> (lines 13–14)

Furthermore, by giving the job, Frost in effect concedes that values do often exist "in twain"; the tramps, for one, simply *have no choice* about uniting values such as love and need, work and play. The narrator's giving thus signals the fact that his ideal realistically admits the tramps' view yet qualifies it without simply negating it: narrator and tramps are thus unified again in their separation. What Frost has done, in sum, is to equip us not with Christian, liberal, or any other kind of determinate doctrine, but with a language and experience requiring innovative

thought and feeling, practical "wisdom" that completes and finally becomes our "delight."

### Are You Experienced?

Lawrence Perrine is right to maintain that "Two Tramps in Mud Time" is about writing.[28] It is not only about writing—its central topoi are purposefully too large and ambiguous for that—but writing is preeminently one of those "deeds" a poet wants "really" done, by combining, as Frost has combined in this poem, love and need, work and play, vocation and avocation. This fact needs to be stressed, for it means that the poem speaks to Frost's poetic ideal by enacting that ideal within itself.

As for what it means to combine love and need, work and play, avocation and vocation in writing generally, and in Frost's poems in particular, we might mention one critic's observation that "one of the most fascinating pairs of opposites in Frost's poetry is . . . Work and Play (otherwise to be identified as the Practical and Poetic)."[29] The Practical and Poetic: probably nowhere in the Frost corpus is this combination more telling than in "Two Tramps in Mud Time." On the level of content, Frost unites the practical tramps and the poetic narrator; the practical woodchopping and the poetic loosing of the soul; the practical facts of nature and its sylvan scenery; the practical moral of the ninth stanza and the poetic story it generalizes. On the level of form, he unites that practical message and the vehicle of the poem itself until there is finally no telling which is which: is the poem a self-sufficient whole, a well-wrought urn (love and play), or a moralized "editorial" (work and need)? Is it vocation or avocation? Or are we not more accurate to conclude that the poem as work of art, *like* the woodchopping, is that "play for mortal stakes" Frost praises—not "art for art's sake" but for "Heaven and the future's sakes?" It is true that, abstracted from the playfulness of the poem, these maxims are banal and sententious. But then to abstract them is just the thing Frost has tried to teach us not to do.

Lawrance Thompson also invokes this combination of the practical and poetic but in terms closer to those that can be of service in reading Frost: "The restrictions which Frost accepts in his theory of poetry save him from the dangers of two extremes: nothing of content (pure art), and nothing except content (pure propaganda)."[30] Applied to poetry itself, then, love and need, work and play signify Frost's ideal of the "philosophic poet" as one who unites knowledge and action in the unity of art and propaganda, poetic, and rhetoric. The poet as philosopher just is the rhetorician, not in any narrow partisan sense but as one seeking to stimulate inquiry, transform commonplaces, and move to new perceptions of self and world. It is the classical rhetorical ideal of Cicero, Horace, and Sidney, for whom the offices of poet, as of orator, were to teach, move, and delight. For too long critics have one-sidedly favored the poetic against the rhetorical, and the

romantic I against the more pragmatic we, and in consequence have failed to do justice to one of Frost's most representative poems.

## Epiphansis and Epideixis

Consistent with that last point has been the long-standing commonplace that most romantic and high modernist poetry and fiction, in succession with Wordsworth's famous descriptions and enactments of those special "spots of time" in *The Prelude* (1805; book 12, line 208), is written in what Robert Langbaum has called "the epiphanic mode." In a seminal essay, Langbaum has noted that literary epiphany has gathered unto itself various, but more or less convergent, meanings: an "intellectual and emotional complex in an instant of time" (Pound); "one of those rare moments of awakening" in which occurs "everything in a flash" (Conrad); an "involuntary memory" in which the past is suddenly recaptured (Proust); and, in one of many of Joyce's renderings, "he [Stephen Dedalus] meant a sudden spiritual manifestation, whether in the vulgarity of speech or of gesture or in a memorable phrase of the mind itself. It was for the man of letters to record these epiphanies with extreme care, seeing that they themselves are the most delicate and evanescent of moments."[31] To William Faulkner, the writer seeks "to arrest for a believable moment" a particular life experience, and F. Scott Fitzgerald writes that he, Wolfe, and Hemingway each strove "to recapture the exact feel of a moment in space and time," precisely, in his view, "what Wordsworth was trying to do."[32]

That last point has been more finely adjusted by the philosopher Charles Taylor, who makes an important distinction between what Wordsworth was trying to do and what most high modernists wanted, namely the distinction between a romantic "epiphany of being," in which some superior reality or order antedating the self is symbolically expressed or pointed to, made manifest; and a more ironic, high modernist "epiphany of form."[33] In the latter, semantic implications of the romantic Symbol have given way to far more plastic manifestations of formal energies—for example, those emotional and visual condensations to be found in Pound's imagism and vorticism and in Williams's dramas of desire; or the *Nichtigkeit* lurking throughout the works of Kafka, Musil, Beckett; or, again in the American grain, rumors of order inseparable from, ingredient in, the formal architecture of the work itself, as in Stevens's "The Idea of Order at Key West."

In either case, of course—whether of being or of form—"epiphany" dutifully serves both the romantic and the modernist reactions against Enlightenment rationalism. The romantic reaction, virtually co-opting Kant's *Critique of Pure Reason* (1781) in order to effect what his transcendental Categories could not, empowered individual psychology almost to the point of animism. While Kant insisted that Order and Law are noumena that man could only (indeed, "must") posit *"als ob"* (as if) but can never know in themselves (*CPR* 257ff.), Coleridge in

particular, and at times Wordsworth, treated Kantian "manifestation" or "appearance" *(epiphansis)* of phenomena or freedom rather as a "visitation" *within* phenomena, as it were an inroad of Being that circumvents the limits set by philosophy in a special, emotional "spot of time."[34] The modernist reaction, in its turn, recast such romantic visitation as an "eruption" (so to speak) of strictly *human* powers, "epiphany" now not as an inroad of anything, nor as a necessary "as if," but rather as a *willed* "as if," willed as a "Supreme Fiction," a fashioning, and self-fashioning, accomplished in the form of the modern work of art.

It is, however, in the modern work of art that epiphany's claim to its momentousness is seen to be at odds with its momentariness, its historicity. In this regard, a nuanced essay by Herbert Tucker has recently sought to "rehabilitate" epiphany, as Tucker puts it, that is, to prise it free from its *ahistoricist* essentializing by New Critics and their epigones.[35] By resituating the epiphanic moment within larger historical, narratival, and social structures, using Browning as his example, Tucker opens up a passage into what I propose only programmatically here, namely that a much-needed *complement* to the literary notion of epiphany is currently lacking, and that one is to be found in reconsidering the theory and practice of the historical genre of rhetoric called epideictic.[36]

Compared to "epiphany," the nominative form of epideictic—an "epideixis"—sounds unpleasantly neologistic; yet the category of epideictic, however we choose to name it, can help us locate an important but neglected development in literary modernism. The advantage of my insisting on what at first may seem an anachronistic conceptual genre—one merely parasitic on Tucker's reworking of an equally venerable and more venerated term—resides not only in suggesting a distinct category better suited specifically to Robert Frost but to what I have alluded to as "low modernist" writers. In other words, I am looking to enable others to plot a graduated scale between the points of epiphany and epideictic, one whose characteristics can be better shaded ad hoc to suit particular cases of theory and criticism.

In *Epiphany in the Modern Novel* (1971), Morris Beja offers two criteria for identifying epiphany, and in subsequent work Robert Langbaum adds four more, so that it will be these six that provide me with my own rhetorical point of departure. By first briefly recalling, however, some historical facts about epideictic as genre and, more important, as the genus of rhetoric itself, we will improve our chances of making specific contrasts between the epiphanic and epideictic. These contrasts should be helpful in identifying the epideictic impulse in many lyrics of Robert Frost. My only caveat is that my summary here is intended only as topical directives or exempla for further invention and judgment, and not as my own final position on Aristotle's *Rhetoric* or rhetoric as such.

1. *Genre.* In Aristotle's *Rhetoric*, first of all, epideictic is one of the three genres of civic speech. Deliberative oratory—afforded by Aristotle five of the fifteen chapters in book 1—exhorts and dissuades with respect to some course of future

action in political matters. Forensic oratory, given six chapters in the first book, accuses and defends individuals regarding past actions in legal matters. And the indefinite genre of epideictic oratory, sandwiched between the other two in only one chapter, awards praise and blame in the present with regard to some person or institution or practice, often as part of some public ceremony or ritual: Pericles' "Funeral Oration" addressed to the grieving Athenians in Thucydides, or, in the American context, Lincoln's "Gettysburg Address," are obvious examples. Bracketing for a moment Aristotle's apparent slighting of epideictic, we can note that this is the oratorical genre historically closest to literature, especially to lyric poetry. "In epideictic oratory every device of literary art is appropriate, for it is a matter of combining all the factors that can promote this communion of the audience,"[37] that is, communion in the shared values of the noble and ignoble as these appear in a public, civic context. When these contexts suffer periodic eclipse, as they did, for example, in the English Renaissance lyric, civic virtues and vices often reappear in more private contexts of seduction and love, while the public or communal function is transmuted into the *poet's* appearing as "civilized" and "appropriate" to the situation occasioning the verse. "Decorum" then narrows from its having been a sweeping rhetorical principle among the Romans to being a self-conscious "showing" of "civil" speech and behavior, all suitably dolled up, of course, in appropriate wit and conventional styles.

This last point hints at a characteristic ingredient in all epideictic oratory and literature, namely the opportunity it affords the rhetor for self-display. Since the audience already identifies with many or most of the virtues and vices praised or blamed by the rhetor, greater attention can be given to the artifice with which the orator or writer achieves his aims. The Renaissance lyric, as is known, showcases all manner of wit metaphysical or otherwise, and it often assumes highly wrought forms such as acrostics or typographical patterns or anagrams, or lesser extravagancies such as the sonnet, the poet doing his best to manifest his own *virtù* in the performance.[38] Indeed, Frost himself often speaks in just this way about his poems: "I look at a poem as a performance. I look on the poet as a man of prowess, just like an athlete. He's a performer. And the things you can do in a poem are very various. . . . Every poem is like that: some sort of achievement in performance" (*CPPP* 890). But this same opportunity for self-display runs the risk of deliquescing into crass showmanship, false posing, hollow oracularity, empty verbiage, as it does, for example, in the Roman period known as the Second Sophistic and does again in Frost's weakest poems ("cracker barrel" wisdom, clever trivia; to some high moderns the unsavory odor of the ordinary). This remains a standing temptation to any epideictic rhetor,[39] and marks an extreme distance from epideictic's original concern with the health of the civic polity.

2. *Genus.* A second, larger perspective on epideictic is, in my view, more important than the historical vicissitudes of the genre. In fact, long before the

Renaissance, in Cicero's *De oratore* most notably, the debate is already underway whether epideictic *(laudationes)* is properly conceived strictly as a genre on the level of deliberative and forensic at all, chiefly because its characteristic concerns differ in important ways. First, epideictic activity is less tied to the urgencies of concrete situations than the other two. Second, epideictic possesses a considerable indefiniteness of subject matter, functioning in many ways as a miscellaneous category capable of handling *any* matter in need of amplification, a task virtually synonymous with rhetoric as such. Third, epideictic speech aims less to persuade than to impress or reinforce or acknowledge shared actions, values, and beliefs, the need for which occurs across all rhetorical situations and genres. As we have said, epideictic normally avails itself of a far wider, "literary" range of appeals than does deliberative or forensic rhetoric, seeking to amplify, evoke, and realize its subject. Eugene Garver concludes that epideictic, even in Aristotle, is better conceived in its relation to rhetoric on the order of genus rather than genre, inasmuch as "the characteristic method of epideictic is the method of the genus as a whole—arguments concerning the more and less, maximizing and minimizing. . . . The existence of epideixis [as genus] provides a mooring in goods independent of particular desires and particular situations. So it is important to our understanding of rhetoric and of its role in ethical life, even though epideictic practice [as genre] is itself not very interesting from the point of view of practical rhetoric."[40] Thus Aristotle devotes no more than one chapter directly to epideictic because, from this perspective, his entire book on rhetoric is given over to it.

Something similar can be seen in Frost's poetry when we approach it with, not (pace Tucker and Langbaum) criteria of epiphany but criteria of epideictic. For invention's sake, we can follow Langbaum in listing six criteria of epiphany in two groupings of three characteristics each. The first set pertains to the existential relationship between the precipitating outward event and the realization it brings about. An epiphany is (1) a sudden change in outward conditions that produces a shift in perception, (2) a shift that is instantaneous, a privileged moment of insight, and that is (3) incongruous with the quality of what produced it, outstripping it in depth, importance, value. The second set of criteria considers that precipitating event itself, the literary (grammatical and rhetorical) relationship between it and the subsequent realization, and the realization itself. Thus the event is not only incongruous with the insight but (4) trivial or insignificant in itself, regarding which (5) an intellectual and emotional leap is necessary on the reader's part, a leap beyond the fragments of the text to (6) a private psychological insight to be achieved by character or reader or (typically) both.

Though any example is almost an arbitrary choice here, and though I happen to consider the narrator in Joyce's "Araby" not altogether reliable in the account of his transit from preepiphanic to epiphanic realization,[41] there can be little

doubt that *this* ending of a story (endings being one likely place for epiphanies) is the sort of thing we call an epiphany. At the end of the tale, the narrator recalls the moment in his boyhood, when having departed a bazaar at which he arrived late in pursuit of a gift for a girl he is abashed, and concludes: "Gazing up into the darkness I saw myself as a creature driven and derided by vanity; and my eyes burned with anguish and anger."[42] Throughout the story, the author has prepared us for this insight, whatever one decides it means, and it is certainly an epiphany rather than (say) any kind of spiritual vision (for it is precipitated and sustained by the physical senses—"Gazing up into the darkness," "my eyes burned,"—not by their suspension). And it fulfills all six of the criteria we have mentioned: it is (1) a sudden shift in his outward conditions (he is too late!), that (2) sparks a rare brief moment of revelation and insight (from boyish naïveté to a more adult "vanity"), (3) the boy's self-awareness far outrunning (incongruous with) the meretricious midway in which it occurs. In addition, all of the events that culminate in this moment are (4) trivial in themselves, even to the boy, and (5) scattered in such a way that the reader must assemble the fragments of external events and internal reactions, in effect making a "leap" to his or her own experience of (6) psychological sympathy with the boy's change ("anguish") and intimations of changes still to come ("driven and derided by vanity").

Though technically and formally a more traditional poet than other modernists, to be sure, Frost himself has written masterful ersatz-romantic, epiphanic poems. One of the better of these is "Iris by Night" (1936), a lyric about his and a friend's—the poet Edward Thomas—wending their way "one misty evening" (line 1) through "wet fields and dripping hedges home" (line 3), when of a sudden "There came a moment of confusing lights" (line 4), "a scene / So watery as to seem submarine" (lines 10–11); "then we were vouchsafed the miracle" (line 20)

> That never yet to other two befell
> And I alone of us have lived to tell.
> A wonder! Bow and rainbow as it bent,
> Instead of moving with us as we went,
> (To keep the pots of gold from being found),
> It lifted from its dewy pediment
> Its two mote-swimming many-colored ends,
> And gathered them together in a ring.
> And we stood in it softly circled round
> From all division time or foe can bring
> In a relation of elected friends.
>
> (lines 21–31)

Like the epiphany in "Araby," "Iris by Night" presents what may be called a retrospective epiphany (assuredly not, again, an unmediated vision) of requited friendship. Speaking more generally, epiphanic realization in Frost as in Joyce

frequently offers intimations, at least, of different and sometimes new criteria for assessing psychological and spiritual states. Thus the narrator in "Araby" seems to intuit alternative ways of understanding his plight, grounded in alternative, perhaps more realistic ways of defining "courage," "adventure," "maturity," and related concepts, while Frost redefines the nature of the particular relation with Thomas.

Like the epiphanic, the epideictic mode of realization can also establish or reconfigure criteria and even evoke something more basic than conceptual criteria, what we have learned Cavell and Wittgenstein call the "acknowledgments" underwriting criteria as such. But epideictic does so in a different way. "Showing forth" the acknowledgments of a community is not gesturing to something noumenal or irrational (much less dumbly mouthing what everyone already believes without reflection). On the contrary, what we acknowledge may be so "in eclipse" and dispersed as to require investigations that appear, at first sight, merely quotidian and uninteresting (and so Frost has appeared to many discerning critics enamored of the epiphanic lyric). Epideictic as genus can outrun praise or blame of settled values. It can function philosophically, transforming criteria and reconvening a community, clarifying what the community may not have known it knew, or convening a new community by virtue of what readers learn about how they might come to order themselves, however provisionally. I propose, then, that we follow Langbaum's lead in generating six criteria of the epideictic, and I suggest that some of Frost's poems, typically cast by critics in the language game of epiphany, fare better when placed in the different language game of *epi-deixis*.

First, then, whereas the epiphanic presents a prepared-for but nevertheless *sudden* change amidst outward conditions ("*then* we were vouchsafed the miracle"; "Gazing up into the darkness"), epideictic literature practices what Pound once predicated of Joyce's *Ulysses,* namely a "circumambient peripherization," a more *gradual* but also more overt evocation of the background patterns and premises of a position, gathering the rhetorical *copia* that no single moment of insight, even if covertly persuasive, expresses in that way. The flash of a firework may be momentarily as bright as daylight, but it is not the same as sunrise, for in the latter "Light dawns gradually over the whole": "When we first begin to *believe* anything, what we believe is not a single proposition, it is a whole system of propositions" (*OC* § 141). To give an example, when Frost declares, in the last stanza of "Two Tramps,"

> But yield who will to their separation,
> My object in living is to unite
> My avocation and my vocation
> As my two eyes make one in sight.
>
> (lines 65–68)

Most critics read these lines as extrinsic to the preceding stanzas, hence as no epiphany at all, which of course is correct. They then further mark the poem as a

failed *epiphanic* lyric, a "just-so story" with an editorial tacked on, which is not correct at all. I have taken pains to show that the "insight" that the poet's two "I's" devise at the end must be referred back to the competing exempla accumulating *throughout* the poem as we read. Nothing happens suddenly at the end that hasn't been happening from the beginning. In terms we can apply directly to Frost, Jeffrey Walker suggests that "the difference [between epideictic and epiphanic] is that an overt . . . argument [including argument by example] is able to make its premises explicit, or to draw the attention of its audience to premises that may have been overlooked (or not connected to the issue-at-hand in *this* particular way), or to question and revise the premises the audience habitually brings into play—and thus to create new grounds for new conclusions the reader/listener would not initially grant."[43]

Second, in epideictic, the "privileged moment" belonging to psychological epiphany becomes the *kairotic* opportunity of appropriate speech. The difference here is that the "appropriate" cannot be conceived except as relative to *all* of its attendant temporal circumstances, its occasion, audience, their aims, the constraints of time and place, relevant events and actions—not (not exclusively) as these may have been read in the original contexts of their appearance but as they become re-imagined in new readings, in the fusion of past, present, and future.

From this it follows (the third criterion) that, because the epiphanic insight stands *incongruously* against its background, it *cannot* ultimately be rationalized, it runs an *unaccountable* (unreasonable) surplus of energy or suggestion. By contrast, while epideictic is not in any way simply "accountable" in the sense of answering to a standing morality or aesthetics or philosophy, it provides new criteria or acknowledgments, establishes as it were the very means of accounting for meanings and actions. In "Two Tramps in Mud Time," the ninth stanza can be read as a timely and fitting *(kairotic)* accounting when taken in the context of its preceding examples. *Then* nothing incongruous stands between its claims at the end and its preceding actions, and neither is reducible to any simple propositional meaning or fixed morality. In "Iris by Night," on the other hand, no analysis in the poem of the given circumstances instantiates or in any way "justifies" the unsought relation of friends, and whereas any wisdom attained in "Tramps" has been lifelong in coming ("The blows that a life of self-control"), in "Iris" the relation of "election" feels not only rare but, unaccountably, not belonging to time at all.

To make the second and third criteria clearer, consider Frost's brief lyrics (brief lyrics being the unlikeliest place for the epideictic because they allow so little room to display argument) "Dust of Snow" and "Nothing Gold Can Stay." The first poem reads:

> The way a crow
> Shook down on me

> The dust of snow
> From a hemlock tree
>
> Has given my heart
> A change of mood
> And saved some part
> Of a day I had rued.

And the second reads:

> Nature's first green is gold,
> Her hardest hue to hold.
> Her early leaf's a flower;
> But only so an hour.
> Then leaf subsides to leaf.
> So Eden sank to grief,
> So dawn goes down to day.
> Nothing gold can stay.

Epiphanies? Very like epiphanies. In each a psychological change ("a change of mood"; resignation to seasonal change) seems to be brought about by a brief, insignificant event ("shook down on me / the dust of snow"; "only so an hour"), an event more or less out of proportion with the effects the reader must gather from assorted details. On the other hand, the events are not so much rare or privileged (epiphanic) as they are surprisingly timely and apt (epideictic, *kairotic*): that is, the only way to grasp just *how* a crow distinctively shook down the snow is not by participation in that event as it gets dramatized in the lyric, for it has not been dramatized at all, but instead by careful attention to the way Frost *himself* distinctively casts his images, meters, and rhymes, thereby giving the reader her own "change of mood" accountable in poetic and rhetorical terms; and the only way to appreciate time's passage in "Nothing Gold Can Stay" is not by sharing a sudden intuition, for there is no sudden intuition, but rather by complex inference from preceding exempla (leaf, Eden, day) that culminates less in an "aha" experience than in an accumulating proof via argument-by-examples.

Fourth, while both epiphany and epideictic use what is at hand, the trivial objects and behaviors of (say) a given day in Dublin in 1904, in epideictic the trivial is significant in itself, however occluded custom and convention may have made it. For Joyce and others, epiphany reveals the essential quiddity or whatness of a thing, as it were the mind's drawing nearer, however briefly, to some passionate aspect of the real. In "Araby," for example, neither the bazaar nor the girlfriend nor the gift nor the boy's arriving late is, in itself, significant. What matters is the gulf that opens up at the end between boyhood before and that which ineluctably comes after. In "Two Tramps in Mud Time," by contrast, the "unimportant wood" on which the speaker spends the labor of his ax is just as meaningful as

anything else in the poem, inasmuch as the narrator spends *himself* on an activity that combines his "avocation and . . . vocation." The generalizations in the ninth stanza are not isolated maxims or summational "truths" but necessary topoi by which we retrospectively organize and interpret the preceding examples and deeds in the poem as a whole.

Finally, where epiphany tends to be disjunctive (the fifth criterion, a leap from fragments to whole) and psychologically private (the sixth), epideictic—though sometimes equally fragmented—requires an accumulative assemblage of materials rather than a leap across gaps. And though it will also eventuate in psychological effects on individual characters and readers, epideictic aims further than these at *communal* realizations and changes, as Erich Auerbach has noted: "The more numerous, varied, and simple the people are who appear as subjects of such random moments, the more effectively must what they have in common shine forth."[44] By this time the contrast between the leap effected in "Araby" and the accumulation I demonstrated in "Two Tramps" ought to need no comment, except perhaps to concede that Frost's readerly requirement to accumulate subtle examples may well be oversubtle in this poem (rather as the ironic "The Road Not Taken" also fools admirers into complacency and critics into charges of self-complacency on the part of the poet). Unlike self-complacency, however, occasional oversubtlety in a poet is a fault with which academics, at least, might be expected to sympathize. Most important, I think, is that epideictic is a communal, not an exclusively personal, undertaking, and that community may be called into question as well as into being, not merely ratified with a stamp of approval but evoked and brought out of its eclipse. Jeffrey Walker precedes me on this crucial point: "Clearly, epideictic argument [including examples] in poetry and prose frequently will be concerned with displays or with critiques (praise or blame) of ethos and emotion, but not necessarily, and not always; it could also be concerned with basic *philosophical* issues. . . . Epideictic argument belongs, in sum, to the domain of theory, and it invites its listener/spectator *(theoros)* to an act of contemplation, evaluation, and judgment."[45]

From this perspective, it is not difficult to see how "Leaves Compared with Flowers" fits a distinctly modernist sensibility, eluding the criteria of high modernist epiphany while it fits the criteria of low. It is modernist—not "premodernist" (only appearing to be so) and much less antimodernist—in more ways than I can elaborate here: its irony, its multiple perspectives, its ironic lack of controlling authorial ideology, its troping of traditional subjects and materials, its "darker mood," and so on. It is impossible, however, to bend or turn the poem to fit the experimentalism and sense of crisis (epiphany) endemic to high modernist authors. Hence the need for a category, like "low modernist," and for a specific account of its method, like "epideictic." What, then, of the latter?

First, the sudden change in outward conditions belonging to epiphanic (for

example, in "Araby" the narrator's arrival too late at a fair far more tawdry than he could possibly imagine) gives way in "Leaves" to (second) a gradual accumulation of observations and generalizations culminating in a dawning (wry, quiet; humble?) realization, while epiphany's privileged insight Frost almost (almost, but not quite) lampoons with a riddle and a mock-public display of his own wit. Third, in epiphany, outward condition and privileged insight are incongruous, while (fourth) the condition(s) is intrinsically insignificant and trivial. In epideictic, by contrast, (third) the precipitating event is both significant (indeed, its significance is often being rescued from invisibility), hence (fourth) condition and realization are congruous, "apt," timely, *kairotic*. Fifth and sixth, whereas in epiphany a reader assembles fragments in an instant of his or her own private insight, in epideictic the reader is required to work through the *copia* of the poem (in "Leaves" the varying exempla) toward a personal but by no means private knowledge: above all, epideictic is public, copious praise or blame, an *amplificatio* designed to undo estrangement and undue irrationalism. Epideictic is the activity not of the nervous or enervated but of the energetic, not of the alienated but of the ambulant and ambitious.

BOOK

II

FOUR BEGINNINGS FOR
A BOOK ON ROBERT FROST

CHAPTER

# 5

## LESSONS IN THE CONVERSATION THAT WE ARE
*"The Death of the Hired Man" (Invention)*

> It would seem soft for instance to look in my life for the sentiments in the Death of the Hired Man. There's nothing to it believe me. I should fool you if you took me so.... The objective idea is all I ever cared about. Most of my ideas occur in verse.... I think they have been mostly educational ideas connected with my teaching, actually lessons.
>
> —Robert Frost, letter to Sidney Cox, 1932

### Conversation in Its Turn

IN *After Virtue,* Alasdair MacIntyre is surely correct in noting that "conversation is so all-pervasive a feature of the human world that it tends to escape philosophical attention."[1] And yet, considered both as an activity of and metaphor for understanding, conversation has fired the literary-philosophical imagination of our own time almost as powerfully as "text," "reading," and "representation" have managed to do. Although these and related terms are essentially contested concepts historically aligned with competing traditions of discourse and thought, it is insufficiently appreciated to what extent diverse contemporary philosophers (MacIntyre among them) converge in placing "conversation" and "dialogue" within the related disciplines of rhetoric and hermeneutics, albeit more or less implicitly and often to contrary effects. The early Heidegger resists *Gerede* (chattering, idle talk, gossiping) as a constant downward pull on our authenticity, while Derrida sees conversation as rhetorically fissured with the deferrals of meaning and presence in the way that, for most contemporary thinkers, all communication is fated to be.[2] As a result, conversation expectedly fails to prevent understanding from slipping its moorings and drifting off into unbounded contingency. For Gadamer and others, on the contrary, understanding and interpretation—the dual tasks of hermeneutics—bring the world to presence only *by virtue* of our ongoing, back-and-forth conversation or dialogue with those texts and traditions by which we live and have our being. For Bakhtin, all thought, language, and action are invested with the thought and language of others. For Paul Ricoeur and Charles Taylor, the autonomous ("monologic") Cogito surrenders in our own time to the

"dialogical self," whose very medium is that conversation in which one "gradually find[s] one's own voice as an interlocutor."³ For Ludwig Wittgenstein and Stanley Cavell, all understanding stabilizes itself in our "acknowledgments," "agreements in judgments," and "mutual attunements" of so-called ordinary language and practice, perhaps the most important of which are our conversations with each other. And for de Certeau, "conversation is a provisional and collective effort of competence in the art of manipulating 'commonplaces' and the inevitability of events in such a way as to make them 'habitable'" (*PEL* xxii). If we will allow that language might be the "house of Being," then conversation makes that house a home—which is to say, our own.⁴

What remain relatively neglected in this philosophic (hermeneutic) turn homeward of ours, what can enliven our understanding of dialogue and conversation as an activity of, and metaphor for, being human as being-with-others, are its rhetorical possibilities. Despite the fact that, historically, conversation has been considered far removed from, and even opposed to, the agon of public debate, nevertheless both everyday talk as well as the more organized types of conversation valued by Plato, Cicero, and Augustine constitute distinctly rhetorical activities. Chaim Perelman has observed that "it is indeed in the course of daily conversation that the opportunity to engage in argumentation most commonly presents itself."⁵ His point aligns with that of Cicero, who elevated (Plato would have said demoted) leisured conversation *(sermo)* on abstract issues—for example, "What is the best education?" the subject of *De oratore* and by far the rhetorician's favorite question—to nothing less than a fourth genre of rhetoric, on a level with and often borrowing the topoi and strategies of deliberative, epideictic, and forensic (*De orat* 1.37). After Cicero the meaning and importance of dialogue and conversation ebb and flow. Walter Ong has documented the progression of the rhetorical tradition in the sixteenth century as a "decay of dialogue," while Nancy Struever has argued that, in Hume's phrase, the "conversable worlds" of Jane Austen's novels effectively rearticulate, at the end of the eighteenth century, principles of the rhetoric of Aristotle and Cicero newly configured as "discursive sensitivity," "a decorum of equity," and "a rhetorical access to social truth."⁶ The sensitivity needed to negotiate relationships among speakers, hearers, and readers in Browning's dramatic monologues in the nineteenth century hardens in the hands of later New Critics, who fictionalize the speaker and hearer and hermetically seal off the reader from persuasive effects. Yet in our time the ultrarhetorical Stanley Cavell finds romantic legacies of Austen's rhetorical values in the 1930s Hollywood comedy of remarriage.⁷ More recently, rhetorical scholars have begun to show how Bakhtin's and Gadamer's literary and philosophic interests in the "dialogical" comport with similar elements of the rhetorical tradition deriving from antiquity.⁸ In sum, while the rhetorical tradition has historically featured argument *in utramque partem* (on either side of a question) in *controversia* and

public debate, it remains a tradition whose orientation to shared understanding as an art of topical inquiry, probable reasoning, interpretation, and judgment in commonplace matters encompasses, like contemporary hermeneutics, many of the cooperative efforts of individuals in moral conversation with each other.

By exploiting these family resemblances among rhetoric, hermeneutics, and conversation, we can, I believe, inhabit our inherited residence in and around Robert Frost's poems. Responding to a question about "Mending Wall," the lead poem of his second book, *North of Boston* (1914), Frost wrote in 1927: "My poems— I should suppose everybody's poems—are all set to trip the reader head foremost into the boundless. Ever since infancy I have had the habit of leaving my blocks carts chairs and such like ordinaries where people would be pretty sure to fall forward over them in the dark. Forward, you understand, *and* in the dark") (*SL* 344). Of all such ordinaries, perhaps the most ordinary is that relaxed conversational gossip of the sort that one glides past without really hearing, in the dark about its upshot or drift until a word, a tone of voice, a turn of phrase or argument deviously "trips us into the boundless," which is to say into the inexhaustible plenitude of (still more) talk about what has been said about what, and how. I propose that we identify this talk of Frost's in *North of Boston*, specifically in "The Death of a Hired Man," as a Burkean "representative anecdote" for Frost's work as a whole. Frost's poems pose, I want to say, as rhetorical guides to our losing ourselves amidst the overlooked places and turnings, the topics and tropes, that we are calling Frost's rhetorical home, which is to say our own human everyday talk and gossip.

As a way of handling the complexity regarding this conversational rhetoric, I wish to posit two formal possibilities of conversation as termini for a broad continuum of rhetoric. At one end resides Cicero's ideal of leisured, educated discussion *(sermo)* on abstract issues, in effect the precursor of that cultivation of "social tact and true taste" that Struever recovers from Hume's aesthetics and Austen's fiction.[9] At the other end is Frost's ideal of relaxed everyday talk and gossip (for example, in marriage), whose nature has undergone, since the eighteenth century, radical shifts in standards of propriety, subject matter, and style, and whose neglected ethical role in literature, for example, Patricia Meyer Spacks has illuminated.[10] Sometimes Frost fails in his efforts, of course, but when he succeeds, as in the edifying model for speech that is "The Death of the Hired Man," his conversational rhetoric broaches an "ethical space," in Charles Taylor's phrase— what I am calling that rhetorical "place of places," what Frost in this poem calls "home"—that we humans require to live and thrive with others, finally to enter more fully with others into "the conversation that we are."

Naturally not everyone has endorsed this recent "conversational turn." In his now outdated but useful essay, "Robert Frost: or, the Spiritual Drifter as Poet," Yvor Winters begins what amounts to a protracted assault on Frost by alleging

the intellectual, ethical, and spiritual scandal for poetry of just Frost's indulgence in gossip and conversation. It would appear that poetry, according to Winters, "is not conversation, and I see no reason why poetry should be called upon to imitate conversation.... The two forms of expression are extremes, they are not close to each other,"[11] there being, apparently, no middle ground. To the rationalist Winters, the "mere rhetoric" of everyday argumentative and emotional conversation that Frost celebrates can only amount to the small, vexed, unsystematic, and self-contradictory (which is to say "irrational," *"adrift"*) opinions of *das Man*, the crowd. Such allegations are serious, surely, and if true might prove fatal. But they are no longer plausible. Indeed, they are *systematically* in error, received from a Platonic tradition of dialogue and conversation inappropriate to Frost's thinking. Yet Winters had one thing right—the metaphor of "drift" as a label for Frost's general poetic pose and position. Like all metaphors, drift is limited, but within its limits, drift evokes that associative surface rambling characteristic of conversation—"feats of association," as Frost describes it in a late interview (1960) reflecting on his life-work, making connections or "putting this and that together."[12] "Drift" also suggests that deeper, unsystematic inquiry involved when people actually work out (or fail to work out) their problems in conversation with each other, what I called, in the previous chapter, "topical drift." What I am after here is also sighted by Stanley Cavell, who refers to the philosopher (of whom Frost's heroes, Emerson and Thoreau, are exemplars) as a "hobo of thought" (*NYUA* 116), and earlier by Wittgenstein: "But do you really explain to the other person what you yourself understand? Don't you get him to guess the essential thing? You give him examples,—but he has to guess their drift" (*PI* § 210).

The ideas I am shaping here signal a fulfillment, then, not a jettisoning, of previous treatments of Frost's fascination with talk, in which most of the critical interest has fallen on tones of voice, sentence sounds, the sound of sense, and the like. While many, even most of Frost's early poetic dicta (chiefly to be found in his letters) encourage this approach, nevertheless he sought something further and deeper: "I made the discovery in doing The Death of the Hired Man [*sic*] that I was interested in neighbors for more than merely their tones of speech—and always had been" (*SL* 159). Here I am seeking to specify that indefinite "more" behind or beneath sound, voice, speaking tones. Now we are asking: What, precisely, can be the moral and philosophic value of the reader's experience of spiritual drift in the gossip, the rhetorical conversation, that Frost himself understood his poetry to portray and perform?

## Gossip: Our Interest in Each Other

"The Death of the Hired Man" is a paradigm of gossip in the familiar sense (two people talking about an absent third person); of conversation and dialogue in the

hermeneutic (Gadamerian) sense (two people coming to understand a shared subject matter); and, superficially anyway, of rhetoric in its classical sense (two people arguing over a disputed ["deliberative"] issue). Here, that issue is what to do about that third person under discussion, namely Silas, the ailing and elderly former hired man just returned to Warren and Mary's farm, it so happens—as the title alerts us, as Mary reminds Warren, and as Warren confirms—to die. It is presumably with Frost's propensity for argument in mind that critics enlist behind Reuben Brower in categorizing this poem as "a debate between opposing temperaments."[13] Unfortunately, the resources of the rhetorical tradition never get so much as mentioned in any analyses of this "debate," so that even the most discerning Frost critic has concluded that the debate never gets off the ground because, among other things, "the dialogue registers mere differences of opinion and not differences of speech, not differences in the way something gets said."[14] This objection typifies, I think, a settled inability among most Frost critics to distinguish different rhetorical modes of thinking and speaking behind otherwise similar tones of voice. To develop our sensibilities for the former within those for the latter, to the enrichment of both, we need to undergo a different discipline, practice a new rhetoric that would have us not merely listen to but actively *engage* in this "debate" between Warren and Mary, in order to cultivate our own thinking and speaking appropriately.

Because thinking is a process, we need some opportunity to enter upon its drift, as I have chosen to call it, at some point other than its inception, where the issues are least developed. I submit that we embark at the point of the rhetorical (not dramatic) climax of the poem, the well-known moment (lines 113–20) when Warren and Mary propose competing definitions of the disputed topic "home," and then patiently work our way back (and forward) from this point. Rhetorically something occurs here that, were it not part of a pattern, would remain insignificant and unnoticed. When Mary responds to Warren's gentle mocking of the word she had used in speaking of Silas, "It all depends on what you mean by *home*" (line 114; my emphasis), Warren construes what he takes to be a sort of challenge from her as an "indefinite" issue, one that Cicero and other rhetoricians named a "thesis," that is, an abstract matter cut off from the concrete circumstances (Gr. *peristaseis*; Lat. *circumstantiae*) of time, place, person, occasion, and so on that normally constitute rhetorical situations: "'Home is the place where, when you have to go there, / They have to take you in'" (lines 118–19). Mary, it will be noticed, also responds abstractly—"'I should have called it / Something you somehow haven't to deserve'" (line 120)—but her emphasis falls indefinitely on *particulars* of the individual case ("*somehow* haven't to deserve") against Warren's appeal to general rules ("have to take you in"). By dwelling on this difference, we should gain a livelier sense of what is intended in the use of the topos of "home."

As a beginning stimulus and guide, we can advert to Carol Gilligan's aptly named *In A Different Voice*, where, as is by now well known, the author exposes hidden male bias lurking in the moral theories of men like Freud, Erickson, Piaget, and Kohlberg.[15] Gilligan aims not to contest the ways in which (Western) males are morally socialized but to identify and value alternative mode(s) of thinking and feeling for which women have been devalued in the past, devalued because tested against an inappropriate (masculine) measure. In a now widely accepted narrative, Gilligan argues that prevailing moral theory features abstract concepts and categories, universal rules, and a rights-based system of valuation and justice putatively based on the "rationality" of the autonomous individual but demonstrably founded on "*male* life as the norm" (*Voice* 6; my emphasis). In contrast to this view, Gilligan cites research of her own and others revealing a different, recognizably "feminine" orientation (based, again, on social roles). This alternative (complementary) orientation—"practice," "method," "way" of moral thinking and speaking—embraces virtues such as intimacy, responsibility, receptiveness, and care for the community. Gilligan writes: "The ["feminine"] conception of morality as concerned with the activity of care centers moral development around the understanding of responsibility and relationships, just as the ["masculine"] conception of morality as fairness ties moral development to the understanding of rights and rules" (*Voice* 19).

Gilligan is not asserting (nor is Frost) that one moral orientation belongs exclusively to one gender, nor that one fulfills the good and the other exhausts the bad, nor that one is superior and the other inferior. Perhaps only an unconscious male bias would incline so many critics to project onto a Gilligan or Frost such ranking, "rules," and corresponding "rigor" of a certain type (in literature, psychology, morality, literary criticism) rather than attending to *how* a new and individual situation, or a specific and unique poem, teaches us to appropriate and apply ethical formulae in innovative ways. (This teaching, incidentally, would explain how poems similar to "The Death of the Hired Man" could strike a critic like Winters, enamored as he is of rules, as morally adrift.) Nor are matters improved much when a majority of Frost's other, equally well-intentioned "moral" critics look to trump Winters's critique by observing that, after all, Warren is concerned with "justice" and Mary with "mercy"—as if the rhetorical-philosophical meaning of these concepts were already sufficiently formulated and established. In fact, this way of summarizing the poem (Justice versus Mercy)—true as far as it goes, even obvious—is true and obvious only in the way that Frost mischievously enjoys, for on reflection it constitutes one of those complacent abstractions that this selfsame poem and poet warn us against. For it secretly avoids (as Warren is tempted to avoid) the difficulty of how to speak in, and to, *this* situation in the poem or *this* community of readers.

Consider once more Warren's initial resistance to the rhetorical drift of things

in the way he adheres throughout much of the poem to a moral rhetoric of rules, concepts, and fixed standards, enthymematic deduction from these, and a metaphorics of morality based on a kind of "social accounting" wherein goods and utilities are balanced, traded, owed, and paid. Mary, in resisting his implication that home *ought* to be earned ("deserved") but normally isn't, upsets not only Warren's tacit metaphor of balanced accounts but the benevolent dictatorship of a standard or rule to be satisfied. Warren reasserts just this (implied) rule later when he grudgingly concedes to her what *he* characteristically thinks of (interprets) as a quasi-moral "claim" (line 124) that Silas may have on them both (the rule, of course, is that Mary and he need to honor all such claims). And all of this Warren does in reliance, be it noted, on what he takes (correctly enough!) to be a rhetorical commonplace. That is, as John C. Kemp has suggested, not Warren alone but the entire community in which Warren lives assumes that the scales of justice are reconciled when labor is fairly bought and paid for.[16] This point, however, then raises the further, unasked question as to where *Mary*, who resists Warren and the community, may be said to reside—where *her* ethical "home" might be situated.

Perhaps Warren's version of the ethical problem that Silas presents can be seen most clearly in the arguments to which he turns, even in the fact that what he turns to is argument, in lines 11–31 and what follows. In this passage, he is at his most voluble in his Yankee reticence, and, though he remains within the contingency central to a rhetorical problematic, his most Kantian in tendency. Having been informed that Silas has returned, for example, Warren instinctively reacts to his wife's first words ("'Silas is back. . . . Be kind'" [lines 5–7]) by defensively shifting some supposed burden of proof back to his "accuser" by asking in effect for evidence: "'When was I ever anything but kind to him?'" (line 11); his subsequent line of thought then characteristically turns to calculations of cost according to strict logic. A commonplace list of arguments, well-suited to Warren's pragmatic-moral bent, begins at line 12. Take the first of his five or six enthymemes: "'I told him [that he wouldn't have Silas back] last haying, didn't I?'" (line 13), he asks Mary rhetorically, as though—the proposition (the rule) having been laid down ("'If he left then, I said, that ended it'" [line 14])—the case at hand (Silas left and wishes to return) may be slotted under it and the conclusion derived ("'I'll not have the fellow back'" [line 12]). (One can then easily diagram the enthymemes that follow: "'What good is he?'" [line 15]—that is, Major premise implied: If a worker is no good, get rid of him; Minor premise: Silas is no good; Conclusion: Get rid of him ["'I'll not have the fellow back'"], and so forth).

In short, Warren's rhetoric is rule-governed and abstract, and much of the remainder of the poem may be said to be about the adjustment needed in Warren's *way* of thinking in order to be able to acknowledge not merely the "change" Mary sees in Silas (line 38) but Silas himself, as if Warren were to come to see

him for the *first* (as well as the last) time. Thus Sidney Cox wrote: "He [Frost] spoke of the latter ["The Death of the Hired Man"] as a little drama in which the gradual change in Warren is shown. It has four distinctly drawn characters. It has climax and surprise; and it perfectly observes the old unities."[17] What the "surprise" involves I will have occasion to explain. What are now in question more generally, I submit, are not Warren's rules, standards, or calculations as such, but the matter of their relevance and application *here,* in Silas's unique case. To grasp an alternative "way" (method) of approaching things, therefore, we need to make two further turns: to Mary, whose response to Silas expresses a related but quite different ethical-rhetorical performance and, briefly, to rhetorical theory for the background necessary to appreciate it.

## The Debate That Never Was

Just what is Mary considering, for example, when she sits "musing on the lamp-flame at the table, / Waiting for Warren" (lines 1–2)? Not arguments, presumably, at least not arguments of the sort that Warren falls into so unself-consciously. Mary does argue, in her way—this is a "debate," after a fashion—and she can reasonably be imagined here to be gathering her appeals before Warren arrives, as if anticipating his familiar contentiousness (as in her proleptic opening, "'Be kind'"). But others have rightly remarked that Frost's choice of "musing" bespeaks a poetic strain in Warren's wife, one that is echoed in the famous lyric passage beginning, "Part of a moon was falling down the west" (lines 103–12), where Mary "put out her hand / Among the harplike morning-glory strings, / . . . As if she played unheard some tenderness / That wrought on him beside her in the night" (lines 109–10). For Richard Poirier, this passage (this entire poem) is a put-up job, the moonlight and music mere "props"—as it were a *mock* debate inviting us to languish in "hygienically fine feelings" kept pure from the start by the marital felicity of husband and (all-feeling) wife.[18] Where Winters had located philosophic, moral, and poetic truth *above* mere marital gossip, Poirier purports to expose Frost's sentimental ideology of marriage *behind* such talk, the poet's systematic distortion of more "genuine" communication between the characters (and author and reader). However, neither criticism, it should be observed, requires us to *listen* to the conversation itself as a possible mode of truth-telling and just (appropriate) conduct. While Poirier does make an important point—that the easy adulation afforded this poem by readers and critics has long been a mistake—the explanation for that mistake lies not (I maintain) in Poirier's claim that the poem lacks "intellectual rigor"[19] but rather in the fact that Poirier and others have missed the specifically *rhetorical* sort of intelligence displayed by the poet. What happens if, rather than construe this lyric passage, for example, as either a sophistic substitute for "reason" (Winters) or as the poet's sentimental

distortion of more genuine ("rigorous") thinking and speaking (Poirier), we instead return it to the larger, fluid conversation of which it is part, asking how that conversation might have motivated the poetic scene (rather than the reverse), and how both require from the reader, not rigor, assuredly, but the opposite—an even more difficult *agility*, let us say an adeptness or, rhetorically, what Cicero and others called "propriety" (decorum) of feeling, imagination, and thought?[20]

When we do so, we can begin to hear Mary's well-wrought silent music as the counterpart, or better the effect, of her equally well-wrought rhetorical address to Warren present from the very beginning. Taking the critical tradition at its word, by treating this poem rhetorically (initially, as a debate), we are able now to remark two obvious but unnoticed differences between Warren and Mary, differences that help to cultivate Brower's correct but inadequate characterization of these "opposing temperaments." These are (1) the difference between Warren's *deliberative* rhetoric of argumentative persuasion and Mary's quite different, *epideictic* rhetoric of "realization" or "evocation" (*epi-deixis* = "showing forth"); and (2) the difference between the issue as Warren seems to be thinking of it— "What will we do about Silas?"—and the related (but in the end impressively different and more philosophic) issue in Mary's mind—"How is it with Silas?" or better: "*Who* is 'Silas'?" and, by extension, "Who are *we*?" "What is our marriage?" and thus "What do *we* mean by (our own) 'home'?" Perhaps this is *not* a debate, after all, but something else (in part, say, a conversation with philosophic implications).

Mary's kind of rhetorical thinking, then, in keeping with the alternative moral sensibility that Gilligan describes, does not produce, from the outset—what a debate would require—a manner of speaking and a purpose (issue) for speech *on the same interactional level* as Warren's. Instead, Mary's epideictic appeals *precede* (even, paradoxically, *support*) the arguments Warren makes, showing forth the premises or grounds (the "home") from which their joint thought and feeling arise in the first place. Her appeals (like Frost's) are not "rigorous" (hard), *not* because they are sentimental (soft) or merely sophistical (adrift), but because they play back and forth across this ground called "home"—adept, appropriate, even (if we insist on the word) reasonable, but in ways that Brower's, Winters's, and Poirier's masculinized slant on this notion must fail to acknowledge.

That is, when "epideictic" is taken in one of its larger acceptations surveyed in the previous chapter—meaning here as that element or function of (narrative and contextual) amplification and reinforcement of values—it exhibits qualities especially pertinent to the analysis of the purposes of a speaker like Mary. First, epideictic presupposes a fundamental identity of values and beliefs with one's interlocutors, so that it is not an adversarial relationship but a cooperative understanding that the speaker enjoys with (or presupposes regarding) the audience. In epideictic, both speaker and audience begin (and end) by acknowledging much

the same things. Second, in addition to explicit enthymematic arguments of the sort Warren employs, epideictic normally has recourse to a far wider range of appeals than deliberative or forensic rhetoric, to "amplify," "evoke," and "realize" the subject. Last, the end aimed at by the epideictic speaker is not persuasion but an "evocation" or "realization" of the subject, an intensification of the audience's "acknowledgment" of some reality, and thereby their own "transformation." Perelman and Olbrechts-Tyteca write that "the argumentation in epideictic discourse sets out to increase the intensity of adherence to certain values, which might not be contested when considered on their own but may nevertheless not prevail against other values that might come into conflict with them."[21] Given this orientation to "reality" and "values," then, we ought not to be in a hurry to conclude that Mary (that Frost) is being "irrational" here. "In this conception," Gilligan writes, "the moral problem arises from conflicting responsibilities rather than competing rights and requires for its resolution *a mode of thinking that is contextual and narrative rather than formal and abstract*" (*Voice* 19; my emphasis).

## A Claim to Community

Consider then, in its context and particularity, Mary's talk with Warren, now within our expanded sense of a contextual and narrative ethics and our more nuanced epideictic and dialogical rhetoric and hermeneutics. If we return to what I marked as the rhetorical climax of the poem—Mary's "'It all depends on what you mean by home'" (line 114) and their attempts to respond, where "it" is unspecified and "you" obviously means Warren and Mary themselves (but also, I suggest, we readers)—if we take this passage seriously, as the rhetorical pivot, then the entire exchange preceding and even following this climax, back to and including Mary's meditative "musing" in the first line of the poem and forward to the last line, might be said to comprise the couple's search not simply for whether or not their home will also be said (by themselves) to be Silas's (as if it were merely a matter of their coming to see what they will choose or do by mere fiat), but also, more broadly and deeply, for "criteria," for "agreements" and "conventions" by which to identify what it is they *can* (rightly) call "home."

What are we after here? It is an abiding theme of Wittgenstein, and of Stanley Cavell in regard particularly to Emerson and Thoreau—Frost's own models—that "home" is the place, and symbol, of the everyday and ordinary, and not least the symbol for and the place of our *use* of ordinary language in, for example, talk and gossip (hence Frost's "such like ordinaries," quoted earlier). In Mary's directing the conversation, it should be noted, *not* to "home" as some completed project or (the same thing) some universally valid concept but rather to what is *meant* by the concept "home" now, at *this* particular time and place, meant by Warren, by herself, perhaps even by others—in directing us, that is, to the contingencies and

actual real-life values, actions, and choices of those who (themselves) will do the defining here, Mary begins to answer her own question by turning away from abstraction and toward the unique circumstances that now impinge on whatever their "home" has been or will be said to be. Mary seeks a *flexible* concept of "home," seeks, in other words, a language use sensitive to the changing particulars of the moment (here the very finitude of Silas, sickness, death) without foregoing the abiding practices (linguistic and otherwise) that she and her husband have subscribed to and share. "Home" signals this intersection of what abides "appropriately" *by virtue of* its ability to change, what Wittgenstein means by "grammar" and "rules" ("conventions," "criteria," and so on). Thus "home" includes the "criteria" of language that enables them (or us) to identify something (like a home) *not* because it is stable but because real people use the term in certain ways to effect certain things. Mary seeks the *grammar* of "home" here, by virtue of which she and Warren will be able to say not only what their (specific) home is but who *they* are, as ones who inhabit that home, dwell in that language use.

Thus Stanley Cavell reminds us that "the philosophical appeal to what we say, and the search for our criteria on the basis of which we say what we say, are claims to community" (*CR* 20). Among other things, this means that Mary's and Warren's search for what they are willing to say about that essentially contested concept "home" (and the basis on which they are willing to say it) is a philosophic search for two interconnected matters: first, for the agreements they share as the would-be community of definers of "home"; and second, since theirs is a search for (dynamic, contingent) criteria to identify their own home, a search for *themselves*, as that which they are trying to identify: their "form of life" as the "place of places" upon which "all" (as a matter of grammar) does depend. But then what, exactly, has Mary been epideictically "showing forth" to Warren all along? What shall we count as *her* contribution to this search for their home, for themselves? What does she wish Warren to *see* that he doesn't see? What do *we* see, or rather hear? We can answer these questions by overturning the conventional wisdom on the matter, without, however, letting go of our hold on it.

The conventional (commonsensical) view, for as well as against the poem, falters, I think, in taking up only one of the two perspectives involved, namely Warren's view (or variants thereof), to the effect that (1) what is at stake here is a practical difficulty (what to do about Silas—as if it were already settled that something must be done about Silas), in need of resolution (2) by explicit, deliberative argument or its "opposite," emotion (that is, "pity"). Like Warren's, the critics' collective head is oriented by, if not turned toward, the *end* of this "debate," to the solution of a perceived problem in some action to be taken: either a final refusal (in all "justice") to have Silas back or an acceptance (out of "mercy") to "have some pity on Silas" (line 135) by taking him in. Of course, Mary appears to "win" this debate,[22] which naturally means opposite things to the two factions.

To those unimpressed with Frost's effort, like Winters and Poirier, Mary's "triumph" here, particularly over Warren's skepticism (see his condescending "smile" at Mary's mention of "home," his "'I'd not be in a hurry to say that [Silas's working days are done]'" [line 154], not to mention his earlier arguments against Silas)—her triumph, again, seems simply to underline both her unreasoned and unrigorous sentimentalism and (worse) Frost's "obvious" rigging of the whole affair in her favor. For those who come away edified by the poem, on the other hand (among them Brower, Pritchard, Cox, Marcus, Kemp, and most others), Mary's victory of mercy seems equally obviously the single decent response to Warren's blind justice. *Either way*, interpreting the poem as deliberative debate more or less forces the reader to interpret all of the details in light of opposing, fixed positions—as if, for example, Mary's extended passage in lines 56–87 is nothing more than the outpouring of an individual disposition or "temperament" or set of feelings (endearing or not) opposite that of her husband's. Construing the poem in this way, furthermore, relegates the reader to the position of "judge" of these competing positions in the way that Aristotle describes the audience for deliberative argument (*Rhet* 1.3; 2.1), suggesting that Frost's goal was (paradoxically) to *persuade* us judges rationally of the moral superiority of feeling over a culpable, mere "reason"! (On this reading, one can begin to understand what Winters was skeptical about.)

Of course, since something like this view does in fact comprise part of this poem, it is, not unexpectedly, illuminating as far as it goes (true, and to a degree relevant; above all obvious). But the critics' versions of Warren's view of what is under discussion, and how and why it is to be discussed—the view exclusively characterized by opposition, debate, deliberation, future action—is demonstrably *not* Mary's view, and all the more not Frost's. In part this is because what we are calling "Warren's view" is not, in the end (nor ever was without remainder) Warren's view, nor Mary's Mary's. By this I mean that the view that I have said the critics attribute to Warren is never *exclusively* Warren's—it is shared to a degree by Mary, even, as we will see, by Frost—nor is it *exhaustively* Warren's, since he also participates in what I outline below as Mary's alternative view, or better, voice: not a competition but collaboration in community. (In this regard note that the couple is twice set "beside," not facing, each other [lines 10, 110]. Nor ought we to put it beyond Frost that the initials of their first names are inversions of each other.)

We will see presently how and why Warren can be said to share in Mary's alternative viewpoint. Here it is more urgent to explain how Mary can rightly be said to take up what we are provisionally calling Warren's view (including among other things his desire to speak of Silas as [farm] implement, tool, hired hand), acknowledging Warren's arguments and their telos in action without, however, finally capitulating to this view, a fact that will enable us to explain the plausibility of the commonsense interpretation while also explaining why it is in error.

For it is apparent that Mary, too, looks toward the "end" of their discussion in action: no fewer than three times she tells Warren "'Wait till you see'" (line 39), "'You must go in and see what you can do'" (line 149), "'Go, look, see for yourself'" (line 155). In fact, her insistence on physical sight, at least at the beginning and end of her talk, would seem to be at once a recognition of the limits of what mere rhetoric can do while yet, within those limits, a successful example of using the standard resources of rhetoric for evoking pity by means of visual appeal, as in lines 33–39 or 147–50.[23] In fact, if we follow through this line of argument (as though we were helping to gather evidence to buttress the critical hypothesis that this is rhetorical debate), we can go all the way and point out (what is true and obvious but, again, wholly neglected), that Mary *concedes* all of the claims and arguments that Warren has "warranted" when she says, "I'll see to that"—see to contacting Silas's brother to help care for Silas—"if there is need" (line 132).

In overlooking this concession, the critics miss what would no doubt seem to them an opportunity to buttress their reading. But in my noting it, I subvert that reading altogether. For Mary's concessions amount to this: not that Warren "wins" any debate, but that Warren's entire approach is something less than altogether relevant. "If there is need" underlines the fact that there is not need and, in context, not likely to be need, hence that there is nothing to debate by way of "what to do about Silas." Silas, after all, it is clear to Mary, "'has come home to die'" (line 111). (In this regard, Mary's urging that Warren go "'see what you can do'" more plausibly pertains to making Silas comfortable, not planning his retirement; Mary's talk about Silas's "plan" [line 158] is ironic and is intended to shelter that plan against Warren's irony.) Or rather, to insist that there is something to argue over here is, again, not flatly wrong—for there *could* in principle turn out to be need to care for Silas after all: "'if there is need'" (line 132)—but is instead rhetorically inappropriate, in this case a speaking askew to the time, place, occasion, and purpose (as when Mary earlier cautioned Warren: "Sh! not so loud: he'll hear you" [line 31]).

We might say that (what we are provisionally allowing as) Mary's view is not an opposed alternative for Warren's perspective but rather something that precedes or underwrites it, even that which makes it possible in the first place—not deeper criteria for identifying something but the very basis in action of all of our criteria of thought and speech. If "Warren's view" invites us to look forward, as it were, toward some set of practical provisions to be justified or "deserved" (a view that, under different circumstances, might be perfectly appropriate), "Mary's view" brings us back or "down" ("drew him *down* / To sit beside her" [lines 9–10; my emphasis]) to the equally practical (but finally unprovable) "beginnings" or "grounds" of this conversation, the *premises* that the couple already occupies (their "home"). So in the statement "'It all depends on what you mean by home'" (line 114), "it" refers most immediately to Silas's plight, to be sure. But "it" refers

no less to *all* of the other values, words, actions that the couple has embraced, undertaken, and will undertake there—in short, their life together. In the same way, "home" for Mary refers to some physical sanctuary for Silas, certainly. But "home" refers even more to an *acknowledgment* of two things.

First, Mary acknowledges Silas's (and hers, and Warren's) humanity, as just that very "'something you somehow haven't to deserve.'" For we never say that we "deserve" humanity, but instead that we "have" humanity or "are" human *simpliciter,* regardless of any possible criteria the skeptic might demand to "prove" this "knowledge" we have. Another just is human—that is, is "acknowledged" by others, by us, as human, not proved to be such, however anxious we may be about it—for here we bottom out at a level too deep for proof, hence for (mere) knowledge. Second, since "it" also depends (as Mary puts it) on what one *means* by "home," that is, on what one *says* about it; and since "home" (here as an emblem for ordinary language) is also the very place where one undertakes such saying or speaking (as Mary and Warren do now), it follows that "home" includes the acknowledgment not just, for example, of Silas's humanity, but also of one's own ability to acknowledge such things *in the saying, in the speaking*—to acknowledge the act of acknowledgment as that which manifests (shows forth) the conventions, the "form," of a community's life, in ordinary language (such as gossip). Thus Wittgenstein, "to imagine a language means to imagine a form of life" (*PI* § 19). This is what Warren does not yet (or presently) see.

I am proposing in short that Warren, himself oriented by the rhetorical conventions of his larger community to debate a *deliberative* issue of practical action, fails to reflect sufficiently on the conventions that underwrite his view, on their content and form, and fails all the more to *reflect*—rather than to debate—on "convention" (criteria) as such. (It turns out that it is *he,* not Mary, who has been in a hurry to say things; line 154.) And I am proposing that the critics—detractors and supporters of the poem both, biased in Warren's favor, caught up in their conventional thinking as they hurry by this conversation and so missing the drift of it—have simply not caught the point of *the importance of speech conventions,* of "grammar" and "rhetoric," to constitute a life, a home, a poem. Warren is hardly wrong when he takes "home" literally, abstractly, and pragmatically (on the contrary, his meanings are perfectly commonplace); but he is inadequate to the moment. When Mary takes "home" *both* literally *and* metaphorically, abstractly and personally, pragmatically and philosophically, she speaks more appropriately to *this* situation, to the meaning of *this* life, *this* death—which is to say that she speaks with rhetorical propriety.

But now we need to shift from our visual metaphors of "forward" and "back" and "down" at just the point where Mary's own "audile imagination" (*SL* 80) takes over (as Frost says, "*The ear does it*" [*SL* 113])—I mean in lines 48 to 145, the very heart of the poem whose details, we will see, simply fail to engage us when taken

as evidences of a "temperament" or psychology but are fascinating as the material of Mary's (and of Frost's) interest in the rhetorical as such—in speaking, in conversation ("The living part of a poem . . . is only there for those who have heard it previously in conversation" [*SL* 107]). And here I can reassert my thesis: The issue of the poem as Mary presents it is *not* "what to do about Silas" (we know from Mary, as well as from the title, that Silas is dying), but how she and Warren will speak about his death and life, his humanity, and thus manifest themselves as the very (human) speakers of and listeners to such matters. As a way of encouraging us to hear and respond to her talk with her husband, I divide the remainder of this chapter into four brief and overlapping reminders: "acknowledgments," "epideictic celebration," and "topical drift" in the next section, followed by an unconcluding rhetorical postscript.

## Reminders

(1) *Acknowledgments*. I have argued that Mary's statement that "home" is something one doesn't have to deserve ultimately functions as a reminder about *who they are*, more precisely about the underlying assumptions that both of them have always depended on—quite as though Warren *already* agrees with Mary (which, of course, he does, though he is preoccupied and momentarily avoids, is even in flight from, the fact). And I have argued that Mary, herself *not* in a hurry to say things but rather willing to take up the particular drift of a problem, not only questions Warren's criteria (conventions, agreements, rhetorical topoi) but also, in calling attention to what one *means* or *says* about a thing like "home," at least opens up the issue of conventions *as such* and what their basis might be. In short, she broaches this as a philosophic problem. This comprises a complex nexus of ideas that Frost makes the subject, as it were, of the poem itself: we are not only *what* we say we are but the *way* we say it, that is, we must speak appropriately to the occasion, audience, time, and place. It is not that *what* Warren said was wrong but that *his generalities do not (cannot) touch the present case*, which is equally a failure of form (application, timing, genre) as of content. Hence one needs a different way of speaking, both a complement to Warren's rhetoric and a return to the grounds of it. Gerald Bruns has put this point well: "As Wittgenstein says, to know the meaning of a word is to know how to use it—and also *when* to use it, and, above all, when *not* to use it. Rules of usage are not simply rules of grammar or semiosis but also rules of suitability and decorum."[24]

What I am after has been identified by Wittgenstein and Cavell: "Knowledge is in the end based on *acknowledgements*" (*OC* § 378; my emphasis).[25] Eventually knowledge ("justifications," "reasons") for things *comes to a stop*, in what we *ac-knowledge*, that is, in what, in grammatical fact, we human beings say and do (not only our criteria but our recognition of the limits of these) within our

universe of discourse and practice, what we shunt onto a siding, away from all doubt. In this sense, "justice" comes to a stop (is "without why") in "mercy," where "mercy" points to (1) the practical supplement of justice in pity, but, more important, (2) the ground of justice in "humanity," *itself neither justifiable nor unjustifiable* because it comprises the very framework for such concepts, the re-cognition of what it is to be human in the first place, including how we act as well as what we believe. Stanley Cavell calls these acknowledgments our "mutual attunements" in our ways of acting together, including our ways of speaking together, our "agreements in speech." And what I want to insist upon is that Mary (and finally Warren!) directly evokes ("shows forth") one set of acknowledgments, and Frost a related (and more fully developed) set.

The first set of acknowledgments, adumbrated above, at stake in "The Death of the Hired Man," is summarized in a letter by Frost to Edward Thomas about the time of publication of *North of Boston*: "We extend sympathy on the grounds of *humanity*" (*SL* 166; my emphasis). Compare this to Wittgenstein: "Only of what behaves like a human being can one say that it *has* pains"; "How am I filled with pity *for this man*? How does it come out what the object of my pity is?"; ("Pity, one may say, is a form of conviction that someone else is in pain") (*PI* § 283, § 287). In this poem, Mary reminds Warren of what they both have "always already" acknowledged at home, that humanity is not deserved but is the ground of deserving (of justice no less than "pity" or "mercy"). Warren, we saw, freely trades in the commonplaces of his community. But then *so does Mary*, who agrees, for example, that Silas's brother should help (lines 131–33). Or, to give another example, so I hear Mary's remonstration of her husband as her re-calling him home to what they mutually share. Against his effort to elicit from her whether Silas "'said he'd come to ditch the meadow for me'" (line 46)—this would amount for Warren, himself ever the arguer, to a self-evident *reductio ad absurdum*—her incredulous "'Wárren!'" (line 47) is spoken (stress on the first syllable) as if to jolt him back to who he is, who they are, namely ones "'who wouldn't grudge the poor old man / Some humble way to save his self-respect'" (lines 49–50). And so I also hear, to give one more example, her "Of course" (line 48) and "Surely" (line 49): these are felt sentiments held unequivocally as assumptions that later get echoed (hence affirmed) in Warren's own "I know" (line 85), and "We know it, though" (line 130), and "I can't [possibly] think Si ever hurt anyone" (line 145). With all of these Mary naturally agrees.

But Mary then further evokes the commonplace that those commonplaces rest on, to the effect that our humanity is not a matter of justice-as-fairness, hence that Silas's humanity (his life) needs to be acknowledged as such, particularly in the face of his "worthlessness" (line 144) and death. How is that acknowledgment accomplished?

(2) *Epideictic Celebration*. In a previous chapter, I had occasion to cite a letter

of Frost to his friend Thomas Mosher, in which Frost, anticipating the publication of *North of Boston*, wrote: "The language [of the poems] is *appropriate* to the virtues I celebrate. At least I am sure I can count on you for knowing what I am about" (*SL* 83–84; my emphasis). Now, to "celebrate virtues," as Frost puts it, to acknowledge at some appropriate moment (say, of commencement [a marriage toast], or transition [a graduation speech], or completion [a funeral oration]), to celebrate what a community always already values, with an end to reinforcing that community, is not (necessarily) sentimentalism but instead may be a wholly acceptable celebration of identity and purpose. And this, as I have said, is precisely the function of epideictic oratory,[26] and it informs equally (as I have suggested all along) Frost's purpose as well as Mary's (note his concern for "appropriate" speech in the letter just quoted). What then does Mary's epideictic oration celebrate? Remembering that her purpose is to remind Warren that our humanity is not deserved, we can say that Mary celebrates precisely the "worthlessness" of Silas's life, which is to say nothing other than his life itself—a celebration in which Warren himself, already partly sharing her view, comes narratively to join, in lines 88–95:

> "I know, that's Silas' one accomplishment.
> He bundles every forkful in its place,
> And tags and numbers it for future reference,"
>
> (lines 88–90)

In effect, their joint reminiscence amounts in the end to nothing less than an epideictic funeral oration, or if that is too grand a eulogy (*eu-logos* = good word), spoken at the moment of judgment or crisis (there on the threshold), when their own identities are held in the balance and they momentarily falter not only in recognizing Silas as one of their own ("'Be kind'" [line 7] = "of a kind, kindred") but in recognizing themselves as properly human. Hence Frost's placement of the couple on the *threshold* of their house (lines 4–10). Their celebration is, to be sure, Frost's troping of the standard topoi of epideictic (normally the virtues and deeds and accomplishments of an individual's life) by adjusting to the present situation and purpose, meaning both Silas's lack of such standard "virtues" and his intrinsic human worth without them. So that it can be said of Frost what Frost said of Emerson: "He blended praise and dispraise of the country people of New Hampshire" (*SP* 113). And this explains why, despite our awareness that it was imminent, we feel surprise at Silas's death at the end of the poem. It is precisely because Silas had just been so *alive* in our imagination *by virtue of* Mary's and Warren's talk. Mary's talk in particular had brought Silas so successfully to life by virtue of her own having, rhetorically, listened in the past to that life as itself a product of conversational rhetoric (for example, Silas's interminable discussions with the college boy, Harold Wilson)—I mean her ongoing invocation

and double-voicing of Silas's words, tone of voice, poor arguments, and conversational rambling. Her double-voicing itself signifies the intrinsic conversational nature of all such talk—its susceptibility to continued life, and to giving life, elsewhere.

The fuller implications of Mary's and Warren's gossip may thus be drawn by asking: what virtues is Frost himself celebrating in this poem as a whole? By now the answer is not difficult. When like Warren we move, with Mary, to a place (topos) behind or beneath deliberative "debate," to epideictic "showing forth" of the grounds of not just this but *all* speech, the poem itself can be understood as having us readers function not as critical judges but (as Aristotle says regarding epideictic) as "spectators" of a performance—meaning both community members who acknowledge the virtues Mary and Warren acknowledge (our humanity, our "home"), and as ones who can appreciate how they (and thus how we) do so. We have said that Silas comes alive by virtue of their talk; but it is precisely *their talk* that is the virtue Frost is celebrating in this poem, for only in such talk can we acknowledge what we already value, remind ourselves of who we already are. Said otherwise: it is precisely by tipping us off ahead of time, to the death of the hired man, and by keeping him "off-stage" (thereby rendering "Silas" a function of talk and interpretation, not physical sight), that Frost focuses our attention on his life as this is evoked in Warren's and Mary's conversation. It is finally their life in and "as" such talk—our life to the extent that it approaches such talk as rendered in Frost's poem—that Frost would celebrate and reinforce: a lesson in the conversation that we are.

(3) *Topical Drift*. It remains for us to understand why and how rhetorical (topical) drift—in the form here of conversation, talk, gossip, in another guise the question of rhetorical invention, of thinking of something appropriate to say (for example, when someone dies), just Mary's "I know just how it feels / To think of the right thing to say too late" (lines 76–77)—how and why topical drift should be an appropriate form for Mary's epideictic task. Of course there can be no doubt that it is a dimension of Mary's (and even Warren's, hence of Frost's) talk throughout. Mary's talk in particular drifts in two ways: (1) from topic to topic: from what Silas said, to commentary on him, to memories of him and how he had (for example) argued in friendship with the college kid, Harold Wilson, to how Mary herself knows "'just how it feels / To think of the right thing to say too late,'" in context a warning to Warren (lines 76–77), to the observation that Silas has come home to die; and (2) from trope to trope: visual detail to double-voicing Silas's words to anecdote and simile about him to commentary to rhetorical question to direct address of her audience, and so on. Mary's talk drifts not only because she sympathetically participates in the drift of Silas's delerium (hence suggesting her own link with madness—"'He ran on'"; line 58), but because she is fundamentally *open* to the wayward desire and truth of what she speaks:

namely, Silas's life. This is the same (by other means) as Gertrude Stein's lifting the repression of desire in objectivists like Eliot or early Stevens, so that language, rather than being rushed into the salvific work of scrubbing the masses, can be allowed instead simply to *wander:* "Error, errancy, drift, sensual 'wandering': these are qualities quite opposed to what Stein later calls 'Patriarchal Poetry.'"[27]

Thus Mary's (and Frost's) concern with "home" is no less the courage to journey away from home (here as deadening convention, sterile argument, abstract morality), in search of what is real and good in this case, at this time. Perhaps nothing less than such topical drift in epideictic celebration of a life, what Wittgenstein calls listening to the "*possibilities*' of phenomena" (*PI* § 90), acknowledging what they already (implicitly) acknowledge, is the appropriate kind of speech to nudge Warren away from his superficial logic and narrow reason, to bring him back "home" to acknowledge Silas as a person—perhaps for the very first time. In *this* case, I submit, Mary has thought of just the right thing to say after all.

That her rhetoric is not, therefore, philosophical or psychological "irrationalism," that it is an achievement of propriety in speech and thought, may be ascertained by noting what ought to have been obvious to Frost's critics but that, perhaps for that reason, they have overlooked. Mary is the more (not less) intellectually astute and right thinking, in these circumstances at least (note how the poem as a whole warns us against generalizing about either of the couple one way or another). She shows, for example, not the slightest avoidance of Warren's arguments, just the opposite. In the beginning, she aggressively takes *him* by the hand (the big baby) and sits him down to talk, and by the end, far from resisting or misunderstanding his claims and grounds (such as they are—she often gently rephrases them more clearly [lines 131–45]), Mary has fully appreciated the real cogency of those arguments and conceded their force. In fact, this partly answers our earlier question as to where Mary lives: she lives *with Warren* in a shared community that values justice as fairness but also values justice as its own unprovable sympathy with, acknowledgment of, humanity (we can now call this "mercy" in our extended sense if we wish, as that which underwrites justice-as-fairness, for at last these terms have been given concrete meaning).

To give another example: Mary herself knows perfectly well how to argue: "'I think his brother ought to help, of course / . . . He ought of right / To take him in'" (lines 131–33; also lines 48–53 and 71–87). The notion that Mary is given to emotional "languishing" has it exactly backward, for it is Warren who is buffeted by his (perfectly understandable) anger against and disappointment with Silas, not Mary who succumbs to some unaccountable pity.

Again: Mary demonstrates throughout that she is nothing less than a quick and shrewd rhetorical critic. She gently dismisses Warren's arguments as irrelevant (the situation to which they apply no longer, or does not yet, exist); and she

has little trouble sweeping aside his, as well as Silas's, jejune failures to reduce their opponents to absurdity: "'confess / He said he'd come to ditch the meadow for me.'" / "'Warren!'" (lines 45–46); "'He asked me what I thought of Harold's saying / He studied Latin, like the violin, / Because he liked it—*that an argument!*'" (lines 79–81; my emphasis).

In the end it is only by keeping both Warren's and Mary's voices in play and by refusing the temptation to reduce them to static positions, and oppositions, that the reader can understand what Frost meant in a letter to Sidney Cox shortly before "The Death of the Hired Man" was published: "I never entertain arguments pro and con, or rather I do, but not on the same subject" (*SL* 135),[28] a remark that points to the way in which Mary and Warren begin within different places (topoi) and slowly converge, find their way home by redefining it: as Wittgenstein has put it, "If you want to go down deep you do not need to travel far; indeed, you don't have to leave your most immediate and familiar *[gewöhnliche]* surroundings" (*CV* 50e). Or again, it is only by recognizing not only Frost's deep involvement with arguments but their juxtaposition with something still deeper—with those "mutual attunements" of judgment that constitute a person, a home, a marriage, finally a culture and a form of life—that the reader can further grasp the rhetorical-hermeneutic (as philosophic) rationality of Frost's next statement: "Really arguments don't matter. The only thing that counts is what you can't help feeling" (*SL* 135). I take it that what one cannot help feeling are precisely those acknowledgments that constitute a form of life, a "home," and that locate what will "count" as our criteria. Arguments may not matter, but *not* because all arguments are somehow shallow or irrelevant when compared to "feelings." At another time it would be precisely *not* Mary's felt, philosophic reflections but Warren's practical arguments (arguments, after all, that Mary, who also has a farm to run, might share)—arguments that would be thought, by them, decisive. Arguments, rather, "do not matter" in this more restricted sense for two reasons: because they do not, *can not,* do the work of "grounding" those feelings, those acknowledgments, and thereby simplifying life in the way that Warren is (economically and otherwise) constrained to desire; and they cannot do the work of *evoking* them, showing them forth in an appropriate way of speaking. What does evoke them, we have seen and heard, is conversation of just the sort that Mary and Warren practice, and that Frost, most deeply in this poem of all of his poems, celebrates.

## Speaking of Speaking

Earlier I asked, What is the moral and philosophic value of the "spiritual drift" of such conversation as Frost portrays? What does it mean, more exactly, for Frost, as poet, publicly to celebrate the ability to talk or "speak well," to speak "appropriately," this latter term borrowed by me from traditional rhetoric to include

here the intimacy of, for example, friendship in marriage, in conversation, and in poems? The question is complex, for it all depends on what we mean by "celebrate" (*epi-deixis*, "showing forth") and by "speaking well." Whatever this latter term signifies, it is not simply equivalent to "conventional" speech, "clear communication," "clear and distinct ideas," and the like, at least not in any obvious way. Mary speaks so that that Warren can come to hear, to understand—but only gradually, by indirections. Her speech, we have seen, is multivalent and polysemic, the very exemplification of what Thoreau in *Walden* meant by objecting, "It is a ridiculous demand which England and America make, that you shall speak so that they can understand you" (Walden 324). Similarly, it is Wittgenstein who says in introducing *Philosophical Investigations*: "I make them public with doubtful feelings. It is not impossible that it should fall to the lot of this work, in its poverty and in the darkness of this time, to bring light into one brain or another—but, of course, it is not likely" (*PI* vi). Thus it is Frost—also framed by the very poverty of the everyday (including everyday language) that is the background to this and all the poems in *North of Boston*—who is misunderstood even by sympathetic readers and critics, not because he cannot or will not "communicate," but precisely because *what* he would communicate challenges both our commonplace conventional wisdom about communication and language, as well our advanced "literary" knowledge. In comparison to these, the flat-footed "demand" that he (that we) speak always, at all times, *in some one way or another*, that we may be understood easily, simply, because we speak without (or with!) manifest difficulty and sophisticated complexity (as if communication were always one thing or the other, as if what we needed were universal "rules" about how to speak): this demand is, as Thoreau says, "ridiculous." The proposal here, about "speaking well," neither resists ease nor embraces complexity of talk. The matter lies elsewhere, in how we actually do speak "appropriately."

Now to turn to our terms "celebrate" and "epideictic." Historically, we know, the Greek eulogy or epideictic funeral oration (for example) was tied to praise of well-known, virtuous public men, evoking their achievements and works for the edification of all. As Nicole Loraux has shown, the funeral oration functioned ultimately to praise the civic body itself, the political home that gave birth to such a figure.[29] In "The Death of the Hired Man," this civic orientation appears entirely reversed. Silas is unknown, unvirtuous, and, much like Warren and Mary themselves, deeply private. Here, it would appear, the larger political community is "in eclipse," to use John Dewey's phrase to refer to the anomic conditions of modern life, conditions that prevent members of society from truly communicating with each other over shared issues of concern. Or it may be (even worse) that such a larger society is, in effect, a self-consuming artifact, a voracious beast of capital that privatizes individuals, reduces them to their use value, and cavalierly dispenses with them when that value no longer pans out. On such an overtly

political reading it might be suspected that, for all of their solicitude in allegedly "acknowledging" Silas's humanity at his death, Frost has had Mary and Warren more or less concede Silas's life to the looming economic leviathan that surrounds them all, symbolized no doubt by Silas's alienated brother, "'A somebody—director in the bank'" (line 128). It would then follow that Frost has merely sentimentalized both that death and life, nostalgically inviting *us* to an apolitical "celebration of a community," now only of two, in marriage, quite as if Frost were in flight from both the crisis of modernity and the modernist poetry and art that attempts to find, it is said, real solutions to our problems—or at least something we can authentically experiment with if not wholly celebrate. Frost's poem then becomes, on this reading, not praise of a political structure that makes greatness possible, as in antiquity, nor a poet's rigorous critique of outmoded bourgeois conventions, as in modernism, but rather the private and somewhat pathetic query of what to make of a diminished thing, meaning now both Silas *and* the larger body politic that can no longer ritually celebrate itself for lack of both ritual and anything to celebrate.

In this way Frost is often said to be, if not antimodern, then "premodern"—in any case quaint, above all anachronistic: "Nevertheless, whatever else it does, his poetry pleases like a Currier and Ives print. It engages the nostalgic interest of readers in a lost way of life, enjoyed in imagination and thought of as quintessentially American."[30] No doubt the same can be said of much of Emerson and Thoreau, whose preoccupation with (the rhetoric of) ordinary people and language contrasts so obviously with the overt difficulty of modernist experimentalism, with New Critical fascination with lyric feeling and well-wrought urns, and with the postmodernist turn to what seems to many not only an irrepressible but an irresponsible play of signifiers—nothing less than a "celebration" of "homelessness."[31]

But the drift of the present chapter has been almost if not exactly the opposite. Far from Frost's beckoning us "back," or elsewhere than where we are, "The Death of the Hired Man" functions as a rhetorical *investigation* of the everyday and its ordinary language here, in front of us, beneath our feet, and over which we, like Warren, stumble and are precipitated headlong for lack of attention to something so ordinary—which is to say, our own experience. As Rita Felski has recently noted, "contemporary theory tends to overpoliticize the routines of everyday life in presenting the 'natural attitude' as nothing more than a vehicle of ideology. At its most extreme, this results in a denunciation of any form of fixity in favor of permanent flux. Habit becomes the enemy of an authentic life."[32] In "The Death of the Hired Man," by contrast, Mary stops Warren at the *threshold* of their own home (which is to say, therefore, not quite at home, but rather, deconstructively, homeless), the one person in a position to imagine how his words might be "idling" (*PI* § 132), as though theoretically floating,

untethered, over the form of life and language games always already in progress. Just as, with her own talk, Mary succeeded by not making sense in conventionally obvious ways, so Warren "makes sense" but does not succeed with Mary or himself, for the reason that the sense he makes merely drifts away overhead. Cavell makes the point: "What is left out of an expression if it is used 'outside its ordinary language game' is not necessarily what the words mean . . . but what we mean in using them when and where we do. The point of saying them is lost" (*CR* 207).

Like the work of Emerson and Thoreau, then, and like the other poems in *North of Boston*, "The Death of the Hired Man" poses a distinctly *philosophic* problem, namely that regarding the grammatical and rhetorical foundations ("premises") involved in defining a world, a home, ourselves. Among other things it is itself rhetorically intended to redefine poetic speech at the turn of the century as an apt place to study the vicissitudes of ordinary language—hence to study communication in a cultural situation of communication in peril and eclipse.[33] What even admirers like Perkins and others overlook, therefore, part of that indefinite "whatever else" that Frost's poetry accomplishes (and note that "It is not a *stupid* prejudice" [*PI* § 340] that leads them to do so), Wittgenstein identifies: "A philosophical problem has the form: 'I don't know my way about'" (*PI* § 123). "The Death of the Hired Man" reflects on this very problem of not knowing one's way about. Expecting so little of so poor a figure as Silas, Warren discovers that he doesn't quite know his way about until he begins to listen to the ways words are being used, how he himself is misusing his own language. As Mary reminds him, "It all depends on what you *mean* by" and "I should have *called* it" (lines 114, 119; my emphases). Thus Wittgenstein remarks: "One cannot guess how a word functions. One has to *look* at its use and learn from that" (*PI* § 340). Expecting so little of a poet like Frost, we readers need to be put in our place or ourselves *find* a place from which we can get new bearings in tangled terrain.

In the end, accordingly, the lesson Frost teaches us amounts to nothing by way of universal concepts or precise rules of language use. We take away no diagrams, notes, answers, nothing other than the exemplarity of our *own* as well as Frost's practice of listening and speaking. It is a matter of education in the broadest sense, of *Bildung*. It should come as no surprise, therefore, that the question "What is the best education?" is the very issue that exercised Silas and the college boy Harold Wilson during the long summers they worked together (as it does also the narrator and Baptiste in "The Ax-Helve," and Dick and Pike in "From Plane to Plane"). Who am I? What, who, should one—should Harold, should Silas, should we—become? How do we become that? If Silas seems (ironically) somewhat overly practical about the means to a "useful" self-formation, or Harold somewhat overly complacent about a more "liberal" end, nevertheless Silas is eager to talk and argue "because he likes it" (line 81), and Harold to labor

while they talk. As usual, for a rhetorical thinker like Frost, such positions lean on each other. In fact, Frost echoes Cicero's subject matter and method in *De oratore* (on what can be called the liberal education of the ideal speaker) in posing this abstract question, What is the best education? as both the subject matter and the medium (method) of Harold and Silas's relationship. In fact, in this way Mary's and Warren's own talk about "home" can now be heard to echo or double-voice the talk about education pursued so tirelessly by Silas and Harold Wilson.

And if, at the very end, at the still point of our disembarking, all conversation finally runs aground in Warren's last, respectful pronouncement, "Dead" (line 166), thereby marking the outermost bound of effective rhetorical drift; if the characters and poet acknowledge an appropriate time and place to quit all rhetoric, leave off talk, acknowledge what talk can never fully say: nevertheless conversation, we can be sure, will soon revive, for surely Frost has tripped us into the boundlesssness of language about the death, and life, of an ordinary hired man, which is to say our own tireless conversation about ourselves.

CHAPTER

# 6

## NAMING BEING IN "WEST-RUNNING BROOK"
*(Judgment as Acknowledgment)*

> If you want to go down deep you do not have to travel very far; indeed, you don't have to leave your most immediate and familiar surroundings.
>
> —Ludwig Wittgenstein, *Culture and Value*

EXISTENCE, origins, change, identity, nothingness, death—"time, strength, tone, light, life, and love / And even substance lapsing unsubstantial" (lines 54–55): such a large number of Big Themes in "West-Running Brook," and the authoritative voice of the philosopher in which they get expounded, fit Frost's figure of the poet as educator and sage who "begins in delight and ends in wisdom" (*SP* 18) and warrant, at least superficially, the work's designation as "Frost's most effective philosophical poem."[1] In the midst (or mist) of the poet's airy abstractions (lines 38–72), however, it has been easy for critics to overlook the concrete activities recounted in, and exemplified by, the poem itself: the questioning, naming, asserting, denying, analogizing, interpreting, and (counterfactual) remembering—activities that are all nowadays themselves vexing philosophic themes. Even easier to miss have been the larger rhetorical forms in which these activities occur—dialogue, narrative commentary on the action, a speech of sorts, paradox and metaphor, rhetorical "hypothesis" (abstract issue or "thesis" in concrete fictional form), and the rhetorical status or point at issue—Cicero's *quid sit?* (what is it?)—of the central issue being investigated. Because all three—these particular philosophic themes, verbal actions of author and characters, and rhetorical forms—repeat throughout Frost's poetry, our experience of their confluence in "West-Running Brook" should help us to appreciate much that is central in Frost's work as a whole and to determine just how vital Frost's concerns may still be to our own.

As a point of departure for considering this most philosophic Frost, more than a few have found it useful to turn to the pragmatism of William James, whose own image for human consciousness as a "stream" appears to be reflected in Frost's "stream of everything that runs away" (line 44) that is West-Running Brook.[2] For James, the creative human act is to cut into and against the flow with concepts carved from human interests and purposes—that is, to interpret it. And

in Frost's characters, we can make out a similar "resistance" (line 58) to the "natural 'drift of things'"—a refusal to accept thoughtlessly the flow of existence—in their attempt to fathom, to interpret, and to name just what the brook's own resistance might mean. In a general way, this "resistance" to self and others, to the flow, this "going by contraries," has long been understood to furnish the prevailing image and theme of the poem. According to Frank Lentricchia, the brook "is emblematic of death and of the life-force of resistive will," and to John Kemp, "the burden of [Frost's] argument is that in the 'universal cataract of death' human life must be a contrary force, a 'backward motion.'"[3] No one can honestly quarrel with this, but we might question whether these general observations reach down deep enough to our insight that Frost's characters, in a Jamesian sort of way, "resist" the brook (and death, time, themselves, and so on) precisely by interpreting it.

Previous critics can be helpful on first beginning, among whom the two best are Reuben Brower and Richard Poirier. Brower has caught, in Frost's poem "The Mountain," something of what I am after: "Like the farmer [of the poem] with his spring [for whom 'all the fun's in how you say a thing'], Frost is much more consciously a *reader* [that is, interpreter], not a discoverer, of reality." In what I take to be the most recent great book on Frost (a book now more than twenty-five years old), Poirier explores more thoroughly the notion that Frost "seems . . . of vital interest and consequence because his ultimate subject is the interpretive process itself" and remarks of "West-Running Brook" in particular: "The poem . . . suggests that speaking or saying is a true measure of time, that human exchange [communication], like poetry, is a manifestation of life resisting any unimpeded movement toward death."[4] Poirier, unfortunately, like Yvor Winters, proves something less than a fan of what he calls this "over-clarified and relatively complacent poem,"[5] and he thus chooses a path parallel to that of more admiring critics who, well-satisfied with Frost's grandiloquence, have simply failed to notice or explore how "West-Running Brook" not simply suggests but rhetorically and hermeneutically makes an issue of interpretation itself.

For a profounder account of understanding and interpreting, and of those related existential themes of existence, death, origins, and so on in the poem, we would not be the first to try to bridge the distance between William James and so initially implausible, even impossible a figure in a discussion of Robert Frost, as Martin Heidegger.[6] Others before me, it is true, have brought out what had long been an overlooked connection between pragmatism and hermeneutics in Heidegger, a connection forwarded again most recently by Hubert Dreyfus: "Heidegger can be viewed as radicalizing the insights already contained in the writings of such pragmatists as Nietzsche, Pierce, James, and Dewey."[7] The Frost reader may object—correctly enough no doubt—that Frost himself would have been the first to resist this hermeneutic turn, particularly to so systematic, so

technical a thinker as Heidegger.[8] Frost's personal (and cultural) preference for "old ways to be new" over "new ways to be new" (*SP* 59),[9] his nativist distance from that Eurocentric modernism of Pound and Eliot, his antisystematic, catch-as-catch-can modes of poetizing, not to mention his reluctance to being personally "found out," are well known and have provoked no stampede to illuminate them further via continental phenomenology. And yet, Frost notwithstanding, the interpretive issue at least is simply whether sustained meditations on philosophic hermeneutics in Heidegger (or Gadamer, Ricoeur, and others) can contribute as much as (say) Jamesian or Heraclitean or Bergsonian readings of "West-Running Brook."[10] While one does not strictly require a Heraclitus or Heidegger to read the poem well, some such knowledge is needed to measure the depths in which the poet is working.

In fact, the similarities between this particular philosopher and poet encourage a closer scrutiny. The reader may recall that in *Being and Time* (1927) Heidegger began precisely as a philosopher of just that unsystematic "everydayness" *(Alltäglichkeit)* of human "being-in-the-world" *(in-der Welt-Sein)* that Frost saw as particularly poetic in both material and method (for example, his home-grown variant on the theme of a vernacular poetry, the "sound of sense"). Every bit as much as Frost, Heidegger was poetically-philosophically captivated by farm and brook, mountains, and woodland paths, and, like Frost in resisting modern technologism, came even more mightily to extol the pastoral role of the poet as thinker (as "shepherd of Being").[11] Heidegger himself mined the pre-Socratics—in particular Heraclitus—as unique interpreters of Being in the way Patrick Morrow has indicated that Frost, less thoroughly and less systematically, had also done.[12] And "West-Running Brook" (published in 1928, one year after *Being and Time*) has been called not only Frost's most effective philosophical poem but his "most witty 'ontological' poem" on "the essential character of what is"[13]—ontology, of course, the study of what is (of Being), having motivated all of Heidegger's philosophic efforts. Though this comparison might be extended, Heidegger's concept of hermeneutic "retrieval" *(Wiederholung)*—or, if we prefer, the better-known "hermeneutics of restoration" and "appropriation" in Ricoeur, or "effective-historical consciousness *(wirkungsgeschichtliches Bewusstsein)* and "application" in Gadamer—speaks to something central in Frost's brand of intellectual (though not political) conservatism in ways that "West-Running Brook" will help us retrieve and, it may be, admire or value. "Retrieval" indeed (or "repetition" in Kierkegaard)—retrieval not only of texts and traditions but of one's experiences and thus of one's self—will provide us with our own hermeneutic, circular motion "back toward the source," a source that is at once Frost's poem *and* his philosophic stance.

Finally, while it is true that interpretation theory can illumine hidden depths in Frost's poem, it remains no less true of "West-Running Brook" that it is, as

hinted earlier, a consummate rhetorical performance as well. Without being able to recount here the close ties between hermeneutics and rhetoric, we might venture the claim that the hermeneutic emphasis on understanding and interpreting needs to be countered (complemented) with a rhetorical emphasis on addressing audiences, arguing persuasively, and teaching topical thinking, and that the acknowledgments and commitments that underlie both rhetoric and hermeneutics are just what constitute "philosophy" as we find it in Frost. From this perspective we may come to see that going by contraries discussed and enacted in "West-Running Brook" (and throughout the Frost corpus) is meant to comprise our own education by and to a poetry that is a counterpart to that poetic thinking ("at the end of philosophy") celebrated by Heidegger. To see how, we need to sort out what a hermeneutic-rhetorical approach to the poem reveals (part 1); then to work through what I take to be the poem's major themes and activities, correlated, for expository purposes, with the three major sections of the poem: naming (part 2 of this chapter; section 1 of the poem, lines 1–37), repeating or retrieving (part 3; section 2, lines 38–72), and time and being (part 4; section 3, lines 72–75); and then briefly to reflect on the rhetorical nature of the whole (part 5).

## Circling the Circle

Most of the basic tenets of postromantic hermeneutics are by now widely accepted, although their implications for interpretation and its validity remain widely contested. That there is no presuppositionless understanding; that all "facts," including texts and text-analogues, are theory-laden; that understanding proceeds from the "disciplinary matrix" (Kuhn) or "fiduciary framework" (Polanyi) or "horizon of understanding" (Heidegger) or "cultural history" of the interpreter encountering the text and then doubles "back" again from the text to the horizon, as well as from part to whole and from whole to part in a dynamic "hermeneutic circle" of understanding; that human beings are self-interpreting—these, we can agree, are givens, bracketing for now the familiar literary-critical problems as to what meaning is or where it resides. Bringing these tenets to bear in a preliminary way on "West-Running Brook," inquiring what questions a hermeneutic-rhetorical reading encourages us to ask, we should be led to ask: How, for example, should we read specific "parts" of the poem in the light of which "whole," and how read the whole in light of which parts? In what tones of voice are we to take "'Fred, where is north?'"; "'North?'"; "'What does it think it's doing running west?'"; "'What are we?'"; "'Young or new?'" What "mode-of-being-in-the-world" is enacted "in front of" rather than "behind" the text?

Perhaps these problems are easily enough solved, perhaps not so easily, but if they can be solved at all it is only because one is operating *immer schon* within a working conception of the whole and within a larger set of questions and coordinates

that give the whole and the parts some measure of meaning. Presuming for now that the poem is unified around some general theme such as "the life-force of resistive will" (Lentricchia), consider briefly the parts, the "story" (or "thesis") they relate. In the first section (lines 1–37), a married couple has come upon a brook that interests the wife for its unexpected flowing west rather than east and that she promptly names on that account. As the brook interests the ("nevernamed") wife[14]—it even appears to wave to her "in an annunciation" (line 31) of some sort—so in the next section (lines 38–22) the brook also attracts her husband (Fred by name) for the manner in which a wave in the brook "runs counter to itself" (line 39). Here again, as the countermovement of the self-trusting brook against the other brooks reminds the woman of herself and her husband (their mutual trust), so the countermovement of the ripple against the brook prompts the husband to reflect (in his own contrary motion) not on the couple's marriage but on nothing less than the human condition itself, and, in particular, not on its self-trust but on its intrinsic instability (lines 38–72): "It is from that [the brook's self-resistance] in water we were from / Long, long before we were from any creature'" (lines 40–41). "Here" (line 42)—that is, in this brook, and in this very notion of instability—"we" (the couple, but also we readers) arrive at "the beginning of beginnings, / The stream of everything that runs away" (lines 43–44). In a speech of some thirty-four lines composing virtually half of the poem, Fred meditates on all "existence" that "'spends to nothingness ... unresisted, / Save by some strange resistance in itself, / Not just a swerving, but a throwing back, / As if regret were in it and were sacred'" (lines 57–60):

> "It is this backward motion toward the source,
> Against the stream, that most we see ourselves in,
> The tribute of the current to the source.
> It is from this in nature we are from.
> It is most us."
>
> (lines 68–72)

In spite of Fred's confidence here—the authoritative tone in which he delivers this philosophic address—we have to admit that it is countered (hence undercut?) by the relative indeterminateness, the instability, of his conclusion. By the end of the poem (lines 72–75), we have not gathered from anything explicitly asserted just what "going by contraries" much means, or how it relates to the "backward motion toward the source," except in the most general of terms. Just what is achieved by "resistance," and how, exactly, one resists, are left in the poem (and in the critical literature) thematically indeterminate. As for Frost's other Big Terms— "abyss's void" and "emptiness" (line 49), "substance" and "unsubstantial" (line 55), "universal cataract of death" (line 56) and "nothingness" (57), "beginning of beginnings" and "source" (43)—it may be agreed that together these tell the tale of man's

life as struggle and resistance to "the drift of things," but it may finally prove to be a tale saved from the commonplace (if one can call it saved) by mere technical display alone.

And that may not be the worst of it. No one has yet demonstrated how or even whether these themes, composing a statement of the whole, organize the other parts of the poem. Or shall we, after all, conclude with Poirier and Winters that this is yet another case of Frost's philosophic tenor outstripping his poetic vehicle? On this view, the countermotion of the brook has presented the poet, and the poet us, with the merest "pretense"[15] for a philosophic poem, in which case any charmed hermeneutic circle of our own will itself go west-running away like water before our eyes. In order to try to reconvene this threatened hermeneutic unity—as a way around within the charmed hermeneutic circle—I propose that we advert from the poem's philosophic themes, which on their surface at least are as (deceptively) obvious as Frost could make them, and bend to Frost's far subtler philosophic activities exemplified by the characters and the author in the poem itself. Poirier vaguely gestures at all this: "Apparently they [the husband and wife] are supposed to dramatize the kind of agitations inherent in the movement of the brook."[16] I think this is right—in which case we need to look into how husband and wife do so, how they themselves resist "backward . . . toward the source." More specifically, if "going by contraries" "with a backward motion toward the source" is that which is "most" human, then how is that which is most humanly the husband and wife in the poem—their naming, calling, saying—a going by contraries and a backward motion toward the source, as they would have to be on the assumption that they are dramatizing its theme? Though all of the big philosophic terms are indeterminate, providing no answer, the activities in and of the poem are not. And just as the statement of the whole has directed us to these, and not other, parts, so the parts provide us with quite specific means to grasp the whole.

## Naming, Calling, Saying

> "West-Running Brook then call it."
> (West-Running Brook men call it to this day.)
>
> (lines 2–3)

What are the central activities of the characters in the poem? Since the poem is their dialogue (with two brief interpolations by a narrative voice), these activities are all symbolic actions in Kenneth Burke's terms—questioning, naming, asserting, analogizing—which is to say that they are both verbal and emblematic of something beyond words alone, arising from choice and aimed at affecting the world in some way. All of them gravitate toward the central activity of naming something, or at least "saying" what it is to be "called," or asserting what is the

case, or saying what something is, not in any scientific or categorical way but in a manner that respects the multiple perspectives from which one can encounter the real and in a way that welcomes the ambiguity involved in disclosing it. (Just this is the problematic of phenomenological hermeneutics and, in a less rigorous way, of rhetoric in both their methodological and existential senses.) These hermeneutic activities lay out, in fact, an insistent pattern throughout, and together exemplify, hence enable us to interpret with some intelligence, just what it means to "go by contraries." Here we need not reject past readings of the poem so much as carry them further "back toward the source" by identifying the poem's major moments, at least five in number, of the all-important "naming" or "calling" or "saying."

In the first few lines, we have noticed, the woman names the brook or, more accurately, decrees, in a sort of Edenic moment, what the brook is to be called. This act of naming has the immediate result of itself "calling" this brook out of anonymity by bestowing on it an identity, something "all the other country brooks" (line 5) individually or ensemble never manage to earn, chiefly because nothing distinguishes them from each other—they all as if conventionally flow eastward. The woman's desire to name is not, moreover, any isolated (though it may yet be a "momentary") "stay against confusion." For only a few lines later, having glimpsed in the brook's (self-)trust some resemblance to the relationship she and her husband share, the wife again turns to assert what she and her husband "are." But at this she falters: "'The way I can with you—and you with me / Because we're—we're—I don't know what we are'" (lines 8–9), posing to her husband the more difficult, the ultimate question: "'What are we?'" (line 10). Clearly she is seeking not a name but some account of their life together (what we would call, after *Being and Time,* their "world").

But the question "What are we?" is momentarily set aside as the woman, not yet done with naming, now (as a second instance of the poem's preoccupation with that activity) metaphorically identifies the wave as a "waving"—an identification her husband immediately, though only teasingly, rejects. And the wave, in turn (a third instance of naming or saying), seems to her to call with some message of its own, "waving to us with a wave" (line 16) "in an annunciation" (line 31) (*nuntiare,* to proclaim or say; *nuntius,* message, messenger). Unlike the woman's calling, however, this annunciation provides no specific name for the woman— no "Hail, Mary"—and no specific message, at least not immediately. For if the wife cannot (or simply does not) articulate what she and her husband are, nor translate what it is the wave is announcing, her considerably more loquacious husband can and does. For in his turn (the fourth instance of naming), he too carries a *nuntius* about what things are: (1) in further specifying "going by contraries" to be, additionally, a "backward motion toward the source," the husband advances his wife's act of naming and defining the brook, as well as the brook's

own message to them; and in so doing he (2) names or identifies, by metaphor, (*a*) his wife and himself, (*b*) human beings as such, and, it appears, (*c*) all "existence." It is this contrary, "backward" resistance (whatever exactly that may mean) to self and others, he concludes, that is "most us" (line 72)—most him and his wife, and most human beings. And here, of course, the poem draws to a close, though not without yet a fifth naming or calling, this time by both the husband and wife—summarized in the wife's naming of the very day on which they have done all this naming: "Today will be the day of what we both said" (line 75).

Hermeneutically it may be thought easy enough to say what all this amounts to: all interpretation involves the circular back-and-forth movement or "play" of self and other, part and whole, past and present. Interpretation is intrinsically a "contrary" motion in the sense that all attempts to name something require that we risk our presuppositions against the recalcitrance of what we would name, that we hazard hypotheses about the whole to identify parts and about parts to confirm the whole, that we draw on tradition to negotiate the present in light of a projected future, and so on. Precisely because that is so, however, the principle of the hermeneutic circle may seem to promise to say little about the specific naming and saying in "West-Running Brook," since it would hold equally of all of Frost's (all of anyone's) poems and so be unable to distinguish this poem from any other. The difference, I am arguing, is that "West-Running Brook" itself thematizes the circle of understanding in its central metaphor (the wave circling back on itself), activity (naming, saying, calling), and subject matter (human resistance to a thoughtless drift of things) by means of what Lentricchia calls the "humanizing imagination" and what Nitchie calls man's "making his own patterns."[17]

As an instance of this alleged hermeneutic preoccupation of Frost, deftly hidden within the poem's surface simplicity, consider how obvious it is (so obvious that Frost's achievement here has gone unnoticed and unremarked) that the wife's initial question, "Fred, where is north?" seems to be, at first blush, nothing more than naïveté or some theoretical curiosity, perhaps "idle talk"[18]—at best a bid for some useful bit of information (perhaps to get one's bearings in the world in an "equipmental" way, to stretch a Heideggerian term). Yet a little reflection quickly dispels this idea. Followed as the question is by her attuned naming of something before her, the wife's question is shown in fact to have been acutely motivated by her intuition of something not right, something unexpected and interesting—an intuition that, once confirmed by her husband ("The brook runs west"—hence he sees just what it is she is pondering), immediately merits that "something" a title of sorts, a name: "'West-Running Brook then call it.'"

Far from thoughtlessness or distracted idle talk, in other words, the wife's initial question—"where is north?"—presupposes a context of focused attention and concern on her part, in this case a literal as well as figurative *Horizont des*

*Verständnis* (horizon of understanding) from out of which her own knowledge of other country brooks, east flowing, can be drawn on to "place" this disturbance, specify its character, and bring into presence what moments before was mere water and now is this unique brook. Like Dewey and James, Heidegger held that such reflection begins only with a problem, a disturbance or "breakdown" that can be recognized as such only against a background in terms of which to interpret it.[19] The process of recovering her bearings, of recovering where and even "who" she is, is dialogic and indeed circular—attending *from* one's background horizon *to* the other, which "other" in turn confirms or challenges one's prejudgments, then back again with a revised account and a new circumspective attention, and so on in a contrary play of self and other and part and whole.

And this point pertains a fortiori to the other questions the wife asks— "What does the brook think it's doing?"; "What are we?" The wife poses these questions out of similar horizonal understandings: what the brook is doing from the perspective of who she and her husband are, and who they are from her understanding of the brook. Hence, what the brook "think[s] it's doing / When all the other country brooks flow east" is what the wife interprets it to be doing, for, clearly—this again would seem to be obvious but has been overlooked—she could have defined the brook in a dozen different ways. And yet her interpretation is the product of neither carelessness nor arbitrary willfulness, for the couple is promptly drawn to "marry" the brook (lines 12–15)—that is, symbolically, to unite mind and thing, knower and known, interpretation and world—a union whose success is actually "witnessed to" by the fact that others come to accept just this interpretation of the brook as true ("West-Running Brook men call it to this day"). Nor, indeed, should this marriage of minds, as it were, surprise us, since she too (and so her husband) is one who, like the brook, trusts herself to go by contraries. This claim about her nature is supported by her own evident resistance to the thoughtless drift of things in her naming of the brook, by her mock indignant "what does it think it's doing?" and later by her playful give-and-take with her husband. While this marriage between couple and brook can hardly be said to make the poem an epithalamium, still we can later ask what small part this "marriage" plays in the larger economy of the poem as a whole.

To name the wife's naming hermeneutically is to introduce something about the text hitherto hidden in its very obviousness and crucial to the poem's interpretation: the poem is both an act of, as well as about, interpretation; and the poem is—we shall see presently—implicitly and explicitly about interpreting or disclosing what is hidden in what is obvious, what is absent in what is present. In this way, "West-Running Brook" closely resembles Frost's later sonnet "Never Again Would Birds' Song Be the Same" (1942), a poem Robert Kern has called "a good example ... [of] his [Frost's] more advanced modernist thinking ... insofar as the poem raises problems of reading and interpretation that are normally less

obtrusive or visible on the surface of his texts."[20] Before we can quite grasp this notion, we need to bring forward in passing two other features of this complex opening that also have gone unremarked by commentators: Frost's use of questions (no fewer than five questions in the first ten lines) and the significance of the narrative interruption in line 3 ("West-Running Brook men call it to this day").

As Gadamer explains in "The Hermeneutical Priority of the Question" in *Truth and Method*, first of all, "openness" to the other (here the brook) as something novel and unexpected is made *possible* by questioning (for Heidegger questioning is the very "piety of thought").[21] Gadamer writes: "The recognition that an object is different and not as we first thought"—(for example, the question "what does it think it's doing?" signifies a disturbance, as though the brook is brooking all conventions of brook behavior)—"obviously involves the question whether it was this or that" (that is, is the brook really going west, as it seems? Which way is north?). "To ask a question means to bring it into the open" and to see it as indeterminate. And while such indeterminacy is, we know, a precondition for interpretation, it need not be simply endless: the "openness of the question is not boundless. It is limited by the horizon of the question" (*TM* 325–26, 327). In fact, it is this horizonal limitation, second, that points again to the real indispensability of the narrator's interruption in line 3. By acknowledging that the wife's name for the brook has been accepted and taken up by others, by confirming a shared horizonal understanding, the poet dispels any potential suspicion on our part of solipsism on hers: here is an honest and true naming—for the couple, for others, and, perhaps, for us.

What then of the remainder of the first section of the poem? To further extrapolate its hermeneutic motion as a play of contraries, we might consider next the wife's naming, by metaphor now rather than denomination, of the wave as a "waving" "in an annunciation" (line 31). In Heidegger's terms, this is but another example (the first was the wife's naming of the brook) of the "hermeneutic 'as'," that is, of the necessity, in naming or defining or simply in coping with the world, of placing a thing in a context, a horizon, of considering or speaking of it "as" or in terms of something else, and thereby in terms of what it itself is not.[22] Its contrary, the "apophantic 'as'," also asserts or defines a thing by placing it in context, but it is a context abstracted from the circumstances of any particular case in favor of what is common to all cases of the same type. The "hermeneutic 'as'" seeks some selection of the unique circumstances composing the context of the thing under scrutiny. For example, to be able to understand that the brook runs west involves a contrary, paradoxical question like "where is east?" (But note Frost's own cunning here in having the wife ask, not "Fred, where is east?"—this would be rhetorically too conventional a contrast for them and us, hence next to none at all—but the more rhetorically puzzling, hence contrary "where is north?" Of course, magnetic north is *the* "common ground" for all of us.)[23] Though this

geographical context itself may seem abstract and impersonal, it is inextricably bound up with the anthropomorphized, hence personal particulars of this brook and with the quite interpersonal, "worldly" *(weltlich)* understandings of words like "west" and even "north," not to mention the religious connotations lurking in such terms as "annunciation" and "lady-land" (the first of May, the day celebrating Mary, has widely been known as "Lady-day").

Here, moreover, in metaphor as a rhetorical device, the contrariness deepens. Not only does the wife once more "resist" the thoughtless drift of things by identifying this wave "as" a waving, an annunciation, thereby lifting the brook out of both literalness as well as anonymity and concealment. In addition, the metaphor with which she does so is itself, in its form, a going by contraries. As Ricoeur, loosely following Frege, has argued, metaphor contains within itself an intrinsic "split" on two levels. First, on the level of "sense" *(Sinn)*, metaphor, in its creating a "semantic incongruence" by ascribing a literally inconsistent predicate to a subject (for example, the wave is not *literally* an annunciation or a waving, as Fred himself reminds us in line 29) also reestablishes an innovative semantic congruence precisely through the "predicative assimilation" of that incongruence: "To see the like is to see the same in spite of, and through, the different. This tension between sameness and difference characterizes the logical structure of likeness."[24] Second, at the level of "reference" *(Bedeutung)*, metaphor is, though it is not merely (as Brower would have it), "illogical," even if nicely illogical.[25] Rather, it works through a "split reference"—that is, through the tension between the suspension of the literal referent and the figurative claim (the wave is and is not announcing a message). In apt illustration of his point, Ricoeur cites the preamble of Majorcan storytellers: *Aixo era y no era* (It was and it was not)[26]—just the wife's forbearing "It wasn't, yet it was" against her husband's initial but no doubt teasing literal-mindedness.

I say "no doubt teasing" since otherwise—on the more common assumption that Fred is *not* teasing,[27] that he genuinely resists his wife about the wave's having some message—Fred's lengthy meditation on the symbolic value of the wave immediately following, readily delivered at his wife's first encouraging words ("Go on. You thought of something"; line 37), is in all ways poetically a failure, as Poirier has said. It is dramatically unmotivated, logically self-contradictory, rhetorically confused and confusing, and psychologically inept, elicited by a wife who misinterprets him by treating his resistance precisely as teasing ("Yes, you have, too. Go on"—or shall we read this as a nagging command?), which he in turn misinterprets as just such a nagging command for self-justification (!). Yet all of these alleged false steps dissolve when we read the contrariness of these two characters as playfulness born of a very serious intent—just the way Frost would have us read him.[28] It is the richly nuanced, psychologically sophisticated, rhetorically deft "fooling" of just the sort we would expect from an intelligent, recently

wed (to the brook), and by all tokens happily married couple. In short, what most critics have overlooked is that sound of sense, that tone, with which the lines need to be read if they are to make dramatic, psychological, rhetorical, and philosophical sense.

On this interpretation of the poem's opening and first section, it becomes possible to see that the husband's meditation immediately following (lines 38–72), in its contrary mode of philosophic speech, while it further counters his wife's intuitive bringing-to-presence of the brook and wave, also completes it. Among other things, it is the husband's contribution to extend his wife's remarks beyond the context of marriage alone, to existence as such, and to specify that the brook's outgoing contrariness has, in addition, a "backward motion toward the source." Only both of these points together will clarify how interpretation is as much an *existential* as it is a methodological or hermeneutic concern—how it bears on life's daily tasks and rounds, on who we are, on our character and *Bildung,* just because it involves naming, saying, calling—and thus how the two main sections of the poem in part mirror each other, as likenesses reversed. In words regarding a different Frost poem that apply equally to "West-Running Brook," "despite its innocent guise of a pleasant just-so story, it actually constitutes . . . a meditation on origins, both linguistic and poetic,"[29] or more fully, on origins linguistic, poetic, and philosophic (existential-ontological).

To see how Frost achieves this, we need to shift our attention to this existential dimension of hermeneutical thinking (to the question "What are we?") and to inquire specifically: How do the interpretive activities of the wife link up with the more obvious existential themes of the husband, and how does "going by contraries" compare with "a backward motion toward the source" (we have seen how the wife's namings have exemplified the former, but how the latter)? Since interpretation as method and self-interpretation as existential problematic are two sides of the same coin, all of the poem's interpretive activities and existential themes should be methodologically and existentially both "contrary" and "backward." Are they?

## Retrieving

"It is from that in water we were from
. . . . . . . . . . . .
It is from this in nature we are from."

(lines 40, 71)

The initially explicit concerns expressed in the intuitions of the wife in section 1 (what are we? what is this brook, this wave?), treated there in the form of questions and metaphors, provide for the husband in section 2 an implicit source of insights and answers, formally treated in more discursive philosophic verse that

extends the metaphors but in a manner different from the wife's, and extends also the wife's "we two" to include "we humans." This taking up by the husband of previous possibilities as the poem runs on ("sending up a little"; line 63) suggests that nothing in the poem simply stands "forever in one place" (line 46)—all is in Heraclitean flux. Yet not all simply runs away "westward" in Derridean indeterminateness. To grasp why and how is not a simple business, but we can chart our way by recovering the concept of "retrieval" from Heidegger's *Being and Time*. While care will be taken to use Heidegger's terms only when necessary and thus to avoid crudely aping him, the reader is cautioned that what we forego in the precision of our account of Heidegger (and of only the "early" Heidegger at that) we may hope to regain in our own retrieval of "West-Running Brook." Said otherwise, Frost himself in this poem is not, unlike Heidegger, laboriously splitting metaphysical atoms, though he does intuit profound issues in an insightful way. Although the technical language and rigor of Heideggerian hermeneutics could not be more alien to Frost, it may be that this hermeneutics offers a contrary medium in which, paradoxically, "West-Running Brook" can best move. While this long way around by way of Heidegger (and Ricoeur and Gadamer) may well test the reader's faith and patience at first, the pragmatic value of this approach will be evident, I believe, when we apply our findings to Frost.

## The Activity of Retrieval: Appropriations

For the early Heidegger, the problem expressed in the concept of retrieval presents in many ways the problem of human existence itself, for it speaks to the task, the "project" *(Entwurf)* of each individual Dasein,[30] taking responsibility for those particular historical possibilities belonging to it—in short, becoming what one (in some sense already) is. Far more than he acknowledged, Heidegger was himself retrieving the concept of retrieval from Søren Kierkegaard's early "aesthetic" and pseudonymous writing, *Repetition*,[31] the fictional account, on the one hand, of the struggle of its narrator to "repeat" totally (literally, to have once more as they had been in the past) a nexus of pleasures epitomized in one of his trips to Berlin, and of his having been brought to grief, on the verge of fulfillment, by "an eyelash, a speck of something, a bit of dust" (173) in his eye (the less significant the cause of his failure, the more preposterous we are to find his attempt). On the other hand, *Repetition* also recounts the success of an acquaintance of the narrator's, a young man in love who manages in a quite unexpected way to "get his fiancé back," not as a flat-footed repetition-of-the-same (which would only be that impossible "repetition backward" of the sort the narrator foolishly sought) but as a genuine "recollection forward"[32] into a new situation, of their own concrete possibilities for love as unique, individual human beings. Ultimately, for Kierkegaard, repetition is a religious act, an act in which the individual enters the paradox that is ultimate truth by repeating the infinite (the eternal) in the

finite by means of an *imitatio Christi* (a trace of which theme [the Incarnation] we can see ever-so-lightly touched on in the poem's allusion to the Annunciation and thus, by implication, to the paradox of the Incarnation, the infinite in the finite, in lines 31 and 60).

For a secular analogy, we might consider the situation of the judge in a court of law, for whom a statute previously laid down and interpreted does not now dictate his decision in the case at bar but is rather "repeated" anew (that is, retrieved as a set of possibilities or re-sources and reinterpreted in the light of the present problem and the interpretive history of the law). Regarding such possibilities for retrieval, we can say that they are both infinite in the sense that new situations for legal interpretation, like the implications of the established law, are in effect endless and yet also finite in the sense that such interpretations will be channeled and constrained by the interpretive history of the law and the new situation in which it is to be applied. In a similar way, an individual is infinite (though not necessarily in Kierkegaard's ultimate religious sense) in his or her capacity for becoming, yet no less limited by personal history and the factual situations in which he or she operates. Repetition is the carrying forward of personal possibilities as resources that guide, not dictate, new acts: "Because of the situated character of human existence, the retrieve *(Wiederholung)* is never a simple reiteration of something past but is also a revision and adaptation which explicates the possibilities that are relevant to the new situation."[33]

Gadamer and Ricoeur provide useful textual analogues for Kierkegaard's repetition in their concepts of "application" and "appropriation,"[34] emphasizing in turn the two inseparable dimensions of "bringing-forward" some distanced text and its history and "applying-anew-now" formerly hidden (that is, unseen because unthought) possibilities for meaning. Like Kierkegaard, each argues that all understanding and interpretation are not "repetitions-of-the-same" (for example, "repetitions backward" of authorial intentions, the author's *Sitz-im-Leben,* or the response of the original audience) but are rather "recollections forward," interpretations of the past in light of a present-shaped-by-that-past: "Understanding here is always application" (*TM* 275). For this reason, "meaning" is never frozen *sub specie aeternitatis* but is always in part lurking, absent, or hidden though retrievable by new readings. That is, readers "fuse" their own horizons with those of the text by means of a play "to and fro" *(Hin und Her)* of possibilities, a movement from present to past and past to present, self and other and back to self, and so on. In one of Frost's own formulations, "we are always hurling experience ahead of us to pave the future with"; or again, "the new thing with me has always included the old."[35]

In *Being and Time,* Heidegger casts repetition/retrieval not as a textual (much less a religious) concern but as an ontological-existential problem of the "Being" of human beings—of what it is "to be" a human being: "Dasein is the possibility

of Being-free for its ownmost potentiality-for-Being" (*BT* 183/144). This possibility is realized in retrieval: "In anticipating, Dasein *brings* itself *again forth* into its ownmost potentiality-for-Being. If Being-as-having-been is *authentic* [my emphasis], we call it *repetition*" (*BT* 388/339). What does this mean? First of all, to be human for Heidegger is to be "thrown" *(geworfen)* into existence, not as some relatively independent, autonomous consciousness *(res cogitans)* over against equally autonomous, value-free objects *(res extensa)*, as in Descartes, for example, but rather as one for whom subject and object, knower and known, already make up the interpreted, engaged, value-laden realities of one's "world." In lectures given at this time (1928), Heidegger wrote: "Self and world belong together in the single entity, Dasein. Self and world are not two entities, like subject and object ... but self and world are the basic determination of Dasein itself in the unity of the structure of being-in-the-world."[36] For this reason we humans are intrinsically interpreting ("naming") beings who cannot know the world except from our own historical situations and from within what Cavell calls an "attunement" with each other and Heidegger calls "mood" *(Stimmung)*. In fact, it is just our being-in-the-world in this mode of engaged, interested "everydayness" that Heidegger argues is the overlooked starting point for the recovery of the question of Being, since such engaged everydayness simply is Dasein's fundamental mode of being-in-the-world.

Such everydayness presents us human beings with both negative and positive circumstances for self-becoming.[37] Positively, we manage to achieve an "authentic" way of being precisely in and through the shared, "public" character of the everyday: "Dasein finds 'itself' proximally in *what* it does, uses, expects, avoids—in those things environmentally ready-to-hand [*vorhanden*, that is, personally taken up by us in its network of relations and values] with which it is proximally *concerned*" (*BT* 155/119, 296/252). Negatively, however, our "thrownness" ineluctably entails also our "falling." In a religious author like Kierkegaard, "falling" signifies original sin. In Heidegger, it is rather that tendency (*Zug* [current] [!]) to "absorption" in Dasein's everydayness—in our daily, our hourly distractedness by people, events, things, activities, and especially by what "others" *(das Man)* say, until one's "ownmost" possibilities are neglected or forgotten altogether. For this reason, Heidegger strongly indicts "mere curiosity" and "idle talk," the gossip of our daily comings and goings among *das Man*. Heidegger summarizes human beings thus: *"Dasein's 'average everydayness' can be defined as 'Being-in-the-world which is falling and disclosed, thrown and projecting, and for which its ownmost potentiality-for-Being is an issue'"* (*BT* 225/181).

As everyday "thrownness" or "being-in-the-world," finally, human beings (as interpretive) are not resourceless, not merely adrift or falling. According to Heidegger, each of us is called by conscience to a "Care" *(Sorge)* about his own thrownness as a project directed "toward" the future (*BT* 227/182). We are called

to "authenticity," that is, to assuming our freedom for our own possibilities through the interpretation ("naming," "calling," "saying") of our own historical Being—a Being that is necessarily an "issue" for us. But this authentic commitment to Care, this issue of our Being, is formal or empty in the sense that it does not reveal (as we find in Plato or Aristotle) a predetermined teleological principle of rationality nor acquire (as in Hegel) its intelligibility only within some historical unfolding of *Geist*. Rather, in committing "resolutely" to one's own freedom, one remains open to the ongoing challenge of interpreting one's historicity. In this sense, Care refers to man's own indeterminate place, or topos, for questioning Being, and in particular his own Being.[38] Understood in this way, our Care for our ownmost possibilities (that is, our questioning interpretation of Being) "is" the Being of Dasein. Dasein "is" that being that seeks to interpret (name, say, call) the Being of beings. In saying so, however, we do not exhaust the meaning of Dasein's Being; on the contrary, we open it for exploration.

In brief, then: first, human being is the being that interprets Being; second, a human being's understanding as such, brought to articulate language in interpretation, is the "counterpull" *(Gegen-Zug)*—the "going by contraries"—against an otherwise unintelligible existence; and third, "retrieval" is the authentic, "backward" bringing-forward, through a reciprocating, dialogic interpretation, of human being's own past possibilities, traditions, heritage, in resistance to absorption in a potentially intelligible but also potentially distracting "world."[39]

For now the question at hand is, How shall we ourselves "apply" this notion of retrieval to "West-Running Brook?"

### The Activity of Retrieval: Applications

We can apply it by proposing that the image of the backward ripple in the outgoing brook that so fascinates Fred signifies just this concept of "retrieval" and its hermeneutic cousins "appropriation" and "application." This image of retrieval in Fred's disquisition in section 2 introduces, in an explicit thematic way, the existential dimension of the wife's (and Frost's) hermeneutic, present but hidden in the verbal activity of section 1. On this understanding, Fred himself is engaged in retrieving hidden possibilities-for-being in his wife's naming (and in the wave's "annunciation") by making explicit hitherto unthought meanings. By analyzing the image of the wave in these terms, we can, I believe, deepen our understanding of the significance for "living" of the interpretive activity of "naming" in that first section (and indeed throughout the poem) and in so doing ourselves retrieve hidden significances and meanings "in front of" the text, applicable to this as well as to many other Frost poems. Before we consider in detail Fred's discourse, however (the third and fourth sections below), we would do well to consider, as a whole, the architectonic image of the brook, first (in section 1) as that going west "by contraries" against the other country brooks identified by the wife and briefly

analyzed earlier, and second (in section 2) as that "backward motion toward the source," identified by Fred in section 2 of the poem. In fact, it is only by holding these contrary images in tension that we ourselves can retrieve what Frost is saying and doing. It is when we "apophantically" abstract theme from activity, content from form, image from context, that we ourselves fail to enact the education Frost would bring us to, and only when we hermeneutically hold them in tension that we become, as readers, "most us."

1. *The image of the brook running westward.* In the first place, then, the ripple hearkens back, though we need constantly to remind ourselves that it does so within a current that goes forth or out, so that the backward ripple is at best a "tribute of the current to the source" (line 70), not any attempt to get back to the source itself as is often claimed. The view of one critic that Fred's meditation is a Platonic longing for pure essence could not be more mistaken, though it rides on a swift surface plausibility. Why is it mistaken?

Viewed as it were negatively, first of all, we might say that, unlike the other country brooks that do seek to get back directly to the "beginning of beginnings" (line 43) in flowing east, to the source of all things in the ocean (not at its headwaters, as some would have it), Frost's brook avoids the error—the philosophic fallacy—of the much-feared "metaphysics of presence" (that is, the belief that one can achieve indubitable knowledge of the "essence" of things [or be such an essence oneself] beyond all change and becoming). In this way, Frost's metaphor of the brook, like the thought of James, Dewey, and Heidegger, is rigorously antifoundationalist. More positively said, the brook's west-running parallels Heidegger's own concept of "fore-running" *(Vorlaufen)* (that is, Dasein's anticipatory being-ahead-of-itself in its projection of its possibilities into time, away from its beginning and toward expansion and life). In Samuel Johnson's less crabbed terms, but now deepening his thought, not only do human beings live "from hope to hope"; life itself from moment to moment is *constituted* by hope, by the possible. Singled out and identified (named) by the wife, "west-running" is clearly associated with her intuitive "forwardness," her sexual energy (her Amazonian connections; line 33), and her metaphoric-poetic "wildness" (the Wild West, and so on). On the other hand—and from an opposing angle—"west-running" is also associated with accepting our human lot in time as finite creatures "ventured"[40] into the unknown, away from our beginnings and ultimately toward our end (for example, the setting sun; the theme of death is treated below). It is to accept that we are what we become and become what we have been but differently (for repetition is not a photocopy of the past) and only as we "apply" ourselves. Thus to "run west" is to be finite creatures, whose essence is our futurity, our forwardness.

But how, then—this is really our primary question: How does this existential theme of becoming-in-time, this "vaguely realizing westward," as Frost expressed

it in "The Gift Outright," how does this *theme* link up with/retrieve the interpretive *activity* of the wife, and specifically with her naming of the brook? How do these two diverse, even contrary movements go together? As a way of answering, we might recall Poirier's sharp but unexplained insight that "saying is a true measure of time." What can we make of this?

Can we not agree that the significance of *this* brook's getting named and of the other brooks in the poem going nameless is this: that only in the venture into time can the world be named at all and only in such naming or saying can time, world, Dasein (the one who names), and indeed any other beings, enter into their respective possibilities at all, hence have their "measure" taken?[41] Surely this will account for the conscientiousness with which the wife names the brook, for it is only by virtue of the name "West-Running Brook" that the brook can be interpreted "to be" what it is—west-running—since only that name (which includes of course the dynamic horizonal wholes, public and private, for which the name stands) provides the coordinates (Emerson's "circles") by which the brook can be said to be that, hence to be itself—indeed, symbolically to have a "self" at all. In this way, the speakers in "West-Running Brook" more obviously succeed where that lone voice in Frost's "The Most of It" initially seems to fail: "He would cry out on life, that what it wants / Is not its own love back in copy speech, / But counter-love, original response" (lines 6–8), but for whom (at first) "nothing ever came of what he cried" (line 9). Here what comes of counterlove in counterspeech is no less than life and love themselves.

By contrast, the absence of individuality that marks the "other country brooks" is due first of all merely to their not having been made focally present. Here we might be tempted to argue, rightly as far as it goes, that they "exist" as much as their west-running counterpart in the context of the poem, are even "horizonally" interpreted by us readers as "east-flowing." In terms, however, of "Being" and not mere existence (that is, in terms of selfhood, that unique mode of Being of human beings that "West-Running Brook" symbolizes) the failure of those east-flowing brooks to be named is just their failure philosophically to try to become in time what they might have been interpreted to be (since all beings "are" only insofar as they are disclosed by Dasein's interpretive understanding). Though it is true that "east-flowing brooks" is an inferable name of sorts, it is a name inferior to the name the wife bestows on the west-running brook; it is a mere "apophantic" assertion of our own, cut off from the larger nexus of values of husband and wife.

The disclosure, therefore, such as it is, of the Being of those east-flowing brooks in the poem is truncated to the extent that they symbolically deny or refuse time, existence, becoming, and hence refuse further interpretation out of their own "impatient" desire for pure presence (as in line 42). Such a desire may become second nature because more conventional, in the way that foundationalist

ontology in Plato, Aristotle, and Descartes has furnished a like convention in the history of Western philosophy. But it is, on this Heideggerian reading, no less a philosophic error, and it is, in this most Frostian poem, no less a human failure, on the order of the wife's refusal in "Home Burial" to take up again the burden of living in good part by talking (hence, to her husband: "You—oh, you think the talk is all"; line 112). In short, then, the brook's symbolic flowing west "into" existence and the wife's naming of the brook on that account are mutually constitutive: the brook disturbs her with its momentary "breakdown" of conventions and in so doing forces her, so to speak, to interpret it out of her horizonal re-sources (a retrieval) and thus to bring it to presence, hence to Being, "as" "West-Running Brook."

2. *The image of the brook doubling back.* In the second place, although the brook flows west, it does not flow only west. The view of more than one critic that the brook represents matter slowly degrading is thus simply one-sided. If we consider the brook's doubling-back negatively once again, we can say that in falling back against its outward current, the brook symbolically avoids *(a)* the *ontological* error of the paradox of "pure" existence, in which the "what" that is supposed to exist disappears into the very flux that is its existence;[42] and *(b)* the *existential* error of falling into the current *(Zug)* of total absorption into everydayness, into the "leveling" of *das Man* (not to mention *[c]*, the *epistemological* error of skeptical relativism and historicism). More positively said, the brook avoids these errors precisely by reaching back toward the source of being in an "appropriation," a retrieval, of what has been and yet also still "*is.*"

Frost is talking, in other words, not of some "pure" fixed presence at the source—for the brook does not get back to the source, only "toward" it (line 68)—but of the source "as" (re)-generative and ongoing origin ("Raising a little, sending up a little"; line 63) and "as" what the brook itself has been "from" this originating source. It is not possible to explore this point here, but Frost is playing ironically with the image of the "circuitous journey" so crucial to a wide range of romantic poetry, in which life is an educative lesson ending where we began, only now having reconciled the various oppositions that life itself has thrown at us.[43] In Frost, by contrast, we do not go home again, but rather go back and forth, again and again, in a process of never-ending regeneration and assimilation—in a word, retrieval—from the ever-present source. Of course, we are not discussing anything the brook has literally retrieved (such as water) but of what its retrieval symbolizes. Singled out and identified (named) by the husband, this "backward motion toward the source" (line 68) is associated with his philosophic turn to (nonfoundationalist) first principles, his deliberate conscientiousness (care), and what might be called his scholarly or intellectual conservatism. It stands for time ontologically considered and also for "tradition" in Gadamer's large sense of the word: that heritage of possibilities for self as re-sources upon which all may draw.

Yet this backward motion is no less a retrieval forward, since the husband's "tribute to the source" only occurs (only *can* occur) within—in contrary tension with—the wife's forwarding current: together these compose at once an "appropriation" (backward) and an "application" (forward).

In fact, this way of putting it is not yet contrary enough, for any appropriation itself entails an application (otherwise how can it become one's own?), and any application entails an appropriation (otherwise what is there to apply?). Trading on these distinctions for a moment, we might say that the husband's "appropriation" of the "beginning of beginnings"—symbolized in the backward motion toward the source—entails his own application to his present circumstances (otherwise how would he know what to retrieve?); and that his wife's "application" of a name to the nameless water—symbolized in the brook's own "contrary" westward flow—must be placed within the context of the husband's backward wave, that is, her appropriation of her own past horizons (otherwise how could she interpret the significance of the brook?).

It is here, plainly, that all talk of what is "the wife's" and what is "the husband's" proves internally tensional and contrary, for what belongs to one belongs also to the other (but differently). And it is here also that all dualisms of "matter" (for example, the brook, the sexual wife) versus "spirit" (such as the source-seeking wave, the intellectual husband) must make way for that profounder unity-in-opposition, a discrimination-without-division, for all dualisms must miss how the brook that is existence is equally and at once both "spirit" and "matter"; how going west is as spiritual (for example, in the wife's "intuition") as going east is material (as in the husband's surface literalism); and thus how "west-running" is not only the degradation or mere running down of matter but also its (always incomplete) spiritual realization.[44]

As a preliminary way of suggesting concretely what we shall grasp more fully when we analyze the "substance" of Fred's address below, namely, the existential import of retrieval as both an appropriation and an application, we can advert once more to the wife's naming of the brook as her retrieval of her own past possibilities ("potentiality-for-Being"; *BT* 225/181). The wife's denomination of the brook draws not only on the public, relatively impersonal spatial coordinates she shares with others but on the private life she shares with her husband, which we readers also share by virtue of those of our horizons that overlap theirs. What the name "West-Running Brook" comes to mean, as a result, includes all that can trust itself: trust itself to go against conventions, to go against the leveling of others *(das Man)*, and to go its own way into existence. This set of meanings is precisely the net result of the wife's repetition/retrieval, her movement back to her and her husband's past possibilities for life and love, brought forward in her naming of the brook, repeated yet again in her husband's similar (but different) namings, and symbolized throughout by this backward (and forward) ripple in the brook.

Thus the *theme* of retrieval, overtly introduced in, but also put at risk by, the imagery of sheer backwardness in the husband's wave, is covertly already completed and saved by the forward *activity* of the wife's naming, itself therefore a recollection forward figured in the westering of "West-Running Brook."

We can see how Frost's various contraries are held together if we draw closer now to the linguistic texture of the poem, and particularly in section 2 (lines 38–72): first to the overarching framework of Fred's discourse, and next to its (un)substantial center (lines 48–63). Specifically, we shall do well (in fact, we shall be the first) to scrutinize under the first problematic (the framework): (*a*) the ungrammatical "from . . . from" lines at the beginning (line 40) and end (line 71) of Fred's talk; (*b*) the question "Young or new?" stated earlier (line 10) in the poem but only now, in this second section, accorded its full value; and (*c*) the imagery of stasis in tension with the imagery of kinesis. Following this, we can turn to Fred's discourse itself.

3. *The framework of Fred's discourse.* First, Frost's well-known willingness to abrogate the rules of grammar is neatly illustrated in his twice invoked "It is from . . . from" line beginning and ending Fred's meditation: "It is from that in water we were from" (line 40); "It is from this in nature we are from" (line 71). In the lines taken singly, then together, meanings interweave in rich ways, enacting in their form what they say abstractly ("apophantically") in content. Taken singly, for example, each line requires that we read its two "froms" in contrary ways, the first "from" stressing source, origin, the "beginning of beginnings" *from which* we are derived, and the second stressing that derivation itself, that novel *what* deriving "from" the source: our attention shifts internally within an (ungrammatical, hence "contrary") locution that holds both perspectives in tension and in which both perspectives are necessary. Taken together, the two lines constitute a genuine retrieval, not merely a "repetition-of-the-same." By dint of its shift in indefinite pronouns ("that" to "this"), verb tense (past to present), and subject ("water" to "nature"), the second line brings what is being talked about (source, origin, beginning) "closer" to the couple, without, however, denying their inability to achieve any total unity with that source of things. For while they "Get back to the beginning of beginnings," this beginning is existence itself, the "stream of everything"; and this, we shall see shortly, is paradoxically present and absent at once—something one can, and cannot, get back to (not only because this stream "runs away" but because one is already in it). It is just these tensions—proximity/distance, permanence/change, presence/absence—that recapitulate the tension in each "from . . . from" line and again the tension in the "wasn't/was" of the wife's metaphor. Of course, the reality of this tension is just what both lines are asserting: the source of all things, that "that" which is "most us," just "is" a contrariness of forces, symbolized by the two motions of the brook outward and back—in short, identity-in-change, absence-in-presence, past-in-future, opposition-in-unity.

Second, in much the way that the second of the two "from . . . from" lines is a retrieval of the other, both taken together retrieve Fred's first line from section 1, his question, "Young or new?" (line 10), offered in response to his wife's query, "What are we?" The contrary possibilities he seems to hesitate over here ("young," "new") are, we can see plainly, those selfsame values of "source" and "derivation-of-the-new" repeated in the later lines, for something is "young" only relative to some ongoing identity, and something is "new" only as a departure from or interruption of something else. Here, as later, Fred hesitates over these possibilities as to how to name himself and his wife, holding two contrary movements in tension.

Finally, these same values/tensions are repeated once more in Fred's invocation, then rejection, of Pirouot and Pirouette "forever in one place" as an adequate account of "existence." This image itself extends the earlier images of the white water of the wave riding the black "forever," "Not gaining but not losing, like a bird" (line 22). The irony is easy to miss here, for these earlier images are offered by none other than the narrator (ostensibly Frost himself) and apparently ratified by Fred, both of whom are thereby identified with those "others," that is, with those "some" who say existence "forever in one place, / Stands still and dances" (lines 46–47). Now, however, in countering these images with the images of the running brook and its doubling back, Frost/Fred resists the leveling of what "others" say, therefore resists any easy identification of Frost's own position and thus asserts a double contrariness of stasis "in" but also "against" kinesis.

4. *The central (non-)substance of Fred's discourse.* By far the most involved expression of these tensions occurs in lines 48–63, the thematic center of Fred's "philosophy" and by all accounts the most difficult to understand. Consider:

> "It [existence] seriously, sadly runs away
> To fill the abyss's void with emptiness.
> It flows beside us in this water brook,
>
> . . . . . . . . . . . .
> And it is time, strength, tone, light, life, and love—
> And even substance lapsing unsubstantial;
> The universal cataract of death
> That spends to nothingness—and unresisted,
> Save by some strange resistance in itself,
> Not just a swerving, but a throwing back,
> As if regret were in it and were sacred.
>
> . . . . . . . . . . . .
> So that the fall of most of it is always
> Raising a little, sending up a little."
>
> (lines 48–63)

Here the dialectic of permanence and change is transposed into the more perplexing talk of substance and nonsubstance, absence and presence. How can

an "existence" equated with "time, strength, tone, light, life, and love" also "be" an "emptiness," much less an emptiness that "fills" the "abyss's void?" How can such an ontological-existential emptiness also "be" "substance" (line 55), much less a substance that also "laps[es] unsubstantial"? (What does that mean, to "lapse," and to lapse "unsubstantial"? Merely water into mist?) How can existence also "be" the "universal cataract of death" (line 56)? Previous attempts to answer these questions have resulted in either vagueness (just "one of those 'immedicable woes'" that Frost expressed a liking for) or one-sidedness ("The brook represents the working of natural forces that are wearing out").[45] In fact, neither of these approaches is sufficiently contrary to capture that sort of tension of which Frost wrote in a light piece entitled "The Armful": "Extremes too hard to comprehend at once, / Yet nothing I should care to leave behind" (lines 4–5); or to capture what Poirier has written of Frost's "The Onset": "But we would misread the poem, and Frost, if we decided that he wants us to 'take sides' against one of the sides given voice by the poem."[46] As hinted earlier, in other words, the central topoi here—"presence/absence," "substance/nonsubstance"—have in fact been present to us all along, though themselves in a hidden, absent, insubstantial way, for they represent in another guise the selfsame problematic as that found in the "hermeneutic 'as'" of the wife's namings analyzed above, the same problematic that Kenneth Burke calls the "paradox of substance."[47] To really gauge the depth of *Frost's* insight here, therefore, we would do well to recover briefly what these expressions mean.

For Heidegger, we recall, the mode of Being of Dasein is never a completed or pure presence, inasmuch as a person's essence is dissolved into the ongoing recovery in time (repetition by means of resolute Care) of past, absent possibilities. As finite, in other words, we are never whole. As a "project" whose meaning and Being are oriented toward the future, Dasein "is" its Care for its "ownmost" possibilities within the indeterminacy of its temporal existence. This indeterminacy Heidegger at times calls "abyss" *(Abgrund)* and "nothingness" *(Nichtigkeit)* (*BT* 194/152, 331/285). A similar (though hardly identical) argument is advanced by Burke: Because (in the first place) any attempt to speak of man's essence or substance entails the paradoxical need to speak of it in terms of what it is not (including, at the extreme, what it is "most" not, that is, "Nothing"), and because all of that which man is not is virtually infinite, any attempt to name this substance once and for all is impossible, forever deferred (in this way Burke deconstructs the traditional philosophic category of "substance" quite in the spirit, at least, of *Being and Time;* and in this manner Kierkegaard speaks of the "paradox" of the eternal in the finite that is the Incarnation). The vertigo that such a recognition can bring on Burke too associates with an "abyss": "however important to us is the tiny sliver of reality each of us has experienced firsthand, the overall picture is but a construct of our symbol systems. To meditate on this fact until one sees its

full implications is much like peering over the edge of things into an ultimate abyss."[48]

The figure of the abyss, then, as both a linguistic and an ontological empty place, not located at the end but *within* existence ("It flows between us, over us, and *with* us"; line 53; my emphasis) is a commonplace for Heidegger and Burke—as it was also for the romantics and is also for Frost, for whom existence "runs away / To fill the *abyss's* void" (lines 48–49; my emphasis).[49] Yet the message from each of these thinkers is not simply suspicious and deconstructive, not an endless deferral of meaning or Being; it is restorative. That is, while man's indeterminacy (linguistic, ontological) is an "infinite" openness to the new (in Frost, "the white water rode the black *forever*"; line 21), it is no less inseparably bound to man's finite, historical possibilities (hence existence "seriously, sadly *runs away*"; line 47). To exist is thus to take up again in time (to appropriate) and to become (to apply) one's own possibilities—it is the repetition, the retrieval, man achieves in understanding and interpreting (including, to be sure, the poet's own retrieval of literary precedents for further use).[50]

Some of the latent difficulty of this passage, and of the problem with which Frost is wrestling, is rightly perceived by Brower in his noting that "Frost . . . finds no easy classification for the essential character of what is."[51] In all ways, of course, this conclusion accords with Heidegger's essential point that no classifications (in the strict sense) of Being are even possible, never mind easy. Brower's assessment is in keeping also with our earlier characterizations of Fred's discourse as a message about, and exemplification of, the instability at the heart of naming and being. What this means is not that Frost is floundering in his attempt to express an elusive Being, but that he is succeeding in expressing the elusiveness of Being.[52] We ourselves, therefore, ought to try to follow Fred/Frost in considering several of his other classifications, namely, those of death ("the universal cataract of death / That spends to nothingness"; lines 56–57), time, and darkness/light, three further perspectives of Frost's discussion that can be seen to implicate each other.

The importance of death as a "no-thingness" in Heidegger's discussion of the Being of Dasein cannot be overestimated, for, as one commentator has put it, "In death man sees the possibility of his not being and thereby alone death introduces the element of possibility into Dasein."[53] What Heidegger chiefly has in mind when he speaks of death in this way is not that "ontic," "factical" death whose signature marks the end of a life, though factical death is of course the necessary point of departure for his thought. Much less should death be taken to be some intrinsic degenerative process in life itself. Rather, what is intended is the fact that only in death does a person recognize just what "possibility" is, for only in death resides the possibility of not-being, the possibility of no-possibility, of nothingness. It is this recognition that makes death not an unfortunate extraneous "end" tacked onto, but an omnipresent revelatory structure within, life itself.

Now Frost, too, like Heidegger, treats death and its relation to being (and to time) in just this way. That is, Frost is not speaking here chiefly of death as that mere empirical ("ontic") end of a life, though it is naturally that also, nor does he intend death as some dark "nothing" tacked onto an otherwise bright "something" (existence) at the end, as if it were either an unfortunate cessation of activities or the bittersweet, inevitable term of life's wearing out. Rather, Frost asserts that somehow, paradoxically, the "cataract of death" just "is" existence itself (lines 54–56) or at least inextricably part of its flow, and that both death and existence in turn somehow just are "time" (as well as "strength, tone, light, life, love"). The suggestion is not ontic but ontological: death signals that nothingness within which all our naming and doing appear (all our light, life, and love), embracing this very nothingness (this death, this abyss) as the very possibility of being and time.

The real challenge in following Frost here and throughout the poem is to hold on to this play of contraries—existence/death, time/out-of-time, possibility/nothingness. Frank Lentricchia, for example, has noticed the tension in life/death but has one-sidedly construed it as a mere "maneuver of wit" conjured up by Frost to "relieve" the alleged "philosophic darkness" of the poet's thought: "Existence does not simply flow over the edge of fullness into the abyss of emptiness—that would be bad enough. The flux of existence is itself generative of nothingness," and again we are to understand this as one more of the miseries of life. Actually the "darkness" here for Lentricchia is twofold: (1) time itself is an "unrepeatable flow . . . that saddens," and, worse, (2) there is an "emptiness within the core of substance, the emptiness within love that binds [the couple]." Indeed, for Lentricchia, "darkness" here "has no equal in Frost," though presumably it is akin to that "design of darkness to appall" that Frost elsewhere has it in him to scare us with[54] (perhaps Lentricchia is thinking unqualifiedly of Job's remarks in *A Masque of Reason*—"I hold rays deteriorate to nothing: / First white, then red, then ultrared, then out" [lines 345–46]).

The problem with such a reading, and with the other readings of this passage more or less like it, is that they do not square with what Frost says and does. True as far as they go, they do not go far enough; they let fall that imaginative holding-in-tension Frost achieves and seeks to impart. Aside from the obvious objection that such "wit" could hardly be said to relieve something purportedly so dark (and, in fact, it is this "maneuver" of Frost's wit that makes the passage so "dark" in the first place, though not so dark as Lentricchia alleges)—aside from this objection, we must consider a more substantive difficulty with such a reading. While it is true, as Lentricchia says, that empirical clock time passes away, and true also that it is sad that it does so ("It seriously, sadly runs away"; line 48), nevertheless, by "time" in this passage Frost does not chiefly mean clock time, that series of discrete passing nows that, in passing, darken our lives until death ends it all. Brower makes this same error when he notes that "our life as measured by

the clock, by time, seems to be passing out of existence" (though he too would lessen the darkness by noting, "but its passing makes the clock go, gives the clock something to measure)."[55] The correction to make here is not that clock time is not passing and is not part of Frost's meaning, but that empirical time is inadequate to the extended uses of terms like "abyss," "emptiness," "death," and "time." We should rather say that, as with the concept of "death," which referred in part to an empirical end but more deeply to the omnipresent fact of "possibility/no possibility" resident throughout life itself, so "time" includes empirical, "ontic" clock time but aims more deeply at the omnipresence of past, present, and future as we find it most notably in the concept of "retrieval." As Brower has put this last point, "Although he [Frost] talks of 'the beginning of beginnings' as back in time, he is also talking of a 'beginning' that is always present, a primary form of being."[56] (We shall see that this holds also for time future.) In short, ontic clock time must be held in tension with ontological "temporality."

It follows from this more philosophical reading that any "philosophic darkness" must be held in tension with "philosophic light," precisely as Frost himself indicates that it should: "And it is time, strength, tone, *light*, life, and love" (line 54; my emphasis). Although this light does not snuff out the darkness, the darkness cannot (as Lentricchia confidently claims) be worse than, it cannot be the same as or even be equal to, that "design of darkness to appall" we find elsewhere in Frost. And far from time's being "unrepeatable," as Lentricchia also claims, time is our "light" precisely because it *is* repeatable, by virtue of what we have called retrieval. Thus darkness and light together constitute retrieval,[57] for it is only by virtue of absence ("emptiness" [line 49], "death," "abyss," "nothingness") that we exist "as" a possibility that can be temporally retrieved, since any claim for pure presence chokes off just that possibility of possibility. In Heidegger's terms, there would be no clearing *(Lichtung)* within which beings could come to be.

To state it this way is to explain how the "stream of everything" that is existence is also at the same time a "substance lapsing unsubstantial" (line 55). It should be clear by now that this lapsing is not an occasional falling off or wearing away, much less the terminus for the flow of life; it is the emptiness resident within, and thus partly constitutive of, life itself. As Kierkegaard has said, "Whatever is in a process of becoming is in a state of alternation between being and non-being."[58] It is this paradox that is also for Frost intrinsic to symbolic "naming"—the paradox that indeterminacy (insubstantiality, absence) attends all our positive definitions—and in so doing makes man's Being-as-possibility possible. Such "lapsing" is a continual playing of contraries that is also a mode of being in the world. The anxiety *(Angst)* this creates in human beings Frost even seems to capture in the "panic" (line 52) the couple feels in the (momentary but no doubt recurring) recognition of their separateness-in-unity and in the momentary disorientation of the wife at the beginning of the poem. Nor does Fred's speech

seek to do away with their panic. On the contrary, Fred/Frost turns anxiety this way and that, variously figuring the direction in which it points (abyss, emptiness, death, nothingness, but also "time, strength, tone, light, love"), and in so doing strengthens the couple's resolve not to flee but to exist within, even to be part of, anxiety's grasp and loss. The Being of Dasein, after all, just is its resolute Care in that deeper sense Heidegger gives the term, and this arises only in anxiety. Care, moreover, is not unconnected to that promise to love and to cherish that the couple vowed when they married and that here perhaps they can be said implicitly to vow again in their marriage to the brook: "The figure is the same for love. No one can really hold that the ecstasy should be static and stand still in one place" (*SP* 18).

This conceit of the wedding vow, though not at all far-fetched, nevertheless does not quite reach the larger question of the Being of human beings, and perhaps of all beings, nor does it enable us to explain "what" gets retrieved in the couple's actions and in the poem as a whole—retrieved by, and for, the characters, but retrieved also by Frost for us, his readers (and shall we further say, retrieved by us readers from Frost, one of our sources?). To determine this, we need to turn to the poem's final section (lines 72–75) and its further thematization of time.

## Time and Being

"Today will be the day …"

In the third and final section of the poem (lines 72–75), the husband and wife continue to counter each other by vying over how to "name" the day. After Fred has finished his disquisition on the past, the wife responds, "Today will be the day / You said so." The husband retorts: "No, today will be the day / You said the brook was called West-Running Brook." And the wife, compromising, and closing (for now) the hermeneutic circle she was the one to open, concludes: "Today will be the day of what we both said" (line 75). Bracketing for a moment the evident importance these two place on their various namings, we are in a position to see that the hidden (and neglected) feature of these lines is their orientation to the future ("will be"), an orientation wholly in keeping with our analysis of the symbolic—the human—value of the brook "as" temporal disclosure ahead-of-itself, in possibility. In other words, what is being asserted at this place in the poem is what has been enacted (by the reader) throughout, namely, that a time will come when the couple will retrieve this day as a set of significant possibilities for future namings.

Before we can understand why these namings on this day should be considered so significant as to merit the couple's retrieving them in some unspecified future, we would do well to reflect on the fact that this orientation to the future of the couple at the end of the poem has already been countered, as it were, by the reader's own orientation to the past at the beginning. Not unlike the "circuitous

journey" of Wordsworth's *Prelude* or Proust's *A la recherche du temps perdu*, "West-Running Brook" looks forward at the end to the event that we readers engage at its beginning, namely, our own retrieval of what has been said by the couple in the past. Said otherwise, the present "now" at the beginning of our reading makes definite the indefinite "future" of the couple projected at the end, since the narrator in line 3 ("West-Running Brook men call it to this day") has placed the day of the couple's naming indefinitely in the past. In this way, the poem itself is a retrieval of their past, and one in which the reader is invited to participate—that is, to take up as significant the couple's set of namings (but namings of what?) for his or her own edification, in the way the couple intend to do at the poem's end. "In my beginning is my end," wrote Eliot in *East Coker*; and again in *Burnt Norton:* "Time present and time past / Are both perhaps present in time future / And time future in time past." In Gadamerian terms, what the wife anticipates for her husband and herself at the end is a "fusion of horizons," of their own (projected) future and their (now-present but then) past, a fusion the likes of which we readers enact now in retrieving the past horizons of characters and poem. This retrieval, our own interpretation-as-application/appropriation, itself fuses our presentness with our own past-future in the act of interpretation, and from this perspective, the beginning of the poem closes (thus counters) the hermeneutic circle opened in anticipation at the end—and vice versa. And each, in addition, is equally a going by contraries with a backward motion toward the source, that is, a retrieval.

But what, finally, is retrieved? It would be comforting to say simply either that (1) in the mimesis that is the poem, in the poem as "just-so story," the couple becomes clearer to us as people because they retrieve some aspect of themselves, some possibility that we ourselves can appropriate "equipmentally" (as Heidegger would say); or that (2) not only the couple but we readers retrieve a philosophic truth, some sort of doctrine hitherto overlooked by ourselves and others ("Some say . . . But . . ."), that we can also then use as "equipment for living" (as Burke would say). In fact, both of these conclusions are true as far as they go. Paradoxically (but not unexpectedly), however, the inadequacy of these accounts of what we may have retrieved lies in their very clarity, in the stability of their formulation. What has been retrieved, we have learned, is not stable, cannot be self-transparent, precisely because it is not a "what" at all. As Frost said of a similar search for Being in "For Once, Then, Something": "Water came to rebuke the too-clear water." On the other hand, what we retrieve is not merely the opposite of clarity, not merely opaqueness and confusion. It is rather the tension of unconcealment/concealment, of presence/absence, of stability-instability: what we have retrieved is the very fact of indeterminacy and instability itself, of being-in-the-world "as" change, flux, motion, "west-running," the "universal cataract of death" that is also and no less (equiprimordially) "time, strength, tone, light, life, and love."

We require, therefore, a way to discuss "what" has been retrieved in terms of a "how" enacted by characters and author as we read. As Willard Spiegelman has put it, "Teaching, in the final analysis, does not take a direct object: the poets teach us how."[59] In Frost's words, "The breathless swing is between subject matter and form"—"breathless" precisely because inspiration and expiration (death) are in equipoise.[60] From this perspective, we might speculate that what is repeated or retrieved in "West-Running Brook" are possibilities for naming self and world, where "possibilities" and "naming" are not self-contained concepts or doctrines so much as malleable, dynamic "re-sources," and that whatever we readers come to name our own selves and our own worlds is not to be abstracted from our own situations of naming. We listen, analogically, through these fictions and figures to our own situations, and we learn how.

Thus, while it may be admitted that we do get some sort of philosophic truth about naming and being, still it cannot be as a determinate ("apophantic") doctrine that we do so. The very lesson Frost has pursued is that, finally, we cannot name the source (Being) at all, or at least not once and for all! The reason is that the source is that "behind" us, as it were, that which is unreachable; yet it is also that which sustains us and that within which we move and have our being ("'It flows over us. It flows between us'"; "'It flows between us, over us, and or *with* us'"; lines 51, 53). Being is not some fixed tableau suitable for conceptual framing but an ongoing mode of acting and interpreting, never fully disclosed in the storytelling (and reading) that constitutes our own lives. It is flux, it is "west-running" in the very moment we are reaching back for it. Hermeneutically said, it is that horizon of understanding that is also our preunderstanding of Being. As John Caputo once put it, "The horizon within which Dasein moves about is its understanding of its own Being (and of Being in general), an understanding *(Verstehen)* which does not get to be a concept *(Begriff)*, which remains anonymous, even though its effects are felt in every corner of our experience."[61]

"Does not get to be a concept," "remains anonymous"—this is exactly the kind of "contrary" conclusion we have learned to expect from so hermeneutically adept a poet as Frost, and exactly the justification for Fred's/Frost's (though not for the critics') indeterminateness about "the beginning of beginnings." Later Frost will quip, "We dance around in a ring and suppose, / But the Secret sits in the middle and knows."[62] This ability of ours to "suppose" is just our opportunity to retrieve the Secret. But we can retrieve it only "as" a figure, a supposition—an image, character, metaphor, narrative, or naming whose essence is that going by contraries that we have learned to associate with the mode of Being of our own being—with change, adaptation to circumstances and audience, openness to the novel and indeterminate, and the playful opportunism that seizes the unique qualities of this moment: "[Our] hermeneutic forestructures [of understanding] then are 'guided and regulated' by this preunderstanding [of Being]. Their role is

to explicate it, and bring it out into the open, to give it explicit, thematic shape where previously it remained anonymous and pre-thematic. The work of hermeneutics is *aus-legen, ex-poenere,* to lay out in the sense of drawing out into the open, to make explicit what we all already understand."[63]

For Frost, as for Heidegger, this is the proper work of poetry: "The figure a poem makes. It begins in delight and ends in wisdom. The figure is the same as for love ... a momentary stay against confusion" (*SP* 18).[64] It is a "momentary" stay, both because all namings/retrievals are momentary, finite, situated, thus rhetorically "strategic" in Burke's phrase; and because in poetry, as in all hermeneutic insight, everything comes down to the moment of vision, to what the later Heidegger called *Ereignis,* "where being as a philosophical concept is effaced and rethought as 'the event of appropriation'"[65] and "re-cognition": "A knowing again, renewing our primordial acquaintance with ourselves. Everything comes down to our capacity for retrieval and repetition; there is no proving and disproving in hermeneutics but only a self-examination, a self-discovery, in which we find ourselves in the account or fail to do so."[66]

As doctrine, then, poetry generally and "West-Running Brook" in particular are empty.[67] But as a place for "actional thought" (for situated interpretation and appropriation of self and world), it is precisely as indeterminate and empty that Fred's conclusion is valuable, indeed something that merits retrieval. But note that this is a retrieval of the truth of Being-as-concrete-possibility—that is, for us, the retrieval of our own Being through the concrete beings of the characters and poem, as selves who name themselves and world: as interpretive beings. And if we as readers are genuinely to retrieve *this* truth and not merely to parrot the same in imitation of Fred/Frost, then what we retrieve cannot be abstract paraphrase or doctrinal summary of the poem as critics have offered in the past, but a "no-*thing,*" rather a personally appropriated activity of retrieval-of-possibility through the very retrievals of the characters and author in the poem. Here form and content fuse together and work by contraries: the couple presents an exemplum of a thesis, whose enactment (in form) of temporal perspectivism (message) prevents us from reifying either the story or the message. Rather, we take on a hermeneutic equipment for living in living through the totality of the poem. We learn, in effect, analogical, metaphorical extensions of what has (and has not) been: "It wasn't, yet it was."

"West-Running Brook" thus opens up an absence that is a momentary presence, a topos or null set that is not meaningless (nor merely equivocal) but the space of meaningfulness. It is the moment of vision that is also the moment of poetic-rhetorical invention (*inventio*)—rhetorical as well as poetic because Frost as poet faces the problem of "how" to communicate the activity—the "how" of naming and retrieving—to a finite, situated, historical audience. It is to this problem that we turn as a way of encompassing and closing our own hermeneutic retrieval.

## Poetry, Rhetoric, Truth

Lawrance Thompson has said of Frost that "he often prefers to reveal-conceal some of his most intimate and personal beliefs through poetic indirections"—which is to say that Frost is often most present when he is seemingly absent, a point Poirier has observed also works in reverse: "he is likely never to be more absent than when he sounds most assertively and publicly present."[68] It has been the argument of this chapter that "West-Running Brook" is a culminative enactment of these themes of presence-and-absence, of concealment-and-unconcealment, indeed of the truth that truth itself, like Being, essentially escapes the concept of a stable essence, that it is, in Heidegger's words, "a presence sheltered in absence."[69] In noting these similarities between Heidegger and Frost's critics, however, we ought not to underplay their differences. When Thompson and Poirier, for example, speak of absence and presence, their emphasis is on the self of Frost, on the poet as expressive agent.[70] Poirier is interested in the ways in which the poet, like the child, comes to play with the multiple possible ways in which "objects" (things, people, events) can be constituted—in short, with the "conflict of interpretations." (In a similar way, Lentricchia focuses on the way the poet creates what Stevens called "supreme fictions.") By contrast, in his later work Heidegger sees the truth of poetry as the gift of Language, of Being itself, and not the expressive (much less fictive) powers of the poet's mere self.

While both of these positions—that of Frost's critics as well as that of Heidegger—reveal something important about Frost's poetics, they conceal something equally central, namely, the rhetorical, communicative, and educative dimensions of Frost's work. On the one hand, without needing to deny that the poet creates "fictions," or that these fictions help to constitute what we think is real (in this way Poirier extends and corrects Lentricchia), we need to remember to explore how the poet creates with and among and for others. This is the very point of D. W. Winnicott's object-relations theory that Poirier employs in other ways to illuminate Frost, namely, that the self is a "field of selves," as Wayne Booth puts it, or in Heidegger's phrase, that Dasein is always "with others" *(das Mitdasein der Anderen).*[71] Thus the various retrievals portrayed, enacted, and taught in "West-Running Brook" are aimed at readers who are invited, even required, to appropriate them as abilities (and not only objective doctrines or concepts) and as members of communities (even if ostensibly only of two, as in marriage).

On the other hand, without needing to deny that Being is not controllable by man ("It flows between us, *over* us, and *with* us"; line 53; first emphasis mine), still we need to remember to explore what Heidegger also did remember though not develop, that all namings of beings are historically situated, humanly locatable,[72] and therefore subject to ideological forces and ideological analysis. Frost himself seems unwilling to go so far as Heidegger in stressing the otherness of Being and

even concentrates on the Being of *human* beings, that is, on naming human beings as the "naming being" (we see this concentration also in "Directive," "For Once, Then, Something," and numerous other poems). The retrievals in "West-Running Brook" remain human resources for the couple and for us readers, whereas the later Heidegger leaves behind the notion of retrieval altogether, and even of the poem in its own right, in favor of an almost mystical moment of "appropriation" of man by Being. In this regard, Frost stands closer to Kierkegaard, a thinker for whom communication was of paramount importance (and especially "indirect communication," as in Thompson's point about Frost's indirections quoted above), and we can conclude of Frost, the philosophical poet, what has been said of Kierkegaard, the poetic philosopher: "Kierkegaard's writings, as a presentation of possibility, are at once poetry and rhetoric."[73] Here poetry, rhetoric, and philosophy-as-hermeneutic combine in the truthful enactment of possibilities for naming that is "West-Running Brook."

In keeping with this neglected insight into Frost as communicator and rhetorician—one who resists romantic expressivism and transcendentalizing in favor of a nonessentialist account of self and Being, and Heidegger's postromantic elevation of Being over man in favor of man's naming of being, and does so precisely by holding these (and other pairs) in tension—it is useful to think of Frost's performance as the use and even thematization of rhetorical devices for achieving in the reader, not persuasion per se, much less religious conversion (as in Kierkegaard), but rather an attitude of questioning, of exploring (as rhetoricians are trained to do) "both sides of the case," those possibilities for naming self, other, world, even Being. More or less hidden in their obviousness throughout the poem are the forms and activities of dialogue, of rhetorical questions, of competing genres of the characters' discourses, of the characters' activities of naming and retrieving as "exempla," and of the rhetorical "question" of the poem as a whole: namely, What is it, to be? We may recall that Brower has hinted that in Frost's "Masques" of Reason and Mercy, the poet retrieved the didactic habits and strategies of Renaissance rhetoricians.[74] I propose here, with respect now to "West-Running Brook," that what Joel B. Altman has to say about the rhetorical "Tudor play of mind," for example, speaks directly to Frost's own seriocomic aims: "The [Elizabethan] plays functioned as media of intellectual and emotional exploration for minds that were accustomed to examine the many sides of a given theme, to entertain opposing ideals, and by so exercising the understanding, to move toward some fuller apprehension of truth that could be discerned only through the total action of the drama. Thus the experience of the play was the thing." Frost's own circumspective "circumnavigation of the topic" of Being by means of a dialogic play between characters, viewpoints ("Some say . . . but"), modes of saying, naming, and thinking, and his thematization of the rhetorical theme of *inventio*, of persuasive naming—all of these are of an "explorative character, one

that teaches and delights by examining through *exempla* which engage the emotions the diverse existential claims that govern human life."[75]

Much more remains to be explored regarding Frost's rhetorical-philosophical poems, not the least of which is the fact that the various governing pairs of terms in a work like "West-Running Brook"—substance/nonsubstance, presence/absence, man/woman, east/west, and many others—can be seen to function as open-ended, even relatively "empty" rhetorical topics that delimit meaningful possibilities for discursive action. By analogically taking up the topical drift, as it were, of these terms, by stepping into the gaps they open, the reader is taught to appropriate, to retrieve, his or her own possibilities for naming.

Yet just this notion of topical drift, and the complacency of mind that the phrase can imply, lead me to conclude the present chapter in a way that may be truer to the spirit (if not the performance) of "West-Running Brook" than any simple acceptance of its "ideology," as we may wish to call it when we turn in some degree to resist it. What we would resist is not what Frost says about resistance and naming as constitutive components of (human) being; these I believe we should and even, epistemologically, must follow. Rather, we would resist what Frost does not say, or what he fails to say and the manner in which he says what he does say and does what he says—in short, his too-sanguine demonstration of his own, as well as others', rhetoricity. In fact, it may be objected that the present chapter, in agreeing to play Frost's rhetorical-hermeneutic game, is equally guilty of Poirier's charge against Frost: complacency of mind and attitude (and extrapolating from this), untroubledness of view, seeming self-transparency of motives, a claim for pure self-presence—in short, just the beliefs the poem demonstrates against but, perhaps, unknowingly practices. This charge is a commonplace in the resistance to Gadamer's own complacent invocation of "tradition" and "application" in hermeneutic theory as it is to Heidegger's starry-eyed removal of the poet from his or her historical time and place.

Nor is it difficult to locate, as Poirier began to do, persuasive arguments for some such critique of the poem: the sheer inadequacy of Frost's using the play, and the playful banter, of a young married couple to convey the seriousness, even the horror, of death, absence, concealment, and the abyss of naming; Frost's failure to include in his "demonstration" how hermeneutic consciousness can be (invariably is) constrained and even systematically distorted by social, economic, and other extraverbal determinants; Frost's self-satisfied tone at the end of the poem (in the wife's admiring "Today will be the day of what we both said"); Frost's oftentimes narrow political commitments to individuals apart from larger communities and their histories; and so on.

Such critique could, I think, be performed to good effect. Without falling into a reductive dismissal of the poem's hidden complexities, still we might agree with, and profitably explore, Poirier's complaints about "complacency." But if we

are inspired to resist the poem and the poet, we must not lose sight of the fact that it is "West-Running Brook" that has invited us and helped teach us to resist, that it is Frost's own rhetorical consciousness teaching us to undo any undue stabilities in the poem itself. Though "West-Running Brook" may not on analysis take us anywhere far enough—at least not far enough "forward" (as some today might put it) into new and concrete thought about praxis (especially political praxis) to satisfy the contemporary hunger for worldly action—still the poem does, I believe, take us deeply down and back into our sources and philosophic origins as human beings, opening up by its own action a space within which we can, for now, imperfectly, name who we are, and reminding us that only some such actional thought about our sources will sufficiently resist and restrain that west-running current (*Zug*) toward absorption in things, that "falling" that calls forth mankind's "sending up" (line 63) from somewhere below, if only "a little."

CHAPTER

# 7

# GIVING EVIDENCE AND MAKING EVIDENT
*Civility and Madness in "Snow" (Proof)*

> Let us not take it for granted that life exists more fully in what is commonly thought big than what is commonly thought small.
>
> —Virginia Woolf, "Modern Fiction"

A SORT OF self-indulgence, as it might be called, in which readers and critics frequently engage in their interpretations of Frost's dramatic dialogues, is their presuming to know ahead of time how to speak the language spoken there. It is an obvious danger if you think about it, one that they, one that *we*, might have thought ourselves less susceptible to embracing. It is as though, having lived a long time among the people who inhabit "The Black Cottage," "The Fear," "A Servant to Servants," "The Death of the Hired Man," "West-Running Brook," "The Code," what we had learned from these works is not how Frost casually mixes the hidden in the obvious, the strange in the ordinary in unique combinations in each, but merely the obvious fact that all of these folks speak English—obvious, as if we know everything we need to know about speaking English. We seem naïvely to have concluded from our encounters with some of Frost's neighbors that they will all answer our questions readily so long as we treat them with civility, assuming, again, that we already speak their language and know what will count as civil. Theoretical contentment with thin descriptions of poems like "The Death of the Hired Man" or "West-Running Brook" suggests that we cannot very well be heeding their author's stated aim to look obvious yet be difficult.[1] Worse is our having allowed ourselves to fall critically silent altogether, in effect to have fallen asleep over a dialogue like "Snow" as though the poem speaks for itself. Even the most successful of Frost's critics have no more than glanced at this poem in the reflected glare, amounting to a blindness, from other Frost poems they prefer. Though it may be true that "Snow" fails to measure up to Frost's best dramatic monologues and dialogues, still at any moment we meet with designs as wrought as a million snowflakes to take our breath away, while the poem as a whole is bemused at the self-complacency of our critical posturing. Yet to my knowledge no one in more than eighty years has written even a single article-length study of this poem.[2]

The reasons for this neglect are not obvious. Consider our American impatience with philosophy in general, our traditional moral naïveté and self-righteousness, our utilitarian progressivism, and our abiding sense of cultural inferiority to Europe, and we begin to grasp why sitting at the feet of the home-grown and low has not been something the cultured among us have rushed home to do. From this angle we begin to understand why Meserve's midnight visitation to the Coles has about it something of the uncanny, what Freud described as the return of the repressed familiar.[3]

Like Emerson and Thoreau, Frost himself bemuses the sophisticated, who nevertheless are willing to concede his genius for form, while he becalms general readers, some of whom, in spite of themselves, remain haunted by his poems years after learning them in school. By "haunted" I am alluding only indirectly to Lionel Trilling's discussion of Frost as a "terrifying" poet, since that particular line of thought has more or less been absorbed, at least by those in the know.[4] I am directly alluding rather to a rhetorical mind and method that puzzles even while it impresses. As argued throughout this book, Frost's mind and method are the first to create an alternative American low modernist lyric composed from everyday conversational materials taken for granted by everyone else. These materials and methods are steeped in the conventions of the ordinary, in our form of life and its emerging and disappearing common sense, whose grammar and logic and dialectic have been rhetoricized in a thoroughly modern manner. What remains to be explored is how distinctly rhetorical principles of thought and sensibility give shape and direction to Frost's logic or proof, in particular to his art as argument by example.

That this poem is a dramatic dialogue open to the familiar and ordinary is, of course, obvious. Less obvious is that "Snow" is itself a rhetorical investigation of the ordinary, and not least the ordinary language of Meserve and of Helen and Fred Cole. I am not claiming that distinctions between literature and philosophy, or ordinary language in everyday life and ordinary language in poetry, are otiose (much less odious). On the contrary, I am trying once more to make specific sense of what it means to call Frost a philosophic poet. The task is to sound the depths of Frost's philosophic register and to get clearer about how he thought those depths are expressed in a literary language beholden to everyday conversation suffused with rhetorical tactics and strategic appeals.

Thus we need to account for, among other matters: the poem's dramatic occasion, a midnight visitation; the characters' interpretive and persuasive conversational habits and skills; the rhetorical effects of time, place, personae, situation, and context on what is said, including what may have gone unsaid or unheard, or what remains unthought in the words of Meserve and his wife, and of Helen and Fred Cole; the simultaneous unbounded banality and controlled fantasticality of Meserve's rambling, its uncanniness; Helen Cole's polite incivility and Meserve's

uncivil enthusiasm and playful posturing; above all, Frost's requirement that readers read the everyday as exemplary. Much as Thoreau does in *Walden*, Frost in "Snow" offers ambiguous images of the outsider as neighbor-antagonist to question what it means to be—and, more important, to test and strengthen our *capacity* to be—"understanding" and "civil."⁵

## A Momentary Stay

We know in general that in designing such matters, Frost winks at us a good deal. We have also had occasion to discover that we are not always accomplished at saying specifically when. The question here is how it is helpful to say that "Snow" as a whole can be taken as, seen as, just such a rhetorical-hermeneutic wink, at once a promise of, and a making-good on, unsuspected meanings in words right in our faces. It would hardly be Frost's first such hint of fooling around in this way, for he had said of no fewer than seven of the fifteen poems in his previous book, *North of Boston*, that they were "almost humorous—four are almost jokes."⁶ Is it accidental that the highest condition to which Frost aspired as a poet—that his poems achieve what he termed "a momentary stay against confusion" (formulated possibly in reaction to Matthew Arnold's claim that "in poetry our race, as time goes on, will find ever surer and surer stay")—is just the situation portrayed, dramatized, in "Snow"?

Consider how the fundamentalist preacher Meserve is forced one middle of the night to the farm of his neighbors, the Coles, in a momentary stay from a blinding snowstorm. By the time the poem opens, Meserve has been there awhile, talking no doubt; then he phones ahead to alert his wife that he's late and on his way (lines 11–30). Helen Cole half-fears Meserve's losing his way, *dying*, in the deep snow, but her several pleas that he stay where he is, like those of Meserve's wife in lines 19 to 27, seem to fall on deaf ears. Meserve talks at some length to the Coles about this and that (111–240), then abruptly departs. And Helen and Fred are reawakened by a call hours later from Meserve's wife, worried over his whereabouts and somehow blaming the Coles. As it happens, Meserve arrives at this time, reporting back that he's home safe and sound. And the drama, such as it is, closes with comments by the Coles as ordinary as those with which it began.

If my account is understated, it cannot be by much, for the narrative details are equally unprepossessing. But then the obviousness, the characteristic plainness of the story, may be providing just the sort of scene necessary for our considering Frost's movements a knowing wink. And its details, rightly taken, might give us more than sufficient reason to think that the entire piece is under the influence of his winkfulness. On this slant, "Snow" would not be a joke or prank in Frost's sense so much as a Wittgensteinian game or Gadamerian play, a performance in which the attempted back-and-forth drama of the characters is taken up and

completed in the event of interpretation by the reader, in an unfolding engagement with what had hitherto been unseen or unheard possibilities for meaning and being. If "Snow" dramatizes one of Frost's central poetic nostrums ("a momentary stay against confusion"), its weight on us is belied by the fact that it looks as weightless and blameless as driven snow. In fact, no one, it seems, has noticed much of anything going on amidst all those falling flakes.[7] We will have to *listen* more alertly (the poem begins, after all, "The three stood listening"; line 1), listening for what Frost's faithful wink might indicate is present in the benighted absences of "Snow." For the poem is both a complex rhetorical transaction among its characters and also Frost's attempt at cultural and ethical (even, obliquely, religious) transformation of the reader.

## Reminding

When we do look and listen, we may be reminded again of Wittgenstein, who speaks to the kind of paradox registered in this and many other Frost poems: "The aspects of things that are most important for us are hidden because of their simplicity and familiarity. (One is unable to notice something—because it is always before one's eyes.)" (*PI* § 139).[8] Wittgenstein's particular concern is with questioning how ordinary language functions when not abstracted from the language games that are its original home. This philosophical impulse to redeem or release ordinary language from the grip of philosophical reifications ("bewitchments"; *PI* § 109) is intended to release our lives as well as our words. Cavell, similarly, notes that "Thoreau is doing with ordinary assertions what Wittgenstein does with our more patently philosophical assertions—bringing them back [home] to a context in which they are alive" (*SW* 92). But Cavell also hears that the particular way Thoreau, in *Walden*, returns our words home is by taking us ordinary speakers away from home, estranging his voice from our words to make evident the routinization of our own lives: "Thoreau's withdrawal is more elaborately dramatized [than Emerson's], its rebuke more continuous. . . . the writer who inhabits *[Walden]* asserts the priority of writing over speaking (at least for the present) in order to maintain silence, where this means first of all to withhold his voice, his consent, from society. Hence the entire book is an act of civil disobedience, a confrontation which takes the form of a withdrawal" (*Themes* 50). This same self-exile homeward is available in "Snow" only when we recall that Frost has also beckoned us readers *away* from home, *north* of Boston, while Meserve spins the Coles out of the tired orbit of their ways, which is to say into the uncanniness (*Unheimlichkeit*, the "not-at-home-ness") of a madness whose method is a patient and civil disobedience.

From this perspective, many of the specific Wittgensteinian themes that Cavell finds in Thoreau and Emerson are found in Frost's philosophical impulse

to quest for and redeem the ordinary in all of its senses, especially in the rhetorical situatedness of ordinary speech and action. Cavell asks: "Does the writer of *Walden* really believe that the manner in which one conducts one's affairs can redeem their external meanness—that, for example, one could find one's Walden behind a bank counter, or driving a taxi, or guiding a trip hammer, or selling insurance, or teaching school?" (*SW* 110). The perhaps not-so-obvious answer is "Yes." When Frost was similarly asked whether he wouldn't like it if some foundation or other underwrote a year at Walden Pond, he cannily responded: "To qualify as a good Thorosian I might well offer them in reply some good reasons for staying where I am [at home] in Vermont and refusing the chance to go anywhere else" (*Interviews* 143). "Walden" seems to be where you find it, or make it.

Wittgenstein insists that redemption from external meanness is not to be achieved, in philosophizing as in everyday living, by what he calls explanation, meaning empirical theorizing about concrete cases, which attitude is a pretty good gloss on what Frost means when he urges that "the poet's instinct is to shun or shed more knowledge than he can swing or sing" (*SP* 50). Wittgenstein turns instead to description, to directing our attention to the deep conceptual patterns of linguistic surfaces in imagined actions and scenes, stabilizing causal propositionalism in what we know how to do and which we already acknowledge. Further, this method of description is available in a different form to the poet as much as to the philosopher or literary critic, in fact to any thoughtful, rightly disposed speaker, as Meserve himself demonstrates. Wittgensteinian description occupies the same continuum as Geertz's thick description of something so deceptively superficial as a cockfight. So that, when Wittgenstein boasts, "What is hidden . . . is of no interest to us" (*PI* § 127), he, like the others mentioned, returns the erudite and recondite to those hidden depths on the surface of a language or culture or pond, the deep play that Frost called a poet's style and that constitutes part of what we are calling its grammar and rhetoric. For Wittgenstein also says: "The problems arising through a misinterpretation of our forms of language have the character of depth" (*PI* § 111), a statement akin to Frost's belief that the poet's "depth is the lightsome blue depth of air" (*SP* 50) before our upturned faces, right in front of our eyes, and to William Carlos Williams's claim that "the thing that stands eternally in the way of really good writing is always one: the virtual impossibility of lifting to the imagination those things which lie under the direct scrutiny of the senses, close to the nose."[9]

Hence Thoreau's pun, "Will you be a reader, a student merely, or a seer?" a question we need to read as a commentary on Emerson's familiar lines from "The American Scholar": "I embrace the common, I explore and sit at the feet of the familiar, the low."[10] When we learn in the *Investigations* that "philosophy simply puts everything before us, and neither explains nor deduces anything.—Since

everything lies open to view there is nothing to explain" (*PI* § 126), we are hard put to find a more apt account of Frost's own rhetorical method in the dramatic dialogues and many of the lyrics. Wittgenstein's next entry—"The work of philosophy consists in assembling reminders for a particular purpose" (*PI* § 127)—helps us to recall Frost's claim that poetry provides "the surprise of remembering something I didn't know I knew" (*SP* 19). It also recalls the fact that *Mountain Interval*, in which "Snow" first appeared, is dedicated "TO YOU, who least need reminding . . ."

## Making

In the talk of Meserve and the Coles at midnight, what surfaces of ordinary language and its forms of life and culture has Frost set before us in order to remind us of what depths? Reminded ourselves of Frost's Wittgensteinian designs, we should find it more difficult to miss or dismiss the fact that to make something, and how to make something, of the ordinary and obvious are just Meserve's primary preoccupations in his lengthy holding-forth to the Coles in lines 116–97 ("'*The least thing* set him going'"; line 259; my emphasis). Having phoned his wife and returned from tending the horses, and now either blatantly ignoring or simply not hearing a question directly put to him by Helen (line 110), Meserve launches into a rambling disquisition, "heed[ing] nothing but the lamp / Or something not far from it on the table" (111–12). What he studies turns out to be a single page of an open book standing upright between the overturned pages on its left and those yet to be turned on its right. These are ordinary items surely, a book page and a lamp and a table,[11] even if remarkable enough to Meserve (he thinks the book page may have moved by itself) to go on at length about such everyday things and how they can "expect to come in front of us / A many times . . . / before we see them" (126–28).[12] How is it that we do *not* see them? Some lines later the lamp and page come in front of us again, now in view with the Coles' collie in the room that the couple occupies:

> "You make a little foursquare block of air,
> Quiet and light and warm, in spite of all
> The illimitable dark and cold and storm,
> And by so doing give these three, lamp, dog,
> And book-leaf, that keep near you, their repose;"
>
> (lines 142–46)

Barely in evidence throughout what becomes a lengthy rambling of Meserve, to which the above passage could be a climax but to the Coles seems like just more talk, is an analogical (not logical) ratio of terms, in which to give repose to ordinary things by the making of a room or home is roughly equivalent to experiencing their "redemption from external meanness" by having them repeatedly come before

us until we "see them" (128)—until, that is, "we answer from within" (134) by appropriating them as our own. Meserve is not very clear about what constitutes a home or how one goes about making a room a home. In any case, the active voice in which he frames this notion ("You make") ill fits the supposed passivity involved in our just *waiting* for "things" to come before us, in our coming somehow, it could be only after the thousandth time (128), to "see" them:

> "One of the lies would make it out that nothing
> Ever presents itself before us twice.
> Where would we be at last if that were so?
> Our very life depends on everything's
> Recurring till we answer from within."
>
> (lines 129–33)

Meserve is also vague about how this seeing is supposed to occur on the thousandth time if it hasn't yet occurred on the first or fifth or five hundredth, though he is correct, surely, that it sometimes does so. We also might wish to ask what, in this setting, in these circumstances, "seeing," "making," and "repose," otherwise ordinary words, *mean*. We have said that what binds these activities together is the thought that the ordinary and familiar can be appropriated as something possessed of more than mere meanness, and as something one's own. But the issues remain what and how.

Answer these questions as we will, what is immediately obvious on Meserve's concluding his rambling talk (line 152) is that the Coles at least do not answer or even raise these questions, for the simple reason that they really haven't been listening. If they have raised anything, it's their eyes, or eyebrows. "'I shouldn't want to hurry you, Meserve, / But'" (153–54). And it becomes increasingly plain after Meserve leaves that, though what he observed had been familiar and ordinary, though his topos had been the familiar and ordinary, the Coles find his speech passing strange. Bad enough is the strangeness they find in the content of Meserve's talk (at best it is self-contradictory [lines 197–200], at worst frightening, even a bit mad ["nightmare talk"; line 168]).[13] The more serious problem as they express it resides not in what he says but in *how* he communicates, or fails to. How he talks, its forms and conditions, seems peculiar to them, even extraordinary. Indeed, when Meserve is gone the Coles trade a number of objections to his rhetorical bearing and the peculiar language games he is (self?)-absorbed in. They note that his talk is out of all proportion to his occasion and audience (line 259); that he never stops talking (line 64); that he's closed-minded even to the notion of differing views (line 65); that he doesn't listen (line 66); that he's oblivious to others, "inconsiderate" (line 345); that he doesn't answer people's "civil questions" (line 251); and that he requires others to do his thinking for him and then ignores what they have to say (lines 346–47).

In Wittgenstein's notion of language games, we are meant to appreciate to what extent the meanings of words are controlled by grammatical criteria, often circumstantially conceived and related by family resemblances, instantiated in their employment, in a specific practice, context, and language game—ultimately in the hermeneutic and rhetorical moves of individuals in (or out) of community with each other. This context-specific understanding of meaning is a point the Coles here, like the rest of us, at least feel instinctively, for it is just their objection to Meserve that he respects *none* of the parameters, the rules, governing ordinary speech and behavior. He doesn't play, or worse doesn't seem to know how to play, everyone else's language games. He fails to observe what Grice calls the "Cooperative Principle" and its attendant maxims: "Make your conversational contribution such as is required, at the stage at which it occurs, by the accepted purpose or direction of the talk exchange in which you are engaged."[14] For Helen Cole especially, this purpose or direction of their talk is whether or not Meserve should venture back out into the snow. That Meserve will not cooperate, doesn't *want* to play their language games, doesn't seem to occur to them.

As far as that goes, we too, identifying initially with the more familiar and sensible Helen and Fred Cole, are alert enough to list rhetorical miscues of Meserve in addition to those of which the Coles complain. For one thing, it's awfully late at night to be initiating such philosophical flights of fancy. Worse, Meserve's speech has no clear introduction—"the least thing *set him going*" (line 259; my emphasis)—and no clear conclusion—his sudden and unexpected "Well, now, I leave you people" (line 197). Nor has his speech any evident *point*, given the way he shifts from the page of a book to the room they occupy to the snow outside figured as a "pallid thing" to memories of a neighbor's clever city-bred visitor and then aimlessly back to the room once again.

Of course the Coles' perspective on Meserve is not the only one provided of either Meserve or themselves, and while true enough as far as it goes, Helen's and to some extent Fred's limitations render their views unreliable if taken alone. At least one other perspective on these and other issues is, of course, Meserve's own (Frost's transgredient presence being the all-important, corrective middle term), to which we now must turn. Given, however, the length and obscurity of Meserve's talk in lines 116–242, my own talk will be a lengthy, though I trust not altogether obscure discussion.

## Playing

Having suggested that making something of the ordinary and obvious, more specifically what to make and how to make it, is Meserve's double theme in conversation with the Coles, we might recast this thematic what and how as two sides of

the same coin, or the same book page, adding that Meserve's theme of redemption of the ordinary is echoed in his practice here of speaking, elsewhere of preaching. In order better to understand what making, seeing, taking, repose, and similar terms mean—hence in what this alleged redemption consists—I begin by looking at how Meserve himself makes something of the everyday, how he sees things (how he takes them), including the Coles and himself, and thereby what he makes of them. And I ask whether, in whatever he makes, he somehow gives of himself, and in so giving gives others and himself, repose.

In obvious ways the first hundred or so lines of the poem provide an important expository introduction to the more important symbolic action that follows. I subordinate comment on these, as well as on the final section (the last eighty lines), in order to concentrate on the middle part, especially Meserve's speech in lines 111 to 197, itself divisible into three sections and the most significant part of the poem.[15] In due course I will attend to the beginning of this speech (lines 111ff.), where Meserve makes a considerable fuss over a simple page in a book, but on beginning it seems best to avoid getting as bogged down as the Coles manage to get about just *what* Meserve might be saying (I have suggested that in part it is a celebration of the ordinary) by getting clearer about *how* he practices what he may be preaching. And this how is especially salient toward the close of his speech, in section 3 (lines 172–96), where memory and language enable him to "play [his] fancy" (line 190). It may well be that this unassuming passage has gone by a thousand times without one reader seeing what Meserve is doing, who he is, when he recalls the delight Avery's boarder felt in the way he (Meserve) banked the snow one day:

> "The snow against the window caught his eye.
> 'Hey, that's a pretty thought'—those were his words—
> 'So you can think it's six feet deep outside,
> While you sit warm and read up balanced rations.
> You can't get too much winter in the winter.'
> Those were his words."
>
> (lines 180–85)

Now, when Meserve twice observes that he is double-voicing these words of Avery's boarder, turning them and his own recollection forward toward the snow now banking itself up against the window as they speak, what else is he doing but himself "making" the room they sit in cozier (see lines 188–89)? He is helping to make over the room in which they sit and talk by reinterpreting it in terms of someone else's (the boarder's) language and "pretty thought" reappropriated for the purpose, and with the not-incidental irony that the snow really *is* six feet deep outside all by itself, threatening precisely to be "too much winter in the winter":

"And he went home and all
But banked the daylight out of Avery's windows.
Now you and I would go to no such length.
At the same time you can't deny it makes
It not a mite worse, sitting here, we three,
Playing our fancy, to have the snow-line run
So high across the pane outside."

(lines 185–91)

In asserting this claim we need not make more of Meserve's act of interpretation than it is, for the three are engaging in nothing more than ordinary conversation, "playing our fancy" (line 190). But, then, it is nothing less. "In conversation," Ricoeur reminds us, "we have an interpretive attitude."[16] If we ourselves play with another of Meserve's terms, his "playing" (here; and earlier: "I used / To play . . ."; lines 41–42; and later Helen's reference to his "fun"; line 338)—his playing can be seen to be a hermeneutic re-posing of his world, a rearranging or re-positioning of a situation and those in it through a reinterpretation of its several components. This reposing, moreover, aims to give a measure of repose, meaning (here) settlement and satisfaction, at least to Meserve if not to the Coles. (*Not* that Meserve has repose in him to give: he is physically and spiritually restless, a spiritual drifter who never seems to stay with any interpretation for long.)

There is, in addition, a decided connection here between grammar-as-hermeneutics and rhetoric, since Meserve is also making a claim and amplifying it with narrative and other appeals within the overall economy of an epideictic speech of praise ("The ways you found to say the praise of comfort / And being where you are"; line 199).[17] Most readers, on the other hand, are more likely to notice the connection with the figure of the poet and not the orator as preacher. "Playing his fancy," graced with the "gift of words" (lines 190, 249), Meserve interpretively plays with everything he sees: "'Was ever such a man for seeing likeness?'" (line 250). Language and memory provide new persuasive interpretations of common objects uncommonly taken, as in narrative or metaphor, and new projections of familiar words like "repose."

Of course, Meserve himself earlier asserted just this point, for he sees the page of the open book as a metaphor for one who is eager to see how others "take" things, interpret their world as they go, re-appropriate what they have otherwise taken but may have failed to understand. In fact, interpretive understanding proves to be one of Meserve's explicit themes when he figures the snow as a beastlike thing that fails to understand ("its own stupid lack of understanding"; line 164) because it doesn't know what to make of people talking together, *how* to take them. The snow fails presumably because it has no words to take them with or as, but also, more important, out of well-intentioned but destructive "overeagerness" (line 161), the intellectual's form of impatience and pride (as

in lines 321–22, 342). We can even conclude about all of this playfulness that, whereas Meserve may seem to be rambling throughout his speech as if abstracted from time, place, and occasion, in fact he is purposely, purposefully, unpredictable in his playing with language and interpretation, and with the others as potential players themselves.

## Recurring

Some such open-ended (because shifting, even shifty) "moral" as Meserve concludes with, however—to the effect that *no* conclusion is stable, much less final, hence is not moral in any conventional way—is still barely even a beginning for us, for Meserve earlier offered much more to think about in that image of the page of a book midway in its turning, as if balanced, "so sensitively poised" (line 138) between future and past, a midway point, as it were, in someone's reading. It may be helpful to be reminded that this image is not the only such balance of opposites in the poem. Meserve, for instance, is placed by Frost in pronounced tension with Helen Cole, just as Fred and Helen may be said to resist and balance each other and Meserve to counter his own wife and vice versa. Again, the snow at the window is on one side threat and on the other comfort. Meserve, likewise, wavers between "Good night" said at the Coles's and "Good morning" said at home. Indeed, this midway in its turning of the page of the Good Book, as it may be, reminds us that Meserve too is midway in his journey home (hear the Dantean echo), between his departure at nine from the village store where he was preaching and his arrival home at three (it is now, thus, the temporal "standpoint" [*stasis*] of mid-night), the Coles' farm being roughly midway ("a halfway station"; line 214).

These passing observations can remind us, as I say, of that other traveler midway in life's journey, though it is true that Meserve is not lost, in his discursive rambling, in the same way that Dante finds himself lost. Meserve, after all, is able to refer to some writing in the shed "to tell me who I am / If it don't tell me where I am" (lines 40–41), suggesting that Meserve already knows, doesn't need to learn, *where* he is. Of course he is already (nominally) aware of *who* he is also, but to press this against the comparison to Dante is to overlook the fact that persons carve their names or initials in shed posts, marking a moment in the flux of time, not to inform (themselves at least), as if to record "knowledge," but to *remind* themselves (as Virgil repeatedly reminds Dante) and to *acknowledge* what they already know.

When, accordingly, Meserve tells the Coles that his own carving tells him *who* he is, the lack of which understanding is, we know, Dante's very theme, we may speculate that it can do so just because, poised as Meserve is between his own past and the future he always fronts (how he will take things, including how

he will take the Coles), such a reminder helps him place himself morally, culturally, even religiously, in a present imbued with both past and future.[18] "I used / To play" (line 41), Meserve muses, beginning to recall not only who he was but also, playfully, still is, and even implying that *his* memory of the Coles' place antedates the Coles' own. In a word, it is *he,* not the Coles, who is the native here, the one really at home. Here memory provides a resource for constituting identity quite in the way, some lines later, we saw that Meserve's memory of Avery's boy is troped to define not only where Meserve and the Coles now are but *who* they are, namely ones, if only they knew it, who can invent by appropriating the past anew.[19]

If the drift of my present description sounds like my own Meservian rambling, or worse, like a critic's imposing a conclusion, it may be because, as Meserve warned, we readers and critics are individually too impatient—whereas *some* impatience, like Meserve's own (lines 121–22), may indicate something else, call it enthusiasm (*en-theos,* God within, as it were under wraps in the "great skin coat" Meserve wore [line 5]).[20] To be "overeager," in other words, is so to desire to *take*—not to interpret but conceptually to seek to theorize, grasp, master, control whatever lies ahead—that, like the brute snow pressing too hard against what appears to be simple unmediated reality but is in fact an invisible interpretive window (line 161), we in our reading inadvertently hold our eyes wide shut and fail to understand, fail to see our way clear ("What is your aim in philosophy?—To show the fly the way out of the fly-bottle"; *PI* § 309). To be overeager is to risk missing why the ordinary is already in order (ordinal) as it is, to grasp at it as though it were a moveable object rather than an inhabitable world, to im-pose our own windowed framework of preconceptions onto it while not minding, not seeing, that our noses smear the glass. Whereas to linger within this world, as Meserve does, taking time to talk and visit (line 339), is to enable one to see, to acknowledge, what may be present in its absence, to take, even to be taken, as if charmed, by it and with it.[21]

Consider then, once again, that book leaf Meserve begins with. Positioned as it is between past and future, it may remind us of the image in "West-Running Brook" of the ripple in the outgoing stream thrown back against its own west-running current. These contrary movements create what has often been interpreted to be a *stasis* of the wave above the flux of the water *(sub specie aeternitatis),* but the solution of the poem resists so simple a fix. On the contrary, the wave images the ever-present moment of the interpenetration of past and future, for the wave thrown back east toward the source is part of the same outward current running westward into the future. The wave thrown back is not above time but just is the moment of time's intersection in itself, the figure a hermeneutic circle makes in symbolizing human understanding. In this same way, the image of the leaf in the book requires to be read under the aspect of human finitude, social mores and manners—*sub specie moris*—not eternity:

> "That leaf there in your open book! It moved
> Just then, I thought. It's stood erect like that,
> There on the table, ever since I came,
> Trying to turn itself backward or forward,
> I've had my eye on it to make out which:
> If forward, then it's with a friend's impatience—
> You see I know—to get you on to things
> It wants to see how you will take; if backward,
> It's from regret for something you have passed
> And failed to see the good of."
>
> (lines 116–25)

The original temptation, again, is to read this as an image of *stasis* beyond change, whereas, returning to it now in the light of Meserve's theme and interpretive practice, the sense is quite the opposite. Like the wave thrown back against its current, the image of the book leaf is not one of abstraction or transcendence but of a consummately ordinary (yet strange, charming, even magical) moment in an ongoing process. For the analogy Meserve is drawing here is not to the effect that the activity of daily living is like words frozen on a page, or like a page frozen in time, or like time stopped in a place out of time, but rather like reading, where a "page turning forward" means (as if paradoxically) its falling back on pages already laid down so that the reader can interpret the new in the light of what he has already read; and where turning "backward" means pages falling forward on those yet unturned to allow the reader, in the light of an emerging whole, to re-appropriate what had been read but is now seen to have been read shallowly or wrongly, missing the depths *there* on the surface.[22] In such an image, past and future, part and whole ambiguously conflate in a hermeneutic circle that analogizes this very encounter of Meserve with the Coles, who, in having seen Meserve pass by a thousand times, have never really seen him at all, not even once.

Such an image characterizes the understanding Meserve aspires to within its temporal horizon, for Meserve himself professes a friend's impatience ("You see I know"; line 122) to "get the Coles on" to "things"—himself, this evening's visitation, whatever is to come—to see how they will interpret them; and to *acknowledge* that. This is just what his allusion some lines later, to the snow's failing to understand what "[they] found so interesting / In one another" (161–62) indicates *he* is doing, and just what his own interpretive activity reiterates. While the Coles for their part come to reconsider this strange neighbor of theirs by revising what they had thought of him over the years in light of what they come to learn in a night: "What? We've found out in one hour more about him / Than we had seeing him pass by in the road / A thousand times" (lines 252–54).

## Taking

In the dramatic setting of the poem, how do these grammatical themes and rhetorical activities epideictically show forth the ways the Coles and Meserve speak to (as well as "read") each other, possibly even give repose? Recall that we are trying to understand what Meserve is talking about (the ordinary) by investigating *how* he talks about it. Thus far his manner (how) has circled around the activities of seeing, reading, taking, metaphorizing, as projections of our concept of understanding. And thus far we have found reason to believe that Meserve approaches the Coles with some understanding and enjoyment, even enthusiasm. How then do specifically rhetorical principles—including now the grammatical criteria employed to measure the world, as well as the full range of strategies and appeals and the rules of propriety they observe or break in doing so—how does rhetoric in this more philosophic sense illuminate Meserve's and Helen's modes of speaking as a component part of their understanding and interpreting? What part does the very event of speaking play? How do the Coles read, take, see, specifically in speaking to, Meserve?

That this last question, to begin with, is not willfully imposed on the Coles here is supported by the fact that no fewer than six times in various forms throughout the poem the Coles pose the same question to themselves: "what kind of man / Do you call that?" (lines 247–48). At least for Helen Cole until this evening it had been transparent what kind of man Meserve is: "one of those pious scalawags" (line 92) eternally hauling God into civil society, "even the thought" of whom she "detests" (line 51); a member of "his wretched little Racker Sect" (line 53); a sanctimonious bigot; a man blithely unconcerned with the effects on his wife of his prodigal paternity. To this "small" (line 70) man she feels she may condescend with impunity because, she seems to think, he is out of it, too socially and culturally oblivious to notice. In short, she thinks Meserve a man she sees *through*. Rudely interrupting his talk with her order, "You tend your horses and come back" (line 42), for example, she gratuitously adds that "You can judge better [of the snow, of the horses' condition] after seeing" (line 35)—as if Meserve's innumerable comings and goings on behalf of others ("I serve") stand in need of such counsel. Fred helps us to recognize that for all her impatience and bluster, Helen is more than intrigued by Meserve, even cares for him in spite of herself ("You like the runt"; line 94), and herself tempers, without ever quitting, the severity in her voice as she comes to know him better. Nevertheless, if we are to test Meserve's ideas about "taking" and the rest, we need to ask how Helen's way of taking and seeing as she speaks, how her own rhetorical habits and underlying unstated grammar of our leading concepts, manifest her own thought and understanding, how they play against Meserve's, ultimately how they help inform us of Frost's.

(1) Consider the logical form, first of all, of Helen's questions and references

to this stranger before her. She speaks of him not by identifying an individual but by means of abstract categories deductively imposed a priori without regard for the concrete circumstances of this unique person in this particular situation. She speaks in terms of "the kind" (line 83), "one of those" (line 92), "the kind of man" (line 215), "what kind of a man" (line 247), "such a man" (line 250), which is to say in terms of various characteristics *abstracted* from the real individual and constructed into general classes or logical types. This is that language use John Henry Newman calls "notional" as distinct from "real," that the early Heidegger calls "apophantic" as distinct from "hermeneutic," and that Kenneth Burke calls "semantic" as distinct from "poetic" or "rhetorical." It is a form of expression derivative from ordinary language, useful for abstract generalization and logical argument, that depends upon avoiding or suppressing the ordinary, real-life contexts from which it springs, those contexts that provide the grammatical as-structures and rhetorical settings of our meaning here and now, in a human form of life. Abstraction distorts the epideictic question, what kind or quality of thing is it? (*quale sit?*), replacing it with a conception of truth as adequation, and ends in Nietzsche's (at least Heidegger's version of Nietzsche's) will-to-power.[23] For all of her considerable virtues, Helen here is not enthusiastic, as Meserve is; she is overeager to take and master in a quite different way, not by lingering over circumstances but by manipulating abstract categories in order to control. "Take" here is an act of coercion, seizure, ultimately violence (the modern prototype of which, not to beat a dead horse, is Raskolnikov, whose "new word" is the imposition of a new order, the superior, the extraordinary, over and against the ordinary).

While otherwise this mode of speech of Helen's has obvious uses, she herself unwittingly concedes that the formal types and categories she employs are really untested social prejudices: "his wretched little Racker Sect, / All's ever I heard of it, which isn't much" (lines 53–54). In taking up uncritically from the very beginning the standpoint of others, Helen manages to *avoid* who Meserve is. Her words are idling, she fails to reformulate case from case, she cannot find the words to speak the language Meserve speaks.[24] Such thin descriptions of Meserve's community as Helen holds cannot constitute an adequate "tradition" for interpretation. It is in fact just this danger, abstraction from the real, that Meserve himself avoids in turning to the everyday, ordinary contexts that redeem the external meanness of the notional or apophantic. He avoids this danger by reappropriating circumstances of time, place, occasion, persons from which the general and abstract are derived, in a rhetorical and poetic language that makes evident the world by image and trope, analogy and narrative, double-voicing, and the projecting of words into new contexts. For this reason, Meserve proves to be what we readers may have suspected all along, Helen's repressed double. Where Helen unselfconsciously abstracts herself from the real, her own language game an assault on this estranged neighbor and the life he presents, Meserve is concrete, nuanced,

inventive, "extravagant" in imagination, attentive to the ordinary occasions of language use without slavishly deferring to conventions. The lesson we recall from chapter 4 is hardly that the concrete case is "better than" the abstract, for any given concrete situation may be simply abnormal, aberrant, while what is normal can only be known by virtue of our ability to compare and contrast and to generalize. The point is rather that Meserve shuttles between both, allowing one to open up, and thicken, the other.

(2) Now consider, more tellingly, the larger rhetorical form and orientation, both the philosophic conditions and presuppositions and the particular way these are instantiated here in Helen's encounter with Meserve. As with so many of Frost's characters, Helen would debate with the best of them given the opportunity, fully-equipped as she is with rhetorical topics and their premises for arguments and an ample supply of tools, tactics, and tricks. Earlier she had, for example, been dismissive of Meserve (line 42); later she grows more aggressively manipulative, expressing part-concern, part-condescension thinned with pseudocivility:

> "Mr. Meserve, I'll leave it to *your* wife.
> What *did* your wife say on the telephone?"
>
> (lines 109–10)

She knows full well of course what his wife said; she was there when he called. She can infer that the answer Meserve *now* fails to give her (line 111) (he hears her question but refuses it, turning away as if distracted) will support *her* side of the *stasis,* the point-at-issue, as she has framed it, namely whether Meserve should stay or not. (Her providing the answer to her own question later proves the point: "But why, when no one wants you to, go on? / Your wife—she doesn't want you to" [lines 233–34]). Exasperated at last, Helen implies that Meserve is driven by selfish motives ("take my advice / And for your family's sake stay where you are"; lines 216–17) of stubbornness and probably stupidity. (And in her "But what good is my saying it over and over?" [line 218], Helen shows again that she is one of the "they" who denies the efficacy of the recurrent or repetitive [lines 129–30].) As a last-ditch effort, Helen admonishes Meserve for his sheer willfulness and lack of reason (lines 233–35). To this Meserve, as if recognizing the limits of his own arguments in this regard, flattering and condescending in turn, can only reply to himself, to Fred, to heaven, "Save us from being cornered by a woman" (line 236).

In addition to the reversal of gender stereotypes, what is rhetorically significant here is less *what* Helen says—she has at least as good a cause and has better reasons than Meserve—than the fact *that* she debates at all, that she (like Warren in "The Death of the Hired Man") construes the matter and occasion as suitable for deliberation and advice-giving, in a word for argument, and construes her interlocutor as a debate opponent ("'he's thinking / He'll make a case of it if he

succeeds'"; lines 85–86). What is significant is that she sees and speaks to others in a way that may fairly be called—thinking now of the main-line rhetorical tradition—Aristotelian and Ciceronian.[25] And it is significant that Meserve counters with not merely the opposite side of the *stasis* Helen is working but an *alternative stasis* and manner of speaking, a different kind of rhetoric altogether.

For Meserve, it is clear, will *not* debate, and does not much argue, at all. (It is a nonissue whether or not he'll go. For him there is never any question that he's going. His is a momentary stay almost in the nature of things, at least in the nature of men: "I must go on / . . . Ask any man"; [lines 138–240].) Meserve inhabits a different philosophical, rhetorical, and cultural world from that of the Coles, one not flatly incompatible with theirs but challenging it, testing it. Whereas, on the one hand, Helen epitomizes Yankee pragmatism and the rational thought and speech that conduce to prudent practical action, a familiar enough theme in Frost, Meserve on the other models a receptiveness to the moment almost passive, what Gadamer identifies as playfulness marked by "absence of strain" and "constant repetition" (*TM* 94, 93). From within this state, Meserve patiently *waits* to see which way the book page falls, if it falls. Hence he can defer closure—"Who cares?" (line 152)—since, after all, the upright page is a metaphor for the fact that "things must expect to come in front of us" (it is not we who make them come) *many* times, until we "see" them. Meserve's point seems to be that we need to resist overeagerness, to wait (but wait for what?). In opposition to received opinion to the contrary, Meserve implies that we are not wholly masters of our selves or our fates, that we are dependent on everyday things appearing, disappearing, and reappearing: "Our very life depends on everything's / Recurring till we answer from within" (132–33). Answering in turn seems to depend on some magic spell, some charm or even witchcraft (another familiar theme in Frost), enabling us somehow to see: "'The thousandth time may prove the charm'" (line 134). In the mouth of an Evangelical preacher like Meserve, a passing allusion to magic charms is barely even a figure of speech, merely a dead metaphor. But on the breath of a real-life poet like Meserve, it hints of powers we do not control, including the power of suasive speech. In contradistinction to Helen's rational arguments and abstracted logic, Meserve seems to them rhetorically *ir*rational, himself "taken" by rhetorical images, metaphors, analogies, oblique arguments, narratives, and ironies—by Emerson's list.

But then: to what purpose? "The whole to-do seems to have been for nothing," Helen concludes (line 337), almost as if Meserve were a little unhinged (not unlike the book page). He is a Christian in any case, and the manner of his allusion to unseen powers here may be but one more of his discreet, even rhetorically decorous ways of encountering the Coles (and Frost's confronting us) with the mystery of an unacknowledged Other. I am thinking specifically of Meserve's not "dragging" (line 81) God into things, the point of which, incidentally, is not

Helen's point, that Meserve "didn't consider it a case for God" (line 82). To Meserve, everything's a case for God; Meserve's very first words refer to the "great scroll upward toward the sky, / Long enough for recording all our names on" (lines 10–11), telling us the temper of his thought right up front. The point is rather that Meserve doesn't "drag" anything anywhere but rather, civilly, allegorizes his meaning. I am thinking of how he earlier (line 111) chose to ignore, acting as if he simply hadn't heard, Helen's question ("What did your wife say?"). And I say "civilly" in view of the rude, barbarous (etymologically "unspeakable") way Helen treats him, misinterpreting his decorousness and civility as rudeness if not quite genuine madness, much as his earlier discretion comes as a cause of surprise to her because she had been expecting just the opposite all along.

How then are we to account, if only briefly, for Meserve's rhetorical position and positioning, posing, re-posing, and im-posturing? Two matters are at stake: first, the meaning of the metaphor that Meserve gives us, that knowing another is not a logical grasping of an object but a rhetorical seeing (acknowledging) of another, one who has a rhetorical claim on us to respond; and second, that only the appreciation of *both* modes of speaking and being, both kinds of rhetoric— Helen's no less than Meserve's—will bring us to the sort of repose Frost holds out for the taking. In order to identify what those modes of rhetoric are, I propose that we rest our horses, so to speak, and play with certain historical possibilities. In advancing these I am not making an argument about influence on Frost but trying to reposition the reader to see how Frost places logical proof (giving evidence) in conjunction with the rhetoric of seeing or acknowledging (making evident), by playing with certain possibilities of time.

## A Momentary Interlude: The Rhetoric of Time

> Around them boomed the rhetoric of time ...
>
> —W. H. Auden, "*Kairos* and *Logos*"

Anyone familiar with the several streams of the rhetorical tradition—the sophistic and its contemporary deconstructive tributaries, the Platonic, Aristotelian, Ciceronian, Vichian, and others—and anyone driven, as we have been, to find some alternative to the commonsense Aristotelian rhetoric of the Coles in order to account for the uncommon Wittgensteinian non-sense of Meserve, may initially be impressed with the similarities of Meserve's manic (or mantic) ramblings to those of Socrates, particularly of Socrates' performance in his second speech in the *Phaedrus*, the subject matter of which is love and the power (and weakness) of rhetoric—in many ways the two themes of "Snow." Like the highest form of love, genuine rhetoric in that dialogue is portrayed as a form of divine madness. There the genuine lover Socrates—dramatizing his own point in a Meservian plurality

of arguments, styles, and mythic narratives, in a complex speech to his beloved and admiring Phaedrus—speaks in a manner not to win some debate (as Lysias had, as Helen does) nor to manipulate the demos for favors or control, but to please the gods by moving his auditor toward eternal rather than human truths, beyond the control of the individual or the crowd, beyond the mere *doxa* and self-deceptions of men, ultimately beyond language itself.

Such a connection to Plato is tempting because it helps us to see *through* the sophist's blizzard of words toward a safer haven of eternal truths. A less eager student of rhetoric, however, may be able to make out a far closer match between Meserve's mode of speech and that of the sophist Gorgias, specifically with the complex doctrine of *kairos*. Had Frost not known the pre-Socratics, whom, as we saw in the previous chapter, he did know well, it would be simply uncanny how *kairos* responds in all of the pertinent ways to our present need to account for the interplay of word and world, self and time, past and future, in "Snow" and in Frost generally, in ways ontological and hermeneutic, ethical, rhetorical, and poetic. But then, appreciation of the value of uncanninesss is the basis of the experience that Frost's use of *kairos* would teach us.

Briefly then. In Greek drama and literature, *kairos* embraces various meanings: brevity, proportion, or moderation (as in the proverb attributed to Hesiod, "Observe good measure, and proportion *[kairos]* is the best of all things"), what is suited to the moment, the expedient, effective, appropriate, correct.[26] Particularly in pre-Socratic philosophy and rhetoric, *kairos* is central to such thinkers as Pythagoras, Empedocles, Protagoras, and Gorgias, and implicated in a rich grammatical field with concepts like *apate* (deception), *epideixis* (showing, shining forth), *pistis* (persuasion, belief), and others. Since it is not possible to do justice here (this is yet another sense of *kairos*) to the term in its Greek setting, much less to follow its fortunes in later Christian thought in the New Testament and elsewhere, I can speak to the moment by isolating our two primary senses of *kairos*, "the opportune [timely] moment" and "the fitting or appropriate measure," and focus on sophistic rhetorical thought, specifically that of Gorgias.

Any rhetoric worthy of the name more or less turns on a conflict of interpretations. The distinction we seek at this time between different rhetorical theories and practices, between Helen's and Meserve's rhetorics, depends, accordingly, on how one resolves such conflict. As we have indicated, in Aristotle and in similar ways in Cicero, the rhetor draws on a vast range of more or less tacitly known and publicly available topics as well as on the facts of the case at hand, seeking major and minor premises with which to assemble enthymemes and other appeals to arrive at *krisis* (judgment), or better, *euboulios,* good decision. Helen conducts herself in just this way. But there are, I have hinted, alternative ways of dealing with conflicting arguments or principles (what Protagoras called *dissoi logoi*), one of which we have just mentioned: the Platonic subordination of time and rhetorical

persuasion to a superordinate dialectic and a transcendent (timeless) order of truth, and an eclipse of the clash of popular images, ideas, opinions, the *dissoi logoi* produced by the contingency of human life and finitude, by way of transcendence into a realm of eternal Forms.[27]

In Gorgias,[28] however, these philosophic themes are transmuted into a third possibility: a relativistic philosophic rhetoric in which the *stasis* produced by contending *logoi* (propositions, arguments) is neither overcome by dialectical transcendence, as in Plato, nor resolved by a predominance of the probable, as in Aristotle, but rather settled in the sense that an orator or speaker achieves persuasion for the moment only, by an exemplary but unrationalizable or non-rule-governed power of invention. *Kairos* refers to the principle and power by which the opportune moment calls forth a response appropriate to the moment—almost literally a momentary stay against the confusion of the clash of *logoi*, at the midpoint that demands action. In Gorgias's view, the orator is open to what he calls the "magic" *(goetia)*, or witchcraft, that produces a beguiling speech, inasmuch as he or she persuades the auditor to choose what at the moment appears the more attractive logos. It is irrational, even magical, for it has nothing to do with popular opinion and the probable. In this regard, *kairos* has direct affinities, it is true, with Plato's divine madness (now without the Forms), as well as with romantic imagination and "genius" (but now without the stress on self-expression). Yet such beguilement as Meserve's is also "deceptive" in the way that these others make it a point to avoid, at least to the extent that the audience is led to believe that only one *logos* is "true," whereas on reflection it will be seen to be but one possibility contending with others for configuring our lots, one *fictio* within the supreme fiction, namely, that all we have are contending fictions.

Now it does not follow from this that such fictions are Nietzschean (Lentricchian) impositions of will; Meserve's certainly is not this. As I have suggested, in a restricted but not Platonic sense the sophistic orator transcends personal needs and interests. Witness Fred Cole on Meserve: "I doubt he's thinking of himself" (line 78). This is precisely right, for Meserve is open, receptive to what classical rhetoricians called the *peristaseis*, the "circumstances" (the time, place, personae, situation, context) of the moment. The orator's (Meserve's) task, ability, and achievement, accordingly, is to improvise a beguiling, charming, uncanny word that will show forth *(epi-deixis)* rather than argue, make evident more than give evidence for, what the situated moment seems to be. It is, in short, an *epideictic* rhetoric that paradoxically allows the speaker to *efface* himself at the moment he or she is most imposing, most manifesting abilities of improvisation and performance. Hence the orator's employment of a *plurality* of strategies and styles, Emerson's list once again: "The *ways* you found to say the praise" (line 199; my emphasis), as Helen admiringly puts it to Meserve.[29] Such strategies, once more, repose less on *doxa* and *endoxa*, opinions and probabilities, than on shifty

("sophistic") *para-doxa* beyond strictly rational reach and (it may well be) in opposition to popular views, to one sense of "common sense." Hence Meserve's paradox:

> "Though for all anyone can tell, repose
> May be the thing you haven't, yet you give it.
> So false it is that what we haven't we can't give;
> So false, that what we always say is true."
>
> (lines 147–50)

How, then, precisely, does *kairos* speak to our own attempt now to see what Meserve is saying, what Frost is doing? How does it help us to gain some measure of repose regarding "Snow?"

## Seeing

> "The thousandth time may prove the charm."

In the remaining two sections of this chapter, gathering the opposed rhetorical positions explored by Frost in the figures of Helen and Meserve, I begin by adverting once more to Geertz, who, in his famous paper on the Balinese cockfight, reports how a Balinese will totally ignore a stranger, a visitor ("they acted as if we simply did not exist"), until "in a day, a week, a month (with some people the magic moment never comes)—he decides, for reasons I have never quite been able to fathom, that you are real,"[30] which is to say, he *sees* you. It is a profoundly *kairotic* moment, irreducible to manifest reasons, suffused with magic and charm, crazy in its way, evidently (as in Geertz's account of his own coming to be acknowledged by his Balinese hosts) at once something both active and passive on the part of the one who sees, a "decision" that is not wholly a matter of will nor of sheer luck or circumstance.[31] It is a moment of the kind so subtly made evident by Frost in the ambivalence, the ambidextrousness, of Meserve's sudden yet studied acknowledgment of the snow: "I *like* that [emphasis on his desire, will]—I like *that* [emphasis on the world-as-gift]" (line 196). This binocular focus ("as my two eyes make") belongs to *kairos* itself and can be said to be a more nuanced version of Frost's topos throughout the poem, namely that living involves *both* what to "make" of the everyday, how intentionally to "take" and "give" it, and the felt magic involved in our coming to see the everyday that we make and take at every moment *as* magical, perhaps as sacred. It is the moment at which we utter what Wittgenstein calls an *"Äusserung,"* a statement that something we see has suddenly changed though nothing outward has occurred (the duck-image into a rabbit-image: "Now it's a rabbit!"). Neither "making" (interpreting, re-posing) nor "seeing" (acknowledging, describing) is *alone* sufficient; Frost would *not* have us choose

between the two, though at any given moment one element may predominate, as Meserve predominates throughout the poem. What then is Meserve saying? And how shall we characterize this moment of Meserve's stay with the Coles?

Recall what is overlooked but obvious, what we have repeatedly seen before without understanding it: it is mid-night (lines 55, 346), literally the turning point *(stasis)* of yesterday and tomorrow. This is to say that it is "an uncanny time of night" *(intempesta nocte)*,[32] or, to take Meserve's hint, the witching hour, his metaphor for a rhetorical *(kairotic) stasis* in which time has been made opportune by a quite fortuitous snowstorm, a magic moment, the thousandth time that may prove the charm because it is charming.[33] And, in truth, *something* comes to be seen and acknowledged by the Coles, who for the first time see Meserve:

> "What? We've found out in one hour more about him
> Than we had in seeing him pass by in the road
> A thousand times."[34]
>
> (lines 252–54)

The Coles are not mis-taking here: they do see Meserve, understand him more clearly than before. What has not fully occurred to the Coles, however, is just *how* they have come to understand—which is, after all, just the "what" that Meserve is trying to teach: how to understand, and how to speak. Consider what the Coles notice but fail to understand—that Meserve's speech is itself a midnight manic rambling, an ex-temporaneous, one-sided, epideictic performance in praise of the ordinary: lamp, table, book leaf, dog, snow, gossip, playing one's fancy.[35] The paradox is that Meserve's shooting the breeze—let us say his im-posturing to "snow" the Coles with a blizzard of words—can also show forth their world, themselves, anew. This is a paradox. Playing over every surface, Meserve's speech leaves everything as it is, yet nonetheless, as snow will do, transformed, the world hidden in its shining forth anew.

To assert this, however, is to state a paradox of our own. For how can we say that Meserve's talk transforms anything when it can't even be said to be what it aspires to be, namely "fitting," "timely," and "in proportion" *(kairos)* to the situation? And in support of this objection, note how literally ill-fitted Meserve appears under wraps, "belittled in the great skin coat" (line 5) he wears (we have already noted the indecorousness of the hour and the inappropriateness in the way he speaks). Yet, such arguments notwithstanding, this objection begs the question. As if it were *obvious* to the Coles what their situation is! We would do much better to argue that the Coles have mistakenly presumed to see through Meserve in the way that Frost's critics have presumed to be able to see through Frost. Whereas, if they (the Coles, the critics) do *not* know what their situation is, they (we) cannot conclude that Meserve speaks in even the slightest way out of proportion, inappropriately, to it.

The challenge here resides in seeing what their situation is by seeing how Meserve's words are meant to stir and fan the (aptly named) Coles. We have said that Meserve seeks to bring language home, in Wittgenstein's phrase. Such homecoming does not coerce language into the window frame of familiar conventions, enabling us to possess it at the last, as if by the rules. Nor is leaving one's home a crazy-enthusiastic abandonment of words unto the farthermost edge of will or desire. Rather, both comprise a holding-in-tension of the two, as in metaphor. Frost underlines this point himself: "I would be willing to throw away everything else but that: enthusiasm tamed by metaphor" (*SP* 36). To bring our enthusiasm for language home via metaphor is much the same as Meserve's attempt to bring the Coles' home, via metaphor and word-projection, to language. This is along the lines of what Geertz means by ethnographic thick description of someone else's home and, conversely, of what Thoreau means when he urges us to become "a Columbus to whole new continents and worlds within you, opening new channels, not of trade, but of thought" (*Walden* 321). In Meserve's ability to recreate the Coles' home—at which Meserve is the one (momentarily) more at home—we find metaphors for understanding and speaking, being both away-from-home and most-at-home. Joel Weinsheimer makes the point succinctly: "If we define the literal as what stays at home, the metaphorical, in contrast, has been transferred and finds a new home away from home. The question, then, is why occupying a borrowed home is not just being 'in someone's home,' as Derrida says, but coming into one's very own."[36]

I have, in fact, been pursuing the answer to Derrida's question throughout this essay in Wittgensteinian and Heideggerian ways: we become ourselves only by residing beside, not in, the other. This is what Meserve would teach the Coles by dint of his performative example with metaphors, and what Frost would teach us by the examples of Meserve and the Coles: "Success in taking figures of speech is as intoxicating as success in making figures of speech" (*SP* 96). Whatever else it is, then, such a stance toward language is not equivalent to Helen's own rhetorical-hermeneutic desire to remain indoors, "to contract [herself] into a nutshell of civility," as Thoreau puts it in *Walden* (7), which has all but incapacitated her ability to see, or say, what her situation is. Her various civil superfluities morph into a kind of madness, as Cavell explains: "I understand Emerson to be writing in general in the procedure of what in 'Self-Reliance' he calls self-reliance, which he there defines as 'the aversion of conformity.' Conformity is the state in which society sees to it that its members live—the state, accordingly, in which we mostly do live. This state is characterized by Emerson as voicelessness—or, say, hyperbolic inexpressiveness—and thus a form of madness" (*CT* 66).[37]

By contrast, Meserve's stance toward, and his activity with, language and communication represent several variant orderings, alternative possibilities of the phenomena. I briefly pursue three here.

In Christian terms, first of all, regarding now the very first line of the poem, Meserve may be said to be listening to the Spirit (*spiritus* = breath, wind) that blows where it will. In his own blowing on the Coles this night as he speaks, what Meserve offers is nothing less than a gift of the Spirit, several gifts in fact: the gift of tongues,[38] the gift of words, the gift of re-pose, and ultimately the gift of acknowledgment. The point is summarized by St. Paul (Frost's favorite) in Paul's paradoxical "I live, yet not I but Christ liveth in me," which is to say living in charity or love, most yourself when most surrendered to, acknowledging, and acknowledged by, others.

In hermeneutic (grammatical) terms, second, Meserve listens to *die Sache selbst*, the subject matter, in this case what it means to listen and speak to, and to understand, others. These are matters Meserve poses as questions, as in a book. Hermeneutically, Meserve's gifts of words and self allow him to avoid what we can archly call the "metaphysics of presents," the fallacy that one can simply give to another, as if handing over a box, that which is never objectively possessed in the first place, never commanded, present, but only present and absent at once. For the very point of Meserve's speech to the Coles is that any repose one gives is momentary, precisely because always (infinitely) susceptible to further tropes, contexts, and circumstances.

In rhetorical terms, finally, Meserve listens to the situation at hand, responds to the *kairos* he does not possess but that possesses him. *Kairos* signals this uncanny return of the repressed counterpart to logos. Time and circumstance, contingency and indeterminacy, are thus the conditions for the possibility of human thought. Thus Meserve's is minimally an ontological hermeneutic much like that of Gadamer, both open to and opening the gap or clearing at the appropriate moment of Appropriation, at mid-night: "Only what is thought, said or done at a certain rare coincidence is good" (*Walden* 330). But then this may come at *any* moment: "All change is a miracle to contemplate; but it is a miracle which is taking place every instant" (*Walden* 11).[39] And so Helen of Meserve: "He's getting up a miracle this minute" (line 84),[40] designed to bring them home.

## Repose

But they are not home free, not safe and sound. The rhetorical *quaestio* of the poem as a whole is raised by the cultural strangeness, the uncanniness Meserve introduces to the Coles, and by the familiarity the Coles represent to Meserve and to us.[41] That the Coles sympathize with Meserve is clear enough; in this sense they begin, at least, to understand him. But their failure to understand what Meserve is saying is a failure in the end to understand the matter *(die Sache)* Meserve is speaking about, which is to say the way he is speaking about it. At the same time, although it has the practical effect of almost burying them in a blizzard

of words, Meserve's dismissal of Helen's pragmatic preoccupations serves as a timely reminder to them to wake up and live. His matter and mode of speech, *and* their pragmatism—two sides of the same book page—comprise, therefore, Frost's question to us: What is the logic of understanding and civil speech? Wittgenstein describes this commonsense answer to this question:

> That is to say: we are so much accustomed to communication through language, in conversation, that it looks to us as if the whole point of communication lay in this: someone else grasps the sense of my words—which is something mental: he as it were takes it into his own mind. If he then does something further with it as well, that is no part of the immediate purpose of language. (*PI* § 363)

The passage is instructive, for it can help us to hear two things from which both Meserve's and Helen's talk taken separately distract us. First, though Meserve at least seems eager to engage the Coles in what Frost elsewhere calls "gossip, our interest in each other" (*Interviews* 176); in fact he never really manages to converse successfully with them at all. Whatever else it is, conversation is an ongoing back-and-forth in talk in which two or more take turns with respect to some subject matter. Now, back and forth is just what we have said Meserve does so well in constellating reading and metaphorizing with gossip and conversation, modeling for us the dialectic of unconcealment and concealment in interpretation. Reading, seeing, metaphorizing, re-posing—each activity is shown by Meserve to be a hermeneutic circle for which conversation can then be seen to be an appropriate metaphor. In fact, it is just this metaphor of conversation for understanding that allows us to see that the Coles' and Meserve's failure really to converse with each other is just that, a failure on both of their parts to understand each other. (By contrast, it is also precisely conversation, gossip, however limited, that Fred and Helen Cole successfully conduct in speaking about Meserve.) Yet the event of this failure is also another of the ways that Frost shows us the limitations of the talk of the Coles, or of Meserve, taken alone. In their individual failures, we are required in our reading to imagine what successful conversation with the poem might mean, among other things in what an appropriate valuing of *both* sides would consist.

In the end, the metaphor in "Snow" that best plays the poem's metaphors for concealment and unconcealment, presence and absence toward and against each other, is snow itself. As snow signifies the threat of death, the hiddenness of the world, that which obliterates difference, words that sophistically blind others for extravagant purposes, snow also arrives as a gift from above, plays over all the world there is, renders the scene charming and magical, occasions transformation. In "Snow," snow presents an opportune blizzard of words that finally enables us first to listen, then to look and see, finally to gain a new if momentary re-pose. In this

way, Frost's poem and poetry remind us of what we already knew but had forgotten, that "civility," as Richard Lanham has observed, "requires the acceptance of imposture,"[42] while madness, rightly taken, offers redemption from our self-imposed barbarisms. Frost gives evidence for, as he makes evident, a new civility, one redeeming the external meanness of the ordinary. A momentary stay against confusion.

CHAPTER

# 8

## ORDINARY LANGUAGE BROUGHT TO GRIEF
*"Home Burial" (Dialogue in Disorder and Doubt)*

> It stands to reason that if some image of human intimacy, call it marriage, or domestication, is the fictional equivalent of what the philosophers of ordinary language understand as the ordinary, call this the image of the everyday as the domestic, then the threat to the ordinary that philosophy names skepticism should show up in fiction's favorite threats to forms of marriage, namely in forms of melodrama or tragedy.
> —Stanley Cavell, "The Uncanniness of the Ordinary" in
> *In Quest of the Ordinary: Lines of Skepticism and Romanticism*

> It is a question in marriage, to my feeling, not of creating a quick community of spirit by tearing down and destroying all boundaries, but rather a good marriage is that in which each appoints the other guardian of his solitude, and shows him this confidence, the greatest in his power to bestow.
> —Rainer Maria Rilke, *Letters*

### Introduction: Fronts

"WHY CAN'T a dog simulate pain? Is he too honest?" (*PI* § 250). The questions are characteristic of Wittgenstein's intermittently comic line of inquiry about pain and other so-called inner states (intending, expecting, understanding, and so on) in *Philosophical Investigations*. Perhaps part of what Wittgenstein meant when he said that a book of philosophy could be composed entirely of such jokes runs along the following lines. Jokes presuppose a rich sense of what is conventional (part of a form of life) and what would constitute a breach or breakdown of convention in a specific case. For Wittgenstein, J. L. Austin, John Wisdom, and Stanley Cavell, among others, this understanding of convention and its susceptibilities constitutes, I take it, the very problematic of the philosophy of "ordinary" language and accounts in part for its comic relief.[1] For these thinkers, investigating our conventional boundaries in their breaking down, or in their return after suppression, can free us, as in laughter, to understand and accept our own powers and limits.

Of course, serious breakdowns of communal conventions often break or at least bend those shouldering them; if anyone manages to laugh, it is usually only

long after they, after we, have climbed out of some black hole, unburdened ourselves. For this reason, most readers have naturally resisted Robert Frost's famous "Home Burial," feeling the poem's pull on us, its gravity, and trying, unsuccessfully, to sidestep both its pitfalls and pratfalls. Yet in this poem particularly, I propose, Frost looks to confide most fully in his readers, relying on our recognition of the significance of conventions, chiefly linguistic, taken by all as markers of, boundaries between, obstacles to, limits of, and bridges across lives and worlds. Like a cubist painting whose planes run askew, "Home Burial" places untold confidence in our ability, despite our discomfort, to accept and negotiate the deepest man-made fissures in, and walls around, each human being. (As Frost says elsewhere, "I'm in favor of a skin and fences and tarriff walls. I'm in favor of reserves and witholding"; *LLU* 223). The characters in "Home Burial," by contrast, only fitfully wield and weakly acknowledge, because they avoid or defy, the linguistic conventions normally needed to constitute a self, a marriage, a form of life. They avoid them with good reason, possibly even to good effect, being constrained, it may be, from doing otherwise. Yet Frost hands it to us not to drop their difficulties, to try to bespeak the characters' and our own situation appropriately. He so positions us that, though we are tempted to mouth platitudes or to go mute altogether, as we often do at real funerals, we must—emphasis on the word "must"—take a double perspective on the plight of each character if we are to understand, and accept, not only their limits but our own. In this way, the poet looks to redeem a particular human tragedy as our ordinary mortal comedy.

On any reading this much is obvious, however: nothing in the characters' view of their situation in "Home Burial" is laughable *simpliciter*. Amy and her husband suffer terribly together, alone. By contrast, the method of presentation and paradox that Frost employs may usefully be called comic, or "comedic" in Kenneth Burke's expansive sense of the word. For Burke, the comedic refers to the engaged but ironic acceptance of human limits or boundaries, much as it does in Wittgenstein and Cavell. If, accordingly, we read "Home Burial" from within the larger situation we readers occupy and in the larger context of other Frost dialogue poems—"West-Running Brook," "Snow," "The Death of the Hired Man," each of which exemplifies different orders of ingenuity and success in speech in the context of the romantic interest in ordinary language—the poem can be understood to locate some of the powers and limits of our own form of life. For the poem voices—at the scene of the death of a child—the eloquent refusal to remain in a world of speech on the part of one of its parents, quite as though refusal were a live option. And it poses what may happen when the unquestionable framework of our form of life with one another is shaken at ground zero.

I noted in an earlier chapter that Frost records that he insinuated "no villains" into the poems in *North of Boston* (1914), in which "Home Burial" appears.[2] His observation also recalls a similar remark regarding Robert Browning's purpose in

"My Last Duchess" mentioned in chapter 1, to the effect that the inclination of readers to moral condemnation of the villainous duke offers the least productive approach to the poem.[3] In "Home Burial," we experience similar temptations to contrast the characters' condition with our own and to judge them harshly; or, conversely, to dissociate ourselves from the suffering and grief and moral failings of the wife and husband altogether. What, after all, is there to say? Resisting those temptations to dumb commonplaces or to dead silence is not easy, for we are tempted to think that our critical talk is all or nothing. Instead we need to listen to what the poem says and to respond to the characters appropriately. But, then, "The *appropriate* word. How do we find it?" (*RPP2* § 72). We might begin by asking, How do the characters themselves speak?

Intimations of what I am calling comic philosophic breakdown, of something perversely gone wrong, may be heard in the husband's tragic "I shall laugh the worst laugh I ever laughed" (line 89). Among other things, this is an exclamation of incredulity spoken after his wife harangues him for something ostensibly no more than a breach of rural manners, his bringing his spade into the entryway of their farmhouse. By contrast, his wife speaks as though the coherence of all things in heaven and on earth had been broken by his lapse, shall we call it, regarding these most mundane of matters: shoes, stains, a spade, "everyday concerns" (line 86).

> "Then you came in. I heard your rumbling voice
> Out in the kitchen, and I don't know why,
> But I went near to see with my own eyes.
> You could sit there with the stains on your shoes
> Of the fresh earth from your own baby's grave
> And talk about your everyday concerns.
> You had stood the spade up against the wall
> Outside there in the entry, for I saw it."
>
>                                               (lines 81–88)

These contrasting attitudes register the two chief perspectives juxtaposed in the poem: the extraordinary perspective on everyday and ordinary things provided by death and grief, and the perspective of what can be called ordinary life itself, belonging to those not exigently forced to walk along the edge. The husband is buffeted between both positions—he sees different things under one or another aspect—hence his inclination to laugh (after all, why get upset over a spade, stains, shoes?), a laugh that would nevertheless be his "worst" (for he seems to suspect, at least, that it might be unforgivable to laugh at such a thing, that is, at such a time. We might say that what he ought to be able to *see,* namely his wife's pain, he has to *interpret* to be pain, as though he were an inexperienced reader).

A related expression, this time of self-protective skepticism, can be heard in the wife's more generalized cry of contempt, beset as she is over the death of their first-born infant son, at the moment she stitches her fate to Fate:

> "The nearest friends can go
> With anyone to death, comes so far short
> They might as well not try to go at all.
> No, from the time when one is sick to death,
> One is alone, and he dies more alone.
> Friends make pretense of following to the grave,
> But before one is in it, their minds are turned
> And making the best of their way back to life
> And living people, and things they understand."
>
> (lines 97–105)

"Friends make pretense of following to the grave," which is to say they *simulate pain* (grief) with respect to an event they are said not to be able to understand and wish to flee. Amy's claim marks another moment of the breaking down of conventions and expectations, when the wife redefines a shared ritual as farce, friends as imposters, and the world as evil. Hearing this, we bystanders would prefer, I think, to distance ourselves from the inclusive indictment it records, handling her contempt as either perfectly explainable rage born of grief or as textbook hysteria. In doing so, we fail even to begin to puzzle out the complex argument and role this indictment performs in the poem.

Being able to simulate pain or grief, for example, or to penetrate the masks of simulation in others, as Amy claims to do, presupposes a knowledge of shared pain- or grief-conventions against which faked speech or behavior can be compared, exposed as unreal. This is the reason that only human beings are said to be able to simulate pain, whereas we say that dogs (less perspicuous a representation than in Wittgenstein's time) not only "don't" but "can't" do so: not because they're too honest (!) but because they fail to engage at least certain complex conventions involved in such an act as simulating. Although we do say, it is true, that dogs "obey" or "disobey" us, we do so because they exhibit the ability to follow or contravene their own rudimentary reactions to some of our more manifest desires. And while we now agree that they experience the physical distress of pain, they do not formulate, they can not do anything with, the word "pain," and they cannot entertain possible purposes for pretending or play-acting pain nor appreciate the occasions on which it might be to their benefit to do so. In sum, they do not, because they *can* not, play "Let's pretend pain."[4]

I rather belabor the point here to highlight the notion of pretense or simulation, including the criteria or conditions for its recognition. The charge of pretense, after all, percolates from the pit of Amy's rage against her friends and world. Our own particular challenge is not to understand why Amy may be angry, nor to strike a studied pose as though facing her down, but to take up a position as it were beside, as a neighbor to her and her husband. That would be an accomplishment both coming and going: refusing ourselves the usual consolation of commonplaces about death and facile judgments of the characters (in a phrase,

refusing the thought that our moral "talk is all"; line 112); and refusing the demented pretense that a child's death has nothing on us (refusing the illusion that leads us to say we do not know "how to speak" about it at all; line 46). Far and away the best critical treatments of this poem are those by Randall Jarrell and Joseph Brodsky; but the former represents the overwhelming majority of critics who seem to believe that their talk *is* all, that is, they work under the pretension that we can or need to *explain* Amy's plight, while the latter stands virtually alone in holding that, when all is said and done, no one—characters or critics—will have spoken appropriately: "language, in the final analysis, is alien to the sentiments it articulates."[5] Neither critical approach works, each seriously breaks down, because each violates the other's boundaries, either inadvertently reducing talk to blowing hot air or directly placing oneself beyond the circle of talk entirely. A successful criticism must articulate more adequate language to acknowledge the powers, as well as the limits, of talk.

For it happens in this poem that Frost no less than Wittgenstein scrupulously attends to talk, to "what we say when," to "how we speak" about, for example, pain or grief or its simulation, what Wittgenstein and Cavell term the "grammatical criteria" by which we identify grief in terms of certain behaviors in certain circumstances. This appeal to what we "can" and "can not," "do" and "do not" say in order to mean what we mean, and even to what we sometimes "must" mean when we say what we say, redirects us away from inner consciousness as the mediator of meaning and toward the outer scene of the natural language we already know and share—our language games and their uses that contextualize both what we know about the world and what there is about the world still to be said. Our ability to talk has been conceived more as a "knowing-how" than a "knowing-that," to use Gilbert Ryle's useful distinction, more the ability to do things with words than to theorize about our doings.[6]

As I have argued, only Stanley Cavell, in his juxtapositions of Emerson and Thoreau with Wittgenstein and Heidegger, has thus far given a sufficiently complex *kind* of reading of what I take to be the rhetorical-philosophical themes and activities also to be found in Robert Frost.[7] In this chapter, my purpose is to link grammatical or philosophical analysis—for example, *what* it is to say something of something, what properly constitutes the saying—with a rhetorical sensitivity to what it is to say it, in the language of rhetoricians, "appropriately."

## How to Speak

"We feel as if we had to *penetrate* phenomena."

—Ludwig Wittgenstein, *Philosophical Investigations*

Of course learning, and being taught or trained, how to speak are the very matters that open *Philosophical Investigations*, with the figure of Augustine, as a boy,

listening to his elders name objects, correlate words with the things that are their meanings, and then going and doing likewise (*PI* § 1). In "Home Burial," similarly, the husband speculates that he might be taught by his wife how to speak: "I don't know how to speak of anything / So as to please you. But I might be taught. . . . / We could have some arrangement / By which I'd bind myself to keep hands off / Anything special you're a-mind to name" (lines 46–47; 50–52). In this passage, Amy's husband acts as though he feels himself once again to be a boy, no doubt a very bad boy. He speaks almost as though he were unconsciously seeking to replace the lost infant son about whom, moments earlier, his wife chastised him for speaking (lines 29–30; 36), their own child who will now never learn to speak, tell a joke, befriend a dog, or pretend, say, to be someone else—in short, to be someone else. Previous readers have missed this philosophic preoccupation of the characters, of Frost, with speaking, with its conditions and requirements and its joys and sorrows as one grows into speech among others. To understand and accept these conditions, as Amy's husband appears half-willing to do, contrasts with Amy's refusal to enter or remain in a world whose limits are the possibilities of the language she and her husband have known, the conventions that they can actually handle and that she labors to overthrow or exchange.[8] In her pain, Amy ambiguously struggles to raze, and possibly even to remake, the linguistic boundaries of their world, concluding suspensefully, "How can I make you—" (line 113), presumably make her husband understand, presumably by means of words.[9]

We know further that, for Wittgenstein, Augustine's picture-model of language proves inadequate, since learning most words is not a matter of accumulating in one's mind "logical pictures" of objects or of external or internal states of affairs but rather embraces untold different interactive "games" involving myriad forms and functions—making jokes, asking questions, guessing riddles, play-acting and simulating, and innumerable others (*PI* § 23)—in sum, Emerson's list once more. To understand such games requires a patient reflection on their strategies and tactics and only afterward cautious extrapolating of linguistic rules and testing for a "truth" appropriate to the kind of game each one is. In these tasks, so-called ordinary language philosophy resembles the reading of legal hard cases. As in law, the aim is not to extract fixed and determinate rules purported to be lurking behind the lines but to formulate and apply more rhetorically sensitive rules as "signposts" (*PI* § 85) suggesting, not dictating, how to "go on" (*PI* § 151, § 210) with the case at bar, the game in play, or the poem before us.[10] Now attention gets directed to interpersonal grammatical and rhetorical structures and occasions of our talk rather than to any genealogy of, for example, the wife's psychological motives. For Wittgenstein no less than the ancient grammarians and rhetoricians, and again for Frost, language cannot be prised apart from the circumstances of its use (*PI* § 154, § 164), the contextual practices and forms of life we share with others, including the grief that we suffer, resist, or avoid.

What has effaced these complex philosophic-rhetorical activities in "Home Burial" for so long is the fact that Frost's investigation of them is not obvious. Or rather it is so obvious that previous critics have not noticed them. Critics were not in a position to notice them because, with this poem as with others, they have been trying so hard to look at the "inner" workings of the characters rather than the outer behavior and scene of their speaking, as though straining to penetrate the characters' words to grasp the mental anguish within. Such a model of knowing similarly tempts the characters to try to bypass words in favor of sight: only seeing is believing and only unmediated first-person presence counts as seeing. "We feel as if we had to *penetrate* phenomena" (*PI* § 90), Wittgenstein observes; "'But *this* is how it is—' I say to myself over and over again. I feel as though, if only I could fix my gaze absolutely sharply on this face, get it in focus, I must grasp the essence of the matter" (*PI* § 113)—as if *"The essence is hidden from us"* (*PI* § 92), and words are in the way. It is true, of course, that persons can conceal their thoughts and feelings by not speaking or by baiting their own words as traps for others. Frost records as much in his earlier "Revelation" in *A Boy's Will* (1913), whose opening lines also point to pretense:

> We make ourselves a place apart
>     Behind light words that tease and flout,
> But oh, the agitated heart
>     Till someone really find us out.
>
> (lines 1–4)

But such dissimulation does not entail that others must, much less that they can, somehow get beyond or "behind" another's words altogether, as though "to know a person" required our being able to see, or somehow to get, inside her head. It indicates rather that a different or new set of words or gestures may be needed to spring the trap, or call the bluff, of another set.

Like the husband in the poem, critics have never noticed what everyone has grown accustomed to ("'The wonder is I didn't see at once. / I never noticed it from here before. / I must be wonted to it'"; lines 20–22), that variations on the act of sight, expressed in ordinary words like "look" and "see," occur a remarkable twelve times in just the first twenty-one lines of the poem and four or five times after that.[11] The stress, meaning both the emphasis within the words and the anxiety of the characters, is unmistakable in the first lines of the poem: "He saw her from the bottom of the stairs / Before she saw him" (lines 1–2). Frost subtly links, as the poem proceeds, physically seeing someone or something with knowing and having power over him or her or it: "'What is it you see / From up there always?— for I want to know.'"; "He said to gain time: 'What is it you see?'" (lines 6–7, 10); "She let him look, sure that he wouldn't see, / Blind creature; and awhile he didn't

see" (lines 15–16); "'The wonder is I didn't see at once. / I never noticed it from here before'" (lines 20–21); and later, "'But I went near to see with my own eyes'" (line 83); and "'You had stood the spade up against the wall / Outside there in the entry, for I saw it'" (lines 87–88).

Again like the husband in the poem, readers and critics have also understandably wanted to see and thereby know not merely what the woman sees outside but, more to the point, what she feels inside, which is to say her pain and suffering, her grief. The general attitude is that her outer words are either a front, or a substitute, for the real inner pain. So Amy's husband would find her out the easy way by emptying her words of whatever meaning they have, reducing them to artificial valves for heartfelt feelings, hoping that he might solve the matter, end her pain (and his) by having those feelings aired: "There, you have said it all and you feel better" (line 108). It is, again, as though words here were themselves empty earthen vessels of some hidden toxin. (If he is not flatly wrong in this, he is not just right either.) Even a critic so sensitive to language as Randall Jarrell executes an almost predictable volte-face when he abandons the husband's surface "rhetoric" (his term) to look for the inner pain and suffering of the wife. As if eyeing a way in (and out) for himself, Jarrell proceeds as though inspired, in the presence of the woman's pain, not to respond to her actual words but to lobotomize them, to extract her deep-set psychological mysteries and motives, her secrets and self-deceptions. Relying on an expertise he expects "we all understand," and impatient with what the woman is saying, Jarrell determines that Amy suffers, as some grieving mothers will suffer, from a displaced guilt-complex, a diagnosis he offers strictly along Freudian lines (as he casually observes, "An old doctor says . . . "): "To her, *underneath,* the child's death must have seemed a punishment."[12] But what can "underneath" refer to here if not to the woman's actions and words? And what could it mean to get underneath her actions and words, "behind" situated language-in-use (or, said another way, what force does his "must" have)?

Whether Jarrell could be right or wrong about what Amy "must" be feeling— his suggestion amounts to our viewing the death of the child as the mother's wish-fulfillment, toward which she feels unconscious responsibility and guilt[13]— his proposals collapse in view of the fact that, here, we cannot possibly have any way of knowing. Or shall we summarily *decree* repression, guilt, and punishment as the primary "lesson" of this poem? After all, if even the husband lacks, as he does lack, the sort of knowledge he would need to determine the matter, how much less in a position are we to determine it? Worse, Amy's husband beats Jarrell to the punch when he tactlessly asks aloud (asks himself more than his wife):

> "What was it brought you up to think it the thing
> To take your mother-loss of a first child
> So inconsolably"

(lines 63–65)

The moral here is not that a clinical anatomy of mourning must prove tangential to Frost's effort, but rather that it is not self-evident that, much less how, it might be relevant.[14] The critics' collective impatience has only brought upon themselves a serious bout of "aspect-blindness" to what stands patently before all of us ("blind creature"; line 16), namely, that what the woman says has never before been parsed, dwelled in, followed out for its sense, or non-sense (or both): "'We see emotion.'—As opposed to what?—We do not see facial contortions and make the inference [she] is feeling joy, grief, boredom.... Grief, one would like to say, is personified in the face. This is essential to what we call 'emotion'" (*RPP2* § 570). In effect, the critics metaphysically theorize, overlooking the characters' manifest suffering in ways that are comic almost to the point of tears.

Meanwhile the temptation felt by the characters and critics to toggle back and forth between outside and inside continues to pull at us with a potent attraction: "the difficulty is to remove the prejudice" that tempts us to want, or to think that we need, to guess inner feelings of pain, grief, rather than to listen to what is expressed or done (their manifestations). "It is not a *stupid* prejudice" (*PI* § 340) that continues to tempt us to do so; as Marjorie Perloff has put it, "even today, mainstream poetry often seems trapped in an oppressive circle of self-presence, the 'cry of the heart' designed to convey some sort of unique personal essence."[15] Failing to rush or maintain these defenses, as we must fail, we soon find ourselves entertaining a distant skepticism about people and taking lyric poems as celebrations by definition of skepticism and solipsism. We not only fear that we can never really "know," for example, another person, but we wonder whether that person is even human at all: "As observers, we feel frustrated because instead of reaching the pain itself, we are restricted to observing merely indirect signs and superficial symptoms. In being conventional ... these signs can seem arbitrary: what we hear as a groan might be ... a song or a signal to a pet and not necessarily a sign of pain."[16]

As we have begun to see, the duplicity of these matters requires careful steps, which are laid out as follows. After we have completed our circumspection of the poem in the two subsections following, the chapter divides into three further sections. The second section contemplates all that it means for the husband not to know "how to speak." The third section unpacks the elaborate sustained claims of the wife, culminating in her charges of "pretense" and "evil"; and the final section suggests how natural it is that ordinary language is brought to grief.

## Boundary Disputes

When we stop and look, we notice that the events of "Home Burial" occur on a stairway and at the threshold of a door.[17] These are literally and figuratively pivotal places that provide scenes of instruction for characters in "The Death of the Hired Man" and "The Black Cottage," as well as, less distinctly, for "The Generations

of Men," "A Hundred Collars," "The Housekeeper," and "The Fear"—in sum, nearly half of the poems in *North of Boston*. These and other images common in Frost signal moments of transition and change at the border.[18] As Bakhtin has noted of the "chronotope of the threshold," it "can be combined with the motif of the encounter, but its most fundamental instance is the chronotope of *crisis* and *break* in a life.[19] When we apply this notion to the investigation in "Home Burial" of the self speaking to others, "self," "speaking," and "other" come to be understood as pivot-concepts functioning more as sites of action and crisis (symbolized by stairs and threshold) than as determinate entities or containers, as Frost himself makes clear in the concluding stanza of the poem quoted earlier:

> But so with all, from babes that play
>   At hide-and-seek to God afar,
> So all who hide too well away
>   Must speak and tell us where they are.
>                          ("Revelation," lines 9–12)

What proves unexpectedly important here is, once more, that little modal auxiliary verb "must," for it identifies, not a priori transcendental conditions, but pragmatic ontological conditions for the possibility of being known at all: to be known by oneself as by others requires coming (to use one of Frost's Heideggerian-sounding phrases) "into the clearing" delimited by the conventions of a shared language.

Wittgenstein effectively catches the drift of Frost's "Revelation" in his celebrated dictum that "Nothing is hidden" (*PI* § 445), a paradoxical claim that arguably stands to his thought in the way that Derrida's "Il n'y a pas de hors-texte" stands to his. Just as Derrida does not intend to deny the existence of the external world, so Wittgenstein does not wish to deny the inner reality that partly informs intending, being in pain, expecting, grieving, and so on. Both pronouncements were designed to jolt us into realizing the linguisticality and physicality—there, on the surface—of what others know, feel, imagine, think. As Frost puts it: "Just the surface of it. That's the main thing, isn't it? The physical surface of it";[20] "Get down into things, / It will be found there's no more given there / Than on the surface" (*A Masque of Reason*, lines 281–83). In "The Constant Symbol" (1946), a famous late essay written one year after the appearance in German of the *Investigations*, Frost offers his own strong version of Wittgenstein's "Nothing is hidden": "How can the world know anything so intimate as what we were intending to do? The answer is the world presumes to know. The ruling passion in man is not as Viennese as is claimed. It is rather a gregarious instinct to keep together by minding each other's business. Grex rather than sex.... No more invisible means of support, no more invisible motives, no more invisible anything (*SP* 24). In addition to subordinating the libidinal drive to the rhetorical motive in people to talk,[21] Frost's more telling point, I take it, is that action, and more particularly

speech, in its everyday forms like gossip as well as its poetic forms like dramatic dialogues, are the means by which "an outsider may see what we were up to sooner and better than we ourselves." "The bard has said in effect, Unto these forms did I commend the spirit" (*SP* 24).

## Grievance v. Grief

Previous readings of "Home Burial" form a tight circle around the belief that Frost's poem is centered on the woman's inner grief. John Kemp and William Pritchard refer uncritically to "expressions of grief" and "the grieving wife." Reginald Cook announces that "grief is the key to the situation."[22] This situation is assumed to be as obvious, as "pathetic" and "tragic" (Pritchard; Cook), as the omnipresent and "inconsolable" grief (Cook), and we are brought to conclude that the poem expresses the tragic portrait of a grieving wife. Moreover, grief is thought by all the critics to be something inner, not only for the good reason that the wife is said to conceal her feelings even from herself (her husband says "Let me *into* your grief" [line 59; my emphasis]; and Cook: "Amy . . . wants to hug her grief"),[23] but because it is assumed that grief is equivalent to feelings at best only analogically inferable from words and physical movements, and in itself irreparably sealed away from others, as if we need to look into ourselves in order to see what others might be feeling, as if we must finally guess. As though to compensate for their supposed estrangement from these feelings, accordingly, nearly all critics either express what I take to be pretentious sympathy for the woman's "tragedy" or self-righteously upbraid and even condemn Amy for her self-imposed plight or flight.[24]

All of this is further aggravated by the fact that "grief" is not only the critics' term but Frost's own chosen word for what he is attempting to express in "sad" (*SP* 67) poems like "Home Burial." We can lessen this aggravation, fortunately, by noting how distinctively Frost uses the term. In his well-known introduction to Robinson's *King Jasper*, Frost distinguishes "griefs" from "grievances" (*SP* 61). Griefs are "immedicable woes—woes that nothing can be done for—woes flat and final" (*SP* 67); they furnish the material for what Frost considers the most genuine poetry. Grievances by contrast grow out of the stuff of local urgency, more or less passing (Frost was thinking of political) complaints, which he rejects as poetry's point: "I don't like grievances. I find I gently let them alone whenever published. What I like is griefs." And most tellingly: "Grievances are a form of impatience. Griefs are a form of patience" (*SP* 62). In other words, grievances are temporary and symptomatic; griefs are permanent and ontological. Grievances spring from removable dissatisfactions; griefs constitute indispensable limitations and finalities (boundaries) of some part of the world. Presuming for now that Frost succeeds in his stated aim in "Home Burial," we can conclude from our previous arguments that the specific "grief" it expresses must be: (1) "immedicable,"

ontological, but also, as we learned earlier, (2) visible, manifesting Frost's own "intending" in ways that the world normally does, as a matter of fact, presume to be able to know.

Thus we arrive at the problem we have been circumambulating for some time. The "grief" that the wife is widely said to suffer—"grief-over-a-death"—is a grief that is also said by the critics to be *concealed,* not visible; and it is a grief that Amy wants to dissociate from others, whose boundaries she wants to *change,* if she can ("I won't have grief so / If I can change it"; lines 106–7)—which latter option would, needless to say, render it something other than ontological, other than "immedicable." Precisely what it is about grief that Amy would change and how she might change it we can leave for later. The thrust of the matter here is that throughout the poem and especially in lines 91–107, the wife undertakes so impassioned a "protest"[25] of some kind that one comes to suspect we ought to liken it more to Frost's impatient "grievances" than to patient, forbearing "grief." Thus Richard Poirier observes: "The catalogue of her complaints is a symptom of how for her they have become a way of deadening a deeper grief too painful to be borne. Her list of grievances is no adequate metaphor, that is, for the grief she feels."[26]

If it is a deep grievance against "grief-over-a-death" that the wife airs to protect herself, as it were a means of self-medication, what then is *Frost* doing in the poem as a whole—I mean on his stated instruction that poems such as this one manifest "immedicable woes"[27]—which is to say, grief. I insist here that it will not do to say, as Cook and others say, that the aim of "Home Burial" is to give us a "tragic portrait of a grieving wife." What Frost invites us to attend to resides elsewhere, neither mostly concealed "in" the wife, in her "grief-over-a-death," nor in ourselves, in our sympathy with or judgment of the characters) but concealed, as it were, in the clearing between the two. What can bridge though not close the gap between us and the characters, between one character and another, and between a character and itself, are just those easy, ordinary words, those junk bonds in which Amy accuses her husband of putting too much stock. Thus her "*You—*oh, you think the talk is all" (line 112). Of course, Amy is right as far as it goes—talk is not all. But Amy is right for the wrong reasons: "you think the talk is all" means (to her) that her husband neglects feelings, which is also true enough but not because those feelings are "inner," as she all along implies. In fact what she no less than her husband misses between them is the rhetorical-philosophical effects of their own palpable words. Talk is not all, not because it leaves out inner feelings but because it manifests the inner *in* the outer, in the daily practices, circumstances, and purposes, in interlocutors and audiences and agendas, with which words comport and which speakers and audiences must engage. Together inner/outer embodied in speech and action in a physical world is all that we humans have, or are.

What, then, is Frost's grief and how might it be understood to organize and comprise this poem? Hypothesizing this grief as comprising something other

than Amy's, imagining that it rests its case on the characters' actions and words, I suggest that the critics' directing us "inside" is not wrong absolutely but rather so inadequate as to be gravely misleading, inviting us to overlook the grief *there*, in front of us. And I propose that the pained grievances of the wife are naturally, secretly, against *that* grief, whatever it is. In this case, what Frost said of Edward Arlington Robinson ought to be applied to Frost himself, and to us: "Not for me to search his sadness to its source. He knew how to forbid encroachment" (*SP* 67).

## The Grammar of Grief

### The Weave of Our Life

If the place at which we have arrived is entangled, the way out is arduous and steep, for our working-through must go "by the long road of the interpretation of signs,"[28] there being no short-cut to any essence, to some metaphysical "grief itself." The phenomenon facing us in "Home Burial" is not grief as an inner event behind the behavior and talk but the characters' own approaches to and avoidances of that grief, and their own (and the critics') misunderstanding of its expression as a logical picture or failed representation of the inner—in short, the grammar of grief and the rhetoric of its refusal. When Wittgenstein writes that "'grief' describes a pattern which recurs, with different variations, in the weave of our life" (*PI* pt. 2, p. 174e), he provides us with resources to begin to discern that the pattern in the weave of this poem has been overshadowed by mounds of psychological speculation and mythology. Rather than adding to these speculations we would do better to ask: What is the pattern in the textual weave of "Home Burial?"[29] That is, what do we understand these words "as"? Equally important: how do we recognize variation and norm in grief? What are our own lives such that grief may be said to be constitutive of them, part of their textual weave, rather than something else, say a discrete, extraordinary event?

I said that previous readers have evinced impatience with this language game and missed the complex pattern when they failed to see or remark Frost's insistence on sight in lines 1–21 and following, and when they failed to consider the couple's obsession with speaking and not knowing how to speak, culminating at the end of the poem in the wife's "*You*—oh, you think the talk is all" (line 112) and "How can I make you—" (line 113). As we turn to focus our attention on how the couple does succeed and fail in talk, we overtake another critical oversight regarding the pattern in the weave, for no one to my knowledge has mentioned the unprecedented occurrence in a Frost poem of such a large number of modal auxiliary verbs.[30] I count 78 instances of such verbs, in 116 lines totaling 1,023 words, or one such verb every line and a half, with the amazing ratio of 7.7 percent overall. "Don't" tops the list with 18 occurrences, roughly half issuing from the wife. Of course, numbers alone reveal little since they tell us nothing about

the different language games in which the verbs are employed. Not surprisingly, these verbs exhibit varying meanings, purposes, and effects. "Don't," for example, is sometimes used descriptively, sometimes prescriptively, sometimes conjecturally, and sometimes with moral, with psychological, or with other consequences and causes. When we recall that modal auxiliary verbs have the power of marking off boundaries, limits, and possibilities of speech and action in someone's world, as in the wife's summary "You *can't* because you *don't* know how to speak" (line 71; my emphases), we can begin to see that at least some uses of such verbs can be "transcendental" in the pragmatic sense of linguistically indicating the conditions for the possibility of something. What possibilities of which phenomena (*PI* § 90), then, do these neglected auxiliaries signify?

In addition to matters of seeing, previous readers have also failed to remark that Amy sustains, across the intense moments that constitute this poem, an elaborate argument—or rather several different arguments, in fact different kinds of argument—first regarding her husband's apparent lack of feelings of grief, then the "pretense" of friends at such feelings, and finally the "evil" of the world. More than any other aspect, this escalating outward of her claims alerts us to the conceptual or grammatical-rhetorical, human investments at stake for all of us.

## "'Don't, Don't, Don't, Don't'"

What, then, is Amy so upset about throughout the poem? If we take it as sufficient explanation that her child has died, then what is she so angry about? But then, it will be insisted, how is this not equally obvious? Her anger, even if we finally call it "irrational," even if others label it "hysterical," at least plausibly constitutes, as we have allowed, a normal part of nonpathological grief. Hence we might be tempted to agree with those critics who assert that, *whatever* she is angry about, or whatever she *says* she's angry about, should be held as insignificant in comparison to her husband's willingness or ability to respond to her appropriately. Inasmuch as he fails at this, as he obviously does, he arguably deserves her ire and dismay.

Yet this line of response condescends to the woman and convicts the husband without due process. It misdirects the question, what is she angry about? away from what the woman *has to say*—as if her words "*cannot*" count, so irrational are we to assume her anger to be—and refuses to discriminate her husband's failures from his lack of success, his failures from his mistakes, and his failures and mistakes from hers. For, though what she says she is angry about is precisely his failure to respond *appropriately* to "what was in the darkened parlor" (line 96) and to her as a person, we cannot simply assume that we know what she means or wants here ("One cannot guess what a word means. One has to look at its use and learn from that"; *PI* § 340). Specifically we know up front that she rebuffs him in anger because he hasn't seen what she thinks he ought to see outside (line 19); that he

doesn't "know how to ask" questions (line 43); and that he "can't" speak (line 36) because he doesn't "know how to speak of anything / So as to please" her (lines 46–47). On reflection, however, these grievances bespeak a complexity beyond the many obviously wrong things that the husband does say and do, and beyond the things that he does and says obviously wrongly. Auxiliary verbs like "can't" and "don't" can signal many possibilities, so we need to try to untangle their meanings. What precisely is her husband's mistake, or failure, here?

The question is made more pointed by the profound ambiguity of attitude that we just mentioned: does Amy's anger drive her past the ordinary boundaries of speech and its normal proprieties onto barren land? How, she implies, can one possibly speak about death and grief? How is one's grief possibly to be understood by anyone else? It remains unclear whether Amy wants to keep her husband and others permanently outside her sphere of suffering or to invite or somehow make them breach its outer limits. Perhaps she herself, in her pain, does not know what she wants; certainly her husband does not know. Most likely she wants both at different times and even simultaneously. In any case, the threefold argument she conducts as the poem runs on centers on the claim that her husband does not know how to speak, and that others merely pretend to do so. What does *this* mean?

In the dramatic context of the poem, the husband's "not knowing how to speak" is shorthand for several related failures of communication, verbal and otherwise: not only his (1) speaking when he should not, (2) in a manner and (3) about what he should not (can not, must not) speak; and not only, in addition, (4) his *acting* when and (5) how he should not (digging the grave, mending the fence, standing the spade in the hall, wearing his muddy shoes inside—all of which "speak" or "say something" to her); but (6) his insisting that his wife speak when, plainly, she will not (lines 12–13); (7) that she listen when she turns away to leave (lines 39, 116); and even, in effect, (8) that she shut up ("Amy!") when "There's someone coming down the road!" (line 111).

This is a considerable ensemble of grievances. Even when Amy's husband responds to her direct request to tell her what he thinks she sees outside (line 18), he fails to get things right, not because his answer is factually wrong but because it *is* right and to her intolerable, and because he appears intent on not merely identifying what she sees outside but, first of all, prefacing his belated astuteness with ostensibly idle remarks and, worse, gearing up to say *more*, to elaborate on "the child's mound" (line 30), provoking her to interrupt: "Don't, don't, don't, don't" (line 30). Don't, that is, *go on* about this intolerable reality that he should not have mentioned in the first place (her own request for it notwithstanding). The offense here seems to be his lack of comprehension of her situation, manifested in both his improprieties of speech and action and his emotional failure (fault? inability?) even to recognize impropriety, to recognize that the boundaries

between them are now shifting and different.[31] In a different context, Gerald Bruns speaks to this last point: "As Wittgenstein says, to know the meaning of a word"—a word like "graveyard" (line 23) or "child's mound" (line 30) or even "child" (line 35)—"is to know how to use it—and also *when* to use it, and, above all, when *not* to use it. Rules of usage are not simply rules of grammar or semiosis but also rules of suitability and decorum."[32] Thus Amy's husband unwittingly plays the Augustinian semiotician: words for him get exhausted by reference, not degraded (or renewed) in abstinence or use. For Amy, these particular violations against suitability or decorum (propriety), however, seem to pall when compared to what she takes to be her husband's mortal fault or failure (or both) responsible for them, a fatal lack that (for her) explains those otherwise venial infractions—namely his absence of feelings of grief: "If you had any feelings, you that dug / With your own hand—how *could* you?—his little grave; / I *saw* you" (lines 72–74; my emphasis).

Now, if we pause at this point in the investigation to ask how Amy knows what her husband feels or does not feel, we come into some advantages in our task of understanding what Frost is up to. First, asking this question gives us enough distance from Amy's terrible pain to allow us to reflect that we may not already understand that pain *or* her situation, just because the seeming transparency of his or her ordinary words is belied by the extraordinary context and the multiple uses to which the words are being put. Further, it enables us to wonder what, exactly, it is that Amy does see when she sees her husband do the things he does and hears him say what he says with his "rumbling voice / Out in the kitchen" (lines 81–82).[33] That is, what does she see them "as?" We are not challenging Amy's faulting her husband's lack of feelings—to her that lack, in general, is his shame. But, specifically, how does she know that he lacks feelings, much less what that putative lack involves and what is responsible for it? It as though she, like her husband, sees his movements and hears his voice as physical, even mechanical events, rather than as human actions. The answer is crucial if we want to understand what her argument, hence what much of the poem itself, means. Obviously Amy is furious about this alleged lack, implying from the outset that it is not merely a factual absence of some kind—a failing for which her husband might, or might not, be responsible—but a fault for which, by definition, he bears some presumably moral responsibility. Hence part of the difficulty of answering this question—what is she angry about? what is she accusing him of?—arises from that ambiguous "you *couldn't* care" (line 97) and previous similar charges, that is, from the ambiguous modal auxiliary verbs, to which we now need to turn.

The explanatory sequence that she implies seems to me to go like this: (1) He "can't" speak because he doesn't "know how to speak" (line 71); and (2) he doesn't know how to speak because he "couldn't" feel what he ought to be feeling (line 97); and (3) he "couldn't" feel either because (*a*) he's morally or otherwise unable

(for whatever unexplored causes or reasons, excluding his own moral agency); or (*b*) he's somehow wrongly rendered himself morally or psychologically unable to feel such feelings. Another possibility is that (4) "couldn't care" (feel) is used merely to indicate *that* there are signs that in fact he "doesn't" care (who knows why?). Against the likelihood that these distinctions ring hollow even to the patient reader ("Who *cares* about what she is going on about? What counts is her *pain*"), we may note that the wife might have responded entirely differently, with a stupefied silence, or inarticulate screams, or patently incoherent rambling on about her child. For us not to struggle to understand *this* particular reaction, just these angry words of hers, would be tantamount to dismissing them, excusing ourselves from responding to her and thus to the poem. Yet how would we support such presumption to dismiss them and to excuse ourselves, short of subsuming her situation under a theory of grief we had tucked away for the purpose from the start? Lacking any such theory of grief myself, I must come back to the contexts in which to *listen* to her.

### "'You Can't Because You Don't Know How'"

For present purposes, these contexts begin with her husband's talk and the sequence just mentioned, that is, with what his words may plausibly suggest and, therefore, how decorous they and he may or may not be. "He said twice over before he knew himself: / '*Can't* a man speak of his own child he's lost?'" (line 34–35; my emphasis). Amy's husband suggests here that he "can't" speak because his wife will not *allow* him to speak (see her "Don't, don't, don't, don't"), *not* that he considers himself rhetorically or grammatically unable—not, that is, because he cannot find or does not know the right words, as his wife believes and he himself later allows (line 46). Here the "can't" is normative and prescriptive, not empirical. And he implies that he doesn't "know how" to speak for reasons most likely related to what he takes to be *her* arbitrariness, the unreasonableness of her sanctions upon him, and not, again, at least at this point, his own limitations, failings, or faults. Moreover, his asking this painful question ("Can't a man speak of his own child he's lost?") *twice*, "before he knew himself," is therefore multiply suggestive: before he realized that he was talking (hence oblivious to situation and audience); before he realized the implications of what he was saying (hence not in control of his words); before he himself realized it (hence, perhaps, lagging behind his wife's grasp of things); before he knew the answer himself (hence as if stumped by his own rhetorical question); and also, perhaps, before he could re-orient himself as to who he was *as speaker* (husband, male, grieving father) posing such a question.

    The ambiguity of these verbs matters because it betokens the same lack of control or decorum to which the husband later confesses, the limits or status of which is unclear: are they a social blunder, or a lapse in memory, hence limits to

his world? Thus, by "can't" here *he* may, as we said, mean that he is not being allowed to speak of his child, but he betrays in his complaint that very lack of sensibility, of decorum, of which his wife soon accuses him. Similarly, it matters that the particular language game he is rhetorically playing and losing here and throughout is the one we would call "lodging a complaint" rather than (say) merely asking a rhetorical question, or whining, or inquiring. These latter would turn his words in quite different directions. As a complaint, they suggest that in spite of his own lack of control, Amy's husband hopes the situation, whatever it is, can be rectified, just as, perhaps, Amy does. After all, the speaker is willing to try to *change* himself, whoever or whatever he is, including even curtailing his sphere of male influence, so to speak, if that is necessary: "But I might be taught [how to speak], / I should suppose. I can't say I see how. / A man must partly give up being a man / With womenfolk," (lines 47–49).

Now what is of interest here is twofold: first, the husband's uses of "can't" and "don't" in lines 35 and 46 ("Can't a man speak of his own child he's lost?") differ from Amy's uses in line 71 ("You can't because you don't know how"), for her verbs include but reach beyond mere description or prescription and gesture toward an explanation (that is, he "can't" even if he wants to; he is constitutively unable because of some particular *cause*). Thus we are in the presence of an argument of hers about the moral and psychological limits of her husband, of his world. Second, and more important, her later, philosophic uses of these and similar verbs—"can't" and "can" and so on (lines 71ff.)—will differ from, and even ultimately contradict, her own empirical, moral, and other uses here—bringing us into the region of limits on the world as such: a metaphysical argument. But first, how does Amy know, or better: what is Amy presuming in order to know what her husband is or is not feeling? And is she correct in her surmise?

### "'Friends Make Pretense of Following to the Grave'"

Clearly Amy has to have what all of us tacitly have—a notion of what grief is. For Wittgenstein, we have indicated, any such notion must identify the "criteria" that must be met for her (for anyone) properly to say that it is "grief" that is present, or absent, in her husband's demeanor. But identification of grief may also include what Wittgenstein calls "symptoms" (what classical rhetoricians call *semeia*, certain or probable signs) that are only sometimes present, indicating that some more complex condition does or does not obtain. Thus, for most human beings, two necessary but nevertheless situated and varying criteria of "grief" are that one has suffered some grave loss and that one's zest for life is thereby curtailed; whereas possible (not only varying but not necessary) symptoms of grief are, for instance, tears, a circumspect countenance, a certain automaticity of speech or movement (for example, "'Making the gravel leap and leap in air, / Leap up, like that, like that'"; lines 75–76 ), and so on.[34] Of course, Amy's grievance from the

start has been that *all* of the symptoms suggest (to her) that her husband is not grieving at all—in effect, that he "couldn't" be grieving when he talks, acts, and looks as he does. Once more: "'If you had any feelings, you that dug / With your own hand—how *could* you?—his little grave'" (lines 72–73; my emphasis). Thus Amy seems to have taken her husband's automaticity of movements not "as" signs of grief but as symptoms of lack of feeling altogether, as it were an inhuman mechanics. And naturally enough, Amy has not specified criteria for grief, only relied on them, although her talk implies that the pertinent criteria, whatever they are, are simply incongruent with "everyday concerns" (line 86), that they remain unfulfilled in her husband's demeanor, and that the other signs (symptoms) that are present further indicate a culpable lack of grief-feelings, hence an absence of grief. Ultimately, whether this moral-psychological argument is a good one or not must involve our own notions of grief and the range of its normal expressions, its pattern or weave in life.

We can gain some perspective on Amy's position when we notice that she has no sooner made this first argument than she abruptly shifts gears and picks up a very different *type* of argument, one she had only broached moments earlier, virtually to herself, when she speculated, "I don't know rightly whether any man can [speak of his dead child]" (line 38). Not only are this particular husband and wife playing different language games, but Amy hints ambiguously here ("I don't know rightly whether any man *can*"; my emphasis) at a "grammatical" inability of men *as such* to speak forth, to represent grief, precisely because they *cannot* feel grief properly, and a fortiori a mother's grief, at the loss of a child. This is the second claim that Amy then extends when she alludes to a similar inability in others: "The nearest friends *can* go / With anyone to death, comes so far short / They may as well not try to go at all" (lines 97–99; my emphasis).

Obviously this is a claim of a kind different from the empirical and normative psychological explanations and judgments made by her (and her husband), and we would do well to ask what reasons she gives for it—whether, for example, this claim also rests, like her first, on an inference from physical symptoms, and even whether it has any basis at all (for she had admitted, "I don't know *rightly*" [my emphasis], where the squinting modifier points ambiguously to herself as much as to others). The scope and implications of this second claim are, again, profound, for its modal verbs implicate not only her husband or even all men but all "friends" and, in the end, the world itself. For this reason, it is a grammatical (philosophical) claim concerned with ultimate limits and boundaries of our knowledge of each other.

The drift of Amy's arguments seems to be this: (1) where her husband culpably *failed* to feel, (2) men as such *cannot* feel sufficiently or really. And not only men but—here she gets vague—(3) all "friends," indeed *all* others "cannot" (as she puts it) "go / With anyone to death" (lines 97–98). In lieu of real grief,

"Friends make pretense of following to the grave" (line 102). Of course, on reflection it is not clear whether "following to the grave" and "going to death" are the near-equivalents they seem to be, much less what it is that they mean (exactly what does she want?). Nor, again, is it clear *how* Amy knows that others cannot do these things. Once more she has not specified but only relied on the criteria necessary for us to identify these feats: do they involve the same criteria as those for "grieving," as they seem to do? To keep from falling into the black hole drawing us into the depths of our own home burial, then, we need to inquire into the grammar of "going to death" and "following to the grave." Are they even roughly that of the grammar of grief? What is it, to go, and to follow? Why is the world "evil?" What scheme of rhetorical-grammatical propriety governs this world that Amy declines to inhabit?

## "Myself As One His Own Pretense Deceives"
### Pretending

We have said that in order to know that her husband is not grieving, Amy needed both a conception (criteria) of what grief is and a basis upon which to argue that he is, in fact, not feeling grief. That basis was found in outward symptoms (digging the grave, going about his ordinary work) inconsistent with her criteria, from which she then inferred, by analogy from her own feelings, an inner lack. How then does Amy proceed to speculate that "all men" "can't" grieve, or to argue that "friends" are only pretending to grieve, making a "pretense" of "following to the grave" (line 103)? Again, she needs to know what a pretense of this would look like and needs to have reasons to believe that their behavior is in fact a pretense.

If we consider pretending in general, we are likely to think of outward signs that someone is not really doing what he or she appears to be doing. We may say that someone is "pretending" to be punching someone else when a closer look reveals that those punches are not hitting home, or that a person is pretending to be Winston Churchill when he talks, scowls, and chomps a cigar like Churchill. In his provocative essay "Pretending," J. L. Austin shows us a further, often overlooked way we use the word, as when we realize or say that someone is pretending to wash the windows when he is really casing the joint.[35] In such an instance, the one in question does, in fact, wash the windows—does fully do what is said is being pretended—yet he is still said to be pretending because the action is otherwise known to be part of something else, some larger circle of affairs that leads us in the particular case to account differently for what is usually meant by "washing the windows." Here we know about the pretense, not from outward signs—someone on close inspection not performing some set of actions or performing them inadequately (punches not connecting, the window-washer not really soaping the windows)—but rather from other sources, say from a tip to the police

putting them on the lookout for a cat burglar pretending to be a handyman who says he will "do windows." This is an a priori knowledge about some greater scheme of things to which the activity in question is known to be subordinated. So again the question: How does Amy *know* that others ("friends") are "making a pretense of" going to death, following to the grave?

I should say that she doesn't come to this knowledge in the same way that she concluded that her husband wasn't feeling grief, not, that is, by inference from outward signs. We can say this not because her claim that "The nearest friends can go / With anyone to death, comes so far short" (lines 97–98) *could* not meaningfully be construed as something one can infer from outward signs, but because this is not in fact how Amy infers it. If it were, we could enumerate here the ways those ersatz-mourners betrayed their false "going to death" and "following to the grave." Reading those phrases literally, for example, we would say that "going to death" is already, obviously falsified, not because the mourners do not physically die but because none of them pretends to. Such a literalist reading would be impossible to credit, in other words, in part because this is not what anyone means when one talks of "going to the funeral" or "comforting the mother," phrases rhetorically similar, I take it, to Amy's "going to death" and "following to the grave." If it is insisted that, ordinary language notwithstanding, physical dying is precisely what Amy means, then it may be noted that Amy doesn't physically die any more than the others do, in which case her accusation of pretense doubles back on herself, rendering her complaint against others all the more difficult to understand as anything more than a long moan of pain. Though this is a logically possible line of interpretation, and though emotionally Amy probably does wish literally to die (*is* moaning in pain), still it's a stretch to see how she could conclude that those unnamed "friends" are actually pretending "to die" taken literally. What then does she mean? Nothing at all?

The conventional and most plausible tack is to take her as saying that those who "follow to the grave" only pretend to mourn, that is, pretend to be sad, to be in pain, to feel lost—that they do not really *mean* what they say and do. And not only do they not mean it the way that Amy means it but in any way at all that could be said to constitute "grief." But again, how does Amy know this? We might say, by the signs or symptoms. Perhaps she saw the mourners alternate their haggard looks with funny faces to amuse each other. Or they sent look-alike substitutes to the funeral and their ruse exploded during an intimate moment of hand-holding. Or they invited Amy's husband to play first base in their baseball game later in the day. The problem with these suggestions, of course, is that we never get any indication that Amy in her suffering has pinpointed any such signs of pretense, of betrayal. Just the opposite: because nothing indicates the contrary, we may assume that these friends do in fact do what friends would normally be expected to do, what we would expect ourselves to do, in the face of another's

loss: say kind words, wear sad faces, wear black, remove our hats, tread heavily to the gravesite, perhaps join the prayers. (As far as that goes, even if these friends had made faces or did play ball or dine out later, we may, but we also may not, want to call their previous behavior pretending.) If we try to save the conventional reading by saying that Amy simply means that the others do not, as a simple matter of fact, feel as *she* feels, then we fail to do justice to how harshly she judges them and how she seems willing to act as a result (that is, to shut out the world). Where then is the pretense?

If what I have suggested holds together, it implies that Amy must infer this pretense from some source other than physical signs—in short, that she possesses an a priori knowledge, or what she takes to be knowledge, about a larger scheme of things within which friends' *actual* following to the grave is understood to be belied. Our question, then, becomes, what is this a priori information and how does she use it?

"A Metaphysical Hiding"

What Amy implicitly relies on here, perhaps has long held in secret even from herself, or perhaps has newly arrived at in spite of herself, what her actions and words perceptibly betray when held against the light of more adequate criteria of grief, is her unspoken assumption that no one *can* ever really "know" what another is feeling or thinking just because one is irreparably cut off from others, a body rent asunder from other bodies and left high and dry. One sees a person from across the room, gawks at him, but one cannot be said really to "know" anything since one cannot see what is "inside," which is hidden. So Amy stares and stares at things, at a spade, at shoes, at her husband, and eventually comes to confess: "I thought, Who is that man? I didn't know you" (line 78), quite as though the world were already well lost. And she explicitly concludes: "One is alone, and he dies more alone" (line 101). This hard nugget of common sense is immediately flattened into the golden hook and thread to stitch up her grief-wound with the unbreakable binding of Human Fate. In this way her body, rather than her embodied words, becomes the limit of her world, and she is snagged in the nets of skepticism: "'In hiding something from me, [she] can hide it in such a way that not only will I never find it, but finding it will be completely *inconceivable.*' This would be a metaphysical hiding" (*RPP2* § 586; my emphasis).

Said otherwise, the pain that Amy implies her husband, all men, "friends," and finally the world do not or *can* not feel is not her child's physical pain or death but her own soul-anguish. To her no other *can* touch this pain because, from their beginning to their end, human beings can only stand and stare. To Amy in her plight, we are each as it were island people unsure of our neighbors on the horizon. One suspects the other of being human, but the glass through which we peer is spotted and weak. Thus Amy's claim to knowledge of our human

subjugation to isolation is what Amy implicitly has a choke-hold on, what has a choke-hold on her, as she looks up at her husband on the stairs. Because he does not speak and act precisely as she does, he is said not to be feeling anything; because men are not women they cannot know what women feel and a fortiori what a *mother* feels; because others (friends, the world) act as though they know what they *cannot* know (what another feels), they are, they "must" be, pretending.

This a priori metaphysical assumption—that we humans stand alone, an imported claim dissimulated by Amy to look like a conclusion soberly drawn from experience—shows its true colors when we turn back momentarily to Amy's earlier psychological argument about her husband's lack of feeling and ask: Is *that* argument any good? Does her view of his behavior support the claim that an absence of feelings accounts for his inability to speak and act appropriately? Furthermore, does it support her larger claim about the "evil" of the world, evil because, though each of us is alone and cannot know what others feel, others insist on pretending to do so? In truth, how distorted her inference about her husband is, perhaps how stunned by the burden of loss Amy is, can be gathered from the fact that her husband does (obviously!) suffer. Then why has Amy not seen this?

No doubt we can agree with Amy that her husband avoids and resists feeling more than he does. But his rambling self-absorption about the dead and how weather will rot a birch fence manifest in context both grief for his lost son and anxiety that he may be losing his stricken wife. No doubt he goes about things ineptly and inappropriately, but he goes about them. If at first we miss the fact that more adequate grief-criteria are fulfilled here, it is because we see and hear him chiefly through Amy's distorting scope. After all, the husband importunes his wife, he declares himself "in the face of love" (line 65), he is willing to try to change himself, he coaxes her (unhappily, he bullies her) to express her grief, he somatically displaces his own mental pain through his digging, he dwells on the ravages of time, he distracts himself momentarily by remembering his own "people." This is not what we call pretense and certainly not apathy, for the signs and criteria are, if not unambiguous, at least available on the surface of things: he is in anguish all on his own. For all her looking, her staring, her obsessive spying—"'I crept down the stairs and up the stairs / To look again'" (lines 79–80)—Amy is sadly "aspect-blind" to her husband's behavior, unable in her all-consuming grief to see it "as" grief-behavior, even as human behavior (in Wittgenstein's image one aspect blinds her to another). What Amy takes as evidence of her husband's mechanical coldness is merely the well-known variability of human behavior in the face of breakdown and loss. As a result, moreover, Amy gathers from her observations *no evidence at all* for her larger argument about the pretense of others, because, again, that argument is a priori and not based on evidence at all; it is, instead, itself a pretense of argument ("without calling it a lie"; *RPP2* § 586), of which she may be said to be both perpetrator and victim.

How do we understand Amy's blindness here? After all, she is not physically or psychologically mad (neurotic, hysterical, and so on). Or rather, if she is, Frost has discreetly denied us any superior position from which to speculate about it, not because we lack medical knowledge (in the way that the husband earlier lacked information about her psychological etiology) but because such psychologizing has all along been irrelevant to our leading question, namely, How can she have missed what was right before her eyes? How can she have argued in the way that she has? The questions are philosophically important to us, for the fact is that we, too, suffer periodically from Amy's condition, in our own moments as mad as she (whence the critics' systematic overlooking of this philosophic problem staring at us), mad in the way that Wittgenstein uses the term: "Madness need not be regarded as an illness. Why shouldn't it be seen as a sudden—more or *less* sudden—change of character?" (*CV* 54e) It is the extremity of the variation of Amy's madness from our own ordinary madness that renders hers and her husband's fate so fateful for us, for we see ourselves as in a mirror darkly, and we are uncannily turned around.

We can say, then, that Amy radically misconstrues (not "mistakes") the phenomena of her world and their possibilities due to a more or less sudden and more or less lasting change of character brought on by crushing loss. And it is a change that culminates in her skepticism toward others, that is, her skepticism about the power of words, of talk, to know others as human and as individuals. This skepticism may be read as her positive approach toward reintegration, or as a flight from and avoidance of loss, or, most interestingly, as both (Frost shrewdly makes each reading plausible). What is central is that Amy's high argument about human solitude places in grammatical and rhetorical relief what *we* ourselves mean when we say that human beings, separate from each other, nevertheless can and do come to know each other. It flushes out our own temptation to avoid facing our true separateness from Amy and her husband, either by going silent (Brodsky) or by playing doctor (Jarrell)—in short, by not speaking at all or by not speaking appropriately. In this way, we are likely to miss the chance for our own change of character by overlooking our loss of autonomy, the fantasy of ours and of the characters' of having no limits or boundaries.

The observation I am making, then, is that Amy imposes unreal criteria of "grief"—"going to death," "following to the grave"—onto others, criteria that could not possibly be fulfilled by anyone for two reasons: the criteria require that someone (husband, friends, others) feel someone else's (her) pain; and the criteria occlude how variously, in fact, people grieve, suffer, heal in the world, how we human beings do these things, demanding that this allegedly pretentious variation be reduced to its essence (herself). Separated from her child, Amy craves that oneness each of us is tempted to fantasize as the only surety of knowledge or love. Employed unwittingly, it may be, to protect herself from the grief she cannot

(yet? ever?) face, her criteria derive strictly from the closed circle of her desire, a tightly spun fantasy of ideal unity of self and other within which *(per impossibile)* no boundaries *can* exist. From this circle she excludes husband, friends, and world, all of which are, perforce, always already other than herself. Thus they stand as reminders of the one separation she fights to forget. What Amy hugs unspoken is her unreal desire to erase all boundaries, belie every body, deny all separateness. In this desire she will fail, as she must, for her speech in lines 71 and following is grammatically nonsensical, though it may be, rhetorically, efficacious, either as a hand raised in self-defense or as a hand held out in hope to her husband. In fact, this abnormal separation of grammar, the sense of linguistic possibilities, and rhetoric, or sensibility to grammatical appropriateness, is, I think, itself a symptom of her avoidance of the world, her blindness to their inseparability.

Meanwhile, as a proleptic consequence of her avoidance, Amy treats words and bodies as barricades and borders, though she may also come to use them as bridges. Nor is she alone in her abject desire, far from it; for her husband similarly complains against "things '*twixt* those that love" (line 53; my emphasis), the very limits and boundaries that she cannot abide and harshly imposes, on herself and others, by default if not by fault. This desire for symbiosis with another is of the sort that only a mother might be said actually to enjoy with an unborn child, although a moment's thought reminds us that symbiosis, by definition, involves two beings, and that, in any case, the deceptive desire for such unity belongs to us all.

## There Monsters Be

Thus the skepticism that leads to the couple's obsessive staring also accounts for remarks of theirs entirely ignored by critics: I mean their half-suspecting that the other may not even be human. Amy's husband wants her to "Tell me about [what she feels] if it's something human" (line 58), as though not just her anguish but she herself may not be human at all! This is entirely in keeping with his distrust of what humans do—in particular, talk: for perhaps this talk is alien imposture, a plague of pestilential vapors to be expelled. How, after all, can one know? He continues: "I'm not so much / Unlike other folks as your standing there / Apart would make me out" (lines 59–61), sensing that she too skeptically fears *his* own possible inhumanness. Both seek to prove and explain in the way that philosophers obsess about reasoning, justifying, explaining, proving: "The difficulty here is: to stop" (*Zettel* § 314). Thus, "how *could* you [dig his grave]?" can be heard to be spoken as if the act were something a human being whose child had died "could not," that is, could not *humanly*, do. This is no longer a matter of one's needing "criteria" to determine humanity for, as Wittgenstein and Cavell point out, there are no criteria by which we know the "humanity" of human beings: "Criteria come to an end" (*CR* 412). We do not "know" such a thing as another's humanity, thereby defeating skepticism: in fact no hard and fast criteria are available to us that another has

a human soul, a psychic life, human feelings, a mind. We can only "acknowledge" that another is human by relying on our "mutual attunements" in a form of life; or we can fail, or refuse, or avoid doing so.³⁶ Thus Cavell: "The truth here is that we *are* separate, but not necessarily *separated* (*by* something); that we are, each of us, bodies, that is, embodied; each is this one and not that, each here and not there, each now and not then. If something separates us, comes between us, that can only be a particular aspect or stance of the mind itself, a particular *way* in which we relate . . . to one another" (*CR* 369). "The *nearest* friends can go . . . / comes so far short" (lines 97–98 ; my emphasis), Amy says dismissively. But how near is near?

In his celebrated essay "Experience," Emerson says of his own son's death, "I *cannot* get it *nearer* to me." Sharon Cameron reads the comment as an avowal of personal failure to mourn on the part of the author, but Cavell reads it as the opposite: Emerson can't get grief nearer because it's already as close as he can possibly get it. In contrast, Amy's similar words are spoken not of herself but of *others*, declaring *their* failure and inability to get nearer: even though (on her view) they are Calvinistically preordained to pretense and failure, they are no less culpable for that. But Amy excludes herself from this alleged human plight of pretending to mourn, an obvious contradiction unless we want to suggest she is not human.

In the end, of course, this is precisely what Amy has simulated, what she pretends is true: that she is not human, not bounded, embodied, and subject to loss; that she is not constrained to speak to be known. Hence her contempt: "you think the talk is all." This unfathomable fact of her humanity she avoids, perhaps wisely, for to face such facts would mean not merely facing a fantasy but facing away, finally, from the burial mound of her child who is separated from her by death (as he was by life) and becoming a new person. Instead, she imposes onto others criteria so strict that it looks for all the world like *their* failure, their pretense at grief, and by contrast like her *own* discovery and practical wisdom: "It is as though we try to get the world to provide answers in a way which is independent of our responsibility for *claiming* something to be so . . . and we fix the world so that we can do this. . . . [then] we take what we have fixed or constructed to be *discoveries* about the world, and take this fixation to be the human condition rather than our escape or denial of this condition through the rejection of the human conditions of knowledge and action and the substitution of fantasy" (*CR* 216).

## Schemes of Propriety

> Of course, if water boils in a pot, steam comes out of the pot and also pictured steam comes out of the pictured pot. But what if one insisted on saying that there must also be something boiling in the pictured pot?
>
> —Ludwig Wittgenstein, *Philosophical Investigations*

In *The Claim of Reason,* Stanley Cavell explains Wittgenstein's parable of the boiling pot as exposing "false views of the inner and outer," "between the soul and its society" (*CR* 329). More than a cautionary tale, it invites us to reconsider the (ineradicably) human temptation to skepticism in view of another person's pain or grief, and ultimately in view of another person's humanity or "soul." Perhaps only later, in the philosopher's study, long after we have seen and heard the "steam" (for example, tears, a cry of pain) escape from someone else—after a dog, say, has drawn blood from somebody's leg—does it occur to us to ask, *How* do we know there's pain "inside the pot," an inner pain to go along with those outer, possibly faked tears and cries? Do we really "know" that those "others" around us have an inner life as we do—that they are human? The drift of Wittgenstein's parable is to tease out not only the insolubility of universal skeptical doubt but equally the impertinence of asking what's boiling in the pictured pot—the normal unreality of the question. "'Yes, but there is something there all the same accompanying my cry of pain. And it is on account of that I utter it. And this something is what is important—and frightful.'—Only whom are we informing of this? And on what occasion?" (*PI* § 296).

The problem with such talk about something in the pictured pot, some pain "accompanying" some cry, is not that there is no occasion on which such a statement can make sense. One can imagine insisting on one's own pain to a late arrival who had missed the dog's bite and overlooked the flow of blood and who laughed, thinking the commotion was all in fun. (One can imagine Amy's crying, "I hurt *inside,*" just because her husband avoids acknowledging any hurt at all.) The problem resides rather in just the wanting to "insist" on "something accompanying my cry of pain" in any and all circumstances, that is, apart from any language game, as if one could finally defeat the skeptic's universal threat, to the effect that that the parable of the pot rightly pictures the facts involved in another's failing to know our grief or pain. Wittgenstein, we remember, does not want to deny that there are (inner) feelings but rather to subvert our additional "insisting" on it to others in order to—as if one needed to—"enforce the *connection* between something inner and something outer" (*CR* 338). The "pain itself" *is* part of the account, but "it's not having a dead picture (of any kind)" (*PI* § 455), not as a representation. That insistence is just a barking up the wrong tree, working from the wrong model of what it is to "know" that another is suffering physical pain (or grieving, or pretending). It is a positing of two discrete things, the behavior we see and that which (we suppose) is left out ("the pain itself"), leading us to think that we need to find a way to bridge the two (Amy's "How can I make you . . . ?") when in fact they are already existentially one, albeit unacknowledged. Human tears and cries, in sum, are not a "representation" of inner anguish but its manifestations. And others appropriately *hear* them "as" pain or grief in context and act accordingly, or do not. Of course they (we) can be wrong about another's pain

at any time; even when the criteria for pain are fulfilled, that fact does not guarantee the presence of the phenomenon we are supposing.[37] But then Wittgenstein holds that there are no such guarantees, even when there are criteria, and that in any event guarantees are beside the point, which is the human need for human acknowledgment. When rightly positioned, and equipped, we just "see" that someone is hurt; our seeing is a "seeing-as" or better, a "continuous seeing-as" rather than a "seeing-through" or "into" some opaque object (what was in the darkened parlor, a husband, a grave), and we act accordingly, appropriately, or refuse or fail to.

For his part, Amy's husband helps bring language to grief by mistaking the ordinary for the cheap, oblivious to the value of contexts, audiences, timing—in a word, decorum. Instead his words whirl like exhaust fans, blowing hot and cold. And when he concedes to Amy that "We could have some arrangement / By which I'd bind myself to keep hands off / Anything special you're a-mind to name" (lines 50–52), he transforms a delicate "know-how" into a blunt (not-)"knowing-that," covertly hearkening to the decorum of the disengaged expert: "One thinks that learning a language consists in giving names to objects" (*PI* § 26) or withholding names when the objects offend, as if some determinate list of forbidden words can exhaust the multiple situations of future offense. In other words, Amy's husband reduces infinitely ramified skills in the grammar and rhetoric of a form of life, a propriety needing constant adaptation and sensitivity to the "stage-setting" that stands behind any naming (*PI* § 257), to the itemizing of objects and activities. Indeed, he would if he could reduce words beyond recognition of their uses, either by going silent like his wife ("Don't!") or by indulging her and himself in empty talk: "'all [you] can do is to groan, to weep, to laugh, to rage, to talk, to talk, to talk!'" (*CR* 382). And this misses how natural grief is and thus how natural it is that ordinary language itself should be brought to grief: "The philosophically pertinent griefs to which language comes are not disorders, if that means they hinder its working; but are essential to what we know as language, to our attachment to our language; they are functions of its *order*" (*NYUA* 54).

# APPENDIX

*Frost Poems Discussed*

## The Black Cottage

We chanced in passing by that afternoon
To catch it in a sort of special picture
Among tar-banded ancient cherry trees,
Set well back from the road in rank lodged grass,
The little cottage we were speaking of, 5
A front with just a door between two windows,
Fresh painted by the shower a velvet black.
We paused, the minister and I, to look.
He made as if to hold it at arm's length
Or put the leaves aside that framed it in. 10
"Pretty," he said. "Come in. No one will care."
The path was a vague parting in the grass
That led us to a weathered windowsill.
We pressed our faces to the pane. "You see," he said,
"Everything's as she left it when she died. 15
Her sons won't sell the house or the things in it.
They say they mean to come and summer here
Where they were boys. They haven't come this year.
They live so far away—one is out West—
It will be hard for them to keep their word. 20
Anyway they won't have the place disturbed."
A buttoned haircloth lounge spread scrolling arms
Under a crayon portrait on the wall,
Done sadly from an old daguerreotype.
"That was the father as he went to war. 25
She always, when she talked about the war,
Sooner or later came and leaned, half knelt,
Against the lounge beside it, though I doubt
If such unlifelike lines kept power to stir
Anything in her after all the years. 30
He fell at Gettysburg or Fredericksburg,
I ought to know—it makes a difference which:
Fredericksburg wasn't Gettysburg, of course.
But what I'm getting to is how forsaken
A little cottage this has always seemed; 35
Since she went, more than ever, but before—

I don't mean altogether by the lives
That had gone out of it, the father first,
Then the two sons, till she was left alone.
(Nothing could draw her after those two sons. 40
She valued the considerate neglect
She had at some cost taught them after years.)
I mean by the world's having passed it by—
As we almost got by this afternoon.
It always seems to me a sort of mark 45
To measure how far fifty years have brought us.
Why not sit down if you are in no haste?
These doorsteps seldom have a visitor.
The warping boards pull out their own old nails
With none to tread and put them in their place. 50
She had her own idea of things, the old lady.
And she liked talk. She had seen Garrison
And Whittier, and had her story of them.
One wasn't long in learning that she thought,
Whatever else the Civil War was for, 55
It wasn't just to keep the States together,
Nor just to free the slaves, though it did both.
She wouldn't have believed those ends enough
To have given outright for them all she gave.
Her giving somehow touched the principle 60
That all men are created free and equal.
And to hear her quaint phrases—so removed
From the world's view today of all those things.
That's a hard mystery of Jefferson's.
What did he mean? Of course the easy way 65
Is to decide it simply isn't true.
It may not be. I heard a fellow say so.
But never mind, the Welshman got it planted
Where it will trouble us a thousand years.
Each age will have to reconsider it. 70
You couldn't tell her what the West was saying,
And what the South, to her serene belief.
She had some art of hearing and yet not
Hearing the latter wisdom of the world.
White was the only race she ever knew. 75
Black she had scarcely seen, and yellow never.
But how could they be made so very unlike
By the same hand working in the same stuff?
She had supposed the war decided that.
What are you going to do with such a person? 80

Strange how such innocence gets its own way.
I shouldn't be surprised if in this world
It were the force that would at last prevail.
Do you know but for her there was a time
When, to please the younger members of the church, 85
Or rather say non-members in the church,
Whom we all have to think of nowadays,
I would have changed the Creed a very little?
Not that she ever had to ask me not to;
It never got so far as that; but the bare thought 90
Of her old tremulous bonnet in the pew,
And of her half asleep, was too much for me.
Why, I might wake her up and startle her.
It was the words 'descended into Hades'
That seemed too pagan to our liberal youth. 95
You know they suffered from a general onslaught.
And well, if they weren't true why keep right on
Saying them like the heathen? We could drop them.
Only—there was the bonnet in the pew.
Such a phrase couldn't have meant much to her. 100
But suppose she had missed it from the Creed,
As a child misses the unsaid Good-night
And falls asleep with heartache—how should *I* feel?
I'm just as glad she made me keep hands off,
For, dear me, why abandon a belief 105
Merely because it ceases to be true.
Cling to it long enough, and not a doubt
It will turn true again, for so it goes.
Most of the change we think we see in life
Is due to truths being in and out of favor. 110
As I sit here, and oftentimes, I wish
I could be monarch of a desert land
I could devote and dedicate forever
To the truths we keep coming back and back to.
So desert it would have to be, so walled 115
By mountain ranges half in summer snow,
No one would covet it or think it worth
The pains of conquering to force change on.
Scattered oases where men dwelt, but mostly
Sand dunes held loosely in tamarisk 120
Blown over and over themselves in idleness.
Sand grains should sugar in the natal dew
The babe born in the desert, the sandstorm
Retard mid-waste my cowering caravans—

"There are bees in this wall." He struck the clapboards,    125
Fierce heads looked out; small bodies pivoted.
We rose to go. Sunset blazed on the windows.

## The Code

There were three in the meadow by the brook
Gathering up windrows, piling cocks of hay,
With an eye always lifted toward the west
Where an irregular sun-bordered cloud
Darkly advanced with a perpetual dagger    5
Flickering across its bosom. Suddenly
One helper, thrusting pitchfork in the ground,
Marched himself off the field and home. One stayed.
The town-bred farmer failed to understand.

"What is there wrong?"

              "Something you just now said."    10

"What did I say?"

              "About our taking pains."

"To cock the hay?—because it's going to shower?
I said that more than half an hour ago.
I said it to myself as much as you."

"You didn't know. But James is one big fool.    15
He thought you meant to find fault with his work.
That's what the average farmer would have meant.
James would take time, of course, to chew it over
Before he acted: he's just got round to act."

"He *is* a fool if that's the way he takes me."    20

"Don't let it bother you. You've found out something.
The hand that knows his business won't be told
To do work better or faster—those two things.
I'm as particular as anyone:
Most likely I'd have served you just the same.    25
But I know you don't understand our ways.
You were just talking what was in your mind,
What was in all our minds, and you weren't hinting.
Tell you a story of what happened once:
I was up here in Salem, at a man's    30
Named Sanders, with a gang of four or five
Doing the haying. No one liked the boss.

He was one of the kind sports call a spider,
All wiry arms and legs that spread out wavy
From a humped body nigh as big's a biscuit.  35
But work! That man could work, especially
If by doing he could get more work
Out of his hired help. I'm not denying
He was hard on himself. I couldn't find
That he kept any hours—not for himself.  40
Daylight and lantern-light were one to him:
I've heard him pounding in the barn all night.
But what he liked was someone to encourage.
Them that he couldn't lead he'd get behind
And drive, the way you can, you know, in mowing—  45
Keep at their heels and threaten to mow their legs off.
I'd seen about enough of his bulling tricks
(We call that bulling). I'd been watching him.
So when he paired off with me in the hayfield
To load the load, thinks I, Look out for trouble.  50
I built the load and topped it off; old Sanders
Combed it down with a rake and says, 'O.K.'
Everything went well till we reached the barn
With a big jag to empty in a bay.
You understand that meant the easy job  55
For the man up on top, of throwing *down*
The hay and rolling it off wholesale,
Where on a mow it would have been slow lifting.
You wouldn't think a fellow'd need much urging
Under those circumstances, would you now?  60
But the old fool seizes his fork in both hands,
And looking up bewhiskered out of the pit,
Shouts like an army captain, 'Let her come!'
Thinks I, D'ye mean it? 'What was that you said?'
I asked out loud, so there'd be no mistake,  65
'Did you say, "Let her come"?' 'Yes, let her come.'
He said it over, but he said it softer.
Never you say a thing like that to a man,
Not if he values what he is. God, I'd as soon
Murdered him as left out his middle name.  70
I'd built the load and knew right where to find it.
Two or three forkfuls I picked lightly round for
Like meditating, and then I just dug in
And dumped the rackful on him in ten lots.
I looked over the side once in the dust  75
And caught sight of him treading-water-like,

Keeping his head above. 'Damn ye,' I says,
'That gets ye!' He squeaked like a squeezed rat.
That was the last I saw or heard of him.
I cleaned the rack and drove out to cool off.  80
As I sat mopping hayseed from my neck,
And sort of waiting to be asked about it,
One of the boys sings out, 'Where's the old man?'
'I left him in the barn under the hay.
If you want him, ye can go and dig him out.'  85
They realized from the way I swabbed my neck
More than was needed, something must be up.
They headed for the barn; I stayed where I was.
They told me afterward. First they forked the hay,
A lot of it, out into the barn floor.  90
Nothing! They listened for him. Not a rustle.
I guess they thought I'd spiked him in the temple
Before I buried him, or I couldn't have managed.
They excavated more. 'Go keep his wife
Out of the barn.' Someone looked in a window,  95
And curse me if he wasn't in the kitchen
Slumped way down in a chair, with both his feet
Against the stove, the hottest day that summer.
He looked so clean disgusted from behind
There was no one that dared to stir him up,  100
Or let him know that he was being looked at.
Apparently I hadn't buried him
(I may have knocked him down); but my just trying
To bury him had hurt his dignity.
He had gone to the house so's not to meet me.  105
He kept away from us all afternoon.
We tended to his hay. We saw him out
After a while picking peas in his garden:
He couldn't keep away from doing something."

"Weren't you relieved to find he wasn't dead?"  110

"No! and yet I don't know—it's hard to say.
I went about to kill him fair enough."

"You took an awkward way. Did he discharge you?"

"Discharge me? No! He knew I did just right."

## Two Tramps in Mud Time

Out of the mud two strangers came
And caught me splitting wood in the yard.
And one of them put me off my aim
By hailing cheerily "Hit them hard!"
I knew pretty well why he dropped behind          5
And let the other go on a way.
I knew pretty well what he had in mind:
He wanted to take my job for pay.

Good blocks of oak it was I split,
As large around as the chopping block;           10
And every piece I squarely hit
Fell splinterless as a cloven rock.
The blows that a life of self-control
Spares to strike for the common good,
That day, giving a loose to my soul,             15
I spent on the unimportant wood.

The sun was warm but the wind was chill.
You know how it is with an April day
When the sun is out and the wind is still,
You're one month on in the middle of May.       20
But if you so much as dare to speak,
A cloud comes over the sunlit arch,
A wind comes off a frozen peak,
And you're two months back in the middle of March.

A bluebird comes tenderly up to alight           25
And turns to the wind to unruffle a plume,
His song so pitched as not to excite
A single flower as yet to bloom.
It is snowing a flake: and he half knew
Winter was only playing possum.                  30
Except in color he isn't blue,
But he wouldn't advise a thing to blossom.

The water for which we may have to look
In summertime with a witching wand,
In every wheelrut's now a brook,                 35
In every print of a hoof a pond.
Be glad of water, but don't forget
The lurking frost in the earth beneath
That will steal forth after the sun is set
And show on the water its crystal teeth.         40

The time when most I loved my task
These two must make me love it more
By coming with what they came to ask.
You'd think I never had felt before
The weight of an ax-head poised aloft,                45
The grip on earth of outspread feet,
The life of muscles rocking soft
And smooth and moist in vernal heat.

Out of the woods two hulking tramps
(From sleeping God knows where last night,           50
But not long since in the lumber camps).
They thought all chopping was theirs of right.
Men of the woods and lumberjacks,
They judged me by their appropriate tool.
Except as a fellow handled an ax                     55
They had no way of knowing a fool.

Nothing on either side was said.
They knew they had but to stay their stay
And all their logic would fill my head:
As that I had no right to play                       60
With what was another man's work for gain.
My right might be love but theirs was need.
And where the two exist in twain
Theirs was the better right—agreed.

But yield who will to their separation,              65
My object in living is to unite
My avocation and my vocation
As my two eyes make one in sight.
Only where love and need are one,
And the work is play for mortal stakes,              70
Is the deed ever really done
For Heaven and the future's sakes.

## The Death of the Hired Man

Mary sat musing on the lamp-flame at the table,
Waiting for Warren. When she heard his step,
She ran on tiptoe down the darkened passage
To meet him in the doorway with the news
And put him on his guard. "Silas is back."           5

She pushed him outward with her through the door
And shut it after her. "Be kind," she said.
She took the market things from Warren's arms
And set them on the porch, then drew him down
To sit beside her on the wooden steps.           10

"When was I ever anything but kind to him?
But I'll not have the fellow back," he said.
"I told him so last haying, didn't I?
If he left then, I said, that ended it.
What good is he? Who else will harbor him        15
At his age for the little he can do?
What help he is there's no depending on.
Off he goes always when I need him most.
He thinks he ought to earn a little pay,
Enough at least to buy tobacco with,             20
So he won't have to beg and be beholden.
'All right,' I say, 'I can't afford to pay
Any fixed wages, though I wish I could.'
'Someone else can.' 'Then someone else will have to.'
I shouldn't mind his bettering himself           25
If that was what it was. You can be certain,
When he begins like that, there's someone at him
Trying to coax him off with pocket money—
In haying time, when any help is scarce.
In winter he comes back to us. I'm done."        30

"Sh! not so loud: he'll hear you," Mary said.

"I want him to: he'll have to soon or late."

"He's worn out. He's asleep beside the stove.
When I came up from Rowe's I found him here,
Huddled against the barn door fast asleep,       35
A miserable sight, and frightening, too—
You needn't smile—I didn't recognize him—
I wasn't looking for him—and he's changed.
Wait till you see."

        "Where did you say he'd been?"

"He didn't say. I dragged him to the house,     40
And gave him tea and tried to make him smoke.
I tried to make him talk about his travels.
Nothing would do: he just kept nodding off."

"What did he say? Did he say anything?"

"But little."

                    "Anything? Mary, confess                         45
         He said he'd come to ditch the meadow for me."

"Warren!"

                    "But did he? I just want to know."

"Of course he did. What would you have him say?
   Surely you wouldn't grudge the poor old man
   Some humble way to save his self-respect.                         50
   He added, if you really care to know,
   He meant to clear the upper pasture, too.
   That sounds like something you have heard before?
   Warren, I wish you could have heard the way
   He jumbled everything. I stopped to look                          55
   Two or three times—he made me feel so queer—
   To see if he was talking in his sleep.
   He ran on Harold Wilson—you remember—
   The boy you had in haying four years since.
   He's finished school, and teaching in his college.                60
   Silas declares you'll have to get him back.
   He says they two will make a team for work:
   Between them they will lay this farm as smooth!
   The way he mixed that in with other things.
   He thinks young Wilson a likely lad, though daft                  65
   On education—you know how they fought
   All through July under the blazing sun,
   Silas up on the cart to build the load,
   Harold along beside to pitch it on."

"Yes, I took care to keep well out of earshot."                      70

"Well, those days trouble Silas like a dream.
   You wouldn't think they would. How some things linger!
   Harold's young college-boy's assurance piqued him.
   After so many years he still keeps finding
   Good arguments he sees he might have used.                        75
   I sympathize. I know just how it feels
   To think of the right thing to say too late.
   Harold's associated in his mind with Latin.
   He asked me what I thought of Harold's saying
   He studied Latin, like the violin,                                80
   Because he liked it—that an argument!
   He said he couldn't make the boy believe
   He could find water with a hazel prong—
   Which showed him how much good school had ever done him.

He wanted to go over that. But most of all
   He thinks if he could have another chance
   To teach him how to build a load of hay——"

"I know, that's Silas' one accomplishment.
   He bundles every forkful in its place,
   And tags and numbers it for future reference,
   So he can find and easily dislodge it
   In the unloading. Silas does that well.
   He takes it out in bunches in big birds' nests.
   You never see him standing on the hay
   He's trying to lift, straining to lift himself."

"He thinks if he could teach him that, he'd be
   Some good perhaps to someone in the world.
   He hates to see a boy the fool of books.
   Poor Silas, so concerned for other folk,
   And nothing to look backward to with pride,
   And nothing to look forward to with hope,
   So now and never any different."

Part of a moon was falling down the west,
Dragging the whole sky with it to the hills.
Its light poured softly in her lap. She saw it
And spread her apron to it. She put out her hand
Among the harplike morning-glory strings,
Taut with the dew from garden bed to eaves,
As if she played unheard some tenderness
That wrought on him beside her in the night.
"Warren," she said, "he has come home to die:
You needn't be afraid he'll leave you this time."

"Home," he mocked gently.

                  "Yes, what else but home?
It all depends on what you mean by home.
Of course he's nothing to us, any more
Than was the hound that came a stranger to us
Out of the woods, worn out upon the trail."

"Home is the place where, when you have to go there,
   They have to take you in."

                  "I should have called it
Something you somehow haven't to deserve."

Warren leaned out and took a step or two,
Picked up a little stick, and brought it back

And broke it in his hand and tossed it by.
"Silas has better claim on us you think
  Than on his brother? Thirteen little miles                                         125
  As the road winds would bring him to his door.
Silas has walked that far no doubt today.
Why doesn't he go there? His brother's rich,
  A somebody—director in the bank."

"He never told us that."

                        "We know it, though."                              130

"I think his brother ought to help, of course.
I'll see to that if there is need. He ought of right
To take him in, and might be willing to—
He may be better than appearances.
But have some pity on Silas. Do you think                                       135
If he had any pride in claiming kin
Or anything he looked for from his brother,
He'd keep so still about him all this time?"

"I wonder what's between them."

                                  "I can tell you.
Silas is what he is—we wouldn't mind him—                                140
But just the kind that kinsfolk can't abide.
He never did a thing so very bad.
He don't know why he isn't quite as good
As anybody. Worthless though he is,
He won't be made ashamed to please his brother."                        145

"*I* can't think Si ever hurt anyone."

"No, but he hurt my heart the way he lay
  And rolled his head on that sharp-edged chair-back.
He wouldn't let me put him on the lounge.
You must go in and see what you can do.
I made the bed up for him there tonight.                                           150
You'll be surprised at him—how much he's broken.
His working days are done; I'm sure of it."

"I'd not be in a hurry to say that."

"I haven't been. Go, look, see for yourself.                                            155
But, Warren, please remember how it is:
He's come to help you ditch the meadow.
He has a plan. You mustn't laugh at him.
He may not speak of it, and then he may.

    I'll sit and see if that small sailing cloud     160
    Will hit or miss the moon."

         It hit the moon.
   Then there were three there, making a dim row,
   The moon, the little silver cloud, and she.

   Warren returned—too soon, it seemed to her—     165
   Slipped to her side, caught up her hand and waited.

   "Warren?" she questioned.

       "Dead," was all he answered.

## West-Running Brook

   "Fred, where is north?"

         "North? North is there, my love.
 The brook runs west."

       "West-Running Brook then call it."
 (West-Running Brook men call it to this day.)
"What does it think it's doing running west
 When all the other country brooks flow east       5
 To reach the ocean? It must be the brook
 Can trust itself to go by contraries
 The way I can with you—and you with me—
 Because we're—we're—I don't know what we are.    9
What are we?"

      "Young or new?"

         "We must be something.
We've said we two. Let's change that to we three.
As you and I are married to each other,
We'll both be married to the brook. We'll build
Our bridge across it, and the bridge shall be
Our arm thrown over it asleep beside it.         15
Look, look, it's waving to us with a wave
To let us know it hears me."

         "Why, my dear,
That wave's been standing off this jut of shore—"
 (The black stream, catching on a sunken rock,
 Flung backward on itself in one white wave,      20
 And the white water rode the black forever,

Not gaining but not losing, like a bird
White feathers from the struggle of whose breast
Flecked the dark stream and flecked the darker pool
Below the point, and were at last driven wrinkled
In a white scarf against the far shore alders.)
"That wave's been standing off this jut of shore
 Ever since rivers, I was going to say,
 Were made in heaven. It wasn't waved to us."

"It wasn't, yet it was. If not to you
 It was to me—in an annunciation."

"Oh, if you take it off to lady-land
As't were the country of the Amazons
We men must see you to the confines of
And leave you there, ourselves to forbid to enter—
It is your brook! I have no more to say."

"Yes, you have, too. Go on. You thought of something."

'Speaking of contraries, see how the brook
In that white wave runs counter to itself.
It is from that in water we were from
Long, long before we were from any creature.
Here we, in our impatience of the steps,
Get back to the beginning of beginnings,
The stream of everything that runs away.
Some say existence like a Pirouot
And Pirouette, forever in one place,
Stands still and dances, but it runs away;
It seriously, sadly, runs away
To fill the abyss's void and emptiness.
It flows beside us in this water brook,
But it flows over us. It flows between us
To separate us for a panic moment.
It flows between us, over us, and *with* us.
And it is time, strength, tone, light, life, and love—
And even substance lapsing unsubstantial;
The universal cataract of death
That spends to nothingness—and unresisted,
Save by some strange resistance in itself,
Not just a swerving, but a throwing back,
As if regret were in it and were sacred.
It has this throwing backward on itself
So that the fall of most of it is always
Raising a little, sending up a little.

Our life runs down in sending up the clock.
The brook runs down in sending up our life.  65
The sun runs down in sending up the brook.
And there is something sending up the sun.
It is this backward motion toward the source,
Against the stream, that most we see ourselves in,
The tribute of the current to the source.  70
It is from this in nature we are from.
It is most us."

       "Today will be the day
You said so."

       "No, today will be the day
You said the brook was called West-Running Brook."

"Today will be the day of what we both said."  75

## Snow

The three stood listening to a fresh access
Of wind that caught against the house a moment,
Gulped snow, and then blew free again—the Coles
Dressed, but disheveled from some hours of sleep;
Meserve, belittled in the great skin coat he wore.  5

Meserve was first to speak. He pointed backward
Over his shoulder with his pipe-stem, saying,
"You can just see it glancing off the roof
Making a great scroll upward toward the sky,
Long enough for recording all our names on.—  10
I think I'll just call up my wife and tell her
I'm here—so far—and starting on again.
I'll call her softly so that if she's wise
And gone to sleep, she needn't wake to answer."
Three times he barely stirred the bell, then listened.  15
"Why, Lett, still up? Lett, I'm at Cole's. I'm late.
I called you up to say Good-night from here
Before I went to say Good-morning there.—
I thought I would.—I know, but, Lett—I know—
I could, but what's the sense? The rest won't be  20
So bad.—Give me an hour for it.—Ho, ho,
Three hours to here! But that was all uphill;
The rest is down.—Why no, no, not a wallow:
They kept their heads and took their time to it

Like darlings, both of them. They're in the barn.— 25
My dear, I'm coming just the same. I didn't
Call you to ask you to invite me home.—"
He lingered for some word she wouldn't say,
Said it at last himself, 'Good-night,' and then,
Getting no answer, closed the telephone. 30
The three stood in the lamplight round the table
With lowered eyes a moment till he said,
"I'll just see how the horses are."

      "Yes, do,"
Both the Coles said together. Mrs. Cole
Added: "You can judge better after seeing.— 35
I want you here with me, Fred. Leave him here,
Brother Meserve. You know to find your way
Out through the shed."

      "I guess I know my way.
I guess I know where I can find my name
Carved in the shed to tell me who I am 40
If it don't tell me where I am. I used
To play—"

      "You tend your horses and come back.—
Fred Cole, you're going to let him!"

        "Well, aren't you?
How can you help yourself?"

      "I called him Brother.
Why did I call him that?"

      "It's right enough. 45
That's all you ever heard him called round here.
He seems to have lost off his Christian name."

"Christian enough I should call that myself.
He took no notice, did he? Well, at least
I didn't use it out of love of him, 50
The dear knows. I detest the thought of him
With his ten children under ten years old.
I hate his wretched little Racker Sect,
All's ever I heard of it, which isn't much.
But that's not saying—Look, Fred Cole, it's twelve. 55
Isn't it, now? He's been here half an hour.
He says he left the village store at nine:
Three hours to do four miles—a mile an hour

  Or not much better. Why, it doesn't seem
  As if a man could move that slow and move.     60
  Try to think what he did with all that time.
  And three miles more to go!"

        "Don't let him go.
Stick to him, Helen. Make him answer you.
That sort of man talks straight-on all his life
From the last thing he said himself, stone deaf     65
To anything anyone else may say.
I should have thought, though, you could make him hear
  you."

"What is he doing out a night like this?
Why can't he stay at home?"

        "He had to preach."

"It's no night to be out."

         "He may be small,   70
He may be good, but one thing's sure, he's tough."

"And strong of stale tobacco."

        "He'll pull through."

"You only say so. Not another house
 Or shelter to put into from this place
To theirs. I'm going to call his wife again."     75

"Wait and he may. Let's see what he will do.
Let's see if he will think of her again.
But then I doubt he's thinking of himself.
He doesn't look on it as anything."

"He shan't go—there!"

        "It *is* a night, my dear."   80

"One thing: he didn't drag God into it."

"He don't consider it a case for God."

"You think so, do you? You don't know the kind.
He's getting up a miracle this minute.
Privately—to himself, right now, he's thinking   85
He'll make a case of it if he succeeds,
But keep still if he fails."

        "Keep still all over
He'll be dead—dead and buried."

                              "Such a trouble!
Not but I've every reason not to care
What happens to him if it only takes                    90
Some of the sanctimonious conceit
Out of one of those pious scalawags."

"Nonsense to that! You want to see him safe."

"You like the runt."

                    "Don't you a little?"

                              "Well,
I don't like what he's doing, which is what             95
You like, and like him for."

                    "Oh, yes you do.
You like your fun as well as anyone;
Only you women have to put these airs on
To impress men. You've got us so ashamed
Of being men we can't look at a good fight              100
Between two boys and not feel bound to stop it.
Let the man freeze an ear or two, I say.—
He's here. I leave him all to you. Go in
And save his life.—All right, come in, Meserve.
Sit down, sit down. How did you find the horses?"       105

"Fine, fine."

          "And ready for some more? My wife here
Says it won't do. You've got to give it up."

"Won't you to please me? Please! If I say Please?
Mr. Meserve, I'll leave it to *your* wife.
What *did* your wife say on the telephone?"             110

Meserve seemed to heed nothing but the lamp
Or something not far from it on the table.
By straightening out and lifting a forefinger,
He pointed with his hand from where it lay
Like a white crumpled spider on his knee:               115
"That leaf there in your open book! It moved
Just then, I thought. It's stood erect like that,
There on the table, ever since I came,
Trying to turn itself backward or forward,
I've had my eye on it to make out which;                120
If forward, then it's with a friend's impatience—
You see I know—to get you on to things

It wants to see how you will take; if backward,
It's from regret for something you have passed
And failed to see the good of. Never mind,            125
Things must expect to come in front of us
A many times—I don't say just how many—
That varies with the things—before we see them.
One of the lies would make it out that nothing
Ever presents itself before us twice.                  130
Where would we be at last if that were so?
Our very life depends on everything's
Recurring till we answer from within.
The thousandth time may prove the charm.—That leaf!
It can't turn either way. It needs the wind's help.   135
But the wind didn't move it if it moved.
It moved itself. The wind's at naught in here.
It couldn't stir so sensitively poised
A thing as that. It couldn't reach the lamp
To get a puff of black smoke from the flame,          140
Or blow a rumple in the collie's coat.
You make a little foursquare block of air,
Quiet and light and warm, in spite of all
The illimitable dark and cold and storm,
And by so doing give these three, lamp, dog          145
And book-leaf, that keep near you, their repose;
Though for all anyone can tell, repose
May be the thing you haven't, yet you give it.
So false it is that what we haven't we can't give;
So false, that what we always say is true.            150
I'll have to turn the leaf if no one else will.
It won't lie down. Then let it stand. Who cares?"

"I shouldn't want to hurry you. Meserve,
But if you're going—say you'll stay, you know.
But let me raise this curtain on a scene,              155
And show you how it's piling up against you.
You see the snow-white through the white of frost?
Ask Helen how far up the sash it's climbed
Since last we read the gauge."
                        "It looks as if
Some pallid thing had squashed its features flat       160
And its eyes shut with overeagerness
To see what people found so interesting
In one another, and had gone to sleep
Of its own stupid lack of understanding,

          Or broken its white neck of mushroom stuff             165
          Short of, and died against the window-pane."

"Brother Meserve, take care, you'll scare yourself
    More than you will us with such nightmare talk.
    It's you it matters to, because it's you
    Who have to go out into it alone."                           170

"Let him talk, Helen, and perhaps he'll stay."

"Before you drop the curtain—I'm reminded:
    You recollect the boy who came out here
    To breathe the air one winter—had a room
    Down at the Averys'? Well, one sunny morning                 175
    After a downy storm, he passed our place
    And found me banking up the house with snow.
    And I was burrowing in deep for warmth,
    Piling it well above the windowsills.
    The snow against the window caught his eye.                  180
    'Hey, that's a pretty thought'—those were his words—
    'So you can think it's six feet deep outside,
    While you sit warm and read up balanced rations.
    You can't get too much winter in the winter.'
    Those were his words. And he went home and all               185
    But banked the daylight out of Avery's windows.
    Now you and I would go to no such length.
    At the same time you can't deny it makes
    It not a mite worse, sitting there, we three,
    Playing our fancy, to have the snow-line run                 190
    So high across the pane outside. There where
    There is a sort of tunnel in the frost—
    More like a tunnel than a hole—way down
    At the far end of it you see a stir
    And quiver like the frayed edge of the drift                 195
    Blown in the wind. I *like* that—I like *that*.
    Well, now I leave you, people."

                          "Come, Meserve,
    We thought you were deciding not to go—
    The ways you found to say the praise of comfort
    And being where you are. You want to stay."                  200

"I'll own it's cold for such a fall of snow.
    This house is frozen brittle, all except
    This room you sit in. If you think the wind
    Sounds further off, it's not because it's dying;
    You're further under in the snow—that's all—                205

And feel it less. Hear the soft bombs of dust
It bursts against us at the chimney mouth,
And at the eaves. I like it from inside
More than I shall out in it. But the horses
Are rested and it's time to say Good-night,            210
And let you get to bed again. Good-night,
Sorry I had to break in on your sleep."

"Lucky for you you did. Lucky for you
You had us for a halfway station
To stop at. If you were the kind of man                215
Paid heed to women, you'd take my advice
And for your family's sake stay where you are.
But what good is my saying it over and over?
You've done more than you had a right to think
You could do—*now*. You know the risk you take      220
In going on."

       "Our snowstorms as a rule
Aren't looked on as man-killers, and although
I'd rather be the beast that sleeps the sleep
Under it all, his door sealed up and lost,
Than the man fighting it to keep above it,             225
Yet think of the small birds at roost and not
In nests. Shall I be counted less than they are?
Their bulk in water would be frozen rock
In no time out tonight. And yet tomorrow
They will come budding boughs from tree to tree,       230
Flirting their wings and saying Chickadee,
As if not knowing what you meant by the word storm."

"But why, when no one wants you to, go on?
Your wife—she doesn't want you to. We don't,
And you yourself don't want to. Who else is there?"    235

"Save us from being cornered by a woman.
Well, there's—" She told Fred afterward that in
The pause right there, she thought the dreaded word
Was coming, "God." But no, he only said,
"Well, there's—the storm. That says I must go on.    240
That wants me as a war might if it came.
Ask any man."

       He threw her that as something
To last her till he got outside the door.
He had Cole with him to the barn to see him off.

When Cole returned he found his wife standing 245
Beside the table near the open book,
Not reading it.

    "Well, what kind of a man
Do you call that?" she said.

        "He had the gift
Of words, or is it tongues I ought to say?"

"Was ever such a man for seeing likeness?" 250

"Or disregarding people's civil questions—
What? We've found out in one hour more about him
Than we had seeing him pass by in the road
A thousand times. If that's the way he preaches!
You didn't think you'd keep him after all. 255
Oh, I'm not blaming you. He didn't leave you
Much say in the matter, and I'm just as glad
We're not in for a night of him. No sleep
If he had stayed. The least thing set him going.
It's quiet as an empty church without him." 260

"But how much better off are we as it is?
We'll have to sit here till we know he's safe."

"Yes, I suppose you'll want to, but I shouldn't.
He knows what he can do, or he wouldn't try.
Get into bed I say, and get some rest. 265
He won't come back, and if he telephones,
It won't be for an hour or two."

        "Well then—
We can't be any help by sitting here
And living his fight through with him, I suppose."

. . . . . . . . . . . . . . .

Cole had been telephoning in the dark. 270
Mrs. Cole's voice came from an inner room:
"Did she call you or you call her?"

        "She me.
You'd better dress: you won't go back to bed.
We must have been asleep: it's three and after."

"Had she been ringing long? I'll get my wrapper.
I want to speak to her." 275

"All she said was,
He hadn't come and had he really started."

"She knew he had, poor thing, two hours ago."

"He had the shovel. He'll have made a fight."

"Why did I ever let him leave this house!" 280

"Don't begin that. You did the best you could
To keep him—though perhaps you didn't quite
Conceal a wish to see him show the spunk
To disobey you. Much his wife'll thank you."

"Fred, after all I said! You shan't make out 285
That it was any way but what it was.
Did she let on by any word she said
She didn't thank me?"

"When I told her 'Gone,'
'Well then,' she said, and 'Well then'—like a threat.
And then her voice came scraping slow: 'Oh, you, 290
Why did you let him go?'"

"Asked why we let him?
You let me there. I'll ask her why she let him.
She didn't dare to speak when he was here.
Their number's—twenty-one?—The thing won't work.
Someone's receiver's down. The handle stumbles. 295
The stubborn thing, the way it jars your arm!—
It's theirs. She's dropped it from her hand and gone."

"Try speaking. Say 'Hello!'"

"Hello. Hello."

"What do you hear?"

"I hear an empty room—
You know—it sounds that way. And yes, I hear— 300
I think I hear a clock—and windows rattling.
No step, though. If she's there she's sitting down."

"Shout, she may hear you."

"Shouting is no good."

"Keep speaking, then."

"Hello. Hello. Hello.—
You don't suppose—? She wouldn't go outdoors?" 305

"I'm half afraid that's just what she might do."

"And leave the children?"

"Wait and call again.
You can't hear whether she has left the door
Wide open and the wind's blown out the lamp
And the fire's died and the room's dark and cold?" 310

"One of two things, either she's gone to bed
Or gone outdoors."

"In which case both are lost.
Do you know what she's like? Have you ever met her?
It's strange she doesn't want to speak to us."

"Fred, see if you can hear what I hear. Come." 315

"A clock maybe."

"Don't you hear something else?"

"Not talking."

"No."

"Why, yes, I hear—what is it?"

"What do you say it is?"

"A baby's crying!
Frantic it sounds, though muffled and far off.
Its mother wouldn't let it cry like that, 320
Not if she's there."

"What do you make of it?"

"There's only one thing possible to make,
That is, assuming—that she has gone out.
Of course she hasn't though." They both sat down
Helpless. "There's nothing we can do till morning." 325

"Fred, I shan't let you think of going out."

"Hold on." The double bell began to chirp.
They started up. Fred took the telephone.
"Hello, Meserve. You're there, then!—And your wife?
Good! Why I asked—she didn't seem to answer.— 330
He says she went to let him in the barn.—
We're glad. Oh, say no more about it, man.
Drop in and see us when you're passing."

                              "Well,
She has him then, though what she wants him for
I *don't* see."
              "Possibly not for herself.
Maybe she only wants him for the children."

"The whole to-do seems to have been for nothing.
What spoiled our night was to him just his fun.
What did he come in for?—To talk and visit?
Thought he'd just call to tell us it was snowing.
If he thinks he is going to make our house
A halfway coffee house 'twixt town and nowhere———"

"I thought you'd feel you'd been too much concerned."

"You think you haven't been concerned yourself."

"If you mean he was inconsiderate
To rout us out to think for him at midnight
And then take our advice no more than nothing,
Why, I agree with you. But let's forgive him.
We've had a share in one night of his life.
What'll you bet he ever calls again?"


## Home Burial

He saw her from the bottom of the stairs
Before she saw him. She was starting down,
Looking back over her shoulder at some fear.
She took a doubtful step and then undid it
To raise herself and look again. He spoke
Advancing toward her: "What is it you see
From up there always?—for I want to know."
She turned and sank upon her skirts at that,
And her face changed from terrified to dull.
He said to gain time: "What is it you see?"
Mounting until she cowered under him.
"I will find out now—you must tell me, dear."
She, in her place, refused him any help,
With the least stiffening of her neck and silence.
She let him look, sure he wouldn't see,
Blind creature; and awhile he didn't see.
But at last he murmured, "Oh," and again, "Oh."

"What is it—what?" she said.

"Just that I see."

"You don't," she challenged. "Tell me what it is."

"The wonder is I didn't see at once.
I never noticed it from here before.
I must be wonted to it—that's the reason.
The little graveyard where my people are!
So small the window frames the whole of it.
Not much larger than a bedroom, is it?
There are three stones of slate and one of marble,
Broad-shouldered little slabs there in the sunlight
On the sidehill. We haven't to mind *those*.
But I understand: it is not the stones,
But the child's mound—"

           "Don't, don't, don't,
don't," she cried.

She withdrew, shrinking from beneath his arm
That rested on the banister, and slid downstairs;
And turned on him with such a daunting look,
He said twice over before he knew himself:
"Can't a man speak of his own child he's lost?"

"Not you!—Oh, where's my hat? Oh, I don't need it!
I must get out of here. I must get air—
I don't know rightly whether any man can."

"Amy! Don't go to someone else this time.
Listen to me. I won't come down the stairs."
He sat and fixed his chin between his fists.
"There's something I should like to ask you, dear."

"You don't know how to ask it."

                  "Help me, then."

Her fingers moved the latch for all reply.

"My words are nearly always an offense.
I don't know how to speak of anything
So as to please you. But I might be taught,
I should suppose. I can't say I see how.
A man must partly give up being a man
With womenfolk. We could have some arrangement
By which I'd bind myself to keep hands off
Anything special you're a-mind to name.
Though I don't like such things 'twixt those that love.

Two that don't love can't live together without them.
But two that do can't live together with them."	55
She moved the latch a little. "Don't—don't go.
Don't carry it to someone else this time.
Tell me about it if it's something human.
Let me into your grief. I'm not so much
Unlike other folks as your standing there	60
Apart would make me out. Give me my chance.
I do think, though, you overdo it a little.
What was it brought you up to think it the thing
To take your mother-loss of a first child
So inconsolably—in the face of love.	65
You'd think his memory might be satisfied——"

"There you go sneering now!"

"I'm not, I'm not!
You make me angry. I'll come down to you.
God, what a woman! And it's come to this,
A man can't speak of his own child that's dead."	70

"You can't because you don't know how to speak.
If you had any feelings, you that dug
With your own hand—how could you?—his little grave;
I saw you from that very window there,
Making the gravel leap and leap in air,	75
Leap up, like that, like that, and land so lightly
And roll back down the mound beside the hole.
I thought, Who is that man? I didn't know you.
And I crept down the stairs and up the stairs
To look again, and still your spade kept lifting.	80
Then you came in. I heard your rumbling voice
Out in the kitchen, and I don't know why,
But I went near to see with my own eyes.
You could sit there with the stains on your shoes
Of the fresh earth from your own baby's grave	85
And talk about your everyday concerns.
You had stood the spade up against the wall
Outside there in the entry, for I saw it."

"I shall laugh the worst laugh I ever laughed.
I'm cursed. God, if I don't believe I'm cursed."	90

"I can repeat the very words you were saying:
'Three foggy mornings and one rainy day
Will rot the best birch fence a man can build.'

Think of it, talk like that at such a time!
What had how long it takes a birch to rot         95
To do with what was in the darkened parlor?
You *couldn't* care! The nearest friends can go
With anyone to death, comes so far short
They might as well not try to go at all.
No, from the time when one is sick to death,      100
One is alone, and he dies more alone.
Friends make pretense of following to the grave,
But before one is in it, their minds are turned
And making the best of their way back to life
And living people, and things they understand.    105
But the world's evil. I won't have grief so
If I can change it. Oh, I won't, I won't!"

"There, you have said it all and you feel better.
You won't go now. You're crying. Close the door.
The heart's gone out of it: why keep it up?       110
Amy! There's someone coming down the road!"

"*You*—oh, you think the talk is all. I must go—
Somewhere out of this house. How can I make you——"

"If—you—do!" She was opening the door wider.
"Where do you mean to go? First tell me that.     115
I'll follow and bring you back by force. I *will!*—"

# NOTES

## Introduction

1. George Steiner, *Tolstoy or Dostoyevsky* (New Haven: Yale University Press, 1959), 3.

2. John M. Ellis, *Language, Thought, and Logic* (Evanston: Northwestern University Press, 1993).

3. John M. Ellis, *The Theory of Literary Criticism: A Logical Analysis* (Berkeley and Los Angeles: University of California Press, 1974), 44; my emphasis. For a similar account of literature as communication beyond specific uses, see Charles Altieri, *Act and Quality: A Theory of Literary Meaning and Humanistic Understanding* (Amherst: University of Massachusetts Press, 1981).

4. Cf. *Zettel* § 458: "Philosophical investigations: conceptual investigations. The essential thing about metaphysics: it obliterates the distinction between factual and conceptual investigations."

5. Anthony Cascardi, *The Bounds of Reason: Cervantes, Dostoyevsky, Flaubert* (New York: Columbia University Press, 1986); James Guetti, *Wittgenstein and the Grammar of Literary Experience* (Athens and London: University of Georgia Press, 1993).

6. Stephen Mulhall, *Inheritance and Originality: Wittgenstein, Heidegger, Kierkegaard* (Oxford: Oxford University Press, 2001), 164; first inner quotation marks added. For a more detailed account, see Stephen Mulhall, *On Being in the World: Wittgenstein and Heidegger on Seeing Aspects* (London and New York: Routledge, 1990). As Guetti explains in *Wittgenstein and the Grammar of Literary Experience:* "When in Wittgenstein's accounts a philosopher holds up his hand in front of his face and declares 'This certainly is a hand,' or when another [philosopher] stares fixedly at a tree and says, 'That is a tree; I *know* that,' both, I would claim, are engrossed by [what Wittgenstein calls; *PI* p. 216e] 'experiencing a word' in many of the same ways that we may be in reading literature, [whereas] both philosophers are just as mistaken as we are if we suppose that what engages us in these instances, what so compels and exercises our attention, is certain [metaphysical] 'knowledge' or [practical, empirical] 'meaning'" (3).

7. Warner Berthoff makes the same point in *Literature and the Continuances of Virtue* (Princeton: Princeton University Press, 1986): "Primarily then this is a book of demonstrations, a showing off of certain exemplary acts of literary making and of the central imaginative invitations each projects. I take some such exercise to be the first obligation of literary-critical writing" (4).

8. For sources, see Walter Jost and Michael J. Hyde, eds., *Rhetoric and Hermeneutics in Our Time* (New Haven: Yale University Press, 1997); Gerald L. Bruns, *Hermeneutics Ancient and Modern* (New Haven: Yale University Press, 1992); Gerald L. Bruns, *Inventions: Writing, Textuality, and Understanding in Literary History* (New Haven: Yale University Press, 1982); and Michael C. Leff, "Modern Sophistic and the Unity of Rhetoric," in *The Rhetoric of the Human Sciences*, ed. John S. Nelson, Allan Megill, and Donald N. McKloskey (Madison: University of Wisconsin Press, 1987). Leff writes: "Intellectuals, like the members of all other subcultures, define themselves largely through negation. They conceive of themselves as different from other, ordinary people, and the differences surface most clearly in respect to the way they talk and think. The study of rhetoric, however, totters unsteadily between intellectual inquiry and the mundane transactions of common life. Its objective, at least according to one classic formulation, is to comprehend the way people ordinarily talk and think, and to treat this seriously poses a threat to the identity and solidarity of the intellectual class" (20). For a good philosophical account of the relations among Cavell, Emerson, James, and Dewey,

see Russell B. Goodman, *American Philosophy and the American Tradition* (Cambridge: Cambridge University Press, 1990).

9. Rita Felski, "The Invention of Everyday Life," *New Formations* 39 (1999/2000): 19.

10. Lionel Trilling, "The Meaning of a Literary Idea," in *The Liberal Imagination* (New York: Harcourt Brace Jovanovich, 1979), 272; my emphasis.

11. In *Hearing Voices: Voice and Method in the Writing of Stanley Cavell* (Chicago: University of Chicago Press, 1998), Timothy Gould speaks to my point here on the general reception of Cavell: "The interlocking network of these concepts of voice, style, and personal manner has tended to confine the discussion of Cavell's writing within a series of sterile controversies. Only rarely has the discussion moved on to include even a rudimentary account of the issues Cavell raises about philosophical *method*. Only rarely do such discussions display even the crudest awareness of the categories of literary or rhetorical analysis. And rarer still is any discussion of Cavell's work that moves to include the issue of method" (2; my emphasis). See also 19–20.

12. Richard Ruland and Malcolm Bradbury, *From Puritanism to Postmodernism: A History of American Literature* (New York: Penguin, 1991), 196.

13. Frost was elected to the American Philosophical Society in 1937 at age sixty-three.

14. *"Philosophie dürfte man eigentlich nur dichten"* (*CV* 24e); on jokes, see Norman Malcolm, *Ludwig Wittgenstein: A Memoir*, 2d ed. (Oxford: Oxford University Press, 1984), 29; Ludwig Wittgenstein, *Last Writings on the Philosophy of Psychology*, ed. G. H. von Wright and Heikki Nyman, trans. C. G. Luckhardt and Maximillian A. E. Aue (Chicago: University of Chicago Press, 1982), vol. 1: § 150.

15. Stanley Cavell, "A Conversation with Stanley Cavell on Philosophy and Literature," in *The Senses of Stanley Cavell*, ed. Richard Fleming and Michael Payne (Lewisburg, Pa.: Bucknell University Press, 1989), 314. Cf. Gerald L. Bruns, "Between Philosophy and Literature: Theory, Practice, and Significance in Literary Study," *Renascence* 41 (fall 1988-summer 1989).

16. Yvor Winters, *In Defense of Reason* (Denver: Swallow Press, 1947); Patrick Diggins, *The Promise of Pragmatism: Modernism and the Crisis of Knowledge and Authority* (Chicago: University of Chicago Press, 1994), 7.

17. Newton Garver and Seung-Chong Lee, *Derrida and Wittgenstein* (Philadelphia: Temple University Press, 1994), chap. 3, "Logic and Rhetoric."

18. Walter Jost, *Rhetorical Thought in John Henry Newman* (Columbia: University of South Carolina Press, 1989); see also Walter Jost, "Philosophic Rhetoric: Newman and Heidegger," in *Discourse and Context: An Interdisciplinary Study of John Henry Newman*, ed. Gerard Magill (Carbondale: Southern Illinois University Press, 1993), 54–80. Note that the remarks collected in Wittgenstein's *On Certainty* begin with a reference to "[J.] H. Newman."

19. Eugene Garver, *Machiavelli and the History of Prudence* (Madison: University of Wisconsin Press, 1987).

20. Cf. Renato Barilli, *A Course on Aesthetics* (Minneapolis: University of Minnesota Press, 1993): "Rhetorical discourse functions primarily as an excellent *Mittelglied* between art and science, because it is engaged not only on the front of *docere* (of knowledge, consciousness), but also on those of *movere* and *delectare*" (141). For a Wittgensteinian stress on the centrality to religion (as to aesthetics) of the logic of seeing connections and disconnections, see John Wisdom, "Gods," in *Philosophy and Psychoanalysis* (New York: Philosophical Library, 1953), 149–68. On the *"Mittelglied"* in Kant, see *CJ* 4.

21. Maria DiBattista and Lucy McDiarmid, eds., *High and Low Moderns* (New York: Oxford University Press, 1996), 10.

22. See, for example, Rita Felski, *The Gender of Modernity* (Cambridge: Cambridge University Press, 1995); Karen Kilcup, *Robert Frost and Feminine Literary Tradition* (Ann Arbor: University of Michigan Press, 1998); and, as especially relevant to concerns with the everyday and ordinary, Wendy Steiner, *Venus in Exile: The Rejection of Beauty in Twentieth-Century Art*

(New York: Free Press, 2001), for example, her remarks on the "intimism" of the French "Nabi" (Heb. "prophet") painter Pierre Bonnard, 157ff.

23. In *The Literary Essays of Ezra Pound* (New York: New Directions, 1968), Pound refers to *logopoeia* as "the dance of the intellect among words" (25), part of which phrase serves as the title of Marjorie Perloff's well-known book; Angus Fletcher, *Colors of the Mind: Conjectures on Thinking in Literature* (Cambridge: Harvard University Press, 1991), 3–4; Gary Saul Morson and Caryl Emerson, *Mikhail Bakhtin: Creation of a Prosaics* (Stanford: Stanford University Press, 1990). For important related works, see John Casey, *The Language of Criticism* (London: Methuen, 1966); Gary Saul Morson, *Hidden in Plain View: Narrative and Creative Potentials in "War and Peace"* (Stanford: Stanford University Press, 1987); Michael André Bernstein, *Bitter Carnival: Ressentiment and the Abject Hero* (Princeton: Princeton University Press, 1992); Michael André Bernstein, *Foregone Conclusions: Against Apocalyptic History* (Berkeley and Los Angeles: University of California Press, 1994); Anthony J. Cascardi, ed., *Literature and the Question of Philosophy* (Baltimore: Johns Hopkins University Press, 1987); and especially Charles Altieri, *Act and Quality; Canons and Consequences: Reflections on the Ethical Force of Imaginative Ideals* (Evanston: Northwestern University Press, 1990); and *Subjective Agency: A Theory of First-Person Expressivity and Its Social Implications* (Oxford: Blackwell, 1994).

24. Kenneth Dauber and Walter Jost, eds., *Ordinary Language Criticism: Literary Thinking after Cavell after Wittgenstein* (Evanston: Northwestern University Press, 2003).

25. Angus Fletcher, *Colors of the Mind: Conjectures on Thinking in Literature* (Cambridge: Harvard University Press, 1991), 3–4.

26. Morson, *Mikhail Bakhtin*, 35.

27. Erich Auerbach, *Mimesis: The Representation of Reality in Western Literature*, trans. Willard R. Trask (Princeton: Princeton University Press, 1953), chap. 1 passim.

28. The contrast I am drawing here and elsewhere between grammatical and empirical matters is softened in the recent work of cognitive scientists and those applying their results to literary criticism and theory and to philosophy. In addition to Norman N. Holland's earlier *The Brain of Robert Frost: A Cognitive Approach to Literature* (New York and London: Routledge, 1988), these latter include, among others, Mark Turner (for example, *Reading Minds: The Study of English in the Age of Cognitive Science* [Princeton: Princeton University Press, 1991] and *The Literary Mind* [New York: Oxford University Press, 1996]) and George Lakoff and Mark Johnson (for example, *Philosophy in the Flesh: The Embodied Mind and Its Relation to Western Thought* [New York: Basic Books, 1999]). More recently, in *Shakespeare's Brain: Reading with Cognitive Theory* (Princeton: Princeton University Press, 2001), Mary Thomas Crane writes that her "purpose is simply to look for traces of a mind [= brain] at work in the text" (35). Such a way of reading overlaps with my own refurbishing of rhetoric in a philosophic vein, but the former takes its point of departure from empirical studies of body and brain and thus leaves unchallenged (in order to get its work done) its own philosophical assumptions. Grammar and rhetoric are no doubt effected, in part, by body and brain, but scientific studies of brain activities can not, by themselves, determine the questions of "what counts" where and when and to whom and to what ends; for support, see Lakoff and Johnson, *Philosophy in the Flesh*, 540ff. In my view, rhetoric is a middle term between philosophy and cognitive science, one that stands to teach and learn from both sides. Thus, in *Reading Minds*, Mark Turner uses the term "cognitive rhetoric" in a way that I find helpful.

29. Fletcher, *Colors of the Mind*, 111–12.

30. I borrow this formulation from Joel C. Weinsheimer, *Philosophical Hermeneutics and Literary Theory* ([New Haven: Yale University Press, 1991], 49), who is working from Kant's third *Critique* and Gadamer's *Truth and Method.*

31. Ludwig Wittgenstein, *Tractatus Logico-Philosophicus*, trans. C. K. Ogden (London: Routledge and Kegan Paul, 1981), 6.421.

32. John Dewey, *Art as Experience* (New York: Milton, Balch, and Co., 1934), 6.

33. Cf. Michel de Certeau, *The Practice of Everyday Life* (Berkeley and Los Angeles: University of California Press, 1984): "Everyday practices depend on a vast ensemble which is difficult to delimit but which we may provisionally designate as an ensemble of *procedures*. The latter are schemas of operations and of technical manipulations" (43).

34. And only vaguely, as from afar, Husserl's *Logical Investigations* (1901–2).

35. Cf. Richard Eldridge, *Leading a Human Life: Wittgenstein, Intentionality, and Romanticism* (Chicago: University of Chicago Press, 1997): "Language is . . . both the cause of our bewitchment and the instrument of resistance to it. Language bewitches us in inviting us to seek a metaphysical ground for our linguistic and conceptual practices. It is about the world—assertational and directed at things, not merely subjectively expressive. But it is semantically open: what people notice and talk about is subject to gradual variation" (190).

36. In a collegial and, for me, instructive conversation at a dinner some years ago at my university, visiting lecturer Helen Vendler expressed to me a qualified appreciation for what Frost was up to, double-voiced (as I heard it) with the suggestion that, whatever he was up to, it wasn't so much. The present book may be taken as the mouthful it would have been indiscreet of me to express at the time. For an understanding of Vendler's views similar to my own, see Charles Bernstein, *A Poetics* (Cambridge: Harvard University Press, 1992), 94.

37. Dewey, *Art as Experience*, 18. In "Modern Fiction," Virginia Woolf writes that "Life is not a series of gig-lamps symmetrically arranged; life is a luminous halo, a semi-transparent envelope surrounding us from the beginning of consciousness to the end" (in *The Common Reader* [New York: Harcourt, Brace, 1925], 212).

38. Joseph Brodsky, Seamus Heaney, and Derek Walcott, *Homage to Robert Frost* (New York: Farrar, Straus, and Giroux, 1996), 107; Edward Snow, *Inside Bruegel: The Play of Images in "Children's Games"* (New York: Farrar, Straus, and Giroux, 1997), 6.

39. Martin Amis, introduction to *Lolita*, by Vladimir Nabokov (New York: Knopf, 1992), xxiii. See also Richard Poirier, *Poetry and Pragmatism* (Cambridge: Harvard University Press, 1992), on the Emersonian attitude toward words standing behind Frost: "We willingly live with the fact that by its beneficent betrayals language constantly delivers us to ourselves, and makes us known to others, within a comforting haze" (30).

40. For a succinct account of the role of the "background" in philosophy after Kant, see Charles Taylor, "Lichtung or Lebensform: Parallels between Heidegger and Wittgenstein," in *Philosophical Arguments* (Cambridge: Harvard University Press, 1995), 61–78.

41. Even now, neither Burke nor Frost fits accepted academic-literary molds and for related reasons. (In *Homage to Robert Frost*, Heaney writes that "among major poets of the English language in this century, Robert Frost is the one who takes the most punishment," and he speaks of the literary—which includes the academic—world's "critical resistance" and "punitive strain" [61].) In his chapter "Rethinking Romanticism," in *Byron and Romanticism*, ed. James Solderholm (Cambridge: Cambridge University Press, 2002), what Jerome McGann says about Byron in the nineteenth century—"That Byron did not figure importantly in the representations of the Romantic period of 1945–1980 is not an anomaly, it is a theoretical and ideological fate" (237) based on the fact that "his style is predominantly rhetorical and conversational rather than symbolic or mythic" (238)—applies equally to Frost and Burke.

42. John Bender and David Wellbery usefully exaggerate this important shift of *rhetorica utens* and *docens* more generally in "Rhetoricality: On the Modernist Return of Rhetoric" (in *The Ends of Rhetoric: History, Theory, Practice*, ed. John Bender and David Wellbery [Stanford: Stanford University Press, 1990]): "the new rhetoric is no longer that of the classical tradition; it is attuned to specific structures of modernist culture; its *fundamental categories* are markedly new" (25; my emphasis): "Rhetoric today is neither a unified doctrine nor a coherent set of discursive practices. Rather, it is a transdisciplinary field of practice and intellectual concern, a

field that draws on conceptual resources of a radically heterogeneous nature and does not assume the stable shape of a system or method of education."

43. Cavell works toward blurring the oppositions between grammar and rhetoric in his essay "Must We Mean What We Say?" in the way he sees "semantic" and "pragmatic" aspects of meaning—for example, Austin's constative and performative aspects of language use—as being interlocked (*MWM* 32). For an even stronger recognition of the continuity between grammar (hermeneutics) and rhetoric, see Cavell's introduction to his essay "Existentialism and Analytical Philosophy" (*Themes* 197); "The Politics of Interpretation (Politics as Opposed to What?)" (*Themes* 41–44); and *IQO* 23: "Our philosophical habits will prompt us to interpret the surface of writing as its manner, its style, its rhetoric, an ornament of what is said rather than its substance, but Emerson's implied claim is that this is as much a philosophical prejudice as the other conformities his essay descries, that, so to speak, words are no more ornaments of thought than tears are ornaments of sadness or joy."

44. This is close to Wittgenstein in some of his last writings collected in *On Certainty* (1969), though it takes much of the present book to circumscribe this thought.

45. The close student of rhetoric will recognize that I am drawing heavily here not only from Burke but from Richard McKeon's essays on philosophy and rhetoric collected in *Rhetoric: Essays in Invention and Discovery*, ed. Mark Backman (Woodbridge, Conn.: Ox Bow Press, 1987) and his essay "Philosophic Semantics and Philosophic Inquiry," in *Freedom and History and Other Essays*, ed. Zahava K. McKeon (Chicago: University of Chicago Press, 1989), 242–56. David Richter uses a similar McKeonesque schema in the introduction to *The Critical Tradition: Classic Texts and Contemporary Trends* (New York: St. Martin's Press, 1998), 12–13. Walter Davis also makes extensive use of McKeon in *The Act of Interpretation: A Critique of Literary Reason* (Chicago: University of Chicago Press, 1978), 93–94, as does Walter Watson in *The Architectonics of Meaning: Foundations of the New Pluralism* (Chicago: University of Chicago Press, 1985), esp. 73–78. For good resources on McKeon, see Eugene Garver and Richard Buchanan, eds., *Pluralism in Theory and Practice: Richard McKeon and American Philosophy* (Nashville: Vanderbilt University Press, 2000); and George Kimball Plochman, *Richard McKeon: A Study* (Chicago: University of Chicago Press, 1990).

46. For a brief, useful account, see Rita Copeland's entry under "trivium" in *The Encyclopedia of Rhetoric*, ed. Thomas O. Sloane (New York: Oxford University Press, 2001), 782–88.

47. Cf. Clarence H. Miller, introduction to *The Praise of Folly*, by Desiderius Erasmus (New Haven: Yale University Press, 1979): "The humanist revival, which gained increasing momentum during the fifteenth century, especially in Italy, might be simplistically described as an attempt to regain and restore the rightful roles of grammar and rhetoric" (xi).

48. The most complete contemporary rhetoric of this sort is Chaim Perelman and Lucie Olbrechts-Tyteca, *The New Rhetoric: A Treatise in Argumentation* (South Bend: University of Notre Dame Press, 1969). For an example of attending to topics in this sense, see Sister Miriam Joseph, *Rhetoric in Shakespeare's Time* (New York: Harcourt, Brace, and World, 1962), 308–53; and more recently, James Crosswhite, "Rhetoric in the Wilderness: The Deep Rhetoric of the Late Twentieth Century," in *A Companion to Rhetoric and Rhetorical Criticism*, ed. Walter Jost and Wendy Olmsted (Oxford: Blackwell, 2003).

49. My distinction is that of William M. A. Grimaldi, S. J., *Studies in the Philosophy of Aristotle's Rhetoric* (Wiesbaden: Franz Steiner Verlag, 1972). The literature on topics is immense, but see especially Richard McKeon, "Creativity and the Commonplace" in *Rhetoric: Essays in Invention and Discovery*; J. M. Balkin, "A Night in the Topics: The Reason of Legal Rhetoric and the Rhetoric of Legal Reason," in *Law's Stories: Narrative and Rhetoric in the Law*, ed. Peter Brooks and Paul Gewirtz (New Haven: Yale University Press, 1996), 211–24; Theodore Viehweg, *Topics and Law*, trans. W. Cole Durham Jr. (Frankfurt am Main: Peter Lang, 1993); P. Christopher Smith, *The Hermeneutics of Original Argument: Demonstration, Dialectic, Rhetoric*

(Evanston: Northwestern University Press, 1998), esp. chap. 3; and Walter Jost, "Teaching the Topics: Character, Rhetoric, and Liberal Education," *Rhetoric Society Quarterly* 21 (winter 1991): 1–16, reprinted in *Rhetoric and Pluralism: Legacies of Wayne Booth,* ed. Fred Antczak (Columbus: Ohio State University Press, 1994).

A third kind of topic—those familiar "commonplaces" as fixed themes or purple patches general across many cases and inserted into one's speech or poem as appropriate—is often identified with topics but is not inventional as described above and therefore plays no significant role in the present work. See Grimaldi, *Studies in the Philosophy of Aristotle's "Rhetoric"*: "Seen as mere static, stock 'commonplaces,' stylized sources for discussion on all kinds of subject-matter they have lost the vital, dynamic character given to them by Aristotle" (116).

50. In fact, just this penchant for *listing* topics has often led to mechanical committing to memory of "places" in the first or third senses—for example, in Renaissance "commonplace" books—rather than to the student's really absorbing how topics, especially special topics, may be used to negotiate disparate phenomena, an undertaking that requires more intellectual instinct and agility than can be taught directly. Properly speaking, a "complete" list of topics is impossible since the social scene is always susceptible to alternate interpretations and is always changing. Topical catalogs range from Aristotle's *Rhetoric* to Augustine's *De doctrina christiana* to the *Federalist Papers* to American case law. Cf. Eugene Garver, *Aristotle's "Rhetoric": An Art of Character* (Chicago: University of Chicago Press, 1994): "The diversity of answers given by commentators to the question 'What is a topic in Aristotle's *Rhetoric?*' suggests not confusion but the possibility that what topics are and how they function vary with the purpose for which they are employed and the manifold on which they are used" (82).

51. Francis Bacon, *De augmentis,* in *The Works of Francis Bacon,* ed. James Spedding, Robert Leslie Ellis, and Douglas Denon Heath, 7 vols. (London: Longman, 1858), 4:424.

52. Giambattista Vico, *On the Study Methods of Our Time,* trans. Elio Gianturco (Ithaca: Cornell University Press, 1990), 15.

53. Ultimately "inventing" becomes a kind of "seeing," or even better a "hearing" of voices (as in a consultation), which is to say both a conventional act learned through training and yet a natural act in the sense of "second nature," such as reading becomes. Thus when Wittgenstein asks, "What do I do when I *obey* a rule?" (*PI* § 199ff.)—for example, a "No Parking" sign—and proceeds to reject both a causal explanation whereby the rule dictates what I am to do and an "interpretive" alternative whereby I align my actions with the rule according to some ad hoc choice of interpretation, he suggests that obeying a rule is rather a kind of "continuous seeing-as," that is, an embedded social *practice* whereby we know how to "go on" from the rule by virtue of our ability to take into account the myriad shifting circumstances that custom tells us is part of its application.

54. W. G. Crane, *Wit and Rhetoric in the Renaissance* (New York: Columbia University Press, 1937). See, for example, Boethius, *De topicis differentiis,* trans. Eleonore Stump (Ithaca: Cornell University Press, 1978).

55. Manfred Hoffmann, "Erasmus, Rhetorical Theologian," in *Rhetorical Invention and Religious Inquiry,* ed. Walter Jost and Wendy Olmsted, 144.

56. Paul de Man, "The Rhetoric of Temporality," in *Blindness and Insight* (Minneapolis: University of Minnesota Press, 1983), 187–91. Cavell makes much the same point about de Man (and Stanley Fish) in "The Politics of Interpretation (Politics as Opposed to What?)" in *Themes* 27–59.

57. In studies of Renaissance painting, similarly, Michael Baxandall has distinguished invention via "ratiocinative *loci*" (mainly what I call formal topics) and an "inductive" invention based on *comparisons* of any kind. Baxandall draws a continuum between a trope *(comparatio)* and the function of material topics, as I will do—observing of Renaissance humanists that "it is not characteristic of humanists to use the classical system of rhetorical invention [formal topics]

in a very comprehensive or consequential way," though they used comparison pervasively (Michael Baxandall, *Giotto and the Orators* [Oxford: Clarendon Press, 1971], 32). For related accounts, see Rosemond Tuve, *Elizabethan and Metaphysical Imagery* (Chicago: University of Chicago Press, 1947); Walter J. Ong, *Rhetoric, Romance, and Technology: Studies in the Interaction of Expression and Culture* (Ithaca: Cornell University Press, 1971); and Charles Altieri, "Rhetorics, Rhetoricity, and the Sonnet as Performance," *Tennessee Studies in Literature* 25 (1980): 1–23.

58. This is in line with Cavell (and Gadamer): "Imagination, let us say, is the capacity for making connections, seeing or realizing possibilities, but I *need* not accomplish this by way of forming new images. . . . Imagination is called for . . . when I have to take the facts in, realize the significance of what is going on, make the behavior real for myself, make a connection" (CR 353–54; my emphasis); cf. *TM* 74ff.

59. My thinking here is echoed in a discussion of contemporary pragmatism by Stephen Toulmin: "first, [pragmatism gives] encouragement . . . to the study of practical methods—the "topics," "dialectics," and "rhetorics"—of all these collective arts, in the context of the *Lebensformen* that embody them; and, second—which is what crucially distinguishes our position from Aristotle's [i.e., Aristotle's biology, metaphysics, etc.]—the fact that these *Lebensformen*, and the forms of thought that are "at home" in them, are not static, permanent "essences" that are capable of being known a priori . . . but changing constellations or populations, whose historically evolving forms have to be discovered, by looking and seeing, after the event" ("The Recovery of the Practical," *American Scholar* [summer 1988]: 351).

60. C. S. Lewis, "Wit," in *Studies in Words* (Cambridge: Cambridge University Press, 1960), 86–110; see also *TM* 24–25.

61. Jean-François Lyotard, *Just Gaming* (Minneapolis: University of Minnesota Press, 1985), 16–17. Cf. David Kolb, *The Critique of Pure Modernity: Hegel, Heidegger and After* (Chicago: University of Chicago Press, 1986): "Lyotard resists what needs resisting but perhaps he expresses too much concern to stay ahead of the language of the tribe and belong to the true avant-garde. If the elements of our multiple inhabitation are themselves internally multiple and tense, then there is room for freedom and *creativity without the need always to be out ahead*" (259; my emphasis).

62. For support, see Anthony Cascardi, *The Subject of Modernity* (Cambridge: Cambridge University Press, 1992), 290.

63. Nelson Goodman, *Ways of Worldmaking* (Indianapolis and Cambridge: Hackett, 1978), 6.

64. For accounts, see John Shotter, *Cultural Politics of Everyday Life* (Toronto: University of Toronto Press, 1993); and Michael Billig, *Arguing and Thinking: A Rhetorical Approach to Social Psychology* (Cambridge: Cambridge University Press, 1987).

65. See Thomas Reid, *Philosophical Works*, ed. William Hamilton (1895; reprint, Hildesheim: Georg Olms, 1967); and, for a modification of this view, C. S. Pierce, "Critical Common-Sensism," in *Philosophical Writings of Pierce*, ed. Justus Buchler (New York: Dover, 1955), 290–301, esp. 293–94 on the "Scotch School." For Moore, see Alan R. White, *G. E. Moore: A Critical Exposition* (Oxford: Blackwell, 1958); and Cavell, *Themes*, 210ff.

66. For an account of the British tradition of moral certainty before and after Hume, see M. Jamie Ferreira, *Scepticism and Reasonable Doubt: The British Naturalist Tradition in Wilkins, Hume, Reid, and Newman* (Oxford: Clarendon Press, 1986); on Reid and common sense, see Joel C. Weinsheimer, *Eighteenth-Century Hermeneutics: Philosophy of Interpretation in England from Locke to Burke* (New Haven: Yale University Press, 1993), 135–65.

67. For an account, see John Coates, "A Short History of Common Sense" in *The Claims of Common Sense* (Cambridge: Cambridge University Press, 1996), 14–38; Henning Jensen, "Reid and Wittgenstein on Philosophy and Language," *Philosophical Studies* 36 (November 1979): 359–75; and Frits van Holthoon and David R. Olson, eds. *Common Sense: The Foundations for Social Science* (Lanham, Md.: University Press of America, 1987).

68. Immanuel Kant, *Prolegomena to Any Future Metaphysics,* ed. Beryl Logan (London and New York: Routledge, 1996), 32.

69. Cf. Anthony Cascardi, *Consequences of Enlightenment* (Cambridge: Cambridge University Press, 1999): "Philosophy, as Wittgenstein regards it, is the realm of reflective rather than determinant judgments, and in language-games that reflection takes the form of praxis. Moreover, this reflective praxis is situated within a framework of shared assumptions that, much like Kant's 'common sense', must be both proved and presupposed" (231). I came upon this excellent book of Cascardi's after my own work was all but finished, though I cite it several times in the following chapters. Cf. *CV* 44e: "A philosopher is a man who has to cure many intellectual diseases in himself before he can arrive at the notions of common sense."

70. Goodman, *Ways of Worldmaking,* 129.

71. Gerald L. Bruns, *Tragic Thoughts at the End of Philosophy: Language, Literature, and Ethical Theory* (Northwestern University Press, 1999), 200.

72. Charles Bernstein quoted in Allison M. Cummings and Rocco Marinaccio, "An Interview with Charles Bernstein," *Contemporary Literature* 41 (spring 2000): 14–15.

73. For this problem in the American tradition, see Jeffrey Walker, *Bardic Ethos and the American Epic Poem: Whitman, Pound, Crane, Williams, Olson* (Baton Rouge: Louisiana State University Press, 1989), 239; Michael André Bernstein, *The Tale of the Tribe: Ezra Pound and the Modern Verse Epic* (Princeton: Princeton University Press, 1980); and R. A. Yoder, *Emerson and the Orphic Poet in America* (Berkeley and Los Angeles: University of California Press, 1978).

74. Cf. Frost: "One of the dangers of college to anyone who wants to stay a human reader (that is to say a humanist) is that he will become a specialist and lose his sensitive fear of landing on the lovely too hard" (*SL* 361); "We shall all be judged finally by the delicacy of our feeling of where to stop short" (*CPPP* 808–9).

75. Ludwig Wittgenstein, *Philosophical Occasions 1912–1951,* ed. James Klagge and Alfred Nordmann (Indianapolis and Cambridge: Hackett, 1993), 132–33.

76. Bercovitch, *Puritan Origins,* 177.

## 1. Dialectic as Dialogue

The text of the third opening epigraph to this chapter (the exchange between Sherlock Holmes and Dr. Watson) is a joke in general circulation in various forms with no author attribution.

1. See René Descartes, *Meditations of First Philosophy, With Selections from the Objections and Replies,* ed. John Cottingham (Cambridge: Cambridge University Press, 1996), 21.

2. Isaiah Berlin, "The Pursuit of the Ideal," in *The Crooked Timber of Humanity,* ed. Henry Harvey (Princeton: Princeton University Press, 1990), 15. On the themes of ideology and fanaticism, see Robert Conquest, *Reflections on a Ravaged Century* (New York: Norton, 2000).

3. For further support for this point, see Seyla Benhabib, *Situating the Self: Gender, Community, and Postmodernism in Contemporary Ethics* (New York: Routledge, 1992), 16; and Seyla Benhabib, *The Claims of Culture: Equality and Diversity in the Global Era* (Princeton: Princeton University Press, 2002).

4. W. H. Auden, "New Year Letter (January 1, 1940)," pt. 2, in *The Collected Poems of W. H. Auden,* ed. Edward Mendelson (New York: Random House, 1976), 175.

5. "The Politics of Interpretation (Politics as Opposed to What?)" in *Themes* 54.

6. Cf. Maurice Blanchot, "Everyday Speech," in *Yale French Studies* 73 (1987): "The images of events and the words that transmit them are not only inscribed instantaneously on our screens, in our ears, but in the end there is no event other than this movement of universal transmission" (14).

7. Cf. "Recounting Gains, Showing Losses: Reading *The Winter's Tale,*" in Stanley Cavell, *Disowning Knowledge in Six Plays of Shakespeare* (Cambridge: Cambridge University Press,

1987): "there must be a use of the concept of telling more fundamental than, or explaining or grounding, its use to tell differences; a use of the concept of telling as fundamental as seeing for oneself" (204).

8. Cf. Gilles Deleuze and Félix Guattari, *What Is Philosophy?* trans. Hugh Tomlinson and Graham Burchell (New York: Columbia University Press, 1994): "a concept is acquired by inhabiting, by pitching one's tent, by contracting a habit.... For them [English philosophers, presumably including the later Wittgenstein] a tent is all that is needed. They develop an extraordinary conception of habit: habits are taken on by contemplating and contracting that which is contemplated. Habit is creative" (105).

9. Cf. *NYUA* 46: "Wittgenstein's appeal or 'approach' to the everyday finds the (actual) everyday to be as pervasive a scene of illusion and trance and artificiality (of need) as Plato or Rousseau or Marx or Thoreau had found. His philosophy of the (eventual) everyday is the proposal of a practice that takes on, takes upon itself, precisely (I do not say exclusively) that scene of illusion and loss; approaches it, or let me say reproaches it, intimately enough to turn it, or deliver it; as if the actual is the womb, contains the terms, of the eventual."

10. On the concept of "epistemic gain," see Charles Taylor, *Sources of the Self: The Making of the Modern Identity* (Cambridge: Harvard University Press, 1989), pt. 1.

11. Cavell is drawing on (among other things) Emerson's essay "Circles" (in *The Portable Emerson*, ed. Carl Bode with Malcolm Cowley [New York: Penguin, 1981], 228–40), which begins, "The eye is the first circle; the horizon which it forms is the second" and continues: "Everything is medial" (230); "Conversation is a game of circles. In conversation we pluck up the termini which bound the common of silence on every side" (233). But see also, toward the end (238): "Yet this incessant movement and progression which all things partake could never become sensible to us but by contrast to some principle or fixture or stability in the soul."

12. William James, *Pragmatism* (Cambridge: Harvard University Press, 1978), 102. Cf. *OC* § 140–41: "We do not learn a practice of making empirical judgments by learning rules: we are taught *judgments* and their connexion with other judgments. A *totality* of judgments is made plausible to us": "When we first begin to *believe* anything, what we believe is not a single proposition, it is a whole system of propositions. (Light dawns gradually over the whole.)"

13. Kant is, of course, the most important Enlightenment philosopher trying to find a way to bridge such divisions. In the first two *Critiques*, cognitive understanding is sharply prised apart from our moral interests and obligations lest the latter bias what we claim to be able to know. But because Kant also holds that our experience is whole—that our knowledge of the natural world of causality is amenable to our moral purposes—he needs a way of showing how they fit together. This is the task of *Critique of Judgment*, where the beautiful is said to provide the scene of our affective mobilization of moral purpose in a world of fact.

14. Cf. *SW* 145: "What the ordinary language philosopher is feeling—but I mean to speak just for myself in this—is that our relation to the world's existence is somehow closer than the ideas of believing and knowing are made to convey." Also *MWM* 71: "In confessing you do not explain or justify, but describe how it is with you. And confession, unlike dogma, is not to be believed but tested, and accepted or rejected."

15. See, for example, Andreas Huyssen, *After the Great Divide: Modernism, Mass Culture, Postmodernism* (Bloomington: Indiana University Press, 1985). For a more sympathetic account of the postmodern, see Matei Calinescu, *Five Faces of Modernity: Modernism, Avant-Garde, Decadence, Kitsch, Postmodernism*, rev. ed. (Durham: Duke University Press, 1987).

16. Thomas L. Dumm, *A Politics of the Ordinary* (New York: New York University Press, 1999), 2.

17. Ralph Waldo Emerson, "The American Scholar," in *The Portable Emerson*, ed. Carl Bode with Malcolm Cowley, 69.

18. Dumm, *Politics of the Ordinary*, 21.

19. Dewey, *Art as Experience*, 194–95.
20. For a good overview see Felski, "The Invention of Everyday Life," 23, 20.
21. Gerald L. Bruns, "Between Philosophy and Literature: Theory, Practice, and Significance in Literary Theory," *Renascence* 61 (fall 1988-summer 1989): 237.
22. Stanley Rosen, "Philosophy and Ordinary Experience" in *Metaphysics in Ordinary Language* (New Haven: Yale University Press, 1999). Only after this book was finished did I come across Rosen's *The Elusiveness of the Ordinary: Studies in the Possibility of Philosophy* (New Haven: Yale University Press, 2002).
23. For a much closer analysis of Wittgenstein's example, see Mulhall, *Inheritance and Originality: Wittgenstein, Heidegger, Kierkegaard*, 43–51.
24. *PI* p. ix: "The philosophical remarks in this book are, as it were, a number of sketches of landscapes which were made in the course of . . . long and involved journeyings."
25. Cf. *MWM* 52: "That on the whole we do [succeed in our projections of words and criteria] is a matter of sharing routes of interest and feeling, modes of response, senses of humor and of significance and of fulfillment, of what is outrageous, of what is similar to what else, what a rebuke, what forgiveness, of when an utterance is an assertion, when an appeal, when an explanation—all the whirl of organism Wittgenstein calls 'forms of life.' Human speech and activity, sanity and community, rest upon nothing more, but nothing less, than this."
26. Cavell ultimately rejects Austin's examples of giving criteria as too specialized (relatively too "non-everyday") to handle the philosophical skepticism ingredient in ordinary language as such. Cavell argues that what it takes to recognize a "goldfinch at the bottom of the garden" (Austin's benchmark instance for criteria), rather than the more generic "bird," is too specialized to allow our *failure* to recognize it (the goldfinch) to generalize as skepticism about knowledge as a whole. See *CR*, chap. 3, "Austin and Examples."
27. Stanley Cavell, "In Quest of the Ordinary," in *Romanticism and Contemporary Criticism*, ed. Eaves and Fischer (Ithaca, N.Y.: Cornell University Press, 1986), 184.
28. P.M.S. Hacker, "Criteria," in *Wittgenstein: Meaning and Mind* (Oxford: Blackwell, 1990), 263, 260ff.; and Espen Hammer, *Stanley Cavell: Skepticism, Subjectivity, and the Ordinary* (Cambridge: Polity Press, 2002), chap. 2.
29. Isaiah Berlin, *The Hedgehog and the Fox* (Chicago: Ivan R. Dee, 1953), 26; my emphasis.
30. Austin, "A Plea for Excuses," in *Philosophical Papers* (Oxford: Oxford University Press, 1961), 182; see also ibid.: "Words are not (except in their own little corner) facts or things: we need therefore to prise them off the world, to hold them apart from and against it, so that we can realize their inadequacies and arbitrariness" (184). Cf. John M. Ellis, "Wittgensteinian Thinking in Theory of Criticism," *New Literary History* 12 (spring 1981): 437–52; Stephen Mulhall, introduction to *The Cavell Reader* (London: Blackwell, 1996), 15–16; and Charles Guignon, "Philosophy after Wittgenstein and Heidegger," *Philosophy and Phenomenonlogical Research* 50 (June 1990): 402.
31. For a comparison of these two thinkers on this and related points, see Mulhall's *On Being in the World: Wittgenstein and Heidegger on Seeing Aspects*.
32. See Angus Fletcher, *Allegory: The Theory of a Symbolic Mode* (Ithaca: Cornell University Press, 1964).
33. Fletcher, *Colors of the Mind*, 28. Fletcher is explicit about both his rhetorical and Wittgensteinian commitments (11–12).
34. Cf. "The Politics of Interpretation (Politics As Opposed to What?)" in *Themes*. For an account of knowledge as *self*-knowledge in Cavell, see Richard Fleming, *The State of Philosophy: An Invitation to a Reading in Three Parts of Stanley Cavell's "The Claim of Reason"* (Lewisburg, Pa.: Bucknell University Press, 1993).
35. Mulhall, *Stanley Cavell*, 61.
36. Dumm, *Politics of the Ordinary*, 31. Cf. *IQO* 154: "I might describe my philosophical

task as one of outlining the necessity, and the lack of necessity, in the sense of the human as inherently strange, say unstable, its quotidian as forever fantastic."

37. As John Patrick Diggins has put it in *The Promise of Pragmatism,* "During much of the first half of the twentieth century, Dewey and Lippmann vied with one another to be the voice of modern American liberalism" (339).

38. See *Public Opinion,* chap. 26, "Intelligence Work," 239ff.; 241. For a recent critique of positions similar to Lippmann's, see Giandomenico Majone, *Evidence, Argument, and Persuasion in the Policy Process* (New Haven: Yale University Press, 1989), esp. chap. 2, "Analysis as Argument."

39. Dewey, *The Public and Its Problems* (1927; reprint, Athens, Ohio: Swallow Press, 1954), 208.

40. Similar results, though politically more sophisticated and far-reaching, are pursued by Henri Lefebvre, *Everyday Life in the Modern World* (1971; reprint, New Brunswick, N.J: Transaction, 1999); and Benhabib, *The Claims of Culture.*

41. For support for this claim, see Dewey, *The Public and Its Problems,* chap. 6, "The Problem of Method," esp. 195.

42. Hilary Putnam, "A Reconsideration of Deweyan Democracy" in *Renewing Philosophy* (Cambridge: Harvard University Press, 1992), 189; see also Hilary Putnam, *Pragmatism* (Oxford: Blackwell, 1995), 42ff. Cf. Richard Shusterman, *Practicing Philosophy: Pragmatism and the Philosophical Life* (New York and London: Routledge, 1997), esp. chap. 3, "Putnam and Cavell on the Ethics of Democracy."

43. For a good account, see Stephen Mulhall and Adam Swift, *Liberals and Communitarians* (Oxford: Blackwell, 1992).

44. Dewey, *The Public and Its Problems,* 153.

45. *Beyond Objectivism and Relativism,* 16.

46. Frost quoted in Stanley Burnshaw, *Robert Frost Himself* (New York: George Braziller, 1986), 243. In *Homage to Robert Frost,* Seamus Heaney similarly describes Frost's sonnet "Never Again Would Birds' Song Be the Same" as "an oblique dramatic statement of his own poetic creed" (78).

47. Wilhelm Dilthey, *Das Erlebnis und die Dichtung: Lessing, Goethe, Novalis, Hölderlin* (Göttingen: Vandenhoeck and Ruprecht, 1970).

48. As Hans-Georg Gadamer has put it, "the concept of experience seems . . . one of the most obscure we have" (*TM* 346). For useful background on this concept, see Elizabeth J. Bellamy and Artemis Leontis, "A Genealogy of Experience: From Epistemology to Politics," *Yale Journal of Criticism* (spring 1993): 163–84; and Joan W. Scott, "The Evidence of Experience, *Critical Inquiry* 17 [summer 1991]: 773–97.) On the difference between "experience" as *Erlebnis* and *Erfahrung,* see *TM,* esp. 60–70 and 346–62; see also Martin Jay, *Cultural Semantics: Keywords of Our Time* (Cambridge: MIT University Press, 1998), 44–53, 74–75; Bruns, *Hermeneutics Ancient and Modern;* and Martin Heidegger, *Hegel's Phenomenology of Spirit,* trans. Parvis Emad and Kenneth Maly (Bloomington: Indiana University Press, 1988), 18–23.

49. Robert Langbaum, *The Poetry of Experience: The Dramatic Monologue in Modern Literary Tradition* (New York: Norton, 1957); hereafter page numbers are cited parenthetically.

50. William H. Pritchard, *Frost: A Literary Life Reconsidered* (New York: Oxford University Press, 1984), 99.

51. Gerald L. Bruns says this (wrongly I think) of Wallace Stevens in "Wallace Stevens without Epistemology," in *Tragic Thoughts at the End of Philosophy,* 176. In *The Poetics of Space* (1958; reprint, Boston: Beacon Press, 1964), Gaston Bachelard puts the point nicely: "Overpicturesqueness in a house can conceal its intimacy" (12) (cf. line 11: "'Pretty,' he said."). Elsewhere the minister refers to "an old daguerreotype" of her husband (always referred to as her boys' father) "done sadly" (line 24) in "unlifelike lines" (line 29).

52. Quoted in Pritchard, *Frost: A Literary Life Reconsidered,* 100.

53. Reuben Brower, *The Poetry of Robert Frost: Constellations of Intention* (New York: Oxford University Press, 1963), 229. Cf. *LLU* 212; my emphasis: "I am *against* all isms as being merely ideas in and out of favor." Frost writes tellingly in *SL* 138: "I make it a rule not to take any character's side in anything I write. So I am not bound to defend the minister you understand."

54. Cf. *PI* § 50: "There is *one* thing of which one can say neither that it is one meter long, nor that it is not one meter long, and that is the standard meter in Paris.—But this, of course, is not to describe any extraordinary property to it, but only to mark its peculiar role in the language-game of measuring with a meter rule."

55. Dewey, *Art as Experience,* 41.

56. Ralph W. Rader, "The Dramatic Monologue and Related Lyric Forms," *Critical Inquiry* 3 (autumn 1976): 132.

57. Charles Altieri, "Life after Difference: The Position of the Interpreter and the Positionings of the Interpreted," in *Canons and Consequences,* 313.

58. Cf. Rader, in "Dramatic Monologue," where he rightly concludes: "Now it seems to me that the dramatic monologue is built not just as a generalized image of an 'other' person but specifically as an artificial replication of the structure of interpersonal understanding" (135). See also the similar results in Herbert F. Tucker, "Dramatic Monologue and the Overhearing of Lyric," in *Lyric Poetry: Beyond New Criticism,* ed. Chaviva Hosek and Patricia Parker (Ithaca: Cornell University Press, 1985), 226–46.

59. Mark Krupnick, *Lionel Trilling and the Fate of Cultural Criticism* (Evanston: Northwestern University Press), 9.

## 2. Rhetorical Invention

1. Vladimir Nabokov, *Speak, Memory* (New York: Knopf, 1999), 137.

2. Vladimir Nabokov, "The Art of Literature and Commonsense," in *Lectures on Literature,* ed. Fredson Bowers (New York: Harcourt Brace, 1980), 371–80. That Nabokov's position is itself (naturally!) something of a pose common to many high modernists is registered in Michael Wood's excellent *The Magician's Doubts: Nabokov and the Risks of Fiction* (Princeton: Princeton University Press, 1995): "Of course, Nabokov had a mythology of his own, which precisely needed the masses, the flattened and vulgar backdrop against which his heroes, and he himself, could cut their distinguished figures; so that paradoxically his arguments about uniqueness and the rest have a slightly ready-made, off-the-peg quality " (226). That this is a European pose Nabokov himself notes ("On a Book Entitled *Lolita,*" in *Lolita* [New York: Knopf, 1992], 333), as does Sacvan Bercovitch, *The Puritan Origins of the American Self* (New Haven: Yale University Press, 1975): "the European great man, for all his superiority to the mass, is sadly restricted. His very self-reliance implies an adversary Other, not only the great precursor poet but everyone to whom he is superior, everything from which he is alienated—history, the common laws, the representative men and women that constitute social normality. American intermediate selfhood has no such limits. Indeed, the very concept of 'Americanus,' from Mather through Emerson, advances a mode of personal identity designed as a compensatory *replacement* for (rather than alternative to) the ugly course of actual events" (177). This latter self—as ideally compensatory to, hence as somehow in *continuity* with the community even as it resists it—underwrites much of the present study.

3. Ralph Waldo Emerson, *Emerson in His Journals,* ed. Joel Porte (Cambridge: Harvard University Press, 1983), 265.

4. This list is a more down-home version of what Lawrence Buell calls the "catalogue rhetoric" of Emerson's more orphic pronouncements and means of persuasion used elsewhere; Lawrence Buell, *Literary Transcendentalism: Style and Vision in the American Renaissance* (Ithaca:

Cornell University Press, 1973), chap. 6. In *Sincerity and Authenticity* (Cambridge: Harvard University Press, 1971), Lionel Trilling observes that "the democratic dispensation required them [Americans] to shape their speech not by the standards of a particular class or circle but by their sense of the opinion of the public.... The democratic style doesn't signify an absence of sincerity; it does, however, indicate that the personal self to which the American would wish to be true is not the private, solid, intractable self of the Englishman" (113). A few pages later, Trilling cites Emerson in his journal for 1840: "There is no deeper dissembler than the sincerest man" (119).

5. Cf. Kenneth Cmiel, *Democratic Eloquence: The Fight over Popular Speech in Nineteenth-Century America* (Berkeley and Los Angeles: University of California Press, 1990), on Henry Beecher Stowe: "Again and again he said that the best public speaking sounded like conversation" (59); and also Charles Bernstein, *A Poetics* (Cambridge: Harvard University Press, 1992): "The immigrants of 1880–1900 radically subverted the language environment of the northeast and midwest as non-English speakers began to settle here at an almost geometrically escalating rate. By 1900, according to Peter Quartermain's assessment [Peter Quartermain, introduction to *Dictionary of Literary Biography*, vol. 45, *American Poetry, 1880–1945*, 1st ser., ed. Peter Quartermain (Detroit: Gale Research, 1986)], about one-quarter of the white U.S. population either did not speak English or learned it as a second language—while in the mid-Atlantic states and New England perhaps only one person in four was a native speaker of English" (106–7). See also Hugh Kenner, *A Homemade World: The American Modernist Writers* (Baltimore: John Hopkins University Press, 1975), 160.

6. Alasdair MacIntyre, *Three Rival Versions of Moral Inquiry* (South Bend: University of Notre Dame Press, 1990), 33. See also F. O. Matthiessen, *American Renaissance: Art and Expression in the Age of Emerson and Whitman* (London: Oxford University Press, 1941), esp. 549ff., on oratory as an analogy for poetry in Whitman; Richard Bridgman, *The Colloquial Style in America* (New York: Oxford University Press, 1966); R. Jackson Wilson, *Figures of Speech: American Writers and the Literary Marketplace, from Benjamin Franklin to Emily Dickinson* (New York: Knopf, 1989); Stephen Railton, *Authorship and Audience: Literary Performance in the American Renaissance* (Princeton: Princeton University Press, 1991); and Gerald Graff, *Professing English: An Institutional History* (Chicago: University of Chicago Press, 1987), esp. chap. 3, "Oratorical Culture and the Teaching of English," 36–54.

7. Henry James, *The Question of Our Speech. The Lesson of Balzac. Two Lectures* (Boston and New York: Houghton, Mifflin, 1905).

8. See *De orat* 1.37; and *On Duties [De officiis]*, ed. M. T. Griffin and E. M. Atkins (Cambridge: Cambridge University Press, 1991), 1.132.

9. Cf. Quintilian, *Institutio oratoria*, trans. H. E. Butler (Cambridge: Harvard University Press, 1958–63), who recognizes this point: "There are then in the first place two kinds of style; the one is closely welded and woven together, while the other is of a looser texture such as is found in dialogues and letters, except when they deal with some subject above their natural level, such as philosophy, politics or the like" (9.4.19–20).

10. Tzvetan Todorov, *Theories of the Symbol* (Oxford: Blackwell, 1982), 65.

11. Cf. *IQO* 23: "Our philosophical habits will prompt us to interpret the surface of writing as its manner, its style, its rhetoric, an ornament of what is said rather than its substance, but Emerson's implied claim [in "Self-Reliance"] is that this is as much a philosophical prejudice as the other conformities his essay decries, that, so to speak, words are no more ornaments of thoughts than tears are ornaments of sadness or joy."

12. Mikhail Bakhtin, *Problems of Dostoyevsky's Poetics*, ed. and trans. Caryl Emerson (Minneapolis: University of Minneapolis Press, 1984), 201.

13. Richard Poirier, *Robert Frost: The Work of Knowing* (Stanford: Stanford University Press, 1977); Brodsky, Heaney, and Walcott, *Homage to Robert Frost*, 105.

14. See, for example, Clifford Geertz, "Common Sense as a Cultural System," in *Local Knowledge: Further Essays in Interpretive Anthropology* (New York: Basic, 2000): "In this century the notion of (as it tends to be put) 'untutored' common sense—what the plain man thinks when sheltered from the vain sophistications of schoolmen—has, with so much else disappearing into science and poetry, grown into almost the thematic subject of philosophy. The focus on ordinary language in Wittgenstein, Austin, Ryle; the development of the so-called phenomenology of everyday life by Husserl, Schutz, Merleau-Ponty; the glorification of personal, in-the-midst-of-life decision in continental existentialism; the taking of garden-variety problem solving as the paradigm of reason in American pragmatism—all reflect this tendency to look toward the structure of down-to-earth, humdrum . . . thought for clues to the deeper mysteries of existence" (76–77). See also Charles Guignon, "Philosophy after Wittgenstein and Heidegger," *Philosophy and Phenomenological Research* 50 (June 1990); and Karl-Otto Apel, "Wittgenstein and Heidegger: Language Games and Life Forms," in *Critical Heidegger*, ed. Christopher Macann (London and New York: Routledge, 1996), 241–74.

15. Robert Kern, "Frost and Modernism," *American Literature* 60 (March 1988); reprinted in *On Frost: The Best from "American Literature,"* ed. Edwin H. Cady and Louis J. Budd (Durham: Duke University Press, 1991), 193. But Kern too narrowly restricts ordinary language to Frost's early notions of sentence-*sounds*. Regarding Stein, consider Charles Bernstein, in *A Poetics*: "I think this is the meaning of Stein's great discovery . . . of 'wordness' in the last section of *The Making of Americans* and in *Tender Buttons* . . . a revelation of the ordinary as sufficient unto itself, a revelation about the things of everyday life that make up a life, the activity of living, of speaking, and the fullness of every word, ofs and ins and ass, in the communal partaking—call it meal—of language arts" (143); and Marjorie Perloff, *Twenty-First-Century Modernism: The "New Poetics"* (Oxford: Blackwell, 2002): "her [Stein's] characteristic constructions depend on the placement of ordinary words in what are usually simple declarative sentences that combine in a tightly interlocking paragraph (and set of paragraphs) in which the verbal, visual, and aural are one" (62).

16. The phrase "drama of desire" comes from Peter Nicholls, *Modernisms: A Literary Guide* (Berkeley and Los Angeles: University of California Press, 1995), 198; see also Helen Vendler: *Wallace Stevens: Words Chosen Out of Desire* (Cambridge: Harvard University Press, 1984). On the connection of the gnomic and gnostic (and agnostic), see Angus Fletcher, "Stevens and the Influential Gnome," in *Colors of the Mind*, 265–87. For a revision of Stevens as pragmatist after the fact, see Patricia Rae, *The Practical Muse* (Cranbury N.J.: Associated University Press, 1997), esp. the section entitled "Doxic Dramas," 156–70; and Poirier, *Poetry and Pragmatism*.

17. See Hope Howell Hodgkins, "Rhetoric Versus Poetic: High Modernist Literature and the Cult of Belief," *Rhetorica* 16 (spring 1998): 201–25. On the Platonizing tendencies of high modernist painters such as Mondrian, see Mark A. Cheetham, *The Rhetoric of Purity: Essentialist Theory and the Advent of Abstract Painting* (Cambridge: Cambridge University Press, 1991).

18. Dates refer to first book publication unless otherwise noted.

19. John Stuart Mill, "What is Poetry?" in *Autobiography and Other Writings*, ed. Jack Stillinger (Boston: Houghton Mifflin, 1969), 195.

20. For an instructive contrast, see the treatment of comparison among high modernists such as Pound in Sanford Schwartz, *The Matrix of Modernism: Pound, Eliot and Twentieth-Century Thought* (Princeton: Princeton University Press, 1985), 74.

21. See Anthony Earl of Shaftesbury, "*Sensus Communis:* An Essay on the Freedom of Wit and Humor," in *Characteristics of Men, Manners, Opinions, Times, etc.*, ed. John M. Robertson, 2 vols. (London: Grant Richards), 43–99; and Immanuel Kant, *Anthropology from a Pragmatic Point of View* (The Hague: Martinus Nijhoff, 1974), 96.

22. In *Wit and Rhetoric in the Renaissance,* W. G. Crane notes that "the critics of the seventeenth century attached much importance to comparison as the [very] basis of wit" (14); see also *TM* 19–30 passim.

23. Cf. *TM* 71: "Genius and being experienced, our [the modern world's] criteria of value, are not adequate here. We may also remember quite different criteria and say, for example, that it is not the genuineness of the experience or the intensity of its expression, but the ingenious manipulation of fixed forms and modes of statement that make something a work of art. This difference in criteria is true of all kinds of art, but is particularly noticeable in the literary arts. As late as the eighteenth century we find poetry and rhetoric side by side in a way that is surprising to modern consciousness."

24. Watson, *The Architectonics of Meaning,* 73.

25. Michael J. Buckley, S.J., "Philosophic Method in Cicero," *Journal of the History of Philosophy* 8 (April 1970): 143–54.

26. Andrew M. Lakritz, *Modernism and the Other in Stevens, Frost, and Moore* (Gainesville: University Press of Florida, 1996) puts the first point nicely: "The paradox of Frost's work is that it inhabits the movement of reasoned thought in order to take reason apart" (72). Margery Sabin ("The Fate of the Frost Speaker," *Raritan* [fall 1982]) speaks to the second: reading Brower on Frost, "we are led to expect two things: first, a kind of coherence of personality; second, a sense of personality made coherent in relation to an event. Frost's point about the dramatic vitality of *sentences* promises neither of these things" (130).

27. Two books have begun to document what might be called the more serious alternative rhetorical and civic traditions in modern and contemporary poetry. The first sentence of Willard Spiegelman's *The Didactic Muse: Scenes of Instruction in Contemporary American Poetry* (Princeton: Princeton University Press, 1989), cites our man: "From Horace to Robert Frost ('a poem begins in delight and ends in wisdom') the major current of Western poetics has flowed from the wells of pleasure to the depths of instruction" (3). Spiegelman rightly places the influential Frost (rather than, say, the uninfluential Hardy, who might have worked as well) at the front of a particular class of later poets who, striking an explicitly didactic stance, are, in another critic's formulation, distinctively modern without being (high) modernist: Auden, Nemerov, Ginsburg, Pinsky, Ammons, Rich ("right popular philosophers" all, to use Sidney's expression). For Spiegelman, notably, Robert Frost "prepares an audience for the very points I assert in this book" (5), though the author chooses not to analyze Frost himself. (Not incidentally, Robert Langbaum concludes "Hardy, Frost, and the Question of Modernist Poetry" (*Virginia Quarterly Review* 58 [winter 1982]: "But whether major or minor, Hardy and Frost matter at this point in the 20th century when the mighty modernist movement seems to have run its course and young people are looking for another direction. Hardy and Frost are important just now, because they show how to be modern without being [high] modernist.")

In a similar way, in *American Poetry and Culture, 1945–1980* (Cambridge: Harvard University Press, 1985), Robert von Hallberg analyzes a different group of postwar poets in a Frostian vein who reflect, and reflect on, contemporary centrist American culture: Robert Creeley and John Ashberry; some of the work of Charles Olson, Robert Merrill, and Robert Lowell; Ed Dorn.

28. Walter J. Ong, *Rhetoric, Romance, and Technology* (Ithaca: Cornell University Press, 1971), 8. Again, all of this is perfectly well known within different groups. What often gets ignored in narratives of these movements and reactions, however (the earlier Ong quotation is an exception proving the rule), is the downfall of rhetoric as a complex of methods or re-sources of "common sense" invention, argument, and judgment orienting inquirers in social space. Thus Goethe's injunction in *Faust* (1808–32) to "Give up pursuing eloquence, unless / You can speak as you feel!" (1.4. 535–36) merely shifts into a romantic register Locke's previous injunctions against rhetoric in favor of a neutral scientific speech a hundred years earlier (John Locke, *An Essay Concerning Human Understanding,* ed. Alexander Campbell Fraser, 2 vols. [New York:

Dover, 1959], 2), while Kant condemns rhetorical methods altogether: "Rhetoric, so far as this is taken to mean the art of persuasion, i.e., the art of deluding by means of a fair semblance (as *ars oratoria*), and not merely excellence of speech (eloquence and style), is a dialectic, which borrows from poetry only so much as is necessary to win over men's minds to the side of the speaker before they have weighed the matter, and to rob their verdict of its freedom" (*CJ* sec. 53). Pound echoes this in his essay "Vorticism" when he writes: "The 'image' is the furthest possible remove from rhetoric. Rhetoric is the art of dressing up some important matter so as to fool the audience for the time being"; in *Gaudier-Brzeska* (New York: New Directions), 83. This attitude was anticipated in many different ways in romantics such as Coleridge, Shelley and Keats, Carlyle and Keble (but not Byron), culminating in Verlaine's injunction to "Take eloquence and wring its neck" (Paul Verlaine, *"Art Poetique"* [1884] line 21, in *Selected Poems*, trans. C. F. MacIntyre [Berkeley and Los Angeles: University of California Press, 1948], 183); cf. Ezra Pound, who said of Yeats that he "once and for all stripped English poetry of its perdamnable rhetoric" (*Literary Essays of Ezra Pound*, ed. T. S. Eliot [New York: New Directions, 1968], 11, also 283). By then Arthur Symons could comfortably equate "the old bondage of rhetoric" with "exteriority" and even materialism, in contrast to many of the symbolists' "attempt[s] to spiritualise literature ... to disengage the ultimate essence, the soul, of whatever exists and can be realised by the consciousness" (Arthur Symons, *The Symbolist Movement in Literature* [New York: Dutton, 1919], 5). In his review of Frost's second book, *North Of Boston* (1914), Edward Thomas, the poet and close friend of Frost, praises the poems precisely for their being *free* of "the exaggeration of rhetoric" and "egoistic rhetoric" (Edward Thomas, "Robert Frost," in *A Language Not to Be Betrayed: Selected Prose of Edward Thomas*, ed. Edna Longley [Manchester: Carcanet Press, 1981], 125, 131), while Frost himself has his own versions of antirhetoric in a letter to another friend, Sidney Cox: "You do right to damn grammar: you might be excused if you damned rhetoric and in fact everything else in and out of books but the spirit" (*SL* 99). Thus Ong's observation is more subtle than the commonplace that romanticism simply shut down rhetoric. For a recent revisionist history of the more positive relations of romanticism to rhetoric, see Don Bialostosky and Lawrence Needham, eds., *Rhetorical Traditions and British Romantic Literature* (Bloomington: Indiana University Press, 1995), and Michael S. Macovski, *Dialogue and Literature: Apostrophe, Auditors, and the Collapse of Romantic Discourse* (New York: Oxford University Press, 1994).

29. Nicholls, *Modernisms*, 197. The canonical version, treated later in this chapter, is one that Marjorie Perloff has called "the puzzle which is Modernism" ("Pound/Stevens: Whose Era?" *New Literary History* [1982], 506), and one that is extended in her recent *Twenty-first-Century Modernism: The "New" Poetics*.

30. I should note here that, in predicating rhetoric of low modernism, I am not unmindful that rhetoric, as a general method and existential hermeneutic, applies to high modernism as well—high modernist protestations to the contrary notwithstanding. Even among revisionists of modernism, we have yet to see studies of the roles of the everyday and ordinary in (say) Stevens, Moore, Woolf, or Lawrence.

31. I am thinking here (to give just one example) of Catherine Belsey's deconstructive critique of common sense in *Critical Practice* (London and New York: Methuen, 1980), in part countered by Richard Poirier's version of the divided self in "Writing Off the Self" in *The Renewal of Literature: Emersonian Reflections* (New Haven: Yale University Press, 1988), 182–223; and, of course, Walter Benjamin in "The Work of Art in the Age of Mechanical Reproduction" in *Illuminations* (New York: Schocken, 1969).

32. Cf. Paul de Man, "Rhetoric of Tropes (Nietzsche)," in *Allegories of Reading: Figural Language in Rousseau, Nietzsche, Rilke, and Proust* (New Haven: Yale University Press, 1979), 105; see also *Friedrich Nietzsche on Rhetoric and Language*, ed. Sander L. Gilman, Carole Blair, and David J. Parent (New York: Oxford University Press, 1989), 20–23.

33. Richard Lanham, *The Motives of Eloquence* (New Haven: Yale University Press, 1976), 4.
34. Ibid, 4–5. More recent work by Lanham moderates his earlier views; see Richard Lanham, *The Electronic Word: Democracy, Technology, and the Arts* (Chicago: University of Chicago Press, 1993).
35. Katherine Kearns, *Robert Frost and a Poetics of Appetite* (Cambridge: Cambridge University Press, 1994), 13.
36. Pierre Bourdieu, *Language and Symbolic Power* (Cambridge: Harvard University Press, 1991), 125–26.
37. Brodsky, Heaney, and Walcott, *Homage to Robert Frost*, 62.
38. For background, see Graff, *Professing English*, esp. 55–120 and 247ff.
39. Terry Eagleton, *Walter Benjamin, or Towards a Revolutionary Criticism* (London: Verso, 1981), 106. For a related new account of modernism, see Lawrence Rainey, *Institutions of Modernism: Literary Elites and Public Culture* (New Haven: Yale University Press, 1998).
40. Quoted in Symons, *The Symbolist Movement in Literature*, 66; Charles Rosen, "Mallarmé the Magnificent," *New York Review of Books*, 20 May 1999, 45. For a more nuanced account of this poet's relation to ordinary language and social interests, and to sophistical rhetoric of the sort I am aligning with Frost, see Jacques Derrida, "Mallarmé," in *Acts of Literature* (New York: Routledge, 1992), 126; and Jewel Spears Brooker, *Mastery and Escape: T. S. Eliot and the Dialectic of Modernism* (Amherst: University of Massachussetts Press, 1994): "In particular, Mallarmé's reputation as an elitist, based on what I have called his Calvinist expediency, has obscured the fact that at the heart of his aesthetic is an obsessive interest in what he calls the 'common functioning'" (45).
41. As Allan Megill states the matter, "More often than not, [crisis] is evoked rather than explained or defended" (*Prophets of Extremity: Nietzsche, Heidegger, Foucault, Derrida* [Berkeley and Los Angeles: University of California Press, 1985], 111). See also Robert B. Pippin, *Modernism as a Philosophical Problem* (Cambridge: Blackwell, 1991), 29ff. I am not offering an opinion regarding the question of crisis, merely proposing that Frost's historical understanding of epistemological and aesthetic developments in the first quarter of the century, in swerving away from one set of norms (those belonging to an aesthetic elite), was able to exploit another set of norms (those relatively, putatively, "common to all"). See especially Frost's poem "One Step Backward Taken" (1946).
42. Rosen, "Mallarmé the Magnificent," 45. Cf. Peter Gay, *Schnitzler's Century: The Making of Middle-Class Culture, 1815–1914* (New York: Norton, 2002): "the bourgeoisie was defined by its antagonists, a ferocious and growing sect of avant-garde writers and artists. These enemies of the middle class were a fertile source for facile generalizations that gratuitously discounted the variations among bourgeois—fertile and only too natural: the enemy is always a single recognizable villain, sporting none of the virtues and all of the vices" (28).
43. Frank Lentricchia, *Modernist Quartet* (Cambridge: Cambridge University Press, 1994), 131. Cf. Gay, *Schnitzler's Century*, quoting Flaubert: "Axiom: Hatred of Bourgeois is the beginning of all virtue" (29).
44. T. S. Eliot, "The Metaphysical Poets [1921]," in *Selected Prose of T. S. Eliot*, ed. Frank Kermode (San Diego: Harcourt, Brace, 1956), 64. Certainly Eliot did not have in mind the sort of rhetorical synthesis I am pursuing here, but the sixteenth-century mind was—according to many historians of ideas, including Stephen Toulmin (*Cosmopolis: The Hidden Agenda of Modernity* [Chicago: University of Chicago Press, 1990])—notably rhetorical.
45. Langbaum, *The Poetry of Experience*, 11; see related discussions in Langbaum's *The Mysteries of Identity: A Theme in Modern Literature* (Chicago: University of Chicago Press, 1977). Stephen Toulmin concurs with Langbaum but further proposes a neglected source of modernity in Renaissance rhetoric (quite antithetical to the standard account) that I want to explore below; see Toulmin, *Cosmopolis*: "A century ago, a Catholic traditionalist like John Henry

Newman could write *A Grammar of Assent*, which treated rhetoric as a topic of serious intellectual interest; but, in the first half of the 20th century, his example was not much followed. Instead, the scholarly focus was on the 'text,' which was taken to mean a text as it appears on a page, preferably a printed page: this limitation went with the desire to isolate literary works, as products, from facts about the historical situations and personal lives of their authors, as producers—i.e., to decontextualize the text. Since the mid-1960s, rhetoric has begun to regain its respectability as a topic of literary and linguistic analysis" (186–87).

46. William Empson, "Sense in *The Prelude*," in *The Structure of Complex Words* (Cambridge: Harvard University Press, 1989), 298.

47. Nicholls, *Modernisms*, 53; see also John Carey's one-sided *The Intellectuals and the Masses: Pride and Prejudice among the Literary Intelligentsia, 1880–1939* (New York: St. Martin's Press, 1992).

48. William Empson, "Rhythm and Imagery in English Poetry," in *Argufying in Poetry*, ed. John Haffenden (Iowa City: University of Iowa Press, 1987), 163; also 160: "arguing in verse has always seemed to me a wonderfully poetical thing to do, so I cannot understand the idea that it is prosy to speak up for the human reason. If the modern movement is the revolt against reason then I have never been in it at all, so I have not left it merely because I am an old buffer."

49. Georg Lukács, "The Ideology of Modernism," in *The Critical Tradition: Classic Texts and Contemporary Trends*, ed. David Richter (Boston: Bedford, 1998), 597–611. Thus Helen Vendler writes of Wallace Stevens: "Stevens is one of the last of our writers to experience fully the nineteenth-century crisis of the death of God; and he learned from Shelley and Coleridge the connection of the loss of religious faith with the loss of sexual faith. By linking the poet to the lover and the believer, Stevens aligns the skeptical crisis of aesthetic desire for the beautiful to the more familiar skepticisms attacking religious and secular fidelity; and since his conception of the aesthetic includes a strong intellectual component, an epistemological crisis is linked, for him, to an aesthetic one" (*Wallace Stevens: Words Chosen Out of Desire* [Cambridge: Harvard University Press, 1984], 30).

50. Cf. Poirier, *Poetry and Pragmatism:* "This relative indifference to crises, to any cultural apocalypse, helps explain, I suspect, why writers of an Emersonian pragmatist disposition were, for the most part, ignored or regarded as insular and pleasantly irrelevant during the period from about 1920 to 1960. This was a period when the wasteland ethos . . . dominated the American literary-academic scene" (132); and Coates, *The Claims of Common Sense:* "[Contemporary] thinkers who take common sense seriously do not believe that the failure of our language to meet the demands of extensionalism leaves us in any sort of crisis" (2). See also Charles Olson, *The Special View of History*, ed. Ann Charters (Berkeley: Oyez, 1970): "It is idle to talk of destruction or decadence, either of which are much the gab and guff of contemporary slow-wits" (48); and Kolb, *The Critique of Pure Modernity: Hegel, Heidegger, and After*, 261–62.

51. Ronald Schleifer, *Modernism and Time: The Logic of Abundance in Literature, Science, and Culture, 1880–1930* (Cambridge: Cambridge University Press, 2000), 5.

52. Quoted in Robert Lowell, *Collected Prose* (New York: Farrar, Straus, and Giroux, 1987), 9.

53. Bernstein, *A Poetics*, 22.

54. Frank Lentricchia, *Robert Frost: Modern Poetics and the Landscapes of Self* (Durham: Duke University Press, 1975), 144. Hereafter cited parenthetically.

55. Lentricchia's book appeared just a year earlier than Richard Poirier's *Robert Frost: The Work of Knowing* (1976), and it is fair to observe that Lentricchia's Kantian notion of "play" is the very opposite of Poirier's idea of "work," while Lentricchia's later pragmatism is a benighted version of Poirier's insights in *The Renewal of Literature: Emersonian Reflections* (1988) and especially in *Poetry and Pragmatism* (1992).

56. Cf. *TM* 43: "He [Kant] reduces sensus communis to a subjective principle."

57. See Immanuel Kant, *Critique of Judgment*, trans. J. H. Bernard (New York: Hafner,

1951), 15. Even in determinant judgment, however, as Robert Pippin has argued, Kant is unclear about how the schematism—which is said to partake of both percept and concept—actually manages this subsumption; see Robert B. Pippin, *Kant's Theory of Form: An Essay on the "Critique of Pure Reason"* (New Haven: Yale University Press, 1982): "Explaining the *relation* between 'form' and 'matter' is . . . a problem particularly well illuminated by Kant's theory of empirical concepts. Moreover, it simply *is* the problem of the schematism" (89).

58. Weinsheimer, *Philosophical Hermeneutics and Literary Theory*, chap. 3.

59. Ibid., 52.

60. Anthony J. Cascardi, *Consequences of Enlightenment* (Cambridge: Cambridge University Press, 1999); hereafter cited parenthetically.

61. Cf. *TM* 39: "That means nothing less than that judging the case involves not merely applying the universal principle according to which it is judged, but co-determining, supplementing, and correcting that principle."

62. One naturally thinks of Aristotle's discussion of "equity" in the *Nichomachean Ethics* or in the American common law tradition; see, for example, Kathy Eden, *Legal and Poetic Fiction in the Aristotelian Tradition* (Princeton: Princeton University Press, 1986).

63. Wittgenstein, *Tractatus Logico-Philosophicus*, 6.421. In this way modernism, as Charles Altieri has noted, "remains wed to Romanticism, because it was the Romantics who first felt on a large scale the fundamental problem that still oppresses the arts: How is it plausible to preserve as publicly significant the values in romance, or in the states made available by the lyric imagination, within a culture that grants intellectual authority only to a range of Enlightenment models developed as antagonists to all romance ideals?" (Altieri, *Painterly Abstraction in Modernist American Poetry* [University Park: Pennsylvania State University Press, 1989], 61). Cf. Jean-Marie Schaeffer, *Art of the Modern Age: Philosophy of Art from Kant to Heidegger*, trans. Steven Rendall (Princeton: Princeton University Press, 2000): "at bottom the romantic syndrome is double: on one hand, the experience of a disorientation linked to the ever-greater differentiation of diverse spheres of social life, and on the other, an irrepressible nostalgia for a harmonious and organic (re)integration of all the aspects of the reality that were experienced as discordant and dispersed" (9); and James Logenbach, "Modern Poetry," in *The Cambridge Companion to Modernism*, ed. Michael Levenson: "In the story I tell, modern poetry grew from a sense (already highly developed by the Victorians) that the great claims made for poetry by the romantics were no longer viable" (102–3).

64. Poirier, *Robert Frost: The Work of Knowing*, xxiii.

65. Poirier, *Renewal of Literature*, 9. On page 42, Heidegger and Gadamer come in for a single, though significant, mention.

66. This is just the project pursued in Michael Levenson, ed., *The Cambridge Companion to Modernism* (Cambridge: Cambridge University Press, 1999). Just as there are many variants of high modernism and numerous aesthetic strategies appropriate to them, so there are of low. Of the latter, those figures in the Emersonian tradition mentioned above make up the most important strand, I think, but there are others, not clearly or exclusively Emersonian, both American and British, writers of poetry and prose, who are complex blends of high and low in their interests in the local, prosaic, elementary, common, overlooked.

67. For support, see Cascardi, *Consequences of Enlightenment*.

68. Michael Bell, "The Metaphysics of Modernism," in *The Cambridge Companion to Modernism*, ed. Michael Levenson, 9–32.

69. For an account, see Malcolm Bradbury and James McFarlane, eds., *Modernism: A Guide to European Literature, 1890–1930* (London: Penguin, 1976), esp. 19–94.

70. Poirier, "Modernism and Its Difficulties," in *The Renewal of Literature*, 95–113. See Sanford Schwartz, *The Matrix of Modernism:* "Pound, Eliot, and even many so-called formalists never intended to dissociate art from life. For Pound and Eliot, like Brecht after them, it

is precisely through its capacity to detach us from ordinary life that art performs its existential functions" (112).

71. Poirier, *Renewal of Literature*, 106. Cf. Steiner, *Venus in Exile:* "To assimilate the latest challenge as art does not involve a victory of fellow feeling across the community but a proud gesture of superiority on the part of experts toward laypeople supposedly incapable of such feats of stamina and discernment" (95).

72. Consider Moore's early "The Steeple-Jack" or Auden's "Law Like Love" (1940) as particularly clear examples of what I call (in chapter 4) rhetorical "epideixis." Olson's "projective verse" and Bernstein's "poetics of absorption" have yet to be taken on as the low modernist kinds of rhetorical "demonstrations" (Gr. *epideixis*, Lat. *demonstratio*) they often are.

73. Taylor, *Sources of the Self: The Making of the Modern Identity,* 456ff.; Altieri, *Painterly Abstraction in Modernist American Poetry,* 26ff.

74. Gerald L. Bruns, "Wallace Stevens without Epistemology," in *Tragic Thoughts at the End of Philosophy,* 166; in this book, see also Bruns (in passing) on Charles Bernstein and Ron Silliman.

75. John Wisdom, "Note on Ayer's *Language, Truth and Logic,*" in *Philosophy and Psychoanalysis,* 246; Austin Quigley, "Wittgenstein's Philosophizing and Literary Theorizing," *New Literary History* 19 (winter 1988): 209–37, reprinted in *Ordinary Language Criticism: Literary Thinking after Cavell after Wittgenstein,* ed. Kenneth Dauber and Walter Jost.

76. Auerbach, *Mimesis,* 552.

77. Jay Martin, "Songs of Experience: Reflections on the Debate over *Alltagsgeschichte,*" in *Cultural Semantics: Keywords of Our Time* (Amherst: University of Massachussetts Press, 1989), 40.

78. De Certeau, *The Practice of Everyday Life*; Agnes Heller, *Everyday Life* (London: Routledge and Kegan Paul, 1984).

79. Heller, *Everyday Life,* 47.

80. Ibid., ix.

81. Ibid., 148ff.

82. See *Rhet* 2.26.1403A17: "It is the same thing which I call element *(stoicheion)* and *topos*; for element and *topos* are that under which many enthymemes fall."

83. Mikhail Bakhtin, *Problems of Dostoyevsky's Poetics.* ed. and trans. Caryl Emerson (Minneapolis: University of Minnesota Press, 1984), 81.

84. Cf. Marjorie Perloff, *The Dance of the Intellect: Studies in the Poetry of the Pound Tradition* (Cambridge: Cambridge University Press, 1985): "Postmodernism in poetry, I would argue, begins in the urge to return the material so rigidly excluded—political, ethical, historical, philosophical—to the domain of poetry, which is to say that the Romantic lyric, the poem as expression of a moment of absolute insight, of emotion crystallized into a timeless pattern, gives way to a poetry that can, once again, accommodate narrative and didacticism, the serious and the comic, verse *and* prose" (184). The "return" of which Perloff speaks, I propose, has been present all along in the low modern.

85. For a far more rhetorical Wordsworth, see Charles Altieri, "Wordsworth's Poetics of Eloquence: A Challenge to Contemporary Theory," in *Canons and Consequences,* 131–62. For a less rhetorical Wordsworth, see Gerald L. Bruns, "Wordsworth at the Limits of Romantic Hermeneutics," in *Hermeneutics Ancient and Modern,* 159–78.

## 3. Grammatical Judgment

1. Quoted in Jay Parini, "Emerson and Frost: The Present Act of Vision," *Sewanee Review* (spring 1981): 225–26.

2. Cf. *CR* 32: "The idea of agreement here is not that of coming to or arriving at an agreement on a given occasion, but of being in agreement throughout, being in harmony, like

pitches or tones, or clocks, or weighing scales, or columns of figures. That a group of human beings *stimmen* in their language *überein* says, so to speak, that they are mutually voiced with respect to it, mutually *attuned* top to bottom"; and *OC* § 130: "But isn't it experience that teaches us to judge like *this,* that is to say, that it is correct to judge like this? But how does experience *teach* us, then? *We* may derive it from experience, but experience does not direct us to derive anything from experience."

3. For a good analysis of how parts of the world can be "taken up into" grammar, thereby overcoming the division between sign and thing typical in poststructuralist theory, see David Schalkwyk, "Fiction as 'Grammatical' Investigation: A Wittgensteinian Account," *Journal of Aesthetics and Art Criticism* 53 (summer 1995): "Not all words can be explained by pointing to the world but, contrary to Saussurean theory, Wittgenstein reminds us that some words are indeed explained in this way. In such cases aspects of the extra-linguistic world are appropriated as samples, or rules of representation, for the ways in which [certain] words are to be used" (288).

4. See especially Anthony J. Cascardi, "From the Sublime to the Natural: Romantic Responses to Kant," in *Literature and the Question of Philosophy,* ed. Anthony J. Cascardi, 101–31; and Cascardi, "The Grammar of Telling" in *Ordinary Language Criticism,* ed. Kenneth Dauber and Walter Jost; Michael Fischer, "Accepting the Romantics as Philosophers," *Philosophy and Literature* 12 (October 1988): 179–89; and Michael Fischer, *Stanley Cavell and Literary Skepticism* (Chicago: University of Chicago Press, 1989); Austin Quigley, "Wittgenstein's Philosophizing and Literary Theorizing," in *Ordinary Language Criticism,* ed. Kenneth Dauber and Walter Jost; Guetti, *Wittgenstein and the Grammar of Literary Experience;* and the essays by Fleming, Wheeler, and others in *The Senses of Stanley Cavell,* ed. Richard Fleming and Michael Payne (Lewisburg: Bucknell University Press, 1989).

5. Cf. Wallace Stevens, *Letters of Wallace Stevens,* ed. Holly Stevens (New York: Knopf, 1966), 443.

6. In the introduction to *Disowning Knowledge,* (17), Cavell aligns the masculine side of human nature with skepticism and jealousy and the feminine side with enthusiasm, fanaticism (including madness), and love. The former illuminates my studies of "The Death of the Hired Man" and "West-Running Brook," the latter of "Snow" and "Home Burial."

7. See Ernst Cassirer, *Kant's Life and Thought,* trans. James Haden (New Haven: Yale University Press, 1981), 256. On this problem in Kant, also see Stephen Mulhall, *Stanley Cavell: Philosophy's Recounting of the Ordinary* (Oxford: Clarendon Press, 1994), 156.

8. Cf. Martin Heidegger, "The Origin of the Work of Art" in *Basic Writings,* ed. David Farrell Krell (New York: Harper and Row, 1977): "We never really first perceive a throng of sensations, e.g., tones and noises in the appearance of things . . . rather we hear the storm whistling in the chimney, we hear the three-motored plane, we hear the Mercedes in immediate distinction from the Volkswagen" (156).

9. W. Jackson Bate, *Coleridge* (Cambridge: Harvard University Press, 1968), 185; also Schaeffer, *Art of the Modern Age:* "[The] Kantian conception of the symbol as an indirect representation of the morally good incontestably anticipates the romantic theory of the poetic symbol. And yet the two theories do not refer to exactly the same thing. For the romantics, it is the *Absolute* that must be presented symbolically, because it cannot be *thought speculatively.* In the Kantian theory it is the *morally good* that must be presented symbolically, because it cannot be presented in a direct intuition" (53). But see also Fletcher, *Colors of the Mind,* 175–76, for a kind of relativism compatible with Coleridgean thinking.

10. The first strategy, which leans heavily on Rorty's version of neopragmatism but lacks actual philosophical analysis of form of life, can be found in Mark Edmundson, *Literature against Philosophy: A Defence of Poetry* (Cambridge: Cambridge University Press, 1995), while the second strategy, to which I am far more sympathetic, in Charles Altieri, "Wordsworth's Poetics of Eloquence," in *Canons and Consequences,* 131–62.

11. "I am not a German: a German you know may be defined as a person who doesnt [*sic*] dare not to be thorough" (*SL* 135).

12. See Aristotle, *Metaphysica*, 4.7.1.

13. For a recent contribution to these matters, see P. Christopher Smith, *The Hermeneutics of Original Argument: Demonstration, Dialectic, Rhetoric* (Evanston: Northwestern University Press, 1998). For Smith, reasoning by example in Aristotle is subordinated to reasoning by enthymeme, but the latter, in turn, which he calls "original argument," "reasons by the 'topics'" (4), which are themselves originally grounded in (hence continuous with) tropes (72ff.), as I suggested in my introductory chapter.

14. See Garver, *Aristotle's Rhetoric: An Art of Character*.

15. For a succinct account of the proposition as dealt with by Russell and early Wittgenstein, see *Themes* 207ff.

16. I am drawing here chiefly on Paul Ricoeur, *Interpretation Theory: Discourse and the Surplus of Meaning* (Fort Worth: Texas Christian University Press, 1976).

17. In "The Problem of Speech Genres" (in *Speech Genres and Other Late Essays*, trans. Vern W. McGee, ed. Caryl Emerson and Michael Holquist [Austin: University of Texas Press, 1986]), Bakhtin summarizes Ricouer's kind of thought: "Courses in general linguistics (even serious ones like Saussure's) frequently present graphic-schematic depictions of the two partners in speech communication—the speaker and the listener (who perceives the speech)— and provide diagrams of the active speech processes of the speaker and the corresponding passive processes of the listener's perception and understanding of the speech. One cannot say that these diagrams are false or that they do not correspond to certain aspects of reality. But when they are put forth as the actual whole, they become a scientific fiction" (68).

18. Cf. Bruns, *Hermeneutics Ancient and Modern*, on Ricoeur: "It seems to me that what we have here is a basic Aristotelian theory of the text, and what is Aristotelian about it is the way the text is saved or justified by being systematized and then reconnected to reality according to an up-to-date conception of mimesis" (239); and Gerald L. Bruns, *Heidegger's Estrangements: Language, Truth, and Poetry in the Later Writings* (New Haven: Yale University Press, 1989): "What Ricoeur deplores specifically is the way Heidegger 'severs discourse from its propositional character.'" (196 n. 26).

19. Isaiah Berlin, "The Romantic Revolution: A Crisis in the History of Modern Thought," in *The Sense of Reality: Studies in Ideas and Their History* (New York: Farrar, Straus, and Giroux, 1996), 193.

20. Schalkwyk, "Fiction as 'Grammatical' Investigation," 287–88.

21. George J. Leonard, *Into the Light of Things: The Art of the Commonplace from Wordsworth to John Cage* (Chicago: University of Chicago Press, 1994); see also Arthur Danto, *The Transfiguration of the Commonplace* (Cambridge: Harvard University Press, 1981). Frank Lentricchia makes this last point at the beginning of *Modernist Quartet:* "I understand how odd it must appear to include Frost in modernist company. One of the reasons for the oddity is that we have forgotten the heterogeneous character of modernist literature: Ibsen, Strindberg, Chekhov, Hardy, Shaw, the Joyce of *Dubliners*, and Frost" (xiii).

22. Ludwig Wittgenstein, *Remarks on the Foundations of Mathematics*, trans. G.E.M. Anscombe, ed. H. H. von Wright, Rush Rhees, and G.E.M. Anscombe (Cambridge: MIT University Press, 1967), 81. Cf. *OC* § 378: "Knowledge is in the end based on acknowledgement." In *SW* 145, Cavell writes: "it is not quite right to say we *believe* the world exists (though certainly we should not conclude that we do *not* believe this, that we *fail* to believe its existence), and wrong even to say we *know* it exists (while it is equally wrong to say we fail to know this)." Rather, our "relation to the world's existence is somehow closer than the ideas of believing and knowing are made to convey."

23. Cf. Charles Taylor, "Overcoming Epistemology," in *Philosophical Arguments:* "The notion that our understanding of the world is grounded in our dealings with it is equivalent to the thesis that this understanding is not ultimately based on representations at all, in the sense of depictions that are separately identifiable from what they are of" (12).

24. Arabella Lyon, *Intentions: Negotiated, Contested, and Ignored* (University Park: Pennsylvania State University Press, 1998).

25. Altieri, *Canons and Consequences*, 105.

26. Michael Billig, *Arguing and Thinking: A Rhetorical Approach to Social Psychology* (Cambridge: Cambridge University Press, 1987); John Shotter, *Cultural Politics of Everyday Life: Social Constructionism, Rhetoric and Knowing of the Third Kind* (Toronto: University of Toronto Press, 1993).

27. Coates, *The Claims of Common Sense*, 169–70; and Dumm, *A Politics of the Ordinary*. Cf. C. S. Pierce, "Critical Common-Sensism," in *Philosophical Writings of Pierce*, ed. Justus Buchler (New York: Dover, 1955): "The *vague* might be defined as that to which the principle of contradiction does not apply" (295).

28. Ralph Waldo Emerson, "The Over-Soul," in *The Portable Emerson*, ed. Carl Bode with Malcolm Cowley, 210–11.

29. For an account of this influence, see Albert R. Kitzhaber, *Rhetoric in American Colleges, 1850–1900* (Dallas: Southern Methodist University Press, 1990).

30. Emerson, "Over-Soul," 220.

31. Cf. *CR* III; "Declining Decline," in *NYUA* 33: "The power of this recognition of the ordinary for philosophy is bound up with the recognition that refusing or forcing the order of the ordinary is a cause of philosophical emptiness (say avoidance) and violence." In *De officiis*, 1.40, Cicero defines *"ordo"* as *"compositio rerum aptis et accomodatis locis."*

32. My sense of "law and order" here is the opposite of what is meant by the phrase in Richard Poirier, "A Literature of Law and Order," in *The Performing Self: Compositions and Decompositions in the Languages of Contmporary Life* (New Brunswick N.J.: Rutgers University Press, 1992), 3–26. Poirier's point, however, is the one I wish to make: that a literature like Frost's avoids the high modernist co-optation of character by its willingness to bind "loosely."

33. For discussions of these issues, see Richard Bernstein, "Nietzsche or Aristotle? Reflections on Alasdair MacIntyre's *After Virtue*," in *Philosophical Profiles* (Philadelphia: University of Pennsylvania Press, 1986), 114–40; and Cora Diamond, "Anything But Argument?" in *The Realistic Spirit: Wittgenstein, Philosophy and the Mind* (Cambridge: MIT University Press, 1995), 291–308.

34. Richard McKeon, "The Methods of Rhetoric and Philosophy: Invention and Judgment," in *Rhetoric: Essays in Invention and Discovery*, ed. Mark Backman (Woodbridge, Conn.: Ox Bow Press, 1987), 58. The rhetorical connection between psychology and judgment—and the Cartesian and later high modernist, misogynistic rejection of psychology for a putatively pure and timeless logic—is incisively discussed in Jay Martin, "Modernism and the Specter of Psychologism," in *Cultural Semantics: Keywords of Our Time* (Amherst: University of Massachusetts Press, 1998), 164–80; and Steiner, *Venus in Exile*.

35. Denis Donoghue, *Connoisseurs of Chaos: Ideas of Order in Modern American Poetry*, 2d ed. (New York: Columbia University Press, 1984), 191, 193.

36. In "The Significance of Common Culture" (*Philosophy* 54 [January 1979]) in talking about just such education of emotion by means of exemplary action (that is, within those rough zones of right and wrong), Roger Scruton helps us to appreciate how we can take responsibility for our own (potential) misdeeds and our own education (58). See also Cora Diamond's "Anything But Argument?": "This is a kind of learning to think. It plays an essential role in the education of the emotions and in the development of moral sensibility" (303).

## 4. Logical Proof

1. Allison M. Cummings and Rocco Marinaccio, "An Interview with Charles Bernstein," *Contemporary Literature* 41 (spring 2000): 5.
2. Dewey, *Art as Experience*.
3. Ronald Schleifer, *Modernism and Time* (Cambridge: Cambridge University Press, 2000), 185.
4. Bruns, *Hermeneutics Ancient and Modern*, 183.
5. John D. Lyons, "Circe's Drink and Sarbonnic Wine: Montaigne's Paradox of Experience," in *Unruly Examples: On the Rhetoric of Exemplarity*, ed. Alexander Gelley (Stanford: Stanford University Press, 1995), 88–89; 92.
6. Michael Wood, "Montaigne and the Mirror of Example," *Philosophy and Literature* 13 (April 1989): 4–5.
7. Ibid., 11.
8. Ibid., 10.
9. Brodsky, Heaney, and Walcott, *Homage to Robert Frost*, 100.
10. Ross Chambers, "Strolling, Touring, Cruising: Counter-Disciplinary Narrative and the Loiterature of Travel," in *Understanding Narrative*, ed. James Phelan and Peter J. Rabinowitz (Columbus: Ohio State University Press, 1994), 21. Describing "Les Nuits D'Octobre," Nerval even suggests that he was influenced in his method by a "prolix orator described censoriously by Cicero" (25).
11. Wittgenstein, quoted in Malcolm, *Ludwig Wittgenstein: A Memoir*, 93.
12. Ellis, *Language, Logic, and Thought*, 17.
13. Some readers may recall, as a particularly glaring example, the once-influential "information theory" of Claude Shannon and Warren Weaver, *The Mathematical Theory of Communication* (Urbana: University of Illinois Press, 1949).
14. Lewis, *Studies in Words*, 260.
15. In partial contrast, see *SL* 444: "All criticism must be ad hoc as you [Bernard DeVoto] insist. But it can be all the way ad hoc, I mean clear to the principles in the thing."
16. See, for example, James G. Hepburn, "Robert Frost and His Critics," *New England Quarterly* 35 (1962): 376: "He is primarily a lyric poet; and, as he says elsewhere the aim in lyric poetry is not mainly implication: the aim is song"; see also Poirier, *Robert Frost: The Work of Knowing*, 275. George Nitchie recognizes Frost's strong rhetorical impulse but is too ready to relegate it to "the cracker barrel and the symposium in the country store" (*Human Values in the Poetry of Robert Frost* [Durham: Duke University Press, 1960], 59). What Langbaum says of Frost's best poems applies to "Two Tramps": "Frost's poems often have the completeness of minor poetry. Discursive poems, like 'A Drumlin Woodchuck' and 'Departmental,' are summed up by their final lines. . . . Yet his best poems are, as I have shown, enigmatic—*even when they employ final summing-up lines*" ("Hardy, Frost, and the Question of Modernist Poetry," 80; my emphasis).
17. Reginald Cook, *Dimensions of Robert Frost* (New York: Rinehart, 1958), 124.
18. "The Case against Mr. Frost," part 2, *New Republic*, 111 (18 September 1944), 345; Nitchie, *Human Values in the Poetry of Robert Frost*, 154; Poirier, *Robert Frost: The Work of Knowing*, 273.
19. John C. Kemp, *Robert Frost and New England: The Poet as Regionalist* (Princeton: Princeton University Press, 1979), 222–23; Berkelman, "Robert Frost and the Middle Way," *New England Quarterly* 35 (1962): 347–53; George F. Whicher, "Frost at Seventy," *American Scholar* 14 (1945): 405–14.
20. On this question, according to Lawrence Perrine (in "'Two Tramps in Mud Time' and the Critics," *American Literature* 44 [1973]): "The common misconception is that the

speaker finally keeps the task of woodchopping for himself. The poem's clear implication is that he yields it to the tramps" (671). See also Kemp, *Robert Frost and New England* (196–97), who agrees with Perrine. I agree too, but for reasons that go beyond Perrine's essentially correct but superficial and sometimes misleading analysis.

21. Cook, *Dimensions of Robert Frost*, 24. Cf. Nitchie, *Human Values in the Poetry of Robert Frost*: "But it seems to me that 'Two Tramps in Mud Time,' like most of Frost's poems that propose or seem to propose formulas, suffers by comparison with many of his non-formula poems" (155).

22. In his pairing of this poem with Wordsworth's "Resolution and Independence," focusing on this matter of poetic avocation (play) and its tension with real-world labor (work) in ways continuous with but more subtle than other critics, David Bromwich (*A Choice of Inheritance: Self and Community from Edmund Burke to Robert Frost* [Cambridge: Harvard University Press, 1989], 219–26) argues that "Frost has not finally earned his eloquence" because, though refusing the tramps ("sacrifice of others"), he never shows "the distance between his nature and that of the tramps" (225). Against Bromwich and others, I argue in the following sections that the difficulties and hardships of landscape, labor, and laborers are ingredient in, but also differentiated from, the structure and texture of the "deed" of the poem itself, and that Frost's ability to accept both (against any claim that he refuses the tramps) is just Frost's achievement as poet and, indeed, as human being.

23. It is an indication of their ideological preoccupation with the woodchopping, as job or as symbol of labor, that critics have inadequately accounted for this transformation and expansion. Lawrance Thompson (*Fire and Ice* [New York: Holt, 1942], 211–12) sees the expansion but wrongly reduces "love" to "pleasure." Cook, in *Dimensions of Robert Frost*, records the change but construes it too narrowly: "In effect, it is a political poem" (122). For Whicher ("Frost at Seventy," 413), stanza nine urges a "philosophy of employment," while for Cowley ("The Case against Mr. Frost," part 2, 345) it is a "sermon on the ethical value of the chopping block." Perrine ("'Two Tramps in Mud Time' and the Critics," 674) and Kemp (*Robert Frost and New England*, 196) note the change but unnecessarily restrict its significance to self-reflexive commentary on the craft of writing.

24. Compare, for example, Kemp, *Robert Frost and New England*: "the speaker accepts (with some reluctance) the tramps' 'right'" (197). Kemp does not explain why the narrator is to be heard as reluctant; below I argue that the speaker can be heard as fully accepting of the tramps' view, which he sees as true *as far as it goes*.

25. Thus Frost's irony in opening the "unifying" ninth stanza with the disjunctive "But," and in closing the divisive eighth stanza with the conjunctive "agreed."

26. Cf. Willard Spiegelman, *The Didactic Muse: Scenes of Instruction in Contemporary American Poetry* (Princeton: Princeton University Press, 1989): "A poem is . . . also a piece of empirical evidence from which one moves forward to an inductive conclusion. One proceeds from data to conclusion" (6). Cf. *TM* 102: "in recognition what we know emerges, as if through an illumination, from all the chance and variable circumstances that condition it and is grasped in its essence. It is known as something."

27. See Kemp, *Robert Frost and New England*, 197.

28. Perrine, "'Two Tramps in Mud Time' and the Critics," 674.

29. Berkelman, "Robert Frost and the Middle Way," 349.

30. Thompson, *Fire and Ice*, 20.

31. Quoted in Robert Langbaum, "The Epiphanic Mode in Wordsworth and Modern Literature," in *The Word from Below: Essays on Modern Literature and Culture* (Madison: University of Wisconsin Press, 1987), 35–56.

32. The quotations in this sentence are from Morris Beja, *Epiphany in the Modern Novel* (Seattle: University of Washington Press, 1971), 19. Perhaps Yeats (in "Anima Hominis," in

*The Modern Tradition: Backgrounds of Modern Literature,* ed. Richard Ellmann and Charles Feidelson [New York: Oxford University Press, 1965]) says all of this best: "I think we who are poets and artists, not being permitted to shoot beyond the tangible, must go from desire to weariness and so to desire again, and live but for the moment when vision comes to our weariness like terrible lightning" (763).

33. See Taylor, *Sources of the Self: The Making of the Modern Identity,* chap. 24, "Epiphanies of Modernism."

34. In addition to Taylor, see Schaeffer, *Art of the Modern Age,* esp. chap. 4, "Ecstatic Vision to Cosmic Fiction?"

35. "Epiphany and Browning: Character Made Manifest," *PMLA* 107 (October 1992): 1208–21. Tucker's reworking of epiphany seems to me eminently reasonable in illuminating a poet like Browning; but in stretching the term in the way he does (almost making it synonymous with the fact of the historical nature of textuality itself), Tucker risks underplaying the qualities many high modernists (not just New Critics) cherished: essence, incongruity with the precipitating event, and other characteristics discussed below. Applied to Frost, even such a reworked (historicized) notion of epiphany would entirely fail to capture the kind of "showing-forth" that occurs there, or in poems by William Carlos Williams, Moore, Auden, Nemerov, and many others.

36. Works I have found helpful in this regard are W. R. Johnson, *The Idea of Lyric: Lyric Modes in Ancient and Modern Poetry* (Berkeley and Los Angeles: University of California Press, 1982); and especially Jeffrey Walker, "Aristotle's Lyric: Re-Imagining the Rhetoric of Epideictic Song," *College English* 51 (January 1989): 5–27; and Jeffrey Walker, *Rhetoric and Poetic in Antiquity* (Oxford: Oxford University Press, 2000).

37. Perelman and Olbrechts-Tyeca, *The New Rhetoric,* 51.

38. See, for example, Altieri, "Rhetorics, Rhetoricity, and the Sonnet as Performance," 1–23.

39. Consider the way Stanley Cavell's rhetorical style and stance have come in for censure for what seems to some merely self-advertising. Much of this criticism, in my view, badly misreads, as failed philosophical deliberation, the successful philosophical epideixis that Cavell has been extremely forthright in declaring as the language game he is involved in.

40. Garver, *Aristotle's Rhetoric,* 70–73.

41. From *Dubliners,* begun in 1904 and first printed in 1914, the year of the publication of Frost's second book, *North of Boston.*

42. James Joyce, *Dubliners* (Knopf, 1991), 36.

43. Walker, "Aristotle's Lyric," 15.

44. Auerbach, *Mimesis,* 552.

45. Walker, "Aristotle's Lyric," 8; my emphasis. Walker's essay is a helpful account of epideictic lyric from ancient Greece to contemporary efforts to account for it by poets and critics such as Charles Bernstein, Charles Altieri, Marjorie Perloff, and Robert Pinsky. Walker argues, correctly in my view, that these accounts regularly fall back into the model of what he calls the "apostrophic" lyric (as cri de coeur) and what I am calling the "epiphanic" lyric. See also W. R. Johnson, *The Idea of Lyric: Lyric Modes in Ancient and Modern Poetry* (Berkeley and Los Angeles: University of California Press, 1982): "What strikes the reader of Greek lyric fragments is that the kind of poetry, the expression or imitation of an anonymous cri de coeur, a disembodied extended cry, seems to have had no place in the lyrics of Greece" (30).

## 5. Lessons in the Conversation That We Are

1. Alasdair MacIntyre, *After Virtue: A Study in Moral Theory,* 2d ed. (South Bend: University of Notre Dame Press, 1984), 210. For the importance of conversation to Wittgenstein's notion of natural language, see Raimond Gaita, "Language and Conversation: Wittgenstein's

Builders," in *Wittgenstein Centenary Essays*, ed., A. Phillips Griffiths (Cambridge: Cambridge University Press, 1991), 101–15; and Rush Rhees, *Wittgenstein and the Possibility of Discourse*, ed. D. Z. Phillips (Cambridge: Cambridge University Press, 1998).

2. *BT* 211ff. Cf. also *Existence and Being* (Chicago: Henry Regnery, 1968), 277; and the later *What is Called Thinking?* trans. J. Glen Gray (New York: Harper and Row, 1968), 61.

3. Charles Taylor, "The Dialogical Self," in *The Interpretive Turn: Philosophy, Science, Culture*, ed. David R. Hiley, James F. Bohman, and Richard Shusterman (Ithaca: Cornell University Press, 1991), 313.

4. Cf. Reginald L. Cook, *Robert Frost: A Living Voice* (Amherst: University of Massachusetts Press, 1974): "'Truth,' he [Frost] stated emphatically, 'is a dialogue,' a perspectival position different from that of the dogmatic adherent of revealed truth" (282).

5. Cf. Perelman and Olbrechts-Tyeca, *The New Rhetoric*, 39; Perelman continues: "It is a curious and noteworthy fact that this everyday activity of persuasive discussion has received very scant attention from the theoreticians. Most authors of treatises on rhetoric have regarded it as foreign to their discipline." "Alfonso Reyes has rightly pointed out that private discourse is a field contiguous to that of ancient rhetoric." Perelman also considers "self-deliberation" as a subset of "argumentation" (which includes all rhetorical strategies, not just explicit argument).

6. Nancy S. Struever, "The Conversable World: Eighteenth-Century Transformations of the Relation of Rhetoric and Truth," in *Rhetoric and the Pursuit of Truth: Language and Change in the Seventeenth and Eighteenth Century*, ed. Nancy S. Struever and Brian Vickers (Berkeley and Los Angeles: University of California Press, 1985); cf. David Hume, "Of Essay Writing" in *Of the Standard of Taste and Other Essays*, ed. John W. Lenz (Indianapolis: Bobbs-Merrill, 1965), 38–42; Walter J. Ong, *Ramus, Method, and the Decay of Dialogue* (Cambridge: Cambridge University Press, 1958). See also James L. Kastely, "*Persuasion*: Jane Austen's Philosophical Rhetoric," in *Rethinking the Rhetorical Tradition: From Plato to Postmodernism* (New Haven: Yale University Press, 1997), 145–67.

7. See Stanley Cavell, *Pursuits of Happiness: The Hollywood Comedy of Remarriage* (Cambridge: Harvard University Press, 1981).

8. In addition to Gadamer and Bakhtin, see Don H. Bialostosky, "Dialogics as an Art of Discourse in Literary Criticism," *PMLA* 101 (October 1986): 788–97; Wayne C. Booth, *The Company We Keep: An Ethics of Fiction* (Berkeley and Los Angeles: University of California Press, 1988); Bruns, *Inventions: Writing, Textuality, and Understanding in Literary History;* and Steven G. Crowell, "Dialogue and Text: Re-marking the Difference," in *The Interpretation of Dialogue*. ed. Tullio Maranhao (Chicago: University of Chicago Press, 1990), 338–60. On rhetorical work on Bakhtin, see, for example, Charles I. Schuster, "Mikhail Bakhtin as Rhetorical Theorist," *College English* 47 (1985): 594–607; and the "Critical Symposium" on Bakhtin and rhetorical criticism in *Rhetoric Society Quarterly* 22 (fall 1992): 1–28.

9. Struever, "Conversable World, 94–95.

10. Patricia Meyer Spacks, *Gossip* (Chicago: University of Chicago Press, 1985). *Sermo*, it should be noted, can include the topoi and strategies of deliberative, epideictic, and forensic oratory, reframed in the private and not public domain of the polis. For more on *sermo*, see, for example, John Tinkler, "Renaissance Humanism and the *genera eloquentiae*," *Rhetorica* 5 (1987): 279–309.

11. Yvor Winters, "Robert Frost: or, the Spiritual Drifter as Poet," in *The Function of Criticism: Problems and Exercises* (Denver: Swallow Press, 1957), 160.

12. Robert Frost, "The Art of Poetry II: Robert Frost [Interview with Richard Poirier]," *Paris Review* 24 (1960): 115. Cf. *SL* 343: "I'm less and less for systems and system-building in my old age. I'm afraid of too much structure."

13. Brower, *Poetry of Robert Frost*, 164. John C. Kemp *(Robert Frost and New England: The Poet as Regionalist)* is probably the most nuanced. Cf. Poirier, *Robert Frost: The Work of Knowing*:

"His [Frost's] genius as a narrative poet is in part his capacity to sustain debates between people" (106). See also Mordecai Marcus, *The Poems of Robert Frost: An Explication* (Boston: G.K. Hall, 1991): "As farmer and wife debate whether to take Silas back" (43); and Nancy Vogel, "A Post-Mortem on 'The Death of the Hired Man,'" in *Frost: Centennial Essays*, ed. Jac L. Tharpe et. al. (Jackson: University Press of Mississippi, 1974), 202. Cavell makes a pertinent remark in *IQO* 145: "to take Poe as it were psychologically (I suppose the most familiar way of taking him) is to eclipse taking Poe as it were philosophically."

14. Poirier, *Robert Frost: The Work of Knowing*, 109.

15. Carol Gilligan, *In a Different Voice: Psychological Theory and Women's Development* (Cambridge: Harvard University Press, 1982); hereafter cited parenthetically as *Voice*.

16. Kemp, *Robert Frost and New England*, 106.

17. Sidney Cox, Letter home in Evans 89. The letter continues: "You are not going to make the mistake that Pound makes of assuming that my simplicity is that of the untutored child. I am not undesigning."

18. Poirier, *Robert Frost: The Work of Knowing*, 107.

19. Ibid., 106.

20. On the contrast between the spatialization of the high modernist "grid" in (for example) architects such as Mies van der Rohe and even Robert Venturi, and the image of fluidity belonging to Frank Gehry's Guggenheim Museum in Balboa and (more broadly) to "complexity theory" of the sort Frost would have approved, see Mark C. Taylor's *The Moment of Complexity: Emerging Network Culture* (Chicago: University of Chicago Press, 2001).

21. Perelman and Olbrechts-Tyteca, *The New Rhetoric*, 51.

22. Kemp, *Robert Frost and New England*, 113.

23. See Quintilian's prescriptions about exhibiting the actual scene: Quintilian, *Institutio oratoria*, 4 vols. (1920; reprint, Cambridge: Harvard University Press, 1980), 6.2.32.

24. Bruns, *Inventions: Writing, Textuality, and Understanding in Literary History*, 117.

25. Cf. Stanley Cavell, "Knowing and Acknowledging" in *MWM*.

26. See Nicole Loraux, *The Invention of Athens: The Funeral Oration in the Classical City*, trans. Alan Sheridan (Cambridge: Harvard University Press, 1986).

27. Peter Nicholls, *Modernisms: A Literary Guide* (Berkeley and Los Angeles: University of California Press, 1995), 209–10.

28. Cf. David Perkins, *A History of Modern Poetry: Modernism and After* (Cambridge: Belknap Press of Harvard University Press, 1987), 250–51.

29. See Loraux, *Invention of Athens*; Walker, "Aristotle's Lyric"; and Walter H. Beale, "Rhetorical Performative Discourse: A New Theory of Epideictic," *Philosophy and Rhetoric* 11 (fall 1978): 221–46.

30. Perkins, *A History of Modern Poetry*, 241.

31. Cf. Karsten Harries, *The Ethical Function of Architecture* (Cambridge: MIT University Press, 1998): "To be genuinely home in this [contemporary] world, we have to affirm our essential homelessness, a homelessness illuminated by shifting ideals of genuine dwelling, figures of home, and precarious conjectures about what it might mean to dwell near the center" (200).

32. Felski, "The Invention of Everyday Life," 28.

33. Edward Thomas, "Robert Frost," review of *North of Boston*, in *A Language Not to be Betrayed: Selected Prose of Edward Thomas* (Manchester: Carcanet Press, 1981), 125ff.

## 6. Naming Being in "West-Running Brook"

1. Kemp, *Robert Frost and New England*, 202. Hyatt Howe Waggoner ("The Humanistic Idealism of Robert Frost," in *On Frost: The Best from American Literature*, ed. Edwin H. Cady and Louis J. Budd) calls "West-Running Brook" "one of the most important philosophical

poems of our period" (26). Reuben Brower *(The Poetry of Robert Frost: Constellations of Intention)* calls "West-Running Brook" a "culminating poem in Frost's career" (210): "Taking 'West-Running Brook' as a whole and not detaching the philosophy from the poem, we can see that it is indeed 'most' Frost" (193).

2. William James, *Psychology* (New York: Holt, 1893), chaps. 2, 11. See W. David Shaw, "The Poetics of Pragmatism: Robert Frost and William James," *New England Quarterly* 59 (June 1986): 159–88. Patrick Morrow turns to the Heraclitean "flux" of existence as a parallel to the brook in "The Greek Nexus in Robert Frost's 'West-Running Brook,'" *Personalist* 49 (winter 1968): 24–33.

3. Lentricchia, *Robert Frost: Modern Poetics and the Landscapes of the Self,* 57; Kemp, *Robert Frost and New England,* 204. For Brower *(Poetry of Robert Frost),* "The clue to the movement and to the unity of the poem . . . is the underground dramatic metaphor . . . of tension and union of 'contraries'" (189). For Lawrance Thompson (*Fire and Ice: The Art and Thought of Robert Frost* [New York: Holt, 1942]), the poem "is built around an elaborate metaphor" that in turn "is built around the image of one wave which rides forever above a sunken rock" (33). But Thompson's formulation stresses stasis over kinesis when neither alone is adequate, and Brower's formulation neglects the image of the "backward motion toward the source," an image that is equally (actually more) crucial to the unity of the poem than the more generic "going by contraries."

4. Poirier, *Robert Frost: The Work of Knowing,* xxiii, 225; and Brower, *Poetry of Robert Frost,* 85. Lentricchia, *Landscapes of Self,* makes many of the same claims as Poirier does (and as Brower and Thompson do) for Frost's preoccupation with the shaping imagination, though he sorely neglects what might be called the public and even prudential possibilities of the imagination.

5. Poirier, *Robert Frost: The Work of Knowing,* 225; cf. Poirier, *The Renewal of Literature:* "It is among the most profound expressions ever given to the immensely intricate Emersonian linkages of origins, actions, and creativity" (173). Yvor Winters, "Robert Frost; or, The Spiritual Drifter as Poet," in *Robert Frost: A Collection of Critical Essays,* ed. James M. Cox (Englewood Cliffs, N.J.: Prentice-Hall, 1962): "there is, in brief, very little to it" (70). Louis Untermeyer called the poem "an extended bit of fooling" (quoted in Morrow, "Greek Nexus," 24).

6. For a connection between Frost and Heidegger, see James Knapp, *"The Greek World and the Mystery of Being,"* in Robert Frost: *Studies of the Poetry,* ed. Kathryn Harris (Boston: G. R. Hall, 1979), 176.

7. Hubert L. Dreyfus, *Being-in-the-World: A Commentary on Being and Time, Division I* (Cambridge: MIT University Press, 1991), 343–67; on pragmatism, see Mark Okrent, *Heidegger's Pragmatism* (Ithaca: Cornell University Press, 1988).

8. For Heidegger it was, of course, just such technical thinking that from the beginning bankrupted traditional philosophy and that in time he himself forswore. See, for example, his famous "Letter on Humanism," in Martin Heidegger, *Basic Writings,* ed. David Farrell Krell (New York: Harper and Row, 1977), 193–246.

9. Robert Frost, "Introduction to *King Jasper,*" in *SP* 59–67.

10. For connections to Heraclitus, see Morrow, "Greek Nexus." For connections to Bergson, see Lawrance Thompson, *Robert Frost: The Years of Triumph, 1915–1938* (New York: Holt, Rinehart and Winston, 1970), 301–3; Joseph Kau, "'Trust . . . to Go by Contraries': Incarnation and the Paradox of Belief in the Poetry of Robert Frost," in *Frost: Centennial Essays II,* ed. Jac Tharpe (Jackson: University Press of Mississippi, 1976), 99–111; and John Robert Doyle Jr., *Sources of "West-Running Brook"* (Charleston: Citadel Monograph Series, 1974). For connections to Bergson and James, see Oehlschlaeger, "West toward Heaven," 238–51.

11. See, for example, Martin Heidegger, "Why Do I Stay in the Provinces?" in *Heidegger: The Man and the Thinker,* ed. Thomas Sheehan (Chicago: Precedent, 1981), 27–30; and J. Glenn Gray, "Poets and Thinkers: Their Kindred Roles in the Philosophy of Martin Heidegger," in *Phenomenology and Existentialism,* ed. Edward N. Lee and Maurice Mandelbaum (Baltimore: Johns Hopkins University Press, 1967), 93–111.

12. Morrow, "Greek Nexus," 25ff.; cf. Frost's "Boeotian" ("That wisdom I need not be of Athens Attic / . . . At least I will not have it systematic") and his interview with Poirier, "The Art of Poetry II: Robert Frost," *Paris Review* 24 (1960): "I'm very catholic, that's about all you can say. I've hunted. I'm not thorough like the people educated in Germany in the old days. I've none of that" (101). In Heidegger, see, for example, *Early Greek Thinking: The Dawn of Western of Philosophy*, trans. David Farrell Krell and Frank A. Capuzzi (New York: Harper and Row, 1975), esp. chap. 2, "*Logos* (Heraclitus, Fragment B 50)" and chap. 4, "*Aletheia* (Heraclitus, Fragment B 16)."

13. George Knox, "Backward Motion toward the Source," *Personalist* 47 (July 1966): 378–79; my emphasis; Brower, *Poetry of Robert Frost*, 192. Along these lines, Nitchie (*Human Values in the Poetry of Robert Frost* [Durham: Duke University Press, 1960]) calls the poem a "statement of ultimate values" (127).

14. Morrow, "Greek Nexus," 26.

15. Poirier, *Robert Frost: The Work of Knowing*, 222.

16. Ibid.

17. Lentricchia, *Landscapes of Self* 57; Nitchie, *Human Values* 127; cf. Kemp, *Robert Frost and New England*, 204, who refers to "imagin[ing] meaning in a wave or a brook or a marriage."

18. *BT* 211–17/167–73.

19. *BT* 105–6/75–76.

20. Kern, "Frost and Modernism," 12.

21. Martin Heidegger, "The Question Concerning Technology," in *The Question Concerning Technology and Other Essays*, trans. William Lovitt (New York: Harper and Row, 1977), 35. Cf. *A Politics of the Ordinary* (New York: New York University Press, 1999), 7.

22. *BT* 200–201/158–59.

23. Cf. *BT* 51/29, 201/158; also *GM* 21–58.

24. Paul Ricoeur, "The Metaphorical Process as Cognition, Imagination, and Feeling," in *On Metaphor*, ed. Sheldon Sacks (Chicago: University of Chicago Press, 1978), 141–57. Cf. Paul Ricoeur, *The Rule of Metaphor* (Toronto: University of Toronto Press, 1977).

25. Brower, *Poetry of Robert Frost*, 190.

26. Ricoeur, "Metaphorical Process as Cognition," 151.

27. Thus, Mordecai Marcus (*The Poems of Robert Frost: An Explication* [Boston: G.K. Hall, 1991]) characterizes it as "gentle annoyance" (127); Radcliffe Squires (*The Major Themes of Robert Frost* [Ann Arbor: University of Michigan Press, 1963]) finds Fred's preceding comments about the wave "solemn, almost oppressive" (97); and Brower *(Poetry of Robert Frost)* characterizes Fred's response as "male impatience" (189). Thompson has got the tone right ("pleasantly contrary views") (Thompson 2:301), but he formulates the meanings in far too general terms.

28. Cf. Frost's response to Poirier, in "The Art of Poetry II: Robert Frost": "I like to fool—oh, you know, you like to be mischievous." "Talking contraries—it's in one of the poems. Talk by contraries with people you're very close to. They know what you're talking about. This whole thing of suggestiveness and *double entendre* and hinting—comes down to the word 'hinting'" (112–13).

29. Kern, "Frost and Modernism," 12–13.

30. Literally, "*Dasein*" means "there-being," where there" is the "world" in Heidegger's technical sense. "Dasein" is a locution that does useful, exact work for Heidegger, but I shall sometimes render it into the less stilted (and less precise) "human being."

31. Søren Kierkegaard, *Repetition: A Venture in Experimenting Psychology*, ed. and trans. Howard V. Hong and Edna H. Hong (Princeton: Princeton University Press, 1983).

32. Ibid.: "Repetition and recollection are the same movement, except in opposite directions, for what is recollected has been, is repeated backward, whereas genuine repetition is recollected forward" (131).

33. Theodore Kisiel, translator's introduction in *Heidegger and the Tradition*, by Werner Marx, trans. Theodore Kisiel and Murray Greene (Evanston: Northwestern University Press, 1971), xxi. For a good account of Kierkegaard's *Repetition*, see M. Jamie Ferreira, "Repetition, Concreteness, Imagination," *International Journal of the Philosophy of Religion* 25 (1989): "The concrete is thus the non-abstract, but it is non-abstract in two ways: it is free or becoming (hence inexhaustible) and particular, distinctive, and historical (hence limited)" (30).

34. *TM* 274ff.; and Paul Ricoeur, "Appropriation," in *Hermeneutics and the Human Sciences*, ed. and trans. John B. Thompson (Cambridge: Cambridge University Press, 1981), 182–93. Søren Kierkegaard too calls "subjectivity," of which repetition is always a dimension, the "*appropriation* of an objective uncertainty" (*Concluding Unscientific Postscript*, trans. David F. Swenson and Walter Lowrie [Princeton: Princeton University Press, 1968], 182; my emphasis).

35. *SP* 19 (cf. "The Constant Symbol," *SP* 28); the second quote in Burnshaw, *Robert Frost Himself*, 246; cf. *CV* 40e: "You must say something new and yet it must all be old." "In fact you must confine yourself to saying old things—and *all the same* it must be new!"

36. Martin Heidegger, *Basic Problems of Phenomenology* (Bloomington: Indiana University Press, 1982), 297.

37. Though Heidegger eschews any moralistic overtones to his analysis (for example, *BT* 220/175–76), wide agreement exists among critics that terms like "falling" *(Verfallen)* are heavily normative and prescriptive. See Michael E. Zimmerman, *Eclipse of the Self: The Development of Heidegger's Concept of Authenticity* (Athens: Ohio University Press, 1981), 44ff.

38. On the rhetorical "topology" of Being, see, for example, Otto Pöggeler, "Metaphysics and the Topology of Being in Heidegger," in *Heidegger: The Man and the Thinker*, ed. Sheehan, 173–85, and Otto Pöggeler, "Heidegger's Topology of Being," in *On Heidegger and Language*, ed. Joseph J. Kockelmans (Evanston: Northwestern University Press, 1972), 107–46.

39. Like Kierkegaard before him, Heidegger in *Being and Time* is overthrowing the more conventional concept of Being as found, for example, in Plato, Aristotle, and Descartes, though, unlike Kierkegaard, Heidegger eschews all dualities of eternal and temporal, sacred and secular. For an account, see Michael Wyschogrod, *Kierkegaard and Heidegger: The Ontology of Existence* (New York: Humanities Press, 1954). Heidegger would reconceive the essence-existence dichotomy as a unity of being-in-becoming, in which Dasein is always temporally "ahead-of-itself" in a projective retrieval of its historical possibilities. In this way, Dasein's Being is understood as temporal disclosure, that is to say, not as a determinate "eternal" actuality (Plato's Forms) or as a self-subsistent substance (Aristotle) or as an indubitable self-evident consciousness over against other consciousnesses and the material world (Cartesian *cogito*), but as a temporal "clearing" *(Lichtung)* or indeterminacy within which one is always en route to what one is, for whom one's essence is *an issue* in the dynamic indeterminacies of existence. (On Being as a "clearing" for disclosure, see *BT* 171/133: "When we talk . . . of the *lumen naturale* in man, we have in mind nothing other than the existential-ontological structure of this entity, that it is in such a way as to be its 'there.' To say that it is 'illuminated' [*erleuchtet*] means that as Being-in-the-world it is cleared [*gelichtet*] in itself, not through any other entity, but in such a way that it is itself the clearing.") The Being of Dasein (Care) is thus both the (open, "infinite") indeterminacy that makes "possibility" possible and the (limited) concrete historical possibilities that enter into the clearing that is its indeterminacy.

40. Cf. Martin Heidegger, "What Are Poets For?" in *Poetry, Language, Thought*, 101; hereafter cited parenthetically as *PLT*. There, poets are the venturesome ones who respond to the call of being by naming it.

41. For Heidegger's account of poetry—that consummate naming—as a measuring, see "Poetically Man Dwells," in Heidegger, *PLT* 221ff.

42. See Wyschogrod, *Kierkegaard and Heidegger*, 15ff.; also of interest is Genevieve Lloyd, *Being in Time: Selves and Narrators in Philosophy and Literature* (London: Routledge, 1993).

43. See n. 55 below.
44. Cf. Heidegger, *BT* 280/236: "As long as Dasein is an entity, it has never reached its 'wholeness.'"
45. Nitchie, *Human Values*, 126; Brower, *Poetry of Robert Frost*, 191.
46. Poirier, *Robert Frost: The Work of Knowing*, 188.
47. *GM* 53ff.
48. Kenneth Burke, "Definition of Man," in *Language as Symbolic Action: Essays on Life, Literature, and Method* (Berkeley and Los Angeles: University of California Press, 1966), 5.
49. See Wyschogrod, *Kierkegaard and Heidegger*, 103, 107. Thus Heidegger asserts that the essence of Being is Nothing, that is, not a further *thing* (for one cannot speak of Being as one more being), but the *Lichtung* of "disclosure-concealment" that makes temporal possibility possible.
50. See Monteiro, *Robert Frost and the New England Renaissance:* "It is not far-fetched to see in this 'tribute of the current to the source' an analogue for the kind of tribute Frost's fetching poems pay to his New England predecessors when he draws upon them for substance—thought, symbol, image, and language" (151–52).
51. Brower, *Poetry of Robert Frost*, 192; cf. Okrent, *Heidegger's Pragmatism:* "Being is said in many ways" (177).
52. Thus the poem belongs to the American tradition of what Lawrence Buell calls the "absent center poem," yet differs in its *acceptance* of rather than resistance to ("from a present position of spiritual barrenness") this absence-in-presence; *New England Literary Culture* (Cambridge: Cambridge University Press, 1986), 123–26. Buell links this kind of poem to the "rhetoric of the jeremiad."
53. Wyschogrod, *Kierkegaard and Heidegger*, 103.
54. Lentricchia, *Landscapes of Self*, 56.
55. Brower, *Poetry of Robert Frost*, 191.
56. Ibid., 192; my emphasis.
57. Cf. Martin Heidegger, *An Introduction to Metaphysics* (New Haven: Yale University Press, 1959): "we do not repeat a beginning by reducing it to something past and now known, which need merely be imitated; no, the beginning must be begun again, more radically, with all the strangeness, darkness, insecurity that attend a true beginning" (39)
58. Kierkegaard, *Postscript*, 74.
59. Willard Spiegelman, *The Didactic Muse: Scenes of Instruction in Contemporary American Poetry* (Princeton: Princeton University Press, 1989), 257.
60. Frost, "The Poetry of Amy Lowell," *Selected Prose*, 71–72.
61. John Caputo, "Hermeneutics as the Recovery of Man," *Man and World* 15 (1982): 357.
62. Cf. *IQO* 176: "One might have imagined that this image [of betrothal] is only accidental in Heidegger's essay ["The Thing"], but it is essentially what goes into his extraordinary account of the thinging of the world as requiring the joining of earth, sky, gods, and mortals in what he calls "the round dance of appropriating" *(der Reigen des Ereignes)*; and when he goes on to say 'the round dance is the ring' that grapples and plays, he can hardly not have in mind the wedding band."
63. Caputo, "Hermeneutics as the Recovery of Man," 357.
64. In Heidegger, see, for example, "What Are Poets For?" in *PLT* 91–142.
65. Calvin Schrag, *Communicative Praxis and the Space of Subjectivity* (Bloomington: Indiana University Press, 1986), 145.
66. Caputo, "Hermeneutics as the Recovery of Man," 358.
67. Cf. Thomas Sheehan, preface to *Heidegger: Man and Thinker:* "In a very real sense there is no 'content' in [Heidegger's] topic and legacy, only a 'method'" (xix).
68. Thompson, *Robert Frost*, 28; Poirier, *Robert Frost: The Work of Knowing*, 317, 334. Cf.

Oster, *Toward Robert Frost: The Reader and the Poet* (Athens: University of Georgia Press, 1991): "Frost's poetry is often most elusive when it seems most accessible" (17).

69. Martin Heidegger, "Language," in *PLT* 199; cf. 189–90, against "essence" as a fixed concept.

70. See also Poirier, "Writing Off the Self," in *Renewal of Literature*, esp. 204–12.

71. Poirier, *Robert Frost: The Work of Knowing*, 318ff.; Wayne C. Booth, *Modern Dogma and the Rhetoric of Assent* (Chicago: University of Chicago Press, 1974), 126–37.

72. Cf. Heidegger, "Language," in *PLT* 218.

73. Louis Mackey, *Kierkegaard: A Kind of Poet* (Philadelphia: University of Pennsylvania Press, 1971), 290.

74. Brower, *Poetry of Robert Frost*, 212, 225.

75. Joel B. Altman, *The Tudor Play of Mind: Rhetorical Inquiry and the Development of Elizabethan Drama* (Berkeley and Los Angeles: University of California Press, 1978), 6, 42, 44.

## 7. Giving Evidence and Making Evident

1. Cf. *LLU* 47: "I should like to be so subtle at this game as to seem to the casual person altogether obvious. The casual person would assume that I meant nothing or else that I came near enough meaning something he was familiar with to mean it for all practical purposes. Well well well."

2. After this chapter was written, there appeared Lewis H. Miller's very brief "'Snow': Frost's Drama of Belittled People," *Robert Frost Review* (fall 1994): 47–51.

3. I refer to Freud's paper "The Uncanny" in *The Standard Edition of the Complete Psychological Works of Sigmund Freud*, 24 vols. (London: Hogarth Press, 1966): "if this is indeed the secret nature of the uncanny, we can understand why linguistic usage has extended *das Heimliche* ["homely"] into its opposite, *das Unheimliche*; for this uncanny is in reality nothing new or alien, but something which is familiar and old-established in the mind and which has become alienated from it only through the process of repression" (241).

4. Lionel Trilling, "A Speech on Robert Frost: A Cultural Episode," in *Robert Frost: A Collection of Critical Essays*, ed. James M. Cox (Englewood Cliffs, N.J.: Prentice-Hall, 1962), 151–58.

5. I consider *Walden*, which Frost called "one of the greatest books ever written" (quoted in Reginald Cook, "Robert Frost in Context," in *Centennial Essays III*, ed. Jac L. Tharpe [Jackson: University of Mississippi Press, 1978], 148) an Ur-text for "Snow," and I advert to it throughout this chapter.

6. *LLU* 40; the four poems are "The Mountain," "A Hundred Collars," "The Generations of Men," and "The Code." Cf. Sidney Cox, *A Swinger of Birches* (New York: New York University Press, 1957): "He thought of poetry . . . as a prank" (15–16).

7. Not quite no one: Edward Arlington Robinson, one of the poem's earliest and, it would seem, very few admirers, ranked it with "The Road Not Taken," "Birches," and, most tellingly, "The Hill Wife" (Thompson 2:210). "Snow" also won a prize in 1917 from Harriet Monroe's magazine, *Poetry*.

8. Cf. Frost quoted in Reginald L. Cook, *Robert Frost: A Living Voice* (Amherst: University of Massachusetts Press, 1974): "Being reminded of something you hardly knew you knew—by something that's in front of you, something that's happening to you, or the past emerging out of the very levels of your knowledge. Books and life and all that—that's the material" (158).

9. Cf. William Carlos Williams, *Imaginations*, ed. Walter Schott (New York: New Directions, 1971), 14.

10. *Walden*, III; Ralph Waldo Emerson, "The American Scholar," in *The Portable Emerson*, ed. Carl Bode with Malcolm Cowley, 69.

11. See *PI* § 97: "We are under the illusion that what is peculiar, profound, essential, in our investigation, resides in its trying to grasp the incomparable essence of language.... Whereas, of course, if the words 'language,' 'experience,' 'world,' have a use, it must be as humble a one as the words 'table,' 'lamp,' 'door'"; and *SP* 106–7: "Fortunately, too, no forms are more engrossing[,] gratifying, comforting, staying than those lesser ones we throw off, like vortex rings of smoke, all our individual enterprise and needing nobody's cooperation: a basket, a letter, a garden, a room."

12. Cf. *CR* 211: "Recall what happens when we don't find the same things remarkable or absorbing or noticeable or 'worth saying,' and try to imagine what it would be like if that began to happen all the time. Part of what you would have to imagine is a world in which we were unmoved by one another's remarks, as if born bored. It is not that what we would then say to one another would be false; and perhaps our words would remain mutually intelligible. I think we might say we would become uncomprehensive of one another; or perhaps curiosities for one another."

13. Cf. Michel Foucault, *Madness and Civilization: A History of Insanity in the Age of Reason* (New York: Vintage, 1988): "When man deploys the arbitrary nature of his madness, he confronts the dark necessity of the world; the animal that haunts his nightmares and his nights of privation is his own nature" (23).

14. [H.] Paul Grice, "Logic and Conversation," in *Studies in the Way of Words* (Cambridge: Harvard University Press, 1989), 26.

15. These divisions are, first, Meserve's talk about the book-leaf and its subtle elision into talk about making a room ("a little foursquare block of air"; line 142) and the "giving" of "repose" (lines 116–52); second, his fanciful portrayal of the snow as "some pallid thing" (line 160) that fails to understand the interest he and the Coles take in talking with each other (lines 159–66); and third, his recollection of how Avery's young boarder one day spoke in admiration of the way Meserve banked the snow up against the house (lines 172–97).

16. Paul Ricoeur, "Geertz," in *A Ricoeur Reader*, ed. Mario J. Valdes (Toronto: University of Toronto Press, 1991), 183.

17. In the first lines of the *Rhetoric*, Aristotle reminds us that we engage in rhetoric all the time, and in the *Poetics*, he refers the "thought" *(dianoia)* of dramatic characters, such as Meserve and the Coles, to rhetorical theory.

18. Cf. *Walden* 17: "to stand on the meeting of two eternities, the past and future, which is precisely the present moment."

19. For an account of Foucault's "negative" (nonsubstantive, nonteleological) conception of the self, which is, however, only part of what I take it Frost is hinting at here, see John Caputo, "On Not Knowing Who We Are: Madness, Hermeneutics, and the Night of Truth in Foucault," in *Foucault and the Critique of Institutions*, ed. John Caputo and Mark Yount (University Park: Pennsylvania State University Press, 1993), 250ff.

20. For Coleridge's similar distinction, between "fanaticism" and "enthusiasm," see *Biographia Literaria*, ed. James Engell and W. Jackson Bate (Princeton: Princeton University Press, 1983), 31. For Wordsworth, the poet is endowed with "more enthusiasm" than the normal person. See *SP* 36: "I for my part would not be afraid to go in for enthusiasm."

21. Cf. Bruns, *Hermeneutics Ancient and Modern:* "The hermeneutical metaphor of 'taking' what is said one way or another implies that understanding is not just a state of mind but also a movement or undertaking: understanding only fulfills itself in action" (43)—as when Meserve heads back out into the snow. Cf. Robert Frost, in a talk at the Y.M.H.A. on 22 November 1952, quoted in Lisa Abshear-Seale, "A Lifetime of Thinking Aloud: Reassessing Robert Frost's Public Talks and Readings," unpublished manuscript: "Another expression we have, always amused me: 'He took her to wife.' Now that is a curious thing. 'He took her to

wife.' He took her from what she was to be something else. You might say that of a poem. What do you take that to mean? Now that's quite another thing. To what use—to what use— do you take the poem, beyond itself? Beyond itself, you see" (9).

22. Cf. *TM* 144: "This is why the capacity to read, to understand what is written, is like a secret art, even a magic that looses and binds us. In it time and space seem to be suspended," that is, in stasis.

23. For an account, see Michael P. Sipiora, "Heidegger and Epideictic Discourse: The Rhetorical Performance of Meditative Thinking," *Philosophy Today* (fall 1991): 239–53.

24. Cf. *Walden* 25 on the "they"; also 325: "Sometimes we are inclined to class those who are once-and-a-half-witted with the half-witted, because we appreciate only a third part of their wit"; and 10: "To be a philosopher is not merely to have subtle thoughts, nor even found a school, but so to love wisdom as to live according to its dictates, a life of simplicity, independence, magnanimity, and trust. It is to solve some of the problems of life, not only theoretically, but practically."

25. Cf. Roland Barthes, "The Old Rhetoric: An Aide-Memoire," in *The Semiotic Challenge*, trans. Richard Howard (New York: Hill and Wang, 1988): "Aristotle's rhetoric is above all a rhetoric of proof, of reasoning, of the approximative syllogism (enthymeme); it is a deliberately diminished logic, one adapted to the level of the 'public,' i.e., of common sense, of ordinary opinion" (22).

26. For various accounts of *kairos*, see William H. Race, "The Word '*Kairos*' in Greek Drama," in *Transactions of the American Philological Association*, ed. Douglas E. Gerber, vol. 3 (Chico, Calif.: Scholars Press, 1981), 197–213. Other helpful works include Mario Untersteiner, *The Sophists*, trans. Kathleen Freeman (Oxford: Blackwell, 1954); G. B. Kerferd, *The Sophistic Movement* (Cambridge: Cambridge University Press, 1981); Jacqueline De Romilly, *Magic and Rhetoric in Ancient Greece* (Cambridge: Harvard University Press, 1975) and *The Great Sophists in Periclean Athens*, trans. Janet Lloyd (Oxford: Clarendon Press, 1992); Dale L. Sullivan, "*Kairos* and the Rhetoric of Belief," *Quarterly Journal of Speech* 78 (1992): 317–32; and Eric E. White, *Kaironomia: On the Will-to-Invent* (Ithaca: Cornell University Press, 1987). Given its provenance in rhetoric, it is of course significant that *kairos* does not appear in F. E. Peters's historical lexicon, *Greek Philosophical Terms* (New York: New York University Press, 1967), since the constellation of values that it elevates—time, contingency, invention, adaptation to audience and occasion, persuasion—are just the values philosophers from Plato to Hegel have resisted. For a high modernist discussion of *kairos* that links the concept with the notion of "epiphany," see Frank Kermode, *The Sense of an Ending* (London: Oxford University Press, 1966), 44–50.

27. On the sophistic-operational method generally, see Watson, *The Architectonics of Meaning*: "The sophistic, great and important as it is, has not been well recognized as such either by those who continue it or by others. The principal reason for this is the diversity and elusiveness of the sophistic approach itself. Also, the good sophist is always new and different and without precedent in the earlier tradition; it is the nature of this tradition to be open and creative" (152).

28. This is to say in the few extant orations, and in the doxographical version of Sextus Empiricus of Gorgias's philosophical treatise "On Not-Being," whose theses are that (1) "Nothing" exists; (2) If anything exists, it is unknowable; and (3) if anything exists and is knowable, it cannot be communicated to others ("Against the Logicians," trans. R. G. Bury [Cambridge: Loeb Classical Library, 1933], 1:65). Gorgias was renowned for his innovative exploitation of stylistic devices to achieve persuasive effects.

29. Thus the later permutation of Greek epideictic into Latin *demonstratio*, which George Kennedy describes as a form of literary performance taught in the schools; see George A. Kennedy, *Classical Rhetoric and Its Christian and Secular Tradition from Ancient to Modern Times* (Chapel Hill: University of North Carolina Press, 1980).

30. Clifford Geertz, "Deep Play: Notes on the Balinese Cockfight," in *The Interpretation of Cultures* (New York: Basic Books, 1973), 413.

31. Ibid., 415–16; cf. *TM* 93ff. on the concept of "play" and the "curious lack of decisiveness" involved in it. In *Radical Hermeneutics: Repetition, Deconstruction, and the Hermeneutic Project* (Bloomington: Indiana University Press, 1987), John D. Caputo formulates *kairos* in ways strikingly close to Frost's: "Now whatever this inscrutable, midnight decision making is, it is not Aristotelian *phronesis*" (220).

32. "The Uncanny" in *The Standard Edition of the Complete Psychological Works of Sigmund Freud*, 17:221; also 17:224, quoting Sanders's *Wörterbuch der Deutschen Sprache:* "'The *unheimlich*, fearful hours of night.'"

33. On the orator as one possessed of almost magical charm, see Cicero, *De orat* 2.8.34; and Quintilian, *Institutio*, 2.8.15 and 9.2.6.

34. Cf. Kermode, *The Sense of an Ending:* "This [*kairos*] is the time of the novelist, a transformation of mere successiveness [*chronos*] which has been likened, by writers as different as Forster and Musil, to the experience of love, the erotic consciousness which makes divinely satisfactory sense out of the commonplace person" (46).

35. Gaston Bachelard (*The Poetics of Space* [1958; reprint, Boston: Beacon Press, 1969]) writes in general that "the lamp is a symbol of prolonged waiting" (34). Bachelard's two chapters on the image of the house offer repeated insights into "Snow" and other Frost poems.

36. Weinsheimer, *Philosophical Hermeneutics and Literary Theory*, 71; and *SP* 77: "The estrangement in language is pretty much due to the very word-shift by metaphor you do your best to take part in daily so as to hold your closest friend off where you can 'entertain her always as a stranger'—with the freshness of a stranger."

37. Cf. Dumm, *A Politics of the Ordinary:* "[Manners] are designed to channel communication upward, to prevent certain communication flows and valorize others. This civility is achieved at the cost of candor and the suppression of grievance, at least, and almost inevitably represses the possibility of democratic participation" (100).

38. Not quite the gift of tongues ("'is it tongues I ought to say?'"; line 249). The passage recalls 1 Corinthians 14:1–40, in which Paul prefers prophecy, which edifies others, over speaking in tongues. The reason is that the latter is an "uncertain" speech addressed "unto God: for no man understandeth him; howbeit in the spirit he speaketh mysteries" (2): "Therefore if I know not the meaning of the voice, I shall be unto him that speaketh a barbarian, and he that speaketh shall be a barbarian unto me" (11). Speaking in tongues requires interpretation ("Wherefore let him that speaketh in an unknown tongue pray that he may interpret"; 13)—while prophesy, unlike speaking in tongues, is a kairotic form of Christian speech (cf. Sullivan, "*Kairos* and the Rhetoric of Belief," 325–26; and Richard A. Engell, "Otherness and the Rhetorical Exigencies of Theistic Religion," *Quarterly Journal of Speech* 79 [1993]: 88–90) that edifies, exhorts, and comforts others in ways that challenge their own understanding of their situation (and situatedness). Again, it would be a mistake to think that Frost (or Paul) would have us simply choose between the two: "Wherefore brethren, covet to prophesy, and forbid not to speak with tongues"; 39.

39. Cf. *Walden* 17: "In any weather, at any hour of day or night, I have been anxious to improve the nick of time, and notch it on my stick too; to stand of the meeting of two eternities, the past and future, which is precisely the present moment; to toe that line."

40. "'It's always a kind of miracle. You're in a performing condition, and then you play,' remarks Frost (May 10, 1952)," quoted in Reginald L. Cook, "Frost: The Making of Poems," in *On Frost: The Best from "American Literature,"* ed. Edwin H. Cady and Louis J. Budd, 43.

41. Meserve, in other words, is a trickster figure like Hermes or the Pan-African *Esu*, who is figured forth in the metaphors of both speaking and writing; see Henry Louis Gates

Jr., *The Signifying Monkey: A Theory of African-American Literary Criticism* (New York: Oxford University Press, 1989).

42. Richard A. Lanham, "The Extraordinary Convergence: Democracy, Technology, Theory, and the University Curriculum," in *The Politics of Liberal Education*, ed. Darryl J. Gless and Barbara Hernstein Smith (Durham: Duke University Press, 1992), 48.

## 8. Ordinary Language Brought to Grief

1. This problematic can be quite differently presented, with stress on community and shared conventions or on autonomy and the shattering of conventions. For the first, in addition to Cavell's own works, see the excellent studies by Stephen Mulhall, *Stanley Cavell: Philosophy's Recounting of the Ordinary* (Oxford: Clarendon Press, 1994); and Michael Fischer, *Stanley Cavell and Literary Skepticism* (Chicago: University of Chicago Press, 1989); and for the second, see Henry Staten, *Wittgenstein, and Derrida* (Lincoln and London: University of Nebraska Press, 1984). On the concept of the ordinary as both odd and not odd ("even"), see Stanley Cavell, *In Quest of the Ordinary: Lines of Skepticism and Romanticism* (Chicago: University of Chicago Press, 1988), esp. "The Uncanniness of the Ordinary" (164ff.) and "Being Odd, Getting Even," 105–30.

2. Quoted in Pritchard, *Frost: A Literary Life Reconsidered*, 100.

3. Langbaum, *The Poetry of Experience*, 83.

4. See P.M.S. Hacker, *Wittgenstein: Meaning and Mind*. Pt. 1, *Essays* (Oxford: Blackwell, 1990), 134. Of course it is also true that we speak as though dogs pretend, when we say that they "play dead." We mean that they simulate not pain but the lack of any pain or feeling whatever. If we challenge ourselves on this point, however, we will find ourselves saying that, after all, dogs don't "really" play dead but rather that *we* play that they play dead, and that, to enhance our play, we *say* that dogs play dead, for the most part unaware that we do not fully mean what we say—that is, that we playfully mean something else.

5. Joseph Brodsky, *New Yorker*, 26 Sept. 1994, 84, 82; reprinted in *Homage to Robert Frost*, by Joseph Brodsky, Seamus Heaney, and Derek Walcott, 5–56; Randall Jarrell, "Home Burial," in *The Third Book of Criticism* (New York: Farrar, Straus, and Giroux, 1969), 191–231. Pritchard, in *Frost: A Literary Life Reconsidered*, says (Jarrell-like) that, for Frost, "the talk *is* all" (103); but this overlooks Frost's lively sense of the limits of language.

6. Gilbert Ryle, "Knowing How and Knowing That," in *The Concept of Mind* (Chicago: University of Chicago Press, 1949), 25–61. Cf. *CR* 391: "I am proposing that our access to belief is fundamentally through the ear, not the eye. The ear requires corroboration (and prompts rumor), the eye requires construction (and prompts theory)."

7. See especially *SW, NYUA,* and *CHU.* To my knowledge, only John Hollander has recognized Cavell's specifically rhetorical abilities (*Melodious Guile: Fictive Pattern in Poetic Language* [New Haven: Yale University Press, 1988], 220). Also excellent is Herbert Marks, "The Counter-Intelligence of Robert Frost," *Yale Review* (summer 1982): 554–78. Cf. Robert Frost, "I'm less and less for systems and system-building in my old age.... Give us pieces of wisdom like pieces of eight in a buckskin bag. I take my history in letters and diaries, my philosophy in pensées."

8. Wittgenstein, *Tractatus Logico-Philosophicus*, 5.6. Cavell writes of "the remarkable fact of the presence of the figure of the child in Wittgenstein's thoughts.... It is not a figure one expects to find in philosophical texts.... In my own case, my interest in ordinary language philosophy has from the beginning been tied up with the idea of the child as a necessary figure, however obscure and untheorized, for philosophy's stake (or repression of the stake) in the ordinary" (*Philosophical Passages*, 167). In the afterword to *Robert Frost: The Work of Knowing*,

Richard Poirier remarks on the importance of imaginative play for the child in object relations therapy.

9. Here we are at some distance from Harold Bloom's high modernist belief that "strong poems strengthen us by teaching *us how to talk to ourselves,* rather than how to talk to others"; Harold Bloom, *Wallace Stevens: Poems of Our Climate* (Ithaca: Cornell University Press, 1977), 387.

10. Frost describes education in similar terms in *PP* 419: "But you came to college bringing with you something to go on with—that was the idea from my point of view: something to go on with."

11. Brodsky is observant about the word "see," though he does not treat its larger ramifications.

12. Jarrell, "Home Burial," 220, 221, 222; my emphasis.

13. See Lorraine D. Siggins, "Mourning: A Critical Survey of the Literature," *International Journal of Psycho-Analysis* (1966): 18.

14. Margery Sabin makes the same point when she writes that "[Jarrell's] essay in *Poetry and the Age* remains the most subtle and discriminating appreciation of Frost that we have, but Jarrell does not construct a way of thinking about speakers and speech"; "The Fate of the Frost Speaker," *Raritan* (fall 1982): 129.

15. Marjorie Perloff, *Wittgenstein's Ladder: Poetic Language and the Strangeness of the Ordinary* (Chicago: University of Chicago Press, 1996), 183.

16. Fischer, *Stanley Cavell and Literary Skepticism,* 62.

17. Austin Quigley offers a provocative analysis of the role of doorways in Ibsen's *A Doll House* in *The Modern Stage and Other Worlds* (New York: Methuen, 1985), 92ff.; see also Angus Fletcher, "Threshold, Sequence, and Personification in Coleridge" in *Colors of the Mind,* 166–88.

18. Frost consistently places the reader imagistically and thematically en route, usually at a turning-point on the way, at some boundary or limit of one's world: at the point where two paths diverge in a wood ("The Road Not Taken"); at the edge of an ocean, or wood, or well-curb ("Devotion," "Once by the Pacific," "A Dream Pang," "Stopping by Woods on a Snowy Evening," "For Once, Then, Something"); between heaven and earth ("Birches"); between consciousness and sleep ("An Old Man's Winter Night," "After Apple-Picking"); at midnight ("Snow," "The Need of Being Versed in Country Things") or at noon ("The Vantage Point"); along a boundary or border or wall ("Blueberries," "Mending Wall," "A Time to Talk," "Two Look at Two"); at a window ("In the Home Stretch"); at the point of decision to continue or return ("The Telephone," "The Wood-Pile," "The Bearer of Evil Tidings"); at the surface or horizon ("Neither out Far Nor in Deep"); between seasons ("The Oven Bird," "Two Tramps in Mud Time," "A Hillside Thaw," "A Boundless Moment"); and many others.

19. Mikhail Bakhtin, *The Dialogical Imagination* (Austin: University of Texas Press, 1981): "In literature, the chronotope of the threshold is always metaphorical and symbolic, sometimes openly but more often implicitly. In Dostoyevsky, for example, the threshold and related chronotopes—those of the staircase, the front wall and corridor, as well as of the street and square that extend those spaces into open air—are the main places of action in his works, places where crisis events occur" (248). For a similar view applied to "The Servant of Servants," see Walter Benn Michaels, "Getting Physical," *Raritan* (fall 1982): 103–12.

20. Robert Frost, "For Glory and For Use," *Gettysburg Review* (winter 1994): 96. For an account of surface in Pound, against Stevens's romantic inwardness, see Marjorie Perloff, "Pound/Stevens: Whose Era?" *New Literary History* (1982): 485–514.

21. Cf. *RM* 288: "Word-using is prior to tool-using even in the obscenely punning sense."

22. Pritchard, *Frost: A Literary Life Reconsidered,* 146; Kemp, *Robert Frost and New England,* 118; Reginald L. Cook, *The Dimensions of Robert Frost* (New York: Rinehart, 1958), 130, 129. See

also Philip L. Gerber, *Robert Frost* (Boston: Twayne, 1966): "She clutches her grief," "She can only hate" (120, 121). So Eben Bass ("Frost's Poetry of Fear," in *On Frost: The Best from "American Literature"*, ed. Edwin H. Cady and Louis J. Budd) argues that "several [Frost] poems show the man as outer by instinct, but tied to the 'inner' wife by love," and that in "Home Burial" the husband is "outer and does not see" (78). See also Poirier, *Robert Frost: The Work of Knowing*, 130; and Mordecai Marcus, *The Poems of Robert Frost: An Explication* (Boston: G. K. Hall, 1991), 47.

23. Cook, *Dimensions*, 130.

24. The wife in the poem, for example, has regularly been charged by some critics with being "neurotic" or "possibly neurotic" (Cook; Poirier); and "mentally sick unto death" (Lentricchia); "hysterical" (Brodsky); or "obsessive-compulsive" (Jarrell); or (alternately) defended as being in an "early stage of grief." The basis of such claims seems to be a body of either psychological studies or at least lore (the first variant), or of epiphanies and intuitions (often kept discreetly in the background) regarding inner reasons and motives properly divined (the second variant).

25. Pritchard, *Robert Frost: A Literary Life Reconsidered*, 153; Poirier, *Robert Frost: The Work of Knowing*, 132.

26. Poirier, *Robert Frost: The Work of Knowing*, 132.

27. We could answer that the grief that the poet expresses is just the woman's (human, ontological) desire to *change* grief-over-a-death; this would furnish the "tragedy" the critics are talking about, since, in fact, she cannot change it. The hitch here is that, while grief (-over-a-death) *is* definitionally immedicable, the desire to *change* grief is not.

28. Paul Ricoeur, *The Conflict of Interpretations* (Evanston: Northwestern University Press), 170.

29. See *Lectures* 41: "I [Rush Rhees] spoke of the harm it does to writing when an author tries to bring psychoanalysis into the story. 'Of course,' he [Wittgenstein] said, 'There's nothing worse.'" For a good account of Wittgenstein on Freud, see Jacques Bouveresse, *Wittgenstein Reads Freud: The Myth of the Unconscious*, trans. Carol Cosman (Princeton: Princeton University Press, 1995).

30. Entangled in the texture—heard, as it were, but never seen or registered—are the following (in order of occurrence, excluding copulative forms of "to be"): "was," "will," "must" (line 12); "wouldn't," "didn't," "don't," "didn't" (line 20); "must," "don't" ("don't, don't, don't") (line 30); "can't," "don't," "must," "must," "don't," "don't," "won't" (line 40); "don't," "don't," "might," "should," "can't," "must," "could" (line 50); "[woul]'d," "don't," "don't," "can't," "do," "can't," "don't," "don't," "don't," "[a]'m," "would" (line 61); "do," "[woul]'d," "might," "[a]'m," "[a]'m," "[ha]'s," "can't" (line 70); "can't," "don't," "had," "could," "didn't," "don't" (line 82); "could," "had," "shall," "[a]'m," "don't," "[a]'m," (line 90); "can," "were," "will," "can," "had," "*couldn't*," "can," "might" (line 99); "won't," "can," "won't," "won't," "have," "won't," "[a]'re," "[ha]'s" (line 110); "must," "can," "was," "do," "[wi]'ll"—and the last word of the poem—"*will*" (line 116).

31. Poirier, in *Robert Frost: The Work of Knowing*, shrewdly refers to "violations of decorum" (134–35) but in my view underestimates how the rules of decorum are being redrawn.

32. Bruns, *Inventions: Writing, Textuality and Understanding in Literary History*, 117.

33. See *Zettel* § 225: "'We *see* emotion.'—As opposed to what?—We do not see facial contortions and make inferences from them (like a doctor framing a diagnosis) to joy, grief, boredom. We describe a face immediately as sad, radiant, bored, even when we are unable to give any other descriptions of the features.—Grief, one would like to say, is personified in the face."

34. For $p$ to be a "symptom" of $q$, one presupposes an independent means of identification of $q$. Thus for a fever to be a "symptom" of infection, one needs some independent way of determining that there is, in fact, an infection. This is empirical. But criteria are normative:

"To say that $q$ is a criterion for $W$ [for example, grief] is to give a partial explanation of the meaning of $W$, and in that sense to give a rule for its correct use" (Hacker, *Wittgenstein: Meaning and Mind,* 250).

35. J. L. Austin, "Pretending," in *Philosophical Papers,* 3rd ed. (Oxford: Oxford University Press, 1961), 259ff.

36. Fischer, *Stanley Cavell and Literary Skepticism,* 73.

37. Hacker, *Wittgenstein: Meaning and Mind*: "If a criterion for $p$'s being the case is exemplified in appropriate circumstances, then there are good grounds for judging $p$ to be the case" (250).

# INDEX

"abyss" *(Abgrund)*, 205–6. *See also* "nothingness" *(Nichtigkeit)*
Achebe, Chinua, 128
acknowledgement, 43, 48–49, 56, 95–96, 101–2, 110–12, 151, 160, 167–68, 170, 172–74, 180, 244, 270, 320 n. 22
Adams, Henry, 6
agreement in judgment(s), 40, 95–96, 102, 160, 173, 318–19 n. 2
allegory, 16
Altieri, Charles, ix, 86, 105, 111, 299 n. 3, 301 n. 23, 304–5 n. 57, 310 n. 57, 317 n. 63, 318 n. 85, 319 n. 10, 321 n. 25, 324 n. 38
Altman, Joel B., 214, 331 n. 75
Amis, Martin, 12, 302 n. 39
Anderson, Sherwood, 76
appropriation, 185
argument, 20, 68, 98, 126ff., 144–45, 152, 160, 165, 169, 177–78, 316 n. 47
Aristotle, 13–15, 18, 62–63, 90–92, 102–3, 120, 124–26, 147–48, 159, 198, 233–35, 317 n. 62, 318 n. 82, 320 n. 12, 332 n. 17
"aspect-blindness" (Wittgenstein), 251, 265
"as-structures," 41–42, 109. *See also* criteria; "seeing-as"; "significance"
Auden, W. H., 109, 234; "New Year Letter (January 1, 1940)," 29, 306 n. 4
Auerbach, Erich, 8, 88–89, 301 n. 27, 324 n. 44
Augustine, Saint, 39, 50, 160, 247–48
*Äusserung* (Wittgenstein), 237
Austin, J. L., 40, 243, 308 n. 30; on excuses, 41; on pretending, 262–63, 338 n. 35

Bachelard, Gaston, 309 n. 51, 334 n. 35
Bacon, Francis, 15, 304 n. 51
Bahktin, Mikhail, 64, 92, 160, 252, 311 n. 12, 318 n. 83, 320 n. 17, 336 n. 19
Balkin, J. M., 303 n. 49
Barilli, Renato, 300 n. 20
Barthes, Roland, 333 n. 25
Bartlett, John, 64
Bate, W. J., 100, 319 n. 9
Baudelaire, Charles, 136
Baxandall, Michael, 304–5 n. 57
beauty, 10, 81, 96, 101, 307 n. 13
Beckett, Samuel, 146
Being, 329 n. 39

"being-in-the-world" (Heidegger), 44
Beja, Morris, 147, 323 n. 32
Bell, Michael, 84–85, 317 n. 68
Bender, John, 302 n. 42
Benhabib, Seyla, 306 n. 3, 309 n. 40
Benjamin, Walter, 314 n. 31
Bercovitch, Sacvan, 22, 306 n. 76, 310 n. 2
Berkelman, Robert, 136, 322 n. 19, 323 n. 29
Berlin, Isaiah, 28, 41, 104, 306 n. 2, 308 n. 29, 320 n. 19
Bernstein, Charles, 77–78, 85, 109, 123, 130, 302 n. 36, 306 n. 72, 312 n. 15, 316 n. 53, 318 n. 72
Bernstein, Michael André, 301 n. 23, 306 n. 73
Bernstein, Richard, 4, 50, 309 n. 45
Berthoff, Warner, 299 n. 7
Bialostosky, Don, 313–14 n. 28, 325 n. 8
*Bildung. See* education
Billig, Michael, 305 n. 64, 321 n. 26
Blanchot, Maurice, 129, 306 n. 6
Block, Ed, Jr., ix
Bloom, Harold, 336 n. 9
Booth, Wayne C., ix, 213, 325 n. 8, 331 n. 71
Bourdieu, Pierre, 315 n. 36
Breugel, Pieter, 11
Brodsky, Joseph, 247, 302 n. 38, 311 n. 13, 315 n. 37, 322 n. 9, 335 n. 5, 336 n. 11
Bromwich, David, 323 n. 22
Brooker, Jewel Spears, 315 n. 40
Brower, Reuben, 54, 116, 167, 170, 184, 206–8, 310 n. 53, 325 n. 13, 326–27 n. 1, 327 nn. 3, 4, 328 n. 25, 330 nn. 51, 55, 56, 331 n. 74
Browning, Robert, 51–54, 59, 160, 244–45
Bruns, Gerald L., 34, 86–87, 173, 258, 299 n. 8, 306 n. 71, 308 n. 21, 309 nn. 48, 51, 318 nn. 74, 85, 320 n. 18, 322 n. 4, 326 n. 24, 332 n. 21, 337 n. 32
Buckley, Michael J., S.J., 313 n. 25
Buell, Lawrence, 310–11 n. 4, 330 n. 52
Burke, Kenneth, 5–7, 16, 107, 114, 120, 130, 144, 188, 205–6, 231, 330 nn. 47, 48; *A Grammar of Motives*, 13; *A Rhetoric of Motives*, 12, 336 n. 21; *The Rhetoric of Religion*, 13. *See also* comedy, as comedic; "dramatism"; identification; "logology"
Burnshaw, Stanley, 309 n. 46

Calvino, Italo, ix
Cameron, Sharon, 268

340   INDEX

Caputo, John, 330 nn. 61, 63, 66, 332 n. 19, 334 n. 31
"care" (Heidegger), 41
"Cartesian anxiety" (Richard Bernstein), 50
Cascardi, Anthony, ix, 3–4, 81–82, 299 n. 5, 301 n. 23, 305 n. 62, 306 n. 69, 317 nn. 60, 67
Casey, John, 301 n. 23, 319 n. 4
Cassirer, Ernst, 100, 319 n. 7
Cavell, Stanley: *The Claim of Reason*, 40, 44, 56, 95, 269; "Must We Mean What we Say?," 105; *The Senses of Walden*, 97. *See also* "projecting a word"; "projective imagination"; "transcendental impositions"
certainty, moral, 19, 44
Chambers, Ross, 129, 322 n. 10
Channing, Edward T., and William Ellery Channing, 61
character, 118–21
Chaucer, Geoffrey, 1, 57
Cheetham, Mark, 312 n. 17
"chronotope," (Bakhtin), 252, 336 n. 19
Cicero, Marcus Tullius, 14, 17, 18, 117, 123, 130, 136, 145, 160–61, 182, 233–35, 334 n. 33; *De oratore*, 61–63, 68–69, 149, 163
*Claim of Reason, The*, 40, 56 and *passim*
Cmiel, Kenneth, 311 n. 5
Coates, John, 112, 305 n. 67, 316 n. 50, 321 n. 27
codes, 131–36
Cohen, Ralph, ix
Coleridge, Samuel Taylor, 78; *Biographia Literaria*, 100, 332 n. 20
comedy, as comedic (Burke), 6, 244–46. *See also* humor; jokes
commonplaces. *See* topics (topos, topoi)
common sense, 18–19, 61, 69, 73, 75, 133, 218, 237, 312 n. 14, 314 n. 31
communication, 32, 47, 49, 69, 72; "pipeline" model of, 134
community, 47ff., 61, 63, 69, 72, 168–73, 243–44, 335 n. 1
confession. *See* witnessing-to
Conquest, Robert, 306 n. 2
Conrad, Joseph, 11, 73, 146
conversation, 62–63, 128–29, 159–82, 241–42, 307 n. 11, 311 n. 5, 324–25 n. 1, 325 nn. 5, 8, 10. *See also* language
Cook, Reginald, 253, 322 n. 17, 323 nn. 21, 23, 325 n. 4, 331 n. 8, 336–37 n. 22, 337 n. 23
"Cooperative Principle, the" (Grice), 224
Copeland, Rita, 303 n. 46
*copia verborum ac rerum*, 18. *See also* "Emerson's list" *under* Emerson, Ralph Waldo
Cowley, Malcolm, 136, 143

Cox, Sidney, 94, 159, 170, 178, 326 n. 17
Crane, Mary Thomas, 301 n. 28
Crane, W. G., 304 n. 54, 313 n. 22
crisis, 13, 73, 75–77, 79, 315 n. 41, 316 n. 50
criteria, 9, 18, 27–35, 44, 76–77, 96, 101, 110–12, 171–72, 246–70 and *passim*, 338 n. 37; and accounting or counting or recounting, 29, 39, 51, 60; defined, 40; and telling, 25, 31, 33; and "what we say when" (Austin), 40, 43, 247. *See also* agreement in judgment(s)
Crosswhite, James, 303 n. 48
Crowell, Stephen G., 325 n. 8
Currier and Ives, 180

Dante Alighieri, 227
Dauber, Kenneth, ix, 8, 301 n. 24
Davis, Walter, 303 n. 45
death, 206ff. *See also* "abyss" *(Abgrund)*; "nothingness" *(Nichtigkeit)*
debate, 65, 68, 75, 161, 163, 167, 169, 325–26 n. 13
de Certeau, Michel, 89, 122–30, 159–60, 302 n. 33, 318 n. 78. *See also* strategy; "wig, the" *(la perruque)*
deconstruction(ists), 43
Deleuze, Gilles, 307 n. 8
de Man, Paul, 16, 69, 304 n. 56, 314 n. 32
democracy, 47–49, 62
De Romilly, Jacqueline, 333 n. 26
Derrida, Jacques, 69, 159, 239, 252, 315 n. 40
Descartes, René, 27–28, 35–36, 98, 119, 197, 201; *Meditations*, 50, 306 n. 1
Dewey, John, 1, 6, 10–11, 62, 104, 124, 179, 184, 191, 309 n. 38; *Art as Experience*, 33–34, 58, 302 nn. 32, 37, 308 n. 19, 310 n. 55, 322 n. 2; *The Public and Its Problems*, 44–50, 309 nn. 41, 44
dialectic, 14, 21–23, 27–60, 43
DiBattista, Maria, 8, 300 n. 21
différance, 50, 114
Diggins, John Patrick, 6, 309 n. 37
Dilthey, Wilhelm, 51, 309 n. 47
"discourse" (Ricoeur), 103–4
*disputatio*, 71
"dissociation of sensibility" (Eliot), 73–74
*dissoi logoi* (Protagoras), 235–36
Donoghue, Denis, 321 n. 35
double-voicing, 176, 182
dramatic monologue/dialogue, 51–60, 160, 218, 310 n. 58
"dramatism" (Burke), 6
Dreyfus, Hubert, 184, 327 n. 7
duck/rabbit stereogram (Wittgenstein), 4
Dumm, Thomas, 33–34, 307 nn. 16, 18, 308 n. 36, 334 n. 37

INDEX 341

Eagleton, Terry, 72, 315 n. 39
Edmundson, Mark, 319 n. 10
education, 159, 181–82, 183
Eldridge, Richard, ix, 302 n. 35
Eliot, T. S., 6–7, 65, 73, 103, 185, 210, 315 n. 44
Ellis, John, 2, 134, 299 nn. 2, 3, 308 n. 30, 322 n. 12
Emerson, Caryl, 8
Emerson, Ralph Waldo, 11, 31, 61–62, 77, 92, 101, 111, 118–21, 162, 168, 175, 180, 221, 239, 307 n. 17, 310 n. 3, 321 nn. 28, 30, 331 n. 10; and "Emersonians," 85; "Emerson's List," 62, 68, 122, 126, 233; "The Over-Soul," 113; and "perfectionism," 49, 111
empirical, as distinct from grammatical, 9, 43–44, 97, 105, 301 n. 28, 302 n. 33
Empiricus, Sextus, 12
Empson, William, 2, 10, 75, 316 nn. 46, 48
endotic, the, 25
Enlightenment, the, 28, 44, 69, 74
enthymeme, 103, 165, 168, 320 n. 13
*epi-deixis* (epideictic), 17, 21, 89, 109–11, 146–55, 167–69, 174–76, 179–80, 230, 234, 236, 318 n. 72; criteria of, 151–55
*epiphansis* (epiphany), 86, 146–55, 323–24 n. 32, 324 nn. 35, 45; of being and of form, 146ff.; criteria of, 149ff.
Erasmus, Desiderius, 16, 303 n. 47
*Ereignis* ("event of appropriation," Heidegger), 212
*Erfahrung*, 58–59, 116, 123. *See also* experience
*Erlebnis*, 58. *See also* experience
ethos, 114
everyday and ordinary, the, 4, 12ff., 30–31, 35, 51, 64, 88ff., 107, 110, 114, 217, 300–301 n. 22, 307 n. 9, 332 nn. 11, 12
example: artwork as, 81ff.; teaching by, 5, 59, 126, 133–36, 162, 214, 218, 321 n. 36. *See also* exemplary knowledge; experience; *historia*; parable; rhetoric; tactics
exemplary knowledge, 10, 83–84, 86, 105, 136–46
exemplification. *See* exemplary knowledge
experience, 51, 57–59, 116, 123, 309 n. 48; in Montaigne, 5, 125–26; in morals and politics, 46; in philosophy, 34; related to criteria, 42, 49; in Stevens, 86
expertise, 22; and experts, 46–48, 114, 306 n. 74

Faulkner, William, 146
feelings, 178
Felski, Rita, 8, 300 nn. 9, 22, 308 n. 20, 326 n. 32
Ferreira, M. Jamie, ix, 305 n. 66, 329 n. 33
figures (of rhetoric). *See* rhetoric; tropes

Fischer, Michael, ix, 319 n. 4, 335 n. 1, 336 n. 16, 338 n. 36
Fish, Stanley, 6
Fitzgerald, F. Scott, 146
Flaubert, Gustave, 73
Fleming, Richard, 308 n. 34
Fletcher, Angus, 8–10, 43, 301 nn. 25, 29, 308 nn. 32, 33, 312 n. 16, 319 n. 9
form(s) of life, 95–96, 101, 103, 110, 134–35, 169, 172, 268, 270
Foucault, Michel, 332 n. 13
Freud, Sigmund, 28, 164, 250, 331 n. 3, 334 n. 32
Frost, Robert: "Beech," 48, 94–95, 97, 100–102, 108; "The Black Cottage," 29–30, 50–60, 96, 102; *A Boy's Will*, 50; "The Code," 130–35; "The Constant Symbol," 116, 252; "The Death of the Hired Man," 108, 162–82; "Dust of Snow," 152–53; "Education by Poetry," 35, 83; "The Fear," 132; "The Figure a Poem Makes," 126; "Home Burial," 201, 243–70; "Iris by Night," 150–52; "Leaves Compared with Flowers," 65–68, 86, 112, 127, 154; *A Masque of Mercy*, 4; "The Most of it," 97, 200; *North of Boston*, 54, 131, 174–75, 179, 181, 219; "Nothing Gold Can Stay," 153; "Revelation," 249, 251; "Snow," 217–42; "There Are Roughly Zones," 115–21; "The Tuft of Flowers," 48; "Two Tramps in Mud Time," 67, 136–46, 151–54; "West-Running Brook," 183–216

Gadamer, Hans-Georg, ix, 1, 10, 59, 125, 160, 163, 185, 201–2, 215, 309 n. 48; *Truth and Method*, 79–83, 122, 192, 313 n. 23, 316 n. 56, 317 n. 61, 329 n. 34, 333 n. 22. *See also* "historical consciousness"; "question, hermeneutical priority of the"; *Sache, die*
games, 127–28, 219
Garver, Eugene, 7, 149, 300 n. 19, 303 n. 45, 304 n. 50, 320 n. 14, 324 n. 40
Garver, Newton, 6, 300 n. 17
Gates, Henry Louis, Jr., 334–35 n. 41
Gay, Peter, 315 n. 42
Geertz, Clifford, 221, 237, 239, 312 n. 14, 334 nn. 30, 31
general will (Rousseau), 45ff.
Gilligan, Carol, 164, 167–68, 326 n. 15
Goodman, Nelson, 18, 20, 305 n. 63, 306 n. 70
Goodman, Paul, 10
Goodman, Russell B., 299–300 n. 8
Gorgias, 235–36, 333 n. 28
gossip, 48, 62, 162–63, 166, 176, 197
Gould, Timothy, 300 n. 11
Graff, Gerald, 311 n. 6, 315 n. 38

grammar, 14, 18–19, 21, 37–39, 43, 56, 169, 172, 319 n. 3 and *passim*
Gray, J. Glenn, 327 n. 11
Grice, Paul, 105, 224, 332 n. 14
grief, and grievances, in Frost and Wittgenstein, 243–70; grammar of, 255ff.
Grimaldi, M. A., S.J., 303–4 n. 49
Guattari, Félix, 307 n. 8
Guetti, James, 3, 299 nn. 5, 6
Guignon, Charles, 308 n. 30, 312 n. 14

Habermas, Jürgen, 28
Hacker, P.M.S., 41, 308 n. 28, 335 n. 4, 338 n. 37
Harries, Karsten, 326 n. 31
Heaney, Seamus, 71, 302 nn. 38, 41, 311 n. 13, 315 n. 37, 322 n. 9, 335 n. 5
Hegel, G.W.F., 113; *Aesthetics* (1865), 80, 198
Heidegger, Martin, ix, 3, 5, 30, 32, 41–42, 90, 100–101, 104, 111, 159, 184–85ff., 231, 319 n. 8, 327 nn. 8, 11, 328 nn. 12, 21, 329 nn. 36, 37, 330 n. 57, 331 n. 72; *Being and Time,* 185–98, 205, 328 nn. 18, 19, 22, 23, 329 n. 39, 330 n. 44; and Dasein, 50, 195–200, 209, 328 n. 30, 329 n. 39; *Ge-stell,* 129. *See also* "being-in-the-world"; "care"; *Ereignis;* "involvement whole"; "mood"; "poetic thinking"
Heller, Agnes, 89–92, 318 nn. 78, 79
Hemingway, Ernest, 146
Hepburn, James G., 322 n. 16
Heraclitus, 185, 327 n. 10
hermeneutics, 4, 84, 88, 101–2, 108, 125, 159, 163, 184–216, 226, 240; and "apophantic 'as,'" 192, 199, 203; "hermeneutic 'as,'" 192; hermeneutic circle, 133, 186, 190, 228–29. *See also* grammar; philosophy; rhetoric; "seeing-as"
Hesiod, 235
high modernism, 72, 75, 77–78, 85ff., 128, 326 n. 20
*historia,* 122, 125
"historical consciousness" (Gadamer), 185
Hodgkins, Hope Howell, 312 n. 17
Hoffmann, Manfred, 304 n. 55
Holland, Norman N., 301 n. 28
Hollander, John, 335 n. 7
Holmes, Oliver Wendell, 123
Holmes, Sherlock, 27
Holthoon, Frits van, 305 n. 67
Horace, 145
horizon of understanding *(Horizont des Verständnis),* 186, 190–91, 211
human, the, 97, 172–74, 267ff.
Hume, David, 29, 35, 98, 160, 325 n. 6
humor, 5, 243ff. *See also* jokes

Husseyn, Andreas, 307 n. 15
Hyde, Michael, ix, 299 n. 8

identification (Burke), 13–14, 16
"infra-ordinary" (Perec), 25
*ingenium,* 17–18
interpretation, 183ff., 226, 245; conflict of, 235
invention (rhetorical), 14–18, 21, 61–93, 107, 120, 159–82, 212, 304 n. 53, 304–5 n. 57. *See also* rhetoric
"involvement whole" (Heidegger), 100
Isocrates, 12

James, Henry, 62, 85, 311 n. 7
James, William, 5, 61, 94, 183–84, 191, 307 n. 12, 327 n. 2
Jarrell, Randall, 247, 250, 266, 335 n. 5, 336 n. 12
Jay, Martin, 309 n. 48
Johnson, Mark, 301 n. 28
Johnson, W. R., 324 nn. 36, 45
jokes, 31, 243
Joseph, Sister Miriam, 303 n. 48
Jost, Walter, 299 n. 8, 300 n. 18, 301 n. 24, 303 n. 48, 303–4 n. 49, 319 n. 4
Joyce, James, 106, 146, 324 nn. 41, 42; "Araby," 149–53
judgment, 18–19, 58–59, 94–121, 183–216; aesthetic, 80ff., 95, 106, 306 n. 69, 307 n. 12

Kafka, Franz, 85, 125, 146
*kairos,* 17, 235–42, 333 n. 26
Kant, Emmanuel, 10, 19, 22, 35, 66, 84, 98–102, 146, 165, 300 n. 20, 306 n. 68, 307 n. 13, 312 n. 21, 316–17 n. 57; and reflective judgment, 60, 79–83. *See also* noumena; phenomena; reflective judgments; schema and schematism
Kastely, James L., 325 n. 6
Kearns, Katherine, 70, 83, 116, 315 n. 35
Kemp, John, 136, 165, 170, 184, 322 n. 19, 323 nn. 24, 27, 326 nn. 16, 22
Kennedy, George A., 333 n. 29
Kenner, Hugh, 311 n. 5
Kerferd, G. B., 333 n. 26
Kermode, Frank, 334 n. 34
Kern, Robert, 64, 191, 312 n. 15
Kierkegaard, Søren, 7, 329 n. 34, 330 n. 58; *Repetition,* 195–97, 205, 208, 328 nn. 31, 32, 329 n. 33. *See also* "repetition"
Kilcup, Karen, 300 n. 22
Kisiel, Theodore, 329 n. 33
knowing-how, 90–91, 270
knowing-that, 90
Knox, George, 328 n. 13

Kolb, David, 305 n. 61, 316 n. 50
Krupnick, Mark, 310 n. 59
Kuhn, Thomas, 41, 186

Lakoff, George, 301 n. 28
Lakritz, Andrew M., 313 n. 26
Langbaum, Robert, 146ff., 309 n. 49, 313 n. 27, 315 n. 45, 322 n. 16, 323 n. 31; *The Poetry of Experience*, 51–58, 335 n. 3
language: bewitchment by, 302 n. 35; as communicative (re)circulation, 32, 34, 247; everyday uses, 2–3, 31, 96–97, 103ff.; and noneveryday uses of, 2–3; nonstandard uses of, 2–3; as ordinary, 2, 30, 35, 46, 48, 63–64, 109, 111, 180, 218, 220, 243ff.; standard uses of, 1–2
language game(s), 21, 38, 101; of credal statements, 55; of naming, 104, 108, 188–94, 197, 208–9, 224, 269
*langue* (Saussure), 103
Lanham, Richard, 70–71, 242, 315 nn. 33, 34, 335 n. 42
Lawrence, D. H., 85, 87
Lee, Seung-Chong, 6, 300 n. 17
Lefebvre, Henri, 309 n. 40
Leff, Michael C., 299 n. 8
Leibniz, Gottfried Wilhelm, 98
Lentricchia, Frank, 74, 78–79, 87, 116, 184, 207, 236, 315 n. 43, 316 n. 54, 327 n. 3, 328 n. 17, 330 n. 54
Leonard, George, 107, 320 n. 21
Lesser, Wayne, ix
Levenson, Michael, ix, 317 nn. 63, 66
Lewis, C. S., 17, 134–35, 305 n. 60, 322 n. 14
liberal arts. *See* trivium, the
Lippmann, Walter, 46ff., 62, 69
literature: 43–44, 126ff., 299 n. 7; "experience of meaning," 3; and language, 1–2; as nonstandard language use, 3; as ordinary language, 2–3, 36–44, 101; and philosophy, 1
Lloyd, Genevieve, 329 n. 42
*loci. See* topics (topos, topoi)
Locke, John, 98, 102
logic, 14, 19–21, 43, 122–55. *See also* proof
"logology" (Burke), 6
"logopoetics" (Pound), 8
"loiterature" (Chambers), 129
Loraux, Nicole, 179, 326 nn. 26, 29
Lowell, Robert, 109, 316 n. 52
low modernism, 77–78, 85ff., 147, 218, 313 n. 27, 314 n. 30
Lukács, Georg, 316 n. 49
Lyon, Arabella, 111, 321 n. 24
Lyons, John D., 322 n. 5
Lyotard, Jean-François, 18, 305 n. 61

MacIntyre, Alasdair, 4, 159, 311 n. 6, 321 n. 33, 324 n. 1
Mackey, Louis, 331 n. 73
Majone, Giandomenico, 309 n. 38
Mallarmé, Stéphane, 73–74
Marcus, Mordecai, 328 n. 27, 336–37 n. 22
Marks, Herbert, 335 n. 7
marriage, 1, 209, 243
Martin, Jay, 89, 318 n. 77, 321 n. 34
Marxist theory, 16, 70, 75, 79, 92
Matthiessen, F. O., 311 n. 6
McDiarmid, Lucy, 8, 300 n. 21
McGann, Jerome J., ix, 302 n. 41
McKeon, Richard, 67, 120, 303 nn. 45, 49, 321 n. 34
Megill, Allan, 73, 76, 315 n. 41
metaphor, 100–101, 102, 193, 241–42, 327 n. 3, 334 n. 36
metaphysics, 4, 5, 28, 30–31, 44, 48, 99–100, 102, 130; contextualist, 84–85
Mill, John Stuart, 65, 312 n. 19
Miller, Lewis H., 331 n. 2
modernism, 6, 17, 69, 73ff., 78, 106, 180, 191, 314 n. 29, 317 n. 66, 320 n. 21. *See also* crisis
Montaigne, Michel de, 5, 125–26
Monteiro, George, 330 n. 50
"mood" (Heidegger), 101
Moore, G. E., 19
Moore, Marianne, 85, 87, 318 n. 72
morality, masculine and feminine conceptions of, 164ff.
Morson, Gary Saul, ix, 8, 10, 301 n. 26
Mosher, Thomas, 175
Mulhall, Stephen, 3, 299 n. 6, 308 nn. 23, 31, 309 n. 43, 319 n. 7, 335 n. 1
Musil, Robert, 85, 146

Nabokov, Vladimir, 11, 61, 73, 302 n. 39, 310 nn. 1, 2
Newman, John Henry, 7, 120, 231, 315–16 n. 45
Nicholls, Peter, 312 n. 16, 314 n. 29, 316 n. 47, 326 n. 27
Nietzsche, Friedrich, 7, 69, 104, 184, 231, 236; *The Birth of Tragedy*, 83
Nitchie, George, 136, 322 nn. 16, 18, 330 n. 45
noetics (Fletcher), 8
"normal science" (Kuhn), 41
"nothingness" *(Nichtigkeit)*, 205ff.
noumena (Kant) 78, 99–100

objectivation (Heller), 90
Okrent, Mark, 327 n. 7, 330 n. 51
Olbrechts-Tyteca, Lucie, 168, 303 n. 48, 324 n. 37, 325 n. 5, 326 n. 21
Olmsted, Wendy, ix, 303 n. 48

344  INDEX

Olson, Charles, 85, 316 n. 50
Olson, David R., 305 n. 67
Ong, Walter J., 68, 160, 304–5 n. 57, 313 n. 28
operationalist method, 67
oratory, 61–62
order(ing), 29, 43, 99, 239, 244, 270
ordinaries, 161, 168
ordinary, the: 69, 312 n. 15; and art, 33–34, 221–42, 243; and politics, 34
ordinary language criticism, 4, 8–12, 113
ordinary language philosophy, 4, 8–9, 21, 88, 321 n. 31

parable, 125
Parini, Jay, 318 n. 1
*parole* (Saussure), 103
Paul, Saint, 240
Peirce, C. S., 134, 184, 305 n. 65, 321 n. 27
Perec, Georges, 25
Perelman, Chaim, 160, 168, 303 n. 48, 324 n. 37, 325 n. 5, 326 n. 21
Perkins, David, 181, 326 nn. 28, 30
Perloff, Marjorie, 301 n. 23, 312 n. 15, 314 n. 29, 318 n. 84, 336 n. 15
Perrine, Lawrence, 145, 322–23 n. 20, 323 nn. 23, 28
perspicuous representations (Wittgenstein), 20–21, 37ff.
persuasion, 13–14, 47, 68, 110, 123
phenomena (Kant), 78, 99
*Philosophical Investigations*, 10–11, 35–44, *passim*
philosophy: 9, 27ff., 32–33, 35–36, 38, 67, 77, 98, 102, 122, 181, 220–22, 243, 299 n. 4, 307 n. 8, 327 n. 8, 328 n. 12; and education, 45; limits of, 6; and literature, 1, 87, 148; as pensées, 335 n. 7; as poetry, 7, 300 n. 14; and rhetoric, 6–7, 11, 311 n. 11; as transcendental, 67, 99, 101, 103. *See also* grammar; metaphysics; poetry; rhetoric
*phronesis* (prudence), 17, 102, 140. *See also* common sense
Pippin, Robert B., 315 n. 41, 316–17 n. 57
Plato, 29, 35, 100, 102, 119, 125, 160, 198–99, 234–36; *Republic*, 47; and skepticism, 50
Plochman, George Kimball, 303 n. 45
"poetic thinking" (Heidegger), 5
poetry, 73; and philosophy, 7–8, 43, 64, 218; as philosophy, 7; as "purposeless play," 78ff.; and rhetoric, 7–8, 64
"poetry of experience" (Langbaum [*Erlebnisdichtung* [Dilthey]), 51–60
Pöggeler, Otto, 329 n. 38
Poirier, Richard, ix, 1, 17, 64, 79, 83–86, 90, 116, 143, 166–70, 184, 188, 213, 215, 254, 302 n. 39, 311 n. 13, 312 n. 16, 314 n. 31, 316 nn. 50, 55, 317 nn. 64, 65, 70, 318 n. 71, 321 n. 32, 322 n. 18, 325–26 n. 13, 326 nn. 14, 18, 19, 327 nn. 4, 5, 328 nn. 15, 16, 330 nn. 46, 68, 331 nn. 70, 71, 335–36 n. 8, 337 nn. 26, 31
Polanyi, Michael, 186
Pope, Alexander, 17
posing, 61, 70ff., 130, 219, 234, 310 n. 2
postmodernism, 69–70, 73, 88, 318 n. 84
poststructuralism, 70, 79, 93
Pound, Ezra, 8, 64, 106, 146, 185, 301 n. 23
pragmatism, 4, 6, 31, 55, 79, 84, 88, 184, 233, 305 n. 59. *See also* "reading pragmatically"
"present-at-hand" *(Vorhanden)*, 30. *See also* "ready-to-hand" *(Zuhanden)*
pre-Socratics, 1, 235
pretending, 262ff., 335 n. 4
Pritchard, William, 116, 170, 253, 309 n. 50, 335 nn. 2, 5, 336 n. 22, 337 n. 25
"projecting a word" (Cavell), 36, 106, 230, 308 n. 25
"projective imagination" (Cavell), 91
proof, 19–21, 96–97, 102, 140ff.
propositions, 94, 102–9, 151
Propp, Vladimir, 128
Proust, Marcel, 146, 210
proverbs, 118
Putnam, Hilary, 4, 309 n. 42

Quatermain, Peter, 311 n. 5
"question, hermeneutical priority of the" (Gadamer), 192
Quigley, Austin, 88, 318 n. 75, 319 n. 4, 336 n. 17
Quintilian, 15, 70, 311 n. 9, 326 n. 23, 334 n. 33

Race, William H., 333 n. 26
Rader, Ralph W., 58, 310 nn. 56, 58
Railton, Stephen, 311 n. 6
"reading pragmatically" (Poirier), 1
"ready-to-hand" *(Zuhanden)*, 30
reason, 5, 68
"reference" *(Bedeutung;* Frege), 193
reflective judgments (Kant), 59, 80ff.
Reid, Thomas, 19, 35, 305 n. 65
"repetition" (Kierkegaard), 185, 328 n. 32; in Frost, 194–209
"representative anecdote" (Burke), 161
"retrieval" (Heidegger). *See* "repetition"
rhetoric: as architectonic method, 14ff., 43, 63, 68–69, 88, 300 nn. 11, 20, 302–3 n. 42, 303 nn. 45, 48; attacks against, 313–14 n. 28; decline of, 72–73; defined, 12–14, 186; deliberative, 66, 172; epideictic, 66–67, 147–48;

"flowers" of, 67; genres of, 160; genus of, 148–49; judicial, 66, 114–21; offshoot of dialectic, 103; "rhetorical turn," 47; and romanticism, 4, 64; as tactical, 123; as thinking, 10; tradition of, 163. *See also* hermeneutics; ordinary language criticism; philosophy; pragmatism; strategy; tactics
rhetorical intelligence, 166
rhetorical investigations, 10–11 and *passim*
Richter, David, 303 n. 45
Ricoeur, Paul, 103–4, 159, 185, 193, 226, 320 n. 16, 328 nn. 24, 26, 329 n. 34, 332 n. 16, 337 n. 28
Rilke, Rainer Maria, 243
Robinson, Edward Arlington, 255, 331 n. 7
romanticism, 4, 68, 72, 317 n. 63
Rorty, Richard, 4, 6
Rosen, Charles, 73, 315 n. 40
Rosen, Stanley, 4, 34, 308 n. 22
Rousseau, Jean-Jacques, 44–50
Rubin, David Lee, ix
Ryle, Gilbert, 247, 335 n. 6

Sabin, Margery, 336 n. 14
*Sache, die* (Gadamer), 240
Saussure, Ferdinand de, 103, 134. See also *langue; parole*
Schaeffer, Jean-Marie, 317 n. 63, 319 n. 9, 324 n. 34
Schalkwyk, David, 105, 319 n. 3, 320 n. 20
schema and schematism (Kant), 80, 316–17 n. 57
Schiller, Friedrich, 78, 83
Schleifer, Ronald, 76, 124, 316 n. 51, 322 n. 3
Schrag, Calvin, 330 n. 65
Schuster, Charles I., 325 n. 8
Schwartz, Sanford, 312 n. 20
Scott, Joan, 309 n. 48
Scruton, Roger, 321 n. 36
"secondary imagination" (Coleridge), 100
"seeing-as," 4, 42, 219, 258. *See also* hermeneutics
sense, 75–76
"sense" (*Sinn*; Frege), 193
*sensus communis*, 1, 66, 68, 72, 130
Shaftesbury, Earl of (Anthony Ashley Cooper), 66, 312 n. 21
Shaw, George Bernard, *Pygmalion*, 48
Sheehan, Thomas, 330 n. 67
Shotter, John, ix, 305 n. 64, 321 n. 26
Shusterman, Richard, 309 n. 42
Sidney, Sir Phillip, 145
Siggins, Lorraine D., 336 n. 13
"significance" (Heidegger), 41; as "equipmental wholes," 41; as "involvement wholes," 41
Sipiora, Michael P., 333 n. 23

*Sitz-im-Leben*, 196
skepticism, 3, 12, 31, 34–35, 44, 46, 48, 50–60, 63, 70, 77, 94–95, 99, 101, 111, 170, 243, 245, 266ff., 308 n. 26, 316 n. 49
Sloane, Thomas O., 303 n. 46
Smith, P. Christopher, 303 n. 49, 320 n. 13
Smith, Steve, ix
Snow, Edward, 302 n. 38
social contract theory, 44–50
sophist and the sophistical, 234–35, 241, 333 nn. 27, 28, 334 n. 34
Spacks, Patricia Meyer, ix, 161, 325 n. 10
speaking in tongues, 334 n. 38
Spiegelman, Willard, 211, 313 n. 27, 323 n. 26, 330 n. 59
*sprezzatura*, 71, 117, 126
Squires, Radcliffe, 328 n. 27
Staten, Henry, 335 n. 1
Stein, Gertrude, 64, 177
Steiner, George, 1, 5, 299 n. 1
Steiner, Wendy, 300–301 n. 22
Stevens, Wallace, 6–7, 64–65, 77, 85, 146, 213, 319 n. 5; "Of Modern Poetry," 86–87
strategy (de Certeau), 122–27, 132, 218, 248, 322 n. 15. *See also* tactics
"strife method" (Frost), 72. *See also* debate; rhetoric
Struever, Nancy, 161, 325 nn. 6, 9
supreme fiction(s) (Stevens), 78, 83
syllogism, 102–3
Symbol, the romantic, 16, 78
Symons, Arthur, 313–14 n. 28, 315 n. 40

tactics, 122–31, 218, 248. *See also* rhetoric; strategy
Taine, Hippolyte, 4
taste, 69; aesthetic, 80ff., 106
Taylor, Charles, 4, 86, 107, 146, 160–61, 302 n. 40, 318 n. 73, 321 n. 23, 324 n. 33, 325 n. 3; and "epistemic gain," 307 n. 10
Taylor, Mark C., 326 n. 20
Tennyson, Alfred, Lord, "Ulysses," 52, 59
"thick description" (Geertz), 221
"thinking the poem" (Fletcher), 9–10
Thomas, Edward, 150, 174, 326 n. 33
Thompson, Lawrance, 145, 213, 323 nn. 23, 30, 327 nn. 3, 10, 330 n. 68
Thoreau, Henry David, 11, 101, 111, 130, 161, 168, 180–81, 220–21, 239, 331 nn. 5, 10, 332 n. 18, 333 n. 24, 334 n. 39
time, 208ff.
Tinkler, John, 325 n. 10
Todorov, Tzvetan, 63, 311 n. 10
Tolstoy, Leo, 1, 12, 41

topics (topos, topoi), 15–17, 67–68, 141, 165, 174–78, 303–4 n. 49; defined, 15; dilemmatic, 112; general, 59; as list, 91, 93, 112–13, 123, 139, 304 n. 50; special, 15, 46, 123
Toulmin, Stephen, 4, 305 n. 59, 315–16 n. 45
"transcendental impositions" (Cavell), 5
Trilling, Lionel, 4, 60, 218, 300 n. 10, 310–11 n. 4, 331 n. 4
trivium, the, 14
tropes, 16–17, 67, 69, 129–30, 175–76, 239
truth, 32, 68, 97, 101, 210, 213–16, 325 n. 4
Tucker, Herbert (Chip), ix, 147, 310 n. 58, 324 n. 35
Turner, Mark, 301 n. 28
Twain, Mark, 5, 61

understanding, 226–28
Untermeyer, Louis, 106, 131
Untersteiner, Mario, 333 n. 26
utterances, 94, 103–6

Vendler, Helen, 302 n. 36, 312 n. 16, 316 n. 49
verbs, modal auxiliary, 255ff., 337 n. 30
Vico, Giambattista, *On the Study Methods of Our Times*, 15, 17, 120, 234, 304 n. 52
Viehweg, Theodore, 303 n. 49
von Hallberg, Robert, 313 n. 27

Walcott, Derek, 11, 64, 302 n. 38, 311 n. 13, 315 n. 37, 322 n. 9, 335 n. 5
Walker, Jeffrey, 152, 154, 306 n. 73, 324 nn. 36, 43, 45
Watson, Walter, 303 n. 45, 313 n. 24, 333 n. 27
Weinsheimer, Joel C., 239, 301 n. 30, 305 n. 66, 317 n. 58, 334 n. 36

Wellbery, David, 302 n. 42
Wharton, Edith, 85
Whicher, George F., 136, 322 n. 19
White, Eric E., 333 n. 26
Whitman, Walt, *Leaves of Grass*, 67
"wig, the" (*la perruque*, de Certeau), 129
Williams, William Carlos, 85, 87, 106, 146, 221, 331 n. 9
Winnicott, D. W., 29, 213
Winters, Yvor, 6, 161, 164, 167, 170, 184, 188, 300 n. 16, 325 n. 11, 327 n. 5
Wisdom, John, 88, 243, 300 n. 20, 318 n. 75
wit, 17, 66–68. See also *ingenium*
witnessing-to, 95, 101
Wittgenstein, Ludwig: *Philosophical Investigations*, 10, 35–36, 179, 243, *passim*; *Philosophical Occasions 1912–1951*, 306 n. 75; "seeing-as," 42, 237. *See also* "aspect blindness"; *Ausserund*; duck/rabbit stereogram; grief, and grievances, in Frost and Wittgenstein; perspicuous representations
Wood, Michael, 125–26, 310 n. 2
Woolf, Virginia, 73, 85, 302 n. 37; *To the Lighthouse*, 88–89
Wordsworth, William, 17, 64, 73–74, 92–93, 100, 146–47, 210
work and play, themes of, 145–46
"worldmaking" (Nelson Goodman), 18
Wyschogrod, Michael, 329 nn. 39, 42, 330 nn. 49, 53

Yeats, William Butler, 106, 323–24 n. 32

Zimmerman, Michael E., 329 n. 37